Subina Giuletti

Before you judge me...
try hard to
love m

***

Grant that I may not so much seek to be consoled, as to console;
to be understood, as to understand,
to be loved, as to love.
For it is in giving that we receive.

Francis of Assisi

***

To all, who feel unloved.

Dast Verlag
N. Dippold
Ziegelberg 9
96135 Stegaurach
dast-verlag@t-online.de

ISBN 978-3-00-039725-7

Bibliographic information of the German Library

The German National Library lists this publication in the German National Biography;
detailed bibliographic data can be obtained at the following internet address www.dnb.ddb.de

Dast-Verlag
Printed 2012 in Germany
Third revised edition
Cover image: fotalia / hearts © magann
Cover design and concept: Frank Nowotny, Bamberg

The book's content is based on a fictitious story.

A portion of the proceeds of each book will be donated to children's charities and people in
need.

Internet: www.subina-giuletti.com
Email: info@subina-giuletti.de

*Title: from "Childhood" Michael Jackson, *HIStory* 1995

May your love light shine as brightly as beloved Saint Michael's Divine Aliveness.
For King of Music's eternal brilliance we are forever grateful. He is Prince of Peace!

Ever Being Reverent I Breathe,
Rev. June Juliet Gatlin

Translated from German to English by
Frauke Bruno and Renee Claire
Musubi Translations

His heart was racing. He tensed noticeably. It hurt. He was scared. Everything had developed differently than planned. He was alone. His door was locked. And he didn't know what was going on behind it. Who would open it. What they would do. What to expect.

A hushed unease was palpable. Anxious tension. The only sound he perceived was his heart, which felt as if it was beating in his throat, so hard that it hurts. Involuntarily he swallowed as if he could force down the terrible panic this way, calm his heart.

To the end he had thought, hoped, he could get out of this. Somehow. Everything was going to be all right.

There were plans. His, those of the others ... and there was God. In whom he had always believed ... who had ultimately always been there. Where was he now? Closer than suspected? Close in a different way than he thought? Damn it, where was Jake?

As always, when his thoughts revolved, he forced himself to think of his mantra. He recited it over and over again to condense the thoughts in his head to a single sentence. Calm, calm. He had to stay calm. Air quivered down his throat as he tried to release the oppression with a deep breath. But with the speed of light panic slipped into his mind again and his heart plummeted down fast, like a crashing elevator. He felt bloodless, brain-dead, an indefinable mass in his brain, incapable of response.

Trembling, he lay on the bed.

How many times had he imagined this moment. He had thought of everything just not that the fear ultimately would be so powerful, so uncontrollable. At times when he was thinking about this moment, given his situation and his meager prospects, he even felt something like relief. Finally, this misery would be over! He would be freed. God, free! Finally peace, no more fear, no more heartache - emotions he had felt so often, was tortured by so many times ... oh, my God, all would finally be still. And then...to sink into this silence ... forever ... forever protected, always loved ... liberated forever. There were moments in his life, where the desire for this state overpowered everything else.

And now ... now it was time. But what came up in him immediately before was pure horror. A rising of terror, the debilitating certainty that in a few minutes everything could be over.

Searing thoughts of his children flooded him. How would they do? His heart broke when he thought of them. No, he could not protect them. Not anymore. Had he ever been able to? The most terrible realization he'd had in these last months was that he himself was the biggest danger to his children. That it would be better for them if he left. He couldn't explain these things to them. But he knew of their perceptiveness. It made no sense to pretend -

7

they always knew what was going on inside of him. And they knew that he was suffering, that he was getting worse and worse. They knew he was unhappy. He had seen a selfless consenting in the eyes of his daughter, as if she approved of his moving on. As if she agreed with his leaving, if he wanted to. She loved him so much that she was willing to give him up, if that would make him feel better. Oh, and he wanted to live! Live a real life!

His heart constricted again, out of love, of pain, out of this eternal, never-ending agony that had haunted him for such a long time, stuck to him like tar.

Fear - there she was - as always. The black dragon dog, that guards the entrance of the gate to redemptive salvation.

And yet, in the cold ashes of this fear a tiny spark glowed, an ember of hope, a firefly of folly that kept him from completely surrendering to fate.

Noises at the door. His head turned to the side. His eyes focused in slow motion from close to far. His glance fell on the clock on the bedside table. Five o'clock in the morning.

06/25/2009

As if through a layer of cotton, he perceived how the door handle was pressed down, softly, almost gently.

With tears in his eyes, he stared at the depressed handle. Whoever was out there hesitated to enter. He heard them breathing, procrastinating, felt the metal of the handle, the sweaty hands, as if they were his own. Then: a deep breath. The decision was made. And as if a button was pushed, a majestic calm settled over him.

It was now too late for everything.

All that was, was hereby over.

He briefly closed his eyes.

And the door slid slowly open.

Sun on my face

I like people. Often I sit somewhere, feel the warmth of the sun on my body and watch them.

I observe their features, their eyes, their expression, lips, nose, skin color ... this inexhaustible complex symphony of individual design. And then I wonder why people look the way they do. Why they dress the way they do, why they are comfortable just this way and not any other.

 I look at what they carry with them, how they place their feet, how they talk, run, are silent, how they swing their arms and whether all of that is in harmony. I ponder what brought on all these movement patterns. What people think. How these thoughts produced these exact patterns of behavior. Where their thoughts come from.

And then I always have the desire to go with them, like a fly on the shoulder, want to know how they live, what habits they have and why. Want to know what they were like as babies and children, what they experienced, if there were key moments, and what opinions they have about the different things in life. And if they ever had a different plan for it.

But above all I want to know if they are happy. And if they are happy, what happiness means to them, and what they think brought them to happiness. All of that interests me.

I find people fascinating.

Every one is a never-ending story. And there are billions of stories. It is said that we all come from the same energy, we are all made of the same stuff ...which makes the diverse expression of the source all the more exciting to me.

No matter where I am- I gawk at others.

No matter how unobtrusive I am - it is amazing how quickly people feel observed. And how exactly they know from which direction they are being watched. Even if they can't make out exactly who is observing them, they sense it and turn mostly in the right direction. Despite an overall decline this basic instinct is still working precisely.

And sometimes that's the beginning of a wonderful story.

Apple-Strudel

The woman looked a little annoyed. She was short and plump, and had sturdy legs clad in Bermuda jeans that ended above knobby knees, and a full chest squeezed into a top with the word "Hawaii" printed across the front. Her hair, not quite blonde anymore, was short and curly and she had the face of a typical housewife. I estimated her to be about 55. You could tell by looking at her that she was energetic, and also that her grumpiness was not her usual mood- she seemed too motherly for that.

Uncertain, she kept looking at her list, a wrinkled piece of paper, indicator of her tension. She gazed over the endless selection of different varieties of apples in the organic section of the supermarket while her lips moved in a silent monologue.

After a quick sniff, the woman decided to act. She pulled several bags from the dispenser roll, put on the obligatory plastic gloves and began to layer different types of apples into bags and placed each into her cart. Red, yellow, green, tart, sweet.

I am not sure what drew my attention to this woman. The shop was busy. Many people were pushing their carts through the aisles, and tossing a bag here and there into their baskets. But amid all the lifted and styled faces and bodies in this hip, fancy store she was by far the most normal-looking person. Perhaps that attracted me.

I stood at the exotic side of the fruit stand, with the kiwis, papayas and durians, and did what I loved doing: gawking. Just three seconds later, her eyes turned in my direction. She had spotted me quickly. With an innocent, hunched look I fumbled for a plastic bag and started to attend to my own source of vitamins. The woman did not watch me further. She tossed one bag of apples after another into her cart, and it was half full of them by the time she finished. I could not help but cast her a surprised look, and our eyes met again.

"Wow, you seem to be embarking on an apple crusade," I smiled, and was rewarded with a broad grin, heavily creased with laugh lines.

"You can say that again," she said, pushing her cart a bit in my direction. "I have to bake apple pie, more specifically, this German recipe ... apple ... apple ..." Farsighted, she held the note at a distance.

"Tart ... or strudel?," I helped.

"Exactly! Strudel! Apple strudel! The children had that in Germany and requested it for dessert." She sighed loudly. Her American pronunciation of "strudel" sounded funny. Strooodle.

"Apple strudel is delicious," I said. "And it's easy. I have a great recipe for strudel dough ... where you mix the flour with vinegar, and ... "

"You can bake strudel?" the woman asked, suddenly very interested.

"Sure," I replied casually. "I often made it for my children. Apple pies, fritters, strudel ..."

"Really," she cried happily and pushed the piece of paper close to my face, assuming I would need that. "Can you help me? See ... here it says ... tart apples! Which apples are tart?"

I looked at the purchases in her basket. I certainly wasn't a professional in the science of apples, but at least I recognized a few varieties that did not meet her requirement.

"Okay, these here ... you can take these out of your cart ... but these can be processed especially well... and take enough lemons..."

Together we remixed the assortment in her cart. Color came to her cheeks and her eyes sparkled with joy.

"Could you give me your recipe for strudel?" she asked. "I'd also be happy to invite you to a cup of coffee."

She gestured towards the bistro in the supermarket.

"But, of course," I said. "But you don't need to..."

"Oh, whatever, let's do it now," she answered resolutely. "I'm Linda. Linda Braxton."

She looked at me almost warily, as she said her name, which made no sense to me. But don't they say that a lot of people have their own therapist? Who knew what kind of paranoia we all carry around? But Linda seemed anything but neurotic. Happily, she squeezed my hand.

"Chirelle," I said, and added "Sandler," reacting to her expectant look. "Chirelle Sandler." I pronounced it in English and enjoyed that my first name did not raise eyebrows here in America.

So we stayed together, paid for our purchases at the cashier, looked for a comfortable table in the cafeteria and ordered cappuccino. Linda was personable and friendly. She did not project that superficial mentality of so many people that say," 'I am your friend, but I don't really mean it', which I particularly didn't like. She had a pleasant and genuine warmth.

She told me that she was manager of a large household, part of a family with three children and a lot of staff for the garden and the house, which required a considerable amount of logistics. Her boss was very keen on natural food and insisted on its fresh preparation. No frozen food, no processed food, and very little meat. He especially paid attention to healthy nutrition with the children. She related that he ate so little, that he was very thin and getting even thinner ... even though he had two chefs specialized in Ayurvedic cooking.

"The children don't always like to eat that", she confided, "...and when it comes to German apple strudel ... then the two chefs are just in a fix."

I laughed. "And now you have been entrusted with this."

"Yes and no," she sighed, "I opened my mouth too fast and wide and promised the children apple strudel. But I haven't made one yet, and I'm not responsible for working in the kitchen anyway... to be honest - I can't even cook decently."

I took pen and pad out of my backpack and noticed how the woman started to observe me as if she was only now aware that she was having coffee in a supermarket with a total stranger. I didn't let anything on (I had more than enough understanding for that kind of behavior!) and with distinct letters I wrote the recipe for the pastry.

"You'll have to convert the units," I remarked as I gave her the piece of paper. "That's real easy on the Internet."

"Do you live here in LA?" Linda asked suddenly and eyeing me as if this would confer a different image.

"No," I said "I am here as a tourist and..."

"Where are you from?" she asked, this time almost business-like.

"I'm from Germany," I answered, surprised about the manner of her question. "I'm taking time off, a sabbatical, so to speak, and traveling around a bit. I was in India for a couple of weeks just now."

"India! What did you do in India?"

"I was in a monastery, in an ashram... and went on... you know, a retreat ... that is I did a four-week silent retreat. It felt good."

"A silent retreat? Do you mean you didn't speak for four weeks?"

"No, not a word, - no TV, no radio... and to jump ahead: I didn't miss anything. As far as I was concerned, it could have gone on forever."

"But why would you do something like that?" Linda asked, baffled.

"Because ....it feels good," I said awkwardly. It was hard to explain the pleasure and effect of four weeks of silence to an American with a TV in the kitchen and "Good Morning America" at breakfast.

"But ... but.... what did you do when someone spoke to you?" she asked somewhat mystified.

"Nobody did. The entire monastery was still. It was incredibly still. And incredibly beautiful," I answered her.

Linda looked away, over to the people at the cash register. I was all too familiar with reactions like that. Even, or maybe especially in the 21st century, you are considered a freak if you don't want to follow the hectic prattle of the world. But I must have interpreted Linda's thoughts the wrong way because when she looked at me again she was almost...indeed...excited.

"And you have kids?" she asked in an exuberant and disjointed way.

"Yes, two, both of them are in college. A good opportunity for me to travel... you know... after all these years of being good and staying at home, I needed a change. My husband has work commitments, and so I decided to do this trip on my own."

That was actually more than I had wanted to share, but Linda seemed so honest that I wanted to keep the door open.

"How long are you planning to travel?" she pressed on.

"For a half -year at the most," I said. "My visa isn't valid for longer than that."

"Half a year! That's a long time … long for a relationship … and expensive... I mean you have to be able to afford that … the hotels, transportation… and so on."

She blushed, which I thought was very cute - not a lot of people blush anymore … over trivial things … and to reduce her embarrassment, I smiled at her and answered just as honestly as she had asked.

"Yes, a trip like that has to be well planned and I do hope that my husband will find time to join me for a few weeks. But we have a great relationship - and we are in contact. But still – it's exciting. After all these years together and with the focus on the kids, you define yourself in a different way after taking time out like this."

Linda listened as intently, as if she were my therapist. I could now feel that she was also sensitive. She did not inquire further. Instead, she gestured to my iPod, which I had put on the table, wanting to know what music I was listening to, what I wanted to see in Los Angeles and what my job was. The last two things seemed to interest her in particular and her attention felt strangely good. Going into detail, she asked me questions about my education, hobbies and oddly, my reading habits. I told her that I had just been trying to make friends with the classics and confided that reading was my passion. She asked, "Magazines?" to which I replied, "What do you mean, magazines?" "Well, yellow press," she said. "tabloids..."

No, I explained to her, books, which elicited an incomprehensible grin. When she asked about my job, I told her that I had held a higher position in education, but then because of the children, had stayed home. And that just now I wanted to break out of the rut and travel, so that then I could sort out my life anew with fresh impressions. I didn't tell her that I also wanted to find answers to certain questions about life. Linda's interest was real - that was palpable. And further, she became more and more excited. I almost got the impression that she wanted to join me on my trip, but instead of the expected question: "Where are you traveling next?" she burst out with something totally different:

"Could you use a job?"

"No," I replied, perplexed, "not at all. I'm here to finally be on vacation! And … I don't even have permission to work … I just have a tourist visa!"

Linda nodded curtly, focused on her coffee cup and stirred it silently. Then she drank the last sip, spooned milk froth from the cup into her mouth and peered at the apple bags. It was clear: she would not pursue the matter any further, and for some reason I was disappointed. Hastily and without thinking, I said:

"But, if you need help with the strudel, then..."

"Yes ... uh, no..." she hesitated, "it would not only be for the strudel ... one of the kitchen staff on short notice ... I mean, she won't be... available for an extended period of time ... and it happened rather suddenly, so..." Linda paused - my expression told her everything.

A job as a kitchen hand was pretty much the last thing I had hoped for from my trip: to transition from one household into another! My days were really too precious for that! Still, there was a part of me that refused to let me say a clear 'no'. My mouth started on it's own:

"I can help out, until you find someone else," I offered, while at the same time my internal warning system went off: Man! You wanted to see the city and be somewhere else every week, every day! You wanted out of the kitchen and into real life!

And yet, defying any logic, something drew me towards Linda ... and to what was concealed behind her. What had I said? Help out, until she found someone else? Slowly the meaning of those words seeped into my brain.

Linda's mouth, on the other hand, fell open and shut as if she wanted to consume the message as quickly as possible, before I changed my mind. Her eyes began to shine:

"You would really do that? Oh, that's ... wonderful! You would help me out so much! We'll find a solution to the visa...!"

And then everything happened quickly. She beckoned the waitress, insisting to pay for both coffees, asked me what hotel I was staying at and if I could join her right away, because the strudel was planned as a surprise for this afternoon. Of course, it seemed logical to do it that way - but it went so fast that I felt completely run over. Darn, I thought, here I want to escape from the eternal grind at home and already four weeks later I'm in the same mill! What is it with me that attract me to these stupid housewife duties like this? But since the situation came about due to the strudel, I could hardly refuse my help at this point. In addition: if I didn't feel like doing this anymore, no one could hold me to it. Somewhat comforted by this thought, I looked at my watch.

"How long will you need me today?" I asked. It was eleven clock in the morning and the sun blazed hot on the huge, dusty parking lot, while we carried the heavy bags of apples to Linda's car. Linda was suddenly nervous. "I can't say exactly," she admitted, "I think first of all we'll go to the kitchen, I'll show you everything, you make the strudel, and then I'd like to discuss some more details with you... and familiarize you with a few things..."

Hectically, she pushed the remote control of her car keys. The trunk of a large SUV popped open while we were still 100 feet away. Linda marched in an almost military goose-step toward it.

"Wow," I remarked, "Cool car."

"Yes, Mr. ... " she trailed off and put the bags in the car, "... err ...Mr. J. is very generous," she said, suddenly watching me again with a look that felt suspicious. Did she think I would kidnap her and then disappear with the car? I nodded indifferently and mumbled something about good working conditions, while Linda got in the car, nervous, tense, and without another word. A strange atmosphere spread around us.

"My goodness, Chirelle," I thought as I sat next to the abruptly quiet Linda, "what did you get yourself into this time?"

As Linda drove along Sunset Boulevard towards the triangle of Beverly Hills, Holmby Hills and Bel Air, where all the rich and famous had their mansions, I became a bit uneasy. A huge gate appeared before us, with guards in front. Security measures like these were common in affluent areas, but here there were *four* beefy guys with sunglasses in uniform posted in front of the gate. But it was not only guards who were there. People of all color gathered and started to screech once the car approached, yelling something, and charging towards the car. Then, after they had checked out the occupants, they turned away in disappointment. Wide-eyed, I stared through the windows as the gate opened and Linda drove slowly through. Both sides of the house were lined with trees, yet when the massive steel gates silently closed, it muted all sound.

Linda's eyes were stubbornly directed straight ahead as she rolled toward the entrance. I noted a swimming pool around the side, with lounge chairs around it, lots of old trees and a beautiful, big park, but I didn't have a lot of time to start thinking about this. We had arrived at the house, the sheer size of which bowled me over.

I could not say anything. I just gawked. My favorite pastime anyway. And I got my money's worth.

Linda switched off the engine. Both hands clamped on the steering wheel, she focused her gaze for a few seconds on the dashboard before turning her head and looking at me with a piercing gaze. A notion that knotted my stomach arose in me.

"Linda," I said, turning on the seat towards her, "what, did you say is the name of your employer?"

"Mr. J.," she replied, locking me in her gaze. Shreds of our conversation raced through my brain ... three children ... he was so thin and is getting thinner and thinner...

"Uh ...Mr. J. ..." I nodded and rubbed my ear, "... um ...J... for ...Jackson...?
I mean... THE Jackson?"
Linda said nothing.
"Oh, God, no," I croaked, "that's not true, is it?"
"It is," she said finally, "I suppose it's true. And I hope you can handle it.
We are here at Mr. Michael Jackson's."
Completely disoriented and unable to think, I stumbled, packed with apple
bags and backpack, after Linda. To wherever she was going.

Two minutes later I found myself in the guest bathroom. I needed some
time off within my time off. Linda was sympathetic. "Just slow down," she
told me, and showed me the restrooms. So here I was, trying to get a grip on
myself. Or more precisely, comprehend this. But at the time...at that time I
knew absolutely nothing. There was no comprehension. In those few
seconds I just registered that I was sitting on a toilet seat in the current home
of Michael Jackson.

***

I'm over 40 and not the type who is interested in celebrities. When I'm on a
plane, I'll grab a tabloid newspaper once in a while, only to find that I don't
know most of those who are pictured. But everybody knew Michael Jackson.
Even me. No, of course I had *not* followed his career. Why should I? I liked
some of his songs. I thought he was ... what did I really think about him? I
am afraid that I had no real opinion of that either.
Had I been asked unexpectedly about him, I would have said: "I think he's
cute. I like his eyes. I like how he laughs."
Maybe if I dug around in my memory I would find the following headlines:
Michael Jackson sleeps in an oxygen tent, bought the bones of the Elephant
Man, rarely grants interviews and is getting more and more strange over the
years. He has had surgery on his face, countless times, has a monkey as a
friend ... and yes, wasn't there something else ... some litigation... but I didn't
know what the outcome of that had been or what it had meant for Michael.
If you had asked me about his successes, I would have ultimately fallen
silent. There were so many stars - and he was just one of them.
But still, there was something that connected even someone like me with
him: Michael and his music had accompanied me since I was 14, and he has
not left me to this day, almost 30 years later. And I haven't left him either.
He was always present to me and to the world in an unobtrusive, natural
way. He was there - and somehow it felt good that he was.

So what?

Somewhat composed, I left the luxurious bathroom and found my way back to the huge kitchen. It bothered me that I had reacted the way I had, but the thought that I was going to bake apple strudel for the children of a celebrity made me nervous and I had to pull myself together to follow Linda's directions.

"The cooks won't be here again until tonight - the kitchen is all yours. If you have any questions, here is a beeper that you can use to let me know."

"When is the strudel supposed to be ready?" I said, forcing myself to be calm.

"Three o'clock would be ideal," said Linda, and glanced at her watch just as I did. "For fifteen people with a good appetite," she determined, and I nodded. It was eleven thirty - I had plenty of time to prepare everything.

The preparation of the strudel pulled me into familiar territory and suddenly I was looking forward to my task. I was going to bake the best strudel I could, with the image of children's eyes shining in my heart! This is the most helpful attitude you can have when preparing a dish, and so I set to work assembling the necessary equipment and ingredients, and began to peel the apples. And the thought of whether I would see Mr. Jackson face to face would not leave me.

One and a half hours later, the smell of baked apples and vanilla floated through the house, and it was not long before a boy with dark, long, straight hair came running into the kitchen, an action figure in his hand. He looked like a small, cute North American Indian. His baby cheeks and big eyes with long eyelashes were perfectly formed and made a stunning profile. The boy was an absolute beauty.

"Linda, Linda," he cried excitedly, "it smeeeeeells so good!"

Linda laughed and tenderly lifted the little one in the air; he might have been four years old.

"Yes, my darling," she said, "there's apple strudel – just like you wanted! Look into the oven, it looks so good!"

The little boy looked curiously at the sizzling rolls in the two ovens and marveled.

"Wooow! That's a lot!"

"Yes, and you can eat as much of it as you want, you little devil!" Linda promised.

"Did you make them?" the boy asked.

"No," she replied. "Chirelle did, look ... this is Chirelle. Say a nice hello to her."

She set the little one down again and he went straight up to me, stuck out his tiny, soft hand and even made a slight bow, which made my heart melt.

"Thank you very much for making our cake," he said seriously, and I had to laugh. I crouched down so I was at his eye level. God, was he cute!

"You're welcome," I smiled. "Linda told me you had that in Germany?"

"Yes," he replied proudly. "I was there with Daddy and it came with ice cream and yellow sauce. And a checkered tablecloth!"

I held back another laugh, the little boy bounced away happily, and Linda watched him, smiling.

"My goodness, what a sweetheart," I said.

"Yes, he is," she said with warmth in her voice. "And Mr. Jackson so lovingly cares for the children. They are everything to him."

The little boy's name was Prince Michael II, and they called him Blanket, which I could understand. If you saw the little guy, you automatically thought of something snuggly.

I saw Michael's firstborn, Prince Michael I, and his daughter Paris, at first only through the kitchen window - a huge picture window, which displayed a view of parts of the garden, a large pond and a swimming pool.

After the dessert, all three children came to us in the kitchen and thanked us. Prince was a pretty boy with serious eyes, and his thanks were followed by a brief bow as well. He was quiet and did not push himself into the foreground. Of the three he seemed to be the wise one. Paris, the middle one, had a perceptibly strong personality. Even at her young age, she already seemed to take on responsibility for her brothers. All three children were exceptionally polite and had impeccable manners. They were without conceit and seemed balanced and happy.

Michael did not show up. I did not hear if he ate any strudel, or if he was even at home.

I cleaned the kitchen and Linda showed me around the beautiful estate. The park was a dream: perfectly trimmed lawn with exquisite solitary trees, fittingly and harmoniously planted, and beds full of colorful flowers that lined the path. But what made the whole thing so unique were the playful details, such as picturesque crafted gazebos, fountains, solitary rocks, peculiarly life - like bronze and stone statues ... crooked benches under trees ... and something else hovered in the park that made it special, but my eyes were not able to catch that. I registered only that it was stunning and idyllic without properly seeing the details. It was as if we entered a different world ... a perfect world, full of children's laughter, full of harmony and wonder, full of marvel, imagination and magic. The overall impression was a fairytale-like atmosphere that drew me completely under its spell.

Linda introduced me to the Deputy Head of Security, Bob Brinkman. I would get to the Chief of Security, Michael Amir Williams, who had been with Jackson forever and whom she called 'Brother Michael', as well as with other important security people the next day. While I was still trying to grasp the strange childlike atmosphere of the park, Linda and Bob were discussing how I should get to the hotel and back.

"What's so complicated?" I interjected, "I'll take the bus or a taxi and get back here the same way."

Both lifted their eyebrows, looked at each other, and Linda, it seemed to me, had an almost triumphant look in her face. Did I say something wrong?

"Okay," she decided resolutely. "Today, I'll take you back. Bob, I'll get back to you about this."

She looked at her watch: "Now I have to hurry, the kids want to go away over the weekend and we haven't packed yet."

Together we walked back to the kitchen. The sun was already low and transformed the park into a pink-orange dream. Again and again I looked out the window, and saw lovely details - an ornate lantern, a small stone elf, a dragonfly in stained glass ... all that reminded me of a long-lost world. A world that seemed more real to me than this so-called "normal" life, a world that enchanted me. I would have preferred to stay outside, but Linda pulled me to the kitchen table to finalize formalities and in particular the working hours.

At the end, she showed me a lounge and rest rooms for the staff. These were next to the kitchen, and the only rooms I was allowed to use.

"May I use the garden?" I asked her. In principle, yes, she replied, but I am not allowed anywhere close to the family.

Finally, she drove me back to the hotel. Before I got out, she held me back again.

"Please, Chirelle, I have to say this now: don't tell anyone, promise me that. Tomorrow you need to sign a document that you agree to disclose nothing of what you see, or otherwise notice, to any third party, or to take any pictures... I..."

"It's all right, Linda," I interrupted. "This is a matter of honor. I'll sign that for sure."

She briefly embraced me. "Thank you," she said, and squeezed my arm goodbye again. I waved to her until she was out of sight, then I turned around, went to my room, took a shower and, to make myself think of other things, took one of the city buses to Rodeo Drive. But even the most fantastic displays and stores of the rich were less glamorous to me than the fact that tomorrow I'd be back on the estate of Michael Jackson's.

Although I saw no one in the family on my second working day, I was far from disappointed. On the contrary, I was glad to have the time to absorb this undisturbed atmosphere.

It was nice to be here. The entire property was saturated with something that was not tangible, but was present in all the rooms. As sun flooded the house, everything seemed to be immersed with Michael's being and his music. There was a kind of longing in the air. The lovingly designed park added the rest: the pond, the old trees, the nooks and arbours, and especially the many miniature statues that awoke the forgotten wonders of childhood in me, when fairytale could delight me and we kids could indulge for hours in our reverie, in which the boundaries between the imaginary and real worlds bridged seamlessly into one another. It was a strange feeling for me, an almost bittersweet emotion, between restraint and breaking free, between childlike exuberance and adult control.

This day Linda had me prepare snacks for the family and went through planning for the next few weeks. Then she placed a five-page densely typed document on the table about the required discretion and told me that she would give me an hour to read through it.

"After you have signed we can continue," she explained.

Without hesitation, I flipped to the last page and signed my name. Linda looked at me with a slight frown.

"I want you to read it," she insisted.

"And I will. But you should know that …"

Her frown deepened. "Chirelle," she said, "read this now. And read it carefully. Then you will understand more."

With that she left me alone. Somewhat intimidated, I set to work, and when I had finished reading the pages I felt almost sick. From the sheer number of paragraphs I could see the difficulties that a celebrity had to deal with and how hard it was to maintain privacy. What methods were used just to get information about celebrities?

With these thoughts in mind, I met the rest of the staff. There were the two cooks, the security personnel, lots of maids and cleaning crew. Each had his or her separate work area and was not allowed to be in other rooms. There was hardly anyone except Linda who was allowed to roam freely in the house.

The Vice-Chief of Security, Jason, did not let go of my hand for a long time and looked at me with eyes as piercing as an x-ray machine. A photo of me was taken and given to the guards so I could come and go without complication, and I also met an assortment of drivers and the old gardener Greg. Greg also held my hand in his for a long time and looked at me intensely. He had beautiful, gray eyes in a wrinkled face, whose story I would have liked to hear. His gaze was peaceful and deep, and I was very glad when his calm reached me and I could compose myself a little.

And then there was Grace, the nanny, but based on the scope of her job that was definitely not the right word. She took care of everything around the family, ranging from the private tutors to practice hours - and other plans around air travel and Michael himself. Basically she was something like Michael's personal manager.

Grace was an energetic woman, who seemed loving, motherly and sexy at the same time. She took care of the kids touchingly; she was their mom and behaved that way, too. In the days and weeks that I spent in Michael's house, I often heard her and Michael's voice echoing from the breakfast room, where they argued about methods of education and that sounded all so terribly normal that it was almost comical - as if Jackson, because he was a star, would have different worries about his children than a normal father who went to work from nine to five.

But he was a normal dad. But, no, that was not quite true. His loving attention and devotion to his children, his willingness to make them the absolute center of his life, the way he romped around with them and played is what probably millions of kids would have wished from their fathers. You could feel the love in which he enveloped his children, even from a distance.

Grace, however, eyed me extremely critically and it was clear that she would not readily give anyone her trust.

Finally, I was introduced to Karen, Michael's long-time make-up artist, a beautiful, blonde woman with a warm nature, refreshingly open, who immediately stormed at me and squeezed the recipe for the apple strudel from me.

Diary, 06/20/2009

I have no choice other than to write. Who can I talk to? There's nobody there. Nobody's there. Is there an increase to loneliness? My walls are full. I write because my heart is overflowing. Where is Frank? Eddie? Where's Jake? Has Jake switched sides? It's all so horrible, so horrible. Why must it be like this, why it can't it just be nice and easy and simple?

I love people. I love life. That's all I have left. Love and fear. I'm scared. Damn it, yes, I'm terrified. I feel weak. I can't meet their expectations. Not theirs, not those of my fans. My fans ... I love them, I don't want to let them down, that's what keeps me going. But I feel that I can't. This time I can't, I can't...'they' threaten me. They threaten me with all sorts of things. No matter what I do. There is no escape. No matter where I turn to. That is what they wanted: they have surrounded me.

I've always been lonely. Where does this solitude come from if everything is one? How can you feel this oneness and yet be so lonely? I'm freezing. Oh, I'm so cold. So cold. I can't get warm. All the warmth has left me. I have nothing left in me. Not even for my kids. Oh my children, how I love them! I love them so much, my heart glows, it bursts, when I even think about them. I cry, and the tears are warm. Even more heat flowing out of me, which makes me even colder. God, I'm so cold, for so long I've been cold. I'm scared. My thoughts run in circles.

Can't think clearly anymore. They are holding me tight. They say, after this I'll be done. I think after this I'll be dead. Anyway. No matter how it goes. They are taking everything from me. They want everything…this contract: they say that this is my last chance, and they are the ones who will help, get me out of all of this. But I do not trust them. Everyone says they will help me, and then they just enrich themselves. They take me over. Rowe says that the contract will be my downfall.

But they say if I do not follow their plan - that will be my downfall.

I'll go down one way or the other. But I want to live so much, live so much … really live! Once in this lifetime I want to live right. But what is really living? Is it a mistake not to know? Does my subconscious have anything to align itself to, if I don't even know what it means to live fully? But I want so much. I want to survive the concerts. I want to dance, want to feel my fans, long to sink into the music, be music. And I want a simple life. Everything is so opposing.

Oh, God, I'm so cold. I'm so cold…like I am made of ice. It's 77 degrees outside. I am wearing thick underwear and several shirts and jackets. That makes me look stronger than I am. But I'm freezing. I want to go into the sun, and I can't. Everything is killing me. Sometimes I'm at a point where I just want to give up. No more fighting. No more defending myself. Let death come. There is a kind of sweetness in this giving up. And still I want to live … but not like this … not like this …

***

The days at Carolwood Drive flowed by.

To Linda's tremendous delight I had dedicated myself to wholesome cooking at home, and now I was in a position to spice up the menu accordingly. So I baked granola - and whole grain muffins, multivitamin pies and carrot cake, prepared Bircher Muesli, exotic breakfast cereals and date sweets, which everyone - except Michael - ate with great appetite.

Michael ate so little, mostly in practically homeopathic doses that I could not imagine filling a person. Food did not seem important to him, but rather a necessary evil.

But the staff and the rest of the family really appreciated the healthy snacks and meals a lot and to my delight there were almost never leftovers.

I only saw Michael sometimes from a distance. When he played with his children in the garden. When he had guests and was standing at the front door. Or when he walked through the only corridor that I was allowed to use. Without his children he moved calmly and at a measured pace, almost carefully. His posture was very straight, he was taller than I had expected, and I often had the impression that he only lacked the long robe that flowed from his shoulders to the ground. I did not know then that I was not the only one who felt like that. But every time I met him, I had the vague feeling that I had been transported into a different time, in a different dimension. He radiated something that touched you, whether you wanted it to or not. He exuded something that was completely independent of his star-existence. Something resonated within him and everyone in the house enjoyed his presence.

Indeed, it very soon became obvious that the people around him not only appreciated his presence but were downright happy when he was there. When he didn't leave. As if they wanted to protect him from the outside world and they all felt that it wasn't good for him. Linda sighed every time he left the house. But she sighed, too, when his many advisors arrived that apparently no one liked, and everyone seemed to wonder why Michael bothered with such people.

Celebrity

The atmosphere in the house and the relaxed, kind staff made my work easy. After a cup of coffee with Linda, Bob and Jason, and the presentation of my first German sheet cake, I climbed into the cab that Linda had called for me on my fourth day, and I was not displeased to have spent the day with housework rather than strolling through town. On the contrary: I arrived at the hotel full of energy, decided to go out that evening and was looking forward to a nice dinner somewhere in the city.

I put on something pretty, put money and a book in my purse and went downstairs to leave the key at the reception desk.

The concierge smiled at me and gallantly took my key. While I asked him something about the bus, I suddenly felt eyes at my back. I ignored the feeling. But as I walked through the revolving door, I noticed how a man who had been sitting in one of the chairs in the lobby got up and followed me. My heart stopped, and I was suddenly aware that I was a single woman in a huge city in a completely foreign country. I turned around.

A well-dressed man with friendly eyes and coffee-colored skin, in his mid-forties, looked at me curiously.

"Excuse me for following you," he said with a charming smile. "But I noticed you days ago ... you ...you always go out alone ... and I…"

My suspicious glance silenced him. He ran a hand through his black hair, and attempted to speak again:

"I'm sorry to spring this on you, but I stay here quite often ... and I thought maybe we could have dinner ... of course only if you like ... I don't mean to be pushy..."

I declined, saying: "I really wanted to go on a sightseeing tour."

"A sightseeing tour," said the man. "Aren't you a bit too late for that?"

"You're not telling me that this city shuts down at seven, are you?" I retorted.

"No," the man smiled disarmingly, "...no, of course not. By the way, I'm Carlton, Lewis Carlton."

I shook his hand, but something held me back from giving him my name. It was rude, I knew that, but I couldn't get the words to cross my lips. Mr. Carlton imperceptibly furrowed his brow, and with a short look at my unadorned fingers, he asked again:

"May I invite you to dinner... Miss...?"

"Um...Miller... Mrs.," I said unimaginatively, and unfortunately started blushing. Ever so slightly, Carlton raised his eyebrows and said:

"I know a couple of popular places into which the occasional Hollywood star sometimes stumbles...." Abruptly, I withdrew my hand.

"No, thank you, Mr. Carlton," I replied. "That's very kind of you, but I'm already ... engaged..."

"Too bad," remarked Lewis, believing nothing. "Then how about a drink?" He smiled again, and his smile was nice. I hesitated, uncertain how I should best decline.

"It would make me very happy," he said, and it sounded so sincere that I pulled myself together. All right, I would have a quick drink with him and then be on my way, I thought, and agreed to go with him. Maybe it would be pleasant to have some company for a change. I had been going out to dinner alone for weeks.

His obvious delight and his choice of an upscale pub nearby were somewhat reassuring to me. His joy seemed authentic and the atmosphere of the place was refined.

We took a seat at the bar, I ordered a cappuccino, he a martini.

"Thank you for joining me," he said, raising his glass. I smiled slightly and sipped my coffee.

"So you are staying in the hotel, too?" I asked, still feeling uncomfortable.

"Uh ... yes ... I travel a lot for work ... and then I saw you yesterday and today, and I thought, wow ... what a gorgeous woman..." He kept flattering me, and my discomfort increased to alarm.

I mean, I certainly could not compete with all the D and DD cup sizes and the perfect, twenty-years-younger faces that packed the city. What was this all about? Annoyed, I finished my cappuccino and decided to take off while he continued to deliver trivialities, clearly trying to keep the conversation going.

"Mr. Carlton, thank you for the coffee, but I'd like to be on my way now."

"What, already?" He exclaimed in dismay. "But we haven't really been talking yet!"

"I know, but..."

"Where are you from?" He asked quickly.

"From ... Europe..." I answered evasively.

"Ah ... and you work here."

That was a statement. Fully suspicious now, I looked at him. How did the guy know that I was working? I had arrived here as a tourist and up to this point had behaved as such. And hadn't I just told him that I was out sightseeing? Mr. Carlton, too, seemed to have noticed his misstep.

"I mean ... wasn't that Linda Braxton who brought you to the hotel the other day?" He added quickly. "I thought maybe you were associated with Michael…"

"What makes you think that?" I asked.

"Well, everyone knows that Mrs. Braxton works for Michael Jackson, and that he's preparing... a lot ... and ..." he ran his fingers through his hair and looked at me. "Listen, Miss ...Mrs. ... "

"Mr. Carlton," I interrupted him angrily. "Mrs. Braxton and I met at the grocery store and she was kind enough to drive me home afterwards. That's it. And anyway, it's none of your business."

"And why did you visit her the next day, too? How did you get past the guards? I mean, to get to Jackson ... especially now..."

My jaw dropped. What did he mean by 'especially now'? And how did he know all this?

"What makes you think that I was on Mr. Jackson's property?" I heard myself ask, while racking my brain for clues from the past days. "I wasn't at all."

"Oh, come on," Carlton said patronizingly, which annoyed me even more. Okay, I was stupid, inexperienced when it came to these things. And not prepared. The confidentiality clauses that Linda had told me to take to heart came to mind. One point was: do not talk with others about Mr. Jackson, not with the staff nor with anyone else. Do not answer questions.

"I am a perfectly ordinary tourist," I said helplessly, hoping that I didn't sound that way. "I am exploring the city. That's all there is to it."

And as soon as I said that, I knew from where he had his information: the cab drivers. He must have asked them where they had picked me up. Or they had told him, because they had a deal with him. What did I know. I fell silent and felt even more dim-witted, with Linda's and Bob's words in my ears, about how I could come and go without being noticed.

Mr. Carlton, meanwhile, tried a new strategy: "Have you heard that Jackson is totally broke and has as much debt as a dog has fleas? People are wondering if he has to perform again to make some cash... You must have spoken with Linda or with him or with someone from the staff, right?"

"Mr. Carlton, what's the point?" I snapped back and took my bag. "You are interpreting a bit too much importance into my humble self."

"How does he treat his staff?" Carlton attacked outrageously. "Listen, I know the rules ... and the restrictive contracts that stars like him put together. You don't have to say anything - you can just nod. Is it true that he forces his employees to laugh all day ... and that his children ... "

"No idea." I hissed and slid off the stool. Carlton grabbed my arm, which really made me aggressive, and he gave me a suggestive look. Then he lowered his gaze to the coffee cup, next to which he had placed a couple of hundred dollars. I tore myself away, gave him a foul look and went outside as quickly as possible. I wanted to call a cab, but changed my mind and just walked off, frustrated. I mingled with the crowd, boarded a bus, went somewhere, and looked for a small restaurant. With effort I buried myself in my book to distract myself.

When I looked up, I noticed a man across from me who smiled at me kindly, attempting to connect. Abruptly, I paid the bill and left. The smile on the face of the man went out like a light. On the street, I looked through the window. He still sat there, without making the slightest attempt to follow me. He had just been friendly. Suddenly I realized the absurdity of the situation. How quickly I felt stalked. A single experience. How many had Michael had?

***

To my infinite surprise the experience a'la Carlton now repeated itself almost every night and every morning - in a different form and with other players, but they all knew that I came from the house of Michael Jackson and bombarded me with all sorts of impossible questions.

Before long, I felt observed every second I was outside of Michael's property, and I became suspicious of anyone who glanced my way when I was in town.

My God, I thought, how must Michael feel, who, for his whole life has lived and suffered under such conditions in far more dramatic form?

At first I thought things would settle down at some point, and I could have my usual peace and quiet. But when one of these shady characters stood in front of my door in the morning, offering money for information and indicating that truth was secondary so long as I used my real name, things became too crazy for me. I had to talk to Linda.

"I expected this, sweetie," she said, sighing, "but that this tribe found out so fast... real detectives they are! If only some of them would solve criminal cases, there would be no more crime in America!"

But she was also very serious and thanked me that I had informed her. Then she disappeared for two whole hours, and when she came back her face was set in determination.

Her seriousness scared me. Was that it? At that moment I realized that I didn't want to leave, that I was entirely willing to sacrifice several weeks of my trip, just to stay in this environment that was nourished by Michael.

Silently, I sat down with Linda at the big kitchen table. She poured coffee, stirred sugar and milk, struggled for words, and finally looked up.

"Chi, it's not easy to find good people who can keep their mouths shut" she began. "Many come from agencies that have deals with the press. Most sell photos or information from here along with information distorted accordingly. No matter who applies here, the risk that they are undercover is high. In that sense you were a real find and we would be happy if you would keep the job for a while longer."

I sighed with relief. I was not going to have to leave, and I waited anxiously for Linda's solution.

"There are some secret entry ways here through which you can come and go," she said. "But that's of no help, since they know where you are staying. I suppose you could switch hotels - that would be a possibility. But we would prefer if you were to move in here."

She was visibly relieved to have finally said it and hastened to assure me that the room was comfortable, I'd have a private bathroom and could use room service – like in a hotel.

"And that doesn't mean that you are locked up here either," she declared. "I know you wanted to travel around the country, but ... "

"Linda," I said, "that's all right. If it's necessary, I will stay here for now."

Linda's eyes looked disbelieving of this easy victory, then she beamed. She half rose from her chair and hugged me.

She could not have known that this mysticism around Michael fascinated me more than I liked, even if it meant being drawn into the captivity of his fame. On my part, I couldn't have known that Michael was having a difficult time finding people with integrity who were willing to work for him.

Tagore

I didn't meet Michael for a long time. I often saw him, though from a distance. No matter where he turned up, it was tangible. Suddenly we knew: he's somewhere in the vicinity. And then everyone, not just me, began to stare at him: how he moved, how he stood, how he spoke.

I saw and heard him often when he was playing outside in the park with his children, where I could watch him from the big kitchen window. Those were moments that made me neglect my work. Michael had the ability to lose himself so completely when playing with his kids that there was no telling who the biggest child was. Their laughter echoed across the distance to us through the open window and put a smile on everyone's face.

There was only one thing which rivaled or even outdid this: when Michael sang.

He sang with his children, he sang when he was looking for something in the house or went out into the garden. He sang involuntarily while eating, sometimes even while reading, with a book in his hand, as if giving a melody to the text. His voice was so pure and clear that everyone paused with the clatter from the current work to listen to his voice.

I had always thought that it was the orchestra he was accompanied by, the perfect mixing of his songs that made their effect so strong. But here, in his house, hearing only his voice, I realized that Michael put his soul into every song that something resonated that gave every melody grandeur.

Although I didn't directly encounter him, these were pleasant days in the house of Jackson. His being pervaded the rooms, the park, the souls of the children, and it was something that attracted me in a powerful and inexplicable way.

Ever since I had moved into Michael's house (with a much nicer room than in the hotel), I set out to explore the beautiful grounds. The grounds were huge and I discovered magical places that invited me to linger. My favorite place was a vigorous deciduous tree with its lower branches spread about five feet above the ground and stretched far outward. The trunk was so wide that three people could effortlessly sit against it next to each other. The branches were dense with leaves and soft moss grew beneath the tree. It was kind of cozy down there, a secret hideout. A sufficient amount of light fell through the branches and, lying on a blanket, with a view to the pond, I listened to the wind in the trees, watched the sky and was happy to be there. It was still and quiet in Michael's garden. It was especially still and quiet under this tree. I listened to music or read, wrote about my impressions and indulged in my thoughts. It was a magical place for me. Just visiting this resort compensated me for the other attractions I was missing while spending my days providing for Michael's children.

After the first week I had already established a routine because life in Michael's house turned out to be surprisingly down-to-earth and unglamorous. The children were educated privately, and Michael took their education very seriously. He took everything seriously that had to do with his children. All his activities revolved only around them and it seemed as if he wasn't planning on doing anything else.

Linda had told me (secretly) that in the first years Michael had hardly been able to take care of business. When he had to leave, he already longed for his children terribly while he was still at the front door, and he always tried as quickly as possible to get back to them. He felt like a mother.

But now the children were older, he was in his late forties, and he seemed to want to get back more into his business ... or he had to. Even amongst the staff, words such as "running out of money" and "financial pressure" were heard, and that's probably why those people who Linda looked at frowning and with skepticism were able to come into his home.

These meetings touched Michael's dark side, his so characteristic sad side that was reflected clearly in his eyes. They left Michael gloomy, anxious and edgy. Restlessly, he began to pace around in the house or in the park, lost in endless, dark thoughts. Then he didn't sing a single note. On these days, I could hear his footsteps in his bedroom, which was over mine. He could not sleep.

It was the weekend. Michael was out with his children and I had some time off. I baked a few not quite wholesome calorie bombs for the staff and spent the next few days in the city, busy doing what I had come here for. But over and over again my thoughts went to Michael and the issues that everyone talked about behind closed doors: about the last lawsuit, his unstable health and his uncertain future.

Late Sunday afternoon, I loaded my backpack with books, a blanket and a bottle of water and strolled through the park, in the direction of my favorite tree.

The evening was warm, the sky clear, the sun just setting. As soon as I sat underneath the tree, its majestic calm settled over me. I spread the blanket, feeling secure under the branches, and began to read in the last light of the day. After a while it got dark, and I turned on my small reading lamp. The book was very intense, and I lost myself in it.

"What are you reading?" suddenly asked a voice from nowhere. Torn from my world of books, I looked up, bewildered, and registered two black trouser legs.

Michael stood before me. Hastily, I scrambled into a sitting position, and when I didn't respond instantly, he smiled and that smile was so magnificent that my heart literally dropped to my stomach.

"Did I scare you? I didn't mean to, honestly," he said, and squatted down so he could look me in the eyes. He gazed at me attentively and prickles ran down my spine because of his deep, searching look. He turned to the book.

"Um ... you didn't scare me," I finally said lamely, and my voice sounded somewhat silly. Michael did not notice, at least not visibly. He took the book in his big hands and read the Sanskrit title.

"What is it?" he asked with interest.

"These are the writings of Indian sages," I said, feeling dumb. But my answer seemed to trigger something in Michael.

"What is it about?" he wanted to know.

"It's about their thoughts, about what they've learned and experienced," I cleared my throat, as my voice was failing. "These are Indian philosophies that..."

"Indian philosophies," he interrupted. He crouched in front of me with the book in his hands and I thought he must be quite uncomfortable. Boldly, I patted the blanket and the spot next to me.

"Would you like to sit down?" I asked, smiling at him.

"Oh yes, thank you," Michael said, pleased, although it was his garden. With a smooth movement he settled, completely relaxed on the blanket, asking in the same breath:

"What are these scripts? What do they say?"

His big eyes looked at me, his rouged mouth was closed, and he regarded me with the same intense attention he gave his children when they spoke with him. His charisma bewildered me. For the first time, I was close to him. For the first time, I felt in concentrated form what I had previously sensed only from a distance. He was like a field of vibrating energy, and it took effort to respond to his question. I would much rather have stared at him some more, tried to understand these vibrations, but Michael was probably rather sick of people gaping at him, so I pulled myself together.

"Essentially, it's an explanation for the meaning of our existence here on this earth," I answered. "It's about recognizing how a sage perceives and masters life...well...and much more. It is too complicated to explain in one sentence."

I glanced at him uncertainly. He had closed his eyes and was silent. He was silent in a way that drew me inside, into an almost meditation-like state. He was silent in a way that made every word unnecessary and did not raise any questions. It was a silence that encompassed everything, timeless and beautiful.

The moon, set in a picturesque scene through gray clouds, gently shone on the beautiful landscape, its silvery light reflected in the water. The overhanging branches of the old tree created a nest for us, and its scent enveloped us in an atmosphere that reflected his soul. In those minutes I could let Michael fully affect me, and what I felt then was nearly impossible to describe with words. And it was almost unbearable.

He exuded such an intensity of something I could not initially grasp...an intensity of light and suffering, of love and longing. It was something so bittersweet, so painfully beautiful, that in his presence my heart involuntarily hurt and opened at the same time. It was so peaceful, so deep, and so still. Every sound we perceived emerged from this silence, revealing its origin to us that night. And it seemed as if the silence originated from him.

Defenseless, my heart went into resonance with that light in him, it elevated me and I felt so light, so light, so absolutely weightless, devoid of any burden, and I felt that I was flying, felt a deep sense of happiness spread in me and waves of joy flood me. There were no thoughts, only this void and perfect happiness that left no room for anything else.

I had experienced this only once before, in India, with an ancient master who had invited me to sit with him in his hut. When I had expected anything but that... to feel this in Michael's presence surprised me deeply.

At the same time I sensed a confusing wild pain, sensed resignation and despair, and these strong, conflicting emotions interwove like a necklace of white and black beads, seemingly inseparably connected. This was the bittersweet part: on the one hand I felt the urge to enjoy the love he was radiating without any restraint, and on the other to hold him in my arms and protect him.

Silently, we sat under that tree, I don't know for how long. At some point he turned to me and asked in his soft voice:

"Have you found a meaning for yourself?"

I looked at him. His eyes were like him: contradictory. Complex. Shy. Behind that: a bottomless depth...deep curiosity, a painful striving to know about the meaning of this life. In this moment he felt so open and vulnerable that my heart swelled in a sensation of love on a completely different level. Love, that did not want to possess and had nothing to do with physical desire or the need for any response. I had the urgent feeling to give him everything to make him happy - only to turn those wistful eyes into glowing ones. This emotion spilled over, came out, reached him. The look in his eyes changed. Michael leaned against the tree trunk, looked down, almost guiltily, I thought. Again, I was confused. But he was still waiting for an answer and finally I said:

"I think the purpose of life is to be happy, to understand why I'm here, and to unburden myself from everything that prevents me from being happy."

He swallowed visibly and I would have liked to softly stroke the black hair away from his pale face.

Arms wrapped around his bent knees, he turned his gaze to the water. Individual strands of hair fell over his forehead, over his darkly painted, huge eyes. His cheekbones pressed sharply through the white skin. He appeared so beautiful to me at that moment.

"To be happy," he repeated softly. "Is this obtainable in this world? Isn't this world a place of suffering? Aren't there enough people that prevent happiness? Aren't we here to be tested?"

"Those are a lot of questions," I smiled, "but, yes, I believe that one can be happy in this world. I even believe that this is the highest duty of every human being. A wise man once said to me: 'Happiness is a noble goal.'"

"Happiness is a noble goal," he repeated. "Yes ... you can say that again."

Then he was silent for a while, and I enjoyed this time to the fullest. Being still with Michael was like listening to a beautiful song.

"What else do they say? " he wanted to know then. "What do they say about how you can attain this happiness? And what does happiness mean to them?"

"They say that happiness is something that arises from within," I said, surprised because that was just what he had initiated in me. "A happiness that one experiences because the parameters of one's life are whole is not real happiness. Anything that can change, that can be taken, is not happiness. It's about finding an untouchable, everlasting happiness ... bliss... if you will ... one that nothing can cause to falter. It's about finding yourself, or finding God in yourself."

He looked at me. "Everlasting happiness," he repeated. "Does that mean that when you find it, you don't have to suffer anymore? That bad things don't happen to you anymore?"

"Uh – yes and no," I replied. "Personally, I believe that negative things wouldn't be necessary any longer if we got where we all want to go. And even if they do happen, we wouldn't have to suffer anymore, because you would experience them completely differently. They wouldn't bother you. You would be independent of them."

Michael nodded. "That's a very nice thought. I already talked with some of my friends about this."

"And what," I asked curiously, "was the result?"

"One of them gave me a book from Tagore. Do you know Tagore?"

"I've never read anything by him," I admitted. "What does he say?"

"Well, he says many wise and beautiful things," Michael smiled. "One of my favorite pieces of text is from the Gitanjali, that is a song to God."

A song to God. It sounded so beautiful out of his mouth. I smiled at him warmly, and we felt that we understood each other on a plane where words were not the means of expression. This moment noticeably took down a barrier between us, a barrier that Michael always had up around adults to protect himself, and I was pleased about this unspoken concession after such a short time.

He listened to the night. It was almost tangible. He heard something. He heard something in between or in the sounds of nature, the chirping of crickets, the rushing of the wind, the trickling of water. Sitting so close beside him, I could feel how he received something, how he opened himself to a frequency that was completely foreign to me, how he captured music that buzzed around in the ether in infinite abundance, ready to be received.

Majestically the moon shone in the sky, framed by stars and clouds. The wind sang its song in the trees and together with the tireless cicadas in the grass they were Michael's orchestra backing him up as he started, with his ringing voice wrapped in a captivating, unfamiliar melody, to recite the lines from Tagore that were so dear to him.

When thou commandest me to sing
it seems
that my heart would break
with pride.
and I look to thy face,
and tears come to my eyes.
All that is harsh and dissonant in my life
 melts into one sweet harmony -
and my adoration
spreads wings
like a glad bird
on its flight
 across the sea.
I know thou takest pleasure
in my singing.
I know that only as a singer
I come before
 thy presence.
I touch
by the edge
of the far-spreading wing
of my song thy feet
which I could never aspire
to reach.

Pearls of sounds and words hung in the air as his voice died away, embracing us like a finely spun web of sound. I was caught in it, enchanted – I couldn't say anything. Any word would have been trivial. And I knew that Michael felt the same way. I didn't have to explain anything to him.

With deep connection we sat together, almost shoulder-to-shoulder, leaning on this venerable old tree, until Michael pulled himself up and said he wanted to check on the children. Before he got up, he asked:

"What's your name, anyway?"

"Chirelle," I replied.

"Is that Jewish?"

"Yes," I said, "but it is spelled differently, and I'm not a Jew."

"What does the name mean?" he asked. "All names mean something."

"Chirelle means 'Song of God'," I said.

"Song of God," he smiled. "That's very fitting for this evening, isn't it?"

This time he giggled like a little boy, so infectious that I had to laugh too.

"Good night, Chirelle," he said, standing up. "Sleep well."

And then he was gone so fast that my reply was stuck in my throat.

"You too," I murmured softly behind him. "I hope you dream something especially beautiful."

***

This evening had stirred up more in me, more than I wanted to admit at first. I felt changed and could not say how or why. Again and again, I thought back to the encounter, pondered what alchemy he had set in motion in me. I felt light ... free ... and happy.

I was not in love with him, oh no. That was certainly not the cause of this feeling of joy. You don't fall in love with people like him. You love them. Their presence unwittingly and unwillingly gives a glimpse of an idea about the true nature of love.

In those seconds of our first encounter his mere presence taught me the deepest and most important lesson of life. The solution for everything.

But the penny did not drop until much later.

The next day Linda swept through the house, her face grim. There was a sharp confrontation between a maid and Grace and Linda. A short time later, the maid left the house with her termination papers. A cab had been called for her. Her face was pinched as she got in.

Wide-eyed, I asked Linda what was going on. Wordlessly, she slammed the newspaper on the kitchen counter.

"Jackson marries nanny", it said beneath a photo showing Grace and Michael as they stood side by side, bending down to the children. The photo had been taken in the dining room of the Jackson estate.

Who is he?

After that evening one thing that nobody in the whole world would be able to change was clear: what I had felt within him was more breathtaking than the most spectacular appearance on stage. Michael was not only a man with a huge heart; he was more than that. And I was eager to find out who he was.

And so, in the following days, I found myself collecting any material that I could find about him in the city.

Books, magazines, discographies, reviews, specials, anything that was available. I surfed the Internet, looked at his performances, downloaded interviews, documentaries and footage of fans who had put their material on the web. I analyzed his face and his movements in his different years and tried to put them in context with the relevant events and situations in which he had been at that time. I clicked in to television broadcasts and documentaries, from which I learned out about his marriages and lawsuits. And I kept hoping for authentic material by him. I wished with all my heart for a continuation of our conversation.

But at first, nothing was happening and I was left to my own devices. Armed with my sources and the Internet, I was trying to make a picture of Michael for myself. I bought his stories and poems in '*Dancing the Dream*', a book in which he revealed surprisingly deep, spiritual thoughts. The texts in it were wise and valuable.

But the reports about Jackson distressed me; there had not been a single favorable one in the last two decades. More so, for nearly 20 years he was ripped apart, his appearance and his behavior seemed to be becoming more and more eccentric - something the press shredded him to pieces for. Even his philanthropic events such as benefit concerts, did not seem to find favor in the public eye. All this was in stark contrast to what I had seen and experienced personally. Even his face was different than in the pictures I had seen below bold headlines.

I started making notes and prepared a rough outline of his life, in an effort to understand what created his fascination.

His childhood must have been hard, which he emphasized over and over. At the age of five, Michael was already standing on the stage boards that supposedly mean the world.

At this point the most down to earth would probably count his exorbitant successes: the best-selling recorded music of all time, the most prizes and awards for best dancer, best singer, best entertainer, best performer, choreographer, songwriter, composer. He not only stood out in these categories, but he also had mastered all of these qualities to perfection and put them together with his own personality. This was a mix that was addictive, that fascinated. It also drove countless experts and would-be experts to uninvited analyses, but ultimately nothing could explain what was incomprehensible to the mind.

There were and are many charismatic dancers in this world, there are singers with amazing voices, inspired composers, choreographers and alike – and yet: the mastery of *all* these arts with this kind of perfection was one thing; the passion with which Jackson brought all these components to the stage, with this unique charisma, that something special that no one could decode and therefore no one could copy, that was something else.

The fact was that many could not leave him out of their sight once they saw him. Maybe because they saw more than just him. This losing himself in his action, this stunning fusion of body, mind and spirit awakened a longing for the feeling that dancers must have when they completely surrender to the rhythm. It was a presentation of himself to the world, the still power that comes from complete devotion to the sound, to the dance and to God. When he was on the stage he seemed to adjust to the perfect order of the world, to take the ideal place in the solar system. That's where he seemed to belong. That's where he was supposed to be.

Wherever Michael Jackson showed up, the masses broke out in a frenzy. He moved them, brought them to hysteria, touched them, charmed them, and not only during his concerts. The more I read about him, the clearer it became that the relationship with his fans went deeper than with any other star. By far, they seemed connected with him on a level that exceeded the ordinary. It was as if they perceived something greater behind his stardom.

Throughout his solo career he sang rock songs, he sang soulful songs. But he never sang anything happy. The soft pieces always carried the banner of sadness and melancholy, sung in a voice that spanned three octaves.

And he always wanted to make the world a better place with his songs and shows; drew attention to conditions to be changed. There was always a message included, always the same one, as if he felt a mission that he had to accomplish.

The shows that he offered to his audience at concerts were legendary. Michael Jackson was a synonym for superlatives. Passionate dance, breathtaking backdrops, pyrotechnics and the best backup dancers in the world that practiced his intricate choreography, while for him it was effortless, in his blood.

On stage he exploded when he performed his hard, heavy songs; he melted away when he sang ballads. In these moments, he was not only a man who sang a song - he was a song in human form. Together with his dance style, which he had elevated to professional heights, he was one with his movements, was a perfected expression of the rhythm of nature.

In all of these actions, he seemed so visibly directed by a higher force, that he awakened in many people a vague but niggling feeling of longing. For him? For this perfection? For the higher authority? Thoughtfully I sat at the computer.

The yearning for the source seemed to me the most probable reason, and because it was unconscious, it was the deepest.

This super dimensional fame generated more fascination. I realized to which extent the term "star" applied to Michael. He was one of the greatest entertainers the world has ever seen. Someone like him did not appear every century. He was a once-in-a-millennium star. A prisoner of his talent and charisma. A prisoner of his fame, his management, the press, and - above all – his vulnerability, this heel of Achilles, which made him falter over and over again.

His appearance? His face was painted like a woman's, the dark, intense eyes traced by black, and yet there was no one who seemed more male on the stage than he. His charisma was so complex that he effortlessly connected generations, genders and races, which was another aspect of his unsolved mysticism. He was handsome in his own way, he was special- everyone felt that, he was a self-created exotic. His fans found him attractive even after he had undergone surgery. He was attractive in an eccentric, bizarre way, even if you knew it was make-up, that these were no longer his original looks. But his appearance still had an authenticity that did justice to the inside of him. Michael's face, which changed constantly, but especially his eyes, expressed a vulnerability and beauty that revealed his soul. One that seemed to show us that we are set neither in one shape nor that our form is all that we are.

Up to his thirty-fourth year his career had soared in an almost vertical path, and there were already 29 intense years of work behind him. Intrigued I looked at the screaming masses, saw both girls and boys faint, saw how people reacted to him. He seemed like an outer worldly, hypnotic light source. What was it that attracted them like this? What was it within him? But I had felt it myself ... on that evening under the tree. He only had to show up, and everybody went crazy.

This radiation did not seem rehearsed but innate. He was already the highlight at the age of ten, when he had sung in the family band. In the beginning it had been attributed to the puppy factor - Michael was super cute with his Afro curls and an endearing smile, his then still curious-fearless eyes. But even when he was older, when the pimples came and when puberty mixed up his bodily proportions, people were crazy about him. It became more and more evident that his brothers were talented, but that he was a musical genius.

At 20, he broke away from the family and launched his solo career. His first album, which he produced in 1979, sold surprisingly well.

His second CD, or actually record, because at that time the transition from records to CD was just starting, was the catapult into the star universe. *Thriller*, I read, has sold 100 million copies to date and turned the music world upside down. They praised Jackson as a natural wonder, as a phenomenon, as a piece of art created by God and himself. I was a little queasy: I hadn't known that Michael had this much greatness - instead I, too remembered only the negative headlines. In the past years there had been nothing else to read about him.

Impressed, I researched further.

Now Michael was no longer a superstar, he was a megastar. He was such a great light in the sky of show business that new names and allegories had to be invented for him. He delivered first class work, was a workaholic, never forgot his lyrics, mastered the métier to the last detail. He wanted everything to be perfect. Not only that his songs were good, his creativity breathed into them a dazzling, fascinating life that was enhanced with his dances and elite-choreographed musical short films that had not existed in this form in the music world before.

Deep in thought I took my fingers off the keyboard. Reading the old reports about him had been a real joy. He seemed like a man with values who didn't take drugs, didn't smoke, didn't drink, was careful with his nutrition, disciplined, polite and shy, didn't womanize or slug reporters, applied himself openly to world causes, for children ... It was all so perfect. He was the utmost example, the knight in shining armor, and it suited him. He seemed authentic; you believed his convictions. Nevertheless, the type of coverage changed so drastically after his incredible success with *Thriller* and stayed so persistently and uniformly negative that I couldn't prevent myself from feeling uneasy. This feeling was just there and I read the other reports with mixed feelings.

With the money he had earned, he bought the ATV catalog in 1985, the rights to the Beatles and Little Richard songs and much more. His business - sense was excellent, he founded a children's relief organization and bought a ranch, which was over 2,700 acres and in which he permitted himself what had been denied him as a child. It was his refuge, and the main reason to buy it had been the wonderful nature of St. Ynez Valley.

Never had anyone in the music world grown to these dimensions, and the fact that originally he did not have white skin made the matter volatile. He was the first African American on this level of performance.

But from there on, a cut seemed to surface, a collapse. This in itself would not have been unusual because everyone knows that after a high, a low follows. But Michael did not have a creative slump, like so many in the industry - on the contrary. He drew from sources that seemed to be endless. Ideas poured like a waterfall to him. And yet after the second album you could feel something destructive, as if his success had conjured an equally powerful adversary.

But the question that forced itself upon me at this point was the extent to which Michael had identified with this heroism and how great the danger was that this had caused him to have too high expectations of himself.

Over a period of four years he produced his third CD, *BAD*, which did not sell quite as well as the second, but still in dizzying numbers. But Michael was devastated - he had expected an escalation beyond *Thriller* and couldn't believe that he had not achieved his goal. In America reports also compared the early sales of *BAD* with the ever-increasing ones of *Thriller* and denigrated *BAD*.

The bulk of the tabloid press wrote little about his music. They ridiculed the number of rivets on his leather outfit, the color of his lipstick, his chimpanzee and his zoo at Neverland ... all this seemed to be deadly. Maybe they did it, I guessed at this point, because there were no scandals, no affairs with women. Other than a couple of staged public tete à tetes with Brooke Shields and Madonna, it seemed there was no woman in his life at all.

I clicked videos on youtube of this period. Although in public the shyness dominated, he was still charismatic and full of spirit. Reports of him from that time confirmed a very interesting phenomenon for me: he seemed to draw a clear distinction between what took place on the stage and his true person. He could not really understand why people stared at him after his performance.

'What are they looking at?' he wondered. As if without his performance there was nothing left to be admired. Or as if the higher source that made it so perfect was no longer present.

I watched his performance at the Super Bowl, which was in a class by itself, saw the beauty of his movements, how relaxed he dealt with the crowds, and especially how comfortable he felt in the midst of a group of children in the final number.

I saw how he visited hospitals in India, Ethiopia, Africa, and in the poorest areas to terribly dirty children, scratched bloody. How exactly did this rumor about his morbid fear of bacteria come about when there were pictures like this at the same time? Did we all have no brains? Or did we switch them off when we read headlines?

My next click of the mouse led me to a page with aid organizations that were supported by Michael, and I almost fell over. Pages after pages of organizations leaped out at me - countless millions of dollars had flowed into those organizations and into his own, which he had provided with millions more not even included.

Michael Jackson was listed in the Guinness Book of World Records as the star who had donated the most.

Despite the snide reactions, mainly in his own country following his third CD, Michael seemed at the time exceedingly sexy, almost androgynous, with his painted face and a nose that he had plastic surgery transform to his specification.

This so-apparent sex appeal, and his equally obvious sexual denial in his private life wound the attraction of fans of both genders to intolerable heights. But the downward spiral had begun, and Michael swam against it.

Then, the fourth CD, *Dangerous*, followed by *HIStory*, which were supposed to bring back all his earlier successes, once again had less sales success than the previous albums. The press spoke ungraciously of "loser of the year". True, he was the King of Pop - with this title, he was the godfather of ethereal achievements. But curiously, his music was barely discussed and trivialities about him picked apart instead. They lashed out at his spacious grounds, found it ridiculous that he kept exotic animals there.

It did not make any sense to me at all. There were so many people who kept tarantulas and snakes in terrariums in their living rooms, why should he not treat himself to a small private zoo if he loved animals so much? There were certainly much more useless expenditures, especially since his goal was to bring joy to children. No one got upset when millions were spent on cars, jewelry, pointless handbags and outfits. But a private zoo seemed to be something terrible. And that he opened the gates of his property for sick children and for children in general was greeted with weird comments, too.

And then, 1992/1993, the total crash: Michael, the squeaky clean of the pop stars was accused of child molestation.

Jordy Chandler, a 13-year-old boy, claimed to have been sexually assaulted by Michael, and Mike's image was tainted from top to bottom. He prevented a trial by settling in the double digit millions, which for many proved he was guilty. The damage was done - his image was impaired, and it never recovered. Michael was deeply affected.

Soon - much too soon - afterwards he got married and, so quickly after this indictment, it caused a stale taste in people's mouth. It came across like: "I will prove to you that I am neither gay nor a pedophile."

The fact that the name of his wife was Lisa Marie Presley did not make things any better. It looked so much like image repair that even some fans had doubts about the authenticity of the marriage and thus about the credibility of Michael himself. After about two years, the expected divorce came, but Michael topped it off: to everyone's surprise, foremost to those who had just had a second to breathe a sigh of relief, that the most desired pop star under the sun was single again, a new wife appeared closely after the annulment of his marriage, an unassuming woman who bore his first two children and 'gave' them to him.

At the age of 40, in the midst of a truly turbulent life, Michael had become a father.

People would have understood had he chosen this woman simply as a surrogate mother. But no one understood why he had married her. This all seemed so strange, so calculated and at the same time so rash that I had a lump in my throat just reading the reports and involuntarily compared the image that I got from those with the one I had been able to obtain myself. But how many people had the privilege of making this kind of a comparison? A handful?

After that, it became relatively quiet around him, though he tried persistently to get back on his feet professionally and restore his image. 1997 and 1998, those were the years in which his first two children were born and in 2002 he had another baby by a different surrogate mother. Now he was responsible for a family, and he had to earn money. He produced *Invincible* with high sales success in itself, approximately ten million recordings were sold. Nevertheless, the press spoke to the crowd with their headlines: Michael Jackson is a loser.

And the gossip wouldn't stop. If you read something about him, the words most often used were "wacky, ridiculous and paranoid". Even though he stayed away from the public as much as he could. The reports insisted that Michael would not get back on his feet after the Chandler scandal. Increasingly more newspaper articles appeared, rating his financial status from damaged to completely ruined, calling him extravagant, out of touch with reality, and, someone no longer earning enough money in proportion to his eccentric lifestyle. And it did not take long before they were reporting that Michael Jackson was in debt.

I researched the woman, Debbie Rowe, who gave birth to his first two children. Who was she?

First and foremost, of course, the one who the press was waiting for: the woman who had sold her children to Jackson.

Rationally, she had quite simply provided herself as a surrogate mother for his use. This woman loved Michael so much that she would have given him anything - and she proved it with rock-solid, amazing loyalty.

The longer I studied her, the more I began to admire her. You don't carry a baby twice in a row for nine months without feeling anything for it. Not to mention the prior process of taking hormones and so on. She had not only gifted Michael with children, her gift was much more extensive than it appeared at first glance: she had also accepted all the suffering, the malice and the isolation. Plus, she consciously gave up the man she loved. What good did the money he gave her do? They never lived together. She did not see her children. She did not see Michael. Why had she even married him?

I thought about my own children and how it would have felt if I had been separated from them after birth. Maybe others were wired entirely differently, but I was convinced that it was a sacrifice for her. Despite everything.

Debbie held steadfastly to Michael. In not one single press release did she say anything negative about him. She backed him up in a way that any man could only wish for, and seemed unpretentious and honest. This woman loved him, without expecting anything in return, but perhaps hoping for something.

Confusingly, she was the one who, after barely three years of marriage, filed for divorce. Then suddenly in 2001 there were reports that she wanted her children back. Had it ultimately not been clear to her after all what it meant to give him her children? In the literal sense? Had she hoped to be connected with Michael through them? And after not succeeding this way, to take the opposite path? But that did not fit with her sincerity.

And how must Michael have felt when she suddenly defaulted on her agreement and involved him in an unpleasant dispute like so many before and after her? Moreover during a time in which he could not afford additional stress because disaster loomed over him once more?

This all took place ten years after that drastic accusations of Jordy Chandler - here, again, his fate repeated itself with even greater force and with a horrible prelude.

In 2002, Jackson was duped by a British reporter who had set out to build his career ladder out of Michael's bones. Martin Bashir produced a documentary that portrayed Michael as a pedophilic lunatic. This massive damage to his image dealt Michael a brutal blow that threw him far, far back. Full of trepidation, I read some reports about this and saved the documentation in my now growing file.

And as if this image damage was not bitter enough, Jackson was sued for child molestation again because of it. Once more, a teenager and his family who Michael had invited to his house testified about sexual advances made to the boy.

But this time the blows were dealt to an already wounded Michael - to one that needed to protect not only himself, but his young family, too. And to one who didn't appear to be able to muster the strength after all these years of malice and slander.

Altogether, the second trial lasted a full two years. Half a year of that was spent in the courtroom. When it was over, he was just a shadow of himself.

Pictures of Michael after this trial shook me deeply. In the videos that showed him after the acquittal, where he climbed dutifully onto the roof of his SUV for his fans, I looked in vain for jubilation and gladness. I couldn't even see adequate relief. Only strained composure. Fighting back tears. And immense exhaustion. He looked as if he never wanted to get back on his feet, as if he had lost faith in the world and in humanity forever.

Then: the flight abroad, trying to go into hiding. The curse of the superstar status alone did not allow it. The media found him and adorned the rare pictures of him with spiteful headlines.

There was not one positive thing to read about him. Michael was the nut, the child molester, the vulture, the King of Pop who had crashed terminally and by his own doing.

But still: no matter how much he was denounced by the media, no matter what was written about him in the press: wherever he went, there were screaming, enthusiastic crowds of fans, people who felt his charisma, who felt who he was, there were people with shining eyes. People who told him that they love him.

Dazed, I closed the laptop after this last crushing report.

His past - from his fifth birthday on to his stardom, and a super dimensional one at that, could have been explanation enough for an unusual relationship with children.

No childhood, no youth, no way to grow up in a normal way, no apparent desire for women or sex, but instead much affection for children, preferably boys ... what were you supposed to think?

But ultimately, in both cases the accusations had come from somewhat dubious people who had both demanded money. They came from a hypocritical, prudish legislation whose custodians had no problems to put even minors in jail because they had helped their sister go to the potty. They were supported by an unhealthily growing custom of filing lawsuits over nothing for a chance to come into money.

And then there was what I had sensed in Michael when we had sat together under the tree. There had been nothing sick, nothing paranoid. I had sensed deep pain, sorrow, unhealed suffering, and, almost inexplicably to me after all these reports, an amazing amount of love.

How must he have felt with all this? He who was so sensitive? For all these years of exorbitant popularity seemed to not have made him tougher, but more vulnerable. This last law suit... what had exactly happened to him there?

And the question that I was most burning to find the answer to was: *why* did it happen to him? Why the same thing twice? Why him?

I wanted a spiritual answer. There were enough logical ones. It just did not fit into my worldview. When someone radiated such love, someone who had done so much in his life for others, when someone had such a good heart, then why had such striking key catastrophes happened to him?

I could not stop pondering these questions. I suspected that a secret embedded in this would have meaning for me too.

For minutes I still sat motionless in the chair. My eyes fell on the book that I had with me when I had met Michael for the first time. And like mist in a drizzle, this delicate, subtle atmosphere that he had exuded came over me again. I could feel the inward drawing energy of his presence, and this made me more eager to find out why he couldn't find the key to his happiness.

The clock showed half past two in the morning when I put the laptop aside. It was a funny feeling, knowing Michael was close to where I was. Knowing he was lying one floor above me in his bed. I hadn't seen him in a week.

XX 1984 Somewhere in the world

"WHAT DID THIS ASSHOLE SAY? Who does this fucker think he is? His Holiness the Dalai Lama in person? Does he think he can do what he wants? Does he think that? DOES - HE – THINK - SO?"

A hard fist slammed on precious wood. Objects on the desk jumped into the air in protest, accentuating the tantrum with tinny, ringing tones, while the sound waves, as if wanting to escape their creator, crowded to the walls, to be absorbed by them. The fate of the sound waves made it clear: here's how it is: you can't get out, you will be swallowed. The only one who could hear the eruption felt how sweat formed semicircles under his armpits, felt the drops trickled down his back slowly, noticeably, down his spine, until they were absorbed by the fabric of the pants and the shirt.

"This impertinent arrogant asshole! A nigger! What does the nigger want? He doesn't have a say. He will never have a say in anything."

The only one who could hear the outbreak knew that the tantrum would end abruptly any time. He waited for this end hoping this would not be the end of the one who the upset was about.

Two minutes and a considerable number of foul exclamations later, the time had come and the now incoming atmosphere in the upscale penthouse office seemed to make the air conditioning superfluous.

"He doesn't know the rules," he said as calmly as if he had never been upset. "Well ... we will teach them to him. Nobody grows when we don't want them to. We'll crush him, this little kid, this hypocritical asshole ... this black Jesus!" He spat out these last words like a vile insult.

The job of the only person who attended all this was to take the sick thoughts that were spun and implement them.

And he was not comfortable with that.

Nightcap

Restlessly I rolled from one side to the other. The questions about Michael's state of being and the deeper reason for his misfortunes haunted me. Finally I got up and decided to sit down with a glass of wine at the lake. Linda had given me the next day off; it was an ideal opportunity for a bit of alcohol to ease the mind.

Quietly, I went to the kitchen, looked in the wine cabinet for an open bottle and lucked out. A dark red one gleamed at me. I grabbed a glass, poured generously and went through the kitchen terrace door outside, towards the water's edge.

Jason was back there with one of his guards. I waved to reassure them and kept walking. The night was windy, and I was wearing only a t-shirt and sweats. For a second I considered going back again for a jacket, but I was too lazy. I would drink my glass of wine, stare at the moon, think a bit about things that wouldn't lead to anything and then go back to bed.

Shortly thereafter I arrived at a stone statue of a child, which stood a bit away from the pond. At Neverland, there had been innumerable statues in bronze and granite, I had been told. Neverland. His refuge from this world. How it must have been for him, to lose all of that?

I raised my glass to the moon hidden behind clouds, took a swig and immediately felt much better. The wind was blowing strongly through the trees, rippling the surface of the water and continued changing the formations of the gray-black sky. Tonight the cover of clouds was too thick - the wind could not liberate the moon from them - and after a while I actually shivered in my thin clothes. The glass was still half full, and I decided to sit in a spot sheltered from the wind.

When I got up, I heard mournful, soft singing. Or was it a sob? I paused in my movement.

The voice was unmistakable - it was Michael! He was here! That could only be him! And sure enough - he sat in exactly the arbor that I had chosen for the second location of my nightcap. But then I hesitated to approach him. The man probably wanted his peace and quiet, otherwise he would not be here.

'But you are here, too,' protested my inner voice. 'And you absolutely do not want your peace and quiet!' 'But still', said my good conscience into my other ear: 'someone like him can never have enough peace. Leave him alone and go to bed.'

But, thank God Michael had discovered me. "Hey, Song of God," he called softly. "What are you doing here?"

"Private party," I explained, holding up my glass of wine. "I can't sleep."

"Me neither," he said. "I often can't sleep. Come sit with me."

"Wouldn't you rather be alone?" I asked.

"No," he said quickly. "Absolutely not. Come here."

I sat down beside him and offered him my glass. He shook his head.

"Thank you, I don't like to drink."

I kept silent. He was so untypical in every respect. If he had screwed around, drank, smoked pot, spent his money on big cars instead of saving children's lives, would everyone have been more understanding? Or would he have been easier to control? But as soon as the thought had come, it vanished again.

"Hey applehead," he pulled me out of my pondering thoughts. "Where are your books? Don't you have any with you? Then you could have read something to me."

"Oh, that's too bad," I smiled. "I didn't know that you had such a strong interest in these things."

Then we were both silent. It was so easy to be still with Michael. I can't say what was better: to be still with him or to talk with him. They were equal. He was present in such a high, unusual way. As if he did not belong in this world, as if he was rooted with his heart somewhere entirely different.

But this night he seemed tormented, he looked tired and too exhausted to hide his weariness. And he seemed - not unhappy, no - but inexpressibly sad. So sad that involuntarily the question came to my lips: 'What's wrong?' But I didn't ask it.

He rocked his upper body slightly back and forth. Immersed in a silent melody, he sat with his eyes closed on the bench, in rhythm with himself. I was a bit cold, so I pulled my legs up and folded my arms around them. Startled by this movement, he opened his eyes.

"Did I disturb you?" I asked. "I didn't mean to. Sorry, you were just so nicely immersed in something."

Michael just looked, he said nothing. And he didn't look directly at me, rather a bit past me, almost assessing, and a silent assumption spread through me. Then he leaned back again and stared at the lake.

"You ... you have an enormously quiet aura around you," I said. "Like a black hole, which pulls inward. It's an amazing feeling to sit next to you."

Michael gave me a tentative smile. A few minutes passed.

"Should ... Shouldn't I rather leave you alone after all?" I looked at him uncertainly.

"No, no ...stay, it's okay ... really," he said to my doubtful look. And then I asked him anyway:

"Michael do you need something? Is there something I can do to help?"

He pressed his lips together.

"No ... you can't ... I don't feel so good today ... but there's nothing you can do. Except sit here. Anyway. Thank you."

46

He wrapped his jacket more tightly around his emaciated body.

"Where are you actually from?" he asked.

"Germany," I answered in monosyllables - I was just thinking if I should get him a blanket.

"You Germans are nice and quiet," he said. "I like Germany. People aren't as hyperactive there."

I laughed: "That may be true ... but unfortunately more and more nonsense is sloshing across the ocean towards us."

Michael giggled. "And why are you here in the States then of all places?" he asked.

"Good question. I've never been here. I just wanted to see it ... this land of supposedly unlimited opportunities."

His expression changed, as if I had reminded him of something unpleasant, and as if wanting to distract from that he asked,

"Why do you read these books? How did you get into that?"

"Oh," I said. "That's a long story...at some point you start looking for answers that you can't find anywhere else. The Eastern theme draws me in."

"Do you meditate?"

"I do, yes."

"Why?"

"To get in touch with the essence that makes me who I am." I replied. "To feel this inner happiness ... to be able to anchor myself there and ... in the end, to be free... When I meditate I get an idea of who we really are ... and sometimes what happens during meditation is so beautiful that I wish I could stay in that state forever. And this breath of an idea gives me hope that there is more than what we see ... isn't that what your Tagore writes about, too? *'The time that my journey takes is long and the way of it is long. I came out on the chariot of the first gleam of light...'*"

"Wow," he said with his voice so low and gentle. "Last time you didn't even know about Tagore."

"That's true," I said. "But your verse was so touching that I bought the Gitanjali. She is really wonderful."

"Which religion do you belong to?" he asked.

"None, per se. I am Catholic and I think the basic ideas of Christianity are beautiful. But I don't like what the churches turn it into, and I don't want to believe in a vengeful God who sits up there in heaven, counting my sins and explaining every minute of my life that 'I am not worthy for You to come under my roof' ...really.... nah ... that's not for me."

Michael giggled and sat up. "And what do you believe in then?"

"In the opposite. That everyone is made of God. The sages explain that God exploded and the one became many. The Big Bang, if you will. He has, so to speak, manifested in the form of diversity. And since he is the source, everything must be made of him: universes, galaxies, the earth, plants, animals, people, just everything that exists. And that is what I try to live: to see God in everyone. And in all things."

I faltered and fell silent. Michael had - reluctantly? - moved. His dark eyes looked at me with an expression that I could not interpret. There was hardly any light out here anyway, but his look was so dark, so deep, and I could not read him. This rarely happens to me, and it made me feel insecure.

"Michael," I apologized. "I don't like talking about these things because ... because... it's just my opinion that no one has to share with me..."

But Michael seemed to be stirred up by my words. Forcefully he said:

"I believe in God ... oh, how I believe in him ... but ... there are ... bad people, there are people who enjoy hurting others, people who would do anything for money ... I know Jesus said 'love your enemies' ... but it's ... it ... seems ... a ... difficult practice..."

"It is," I said softly, and all the nasty things that had happened to him came to mind. "But I think there must be a reason that you meet the people that you meet ... and that they do what they do ... I mean..."

"What sense would that make?" he asked, roused. "Why can't we just live in peace, why can't people just leave one another alone...?"

"Don't know, maybe they're here so that we understand something...?" I answered, feeling silly, because it sounded so cliché.

With a toneless voice he asked: "What? How to best deal with beatings?"

"No! Maybe figure out why you are getting them," I replied and looked at him in astonishment. There was hardly anything left of the tranquility that I had so far been seeing. He controlled himself visibly. And that control and the cool wind made him tremble. He shivered. He was trembling like a little child, and I would have really liked to put a blanket around his bony shoulders.

The black eyes looked at me. Oh my God, were they dark! So huge in that pale face! My mothering instinct made a mighty leap - he must have seen it in my eyes and backed away a few inches with his upper body. And then he leaned forward again. I felt his desire to communicate and then ... there was fear again. And it was fear that ultimately took the upper hand. He remained silent.

Distraught, I leaned my back on the bench. His charisma was so ambivalent. There was something about him that I had sensed with masters during my travels, something elevated, supreme, bright, but aside from that there was also this endless pain, this torture, a palpable yearning for another world. Yes, that's how he felt that night: like someone waiting to come home, waiting for his deliverance from this planet.

I didn't know what to say. I didn't want to ask him about all these horrible experiences ... or did he need just that? Frantically, my brain rattled through possible ways to extend the conversation, which all sounded pointless and inappropriate. Finally I heard him inhale deeply - and exhale. Then he asked: "Does that mean you think I deserve them ... the beatings?"

"Oh God, no!" I gasped, "Absolutely not! Especially not you! I mean ... that's the big question that I ask myself! Why you? Why not some idiot who mistreats his children and is an asshole? Why of all people did *you* have to experience something like that? I just don't understand it ... but I want to understand it...!"

"Because perhaps I have skeletons in the closet after all?" He turned his face toward me and for the first time the pain and sadness jumped out without being filtered. And his eyes ... oh my God...his eyes ... they were inconceivable in their expression.

"No," I whispered. "Because you're such a fine person. But that is precisely why there must be a purpose. Some kind of purpose!"

"Maybe it's a test," Michael said calmly.

"For what? What exactly is supposed to be tested?"

"My faith in God. How strong it is. If I am able to believe in him in difficult times, too."

"I don't know," I sighed. "Frankly I believe a God who thinks that is a real pain."

A small jolt went through his body. Michael looked at me curiously from the side. His lips curved upward subtly.

"It's small-minded and petty," I continued. "I can't make friends with a God who says: now my friend, now I'm going to test your love for me and give you a good old torturing. Let's see if you're worthy... no... I don't want to believe that. It's always said that He loves unconditionally. So what's it going to be? Rather, I believe that God wants our happiness, and our happiness alone ... and all the drama around it is our own invention."

"Our own invention? What do you mean?"

"I mean that ultimately we plopped onto this earth so we could see just that: that we make a drama out of our lives. Our job is eternal bliss; everything else is a waste. But we constantly invent some kind of story so that we don't have to recognize the simplicity of that."

"You mean ... the famous ego?"

"Yes, the mind, the ego ... all of these ghosts that we called upon ... that make us believe that we need this and that and distract us from what is essential ... that make us believe that everything around us is crap and so that's why we can't be happy ...Man, we are so dumb, huh?"

I giggled and nudged him. Michael was so destined to horse around and somehow his childlike aura infected me. But he only laughed half-heartedly. Recognizably, he was trying to apply everything that had been said to his situation.

"But there are ... people who think completely differently, that ... begrudge your happiness..."

"That's just it," I said indifferently. "That's just one of those self-invented dramas. I am not saying that those kind of people don't exist, but my experience is that they are only there because we are off somehow... and that they disappear really quickly once you have recognized and figured out the reason for their appearance."

"Disappear?" Huge eyes were looking at me.

"Yes ... poof - as if by magic they're gone!" I took a sip from the wine glass and automatically handed it over to Michael. To my surprise, he took it and sipped.

"How ... explain the part with the disappearing again," he prodded. The subject seemed to be of burning interest to him.

"Well, the principle is simple. A problem comes up ... in different colors again and again... then I try to figure out what the reason is. What it wants to tell me. Because it's something, that stands in the way of my happiness. Because somebody out there is showing me something that I haven't yet solved internally. That is the question of meaning ... an unhealthy pattern that is usually based on a mindset that is invisible to you, one that you don't know about, but is uncovered by that situation or person... the 'problem' is there so you can recognize it. And solve it. It's a process."

"Have you... done this often?"

I laughed. "All the time! I mean one's whole life is a challenge! But it gets easier with time, less complicated ... the more you unravel."

He nodded vigorously and thoughtfully. Suddenly it occurred to me that his life had become more complicated rather than less. For a long time he didn't say anything. Sat next to me with mixed emotions. I felt how great his fear was to open up. How often might he have done that before and fallen flat on his face? At the same time I felt his urgent need to talk and I didn't know what I could do to convince him that I would not abuse his trust. The trouble was that I only had an outline of his life - in the short time it had been impossible to get into the details. I had no idea, not a nano-fraction of a clue, what problems he was wrestling with that night and how great his dilemma was. But what came across to me was pure agony, which I sought to ease. As gently as I could, I said:

"You are very courageous, that you have chosen this life, believe me."

He turned away. His arms lay folded on his knees, he had clenched his hands together and rubbed his chin with his knuckles vigorously.

"Chose..." he muttered. "Would I have chosen this life? If I could have? Maybe I don't want it anymore, not like this, not this ... I endure it for the sake of the kids ... for my children ... and the children of the world ... and if you really want to know ... for me so far everything was a test, that was the only thought that kept me going. I bear it for all of those who haven't lost their magic ... for all those who believe in love and ... "

"... Who love you," I quietly completed the sentence.

"Love me..." He repeated, and for the first time I heard bitterness in his voice.

"Michael," I began, wanting to give him comfort, but he interrupted me:

"Love me ... do people love me? They despise me. They avoid me." He spat out the words like a disgusting lump of slime.

Taken aback, I looked at him. Had these experiences really robbed him of all his faith in himself? I mean, it would have been hell for any one of us, but for someone like him who was so sensitive, and in light of the fact that he lived a life in a Truman Show, the effect must have been multiplied hundredfold.

"Millions of people love you," I protested. "Your kids love you. Everyone who really knows you loves you. Your fans ... I don't know, Michael, to me you are one of the most loved people in the world. Are you the fish now that is thirsty? You of all people? Especially since love just shines out of you?"

His virtually black eyes rested on me. His big hand brushed pensively over his thin leg. "You know, Chirelle," he said softly. "I love my fans. I am deeply grateful to them. I always try to live the love, no matter how bad a shape I'm in ... I ... no matter how people treat me, regardless of what they write about me..." He trailed off.

"People," he began again, "are always ready to make something bad out of something good. They are..." and he used the word, which he had said in several interviews already, "...ignorant." It sounded like, 'Lord, forgive them ... for they know not what they do.'

Scenes of the aforementioned interviews flashed through my mind. Michael had never been verbally abusive, no matter how aggressively the journalists had attacked him. He even remained polite to the police who must have tormented him with glee when they put him in jail; no aggression, nothing - even though it was clear that he was miserable. He even refrained to say negative things about those who had treated him so badly, had made his life hell. I remembered how he had mentioned in an interview that he was trying to imitate Jesus, wanted to be as good as Jesus and to give like Jesus. I just hoped that he hadn't unconsciously decided to suffer like Jesus, too. But right now he was doing just that: he was suffering.

I don't know what he was thinking in this moment, but his pain shot up like a fountain and I jumped, startled.

Tense, he covered his eyes with his hands, thrown back to tormenting memories, and tried to bite back the rising tears. I wanted to put my arms around him, but we were just meeting for the second time. How would he react to such a touch?

Then I didn't care. I moved a little closer and carefully put my arm around his skinny body. Michael was soft, oh God, how soft he was, as snugly as a baby! A baby that needs to be protected...and whom I wanted to protect. My maternal instincts awakened, and I pressed him gently to me. For a moment he yielded to the touch, for a precious moment he allowed himself to be held, and I sensed that this was unusual for him. That he was used to being strong. After a short while, he pulled away and wiped his eyes.

"I'm sorry," he said.

"For what?" I asked quietly. "The touch? I hope it's not what you regret."

"No," he answered and smiled, slightly reserved. I was silent.

"It's always so quiet at night." he said then. "That's when inspirations fall from the sky like rain. You only have to listen to the stars and the wind and..."

He fell silent again, and I snuck a look at him. He had closed his eyes and seemed to be experiencing something beautiful. Perhaps the melody for a new song, delivered on frequencies that only he could perceive because a part of him was so open and ready to receive these messages. From one second to the other, he had dropped back to his bright side and remained there. It was a dream to be immersed there with him.

Silently we sat on our bench until dawn broke. Quietly, I took the wineglass that was still not empty.

"I think I'm going to go now. Thanks for your company, Michael ... I..."

"Wait, applehead," he said, "I'll come with you." and he stood up, too. Together we strolled back to the house. Linda had prepared me for his habit of addressing people with 'applehead'.

"Tell me, what are you actually doing here?" he asked me suddenly and stopped. "You can't have been here for long. Did Linda hire you?"

"Yes, she picked me up at the supermarket," I smiled. "Linda made it abundantly clear to me that the wholesome nutrition of the Jackson children is more important than a trip through the USA, and so I'm here for the time being."

"Oh, so we have you to thank for all these delicacies?" he grinned. "I love your muesli muffins! The ones with the nuts and raisins!"

"Don't tell me you eat them? I mean really eat them, or do you just pick up the crumbs that your children leave on the plate?"

He grinned in his unique way: "I swear, I once devoured an entire one. All by myself! Ate it all up!"

"Wow," I said, shocked. "A whole muffin? How did your belly look like? Muffin-shaped? Were you still able to close your pants? I mean, surely the muffin form must have been visible through your belly right?"

Michael burst out laughing, and it sounded so relaxed and at ease and coming from the heart, as if there had never been anything painful in his life.

All of a sudden he was a high-spirited, cheerful child, in the mood to be cuddled, full of enthusiasm, who saw life as an exciting adventure. When Michael laughed in this way, when his suffering could no longer be felt, he had the energy of an angel.

"Why don't you make pizza muffins?" he suggested. "Or some ... with Kentucky fried chicken inside and ketchup ... or with…"

"Wait a minute, are you serious?" I looked at him dumbfounded. "I thought you were a vegetarian!"

"Sometimes," he said cheerfully. "Sometimes I also eat vegetables ... really vegetarian. But there's nothing like a hot pizza ... and fast food. I love fast food!" He laughed at my expression until I giggled along and shook my head in disbelief.

"Thanks for the time together, Michael," I said warmly. "It's really beautiful to talk to you. And to be silent."

He nodded and said goodbye. "Good night, German granola girl," he gurgled. And I let out a "Good night, American muffin mauler," which drew out another giggle.

Elated I turned around and headed to my room.

"Hey, Chi!" He called after me and took a few steps towards me. At a respectable distance, he stopped. A shy man, struggling for words. And with this so infinite silence around him.

"I would like to know more about your books," he said finally. "…and about your views ... if you're not too tired in the evening ... we could talk ... philosophize ... about what you said ..."

"Oh yes!" I said enthusiastically. "That's a great idea!"

He wanted to say more, but the words did not cross his lips. The pause grew and he took a small step back. Did he feel awkward? Embarrassed? If that was it, I did not want to let him go feeling like that.

"You know what," I said enthusiastically. "As of tomorrow I'll be your Scheherazade! We'll play Arabian Nights! Every evening, a story by the fire ... that's going to be great!"

Michael smiled. "Arabian Nights," he repeated and his eyes began to glow. I could literally feel how he was thinking about a stage show or a song.

"Yes," he said. "I look forward to it. See you tomorrow evening."

Then he left. Singing softly, snapping his fingers.

"*Arabian nights ... Arabian nights ...* " I heard him trill. "*... Thousand and one nights ... the one and only night with you ... can you rescue me ... can you free me ... with your voice. ... with your wisdom ... with your myths… Arabian nights...*"

A song that the wind in the trees had whispered to him.

As mentioned before, I had the next day off. My emotions were on a roller coaster. Michael aroused such deep, unusual emotions in me that I had a hard time sorting them out. At the moment, all possible impressions were coursing around in my head: the very conflicting reports about his person, the bitingly sardonic tabloids, and my personal time with him. I instinctively knew that it was better to let it settle before ... well, before what...? Before I formed a judgment? I didn't want to judge. Of course he was a mystery, so of course this is why you wanted to uncover his secret. Like so many before and after me. And then? Would we have been satisfied once we had finally forced him into one of our many, well-defined boxes? Did he appear so mysterious because he was outside of all norms? Because you couldn't classify him? Because he was from a dimension that we couldn't comprehend?

Hadn't all of these people, who hadn't fit into our pre-made grid been turned into weirdos? Hadn't we always fought the otherness, we, the humans, Homo sapiens, who were further removed from matters such as wisdom and tolerance than a monkey who at least lived in harmony with itself and nature?

I didn't know. I also did not understand, why I kept compulsively buying more books about him from people who claimed to know all about him. But his secret attracted me. Not the question of whether he was a genius or a freak. Not the question of whether he was a pedophile or not. I was absolutely convinced that neither was Michael crazy nor had he committed a crime. And that he was an artistic genius was without question. No, it was the mystery of his being and his destiny that attracted me. The mystery of how so many bad things could happen to someone who was such a fundamentally loving being. There had to be an answer. For him. And for me.

06/21/2009, 2:30 am

I need to talk to them. This is my only chance. Have to tell them how things are going for me. I have a plan. I don't know if it's good. If it will be useful. If it's going to help.
I gotta get out, gotta get out, gotta get out, out, out! Somehow! Do I have to? Do I want to? I don't know if I want to. So many times I thought that things will get better. I'm not Wacko Jacko. My name is Michael. *I am a person with dignity. I want to be loved, just like any other person in this world. All I want is love. And everything I give is love. They give me no love. All those people out there who talk about me and judge but don't know me. But all I can give is still only love. I can't help it. There's something in me that says: love them. That's the best response that you can give.*

Research

By late afternoon I was back at home and put the books in a shelf of my closet. Then I went into the kitchen and prepared some dateballs that I arranged on a bowl and put in the refrigerator.

I had time. And no idea what Michael understood 'evening' to be. When did it begin? Probably late - as he would want to put his kids to bed for sure.

Undecided, I stood at the window and made up my mind to bring some sweets to Chris, who was on duty today. So I packed a few things into a basket, brewed a pot of coffee and made my way to security.

"Hi Chris," I greeted him. "Feel like coffee and a couple of little sins?"

Chris laughed. "Anytime," he said. "And for some good company even more so. The night watches draw out."

I unpacked my goodies and poured us some coffee. It was still light out and we sat in the small cubby so that Chris could simultaneously watch the monitors that hung at eye level on the wall. Below was a simple desk, actually more of a board, on which several different colored phones and two computers stood, along with tons of paper and personal paraphernalia. On the walls Chris had pinned drawings by his and Michael's children.

We had a lively conversation about his family, about life here compared to mine in Germany. And at some point the conversation turned inevitably to Michael. Chris worked for him for a long time already, and was employed by him in 2003 when his legendary ranch was raided for the second time by cops.

"Back then," he said, referring to the period before 2003, "there were times when he was happy. The ranch alone! You should have seen it! This place isn't even a cheap copy of it - at Neverland, that's where he was at home ...that was his world ... that's where he was comfortable and there was a time when he was happy for the most part. Not always, who is - the press alone made sure of that. But ... when the kids came ... he was so ... so embedded in his little family ... I always thought, 'man, now he has found peace at last'. We were all so happy for him! You should have seen him! He was crazy about little Prince. He had his crib in his room and sang constantly. And when he held the baby in his arms ... then his face shone, it ... shone ... you've never seen anything like it ... he was so ...man!"

Chris bit his lip and stared at one of the monitors.

"Well," he continued, "but those bastards begrudged him even that. Even that ... little bit of happiness."

He was silent, lost in thought again. Then he told the monitor: "I've got my own ideas ... my own theory ... you see so much with time ... I ... never had the courage to talk to Michael about it ... but ... sometimes ... when I see him so ... so broken ... and if I compare that with before..." He gritted his teeth.

"Was that really so different?" I asked, astonished. "I mean, he is so loving, he walks through the house and all the time you hear 'I love you, Dad,' and 'I love you, Paris'... all the time ... was it really that different?"

"Yes," Chris said, looking at me glumly. "Yes. There's a big difference. He laughed differently. He moved differently. I don't know." Chris wrinkled his brow and took a sip of coffee. "And I hope he'll make it," he muttered, barely audible. "I hope so much that he'll make it. That he sees through everything in time ... that he comes out of this..."

"What do you mean ... see through all this?" I asked, confused.

But Chris did not say any more.

For a while we sat silently and stared at the monitors. Chris nervously stroked his bald head. We were not allowed to talk about Michael. It had happened too many times that these conversations had been recorded, going to the customary channels with corresponding distortion. That seemed to come to Chris' mind now, and he felt uncomfortable.

"Chirelle..." he began.

"Hey, Chris," I said quickly. "Take it easy. Look here ... " I spread out my arms. "... no microphone, no tape recorder!"

Chris smiled at me slightly tortuous and grateful. It almost appeared as if he wanted to add something, but then the fact that I was a German, unfamiliar tourist, and he shouldn't trust me outweighed his desire to speak. He, like his employer, couldn't trust anyone.

His retreat was obvious, but after everything that I had been through myself, I could not blame him. Michael had already been screwed by people, who had spent years working for him and eventually had been unable to resist the temptation of money. I had heard that there were recruiting agencies that had contracts with the press, and that employees were bribed with large sums of money to recommend staff and infiltrate them, such as contract handymen who used repairs to install mini-cameras in the most unlikely places: some had even been found on Michael's toilet.

How could Michael live with something like that? He always had to assume a camera was pointed at him. He must feel watched constantly. Before long, I understood why I was a bargain for Linda. And yet even those who had good intentions in the beginning could pose a threat. Linda had told me she couldn't even remember how many times she had been offered bribes, with ever-increasing sums, the longer she was with Michael. He could never be sure. People were people. Despite years of loyalty, any minor dispute, a promising offer at the right time, could change everything. That fact alone would make me sick, I thought. It's so easy to say that celebrities live in a fishbowl, but nobody stops to think about what that really means.

Absent-minded, Chris drank his coffee and eyed the choice snacks on the plate I brought.

"No more dateballs," he said, disappointed. I grinned. He had it in for these things.

"There are some more in the fridge," I revealed. Chris looked at me with the expression of a child. His thick lips formed a silent "Oh" and "Please, please, get some more!" while he wrung his fleshy hands.

I snorted out loud. "My goodness, who can resist this look?" I grinned and stood up. "What do I get in return? I'll make some more coffee, while I'm at it."

Chuckling, I reached for the pot, went back into the kitchen and put on more coffee. While I waited, I heard Michael's agitated voice from the dining room.

"That ... I didn't approve that! I didn't arrange that! I... " He quieted, listening into the receiver.

"No!!" he exclaimed, "I'm afraid of him. He controls my life, he is taking over everything ... he cuts me off from my relationships ... I don't know ... anything anymore ... I can't even access my bank accounts...! There's a method... it ..."

He began to sob. His voice was resigned, fearful and it about strangled my chest.

"Call me if there's a chance," said Michael, and hung up.

When I came back to Chris and set the bowl on the table, he immediately pounced on the treats and turned his eyes upward with relish. "These things are amazing," he said, munching and flushing the mouthful down with a swig of coffee. "This is so divine ... mmhhh ... and just look ... I really have something for you...!" he sputtered with full cheeks, "waitasec!"

He waded through the chaos on his desk until he found a DVD that he fed in the computer. My head full of thoughts, I looked at the screen:

The Jackson family was sitting outside in the sun on blankets on the shore of a large lake. Grace was holding Blanket, who had probably fallen asleep snuggling in her arms. His long black hair fell down to the side. Paris laid next to them and read something to Grace, while Michael and Prince, shrieking loudly, were engaged in a water fight with oversized pump guns. They laughed and Michael seemed full of high spirits and energized. Giggling together with his oldest, he pulled something out from under a bush. With a roar Prince and he flung on to Paris and Grace and threw water balloons at them. Loud shrieks erupted.

Grace protected Blanket with her body, Paris complained loudly that her book had become wet and immediately delivered a counter-attack. Michael continued running around like a goblin and laughingly smacked water bombs on the ground.

In the end Grace and the kids thoroughly retorted and the whole family engaged in a heated water balloon battle. The water was dripping down on them, the hair stuck to their heads, everyone was soaking wet and rolling on the ground with laughter and excitement - foremost Michael. He was so exuberant - I would never have expected that of him. He squealed and whooped with joy, jumped and raved and infected everyone with his ebullient mood. When the ammunition was expended, Michael took this youngest in his arms and tickled him. Blanket squealed his irresistible baby laugh and kicked his little feet. Michael pressed him tenderly to his chest and Blanket put his tiny arms around him. I could almost feel the soft child's arms on Michael's skin. This round baby cheeks, nestling in the warmth of the neck, that wonderful scent that emanates from babies and small children ... and Michael, you could see that, enjoyed it to the fullest. With his eyes closed, he danced gentle steps with the little one on the lawn. He conveyed the image of such intimacy, such joy, such a deep love for his children that tears sprang to my eyes.

"Damn, I've never seen the man as happy as that since," Chris said, as he removed the DVD from the tray. "Oh, those bastards...those bastards...!" His voice sounded grating and then he added what at the time I mistakenly thought referred to the press. "If they would finally just leave him alone."

With Michael's high-spirited laughter, Chris' ambiguous messages, and the memory of the phone call, I went back to my room. Finally, I flipped open my laptop and looked at my files of saved reports and interviews. Obsessively, I read the same old stereotypical reports. They always had the same message: Jackson had lost it. He couldn't cope with his success. He couldn't handle his childhood or his life or the world. His mental state - and all reports hinted at that - was unstable. And it was also subtly hinted that this could develop into a dangerous paranoia, with consequences that could not be foreseen. That seemed odd to me because these were reports from 15 years ago. Before any trial.

But even now, after these disastrous experiences, I hadn't discovered a single sign of paranoia in him.

Finally, I logged into a playlist of the mega-interview with Oprah Winfrey in 1992 - the first TV interview that Michael had given in 14 years, whose scenes I often went back to so I could look at his face more closely. Or to listen to some of his answers again. For almost the entire time he appeared attentive and composed, but seemed alive and passionate for only certain questions. Again this contradiction: on the one hand he had caution towards the talk show host, but on the other hand he wanted to communicate. It was a distancing game. He had hoped for understanding in this interview, wanted to present his point of view. But Oprah did not let that happen. What I noticed was that she consistently interrupted him every time he asked the audience not to believe what was written in the tabloids. He started this theme so many times - and every time she cut him off immediately with an unrelated question. Why had she prevented it?

Then his revelation that he was sad. The request in this pronouncement was so strong: 'Please love me.' The typical response of a career-oriented American awaited him: but you had five number-one hits in a row! Why are you sad? As if success and fame could substitute for compassion and warmth. That was the moment when he pulled back completely. He had tried to share himself, and she had quashed it. What would have happened, had she engaged?

Michael remained polite, and the interview shallow and superficial. He felt misunderstood. And not only that: he felt unloved.

Startled, I looked at the clock after the last section. It was ten o' clock in the evening! I registered with relief that Michael was still with the children, made coffee in the kitchen, sat down with my books at the big, cozy bar and waited.

XX / 1983, one step away

"He is sick. That makes things really easy. He'll go to the hospital. Again and again. And anyway – we're in Hollywood. Enough people here who would do anything for money. And have no conscience. Ultimately, it's always his responsibility."

King Schariyar

"Hey, Scheherazade," he said, raising his hand. The fingers twitched as if they wanted to form his peace sign. How many millions of times had he done this before? He smiled vaguely and was wearing sunglasses, even though it was night.

"Hey, King Schariyar," I replied. "Ready for the first reading?"

"Yes," he smiled in his reserved way. "I'm ready."

I slid off my stool. "Would you like to have some tea?"

"Tea?" he asked, puzzled. "Sure ... why not? Let's have tea. Thanks."

I put cups and a teapot on the counter and turned on the kettle.

"Let me help you," he said, fetching a tray. And to my surprised look: "I love housework. It calms me down. I love vacuuming most."

"Well incredible," I said confused. "Can I borrow you? I mean, for my carpets in Germany?"

Michael laughed in a restrained way as he put everything on the tray.

"Um ... not here," he said, motioning with his head toward the door. "Best to meet in the living room."

He was cold - he actually had the fireplace going and sat in his rocking chair close to the fire. Today he'd had meetings in the city and was dressed in one of his uniform-like outfits. His big feet were sticking in black ankle boots and he was still wearing the sunglasses. I could only imagine that his eyes were following me as I poured the tea, and then sat down on the fluffy carpet in front of him.

"Oh, no," he protested immediately with his soft voice. "Don't! I'll get a chair for you!"

"If you don't mind - I feel more comfortable here," I said.

Michael hesitated. But then he stayed seated.

"Okay, what are your plans?" I asked. "Should I really read to you? Shall we just have a go at it?"

Michael smiled involuntarily. "Have a go at it ... sounds good!"

Touched, I noticed that these few words already awakened the playful side in him. I took one of the books.

"Oh, I know what we'll do!" I cried. "We'll let chance decide! I'll flip through the book with my thumb and you put your finger in between somewhere."

No sooner said than done. With vigor I let the pages slide beneath my thumb. Michael stretched out one of his long fingers and slowed the momentum of the pages. I settled back again, opening the book at the place he had chosen for the evening. He leaned back and the fire was reflected in the dark lenses of his glasses - how I would have loved to see his eyes. But my eye fell back to the page and I read the first sentence:

"Your being on this planet is a choice you have made."[2]

Although I didn't look up, I felt an almost imperceptible twitch travel through Michael's body. It was spooky – wasn't this the topic that we had talked about last time?

"Courage is the very membrane that shields your heart. Live your life courageously, knowing that whatever you are faced with is not stronger than you are. Your problem is not greater than you, nor is it smaller. You look at your problem as your equal. Everything, that happens in your life is for your own upliftment."

I didn't feel the need to read on. Not a single movement came from the rocking chair. Michael sat still as a doll, frozen in space.

Now the silence was no longer peaceful - it was tense on both our parts, full of unspoken questions and suppressed feelings. Almost encouragingly, the fire crackled in the great fireplace and sent warm light into the room. Gently I put the book down and took one of the big pillows that were scattered all over the floor, rested my head on it and stared at the ceiling. The shadows of the flames flickered above me, painting restless, ever-changing patterns on the white. My voice was raspy, as I said to the ceiling:

"When I read this sentence for the first time, it was like a slap in the face, like a memory of something that I instinctively didn't want to be reminded of."

"Which sentence do you mean?" Michael asked tonelessly.

"That the existence on this planet was my decision," I replied. At times I felt so at odds with this world that I didn't want to be here. I didn't want anything to do with people; I thought they were exhausting. I didn't seem to know the rules ... felt marginalized. Misunderstood. Unloved. I just thought I didn't belong here."

A log in the fireplace crackled loudly, and sparks flew high, then silently reunited with the fire, as if they had never been separated. Michael was still, but it was an expressive silence. I turned to the flames and directed my words to them:

"I seemed be doing everything wrong. Somehow I had no idea how to behave in this world, everything I did was somehow off. I was too loud or too quiet, compliant or demanding ... my behavior never seemed to be appropriate. Everyone else was always so ... confident ... whereas I felt weird and strange. It was horrible. I felt that I didn't belong to this world and its people."

I looked at Michael. Watched as he took his sunglasses off. Saw his eyes so dark, his face, which was so beautiful with his expression.

"I had that feeling a lot, too," he said softly. "So many times. I still have it today."

Suddenly he stood up and turned off the overhead light in the room. The only light was from the warm glow of the fire. To my immense surprise, he took off his boots, fetched a pillow for himself, too, and settled down on the floor, a bit more than three feet away from me.

Searchingly, the made-up eyes looked at me, an expectant smile on his face, and I was amazed at how quickly he was able to switch from his initially distanced behavior to a childlike openness. Even more than that: now he looked like an inquisitive boy and that's how he sat on the floor: like a child who looks forward to a riddle ... to the solution to an exciting mystery. This change was so abrupt and the layers had fallen so spontaneously and without thought, that I instantly realized how easily he could be exploited. He was still a child who just wanted to play and have friends, who wanted to entrust himself to other people without reservation. It was touching to see him sitting on the carpet like that, with these glowing eyes. A child who looks you in the eye with trust, utterly convinced that you won't harm him and will protect him from all evil.

I was completely overwhelmed by this innocence. It couldn't be called anything else. It seemed as if there were no shades between the distrustful, beaten-down man and the open child. He could only choose one side or the other.

My heart swelled in the need to hold him in my arms, to stroke his cheeks, to do all the things, which he might have longed for as a child and still did.

"How do you feel about that today?" he asked me. "Do you still believe that you've landed here by mistake?"

"No," I replied, "...although it wasn't easy for me. When you are unhappy, the first impulse is probably to escape - in thoughts, actions, addictions - we have a lot of surrogates in this world, don't we? Mental escape had always been my impulse. But this sentence... struck me ... and I realized for the first time that I was running away from my challenges. To be honest: at that time I went from one disaster to another ... and eventually I realized that I was being confronted with the same things over and over again - in different packages - and I realized that this would pursue me until I had solved it ... and that I'm here on earth *in order* to solve all of this. Oh, I was so sick of it! I wanted to be rid of it!"

"Yes, but rid of what?" Michael asked, no longer holding back as he had before. "And more importantly: how can you solve something like that?"

"To explain that I would have to reach way back into my belief system," I joked. "And then I doubt you'll still think I'm all there."

Michael giggled, relieved, I thought. "As far as the whacko image goes, I'm way ahead of you," he kidded.

I laughed and sat up. "So, at the risk that our first evening chat at the fireplace is the last and you'll have my head chopped off like King Schariyar did with all the women who couldn't entertain him properly..."

"You're Scheherazade," Michael said, amused. "The others have already lost their heads before you!"

"Oh, very reassuring! Do you have a cabinet like the one King Henry VIII had in the basement?"

"A cabinet? What do you mean?" he asked astonished.

"Didn't you know? King Henry XIV who was married six times, who's said to have had innumerable liaisons, had the wives decapitated that he didn't like any more, two of them for sure. Evil rumors were afloat saying he had a cabinet in his cellar where he stored their mummified heads... which is probably not true, but..."

I saw a flash in Michael's eyes and realized that he thought that was a good idea for a music video. After all, he was into horror stories and masquerades, and what he turned them into with his dance was fantastic.

"Do you want to write it down?" I asked him.

"No, I'll remember," he answered lightly, and neither of us realized that we had just communicated telepathically.

"So, tell me, what do you want to solve here? What's the meaning? Do you know why you're here? Do you feel there is a particular task for you?"

He asked these questions with such a passion that it was clear: these were his questions. The ones that he wanted to know and understand so badly.

"What's your explanation for all these things?" I asked him.

"No!! You first, you first," he cried, "chickening out is no fair! No fair! No fair!"

He started beat boxing, almost unintentionally, triggered by the rhythm of the words. His head moved in the "No fair, no fair" rhythm, he sang it like a nursery rhyme, and effortlessly words, rhythm and melody fused into something new in his brain. He was pure creativity. It was fascinating to watch. As I started to giggle, he stopped and asked:

"What's so funny? Does this sound weird?"

"No!! Just the opposite! Just the last part ... as if someone is forever burping!"

Michael laughed. "I'll have to tell my children about that," he gurgled. "Stuff like that always makes them happy!"

"Yeah, lots of carbonated water and go! The Jackson-burp-song!"

Giggling, he sat in front of me, seriously considering if this could turn into something. I burst out laughing again, imagining it.

"Speaking of..." he said. "...this shouldn't turn into the topic of the evening, right?"

"No ... my goodness, what a change! From burping to the meaning of it all," I giggled. "It's not too bad! We're just letting out some air!" and in response to his playfully indignant look ... "Okay, okay... I am starting already...our last topic was ... that each of us is made of God."

"Yes, that's what I believe in, too ... but if that's true, why he is doing all this to me? Why is there so much evil then? And ... why me? Why me? Why are there so many contradictions?"

"Maybe they only appear like that ... where do you see a contradiction?"

"What you said yesterday ... I've never, ever done any harm to anyone deliberately ... only did good ... and yet it seems that evil is triumphing. You just don't stand a chance. At first I thought: these are simply troubles that come with success, people are jealous ...greed, power, money, sex ... these are the things that count to people, and if you don't play that game, you're cut down. Why are those things always stronger than the good? Why does God allow it? I can only explain the whole thing as being a test: to respond with even more love, to give even more, not to walk the same path as these ... others..."

I admired him. Already at this point, already then, when I had not read anything but headlines about his life, didn't have the faintest clue what he had already been through. If it really was supposed to be a test, then he had passed with flying colors. He had never lost his faith in God and he never ceased to love. I'd like to see anyone do better - most would have probably ended in bitterness. And what earned my highest respect: he sought and wanted answers. I smiled because he evoked such a warm and powerful feeling in me, and I silently shook my head.

"What?" he asked.

"You're amazing," I said. "God, Michael, you deserve all the happiness in the world."

Michael looked in the other direction.

"There are those who know to prevent that," he said.

"What does happiness really mean to you?" I asked.

"My children ... my music ... the world...nature, she is so beautiful ... there is a lot that is worth living for. I love to transform what I feel into melodies and lyrics, to make God's thoughts visible to others, to pass that on ... to help the children of this world ... the earth is bleeding ... we have to do something, and I feel called upon to do that. God didn't give me this talent for nothing. He gave it to me so I could move things, make others happy..."

"But what about your happiness?" I asked.

"This is my happiness," he replied in astonishment.

"But you're not happy," I said. "You're everything but happy. You are suffering."

He shot me a look as if to say, is that so surprising?

"I mean, what do you do for your happiness?" I persisted.

He looked at me blankly.

"Michael," I began, hesitant to say the next sentences. Then I looked him in his eyes. "You asked me how I solved my disaster ... and one of many realizations was that I believe that God is really not interested in making us suffer ... as in 'to earn our happiness.' That sounds ... so pedantic ... give me your pain and when you have suffered enough, then you receive happiness? Nope, really, no. I believe in a generous, humorous God. In one who loves me no matter how many mistakes I make. I believe that suffering is the real blasphemy."

Michael was 100 percent present, so open and so ... excited. Yes, he was excited, eager for a solution for himself. He didn't say anything, so I continued:

"You know, at the time when everything went wrong in my life, when the bottom fell out, I thought ... okay Chirelle, that's it. You are completely done, financially, socially ... well ... that was the point at which I began to search for other answers instead of blaming other people and circumstances."

Oddly I felt like laughing because all of a sudden and with total clarity I realized how stupid I had been and how much my ego had tried at that time to gain the upper hand: to be right, to find someone to blame, to make judgments. I was really on the verge of laughing out loud and Michael sat in front of me with an uncomprehending, puzzled look, ready trying to get the joke.

"And then what?" he inquired.

"Jeez, my whole life I was doing this utterly pointless thing. I wanted the problem to be gone."

"That's understandable, if that's what causes the pain and unhappiness," he said.

"Perhaps understandable, but still absolutely nuts," I grinned. "Anything that hurts should go. The person who hurts you has to go. The lack of money has to go. The disasters have to go."

"So," asked Michael. "Were you successful?"

"Of course. But then all the crap came back. Only this time it was just green instead of red ... but the same crap..." I shook my head. "...and ... yes, that's when this book that we have this evening fell in my hands. This exact same spot. Funny, isn't it? And ... when I read that ... I felt as if someone had hit me over the head. And it occurred to me: If it's God who lives in me and in everyone else, then everything that happens to me is God, too. In the beginning, you asked the question: 'Why is God doing this to me?' The question should rather be: 'Why am I doing this to myself?' Why are you doing all this to yourself?"

I heard Michael exhale with a disbelieving sound and he turned to the side staring into the fire. His narrow chest rose and fell. He sat there as if he were set in stone. Alarmed, I watched him. It appeared as if he was afraid. Or as if he had just seen something terrible.

"Michael ... is everything okay?" I asked. "I..."

"Go on," he whispered. "Please."

I breathed deeply, focused on the fire, and said:

"My thought was that if it is true that we have chosen this life, then we have also chosen our challenges and the context in which we are here."

"So it's about a predetermined destiny that we sust... obtain?" Michael asked, turning back to me a little.

"That was my first thought, too. But ... no, that's not what it means to me. To me it means: to have the freedom to live a happy destiny, regardless of the challenges I have chosen. Regardless of the horoscope I was born with... why should fate enslave my soul? If I have a problem, then it shows me some dark place I have inside, one that undermines my happiness, you know what I mean?"

"So it's about finding the reason why all of this happens to us."

"Exactly! The famous example: you smear chewing gum over the signal light for the oil indicator because it has lit up. Even when the signal is gone, you still don't have enough oil in the engine. And then it happens what has to happen: the motor blows up."

Michael winced. He took this all very personally.

"And then..." he swallowed. "...if you can't figure it out, can't do it ..."

"You buy a new car..." I teased. But Michael understood the analogy and his posture, his expression told me that he didn't think his present being would necessarily allow him to achieve his happiness. That shocked me deeply.

"You can do it," I said urgently. "Look what it says here: you get the nuts that you can crack." I looked at him imploringly. And suddenly I became aware of his frailty, and I pushed aside a premonition that was trying to force itself on me because I didn't want to feel it.

"There's not much time," he whispered.

"Perhaps time isn't that relevant." I replied, although I felt uneasy.

"You believe in reincarnation?"

"Absolutely," I replied. "Otherwise, all of this would hardly make any sense. Can our soul be compressed into anything so vulgar as time? What do you think?"

Michael hesitated before he gave me his answer in a broken voice - carefully appraising me.

"I know that this is not my first life," he whispered, as if he was ashamed of his views. "So many times I can feel these old, past lives ... and the longing for them. So many times I dream of a life when I was king ... in such a beautiful country and..." he trailed off, uncertainly.

"Yes," I muttered. "I can feel that within you ... this aura of the ancient kings, this aura of greatness ... and the time when a king was still a king..."

"I see pictures," he said, encouraged, "... about how everything was. How I was. I even had a picture painted of it once. And pictures were given to me ... this time as King ... as ... uh ... " He was embarrassed at first to say it, but then he did anyway: "...as a being of light..." and almost desperate and with a deep longing he broke out: "I want to be in that other world again. A more beautiful one... where we can trust one another, where a friend is a friend, where there is no violence ... and no distrust ..." He lapsed into silence.

The aura of Kings. The radiance of a Being of Light. He had brought that with him to this place. And also his unshakable belief in the power of love and his longing for it. He couldn't help it. And that's why he believed in people ... even trusting the evil uncle again and again because something in him was pointing him in the wrong direction. But what?

We were both lying on our pillows, listening to the fire, and again there was this feeling of absolute connection. Even though he carried so much suffering, it was fantastic to come into resonance with him, because his bright side was open and shone like the Holy Grail. After a while he turned his head to me, questioningly.

"If you're here, there's a reason," I reminded him gently. "It was your choice."

Michael pressed his lips together. It was not hard to see what he thought about his choice.

"Maybe God chooses you for certain things," he said.

"That's the same thing," I replied. "If you come from God, it is His and your decision. I think He and you are one. You're not separated from Him. So you've decided to be here, to search for your soul mates here, be with the people you are with, your parents, siblings …friends, enemies…"

Michael paled, as much as one could tell with his complexion.

"Why should I have chosen such a difficult life?" he asked. "Why such…big enemies? What reason would I have to choose all this shit? Doesn't makes sense, does it?"

"The bigger the shit, the greater the development," I joked. "You've got huge potential there, huh?"

Michael made a noise that was supposed to sound like a giggle, but his face said something else.

"And besides," I continued calmly, "Shit is a really good fertilizer … and it's up to you to finish everything by getting it into your head why you are experiencing this and why you provoked it."

"Provoked? I provoked it? Are you nuts?"

"Why not? You are so well read! And spent time with the best spiritual teachers in the world! I mean: it's true: people often tear down big things, turn, what appears too good into something bad … and when someone has success, there *are* the envious and malicious … but you know also of all the laws of resonance, laws of projection…!"

"Yes, but…" I could hear something like panic in his voice, the impulse to flee. I bit my lip as it erupted violently and suddenly from him:

"I didn't do anything wrong! I didn't do anything bad! I'm innocent!"

Shocked, I sat before him. What kind of eruption was that? I was good! I was good! Why did he emphasize that so much? What was he blaming himself for? I gently put my hand on his bony shoulder. Even more gently I said:

"Michael, you didn't do anything wrong … it's about a pattern in you that brings out your drama. Look at the people who have hurt you from that perspective. Everyone is a villain only for as long as you don't need them anymore, everyone is just playing their role, to help you recognize something."

"A role," Michael repeated flatly. "A role … Do you think that everyone has their defined role on this earth, once he has chosen it? I mean … that sounds pretty frustrating…"

He sank into thought, tried to transfer the last sentences to his situation, and it was noticeable how much he resisted what had been said. Then he looked at me. Seeking help, resigned.

"I once had a conversation with someone about Judas," he said softly. "Judas and his role. Nobody talks about Judas and when they do only with contempt. But he just played a role, too ... and he had to play it..."

"Yes, he played a role..." I hesitated. "...but: did he really have to play it? I think: even Judas had a choice, Judas had free will, just like everyone else - if he even did what he was accused of - but ... I don't know, Michael ... no matter what role you've chosen here, why should you not be allowed to be happy? Who in the hell can stop you?"

"There are several who are preventing that," he said again. "My motto is: be loving to all people. To give love ... to help where I can ... the children ... all these years ... all these years ... and..." His voice broke. Sobbing, he continued. "...no matter what happened, no matter what they did to me ... I am playing my role ... but it's a damn difficult role and I can't imagine that I would have chosen a life like this..."

"Maybe this is all a misunderstanding," I said softly, trying to look him in the eyes without having my brain stutter. "Maybe those that hurt you had to because they wanted to make you aware of something. Once you have understood what it is, these people will disappear ... your problems will disappear ... it's not about suffering and a predetermined fate, but simply seeing that our own happiness is very important, and that we deserve it for every second of our lives... our own happiness ...*your* happiness."

Michael breathed in and out deeply. He stared into the flames, and I could clearly see how he was processing. Very softly and full of fear, he whispered: "And what if it ... if it is... just ... too late?"

A chill ran down my spine. He had said it a second time, it sounded so final, so terminal, so hopeless. I didn't want to see him hopeless, not him, not after he had survived all this crap.

"It's never too late, Michael, I'm convinced of that. Look at these words one more time: you know that your problem isn't stronger than you are. And ... don't forget ... you are alive ... you're alive...!"

"Some problems are hard," Michael murmured and turned his head. "some of them are ... really ... huge ..."

"Michael," I interrupted him. "When awful things happen to you, then there is something in you that provokes these awful things. Stop sending signals!"

Distraught, he looked at me. His mouth opened and closed again. His lips pressed together. He was definitely not pleased with my last statement. And I had so much in my heart that I didn't know what to tell him first. This was not a good sign. I didn't want to run him over, was afraid that I had done so long ago already, and I counted my breaths so that my tongue wouldn't get out of check even more. I had just told Michael that he had awful things in him. The Michael who wanted to be perfect, who wanted to be good, and to him this belief was one of the anchors in this life. He sat on the floor, his hands popped up, ready to run.

"Don't run, Michael," I murmured. "This is important now. Please."

I looked at him. My, God, the eyes this man had! My heart was racing again.

"I won't run away," Michael said and his voice had a high pitch. "So many people have told me again and again that it is strength when you endure things."

Did these beliefs come from a rigid religious upbringing? What other dogmas had Michael gotten down the wrong tube, things which threatened to suffocate him?

"Michael," I said gently. "When I said that it is our highest goal on earth to be happy, you didn't contradict me. But look: this degree of suffering and happiness don't really go together, right? We were not plopped on this earth to suffer. That's crazy! If you encounter problems in the outer spheres of existence, then it means something."

"What," he pressed. "What, damn it!"

"To find out could be the meaning of our 1001 Nights."

My heart was pounding when I said that. Michael sat up and looked at me. Searchingly. Then he took the book in his hand, flipped aimlessly through it again and stopped at the page that we had opened originally. He reread the words softly to himself. They sounded like a song, and I could feel that they inspired him.

"'You look at your problem as your equal'," he quoted almost reluctantly. And then, with a rapid movement towards me, he looked me in the eye, and quickly said:

"I have big problems Chirelle, really ... you can't imagine ... " he trailed off, his face turned to the fire. His chest rose and fell visibly.

"Do they appear too big?" I asked quietly. "The bigger the issue, the more powerful the step that you take. Don't be afraid. You are such a courageous soul. Because what you've chosen here, in this context, of this magnitude, that is to say, with the whole world watching you address your problems is huge. And then you also picked such gifts, such a talent! Wow, what a..."

"I always wanted to make the world a better place," he interrupted quietly. "With my voice, my songs, my lyrics, the dance."

"And you are doing that, Michael," I said warmly. "To how many people have you brought joy! But ultimately that's not what it's all about. It's not about making the world better. That's not the first priority. That can't be your first and utmost task! Your most important priority is you."

Michael looked at me as if I were an alien – no - he would have been thrilled about that, but he obviously wasn't about my words.

"Excuse me?" he asked indignantly. I know that my talent comes from God, that I should use it to do good. If all this is..."

"That's very honorable and speaks very highly of you," I replied quickly. "But that doesn't help you progress. And it doesn't help the world progress either. And on top of that..." abruptly I shut my mouth, a thousand words on my tongue.

"Why not?" Michael was upset and I noticed how he was closing off.

"Because this play on this earth is just about YOU," I cried recklessly. "About your life! The point is for YOU to be happy. And if you were, then look what could happen! Then you wouldn't have all these problems that you have today, they would vanish into thin air, because you would not be giving them a breeding ground anymore! But for that you have to have the courage to look at yourself and at no one else. You have to make yourself happy and no one else! And out of this you can help other people! This is the true way to make the world a better place!"

"But ... but..."

"And," I continued impulsively, "...You would have a much bigger impact here on earth, without all the strength, misunderstandings and suffering you have now! What are you doing to yourself that they are beating up on you so much? What is it about you that give people permission to treat you like that? And with this consistency, for all of these decades! Why?"

Startled, I slapped my hand over my mouth after this outbreak. What am I saying? Did it even make any sense? Michael looked at me with an indefinable expression. Angry? Offended? Indignant? Rejecting? Stunned? Knowing? Confused? A bit of all of that.

"Try to see," I said. "How are you going to solve the world's problems, if you're not willing to solve your own?"

Michael drew a couple of inches away from me. His lips were pressed together and his long fingers plucked away at a thick woolen yarn in the carpet.

"You don't understand me," he said, and it sounded like a slap in the face. "You have no idea."

I bit my lip. Seconds of tense silence followed.

"What word did you want to say back then, when I interrupted you," he asked suddenly.

"Did you interrupt me? When?"

"Yes, when you spoke of my talents. You said, what a...?"

I was silent.

"Come on," said Michael. "I want to hear it."

"No, Michael, I've said too much already today ... and..."

"Chirelle! I want to hear it! Please!"

Jeez, I thought. The king has spoken. He was very authentic in this role. I liked that. It suited him. It felt better than the timid.

"All right," I said, challenging. "I wanted to say: what a temptation."

Michael collapsed on his back and stared at the ceiling.

"A temptation," he repeated aghast. "A temptation! Does that mean it was a mistake to perform, to go on stage? Should I not have expressed my talent? That's how I earned the money that I was able to donate. That money helped a lot of people ... and that's my biggest intent: I want to help children, want to be there for them ... they have no voice ... I feel their pain..."

"Not to live your talent?" I interrupted him. "Are you nuts? That would have been quite simply a crime! No, that's not what it means, Michael. It's great what you're doing, and it is marvelous how you can help the children of this world. But it is a temptation, as long as it prevents you from dealing with your issues. When you sing and dance, you're connected to God - it's so noticeable and makes everything you bring to the stage so unspeakably beautiful. But what if you aren't dancing? When you are not singing? Do you know what I mean?"

Michael said nothing. But he retained eye contact.

"There is something else you didn't say," he declared.

"Really?" I asked, amazed at his memory.

"Yes. You said, when it comes to children and about our planet, which is so dear to me ... you said... On top of that...?"

"Oh God," I giggled and plopped down on the pillow. "I can't tell you that, you'll be completely offended! That's too crude!"

"I won't be offended at all," cried Michael.

"Will too!"

"Will not!"

"Will too!" I cried and threw my pillow at him. Michael caught it and I waited for his famous giggle. There it was, two seconds later, and he threw the pillow back. Oh, what a wonderful guy he was! So easy to pull to the fun side of things! He laughed himself silly because his pillow bomb had hit my teacup and the contents spilled on my foot.

"Crap," I grumbled and took off both socks.

"Come on!" he cried. "The word! And on top of that...?"

"And on top of that it is hypocritical!" I blurted, looking at him almost defiantly.

"Hypocritical!" Michael groaned, honestly shocked. "Are you saying I'm a hypocrite?"

"Michael," I said and sat up. "I've hardly ever met a person who radiates such a deep and genuine love as you do. So ... childlike, so immaculate, so pure ... it's just unbelievable! It feels so great to be with you! Wow! I mean ... it's ... just beautiful! Pure delight! I am so excited about you - I can't even express it ... and I have been in the presence of many extraordinary people..."

Michael relaxed, his shoulders moved slightly downward. Oh, he was so receptive to compliments!

"But at the same time I have never met a sadder person," I continued. "Someone who so obviously carries so much suffering inside."

Although he winced, he still looked at me firmly.

"This is a deep discrepancy, Michael," I said. "A discrepancy that people feel. How can a person who is so unhappy make the world a better place? They don't believe you. They can't believe you, because deep down inside they know that's not possible. Maybe that's one of the misconceptions."

"But ... there are people who don't want me to be happy," Michael whispered. "Out of pure jealousy and greed...believe me, there are just horrible people who want to prevent this, they..."

He was petrified. Blindly, he stared into space, into nowhere. It was hard for me to stay focused. Everyone knew that there were sharks in the music business - and Michael knew them much better than a clueless tourist from a provincial German town. Almost reluctantly, I said what came up in me as if I did not really want to believe it myself:

"If you are looking for a spiritual answer ... there is ultimately only one person that can prevent that. And that's you. Everyone else is just a mirror of your soul. Why are terrible people in your life? Why do you let them get to you? Sorrow attracts sorrow. Look inside and you'll find the solution."

Michael sat in front of me, the big feet in white socks, toes clenched, his whole body on the defensive. An unhappy child.

I leaned forward and this time I stroked out of his white face the strand of hair that hung before his beautiful eyes. He began to tremble, and a tear ran slowly down his cheek. My heart ached at the sight. I didn't dare put my arms around him. What I had said was not what he had wanted to hear. He had hoped for a different message... I knew it, I knew which one, too, but I doubted it would have helped him.

Michael sat in an inner trembling paralysis. Inside the turmoil raged, but his face was expressionless, his lower lip pushed forward. Then he took his sunglasses and put them on slowly.

My heart was in my mouth.

"Do you want to be alone?" I asked with a lump in my throat.

Michael nodded.

Dejected, I got up and left.

***

He paced. Part of his bedroom suite was over my room. And so I heard him pace. Incessantly. Clack, clack, clack ... the heels of his boots. Sometimes he seemed to stomp or kick something out of his way. I blamed myself. I had been way too hard, way too direct, something that happened with me all the time. I felt something and expressed it. My guilty conscience grew in me.

Wide awake, I lay in bed and listened as Michael paced. He paced and paced and paced. Back and forth. In a circle. Rotating thoughts that caused his insomnia.

I almost went mad in my room. For how much longer would he pace his circle? Should I go to him? I wasn't allowed in the upper floor. But, heck, if Bob was on guard ...

Spontaneously I threw back the covers. Stood in the room. Listened above. It was quiet. A few seconds later: still silent. Maybe he had gone to bed after all. With eyes closed, I listened for sounds from above. Nothing. I heard myself exhale slowly, feeling my tension. Knew that sleep was out of the question, pulled on sweats and grabbed a blanket. I had to get out.

I quietly opened the door and collided with Michael.

Speechless, I stared at him. Speechless, he stared back.

"Where are you going?" he whispered.

"Under the tree," I whispered back. "You want to come along?"

He nodded. I grabbed another blanket and we left.

It was a silent procession, but I can't describe how grateful I was for this second chance with him. When we arrived at our tree, I spread one of the two blankets as a ground cover and wrapped the other one around Michael's gaunt body. I let my arm rest on his shoulders, to give him extra warmth.

"Michael," I said softly. "I'm sorry. Really. I shouldn't have barged in like that ... I'm terribly sorry, I didn't mean to hurt you."

"You didn't hurt me," Michael said, his voice dark. "You... got to me. For years, I've been trying to understand. For more than two years I've been talking with a therapist, for the first time in my life. It feels good ... but I am still ... unhappier than ever..." He swallowed hard.

"Things are not getting better... he whispered then. And then he tensed and hissed: "And ... I hate what's happened to me ... I hate the people who did this to me. I hate them!"

He quieted. It was so clear how bad he felt harboring such feelings. But then more burst out of him:

"I believe in love. I was convinced that you get out what you put into the world. But exactly the opposite has happened."

He pressed his lips together, and the clenched jaw muscles pressed through the skin on his face. Whispering, he continued, "Today I am sitting here. Everything is destroyed. My reputation, my career, my life is in shambles, everything I love is in danger. The catastrophes aren't stopping. Today, I sit here and want to scream out my rage. I know that hate is not good, but God knows, and may He forgive me, I hate all those people who did this to me ... this child who betrayed me so ... I hate him and his family...!" Startled, he quieted and held his hand to his mouth.

"Oh, good," I said, relieved. "Finally! Keep going!"

Puzzled, he looked at me.

"Don't you have stomach ulcers by now from everything that you've bottled up over the years?" I asked him. "How can you cope with these feelings?"

"I … I imagine … a friend of mine says … in my mind, I should confront these people who sued me." Michael's voice was getting quieter. "…and … forgive them…" he whispered. "And I can't. I can't. Basically, I don't even want to."

"Greetings to your friend from me," I hissed angrily, "Next time imagine giving these bastards the kick in the ass they deserve! And then punch them a couple of times in their lying, greedy faces!"

With an open mouth, Michael stared at me. "Excuse me?" he croaked. "How is that compatible with the teachings of Indian philosophers? And that evil produces more evil?"

"Holy shit!" I gasped. "Michael! That's not what I meant! Oh, my God…!"

Horrified, I grabbed my head, panted deeply and looked at Michael stunned.

"Anyone who has a heart of gold has to protect it." I snorted. "The tragedy is that you aren't doing that! Allowing these people to treat you like that! And then you are supposed to forgive them all gloriously? Throw a grenade at them!"

"Chirelle!" cried Michael.

"Sorry!" I cried back. "But that's what I meant with, make your own happiness!"

"By throwing grenades at others?"

"By creating circumstances that are good for you! By not being worthy of this bullshit! Why do you allow this pack to come into your house? Forgiveness comes later, tell your friend that!"

How do they come up with such lunacy? I mean, ultimately it is about forgiveness, but how was Michael supposed to get there without taking the necessary steps in between? Without ever having vented his anger? This anger would always be the wall in front of forgiveness and in addition give him a sense of failure because he didn't appear as good a person as he wanted to be.

Michael's mouth still hung open and I had to laugh.

"Hey, Michael, buddy," I said, nudging him. "I don't think the point of this experience is primarily forgiveness. After you've seen yourself through this that will come automatically. These people who screwed you are loathsome. Let's face it, that's all it is."

Michael shook his head in incomprehension.

"But you just said that all the people who cause pain have a purpose. And now … now … I hate a child…"

"So what? It will pass. Hate is not good, you're right there. But it's good that you admit that you hate a child. You'll eventually get over that … but give yourself time. You don't understand why all of this has happened to you. How can you forgive, then? That's a long way to go."

"What's good about hating a child?" he asked.

"It is not good in general. It's good for you. Because you always polarized between adults and children. One of them is good, the other bad. If you can even just break through that, you might come out a step ahead."

"Still..." he said. "... in children I see something that I almost never see in adults ... and what I see is there. It's definitely there! I can see it! And feel it! I get along really well with adults who have it, too. I do not polarize."

"What is it that you see?"

"I see their purity, this innocence..."

How often he had already said those words in interviews! How often had the journalists rolled their eyes to the ceiling! Yet, he insisted.

"How do you see that?"

Hesitantly, he said: "It's like a glimmer of light around them. It's like a bright light, it's as if rays are emanating from the children. And that is a form of energy that makes me feel incredibly good. And adults don't have it. Most of them don't. And that's how it is."

"You can see auras," I stated. And when he turned around to me, I realized that he knew that. But it didn't mean anything to him He only knew that the aura of children was the same one that he had around him. It was this energy in which he found peace, where he could recharge. It is scientifically proven that children under the age of five constantly resonate in the alpha mode until their fontanel closes. It was true what Michael said, that children had access to the so-called zero-point or quantum field, which was possible for adults only in a state of expanded consciousness - a state that Michael could easily call on.

"When babies come into the world, this connection with the Divine is so strong," he said. "I'd love to be a midwife ... imagine, these people are constantly immersed in this energy ...babies ... still have it all ... but they only have a few years, just a few years until they lose it."

Tormented, he looked at me. There he was. He, who had never lost this power. A person, who could access this channel that is locked for so many of us, had it so freely available for the messages of the harmonies, the melodies. He, who made this energy visible to us, in music and dance. Who always emphasized that humility is the most important thing. And therefore dismissed compliments because he knew it was God who was dancing in him, it was God infusing melodies into him. And because children were still so close to God, he sought their presence, he sought their and his source. He openly admitted that it were the children who inspired his songs, texts, dances, his creative expression. It wasn't as if he didn't want to grow up. It was more that he didn't want to lose this light, this access.

And then there was us, his audience. We felt more than knew that greatness stood before us. We felt that what Michael brought to the stage was more than the sum of its parts. We snatched a glimpse of eternity, beauty, perfection, when we heard him sing, saw him dance, because, when he did he was in direct contact with what we were all striving to be.

"At some point the children of the world fall mercy to the values of the adults," Michael continued after a long silence. "And then they are corrupt, conditioned by the mind. Most of them forever and ever."

That was true. Many of the adults had lost their inner innocence, their inner child. At some point it was just all about career, self-importance, money and satisfying needs and wants. That's what happiness was pegged by and by that alone. Was it surprising that Michael's inspiration was Peter Pan? And that he dreamed of a world ruled by trust and love? Didn't we all wish for that? Wasn't it very telling for our world that we dismissed these thoughts as ridiculous?

"But you have adult friends," I ventured.

"Yes, these are the few who have retained their child," he answered. "Liz, Grace, Frank, Karen ... a few ... and you ... you have that too."

"Michael…" I said hesitantly. "Even if this was not such a good start today... please give me a chance to understand your life. Let's unravel your story. I don't know what the outcome will be, but there has to be something there that is causing you problems. Maybe we'll find it."

Michael nodded hesitantly. And this reluctance made me realize that he was inches away from switching to distrust. Understandably. I mean, who was I? Someone who bakes muesli muffins, someone he didn't know. Someone, who could go to the press tomorrow.

But a second later, he gave me a warm, welcoming smile. This enchanting smile that contained the charm of the whole world. This time he was the one, who brushed a strand of hair from my face.

"That's what we'll do, Scheherazade," he said. "Maybe we'll really find something. We'll meet tomorrow. Good night!"

***

Grace was rarely seen in the kitchen. Especially around breakfast. This time she came into the kitchen before breakfast, opened the fridge, looked inside, and without taking anything, closed it noisily and went back to the dining room, not without cutting me a long look. And then she came in after breakfast with the used dishes, which was actually Linda's or my job. And again she looked at me. Inquisitively, suspiciously, warningly.

She started a superficial conversation with Linda, choosing a spot that gave her the chance to fix me with her stare. I stood at the window and peeled apples - in the meantime there was apple strudel day once a week. Linda would not have been able to tell whether Grace was looking at me or through the window.

That made me uncomfortable. I knew she was closely connected to Michael - in whichever way - and she had feelings for Michael - who didn't? She had a strong bond because of the mere fact alone that she was practically the mother of his children. Michael treated her exactly that way. He flirted with her, touched her or patted her on the back sometimes - and argued with her.

If there was something I wanted for Michael, then it was a woman who was as strong as Grace, who loved him, who shared his sleepless nights with him, who was there for him, who took away his loneliness. I didn't know if it was Grace that his heart was yearning for. Or whether there was anyone at all.

Grace's eyes were burning on my back and when I'd had enough, I simply turned around and looked her in the eyes.

The expression in hers was openly threatening. Once she was sure that I had perceived this to the fullest sense, she turned around, grabbed Linda by the arm and pulled her outside for a meeting.

Michael had said. "See you tomorrow."

Evening came. The children were in bed, the kitchen was cleaned up, night had fallen. He didn't show up.

I sat in the kitchen drinking coffee, reading books. Nothing.

The caffeine kept me awake. Awake too much. Went outside. Maybe he was sitting at the shore? Under the tree?

Bob was on duty and he revealed that Michael had driven off in the early afternoon. To the airport. To Las Vegas. Could be longer. He hadn't even let me know. Disappointed and unsettled, I went to bed.

The next day was the first one that felt really long to me. Grace and the kids had left to join Michael - which meant I would not have much to do, really. I was restless and frustrated, wondering if I had gone too far too soon. Now this seemed to be his legitimate withdrawal.

Linda assigned work that kept me busy for three hours. She didn't seem to be having the best day herself, was cool and somewhat irritable. With the impulse of wanting to get away from it all, I made plans during the workday for the unexpected free weekend. I wanted off the grounds. Without the chance to meet Michael, I felt trapped in this house.

I could book a domestic flight somewhere ... up to San Francisco ... or visit the redwoods ... or San Diego ... armed with a cup of frustration-coffee I went to my room to gather information about flights.

My eyes fell on my little camera. It was lying on the floor without its protective cover. Then I saw that my backpack, which I had put on the chair was also no longer sitting there. Slowly, my eyes wandered around the room. My computer was on, even though I had shut it down for sure. The closet door was ajar, and as I opened it, I looked into chaos: all the documents that I had collected in the recent past relating to Michael lay in an untidy mess on the shelf. I opened the other closet door: underwear, other clothing...everything had been ransacked. The person in question had not even bothered to hide the search. A warning? Grace's threatening look came to my mind.

I picked up the camera. The display was set to image search - somebody had checked the images on the camera. I had nothing to hide. All the photos were shot in the city, were real touristy pictures. But I was absolutely uncomfortable with someone snooping through my room and drawing God knows what kind of conclusions. And brought them to Michael. What was he supposed to think, when he was told that I kept material about him in my closet?

As unpleasant as it was, I had to talk to Grace.

Tom

One thing was for sure: I needed a change of scenery, which I hoped to find in the city. I embarked on extensive sightseeing and shopping tours, visited the Contemporary Museum of Art, strolled through the streets, sat in cafes, read a lot and tried to think of other things.

I checked off places in my guidebook that I had already seen and decided to explore the beaches of Los Angeles for the next couple of days.

Absorbed in my information pamphlet I left the coffee shop with a large coffee to go. At that moment someone burst through the door, bumped into me, and the contents of the cup poured onto both of our clothes.

"Damn! Sorry! Yikes!" it resonated in German and English from me and from him. The coffee was absorbed within seconds by my shirt and pants.

"Oh my God, I'm so sorry," cried the man, and looked in horror as everything discolored. I pulled a package of handkerchiefs from my backpack and said, "Don't worry ...it'll wash out..." and rubbed away at my clothes, transforming the paper towels into unattractive crumbs that didn't make the mess any better.

Eager to be doing something, the man repeated: "I am so sorry! Wait, I'll get a damp towel!"

"It appears we have emptied our cups... in the truest sense of the word," I joked and finally looked up from my unproductive efforts. I was thunderstruck. An exceedingly attractive, blonde middle-aged man looked at me with very blue eyes that were begging for forgiveness.

"Wow!" I blurted out. "Are you a model?"

The stranger laughed in relief and amusement. "Oh, thank you! No, not at all, but as I said, I'm terribly sorry ... I'll buy you new things ... there's a store over there ... I'll pay for the cleaner ... I'm so sorry..."

"You've already said that several times," I said, detached. "Relax, I'll take a cab home and change. No problem."

The man looked a little perplexed. Then he said:

"Thank you taking this so calmly ... are you sure you didn't get burned? The coffee was probably very hot..."

"What about you?" My eyes traveled down his body and I started to grin. There was a huge stain right at his crotch.

"You seem to have taken quite a hit, too," I giggled.

The man looked down at himself. "Oh my God!" he groaned and held his hands in front of his most precious part, which was rather counterproductive.

I couldn't help it. I laughed out loud. He looked so helpless and the situation was so embarrassing to him that I pressed my little backpack into his hands, which he gratefully put in front of his lower body. That made it look even funnier. He had frantically pulled his arms up, causing the bag to dangle between his legs, and his expression wavered between embarrassment and insult. I laughed even more, and because people started staring at us, I steered him out of coffee shop towards a store.

"Do *you* want to buy something?" I asked. "Then go ahead – I'll certainly not sue you for assault or anything. Shall I walk with you across the street ... because ... the decoy?"

"Decoy? What? What do you mean ... oh!" Colossally the backpack swung between his legs.

He snorted. "You're really not easily fazed, huh?" he noted and looked at me curiously

"Not by spilled coffee, at least," I chuckled "So? Do you want to go over there?"

"That would be good ... would you lend me your backpack until then?"

"That doesn't make it look any better," I teased. "A pendulum like that between your legs..." I giggled again and walked with him to the store. In front of the shops' door he gave the bag back to me and thanked me.

"Well ... then all the best to you," I said and turned to leave.

"Hey, hey, wait a minute!" He exclaimed flabbergasted. "I ... you ... just want to leave like this?"

"Is there something else to discuss?"

"No ... but ... I mean ...may I at least invite you to a cup of coffee since I spilled yours?"

I looked down at myself. The wet spots didn't feel good. The man recognized what I was thinking and grinned impishly. That suited him. Very, very well, indeed. God, was he gorgeous!

"Well ... if you don't mind..." he said as he kept his eyes on me. "...then ... we'll both buy new clothes ... and afterwards ..." he gestured with both pointer fingers and a nice hip rotation to the coffee shop. "...I'll order another cup of coffee for you ... and anything else you'd like... and we'll have a relaxed conversation ... we've already put the embarrassing part behind us."

I hesitated. Michael wasn't there anyway. And I couldn't bring up a lot of resistance because the guy was so cute.

"I'd feel so much better if you would agree," he said.

Those blue eyes were just stunning, the whole guy was stunning, so I said yes. And within the next hour it already became quite clear: Tom was not only incredibly handsome, but was also fun and humorous company.

We went into the jeans-store and with a lot of joking around and laughter picked out a couple of items. Unexpectedly, this turned out to be a lot of fun and was so amusing because Tom cracked one joke after another, made fun of himself liberally, mocked bizarre people in business (inconspicuously of course), so I couldn't stop laughing. In jeans and T-shirt Tom looked attractive in a different way than in a suit. I couldn't say what suited him better. In any case, he looked more boyish and mischievous like this.

Then we looked for a quiet spot in the café and talked animatedly about Los Angeles. He made suggestions for restaurants, bars, in-places and for places rarely visited by tourists. The conversation flowed brightly and vibrantly. It felt so good to just talk away, and Tom was incredibly charming. I admit he brought out the woman in me. It didn't take long before I was bubbling just like he was.

"Just imagine, I haven't even been to the beach yet," I told him, "and that's unusual for me since I love the sea and beach. Which one do you think I should go to first?"

"Why don't we go right now?" he asked.

"Right now?"

"Do you have time? I'll show you Laguna Beach, I think its much more beautiful than Venice, and then you can explore Newport and Huntington beach in the next couple of days on your own..."

It reassured me a lot that he wasn't intending to show me all the beaches. Still, I was very suspicious of potential reporters and paparazzi. And in other ways, too, it was not advisable to go with a stranger. But Tom was simply tremendously personable, and so I agreed for a second time.

Finally, he bought a large ice cream for me and we traipsed out of the café in our newly purchased flip-flops and got on the bus.

It turned into a beautiful afternoon by the ocean. We found thousands of things to talk about, about his job - he was a lawyer - and about my life in Germany. He was attentive, unobtrusive, and a real treat.

"How long will you be in LA?" he asked me when I got ready to leave.

"Oh ... uh... no idea ... not much longer, I think."

"May I invite you to dinner, before you disappear from this part of the country?" he asked, grinning charmingly.

"Sure," I replied. "With you, always!"

"Then I'll pick you up the day after next at the hotel," he said happily. "Which..."

"Oh, wait ... I'll be in town earlier already! If you don't mind, I'd prefer we meet at the restaurant."

Tom nodded surprised, but agreed.

"May I have your number, please?" I asked him. "Just in case something comes up – I'll give you mine as well."

So we exchanged numbers and said goodbye. Should Michael come home and a conversation occur, that would be much more important to me than a date with Tom. As cute as he was.

XX / Again and again in 1999/2000

"Give this journalist some sugar. He would be the first one whose moral values were larger than a pile of money. His shows sure don't look like they are."

***

Michael didn't show up and so for the first time in a long time I spruced up and set out.

Tom was waiting for me at the bar of a wonderful, super fancy insider restaurant. Amazed, I followed him through the tables after our aperitif at the bar. Wasn't that Britney Spears sitting over there? And this guy looked a bit like Will Smith ... and back there ...my knees weakened.

"Hey, where did you take me?" I asked anxiously. "Are you a star lawyer or something like that?"

Tom laughed. "Oh, you know how it is," he said. "You always have to show yourself where your clients are."

"So you turn out to be a celebrity lawyer after all. You hadn't mentioned that."

Why did Tom go out with someone like me when there were all these delightful choices? I was just glad that I was wearing something adequate.

"Well," he said, and let his eyes wander over the crowd, as we sat with a glass of champagne. "Pretty impressive, huh?" His boyish grin didn't make the sentence seem pretentious. Mischievously, he leaned forward, nodded his head to the right towards a round table, where six expensively and flashy dressed people were sitting and whispered:

"What do you think about the table next to ours?"

I leaned forward and whispered back: "Tom, don't be upset ... but who are they? That person back there ... is that Britney?"

"That's not Britney!" Tom said indignantly as his disbelieving glance went to the indicated direction, back to me and then again to the next table.

"You don't know them? Is that a joke?" he asked, rather bewildered. "That's Usher and Chris Tucker and..."

"It's no joke," I said uncomfortably, not daring to ask who Usher was.

"But everybody knows these people," he added.

"So ... even at the risk of totally falling out of your favor, " I said. "...I'd probably walk right past most of them."

"Are you serious?"

"Uh, yes. Is that bad?"

"No ... it's ... just ... unusual," stated Tom, looking at me strangely. "I mean, these people are stars ... they're in every newspaper..."

"... which I don't read."

"But you watch TV."

"I don't."

Tom looked at me dumbfounded. He was truly baffled.

"You don't watch TV? I mean ... not even in Germany?"

"No. Rarely, that is. When I want to know something, I use the Internet to get information, I mean about politics, but that's about it."

Tom was speechless, if not to say shocked. I became anxious. Was he mad that he had invited me to this upscale place and now thought a hot dog stand would have done just as well?

"I don't know," I continued, in an effort to justify my lack of interest in celebrities. "I think it's pretty dumb, what the papers say. The other day I was at the dentist's ... there was one of these rags there and one of the topics, besides who cheated on whom and who said what, was: 'What do stars keep on their bedside table?' They filled seven pages with that! Come on! I need to know so bad to get to heaven."

Tom laughed softly and I thought how stunning this man looked. His blue eyes twinkled and his smile was so charming that it just took my breath away.

"Yes, but there are also important celebrities ... People who move something ... they lead a glamorous life ... an enviable lifestyle..."

"Hey, Tom, now keep your feet on the ground. Ultimately, stars are only human, too and I really doubt that they have a better life than we do. I mean, at least we can make our mistakes in private, but as a star you're doing all them under a spot light - what a nightmare! I think the worst thing that can happen to a person is to be in the public eye!"

Tom looked at me speculatively. Obviously, with this statement I had put my foot in my mouth.

"What's the matter," I asked straight to the point, "is that so shocking to you?"

"No ... uh ... I'm ... just surprised." said Tom, but he was still looking at me strangely. "And there isn't anyone you'd want to meet in real life...?"

"What for?" I asked casually. "To get a photo with both of us? So that the glamour of a stranger might radiate on me? Please."

"But ... there are totally interesting people...!"

"You can find those in the 'normal' population, too, Tom. But you're right. If someone has depth, then that would be a reason to want to talk to him. But not because he's a celebrity. There you are. Can't we just move on?"

"From celebrities?"

"Yes, exactly. I'd much rather know what you like to read and how your life has been so far ... and what your future plans are..."

We became lost in his career path, talked about the different school systems in our countries, about favorite movies and books - and Tom wanted to know a lot about me. Finally, it became a relaxed evening.

"You were in India?" he asked, keenly interested.

"Yes, a couple of times already. It is a fascinating country. But I spent a lot of time in an ashram. I went there to forget about everything for a while. You know how it is, at some point the thoughts spin around in your mind and you can't switch them off. When that happens, I go to a monastery for two to four weeks. I find peace there, read ancient texts and try to shut down the flow of thoughts through meditation."

"That sounds ... exciting," said Tom, somewhat distracted. But I was already familiar with that. Most people were bored when the conversation turned to this subject. Nevertheless, he pursued:

"And what texts do you mean?"

"Oh, there are dozens of texts from wise men, ancient legends, Indian ones, parables, songs and reports on the lives of Zen monks, of gurus, Sufis ... of masters from all over the world that are translated into English. I just love to read their thoughts. They are so old and so true, and so universal and so..."

"Do you have a favorite thought?" asked Tom.

"Several. I'm thinking of one from a movie called *Samsara*. Do you know the movie?"

"No, never heard of it."

"It's about the question: how do you keep a drop of water from drying out?"

"Is that a koan?"

"No."

"Then there's a decent answer?"

"Of course."

"Which is?"

"By letting it drop into the sea."

Tom's look was rather blank. But that didn't bother me either. I was used to that, too.

XX / 1985/86

"People," he said, puffing fat rings of smoke out of his philosophizing mouth: "...have no clue where the real danger is. They are afraid of nuclear war, illness, pain, of poverty ... but the real danger are their desires."

He gazed upward, eyes trailing the smoke that hovered sluggishly in the air.

"Do you know why the music - and film industries are the most powerful of all?"

He didn't want an answer. That was common knowledge. You let him talk.

"Fame," he explained. "Because of fame. That's how you control the masses ... those who want it and those who worship the ones that have it. Fame ... is like anthrax. Insidious. People think that if they are admired, they are loved. It's hilarious ... but everyone falls for it. And when the fame fades, they become unhappy. To them, fame is like the air they breathe. But the one who has the power is the one who calls the shots. The power belongs to the one who can see that. The power belongs to the one who doesn't need love. Do you understand? Everyone is chasing after love and thinks it's synonymous with success. If you want to make someone dependent, make him famous. Then he is forever at your mercy. People will do anything to be gaped at. Scientific studies show that being gaped at is addictive. People feel that something is missing, that something feels wrong if they aren't gaped at any longer. They do everything they can to prevent their success from fading. That's the sticking point. That's how you get most of them. Fame is the most effective, most invisible and deadly drug in the world. And sometimes ... sometimes it leads to death ... a death that can happen to anyone ... and leaves no trace - no one, except the person himself is to blame.

And almost no one abstains. Someone who has lived in a palace doesn't want to move into a hut. Few have this largess. 99% of the population can therefore be manipulated. The masses - the masses are ours."

Smearings

Grace was back without the kids, without Michael. I missed his presence. And worried. I stood undecided in the kitchen; it was late morning. To keep myself busy, I took ingredients for a cake out of the refrigerator just as Grace came in.

"Hey, Grace," I said lightly, before the memory of her last look and the search made me uptight.

"Hey," she replied, measuring me from top to bottom.

"Shall I prepare something for you?" I asked.

"No, thank you, nobody needs that many calories," she said coolly.

Hurt, I stared at the egg carton, heard Grace open the refrigerator and slam the door shut. Let her tell me what she was thinking! And to my face! With an impulsive retort on my lips, I spun around determined and could just see her breezing out the door, slamming it too loudly behind her.

To distract myself and to defy Grace, I baked the cake. It needed an hour to bake and I wanted to walk off my frustration in the enormous park. I could hardly wait to get outside and it felt great from the first moment. The air was clear, the green gleamed intensely and my walk along a path that led to a grouping of large deciduous trees cleared my head. The sun shone on these majestic trees and, in search of a path between them, I came to a small clearing where the trail ended. I was just going to turn around when my attention was drawn to something unusual. Four or five crumpled pieces of paper were scattered on the ground, in grass, moss and leaves.

Curious, I moved closer, looked around. Had the children played here? I knelt down and picked up the balled up pieces of paper. There were five. I sat down in the dry leaves, smoothing the paper of the first note, and leaned against the trunk of the tree.

Sans serif font size 14, bold. The words:

"You know what it's about. We've long since got you. You're dead already."

I felt dizzy. The hope that this was a detective game of children was dashed by the text of the second note.

Sans serif font, point size 14, bold and italic:

"You black paleface can't protect your children. We know everything."

My heart skipped a beat. Had Michael read this? Had he crumbled up the notes? Scenes of his everyday life came to my mind. He never left the children without supervision. He always went along with them or left them in the care of several people and his security personnel. In public, they wore masks. They were educated privately. Gifts were examined closely before they were allowed to be opened. He knew about the letters. I broke into a sweat. What were the conditions he was really living under?

Third, fourth, fifth note, same font, same pattern:

"There are many ways to die. And many levels. Do you notice how you are dying?"

"Do you know what they give you in the hospital? Everything is infiltrated. It is our net in which you are suspended. Give up"

"We'll crush you. We will make your life hell. You will wish for death rather than life."

Horrified, I closed my eyes. What kind of sick people were out there? How did these notes even get here? And above all: in which state of fear must Michael be living? I remembered words from our last conversation: "I've got big problems Chirelle, really ... you can't imagine how big they are..."

And I had thought I could dismiss this with some super clever talk? How could I? How naive must he think I am! It's no surprise that he pulled back! What had I even said to that? That the problems always come from one's self? Groaning, I covered my face with my hands. The power and wisdom of Indian philosophies suddenly seemed inconsequential in the face of these threats.

Completely dazed, I walked back down the path, notes in my hand. A dull emptiness had spread in my head - it made me incapable of doing anything. Finally I took a shower, letting the hot water run down my body for a long time, as if it could flush these issues down the drain. But at least it could ease my tension a bit and I thought about what I should do. I had to give the notes to security ... yeah, that's it! Hastily, I took the cake from the oven, tucked the papers in my pocket and ran to the guard station. But Jason was sitting together with the entire guard personnel in his little room assigning shifts. Glumly I bit my lip. Jason saw me through the window and came out briefly.

"Hey, Chirelle, it's not a good time right now- we have a meeting - today isn't good ... maybe in two or three hours, or better tomorrow?"

"Yes…" I said. "Okay, I'll come back later."

I managed a wry smile and walked slowly back again.

My phone vibrated. Glad to have something to do, I looked at the screen:

'Hi Chi, feel like coming downtown the next day or so?'

The text was from Tom and after thinking about it a bit, I arranged to meet with him again. Tom knew the celebrity scene better than I did. Maybe it was possible to milk him for information inconspicuously. Maybe it was not unusual for stars to receive such morbid letters. But something told me that Michael was actually in danger, the extent of which I couldn't even begin to imagine with my 'all's-good-in-life' experience.

Back in the kitchen, I looked at the clock. The cooks were off - there was hardly anyone there, after all, to cook for and, unlike me, they could go home when unexpected free time like that came up. I threw on the coffee machine, put my cell on the table - Tom wanted to get back to me again - and went to my room to get a book, sticking the wretched notes between its pages. When I came back to the kitchen, Grace was fiddling with my cell phone.

"Hey!" I said sharply. "What are you doing?"

"This thing can't even take pictures," Grace said, unmoved and kept typing on the menu keys. "It can't even take recordings? What century is this from?"

Speechless by her insolence, I stared at her. "Don't you think you're going a bit too far?" I said icily, and snatched it out of her hand.

"Where is the second one?"

"The second what?"

"A second cell phone. This is just a fake! Nobody uses an ancient phone like this!"

"This ancient phone has a great battery and the rest is none of your goddam business!" I hissed.

We stared at each other. She: combative, fully confrontational, fully intent on provoking me to the extreme so I would confirm what she suspected.

"Hey, what's going on here? Cat fight?"

We turned around. Karen, Michael's make-up artist, stood in the door.

"You think you can get a decent cup of coffee, and then this!" she teased, but it was obvious that she was making an attempt to take the edge off the situation. Grace threw Karen a meaningful look and swept through the door. My shoulders slumped down when she was gone, and I could feel Karen's gaze fixed on me.

"What's going on, Chirelle?" she asked.

"Oh," I said with a rough voice and only now realized how much the situation bothered me, "Grace thinks ... she checked my phone ... and she thinks, I guess she thinks..."

Karen sighed, went to the coffee machine and took two cups from the pegs.

"Oh, you've got cake!" she cried with sparkling eyes. "That would go really well together, don't you think?"

"It's still too hot to eat." I said sourly.

"That's fine, coffee will do, too."

"Karen, is it possible that Grace is jealous?"

"Why should she be?" Karen asked cautiously.

"Because she and Michael maybe ... I mean, every time I talk to him ... she's particularly nasty to me."

"What do you and Michael talk about?"

"About literally everything under the sun."

Karen was silent.

"Chirelle," she said, "she certainly isn't thinking that way. I mean we both know why Grace has concerns. You have to understand one thing. She's been working for Michael for over 15 years. Believe me, she saw every piece of shit that Michael had to put up with all this time. And up close. She's just worried, you know? This business is in worse shape than you can imagine and Michael is ... can be very trusting - and that's already cost him dearly ... so dearly that he has endangered his livelihood."

I remembered the notes. I jumped up so quickly that my hip bumped the table and the coffee swashed high in the cups. Karen looked at me surprised "Karen," I cried. "I really have to show you something!" Excitedly I pulled the wretched notes from the book.

"I found these in the grass," I explained. "I was taking a walk and there was this stuff crumpled on the ground... Karen ... where does this crap come from?"

Karen took the sheets and read. Her eyes went dark, her lips pressed together tightly as she read. Her whole reaction told me that notes like this were nothing new. Was this cause for hope?

"Why don't you go to the police?" I asked urgently.

"Police!" she retorted. "They have bags of this stuff!"

"Then ... then that's ... I mean, not to sound stupid ... But then is this ... normal?"

"Normal? Normal? What's normal anymore?" Karen seemed more worried than she wanted to admit. "Normal is that celebrities get this crap. Yes, that's normal." Her intense, gray-blue eyes looked directly at me. "Then it'll be investigated, revealed who did it and the asshole will be punished. Yes, that... that would be normal."

"And how is it here?" I inquired.

Karen ran both hands over her face and through her angelic golden hair. Her eyes fixed on the table, she murmured:

"Here, nothing is normal at all. Anything around Michael is not normal. The police have had this stuff for years. There's method behind it. We find... Michael finds ... these notes in the most unlikely places. On the pillows of his children's beds, in the bathroom ... in his clothes ... in the car ... I mean, how would that make you feel? This guy or these guys get into the house! They are *in* the house! In the kids rooms! Somehow. And for years the police find nothing, absolutely nothing? What's up with that? Instead, they booked Michael with puny evidence for child molestation, put him in handcuffs and treated him like a criminal, while someone who is seriously threatening him is out there walking around freely!"

Clearly upset, the volume of her voice had increased until she was almost shouting at me. Paled, I sank into the armrest of the kitchen bench. Karen's eyes changed and she looked at me, they way Grace sometimes did.

"Karen, you... I ... " I stammered. Now what was wrong with her? She wouldn't believe that I...? But abruptly the tension released. Her anger gave way, and the expression in her eyes switched from suspicion back to their normal, friendly look when she sensed that she was directing blame towards the wrong person.

"Look," she asked resolutely, "how much do you know about Michael?"

"Not much," I replied. "I had to buy biographies to know anything."

Her left eyebrow raised slightly. "What does the name 'Tommy Mottola' mean to you? Tom Sneddon? Tohme Tohme? Branca? DiLeo ... and what is the name Martin Bashir to you?"

"Not much. Bashir ... wait a minute... isn't that the journalist, who..."

"Exactly, that's the journalist, who..." she replied, ironical. "I was there when Bashir swore to Michael with the tongue of an angel that he would make such a super documentary of him! Oh, was it ever super! I would suggest you take a look at that, then I'm sure you'll understand why some people here act a little paranoid. What about the darn cake? It looks really yummy! I'll eat it warm, too."

I laughed and cut her a nice big piece. "Man, you have an enviable metabolism - where do you put that all?"

"Yeah, must be shitty if you can bake all that stuff, and then don't want to eat it," Karen grinned.

As she walked away, she looked intensely in my eyes:

"You have to understand Grace," she said. "We all want to protect Michael, because we... love him very much. He is the child of all of us."

And she meant it not only in the way it sounded at first.

***

I'd had enough for today. The computer stared at me reproachfully when I walked into the room and stashed the book with my notes there. I was tired.

Finally, I opened the laptop anyway, and the Bashir documentary stared at me defiantly, smugly. I hesitated. There were more videos in the sidebar. Shows recorded by fans and posted online: "Michael doing jokes", "Michael's best dance" and so on.

I clicked on these. I wanted to see Michael dance. I wanted to see him happy.

The night dragged on. It was hot. Again and again, I woke up. Thought about going outside, was too lazy. Hauled myself out of bed, drank a glass of water. Woke up from that. Turned on the computer. Scrolled, flicked, clicked ... a page with "rare moments" appeared.

Moments that portrayed Michael's exceptionally compassionate personality. Fascinated, I watched how he interacted with people:

Scene 1: A girl allowed to join him on stage. She hugs him and faints. Michael doesn't just call security. Like a knight, he carries her in his arms to the edge of the stage and ensures - singing - with hand gestures and glances that she is well taken care of.

Next scene: Michael performs his famous Earth Song, during which he rides via a crane above the crowd, first only about three feet above their heads, then high up into the air. A crazy fan manages to climb onto the contraption, God knows, how he did it. He pulls himself up to Michael, stands outside on the railing of the mobile platform, where Michael is singing. Immediately, Michael's arm wraps protectively around the narrow body of the fan. Not one moment too soon: in this instant, the crane moves to dizzying heights. Triumphantly, the fan pulls up his arms, he is not holding on. Michael pushes his arm down, forcing him to hold on, while he wraps his second arm around him. He can't lift the young man onto the platform: it is too small for that. But he holds him firmly until the crane comes back down again, and several security arms grab hold of the crazy guy, pull him away from Michael while he touches the shoulder of the fan, as if he wants to make sure: are you all right? Is everything okay?

During all of this drama he continues to sing his song, with unbridled passion and without the slightest uncertainty.

Scene 3: a zoo. A separated-off room, more like a hall. A girl, who is brought to him. Apparently, she unexpectedly won a meeting with him. She is already screeching and screaming when she sees him from afar. But she is rather running away from him. She is so completely beside herself that she overreacts, becomes completely hysterical. The bodyguard practically drags her to Michael. He stands there quietly, waiting, appears neither impatient nor annoyed. Then her switch: she gets that it really is Michael, who is waiting for her, she runs towards him and slams her body against his (I thought - God, how can he stand this?). He does not move or waver, just holds her. She cries and cries and cries. He holds her until she is all wept out, until she's quiet, then he gently makes her aware of the beauty and humor of the gorillas, trying to calm her. She pulls away from him, relaxed and peaceful. He puts his big hand to her cheek, strokes her hair, looks her in the eye and asks: "Are you are okay?"

He speaks so often of God, of humility, of love, of gratitude, as if to remind us of something. The next scenes that I look at are concert recordings.

I see him on stage, this narrow, shy, loving man who opens his heart to everyone, who wants to give all that he has, who wants to draw attention with his talent to all the evils of the world and, other than that, wants nothing but his peace and quiet. There he stands on the stage of his vocation, in the spotlight. I see how he dances, how he sings, how he carries himself, how he gives...how he turns with a magical movement to the audience. His shirt is flapping, his arms outstretched to meet the people, he is laughing, happy, filled with love and cries: "I love you!"

***

90

The next morning, I had a headache, and I got up reluctantly. When I came into the kitchen, my mood did not improve. Grace and Linda stood together and both looked at me with unmistakable suspicion.

"Good morning," I greeted them, shocked.

Linda ... so far she had always been my support here - it hurt me to see that she was treating me with the same distrust as Grace did. I remembered the ransacking of my room. Was this a good time now- with a headache and two venomous faces staring at me? But without knowing exactly what drove me, I headed over to the two of them.

"I'm glad I caught you together," I said with fake cheer - which made me look even more suspicious because it sounded false. "I would like to address something."

Grace raised her eyebrows. Linda was embarrassed and clearly at a distance, which hurt my feelings. And as always, when trifles like this happened to me, my thoughts went to Michael, whose social exclusion and ostracism had been unparalleled.

That gave me courage. "My room was searched," I explained, "my personal stuff, my wallet, camera, computer, even my underwear..."

Linda's eyes widened and she looked at Grace surprised, but Grace did not flinch.

"Is something missing?" she asked tartly.

"Uh ... no, but ..."

"Then what do you want?" she snapped, then turned and disappeared. I approached Linda.

"Can you tell me what's wrong with all of you?" I asked angrily. "Do I have a contagious disease or something?" I felt stupid when I said it. After all I knew what everyone was thinking. Linda cleared her throat. But she was getting friendlier.

"Chirelle, my dear..." she began, and obviously had no idea how she should address the issue. After a few seconds of embarrassing silence I took the initiative.

"Linda. I know you both believe that I would take advantage of the conversations that Michael is having with me. Please tell me one thing: is there anything I can do to reassure you?"

Linda looked at me with the unhappy eyes of a housewife, unhappy because she did not want to be the one who had brought this potential rotten egg, me, into the house. My proclamation of innocence didn't help at all. Linda took a deep breath.

"Chirelle, you have to understand that we all love Michael very, very much. And we all know what he has been through. We all know that he has reached the limit of his strength. And what we don't know is whether he would still be here today if it weren't for his children. But what we do know for sure is that he won't survive another disaster. And that we will do everything in our power to prevent one from happening."

She had tears in her eyes as she said it, and a maternal need to protect Michael drenched her words.

"Linda," I said, choking, "don't you think I feel the same way? How can I convince you? Tell me what I can do!"

Linda looked at me and wiped away the tears. "Oh," she said, sounding resigned, "in the end all you can do is hope that nothing happens."

"Linda…"

Again, she looked at me. Then she cleared her throat and said with a firmer voice: "I trust you, Chirelle. I can't do more than that. And basically that's already incredibly much."

In the afternoon I went out with Tom and was glad for his uncomplicated company. He was simply funny and cheerful, made me think of other things. He showed me Newport, we sat in the sun, talking about his ex-girlfriends and my marriage and had dinner together. It was so wonderfully relaxing that we immediately made plans to meet again.

"How much longer will you be in LA?" he asked. "Hadn't you wanted to be long gone?"

"Yeah…" I hesitated, "that's right … But the city is huge … let's say, I'm enjoying just being able to do what I want. And right now I'm not drawn to leave."

"That's good," said Tom. "Then we still have plenty of soulful conversations ahead of us – you're good for me, Chirelle." And he smiled at me warmly.

XX / 1985

"Why are you guys just so unimaginative" asked the raspy voice and laughed in the diabolical way that his question was meant. "You didn't understand me correctly: I want his ruin on every level."

The raspy voice trailed off, leaving the other one time to absorb what has been said in its entirety. When he felt no synchrony, he deigned to give an explanation:

"A person has his health, he has his income, his talent, his family, his social life, his reputation, his image… and he has aspirations and dreams. I want that nothing of that remains but a stinking pile of shit."

His counterpart nodded. And swallowed. As he was leaving, the raspy voice held him back once more:

"So I don't forget, I want something out of it. I want to enjoy it. We have time. And if anything comes out of it for us …all the better."

***

After Tom and I had parted ways, I took the bus to a neutral place and called the Jacksons' from the road. I wasn't permitted to take a cab to Michael's house - I had to be picked up by security personnel. Everyone would have recognized one of Michael's limos and they would have followed it and so Michael used, as so many other celebrities did, a classy car company that constantly changed the vehicles. I used these – with Michael's staff, when I wanted to go out.

"Hey, Chi," greeted Jason when I got in, "did you have a good time? Where were you?"

And again this feeling: did he think I had been selling information?

"On the beach at Newport," I replied, and looked for my part in Jason's face for signs of suspicion. Jason glanced at me, saw what I was thinking and looked back to the road, then back to me. "Now it's got you too, hasn't it?" he asked.

"Oh, Jason, I'm sorry!"

"No reason to be upset," he said. "That's normal. We've all gone through this."

Next Day. Hardly any work.

Bashir was still on the computer - document saved. My fingers played on the keys, unsure if I even wanted to see.

Karen had told me that in 2001 after the release of *Invincible*, Michael had been quite depressed and had agreed to this interview for two reasons: first, because Lady Diana, a soul mate of Michael's, had trusted Bashir and second because he had promised Michael solemnly to repair his bad image.

The documentary was broadcast in 2003 and was made in the years 2001/2002. Bashir experienced the King of Pop over a period of nearly three quarters of a year at various locations around the world. Michael opened his door to him and granted him access to his soul. Many reporters had complained that he revealed nothing of himself and this is the reason why the paparazzi made so much up about him. Karen had said that Michael went into this documentary with a deliberately open mind, although his health at that time was not very good, and the dosage of his medication was quite high. She stressed that Michael had to take medication because he was ill. Like someone, who had to inject insulin to survive: "Then somebody who's taking pills to regulate blood pressure is also a pill popper," she had said angrily. But in the meantime the media had turned it into an addiction rather than a necessity.

For five long years, the British journalist Martin Bashir had strived to make a Michael Jackson documentary. He wanted to show Michael in a way he had never been shown before. And he succeeded.

My index finger pressed down, I put on the headphones and the recording began.

A smug face appeared on the screen:

Bashir

As he stood there in the sun, holding a black umbrella in his hand and welcomed Bashir, Michael seemed like a big kid. Once again, I realized that he was not capable of pretending. He could have said what was expected of him, could have done what he knew people would like, but he could only be himself. And since he didn't have an evil streak in him, there was no reason for him to pretend.

After a few minutes I was as if paralyzed. Bashir trampled on Michael's openness with his feet, put him in front of a distorting mirror, ridiculed him with every trick in the book, rolled him in journalistic filth for 120 minutes.

The discrepancy between Bashir and Michael was already palpable at his arrival: Bashir stared so arrogantly into the camera, as if to say:

"Look. I am the great Houdini reporter who gets every interview."

He is unable to absorb the atmosphere of Neverland, shows zero respect, let alone gratitude. Right at the beginning he asks questions like: "What is this?" "Where did you get that?" These rational questions didn't interest Michael that much, because he had acquired the attractions of Neverland to enrich himself and others, not to discuss the year of their manufacture and the cost. But that turns to the basic theme of the broadcast.

Bashir and Michael walk past the carousel. With shining eyes Michael explains how nice it is to turn in circles to classical music and evergreens. Bashir seems overwhelmed already by this response and doesn't have a clue what to do with it.

Bashir wants to know where this Ferris wheel comes from, while Michael tries to explain how to make dreams and visions come free when sitting up so high, directly under the sky. He even confides that often he goes up by himself and lets the magic of the universe work on him. Bashir's response suggests that he already at this point thinks Michael is whacko. His responses to this are merely technical questions that Michael answers dutifully. Bashir then asks if he can take a ride on the Ferris wheel and Michael, happy and as relieved as a child because Bashir is finally doing something according to his mindset, exclaims enthusiastically:

"Of course! Absolutely!"

Why doesn't he get what Bashir is really up to? It goes on:

the journalist wants to know how Michael writes a song, and it would have been best if Michael had handed him a detailed instruction manual. But he points upward and says: it comes from God. It flows through me, all I have to do is listen. Here his face shows small signs of unrest. Does he feel that Bashir can't even begin to understand what he means? But Michael remains polite and for a long time gives the impression of wanting to answer the questions as precisely as possible.

Bashir asks him what he thinks when he dances. Michael tells him it is the biggest mistake of a dancer to think when he dances. You have to feel it, he explains and his hand rises upwards again. Meaning: you have to be ready to receive the information from above - thinking imposes a mere hindrance.

For Bashir this is dumb spiritual chatter. "Ah," he throws out, although this statement from Michael constitutes an essential element of his genius: "You are virtually the physical embodiment of your music."

It's amazing that he was even able to formulate this sentence at all. Typical: he lets dance steps be shown. Technical details. Although Michael had previously explained to him that you have to be open to things, this seemed entirely incomprehensible to Bashir. Michael is patient and shows it to him.

But Bashir has something else in mind than Michael thinks he has. You can almost see how he stands with a shovel in his hand, digging a hole for him. He often asks the same questions and it is not hard to guess that with the next interpretation he hopes to hear Michael say something that he can use against him.

After those first ten minutes, I had the burning desire to jump into the movie and rip Michael out of this nightmare.

Michael says he's Peter Pan in his heart. Bashir consternated reply: "You are Michael Jackson." as if he had to teach a schizophrenic his identity. In the subsequently added commentary, Bashir embraces the idea of the man-child and pushes Michael's statements in this direction for the viewer.

Michael says, "I mean, I'm Peter Pan in my *heart*, I feel child-like in my heart. Bashir raises his eyebrows. Child-like in your heart? What kind of crap is that?

Then Michael shows him something very private: an ancient tree, his Giving Tree, and shares with him that he loves to climb trees and that there, on these secular branches he had received inspiration for his greatest songs. For *"Heal the World," "Black and White," "Will you be there."* That's a message that is way beyond Bashir. Inspiration on a tree? Apparently he considers energy that comes from above and flows through the body esoteric nonsense and people who believe in it deranged.

We are still living in the Middle Ages, in the time of witch burning, when we erect bonfires for dissidents and the earth is flat.

Bashir's witty question to Michael's inspirational secret: "And how high can you climb?"

Michael points his hand upward and indicates the spot.

"Would you like to climb up there?" asks Bashir, and then something happens that makes tears shoot into my eyes. Again and again I go back to the scene, watch it over and over.

Michael gushes a jubilant "Yeeeesss!" hands the obligatory umbrella over to Bashir and *runs* to the tree. He doesn't walk with a measured pace like an adult who knows that cameras are directed on him, no, he bursts with big steps towards the tree, like a happy, liberated child who is sent outside to play. It is easy to guess that he is more comfortable in the presence of the tree than in Bashir's.

Nimbly Michael climbs his Giving Tree, unaware that Bashir is plotting his social downfall with precisely this footage. Michael settles on a platform, ready to receive inspiration and miracles that this man has long forgotten. It is palpable how familiar Michael is with this place... that he meditates often here and is in unison with something that is buried and lost for so many people. And in that moment, when he sits on the protrusion of the branch, he sinks into himself so clearly that one could see the connection. This moment shows the real Michael, the Michael who is so misunderstood by people: someone who can totally connect with his inner source. What a crude contrast to this man who is looking up from below, ready to push him down from this height. It is an image that represents Michael's entire life.

Michael asks him in astonishment: "You don't climb trees?" And Bashir's expression says, "Am I a monkey?" but on Michael's request he tries awkwardly, clumsily, to climb upwards. He is, he says, 'afraid' and I believe him right away.

Michael stresses again how much he loves to climb trees, to go on balloon rides and to have super soaker battles.

Bashir says: "You wouldn't rather go to the theater? Or make love?"

Undertone: Isn't this guy totally nuts?

At the beginning Bashir is still somewhat polite, but with time he becomes rash. With time he realizes that Michael's kindness knows no boundaries. That Michael isn't setting any boundaries for him. And at some point the tone tilts in the direction of the director questioning the schoolboy.

Already within the first ten minutes of his documentary, Bashir puts out the verdict for an audience of millions, by saying:

"Michael Jackson's estate is a paradise for a ten year old boy, but Jackson is 44 years old."

To all of you people who have angel figurines in your homes and gnomes in your gardens, beware of Bashir!

He is a journalist - he knows what sells. He replays every frame he shoots as ungraciously as possible. He takes words out of context and shows Michael from the most unfavorable angles.

Suggestive questions about the number of plastic surgeries follow, why his children can't grow up in a normal way, if it isn't inhumane to let them walk around with masks. The very nature of the questions alone is opinion shaping. The mannequins that Michael has all around are shown in close-ups and -from a very unfavorable camera angle - he shows how Michael tries to bridge his loneliness with interactive video gaming machines: his big feet are clad in socks that slide off a bit on the treadmill of the machine. Bashir has filmed this in a close up and it most certainly has nothing to do with improving Michaels image.

A shopping spree in Las Vegas proves: Jackson loves kitsch and spends uncontrollably. It is palpable that Michael wants to prove with these scenes that he is anything but broke.

The thing is long since tilted when in addition it is suggested to the viewer that Michael is incapable of raising children. A visit to the zoo is on the agenda, which is supposed to be closed for this occasion for a couple of hours. But strangely, every paparazzi and every inhabitant of the town knows that the zoo is far from closed, and the trip becomes a disaster that Michael probably regrets most of all. After all, he had just wanted to make his children happy.

Bashir, strict now, entirely the relentless critique:

"This wasn't an excursion for kids! Your son got an umbrella in his eye!"

The under-tone: he feels so sorry for all of Jackson's children.

Michael, guilty, scolded, sits on the couch and does not forbid Bashir to speak.

He had arranged to close down the zoo for his visit, and that probably cost him a ton of money. He *had* cared for the safety of his children and Bashir knew that.

Another commentary added later to the zoo episode:

"Someone helpfully gave them a tip." One wonders involuntarily: who may this 'someone helpful' have been? For whom was it really helpful?

It increases to a crescendo that portrays Michael once again, and not only, as an inept father: his fans scream themselves hoarseless outside of his Berlin hotel. They want to see Michael. They chant that they want to see the children to lure him out. Michael appears at the window, the crowd shrieks happily and they scream again: "Show us the baby!"

At this point I realize how much Michael appreciates - and needs - the love of his fans. Moreover: he can't live without their love – they are his support in this world. They are what charge him. They are his battery.

He sits trapped in the hotel. He would prefer to be in the streets and bathe in this love. He can't. He sits up there, beyond reach, powerless, but he wants to do something so badly! He wants to feel this love skin to skin that penetrates from below, wants so much to fill that emptiness inside... the emotions overwhelm him and in a spontaneous act Michael takes Blanket, then a few months old, holds a sheet in front of his face and shows him to his fans. And in doing so holds him a bit past the railing of the balcony.

A thoughtless reaction with devastating consequences. And to Bashir a welcome sensational treat for his scandalous documentary. The scene took a second. In media all over the world it's shown in slow motion: Michael with his mouth wide open, dangling his baby over the edge of the railing for several seconds. It looks terrible.

Last but not least, main course and dessert together: Bashir suddenly shifts his commentary back to the old allegations of child abuse, back to 1993 when Michael paid off the alleged victim Jordy Chandler to settle.

Bashir's cynical voice: the allegations were never really proven, for many the settlement was an admission of guilt.

Then - wham: cut to Michael in 2002, who is holding hands with a boy named Gavin Arvizo on the sofa and naively admits that children are spending the night with him as before — in his bedroom, with him on the floor, the kids in the bed.

Shocked, I closed my eyes at this point. Oh, my God, I thought. Why are you doing this? You'd have to know what people would think! And even if you believe in yourself and your innocence, don't believe in a journalist who lives for scandal! There was no doubt in my mind that Michael had not harmed these children - otherwise he wouldn't have spoken about them with such trust and innocence. Which pedophile is stupid enough to talk openly about what might incriminate him? But still, he also was also a veteran of the business: why did Michael speak on camera about it?

That he had paid for the boy's cancer therapy and had saved his life, was irrelevant at this point.

For Bashir and many other people in this world that statement was evidence of wrongful, criminal behavior.

They couldn't grasp Michael's being. They could not comprehend that Michael wasn't interested in sex and was inspired by the thought of helping other people, in his particular case children, in a world in which they had no voice. That's what he told Bashir, who asked him pointedly if he thought that was right.

Michael defends himself and for the first time he comes to life and is - pissed.

"You only think about sex," he exclaims indignantly. "As soon as you hear the word 'bed'! Well, I wish there were more adults who took care of their children, who let them climb into their beds, gave them love, instead of putting them in front of the TV or computer and exposing them to violent games! I give these children love and that's what the world needs! More love!"

"So the world," commentates Bashir vilely, "…needs a 44-year-old man who sleeps in his bed with children."

And although the journalist at this point would have deserved a hefty slap in the face, Michael asks him incredulously, "You would never allow children in your bed, children who never had a childhood, who will never have one and who need love?"

Taken aback, the journalist denies ever having done so, but in those seconds, he asks the perhaps only, sincere question:

"Why does this mean so much to you?"

Michael replies, "Because I feel the agony of these children, their pain. I can feel it, I am connected to them, it's as if I feel what they feel. I want to give them a bit of family, for at least one day, to see them happy for one day, that's little enough! I want to help them ... it hurts me that they don't have a real future."

He says it with tears in his eyes, describes how he reads bedtime stories to the kids, how he gives them hot milk and cookies, and how he brings them to bed with the feeling of a deep sense of security. Everything he hadn't had himself, that he misses to this day, and he knows that this gesture can move something profound in these children's hearts.

"That's important, Martin!" he says urgently, but distraught, perhaps realizing that his impression will once more mount prejudices against him instead of explaining his good intentions. And that's exactly what happens.

Martin wants the exposure: children shouldn't be sleeping in beds of 44-year-olds. The fact that Michael sleeps on the floor is swept under the rug.

Then the crushing finale: the cynical message in the shape of a shriveled report of Michael's social engagement, talks about the fact that every three weeks Michael invites socially and physically disadvantaged children into his house and lets them do anything they feel like. Bashir's spiteful remarks:

"Jackson invites underprivileged children to his estate" - particularly sarcastic: "They can hardly believe their *luck*," and it's made clear to the blindest that these children have landed in the gingerbread house of the evil witch for sure.

Michael had trustingly offered Bashir his hand so he could be pulled up, as was promised, but instead Bashir had stepped on his hand and given him a brutal kick that carried him into the abyss.

***

Shattered, I sat at the computer after this documentary. What a disaster this must have been for Michael!

I remembered our conversation from the other day. My invitation to open up, to unravel his life ... groaning I slapped my forehead.

"Oh, my God," I thought. "How could I have expected that Michael would ever reveal his inner life to even one person ever again? Bashir was not the only one who had abused his trust! But he had done it on a worldwide scale. To a large degree he had initiated Michael's destruction, his crusade and the crucifixion itself:

The direct result of this documentary was the second trial for child molestation in 2003. The trial with the largest media coverage of all time. A trial that had never existed to that extent in the United States before. Not even for a mass murderer. Not even for OJ Simpson. That was also an indication of Michael's greatness, though. If he had really been this miserable wretch that the media consistently tried to portray him as, he would have only been worthy of small provincial court proceedings. But in his case, such a gigantic backdrop was put up that it entailed a disproportionate amount of time, personnel and commercial expenditure.

One thing followed after the other: a second search of his ranch, destruction in the name of a questionable law. Negative headlines without end.

Michael lost his Neverland. It was lost in every way. There was no more Peter Pan-land. He could no longer seek out all those magical places, had to let them grow wild. He was socially, professionally, financially and psychologically ruined.

I choked up. Oh, my God, I thought, how must he have felt?

For a long time I sat in front of the laptop. Unable to think a clear thought except for one:

"In life, what comes around goes around. Life is fair. And I wholeheartedly wish everyone involved justice. Even more, I wish you'd have the insight and the chance to make it right."

I breathed deeply, abruptly closed the computer, pulled on a sweater and ran into the dark park. I had to move so I could clear my head

Apart from Bashir's unfair documentary, there were a couple of nonsensical things that occupied my thoughts.

How was it possible that a documentary like that was aired? With a world-class star like Michael? With someone, who had an entire public relations department working for him? Usually, the final version of anything produced requires a written release. How could this have happened? Where had his advisers been?

So many weak characters were marketed in our society and set into a scene, although often they had little talent and personality. And here ... here there was a serious, decade-proven, socially engaged presence who had, in addition real talent ... and no one was able to make use of it?

That in itself was strange. And not only that.

The scene in which Bashir asked Michael about his father, about the beatings, the loss of his childhood…Michael reacts as if this question had never been asked before, reacts even stronger than on Oprah. In fact, he had seemed more professional with her ten years ago than here with Bashir. What had happened in the meantime?

And oddly enough, I found the justification of his baby-dangles-over-the-balcony-escapade as a key scene:

hyper, super nervous and jittery, Michael sits with Bashir in his room at the Hotel Adlon in Berlin. He is horrified, feels humiliated. The Berlin police and social services had already interrogated and warned him. He holds the baby in his arms, the bottle in his hand. The baby's face is covered with a green gauze veil. Michael's legs, on which little Blanket rests, rock in a rapid staccato up and down, up and down, up and down, and Michael's incredible nervousness transmits to the child. He starts to scream. Michael pushes the bottle between his jaws, the baby calms down to some extent, in contrast to Michael. Upset, he splutters an explanation for the balcony affair: that the baby was in no danger at any time, he loved his children above all, he would never expose them to any risks.

But he *had* put Blanket at risk because something had come up in him that was stronger than he was. Instinctively, he knows that, because in the end he insists, trembling, "I'm innocent!" pushing his lower lip forward like a stubborn child.

Again, this, "I didn't do anything bad! I didn't do anything! I was good!"

Here Michael revealed to me his deepest, darkest fear. And it is typical that what we are afraid of keeps reappearing; no matter how hard we try to suppress it, it catches up with us. We can't do anything other than finally confronting this fear face to face so it can dissolve and reveal what it really is: the illusory guard at the gate to the light.

The scene had to happen. Michael had literally attracted it.

And Bashir, trapped in his own thinking himself, stood behind him with the knife, ready to gut out another person to the very last drop of blood for the sake of advancing his own career.

Had he known that he was thereby opening the gate of hell for Michael?

XX / 1987/88

"What's the problem? He needs doctors, he will always be in the hospital occasionally. And if not, make it happen. There's enough stuff that works fast enough. And long enough."

Michael wasn't there the following day either. And I was even fine with that, because I was still too upset, too undone to be able to approach him with a solid stance. My own belief system in the world had been shaken up quite a bit, in light of the difficulties that he had to contend with.

Michael was not the only one something like this had happened to, but he was the only one who was subjected to this negative publicity with such great fanfare and steadiness. Or did it only last this long because he was still around? Not broken yet?

And in spite of everything he had remained a good person.

The next day I researched Bashir. It was interesting to see what could be found about him on the Internet:

he had already been indicted in England for frivolous reporting. His breakthrough had been with a personality similar to Michael's. Just as loving, just as engaged in charity, fighting against the establishment: Lady Diana. But at the time the people had reacted sympathetically to Diana's revelations of being an unhappy, cheated wife. Perhaps his interviewee was just simply lucky that this shot hadn't backfired.

A fortune not granted to Michael? His comments on this topic occurred to me: "There are people who are preventing this..."

And what had I answered? That there is only one person that prevents it and that is he himself? I wanted to throw up. To see ones belief systems confronted with reality was damn hard.

With astonishment I discovered a counter report from Michael's camera team a day later on the Internet, which proved that the impression made by the Bashir documentary had been distorted by intentional cuts - exactly what Bashir had been accused of in his trial: distortion of facts and manipulation of reporting.

Michael had his own camera filming throughout the entire take. And so the content of the counter documentary was a revelation: here someone was opening himself, someone the world would have been able to understand, a coherent, human and humorous person who spoke warmly from the heart about his most intimate feelings.

When you heard that, it was clear why he had trusted Bashir to the end: in the full context, Michael sounded reasonable and personable. And of course he had thought that he would be presented in that way.

He speaks openly about why he is shy with adults, why he feels more comfortable with children.

"Little children have never cheated on me or betrayed me," he says. "It's not in their mind sets. They don't get that until they are older. They don't judge

102

you, they accept you for who you are, while to adults your status, your role in society, and your money are what count."

Michael tells Bashir that the people who criticize him don't even know him, and explains that they don't want to know the truth, because they are more interested in bad things.

"The stars, the moon, the universe…" he explains, "…are what children mean to me. All children, not just my own. I've always felt responsible to take care of others. I go to hospitals as often as I go to concerts, you know? Wherever I do a concert, I go to the hospital first, to the children. And I don't expect the press to print that − they wouldn't even want to print it. I reach my hand out to the children; I've been doing that for decades. I buy a pick-up full of toys, pack everything up and surprise the kids."

And to be able to fully understand why Michael hadn't doubted a favorable outcome: visibly moved, Bashir tells Michael that this statement was the culmination of the interview, he has tears in his eyes and praises him for having expressed himself so wonderfully - and then he has the scene cut.

When Bashir asks Michael about his aversion to the press and adults, he answers:

"You know, no matter how good your intentions are, there are always some idiots who want to take you down. All you want to do is bring a little more love and joy into this world, but I suppose it's easier to hate, condemn and be cruel, and that shows me that humanity can be ugly … and cruel … judge and hate − that brings out the ugly side of humanity."

How true.

It was shocking for me to see how Bashir was crying during this confession, to hear him sob how much he appreciated Michael's concern for children, how great he thinks his commitment to them is and that he admires him endlessly for what he is doing.

"… I have to cry," he told him, "when I see how you treat your kids … there is so much love, so much love … you are my role model!"

Michael explains to him the meaning and background of his social work and he does it so sincerely and touchingly that Bashir congratulates him afterwards, thanks him and stammers with moist eyes:

"That was really … really special, thank you, Michael. That was really special."

And cut − the scene is out.

The audience of millions in front of the TV, primed for scandal, saw only a chimera.

A few short scenes found by accident, only seconds, reveal a broader perspective of the relationship between Michael and Bashir.

Michael sits on the couch waiting for Bashir's people to finish setting up their camera while his own is already running. He takes a bottle of water and drinks from it. Suddenly you hear Bashir's belligerent voice:
"Why are you drinking from a bottle? Go get a glass for Christ's sake!"
Intimidated, Michael sets the bottle on the floor, his expression fades past too quickly − it seems to me, he feels guilty.
Shortly thereafter: Michael yawns. Bashir scolds. "Why are you yawning? Didn't you get any sleep?"
And Michael put up with all of this.

Oddly, the counter documentary didn't receive the same attention as the Bashir documentary did. Why? The tabloids should have been delighted with such a battle - it could have brought them millions.
So if it was really only about the money, then Michaels' opposition should have received attention. The only reason it didn't was, that it wasn't all about money after all.
I felt hot at the thought because that meant his fears seemed justified − it was about taking him apart.

Chris' words came to my mind. He had said: "If these bastards would finally leave him alone..."
Had he really been referring only to the media?

Inwardly I refused to read more about Michael. I wanted to hear the story, if at all possible, from him directly. Whether I was ever going to get a chance for that, I did not know. He would have to be there for that. But he wasn't there. And he did not come. He remained absent.

***

I continued to go out with Tom, he had become my glittering oasis. We understood each other like brother and sister, by now he knew my entire family and I knew all his ex-girlfriends by name. The days with him were uncomplicated and full of laughter. Tom was so funny and charming, he had become darn dear to me in these few weeks. He had become my true friend, a buddy you could steal horses with.

In the meantime, six weeks had passed and I was homesick. Even though I had been at home for a week between India and the United States, I had been gone altogether for nearly a quarter of a year now. And the more time I spent here in LA, the more I realized how many things I had planned I was missing.

When Tom and I were in a library, I picked up a pictorial of America and sighed involuntarily.

"Man, I had wanted to see all these places," I said, flipping morosely through the pages. "I wanted to have seen this by now."

"What's keeping you?" Tom asked.

"Yes, what's keeping me?" I repeated mechanically. "I suppose it's really time to go."

"Do you really mean that?"

"Yes, why not? I've seen a lot here in LA −thanks to you!"

"Exactly! You're going to miss me!" he said slyly.

"Why don't you join me?" I joked. "Take a vacation!"

Tom laughed.

"Vacation! What kind of a word is that? We're here in 'busy America'!"

"Well, that's exactly why," I replied. "Before you die of arteriosclerosis…"

"What else do you want to see?" he asked, and I couldn't quite read his expression and intonation. There was more warmth in his voice than usual.

"San Francisco … Sacramento and the other direction to San Diego and over to Mexico…"

Tom didn't say anything.

"What's the matter?" I persisted and cuffed him, smiling. "Join me!"

"I can't, you know that … I have too much going on here … have a couple of very stressful cases…"

Tom suddenly looked very tired. He ran his hands over his face and eyes. I looked at him closer and saw that the lids of his eyes were red.

"Are you getting enough sleep?" I asked, worried.

"Yes … sure … can always get four to five hours…"

"Sounds like strong coffee in the morning. What cases do you have right now? I hope no murder case?" I joked.

"No … let's hope it won't turn into one…" he smiled, but he looked almost cynical and the smile vanished from his eyes immediately. Rather hectically he took a book from the stack and leafed through it. Something seemed to have been bothering him this whole time … he had a demanding job after all − and dumb old me hadn't seen that? Where had my sensitivity gone? With a bad conscience, I wandered through the book tables and found myself at the newsstands. Michael's name shone in large letters from several tabloids:

Michael Jackson turns 50 − a man reaches puberty
Michael Jackson broke and homeless
Live tour with the Jackson family planned

Michael Jackson chooses residence next to primary school - parents complain
Foreclosure auction of Neverland Ranch
Michael's sister Janet has to pay her brother's staff

Stricken, I picked up the newspaper with the report about his ranch. His face looked incredibly stupid in it. And I knew: that's not how he looks like at all.

"Hey, I thought you're not interested in stars" I heard Tom from behind me.

"Yeah, that's true ... I don't ... but Michael Jackson was in my time, you know, the '80s, disco ...dancing... the first boys..." I fell silent.

"It is so sad what they write about him ... is it true about his ranch?" I asked then. Tom's eyes were dark as he took the paper from my hand and looked at it.

"I'm afraid so," he said, his voice a shade quieter than usual.

"And the part about these people complaining that Michael lives next to an elementary school ... just look ... it says here that they're afraid that he could watch their children when they get on the bus! Is there a school where he lives?"

Tom looked at me. "No idea," he said, and seemed somewhere else with his thoughts. Then he seemed to pull himself together and continued:

"But with Jackson it's one of those things with the kids ... I mean ... the allegations certainly have something to them... he's not quite right, don't you think? Why does he take little boys to his bed?"

"Does he take them to his bed?" I asked anxiously, and admonished myself to watch what I was saying.

"Well ... after everything you hear... and his obsession with plastic surgery ...he's a total freak, huh?" Tom grinned at me, but this time it didn't seem charming.

"Yes, that's what they say," I answered, and gritted my teeth. "I like him anyway. Maybe you Americans are simply sensitized because of your high crime rate ... but I personally don't believe that Jackson fools around with kids."

The last sentences came out more forcefully than intended, and I turned around so Tom couldn't see the expression on my face. Oddly, I felt violated, as if he had criticized me personally. Blindly, I stared at the pages in my hand.

"Chirelle," said Tom quietly and I could hear that he was standing very close behind me. "I think that Jackson is ... just..."

He broke off. I turned around. Tom looked me straight in the eye and the light that had become so dear to me had left and made room for unusual seriousness.

"Do you know him?" I asked suspiciously.

"No ... yes ... that is ... I've met him a couple of times ... at events ... does that mean you know a person? No ... honestly ... who really knows Michael Jackson?"

He laughed faintly but something about it didn't sound sincere.

"That's true enough," I confirmed. "He is certainly ... very complex."

"He doesn't look good," he muttered, and looked at the magazines. "They say, he hasn't recovered from the last trial."

"Is it my imagination or do you sound... glum?"

Tom turned a little bit away from me, as he stuffed the paper back into the rack. "Jesus ... no, why should I be?" he trailed off.

Astonished, I looked at him. He sounded so strange. Was there a trace of melancholy in his voice? Then his blue gaze lowered to my eyes with a slight smile. "He's a weirdo, Chirelle, to me, he's clearly nuts ... but ... somehow ... I like him."

Two days later, Tom called me and said he had a surprise.

"A surprise?" I said happily. "Wow, thanks!"

"You don't even know what it is yet," he laughed and was back to the old mischievous, carefree Tom.

"No, but thanks for even planning a surprise for me!"

"We'll need a whole day," he said

"No problem ... but I thought you were under so much pressure?"

"Yes, I am, but I thought that's exactly why a day in between would be nice."

"Oh, great! When are we leaving?"

"When are you free?"

"How about day after tomorrow? Shall we meet at our regular cafe?"

"Yes, all right, great, I'm looking forward to it."

"Me too ... and thank you, Tom."

So far I had heard Linda's voice raised only once ‒ when the maid had been fired. But on this day she was literally screaming. She was screaming at a man who had come to the house and wanted access to Michael's files.

"Mr. Jackson isn't here. You don't have any authority!" she yelled in disarray.

"I have permission, madam," the man growled with a foreign accent and held up a densely typed piece of paper. "Here is Michael's signature. I am authorized to look into his financial matters."

"Leave the document here. I'll read it and have the signature examined." Linda said stubbornly, and literally put her foot down in the doorframe. "And in particular, I'd also like to hear that from Mr. Jackson himself...I can't grant you access to Mr. Jackson's records. So leave!"

I admired her courage. The man was boiling, that was clear to see. He was dark-skinned and his face had rough features. A square jaw – somehow not unlike Michael's father, the father who had beaten Michael so many times.

Grace joined in. Standing tall she approached the stocky man, and at that moment her African profile was of royal nobility. She just stared at him, and the man actually withdrew a couple of inches.

"He says he has Michael's signature," whispered Linda, and showed Grace the piece of paper. Grace didn't leave the man out of her sight as she took the document, then glanced briefly at the signature.

"Listen, Mr. Tohme," she said icily, "I don't know how you got this signature. I don't even want to know. It is a fake. This is the signature of a an imposter! And now leave!"

And with that she tore the paper into tiny pieces and threw them at him.

"This will have consequences," the man hissed

Grace turned around with indifference. "It always does," she said. "no matter how it turns out."

The fact that Grace saw my expressions, as I was at my door gaping with dropped jaw, did not improve our relationship.

A beginning?

"Hey, Scheherazade," he said, and made his peace sign.

I turned around. Michael stood in the kitchen door, holding Blanket's hand. It was seven thirty in the evening.

"Hey! You're back! That's great!" I cried, and for a moment my heart skipped a beat with happiness.

"We were in Las Vegas," the little one revealed, and prattled on about what he had seen – of tigers and pirate ships and battles "on the middle of the street!!" of circus hotels and huuuuuuuuge pyramids and even larger mouths of lions that guarded the entrance to the hotel. I made a cup of cocoa for both of them while Blanket bubbled away and gave his adorable childlike enthusiasm free rein. Michael smiled at his son tenderly.

"Blanket," he said softly after a while, "you have to go to bed now. Grace is calling you."

"Yes, but I still want to tell Chi..."

"No, you have to go to sleep now, sweetheart. You said you just wanted to say hello."

"Tell you what," I said. "I want to bake cookies tomorrow – you could help me with that, do you feel like it?"

"Yeah! Yeah!" called Blanket and clapped his pudgy little hands. I looked at Michael. He looked good. Fresh. Rested. Our eyes met.

"I'm glad you're back," I said softly and lifted Blanket off the table.

Michael took his little one by the hand. He hesitated. Then he looked at me shyly. With a beating heart I waited for a few words from him. But he didn't say anything.

"Michael" it burst out of me, "please ... I need to tell you something that is weighing so heavily on my heart…!"

"You can tell me now."

"I…" my eyes went to Blanket, who was watching us with wide eyes. Then I looked at Michael.

"Fine. In the fireplace room then. In an hour? I have to tell you something too."

I swallowed hard. "Yes, that's great. I'll be there."

He nodded. Then he left.

And I pressed the kitchen towel that I had bunched up in my hands to my eyes with excitement.

When I stepped into the living room, I felt queasy. How do you convince someone of your sincerity, if this Someone has already heard that 1,000 times before and it turns out to be a lie just as often? I had to think about my experiences with Mr. Carlton and Co. Those were just a few. A few that had made me suspicious of all the people living in this city. How does someone feel who had already been bitten by sharks several times? I felt insecure down to the bone. But in the end honesty was the only thing I had to counter with.

The now almost usual picture: Michael in a rocking chair, without make up, with a lighter pair of glasses that allowed me to see his eyes.

I approached cautiously, sat in front of him on the floor, and this time the position didn't feel right. Michael realized that at once, got up and wordlessly pulled a chair in front of the fireplace. He was so tremendously sensitive and polite. That alone touched me so much. I had barely sat down when it already bubbled out of me.

"Michael, I ... as far as our last conversation is concerned, I ... uh ... these past few days I watched the documentary with Martin Bashir."

Michael stiffened, but he continued to look at me.

"I am so sorry that I so thoughtlessly asked you to talk to me about your life... after I saw that, I know that you have plenty of reasons to trust no one, least of all a woman from Germany who has only been here for a few weeks. I wanted to tell you that I totally understand and..."

"You didn't know the Bashir documentary?" asked Michael.

"No!! I was completely stunned! What a pathetic...!" I closed my mouth. Michael smiled sourly.

"…I wanted to let you know that I would never pass on anything to the outside … I haven't even told my husband about it. And I know that you just have to believe me… that I can't prove anything … "

God, that sounded so lame! And I had just created the "over-and-out" for our conversation! Discouraged, I bit my lip.

"It's okay, Chirelle," he said. "We'll see what happens."

I nodded. Both of us were silent. This time it wasn't at all pleasant.

Michael was the one who broke the silence. "I've been thinking about a lot of the things you said last time."

I looked at him. Evasively, he watched the flames.

"You said … I attract things. Bad things. I send out signals."

I still didn't move. I wasn't so sure anymore of my so carelessly construed theory. Michael looked back towards me.

"I want to recognize these signals," he told me, and this sentence contained his entire, enormous suffering. It struck me like a super dimensional wave and almost tossed me down. And then, in despair, he added: "And I want to get rid of them."

"Michael..." I said softly. "I'm not sure anymore if I can do that…when I spoke the first time with you, I didn't know anything about you aside from a few performances and songs. And now … now …"

"Now you have gathered information about me and are in doubt," he completed my sentence without rancor. He would have accepted this response, because he had experienced it a thousand times before.

"Oh, God, no, Michael!" I cried, and when, startled at my intense reaction, he turned towards me, "No! Absolutely not! If I am in doubt, then it's about me … I don't know if I can help you … if I am able to draw the right conclusions … if … you know … in the last couple of days I've been starting to see the enormity of the challenges you have to deal with … and … and … in comparison, these spiritual insights suddenly seemed very…"

"Do you think they are of lesser importance just because the problems are bigger than you thought?" he asked. I hesitated. Then I felt ashamed of myself

"You're right, Michael," I said softly. "I'm sorry. Of course, I'll walk with you on this path … if you have the courage to unravel your life…"

"What do you do, anyway?" he asked me suddenly. "Are you a therapist?"

"No, that's just it," I replied. "I can only listen to you and give you my two cents, nothing else. I am not sophisticated. But I know from personal experience that we are often controlled by unconscious patterns that affect us for our whole life. Maybe we can solve one thing or another, by the mere fact alone that you recognize it …"

"That would be enough for me," he said.

We talked for a while about his children. The conversation became relaxed, and Michael even laughed as he talked about the things that he and his children had experienced in Las Vegas. It was well after midnight when he, the perfect gentleman, accompanied me to my bedroom door. He had helped me clean up the tray, put everything in the dishwasher and wiped the counter.

At my door, he was once again the reserved, shy Michael Jackson, who kept at least three feet distance. As I placed my hand on the doorknob, I closed my eyes for a moment and savored this so special energy that surrounded him. Then I turned around to him. He had taken off his sunglasses and looked at me with his incredibly intense eyes. A wave of deep affection rose up in me and flooded us both.

Michael sighed slightly as if bathing in it. He looked at me with kindness and asked. "Are you okay?"

"Yes, I am," I smiled. "… And ready for challenging a lightweight like you tomorrow with my newly created granola!"

Giggling, he asked: "Does it have marshmallows in it?"

"Yucky, gross, do they have them in whole grain version?"

"No Marshmallows?"

"Since when are you into stuff like that?"

"M & M's?"

"What next? This is wholesome food and no Smurf granola! But maybe I'll hide a couple at the bottom of the bowl! Just for you!"

Michael laughed. "No Jelly Belly's for Michael," he sang. "Good night applehead."

"Good night, Michael," I said warmly. "And thank you."

"What for?"

"For your trust."

He hesitated briefly.

"I'm ... busy for the next couple of days," he said. "I'll call you when I'm ready ... Sleep well, dateball."

And then we both giggled like little kids.

Michael was already on his way upstairs and I could still hear his so typical gurgling and giggling until the door closed behind him on the upper floor. I fell asleep with Michael's laughter ringing in my ears. Blissed.

***

It was the day for Tom's surprise and Linda and I had agreed that I could leave after breakfast.

The children had already disappeared with their private tutors into the study. It was my job to clean off the table and tidy up the kitchen. When I entered the room, Grace and Michael were still sitting at the table, engrossed in a controversial issue.

"Oh, sorry," I apologized, "I thought you were already…"

Grace shot me a murderous look and I got out of there. Michael was wearing dark sunglasses and other than his lips pressed tightly together there was little that could be seen of him. He was still in his pajamas.

Back in the kitchen, I breathed deeply. That didn't work for me at all. I wanted to get going, but had promised Linda that I'd take care of everything. She wasn't here today, and the maids had enough on their hands. I went to my room to get ready. At some point the two of them would leave the room, then I would sprint inside, clean up and take off. When I came back into the kitchen with my backpack, the volume of their conversation had increased considerably.

"Are you crazy to give this man power of attorney?" Grace yelled angrily. "You have to revoke that! The man is your downfall!"

Michael responded with something, his voice was softer than Grace's. I could understand only a few individual words.

"Promised. Neverland…" I heard. "Jermaine … but he's my brother…"

"After everything you've been through," I heard Grace rage. "Jermaine got you into shit before! And that one … you can see from a mile away that he's a gangster!"

"Grace!" exclaimed Michael loud and clearly. "He's not leaving … he's just not leaving! And there's nobody else here!"

"That's just it! He's taking you over! These people are running around with fake signatures of yours and closing deals in your name! Here! Look at that!"

She seemed to throw something at Michael. It took some time until Grace's voice was heard again.

"A charge from a hotel manager in Las Vegas, who says you were supposed to perform there last week! Who got the commission for the deal? And they'll take recourse against you!"

There was no response from Michael.

"And yesterday this auction house called – your entire furniture is being sold off! Your entire memorabilia from Neverland! You can't allow that! What did you sign?"

"I didn't sign anything!" I heard Michael, upset. "What are you saying about Neverland? Is that true? He's selling my things?"

"Is it ever true! Everything is ready to be auctioned off!"

There was no sound from Michael.

"Man, Michael … your CFO was here the other day. He wanted to talk to you … he says…" Grace lowered her voice, no longer understandable. Michael's answer wasn't either, but it riled Grace up so much that she became loud again.

"And I'm telling you, you're trusting the wrong people again! Go back to your old lawyer! You're surrounded by vultures! Michael! Wake up! These people aren't doing you any good!"

"My old lawyer cheated me, too!" Michael cried, and you could still hear the pain over it in his voice.

"Maybe he didn't! Maybe he was tricked just like you were!"

Michael didn't respond to that. Then Grace's voice again:

"Damn it, you have to get out of here! You have to relax ... you have to..." she trailed off, discouraged and desperate. When there was no response from Michael:

"There's... there's an offer from a promoter ... they'll pay ten million for a performance."

"Grace ... you know exactly how much of these ten million will be left over for us. A fraction! And I'd be on the road for weeks! They do all of that just to line their own pockets! And they need the puppet who dances for them!"

This time it was Grace who was silent.

"And one more thing, Grace: I'm not stupid. It may be that I still don't have a clear way out yet, but even a net profit of ten million wouldn't be a solution."

"I know, Mike," Grace said softly, and I could understand what she was saying, because I was, plain and simple, eaves-dropping, "We need help ... what about..."

The next sentences were spoken quietly again and after a minute I continued working in the kitchen with a guilty conscience.

The doorbell rang. I looked at the clock. I had to leave in five minutes at the latest. Maybe I could clear the table now.

Grace had left to open the door. Through the open kitchen door, I saw that it was the man she had kicked out last time. With a haughty look on his face that made me want to throw up, he demanded to speak to Michael. He came out of the dining room, saw him and literally cowered as if he wanted to hide. Grace stayed at the door, her posture expressing resignation and despair. Then Michael straightened, approached the man and shook his hand. Together, they went to his office. The door closed behind them. It looked like a march to the gallows.

I ran into the dining room as fast as I could, stacked the used dishes onto the tray, cleaned, and loaded everything in the dishwasher. Then I grabbed my backpack and headed for the door.

To my surprise, Grace was sitting on the stairs, her chin resting on her hands. Was she crying? When she saw me she turned away, got up and left without a word.

Sleeping Beauty

"Where are we going?" I asked Tom, and he looked at me with rebuke.

"It's a surprise! You don't think that I'm going to tell you!"

"But it would be helpful! Do I need a sweater? A second pair of shoes?"

"No ... really ... nothing at all ... just get in!"

I put my backpack in the back seat and pulled out the camera.

"I have to take a picture of you. My husband is really curious. I suppose once he realizes how good-looking you are he won't only be curious but also worried..."

"No pictures, Chirelle, absolutely not!" Tom said rather harshly. Astonished, I put down the camera.

"Why not? Are you worried that my husband will fly over here and beat you up?"

Tom forced a smile. If you didn't know him, you could barely see it.

"Chirelle, just get in, we need to go ... and close your eyes! Then my surprise will work best."

"I'll take that literally," I predicted. "I've got to be the worst passenger in the world. I always fall asleep. It's terribly boring to be in the passenger seat."

"Then take a nap," said Tom. "I have some thinking to do about a couple of cases anyway, so that will work for me."

He pointed to a thick stack of files that he had put on the back seat.

"Do you want to go through these today?" I asked, astonished.

"Well, yes ... I'd planned to, " he grinned. "I think I'll have the time ... But like I said, wait for the surprise."

That was fine with me. I tilted the seat back and enjoyed the heat of the sun that shone through the window as it lulled me to sleep.

After about two hours, he woke me up.

"We're almost there," he said. "How are you doing?"

"Oh, Tom, I totally passed out," I said, rubbing my eyes. "Where are we?" Sleepily, I looked at the watch. "Oh, my goodness I was out for two hours?"

"Were you ever! You were snoring!"

"Oh God, how embarrassing!" I chuckled. "Was I very loud?"

"It was all right," he grinned. "I turned on the radio."

I looked around curiously. He had taken the coastal road to San Francisco and we were close to a cozy and tidy- looking town. Green yellow foliage surrounded us, large expanses, the mountains to the back, a lake glittered in the distance. It looked idyllic but like nothing special. Nothing out of the ordinary.

"Close your eyes for another sec," Tom instructed. "I'm driving into town now and we'll have a cup of coffee so you'll wake up again. But I don't want you to see the sign."

"But Tom, that's silly. There's a reference to the place in every coffee shop!"
"I'll take that risk," he grinned. "So come on: shut eye!"
I did as I was told and he managed to actually find a place in the cafe that he had chosen, which gave me no chance to prematurely discover his secret. He got bagels, donuts and coffee and I thoroughly enjoyed the hot caffeine. Fortified, Tom led me back to the car, held his hands like blinders over my eyes, and told me again to close them.
"Man," I scolded. "Had I known that this was going to be a blind man's walk…"
"Only three more minutes! Can you hang in there?"
I began to peek after what felt like ten minutes. The car slowed down, Tom seemed to have arrived. I heard him turn off the engine. With eyes still closed, he steered me out of the car and put me in position.
"Now!" he said.
I opened my eyes and squinted into the sun. Two huge, red floral wreaths on a wrought iron gate flaunted at me. Distraught, I staggered a few steps back. Tom grabbed my arm.
He had brought me to Neverland.

***

"Considering you're not a fan and don't care for celebrities, you're pretty impressed," he stated. We were still at the gate. I turned to face him. Looked at him. I couldn't understand what was going on inside me. Everything was messed up in me. And I couldn't say a word.
"Okay, honey, I'll drive you inside now up to the main house … and then…"
"You have the keys for the gate?" I asked incredulously.
"Well … connections. Sometimes it's helpful to know the business … " But Tom didn't laugh when he said it.
Dazed, I dropped into the passenger seat again. When Tom started the engine and slowly drove through the gate, it seemed to me as if I were falling through the back of the enchanted wardrobe into Narnia, into an unknown wonderland.

A long, long, winding road through dense groves of trees, avenues, open spaces. The ground beneath the trees was dry, the grass burnt in places.
But still, the beauty and the magic of Neverland could be felt every second. Flowers bloomed everywhere and when we got closer to the main house, I saw Michael's Giving Tree, the tree on which he had received so many melodies and passed them on to us. My heart was pounding.
Tom even had the keys to the house.
"It's empty," he said. "You can look at everything."

Speechless, I stared at him. "Thank you, Tom," I whispered at last, "thanks a million."

"It's all right," he growled. "Don't you want to take your backpack with you?"

"No ... I'll leave it here... Wait a minute, I'll just grab something out of it."

I dug for a tissue and put it in my pocket.

"A tissue?" he asked as baffled as if I had pulled a gun.

"In case I have to cry," I told the astonished Tom.

He sat down on a bench, put the stack of files next to him and shooed me away.

"I've planned for the whole day," he said, "take your time."

I took my time. For a long time I just stood in front of the house, absorbing the atmosphere of the grounds, the enchanted likeness of a fairytale land without its king.

The nature here was breathtaking. Neverland was a scenic gem.

Slowly I walked up the stairs, flanked by box trees up to the main house. There was a huge flowerbed, defined by rocks in the center, and next to it an even larger one, now unkempt and rampant, but you could still make out the word, 'Neverland' and a butterfly made of flowers. Further up, the house in Tudor Style, the grand entrance. The key burned in my hand.

But first my path led me over the grounds.

Large, imposing trees everywhere, winding paths, huge, free areas where all of the attractions must have been: the Ferris wheel, carousel, the bumper cars, the go-cart ... the foundations of their platforms could still be seen, abandoned and useless, ruins of past joys.

Winding paths were put in everywhere, through grasslands or groups of trees, which led to differently themed places.

On an area tiled with stone slabs a red bicycle stood with an empty candy box in front, forgotten and recounting old days. It stood at a small, beautifully constructed pond, the mountains in the background. The red candy bike looked so bizarre, so enchanted, like a talking figurine that seemed to ask me:

"Where are the children? Where is the laughter? The joy? Where did it all go?"

It appeared terribly abandoned the way it stood there, like a symbol for all that had been lost.

The sun shone on the water, the scenery was lovely and idyllic, so exceedingly pretty, but wistfulness wafted like a melancholic scent over it all. Everything was frozen in a century's sleep like in Sleeping Beauty's castle. Just a kiss, given in love, and everything would come to life ... the air would be filled with the laughter of children, with elated shouting, with songs from the speakers and raging water fights ... it was all still here, all that was tangible ... and my throat tightened.

I saw the clock, adorned with a flower-design on the railway, the famous train station, now shut down, walked to the big lake with the three bronze children on the hill, passed small streams, decorated with figurines of children who were sitting on a bridge, talking, past so many sculptures playing in different poses, which seemed to all be asking me: '*Where is Michael? When is he coming back?*'

The many statues made the area appear even more vivid. What I had sensed in the first few days in Michael's house in Los Angeles could be felt here in a more pure, amplified way: not only the atmosphere of a happy children's world, but also the desire for one.

I encountered the Indian forest, with partly caved in tipis, the charred spaces of campfires and a huge banquet table beneath trees at the lake. You could feel the parties that were celebrated here, the joy, the laughter, the exultation and hear the songs ... oh, it was so incredibly delightful to walk through this magic and idyllic kingdom, to feel Michael's spirit and his childlike sense of beauty within it.

I wandered on. Neverland was especially captivating with its wonderful landscape. Of the 2,700 acres of land, only the smallest part was cultivated and landscaped, the rest was undeveloped, wild country - a magnificent piece of land, with unexplored valleys ... a bit of freedom for Michael.

There was so much to discover, so much to see. I would have wanted to spend a whole week here.

It wasn't until hours later that I got back to the main house. When I put the key in the door I felt like an intruder. These used to be Michael's rooms. This is where he had slept, spent sleepless hours, daydreamed, debated with his wives, brought up his children. The dark hardwood floor looked cozy, its pattern telling a story of its own. The whole house was permeated with it. It smelled of sun, dust and wood. The ceilings were very high, and the rooms had floor-to-ceiling windows with many terraces, an oversized kitchen decorated with lots of ceramic and enamel, an equally oversized living room. A huge, golden chandelier hung like the heart of the house in the middle of the open rafter. Everything had been moved out, everything was empty - ready for the next buyer.

I searched for Michael's bedroom and sat there for a while. Unrest could be felt here, nights of sleeplessness and tears. And the violence of wanton destruction. I couldn't bear to stay there for long. Something had happened here that had destroyed the atmosphere of the room completely.

But then I found the dance studio. With the first step over the threshold, I was already overcome. The afternoon sun flooded onto the dark parquet, the entire room, every single panel, every joist exuded music, exuded rhythm, vibrating from the feet that had followed this pulse, that had implemented it in dance, in dynamics, precision and harmony, in hard and gentle movements. I felt the dancer letting go, the dissolution of his self in the sounds of music, the dedication of the body to every single note ... in that room I so clearly felt the connection of the divine with the matter that I became dizzy from it.

Dazed, I leaned against the wall and let my back slide down until I touched the floor, eyes closed, in bliss with the palpable sensation that Michael had left behind here years ago, the awareness of his oneness with the Creator, when he danced.

The day was actually coming to an end when I stepped back outside. I hadn't thought of Tom for one second during this time and was startled when I saw that the sun was setting. But he had said, 'take your time,' and I needed a bit more for the last place that I had saved: the Giving Tree.

It was a dream of a tree. Admiringly I stood before this greatness, before these visible centuries, the branches so gracefully grown that were predestined for climbing. The entire tree was an invitation to sit in him and be with him. How many years old would such a giant be? 100? 200? Crampons had been put in the trunk and it did not take much effort to climb. Within a minute I had arrived at the broad branch, the platform on which Michael had received his most beautiful songs.

Motionless, I sat on this spot. It was gigantic. There were no words for this.

I woke up when the stars were in the sky and Tom was calling for me.

"I'm so sorry, Tom, I'm afraid I took your suggestion to take my time too literally. Can I make up for it somehow?"

I felt terribly guilty. He had sat on the hard bench for eight hours for my sake and had waited patiently.

"No, no, it's okay..." he ran his fingers through his hair, seemed impatient and nervous, which logically I thought was due to the time I had taken. "But we should gradually get back." He wasn't looking at me at all.

"Of course. You must be hungry ... please let me treat you to dinner ... if it's too late today, then another time ... I'd really like to, after this absolutely successful surprise."

"Yes," he said with an almost cynical tone. "Now you really owe me, don't you?"

I looked at him, puzzled. That didn't sound like him at all. Was he really that mad at me? His cell phone rang. He answered it. Hurried, annoyed.

"What!?" he barked into the phone. "No...no...not yet ..."

I walked away a few steps so I wouldn't intrude.

118

"Listen ... that's bullshit. I mean ... sh ... uh ... he checked ... yes ... everything with me ...no, nothing ... I'm sure!"

The caller seemed pretty upset, even though you couldn't understand the barked words, you could hear them - despite the distance between Tom and me.

"No!! Nothing is going on there ... he's one hundred percent pro! Man, I haven't been doing this since..."

Annoyed, Tom paced back and forth. "Okay, okay ... yes ... all right ... I will ... yes... it'll get done."

Pissed, he turned off the phone and took a deep breath. With hands propped on his hips, he looked into the vast night sky. Then he turned to me and said in a husky voice:

"Let's go, Chirelle."

We drove in silence. It bothered me tremendously that Tom, who had become such a friend, was so reserved. He didn't ask me any questions, which was very unusual for him, but when we arrived in LA, he insisted that we go for a drink. Although I was tired, I felt that I owed him at least that. Maybe he wanted to tell me what was bothering him. So we went to a bar.

"Tom, thanks again for this day, for your patience, and this really awesome surprise," I said to him as he sat with a double whiskey and I with a cappuccino. "I'm truly overwhelmed."

His smile was slightly distressed - was I irritating him? But then he caught himself and said it was a pleasure.

"Really," I doubted. I was sure that he was angry because I had taken advantage of his time limit so drastically, but then why had he still wanted to go to this bar?

"Tom, what's wrong? You seem so stressed. Is there anything I can do?"

Tom gave me a nondescript look.

"No, honey, I have to get through this on my own ... these are ... business affairs. "

I nodded. "Well then..."

"But ... but ... I..." Tom looked away, seemed to think about something, seemed to make up his mind, and then turned to me resolutely.

"Listen, Chirelle. Don't ask me how I know, but I know. I know that you work for Michael Jackson. For months now. And I know that you have intimate conversations with him, with Jackson, personally."

My heart was pounding. Should anyone ever again make fun of Michael as suffering from paranoia, then I'll share this little story with them.

"And you're mad because I didn't tell you?" I asked calmly.

"No!" he shouted. "I'm not mad!" He said it almost in a rage.

I had no idea what I should do. So I said nothing. And waited.

"Okay, I would ... I would like to pay now," Tom said abruptly and I didn't understand anything anymore.

"It's on me – that's the least I can do," I said, confused and depressed about this strange atmosphere.

He waited until the waiter finally came. Impatiently, he drummed his fingers on the table. I paid the bill. We went outside and stopped in front of the door of the restaurant. Tom put his hand on my shoulder:

"I'd like to give you something, Chirelle," he said, and looked deeply in my eyes. "And I want you to look at this carefully, OK? Right away. And promise me…"

He stopped and ran his fingers through his hair. This was getting more and more confusing. Again he grabbed my shoulder, pressed it firmly, forcing me to look into his eyes.

"After I've given you this... promise me ... to think about it ... I mean that you *think-about it*... do you understand?" and once more forcefully:

"You understand?"

Distraught, I looked at him. What was going on? I nodded silently several times. Tom let go of me. His hand reached into the inside pocket of his jacket and pulled out a legal-sized envelope. He gave it to me. I took it. Tore it open. There was a check for $50,000 in it for an exclusive interview with a well-known newspaper.

Stunned, I looked up at Tom. He stood there with lips pressed together tightly, eyes focused on me, dark and gloomy, I could feel his heart beat, while mine was in free fall.

"Tell me this isn't true," I rasped. "Tom ... please not you! Not you! Please tell me this is a bad joke ... tell me ... that it's not true..."

I burst out in tears. It couldn't be, not Tom, not after all this time and these carefree hours, not after this wonderful day that he had given me! I shook my head, the envelope burning in my hand, as the key to Neverland had before, the betrayed kingdom, the kingdom that had been destroyed by greed for power and money and envy.

Furious and incredibly disappointed, I tore the check into small pieces, took a few steps back and looked at Tom. He stared back. Then I turned around and ran away.

It was terribly difficult to keep my composure in front of Bob, who picked me up this time. I could hardly wait to get under my tree and cry myself out. Tom had meant so much to me. He had been like a brother to me. It hurt more than I could have imagined.

***

"I have to talk to you! Right now!"

Without much ado Grace grabbed my arm and pulled me towards my room. She opened the door, pushed me inside, then followed, closed the door and leaned against it.

It was the following morning. I had just cleaned up the kitchen and wanted to go for a jog when Grace surprised me with her assault. I looked at her in alarm. Grace was assessing me with her big, dark eyes.

"Number one," she said curtly, "it was me who did this with your room. I wanted to find out what you were up to."

"So? What am I up to?"

"I'm still not quite sure. Are you up to something?"

"Nothing you should be worried about."

"Why do you have so much information about Michael?"

"Because I think he is interesting! Because before I knew next to nothing about him!"

"And why do you want to know everything now?"

I groaned. "Grace, I am not a chick from the press and I'm not a money-grubbing rat that wants to make a profit. How can I prove to you that it's not like this? Tell me what I can do and I'll do it!"

"You could get out of here, and right this moment!"

I paled.

"You see? Not that easy after all, is it?"

With rapid steps she strode towards me and looked at me with wild eyes. "What's going on between you and Michael?"

"Grace," I exclaimed in horror. "How do you mean that? Hopefully not the way it sounds?"

She was silent.

"Jeez, Grace, if it makes you feel better: I am happily married and have two children. And anyway, I can say what I want; if you don't want to believe me, you won't believe me. But I don't want to leave either."

Grace calmed down a bit. Audibly, she let out a breath.

"You're married?" she asked suspiciously. "You're not wearing a ring!"

"My husband and I just didn't happen to exchange any."

"And you have children?"

"A girl, a boy."

"Do you have pictures?"

"On the laptop. Do you want to see them?"

"Y... yes."

Although we both knew that it was absolutely not our real objective to look at pictures, nevertheless, a minute later we were sitting in front of the screen. Grace smiled involuntarily, when she saw the old pictures of babies and toddlers, the yearly changes to my loved ones and my really very happy family. And I felt weak in my knees. I missed them. I showed Grace my house, the neighborhood I lived in, and it was reassuring for her to see how much I lost myself while I was describing the pictures and how ordinary my life was. And how far away from the madness that surrounded her here. But ultimately, that was still no reason to trust me.

"And now the children are all grown up," I said, and started a little slideshow that I had made. "Look, this is my husband."

"He ... he looks really nice."

"He is. I am very lucky. He is a dream come true."

"Then why are you here?"

"I just wanted to get out. My husband's job is very demanding and he couldn't join me."

Grace seemed distracted; apparently she had other questions in mind.

"Why do you want to revisit Michael's past?" she then hissed at me so abruptly that I recoiled.

"It ... it just turned out that way," I stammered. In a helpless move I went to the nightstand and picked up the book that had started all this.

"This is the book that we talked about..." I frantically opened the pages. "And ... these ... are the words that started our conversation."

Grace was silent. But she took the book and bowed her head to read the text.

"That's ... that's how it started, Grace. Totally harmless. And at the time I didn't know anything about him ... I knew a couple of Michael's songs ... but I didn't know him! And after I had that first conversation with him, I wanted to know more about him, wanted to know why a person who is so profoundly good, has to go through this kind of shit!"

Grace's eyes narrowed.

"Have you been able to give him an explanation yet?" she asked sarcastically.

Quietly I said:

"I ... I told him that it must be because of him ... and then we had the idea ... to put his life in relationship with these words of wisdom ... and the day before, Michael asked me to work through his life with him... even though I told him that this is out of my league." I bit my lip.

Grace didn't say anything more. She sat on the chair and stared straight ahead. Then she pulled a USB stick out of her pocket and put it in my laptop.

"Now I'll show you something," she said, almost gently, "grab a chair and sit down."

She opened the file she had loaded. A video recording started. I saw the entrance to the bar where I had been with Tom yesterday. People went in and out.

Then I saw myself as I left the bar with Tom. I caught my breath.

The camera went on zoom; we are both making serious faces. It can be seen abundantly clear: Tom is talking intensively with me, puts his hand on my shoulder. He pulls the envelope from his inside pocket. I nod my head several times and take the letter. The film ends.

"That," said Grace indifferently, "is the version Michael gets to see."

As if struck by a viper, I sprang up. The chair clattered to the floor.

"That's not true, that's not true!" I screamed and burst into tears. "I tore the check up - I didn't take anything! I didn't take anything!"

Grace sat calmly, watching me.

"Keep cool, honey," she said. Completely beside myself I saw Grace's fingers click again - the movie continued:

I tear up the check and run away.

Five seconds - and a world of difference in between. Totally confused, I looked at Grace.

"You get it?" she asked cynically. "That's what's going on here, constantly and incessantly. It drives you crazy and I guess that's what they want."

Never had I imagined walking together with Grace to the pond. After these last horrible couple of hours, it was an absolute blessing.

"Why are you still suspicious of me, even though you knew that I tore up the check?" I asked.

"It wasn't for a lot of money," she replied. "You're still a threat. You're still talking with Michael. How do I know what you'll turn it into? Insights into his private life are worth quite a bit to the press. With pictures, even more. Man, you're really naive. Or I am ... I'm naive ... but ... I'm so sick of this mistrust! Sick of it!" she yelled. "My God, you have no idea how sick I am of this!"

How could I respond to that? Just a couple of weeks had me falling apart already. Grace had been in this circus for over 15 years. And Michael all his life.

"Tomorrow night, Michael wants to talk to you," she said flatly. "What exactly do you want to hear?"

"I have no idea. It will develop."

"Michael said you want to work through his life with him?"

"Yes ... that's right ... that's what we had discussed."

"The trials, too?"

"Yes," I said. "They are the main theme. I mean, they are the consequences of something we hope to uncover."

Grace was silent for a long time. Then she said softly:

"Let me be there ... I mean ... don't do that alone. There are some things you don't know about Michael, and they can make an undertaking like this unpredictable."

"Grace, whenever you want to. But how do you want to go about it?"

"You keep me informed."

"I can do that."

"Are you recording the conversations?"

"Are you crazy?"

Grace grinned. "Sorry, that's my acquired paranoia."

"Which I can now certainly understand better."

I turned to leave. I had work to do.

"Chirelle," Grace said, "I'm sorry about how I treated you."

"Not a problem," I replied. "As long as you're protecting Michael, you have every right."

It was only when we had separated that I began to think of key questions: how did Grace get that video? Both versions? That was only possible if I had been tailed the whole time. An uneasy feeling spread through me when I considered that I had been constantly watched in my spare time. And something else didn't fit, but I couldn't get it. I resolved to ask Grace about it as soon as possible.

Despite the disappointment over Tom, I slept really well again that night. Having come to an agreement with Grace was much more important and meant more to me than I had thought.

Let's begin

Michael came to me around noon the next day, cheerful and in good spirits and whispered in my ear:

"I ate your granola, although there weren't any M&M's in it. Not even at the bottom of the bowl - I scooped all the way down. You were messing with me!"

"I wasn't messing with you," I whispered back. "I was motivating you! And it worked... that's awesome, isn't it?"

"That's great!" Michael giggled. "But I'm not going to fall for it again!"

"Okay," I said, "but tomorrow the joke of the day will be at the bottom of your granola! Isn't that exciting to you?"

Michael grinned broadly.

"The joke better not be bad," he said. "It's going to have to be worth at least a bowl of granola. I already shoved one into me today!"

"A whole bowl of granola! Good grief! Are you going to blow up now? Let me see your belly - heavens! You look like you're pregnant!"

He laughed out loud. He seemed more relaxed than usual.

"Hey, Chi, time to start digging," he said then. "See you tonight?"

"Sure. I look forward to it! When?"

"At seven, I'll pick you up."

"OK, good ... I'll wait in my room ... or in the kitchen."

"No worries, the house isn't very big, I'll find you."

The house had eight bedrooms and eleven bathrooms. I could not help but think of Neverland.

Right on time, at seven, there was a knock at the door. I opened with a beaming smile, which dropped out of my face immediately: an unfamiliar, older man was at the door. He was stocky, had gray hair and blue-gray eyes. The eyebrows were distinctively bushy, the nose bulky and the lips narrow. He wore a suit with a crooked tie. Dumbfounded, I stared at him.

"What's the matter," asked Michael's voice, "I thought, we had a date."

"Michael!" I exclaimed, and my lower jaw dropped another couple of inches. "That's ... Is that you? That's incredible! How did you do that?"

As many times as I walked around him, I couldn't see that it was a mask. Michael laughed himself silly because the joke had worked. He hopped around like a three-year old child and pointed his finger at me, squealing and giggling. An image for the gods! An elderly gentleman, hopping around the room like Rumpelstiltskin! Laughing, I shook my head.

"So, sir, what are your plans?" I asked.

"We're going out," Michael explained.

"Okay ... and where to?"

"I know a quaint little place with private nooks that would be perfect."

"But why a restaurant?"

"Because there, definitely no one can hear," he replied. "Nobody knows where we're going. It'll be only you and me."

But Brother Michael, his bodyguard, patted me down anyway before I got into the car with Michael. He left my purse alone, and I saw that Michael noticed.

The restaurant was plushy. Red upholstery, high leather partitions that concealed guests from each other, dim lighting, dark furniture. It was really perfect.

"Aren't you sweating in this mask?" I wanted to know.

"A little bit, but I love to dress up, that's my freedom. Then I can do ordinary things. I was in a supermarket the other day and was shopping. Thank God Karen was there, because I had forgotten to bring money. Nobody screams, nobody charges at me, I'm in the crowd ... and still free – that's ...awesome!"

"It's such a paradox," I smiled. "That people become famous and want to experience everything of what you want to avoid. And those who are famous want to do what the non-famous are doing. Would you have preferred to not be famous in your life?"

Michael thought about it. "You're right," he admitted, "I love being on stage. I would have just liked to do it without this shit."

"But how about now?" I asked. "Do you want to go back?" I couldn't help wanting this for myself ... a performance by Michael ... there was something magical about it. But he sighed in response to my question.

"Sometimes I want to ... just because I miss the stage. But there are too many reasons that argue against it. A tour would kill me. You can't imagine how stressful it is. I can't eat because my stomach is all knotted up; I don't drink anything either. I just can't get anything down. Within a short time I'm dehydrated and weak. Often I have a fever. In addition, I can't sleep at night. I was never able to sleep well. But after shows it's extreme. My adrenaline is cranked up so much - I can't get off it easily. Then I spend the nights playing video games, with the computer, with something ... I can't sleep."

"Has it always been like this?"

"It started very early. When we went on our first world tour ... that's when it started, I think."

"But don't you get tired after such a huge effort?" I persisted. "Maybe the adrenaline is up for a few hours up after the concert ... but..."

"Believe me," replied Michael, "it doesn't go down. You're full of testosterone and adrenaline. If I had to go on tour now, I'd be dead afterwards. My body ... is ... I mean, I'm not 25 anymore."

"And what are you going to do?"

"Sing. Compose. Make movies. Charity. Connect people that make positive things happen in the world." He was silent.

"That all ... sounds pretty doable to me," I said. "I've read that you've produced 120 songs for each of your albums ... is it naive to ask if you couldn't live off of that?"

"Under normal circumstances I would have been able to live from what I created and built a long time ago," he said, "a long time ago."

"But?"

"That's being prevented. Systematically. I'm being...I am supposed to be destroyed." His voice was extremely quiet, I had to lean forward to understand him and his hands trembled as he picked up his glass. Then he didn't say anything for a while. Beseechingly, he looked at me.

"Michael," I said carefully, "we don't have to do this ... you know that."

"I know that, Chirelle," he said. "I told you - I want to do it."

"Okay, then ... lets start!" Invitingly I looked into the strange gray eyes of a 60-year-old, stocky gentleman and tried to reconcile him with the elfishly-slight figure of Michael.

"Well ... okay..." he said routinely, "where should I start?"

"Right at the beginning. As far back as you can remember. As far back as possible."

He took the glass of wine in his large hand and leaned back. With an almost monotone voice, he reported of the beginning of his career, how he had watched James Brown, Gene Kelly, Fred Astaire on TV, which artists he admired, and how his brothers and he had practiced in the mini-living room under the harsh tutelage of his father.

After a short time I interrupted him: "Mike, to know about that we wouldn't have to stay up all night. Your biography would tell me that."

With big eyes, he looked at me.

"I want to know about the other stuff," I said firmly. "About what you hopefully haven't forgotten yet. I don't want to see the image of Michael Jackson, but you yourself, straight up, you know what I mean?"

His mask annoyed me tremendously. To me it wasn't Michael sitting across from me - it all looked terribly fake and weird. The mask didn't reveal much emotion, but I thought I could feel that my request had caused his stomach to flutter. He was supposed to tell me what he had never told anyone before? His look spoke volumes. Resigned, I slumped back.

"You should have checked my purse before," I said dejectedly. "But I swear that I'm clean."

Michael remained silent.

"I ... I can't do this," he blurted out then. "Chirelle, I'm sorry ... but I can't...! For too long ... too many times ... I..."

And then he started crying. Like a child he pressed his fists to his eyes and kept his head down.

"Michael, let's go to a room in a hotel," I said gently. "Could you take that mask off? Please - I want to see your eyes. Don't be afraid. Maybe it's better if I ask you a few questions at the beginning and you try to answer. And if it gets too hard for you, then we'll stop."

The older man looked at me. Tears ran down his wrinkled cheeks, and he trembled. I got up and sat next to him. Put my arm around the thick waist, felt the padding that stuffed out his middle.

Then I motioned to the waiter. Michael called Karen, who was probably already used to invasions like this. We met her in his luxurious town house that he had bought using a false name. It took one and a half hours before he was presentable again. Yes, and then he finally, finally started to tell his story.

Little boy

"If I remember one thing that I can still feel up to this day," he said, "it was this sound. Sound was everywhere. Music was everywhere. Rhythm was everywhere. As a little kid I lay in bed and heard music throb. I felt like part of it, like everything was alive, everything throbbing all in the same way, in a universal rhythm. I liked to lie in bed. All was quiet there, and I was able to observe the stars, and they were throbbing, too — I can't say it a different way — everything was throbbing, humming, singing and part of an eternal song. Sometimes I could see it, I could hear it, was lost in it… I sank into this infinite silence from which everything is born: every note, every rhythm … I can still hear it to this day — the galaxies, the stars, the moon, the sky, the universe. They are singing! It is such a unifying element, this inexhaustible sound that is the source of everything. These are my best memories. This pulsation. This sound. Everything was sound. The world is sound."

Sometimes he told his mother about that. He tried to explain in his baby talk what he was experiencing. She laughed, stroked his hair and sang to him, to the little boy whom nothing could delight and calm more than a song. He loved it when his mother sang. She sang with something in her voice, which he understood deep down, something that connected the earth and the people. Something he felt inside himself too, the height, this cornucopia of joy and happiness, from which all these melodies originated. He knew this was the origin of all life. He understood what in the 16th and 17th century Johannes Kepler had described as the song of the stars in his "Harmonia Mundi." Yes, to feel this was pure joy, it filled him completely, and in those moments he longed for nothing. Everything was perfect.

He was a bright little fellow, lively, playful, and he saw magic everywhere. He saw the glow of a flower, sensed the magic that lay over the world, and with his child's eyes he saw fairies and elves and felt energies that made him happy.
And he felt music in himself. He could always hear this music. He felt it the strongest when he was quiet, when he closed his eyes and sank into this deep, eternal silence, when he was enveloped in creation and there was nothing that should have been different.
His brothers played with him, romped around with him, they were always there. He always felt close to someone, snuggled to one of his siblings or to his mother. That felt good; that was warmth; that was safety and security.
Like many he was bathing in happy timelessness in the first years of his childhood.

His father and his friends sometimes came to the house and played music. For him that was the most exciting thing ever. How a song was created through instruments, how guitars, drums, bass and voices fitted together. Michael listened carefully. And over time, he could have told them in detail which instrument they should set in with and the intonation with which the songs should be sung.

He would have loved to move with the music, his feet twitched with every beat and in his mind clear images formed when he heard the music. His mother admonished him to sit still, but he couldn't.

He danced when he heard music. His little body moved automatically, easily transcribing each respective beat. His feet tapped the floor, his hands made funny movements, his head swirled to the sound.

Many laughed whole-heartedly when they saw him. He was three and it looked cute. And not only that, he wasn't just cute to look at - there was something different in his movements. Nobody could have known that Michael not only heard the music, he also responded to what was underlying the music.

His brothers played music, too. When their father wasn't playing, they took the guitar out of the closet and Tito and Jackie, the oldest ones jangled around on it. They were talented, soon figured out the chords and tried to recreate what they had heard from their father. They did a good job. Before long, they could play whole songs and they deepened their knowledge in music class at school. In the evening when the father played they sat close beside him, staring at his hands, remembering what they were doing.

Except for Michael, who was still too young, they all practiced on the guitar. It was one more reason to be happy that the father was out of the house.

Michael was confronted with the fact very soon that the world was not all happiness and magic, that there were things that upset this magic. The first time was when he overheard an argument between his parents. It was about money. Katherine, with her soft and gentle voice, was trying to convey something to Joseph. He reacted angrily. When she wouldn't let it go and kept persisting, he yelled at her:

"That's my business! Stay out of it!"

But Katherine didn't stay out of it and that's when he hit her. His hand slapped her hard in the face and Katherine staggered back to where Michael was standing, watching this scene with huge eyes.

And there ... that's when he felt pain for the first time. Not the kind of pain you felt when you fall down and scraped your knee, no, pain inside, where you can't reach with your hand to rub it and make it go away. A huge pain that came from his mother and was transferred over to him. He felt how she was suffering and that she was unhappy. He was fully connected with her and her pain. And with this came the fear. Michael started crying, afraid.

Blood was dripping from Katherine's mouth; limping she took a handkerchief and pressed it to the bleeding spot. Michael stood next to her, crying, anxious and feeling powerless. Katherine cried, too. Seeking solace, she took him in her arms and rocked back and forth with him.

It took a while until he could feel the rhythm again. He got it again. But for the first time ever, he had fallen out from this unity and was thus made aware of the other side of life. A side that made him afraid because it promised pain and that he rejected with all his heart. But he could not ignore it, his permeability was too high. These sensations always seeped into him whether he wanted or not.

And so he instinctively began to look for ways to protect himself: for a recipe that would carry him safely through this life without this pain.

His mother was his role model and she took refuge in something that seemed to be larger than anything else. She always took him to church and at first he did not understand the words that were spoken there. But it was exhilarating when the people sang. That was beautiful, was what he liked and loved so much. But since that first conscious encounter with pain and fear, he also noticed other emotions in the church: despair, suffering, resignation and grief. And another thing, he noted: how much better people felt after they had prayed and sang. Music heals, he thought at the time. She makes people beautiful. She makes you forget about what troubles you.

Soon he also understood the words that were spoken in the church. They were often the same as the ones his mother told him.

"You have to be a good person," Michael, she warned him, "a good person. That's really important. Always be good to others, no matter what happens. Your good deeds will be counted and squared up at the end of your life. Make sure that you remain a pure, good person. God always sees you. The world is bad. But you can't measure yourself to that. You have to do better than the others."

You have to do better than the others. Michael loved her. For her sake alone, he wanted to be a good person. Here was definitely a way to avoid the pain, definitely a solution, because after all it came from God.

He heard this often. He heard that there would only be a few that go to heaven and he was afraid not to be one of them, not to belong, to do something wrong, to not be good enough. He couldn't do anything wrong! His mother was right, and he found her theory that the world is bad confirmed everywhere. All variations of the theme was demonstrated on TV; on the street the younger ones were beaten by the older and he saw firsthand how his father treated his mother and siblings. Why was a person allowed to be so evil to another?

Sometimes Michael didn't understand the teachings of his mother. Doubt clouded his little heart. Why did the father hit the mother, who was so good? Why were precisely those children who hadn't done anything beaten in the street and in the school?

When he was all grown up, he vowed it wouldn't be like that. He would not impose anything on anyone and he didn't want to be powerless. He would make the world a better place. He wanted to determine his life himself.

His mother told him he shouldn't go outside to the other children. He did not understand that. With children he felt safe, he would have loved to play with them. But the parents prohibited it. They wanted no dealings with others.

"You don't take anything outside that happens in the family," they explained. "Never take problems outside. People don't understand it and it's none of their business."

This was Michael's first image-training. What you take outside was different from what you feel inside. To the outside everything had to look good. But still there was a contradiction for him there, because Michael's family was considered weird by the community. Different.

His mother had joined the Jehovah's witnesses after she had heard that the pastor of her former church had cheated on his wife. The strict rules of the Jehovah's witnesses, their belief that only 144,000 people would be admitted to the kingdom of God following the destruction of the present world, and of course their door-to-door preaching, did not contribute to improving the Jackson's image in the community.

Somehow they didn't have the respect of people, because they disassociated themselves. There were no Christmases, no birthday parties, no joy at all was allowed and Michael felt ostracized.

"If we don't interact, there won't be arguing," his parents said. "You are nine brothers and sisters, you have enough company at home."

But there were arguments - like in any other family - too. About money. About work. About the children. And always it was the father who precipitated the argument, because he lost his self- control over little things.

One single person could make life difficult for many others, one person can determine how the lives of others had to be. An aversion developed in Michael. An aversion towards this injustice and this authority, that seemed to prevent this wonderful magic, that did not understand let alone perceive it, and that made life dark.

He was a young child. He could not see how Joseph labored to feed the family. He could not know that Joe wanted to protect them from the rising crime in Gary, where gangs killed neighbors every day. He could not imagine the demands of working two shifts. How much would Joe have loved to dedicate himself to music...had it not been for the duty to care for his family. Joe was a simple man. He acted the way he felt. And when he was angry, he hit. That's what he had learned and that's the only thing he could pass on. But he could also be incredibly affectionate and charming. He loved his wife and he loved his children. And he was hell-bent on giving them a better life. That was his self-imposed vow over which he lost all his reason.

Then came the day that would change their lives. His brothers had once again swiped their father's sanctuary and were making music. Michael was always there when the guitar was in the hands of the brothers and with his little fingers he reverently enticed a tone from a string, listening to the sound until it disappeared into eternity.
"Hey, Mike," called Tito. "Hand it over, now let's make some music!"
Tito took the instrument in his hands and played the blues. The others sang, bobbing their feet, automatically found the background vocals, created the background song - it sounded pretty darn good.
"Again, again!" shouted Little Michael, when the song was over, and he patted his hands together. Jackie laughed and sang a new song. His fingers plucked at the strings, then there was a "ping!" and a string had snapped in two. Shocked, the brothers looked at each other.
"Oh, shit," whispered, Jermaine, and covered his mouth in fear. "Where can we get a new one?"
Tito was barely breathing. "And even if we could ... does anyone know how to string it?"
He received silence.
"Man," Jackie volunteered. "How hard can it be? Put the thing back, if we're lucky, he won't notice and we can buy one tomorrow after school. We have to tell Mom."
Trembling, the brothers put the guitar back.

Joe came home in the evening. Charged because he had been bickered at on the job and to the children's horror, he went straight for his guitar right after dinner.
A short time later, a scream rang through the house, and Joe pulled the belt from his pants.
Michael covered his ears. This discord! How much it disturbed the order of the universe - how disharmonious suddenly everything sounded! Everything was infused by this fear! Michael hated the destruction of his world order. And he hated to have to be afraid of someone. Someone he was in complete subjection to.

The brothers begged for a chance. They screamed that they could play, that they were able to make music, and then the miracle happened: the father put down the belt, and after replacing the string, pushed the guitar into their hands and challenged them to prove what they had said.

And they played. And sang. The expression on the face of the father changed. Suddenly it all became clear to him.

In his mind, viscous dreams of his own music career reformed to a concrete, different vision. If he himself apparently didn't have sufficient talent - his children sure did! With that he would never have to worry about money for his family ever again! He would fulfill his dream. Of a better life. For himself and his kids. They would make it. He was sure.

For Michael, this experience had a much deeper meaning: he was exhilarated and happy afterwards. He thought of his father's face, how it had changed, when the music played. When they had all sung together. Music heals the world, he thought. They play and they sing, and everything is OK. She changes even Joe. Music makes everything all right again.

Joe however, plunged like a madman into his new mission and in his own way he was brilliant. Keenly he studied other bands, was able to analyze mistakes and strengths and gathered information himself about the scene, what hurdles they had to jump, which obstacles they had to overcome to get to the top.

Adamantly, he drilled his children. Jermaine was the lead singer, the others sang background and played the instruments. But Joe wanted the full program. He was more than aware that it was mainly the whole package that attracted people. It was not enough just to play one good song - it had to be perfect. Not only the compilation of the repertoire, the costumes, the choreography, the dancing ... all the embellishments were crucial. With this he demonstrated an infallible instinct and demanded perfection in every step, in every note, in every combination. Spellbound, Michael watched when they practiced, moving with them off to the side, imitating the steps and pretending he was holding a microphone in his hand.

When Katherine came home one day, she heard Michael sing. She had heard him many times before, but that day she noticed how clear and strong his voice was and how angelic. Fascinated, she listened to her four-year-old child, and she knew that Michael had more than just talent.

She told her husband before dinner. He wanted no part of it. A four-year-old? How did that look? How was this supposed to work when they went on

tours? Katherine retorted: "Marlon is five and he is in the band, too. Let Mike sing something to you. When you hear him, you'll know what I mean."
She was right. Joe got it with the first notes that Michael sang. The little boy had something that swept you off your feet! His concerns evaporated and his face shone.

After dinner was the second rehearsal. Jermaine, nine years old, put himself in front of the microphone and cleared his voice, the way his father had shown him.

"Jermaine!" barked Joe, and gestured with a nod to the back. Surprised his son looked up. "Starting today, Mike is the lead voice. You sing with him ... or in the background."

That wasn't a big deal for Jermaine. They were brothers and they all had the same goal. They wanted to become famous, wanted to make it, and if Mike was an asset to the band, there was no reason not to use him. Nevertheless, they were all surprised at how easily he fit right in.

The boy stood there in front with a microphone in his hand as if he was born with it, and from the start he moved like a pro.

***

"One ... two ... three ... four...!"
The music started, the boys began to sing, the first steps were taken ...
"Marlon! You've messed up your step again! How many times have I told you to focus!" yelled Joe. He grabbed the frightened boy and pushed him against the wall. This is about something important, you idiot!"

Marlon rubbed his aching shoulder. To follow the choreography would be very painful, but he couldn't let on under any circumstances. Intimidated, he gritted his teeth, panting deeply, trying to concentrate. But he was tired. Three minutes later his step was too late again.

"Marlon!" roared Joe. This time he pulled the belt from his pants. The leather whizzed through the air and smacked with ugly noises on the boy's back and buttocks. Marlon screamed. The father screamed. Katherine screamed. The little kids were scared and screamed too.

Michael pressed his hands to his ears and cried. Oh, how he hated that, how he hated it! Never, never should this happen to him! He worked himself up to an insane level of perfection to be sure to give no reason for this kind of treatment. And Joe screamed over and over again:

"You have to be the best! There is nothing other than the BEST! There are winners and losers in this life, and none of my children is a loser! Remember that!"

Next practice. Jermaine was beaten because he was off with the key, Marlon messed up the dance, almost as expected, and Joe was livid. The atmosphere was explosive, nauseating and the children trembled from the tension. Then, during a turn Michael lost his shoe and his balance and fell.

Joe had had a hard shift. Out on the street crime was escalating with frightening speed. Gangs sprouted like weeds and violence was commonplace. His boys had already been threatened with a gun on the way home from school. They had to get out of here! West, to California! And the kids couldn't get it together! Money problems were mounting - the instruments and costumes for the children had devoured enormous sums - and Katherine hassled him because he had used up their savings. The last practice had been a disaster and now the brats were screwing up the dance steps again! As if there were nothing at stake! Why couldn't they realize how serious the situation was? Did they think he put himself in front of them three times a day for nothing? Was it not clear to them what it was about? He was fighting against windmills! Rage shot through him like hot steam. His eyes fell on Michael, who was calmly putting on his shoe again ... and this nonchalance was the last straw that made the bomb in him explode.

"You!" yelled Joe, grabbing for whatever happened to be near him to hit Michael on the head with. "Is your nose so fat that you can't even see your feet?"

Despite all the misery, the brothers had to laugh at this remark. Michael's eyes teared up, his head hurt, but he bit back the tears. He would not cry, not in front of his father. Why had he messed up the dance? He had practiced for such a long time and had sworn that it would not happen. If he had not fallen out of step, it would not have happened. He couldn't mess up - he had to be perfect. To be perfect was such a great help against pain.

In the evening he looked in the mirror and studied his nose. And the longer he looked at it, the fatter it became.

Father's ambition left no room for pity. He knew no mercy. The children got up three hours before breakfast and rehearsed. They came home from school and rehearsed. They had dinner, did their homework, rehearsed one more time and fell into bed. The Jackson brothers knew nothing but work.

Praise did not exist. There was no time for tender loving care, attention and affection. What for anyway - they hadn't accomplished anything yet. And Katherine had to take care of nine children. A lot fell by the wayside.

When Michael started school, it was strange for him to sit with so many unfamiliar children in a room. Amazed, he looked around. Some smiled at him, and during the breaks he could even play with them. They had something about them, these children, something he missed for himself, something he didn't have ... but he didn't know what that was.

The teachers were nice to him, so nice that he felt an overwhelming love in himself, and an absolute need to reciprocate. He brought things from home to give to them because he was so grateful for their kindness. Katherine was shocked when she realized that Michael was giving away her jewelry.

"You can't do that," Michael, she told him, "that doesn't belong to you; you can't give away other people's things. Why are you doing this?"

Michael tried to explain that it was such a wonderful feeling to make someone happy and because he didn't own anything himself, he had just reached into Mama's jewelry box.

Katherine said nothing. She couldn't help but suspect that the love of his teacher was very important to Michael and that had been the real reason he had gone into her jewelry box. She suspected that he wanted to give because he wanted to be loved, and he thought this would help.

Michael, however, was sad that he couldn't give anything. If people were kind to him, it seemed like a miracle. He was generous and at some point in his life he would be in a position to give a lot. This he promised himself firmly.

The first time

Every year the school had an event where children were allowed to perform in front of their parents. Michael had informed his teachers he would like to sing a song. He would stand on the stage for the first time! He would have a real performance - like a star! And he craved it, his whole body resonated with the song and he wanted to pass this bounty along to his audience.

Shy, he walked up and down the small school's stage several times to get a feel for it, but when his teacher asked him to practice his songs, he refused.

"Why don't you want to practice?" she asked him. "At the event you might be so excited that you can't bring out a single note."

"Thank you, Mam," Michael said, politely but firmly. "I'll sing, when the time comes."

Katherine smiled at his zeal, and promised to come to the performance. When the day came, she took along Joseph's father, Samuel, a stern, sour man who was difficult to draw out of his shell.

One child after another performed. Their performances were sweet and child appropriate, but Katherine felt Samuel becoming impatient and cantankerous next to her.

"When is this finally over?" he growled. "My ears hurt from this yowling. When is your brat finally on?"

"It's almost Mike's turn," she whispered to him soothingly. "As far as I know, he is the next to last ... it won't be much longer."

"I sure hope so," Samuel spat. "Why did you drag me along? My butt hurts, I can't sit any longer."

With ungracious coughing and throat clearing, he endured another performance without applauding.

Then it was Michael's turn. The first seconds he stood still in the middle of the stage. He'd said not a word and sung not a note, but the room was noticeably electrified. A palpable jolt went through the audience, and his presence alone made them sit up straight, eyes directed forward expectantly.

You could feel the symbiosis of the little boy with the stage, with which he seemed to merge. Michael stood there with the self-assurance, as if this place had been invented for him. He felt the audience more than he saw them. He was full of emotion, full of the song that he wanted to sing, full of the need to give everything he had. This emotion flowed out, spread like a mist, reached every single one in the audience and touched their hearts, before he had even opened his mouth.

And then he began to sing. He put his small old soul into the song. Everything, everything poured out. He could feel it, see it, notice how the audience became resonant with him, feel how he captured them, how they responded to his tune. He filled each letter of his lyrics with emotion and gave them to the people down there below - and they absorbed them - they did not misunderstand; they felt exactly what he meant. It was perfect harmony, perfect understanding, perfect unison.

When he finished, there was a second of silence in the room. A delicious second of silence in Michael himself. Then raging, unending applause for him broke loose. People stood on their chairs. His teachers were crying and almost couldn't contain themselves; the principal clapped his hands until they were burning. Katherine, who was struggling with her own feelings, turned to Samuel, and was amazed to see that he was sullenly wiping tears from his face.

That evening Michael was brimming with happiness. There was something that he could give. That he could give to the world. I made them happy, he kept thinking, I made them happy! He wanted more of that! Perhaps he couldn't express himself that well with words, but he could through music, and through his person. With that thought, he felt comfortable, that seemed right and good. And it was such a lasting feeling that he was still whooping with joy days later.

And his mind told him: if you do that, then you will find your happiness. That's what he believed in. What else could he do?

***

"Jermaine!" roared Joe. "You're out of tune! Can't you hear that! Jesus, children, this is about your future! Is that so hard to understand?"

Living room-rehearsal. Joe was sitting in front of the children and was watching them like a hawk.

"Tito! Your entrance was too early!"

The belt swung in his hand, and threateningly it switched against the floor, as soon as Joe started to scream. He had been disciplined as a child like that and it had not hurt him. It never occurred to him that a blow could cause damage. Of course he did not want to harm his children. His belief was: discipline is everything. Whoever wants to get somewhere in life has to be hard on himself. Must overcome himself. Has to work harder than others. Michael agreed with him about that point, but he despised his father's methods deeply.

"Michael! What kind of a step is that? That's not in the program!" barked Joe, and the allocated amount of mistakes of the day was exceeded. He raised his hand. Michael pulled his shoulders up, stepped back and shouted: "That's how James Brown dances! I saw him on TV!"

Wham! The belt and the hard metal buckle pelted on Michael's back. But before anyone could even say a thing, the boy furiously pulled his shoe from his foot and threw it with full force at Joe.

Like in slow motion, in front of everybody's eyes, this shoe bounced off from Joe's head and fell clattering to the floor.

Shocked silence filled the room. Nobody dared to breathe, and everyone stared at the father. It took Joe five whole seconds to realize that his six-year-old son had thrown a shoe at him. Then all hell broke loose. Joe roared like a wounded bull and stormed at Michael, who tried in vain to get away.

And Joe hit him. He hit wherever he could make contact, he hit and hit and hit, and with every blow he got more aggressive, especially since in the beginning Michael didn't utter a sound. Joe saw red - he worked himself into a frenzy that made him blind to everything around him. Michael was on the floor, doubled over, frozen, tense and crying loudly. Blow after blow landed on his back, on his butt, his face, everywhere. Joe was in a total rage. Slowly, as if through cotton wool, the screams of his wife reached his ear:

"Joseph, stop it! Stop it! You're killing him, you're killing him!"

And at last he stopped, delivered one final bow to the weeping Michael, and rubbed his aching hand.

Michael stumbled away from him. Panicked, flayed, paralyzed with terror, he sought a place where he could not be found. A place just for him, a place, where he could cry, where he could be alone, where he was safe.

138

He locked himself in the bathroom. Leaned against the door. Heard his father banging against it a short time later, ordering him to get back outside. To continue rehearsing. In the background Katherine's begging voice, addressed to his father, saying he should give him a few minutes to collect himself.

"Five minutes!" thundered Joe, emphasizing his words with a threatening punch against the wood.

Michael sat down with his back to the wall, to where the shock of the blows could not penetrate and where contact with his father was no longer possible. He hugged his knees and rocked back and forth. His body was full of pain. The belt and the fist had left numerous bruises and red welts, open sores. After the first shock had ebbed, the effect of the beating covered his whole body, burned like fire. But his heart hurt even more. Oh, that feeling inside! It was full to the brim with this disgusting mess. Where did the magic and love go? Instead hatred spread through him, helplessness ...subjection ... the sadness over having irretrievably lost something that used to be there. Little Michael was crying silently, his mouth open. He had five minutes to cry, to handle this all-encompassing pain. Then he had to go back - to practice. On stage.

Ten pairs of eyes stared at him as he limped back to the living room.

The atmosphere was saturated with repression and fear. Everyone was quiet as a mouse. The eyes of the brothers dropped towards the floor in shock when they saw his face beaten black and blue. Katherine looked at him with compassionate eyes. He looked away. He couldn't take that. If he let himself respond, he would burst into tears and he didn't want that. Not in front of Joe. Tito raised his head imperceptibly and winked. Michael was grateful to him for that. With this wink he had clicked in to the other side, the side that also was still there - the playful side that made life bearable here. Defiantly, he stood with swollen, bloody lips behind the microphone and avoided the gaze of his father.

"You will never do that again," he said, more a statement than a threat. "And now I want to see a kick-ass show, come on!"

And the kids gave it their all. They were *The Jackson Five* - and they had big plans.

At night Michael was in bed.

Katherine had come to him, had stroked his hair and said:

"He just wants your best. He doesn't mean it."

That didn't mean anything to him. Joe meant it, he was sure of that. His body ached like hell. His lip was split open, it hurt when he sang. And his heart ... it was crying quietly, and without anyone allowed to see. His family did not talk about feelings.

He looked up at the stars and felt lonely. In the midst of his brothers that were all around him breathing and physically present, he felt alone. He yearned for lighter energies, the ones he could feel so clearly. Fell into a dream...dreamed that he was surrounded by elves in a mystical forest and everything, everything was good, everything was peaceful and sunny. It was a different world.

***

Tears were running down my face. Next to me stood a Kleenex box and the trash bin was half full with tissues. But only with mine. Michael remained strangely and unsettling calm - as if he had distanced himself from these events. A long time ago.

"How did you cope with it?" I sniffled. "How did you have the strength to get through another rehearsal?"

"I learned to perform even when I was in pain," he said. "To go on the stage, no matter how I felt. Even with a battered body, pneumonia or a nail in the foot... when I sang or danced I could forget. Then I was in my element, then everything was fine."

But he could not sing and dance all his life long, in order to forget.

Even though the episode had certainly left permanent damage in Michael, it also gained him a certain amount of respect. None of his brothers, even though they were older, had ever stood up to Joseph. The brothers as well as Joe were aware of that. For a time he treated Michael with a bit more moderation, which was barely noticeable because he was the one with the least to complain about anyway. Michael was more than a born entertainer, his instinct for doing the right thing at the right time was simply magnificent. He had a fabulous ear and amazing coordination. Every show he watched of other artists with steps that he liked, he was able to imitate in seconds. He saw them, practiced them and mastered them. And he practiced them until he was better than the original, until everything was perfect, until there was no single cause for a punch or a complaint. Then little Michael ran to his brothers, showed them the steps and at the same time made suggestions for a new choreography.

Joe noted with astonishment these extraordinary abilities of his son and never reprimanded him in that regard. If he had realized one thing, it was that Michael and his ideas propelled the group forward.

Maybe it was a kind of apology, but Joe began to say to the brothers:

"Do it like Michael. Take an example from the little guy!" Then he beat Marlon, Jermaine, Jackie and Tito and forced them to follow the instructions of their six-year-old brother.

Even if this could have been a kind of praise or show of respect, it was counter-productive in many ways. The brothers began to get irritated and sometimes felt like the backup band for a child star. And Michael registered and stored in his head that he indeed could avoid the unpleasant with achievement and perfection He felt that it was important to function and to accomplish. That was his right to life. If he was good, everything went well. But if he did not fulfill the expectations of the others, all the bad came to him. He had to function. And with this belief alone he put out several ominous magnets, including one for situations and people who placed exactly this demand on him.

The first hurdles that *The Jackson Five* had to overcome were the contests that were advertised in the district. Joe entered them in every last one. His steely discipline paid off: without exception they won every single competition. Already in those years they performed with such a high degree of professionalism that no one stood a chance against them. That was what Michael grudgingly admired his father for. He knew what constituted success and this was imprinted on him: hard work and discipline.

"No matter what happens," Joe said over and over again, "the show must go on. You owe that to the audience. And if you are just about to croak, save it for later. You can do that after the show. Never disappoint your fans. These are the most important people in your life. Remember that. Never disappoint your fans."

Having no competition in the area left to win, Joe went with his children to Chicago to take it to the next level.

It was truly a tough time for everyone, but also a time of connection.

During the week they rehearsed according to the already described routine. On Friday, the equipment plus the children were squeezed into the VW van and off they went to a weekend full of performances in all kinds of clubs. Some evenings they performed in five different clubs, rushing from one to another. Sunday, late in the night, they loaded the bus for the trip back home. Joe took the wheel and drove through the night while the children slept best as they could packed tightly in the back.

Five o'clock on Monday morning, back in Gary, dead tired and exhausted, they staggered into the house, hugged their mother, fell to bed for three hours, got a full breakfast, and then swayed to the school while Joe went to work for a hard week of shifts.

Clubs

The clubs were a thing in their own right. Chicago was a thing in its own right. It was a different place than Gary and its surrounding areas. Louder, more hustle and bustle, larger, more extravagant. With his fine senses, Michael was aware of this entirely different pace.

Their competition was no longer some small school or provincial bands; no, this time real names appeared on stage. Sometimes names they had already heard on TV and radio. Wide-eyed Michael waited eagerly to see these people perform. He wanted to know what they did, how they did it, what the intricacies were. He was the perfect analyst, standing behind curtains at the side of the stage and soaking up whatever he could. Often he was allowed access to the dressing room of a star and then he lost his shyness - in an intimate conversation he would drill his opponent with endless questions. And most of them answered gladly. Not only were they flattered, they were also touched by the enthusiasm of this little guy. Michael learned a lot during these days. While his brothers went about their pleasures after the shows, he ran star analysis.

For Michael, the performances in the clubs were very influential. Already married to the stage, he now developed real stage experience. He was drawn to the stage-boards: that's where he wanted to encounter that feeling of giving and solidarity. But the better he got, the more his father humiliated him during practice. Did he want to prevent Michael from feeling special? Maybe Joe began to suspect already in those days that the band was worth only half as much without the little guy. And that Michael could use this knowledge as leverage.

Anyone, who saw *The Jackson Five* was fascinated by the boys, but especially by the six-year-old. "Where did he get that from?" Joe kept hearing. "How can such a little guy put so much feeling into the blues ... as if he knew what he is singing about?" and: "Wow, how that little boy can dance! That's divine!"

Always just Michael, Michael, Michael. The others were also noticed, but only with: "The band is very good ... The brothers are really great..." Rarely was someone mentioned by name. Michael was the only one ever mentioned individually.

It irked Joe, and although he was also proud of his little one, he wanted to counter a trend that could jeopardize all of their livelihoods.

He beat Michael more than ever for the few mistakes he made. But what he was not considering was that this treatment activated the leverage he so dreaded earlier than he would have liked.

As Joe's hand once again rose up against Michael, the boy screamed at him: "If you hit me one more time, I will never perform again!"

Two pairs of eyes flamed angrily at one another. Furious, Joe's hand hovered in the air. Michael stood before him, with grim determination, seven years old, with as much authority in his eyes and absolutely equal to Joe. But he, Mike, never realized this for his entire life. And Joe gave in.

"Get in line," he growled, "before I change my mind." He let his hand drop. The brothers looked at each other dumbfounded. And Joe thought: there are other methods, too.

***

The clubs were dark and dreary when they arrived. They stank of male piss, stale smoke, the stages were shabby and the hotel rooms a disaster.

Michael missed his mom, missed her way of giving comfort as she did in the house in Gary. There were no goodnight kisses anymore. There was no cuddling; they had to be successful. Mike felt that his mother wanted that, too. And in turn, he wanted and needed her love. He wanted to see her laugh, and she laughed and smiled every time they came home and told her about their successes. Like so many children in this world, Michael began to believe that if he could meet challenges and achievements, he would in turn receive a corresponding amount of love.

But there were days when he almost despaired. Days when he lay at home in bed, where it was so warm and cuddly. He dreamed of breakfasts that Katherine prepared, had the smell in his nose of waffles and all the delicacies that she conjured. His little hands wrapped around the cup of hot milk in a dream, to which the mother had added a shot of honey, and Michael saw himself sitting at the table in bliss, the day ahead of him. A day he would spend with friends playing games. And on which he could, whenever he wanted to, be with his mother. She was there. He was there.

Then the abrupt cut: Someone yelled at him, he had to get up, hurry! They were late! Torn out of a warm bed, into a cold bus, jammed between amplifiers, guitars and the brothers. No warmth, no security, nothing. He felt lost. A longing in his belly for peace and love.

He found himself in a world that was dominated by sex, drugs, alcohol and egomaniacs. The world of nightclubs. No mother to bring him to bed at night, no peaceful breakfast.

There were days when he was crying in his bed and did not want to go.

"I want to stay here," he wept and pulled the blanket over his head. "I want to stay with mom…"

But: hands that pulled the warm blanket from the body, a wet washcloth slapped in the face, impatient, harsh commands.

He began to hide. He sat in closets, in dark corners, under the bed, where everything smelled of magic and the sense of security that he was so desperately looking for. For that feeling of being safe, not to be found. He did not want to be with these adults who always tore him out of the magic. But they always, always found him.

Who cared about the emotions of a child in those days? He worked hard. He had an 18-hour day. Michael was five when he was torn out of childhood and thrust into a business world where it was about money and power. In a time when many children can't even read and write, he danced and sang like a pro. In a time in which he should have fallen asleep in his mother's arms, untroubled, he was brutally catapulted into the world of show biz and of grown men. The shock was too great, the weaning traumatic. It hooked firmly to his insides almost like a bloodsucking tick - an everlasting sense of loss. The feeling of having lost something permanently manifested itself in a massive way.

And what was going on in the clubs was not likely to dispel Michael's fears. He was confronted with things that he could barely handle.

Joe shooed his kids to their rooms after the shows. But since the hours between performances were the only truly free time they had, the siblings roamed around in the clubs or hotels. Michael was always found in the vicinity of the stage, while his brothers were all over the place. Where Joe was, they did not know.

But one evening, they watched him as he went to his room, two girls of the trade in his arms giggling stupidly and making obscene comments. It was obvious what Joe had in mind. A short time later, a mix of animal groans, moaning and giggles penetrated through the thin walls. Stunned, the children looked at each other.

"Can you believe this?" asked Jackie and looked at Tito. He shrugged. Helpless. What should they do? That was the question that Jermaine posed. He was also dismayed. He was on the cusp between a child and teenager. And his father was in the process of loudly moaning away some of the values that he had considered irrefutable.

"Should we tell Katherine?"

The brothers got into an argument about it, heated discussions followed and in the end they decided unanimously to keep their mouths shut so they wouldn't hurt Katherine.

Wide-eyed Michael had followed the debate. For him, Joe's infidelity made his world collapse. His parents' marriage, this holy alliance, was suddenly only a facade and Joe was to blame. His fear of his father was now joined with a deep contempt, a mix that did not help reduce his feeling of loss. Mike was the last person who wanted to hurt his mom, but it was explicitly she who had emphasized over and over again the importance of honesty. "Don't lie, Michael," she said, "no matter what happens."

And if you didn't say anything? Was that also a lie? He was supposed to be a good boy, he had promised her. But honesty seemed to be something that was not so easy to handle. Michael often felt that he couldn't meet the expectations placed on him. It was so terribly much.

Life in the club was degraded. They had gigs in striptease clubs, in seedy establishments. Joe always looked at the other performances to assess the competition or to get ideas. And these other shows were not only by bands.
Michael sat with his brothers in a corner and watched too. He saw women take off their clothes on the stage, saw how they jiggled their breasts and gyrated their hips, how they made obscene mouth and hand movements...
Instinctively, he put his hands over his eyes, but the brothers giggled and pulled his hands down again.
"You have to see this," they whispered. "Look, what she is doing!"
A garishly made-up woman had a long object in her hand and was making motions with it that Michael did not understand. But there was something wrong and vulgar about it, he could feel that clearly. Nobody could like something like that!
He looked around. Shocked and disgusted, he saw the hypnotized faces of his brothers, the distorted faces of the men that were spread around the stage. He could not believe it: this was the transformation of human beings into animals, into wild, panting, uncontrollable animals! He felt the corporeal, sensed the lust spread like a tangible net over the entire room that trapped people and held them in its spell. The men shouted vulgar things, women responded with rough laughter and even cheaper gestures. They came up to the men, held their breasts against their noses and mouths ... and the men tried to take hold of them, with their hands, their tongues ... the drool was literally running from their mouths. Michael just about threw up.
He got up and wanted to leave - when the stripper noticed him.
"Hey!" she called out from the stage and everyone turned around to look at him. "What have we here?"
He stood petrified. She was naked except for a fig leaf, wore a thick chain that dangled between her breasts, and legs on high heels. The light came from behind and illuminated her figure, came through where her body allowed it: between her thighs, this small gap, where the legs can't close all the way... a lascivious, swaying gait. Like a demon she moved toward him, stopped with legs slightly apart on the edge of the stage.
Paralyzed, Michael stared at her garishly painted face that looked back at him invitingly, diabolically, with a voluptuous smile and half-closed eyes. She made a joke of his stupor. The other people in the room howled when they noticed the little one with the huge afro curls. The woman was standing at the edge of the stage, and Michael was about 12 feet away. She beckoned

with her finger, and as if through cotton he felt men's arms grab him, push him forward, heard men's voices, chanting something he could not understand in his shock.

With dread his gaze fixed on the woman who then put her hand on the fig leaf and shouted:

"Let's see who has the bigger pussy here...! Come here, little one, you'll get a free introduction from Big Lila!"

With that she tore off her fig leaf, which was followed by an outcry from the men, Michael was heaved up brutally, kicking his arms and legs as she tried to sashay her ass towards his afro hair.

It was Tito and Jackie who rescued him. They sprinted to the front and dragged him away, just in time.

Michael had a crying fit and the laughter of the audience on top of it. He felt humiliated down to the deepest place of his soul. They had laughed at him, made fun of him! They cracked jokes about things he did not understand and it was so terribly disgusting, so awfully gross, he hated it. It milled around in him for days and nights, weeks, months. Years.

His brothers did not talk about the incident - it was more or less meaningless to them. Nothing had happened after all. And the only thing Michael could do was to see it their way. And take refuge in his own magical world, where everything was safe and beautiful and idyllic.

Apart from these sleazy events, there were also good times from this period. I was glad that Michael also remembered that.

"We won all the competitions again," he told me. "In Chicago, and then when we did the famous chitlin circuit: theaters that could accommodate up to 2,000 people ... in Cleveland, Baltimore and Washington... St. Louis, Boston ... Philadelphia ... we got them all. And there were great artists ... I saw James Brown live, the Four Tops ... I loved that ... I loved to study them, loved the interaction with the audience and feeling the interplay with my brothers, how music influences, what it can trigger. We were getting more and more successful, professional and I felt more and more comfortable on stage. I loved this giving of my feelings ... I love it today still."

His energy was high, it burst through to the outside, expressed itself in melodies and lyrics. Michael was an old soul, he understood the heartbreak he sang because he found everything deep inside himself. He clearly captured the feelings described by a song. He could pull the sorrow straight out of his own heart, just like romance, love, rage and anger ... the whole range of feelings swung in his soul and transported effortlessly into his voice. Those were frequencies that the audience received subtly, whose authenticity they felt, and against their touch nobody could defend. Michael wanted, like all people all over the world, to be happy. The joys of childhood, the carefree games were denied him. His framework was rigid. And the only chance he had; the only opportunity to feel happiness was when he sang and danced. And he did.

Maybe everything would have turned out differently had Michael been older. But he was a perceptive child who saw things that others did not see. Some of his brothers were already grown or in puberty. And the 70s, and even more so showbiz, were too much for his sensitivity.

This contributed to a further separation within the group that was exacerbated by the fact that his brothers began to exploit the popularity that they'd built for themselves. To Michael's infinite disappointment, they followed in the footsteps of his father.

He was a nine- or ten-year-old lying in the bed of a cheap hotel room and heard how they had sex with groupies. They ordered him to keep his eyes closed, but sometimes he opened them in secret and what he saw then was what he had seen in clubs: distorted faces, out of control, open mouths, rolling eyes ... weird, unnatural voices ... it was disgusting. Michael pulled back into his world. His world was that of harmony and magic. His world was much nicer than the compulsive swagger of adults.

He did not feel he belonged. Felt different. He liked different things, saw different things, felt different things. And he made the profound decision not to want to be that way. He wanted to be a good person. He did not want this bestial way, which seemed to be in stark contrasts with the innocence inside him. He longed for this subtle energy, which he felt deep within, but at the same time he realized that for this in particular there was no place in showbiz. It was a dilemma.

Nights were filled with nightmares that tore him from his sleep, and with him his brothers.

More than ever he adored his mother, who not only preached to him but lived values such as loyalty, honesty and love. He needed something to believe in. Katherine was pure. She was gentle, she was caring, her heart overflowed with love when she saw her children again after a tough weekend. Michael reveled in the energy of the heart and then felt a mysterious longing so intense that he could have cried at the same time.

At this point Michael stopped with his story. He stopped abruptly. When after a few minutes he was still silent, I looked at him.
"Michael?"
He did not answer.

"Enough for today?" I asked him, as gently as I could. He had talked for three hours now - and my heart was heavy from all the impressions.

But the look in his eyes sent chills down my spine; it was so fierce that my brain needed some time to understand why this was so.

Michael wanted to tell me something he had never told anyone before.

And: Michael didn't want to tell me something he had never told anyone before. He stood in front of a black hole. With his eyes he asked me to force him.

And I did.

*****

"I can't even tell you what year it was," he whispered.

"It doesn't matter," I mumbled. "At the time you were too small and too young for everything."

Reluctantly, he started, stopped, tried again, stopped again. Again and again I had to encourage him.

"…I was … as so often … behind … a … curtain…"Again he stopped, tried to find a beginning, started with one syllable, then paused anew.

"What did the curtain look like?" I asked. That in itself was insignificant, but perhaps the description of the details would make him ease into the story more readily.

"It … it was red … red velvet, heavy, old worn…golden, faded tassels…"

"What did it smell like?"

"Like… it smelled … funny … I don't know like what, like smoke … but also like so many other things…"

"You were alone?"

"I thought I was alone."

Michael was doing his very favorite thing. He was watching an artist who was on stage and was delivering her performance. She was lascivious, but in an aesthetic way. He liked her smoky voice and when she stroked with her hands suggestively over her body, there was just a hint of sex. She almost withdrew from the audience more than she offered herself, and Michael was fascinated. With surprise and relief, he perceived that the audience responded too, not with wild screaming, but with silence. With something like dignity. He saw the men swallow, but there was also a glint of admiration, one, that showed class and made them look like knights who wanted to conquer a lady.

"That," Michael thought, "*that's* it. That feels good … that's terrific! How does she do it?"

148

During the break he waited for her in front of her dressing room. She shooed him away. Several times. He persisted in his shy way, until she asked him in after all and revealed her tricks.

Then came her second performance. Again, he was behind the red curtain. Studied her, internalized what she had told him. She winked at him from the stage, and he smiled back, blissful. She was very nice and he liked people who were nice to him.

That night he could not sleep. He stood up and walked around, came back to the red curtain. The stage was now dark and deserted, but Michael saw the lights again, heard the music, saw the show. With his hands he tried to imitate the movement she had shown him. The red velvet moved slightly and Michael suddenly felt: he was not alone.

Frantically he turned around. A stagehand stood before him.

"Well, little one? Are you looking for ladies?" he slurred. He was drunk as hell, and blocking Michael's way.

"Where y'goin," he hiccupped and grabbed him. "Come on an' open your mouth..."

With these words he let down his pants and pushed towards him. Michael screamed shrilly. The man jumped and tried to cover his mouth.

"Shudda fuck up, you...hick ... little prick," he growled and tried to pry the little one's jaw apart. "Open your mouth ... goddammit...!"

Michael felt the hard grip on his jaw, he turned and twisted as much as he could, but the man was big, he was massive. Effortlessly, he pushed him against the wall, his body with the open pants, greasy fingers on a frantically closed mouth. A stifled cry burst from Michael and he turned his head to the side. Everything in him revolved. The guy stunk! Oh, God, his smelled so pathetic...he was so disgusting and these hands, they held him, groped between his legs, pinched him, hurt him, used him.

"You dirty fuck, you're worth nothing, you ass..." mumbled the man, he was angry because he was not getting what he was after and again buried iron fingers brutally into Michael's face.

"What did you feel?" I asked urgently.

"Incredible fear," whispered Michael. "Total humiliation...disgust...he stank...God, how he stank! Of urine, feces, of old grease, alcohol... this smell...! And he was so close ... so close ... it ... I saw his thing ... it was slimy ... oh god ... it was so... "

A strangled sound came out of his mouth before he burst into tears, shook and fell to the carpet. ... "...And then ... Tito came ...Tito saved me ...Tito saved me...!"

"Tito, Tito!" shouted Michael in a blood-curdling scream, risking the danger of having to open his mouth even more. He screamed and screamed and the man cursed, changed his tactics, gave the boy a blow, closed his mouth and pulled down his pants. Horrified, Michael felt how the fabric slid down his legs, how the man grabbed and turned him, how he touched him, how he soiled him. Like an epileptic Michael flayed, kicked and punched until he got a fist to his head.

But when he struck him the man's hand had slipped from Michael's mouth and he screamed again like a stuck animal.

Tito came dashing towards them, his instincts guiding his way, and he understood the situation at a glance. He grabbed Mike, as he had grabbed him once before, gave the big, hulking guy a huge kick and hissed:

"Get lost, you drunken pig and don't you dare ever again...you old bastard...!"

At a run he brought Mike to his room and in his bed. Michael had fallen into a state of shock, he was shaking like a leaf and Tito could not do anything other than to say again and again: "Nothing happened, nothing happened ... Mike ... nothing happened..."

But Michael began to gag. His eyes rolled into his head and Tito was filled with fear. The others stood alarmed around them.

"What's going on? What's happening?" they wanted to know, but Tito brushed them off. He did not want to recount the incident in front of Mike. They dragged Mike to the bathroom where he threw up, heave after heave until only bile came up.

Then they washed him awkwardly and put him back into bed.

And that's where he lay. Alone. After all, nothing had happened.

Forty years later, Michael sat in the same stupor he'd been in then. He gasped. He was stuck in the cement of emotions suppressed for years. Of an unstoppable panic and the principle feeling to have been humiliated and smeared to the very foundations of his soul.

And suddenly he bowed forward, as if someone had stabbed a knife in his stomach. His mouth opened and he uttered such an inhuman sound that I was terrified. With presence of mind, I held out the trashcan.

"Out with it," I whispered to him. "Come on, Mike, spit it out, then it's gone, then you're forever rid of it - it will never follow you again ... you'll be rid of it forever..."

I had no idea that a man who was as thin as Michael could vomit so often. Tears ran down his cheeks, from the mental and physical pain, smeared his makeup and he was crying his eyes out. Finally, finally, finally. Oh, God, I was so grateful for this flood of tears! He wept for a long time...frantically loud, shaking, clinging to me...stammering broken sentences...and along with the stomach contents and the words, old stories broke from him, damaging beliefs, deep wounds, and he sobbed and sobbed and sobbed... until it was over, until he had no more tears and everything had flowed out of him.

Drained and exhausted, Michael sat next to me, shaking, shivering, even though it was warm in the apartment. I spread a blanket over his slim body with one hand as best I could while I held him in my arms. It was very likely that he otherwise would have fallen. Apathetic, he stared straight ahead.

"Mike," I whispered, stroking his head. "It's over ... it's over ... it's gone..."

I said it over and over again, performed healing visualizations, forcing him to participate, until Michael's breathing quieted and he half-opened his eyes. He looked incredibly tired. And this is what he said:

"Chirelle," he murmured, "I ... am tired..."

"That's no surprise," I said with a shaky voice. I was totally exhausted myself.

"But," he whispered, "that is a surprise...I'm tired ... so tired that I want to sleep..."

I sighed in relief and understood. "Shall I put you to bed?"

"I ... stay here ... couch..." he mumbled, half-asleep.

With my help, he hauled himself the few inches up onto the wide couch and I stuffed two blankets around him. Within seconds he was asleep. I quietly disposed of the contents of the wastepaper basket, watching as the muck flowed into the toilet and was neutralized by the pure water, got two more blankets and wrapped one around him to make sure he was not cold.

With the other, I lay down on the floor and was out just as quickly as he was.

***

I woke up because my cell was ringing loudly and demandingly.

"Where are you?" snapped a troubled Grace. "You didn't shown up this morning and Linda thinks you've landed your first newspaper article!" It was supposed to sound funny, but the worry was overpowering in her voice.

"Oh, God, Grace," I moaned. "What time is it?"

I quietly got up and went into the bedroom and sat on the bed. I felt completely wrecked.

"It's one o'clock in the afternoon!"

"Okay."

"Okay, what? Where are you? Where is Mike?"

"He's asleep ... for at least six hours, and I don't want to wake him."

"What ... what did he take?" Grace said softly.

"What ... what did he take? Do you mean booze?"

"No, I mean ...sleeping pills," she said impatiently.

"Not in my presence, and I was here the whole time...Grace, as long as Michael is still sleeping, I can't leave...I'll tell you everything when we get home."

"Why has he been sleeping for so long?"

"Six hours is not really long!"

"Are you nuts? Six hours, without having taken anything are... an eternity!"

I was silent. Mike's insomnia was known to everyone.

"What did you do?"

"Nothing. He did it."

"Yes, but WHAT?" she almost shouted. "My goodness, don't torture me!"

"Grace...I can't tell you in three words over...it was a long night...I'll bring him home when he has had enough sleep, then we'll talk."

Three hours later, she called again. "Don't tell me that he's still asleep."

"He's still asleep."

"And you didn't give him anything?"

"Jeez Grace, what would I have given him? I have never in my life seen a sleeping pill!"

Silence. In Grace's head thoughts awoke, which I could never have conceived, possibilities that would have surely shocked me. Finally, she stated helplessly:

"He's been sleeping for ten hours now."

"He needed it. I suspect he has some catching up to do, approximately 30 years? How long has he not been sleeping well?"

"That's just it, yes," Grace said softly, "wouldn't you be surprised?"

Michael woke up after fifteen hours of sleep. His hair was mussed up, his makeup smeared and stubbles pushed through the pale skin. He looked like Dracula.

In the first few seconds, he didn't know where he was. I sat on a chair across from him and put down my book when he started to move. Confused, he looked down at his left arm, then down his right. They looked perfectly ordinary to me - clad in the shirt and light jacket he had worn yesterday - but apparently not to him. Then he looked around and realized where he was. He saw me and the memories came back.

"Wow," he said with an ever so quiet voice. "Was I sleeping?"

"You were," I replied, smiling at him. "... for fifteen hours. Grace is…"

"Fifteen hours?" He sat up straight. "Fifteen hours!" he whispered then. It took a few seconds, then a smile spread across his face and he raised his arms in the air, stretched and repeated happily: "Fifteen hours!"

A strand of hair fell into his face. He felt his head, then touched his face, jumped and squealed like a diva caught in curlers with cucumber eyes and a clay facial. He got up as fast as he could and ran to the bathroom. A new shrill shout echoed through the apartment. I snorted and fell into a fit of laughter. I was in stitches about Michael's hilarious behavior and laughed so loudly that he came out of the bathroom, insulted, and poured a bucket of water over my head. In outrage, I screamed.

"The poor carpet!" I yelled, and when the comment made him stare at the same in amazement, I took the carafe of water and did to him what he had done to me.

"You squeal so adoringly!" I exclaimed. "Squeal again, please! Squeal for me! One more time!!" And since Michael automatically really had squealed, we both started laughing so hard that we had to hold our sides.

Sometime in the evening we came home. I had sent Grace a text message and she stood at the front door like a mom waiting for her children.

"Hey, Grace," said Mike, grinning at her. He made a beeline for the children, where he remained the rest of the evening.

Grace and I took a walk around the park and I told her what had happened.

"And that was it?" she asked, disappointed.

"That was a lot," I replied.

"But... but... that was a tiny bit! I mean, considering the mountain of grief in his life... that wasn't more than a...a speck of dust!"

"Maybe. But perhaps the speck was one of the foundations of the mountain."

She looked reproachfully at me with her dark eyes.

"Maybe it's not a speck of dust," I explained, "but the source of a chain reaction, you know what I mean? Maybe it was a domino piece."

"You mean, if that's gone even more could go away?"

"Yes... maybe," I mumbled.

"What do you mean, 'maybe'?" Grace exclaimed nervously.

"What do you expect? I'm not a therapist! He really had to suffer a lot! I don't know what's ahead. I can only say: what's gone is gone. That's it."

Grace looked at me almost in despair: "You do realize that you're playing Domino Day?" she asked me and did not look happy.

"Tell me, Grace, do you love Michael?" I inquired spontaneously.

Grace looked at me and shook her head. "I love him in my own way," she said. "But I'm not the woman for Michael."

"Would you like to be?"

Quietly, Grace sighed.

"No," she replied. "But he's got somebody. For some time now ... he's with somebody. He's not alone."

I was so surprised by this statement, that I didn't say anything for a while.

"Is she here?" I wanted to know.

"No ... they don't live together."

Then she breathed deeply, looked straight ahead and went into reserve, dodging any further request to reveal more.

"You're right," she picked up the prior conversation. "What's gone is gone. We must be grateful for every little break."

"Exactly. This humiliation he suffered at the time could actually be the basis for a pattern in his life. Just think about how he has been humiliated over and over again... and if that's gone now... sometimes a lot of things are resolved with just a single issue."

Grace looked at me and closed her eyes. And then she said what I had heard so often: "I just hope ... it's not too late."

And as always, she refused to elaborate.

XX / 1989 somewhere

"Prejudice has advantages," he said, laughing harshly at his own cleverness. "There is a study that shows that people can be more easily influenced by prejudice. If you tell women before an exam that women do worse in math than men, their test scores are lower. If you say the same thing to men, it doesn't happen - because there is no prejudice that supports the thesis. Which logically concludes that all you have to do to easily bring people to believe what you want is to sow prejudice ... that's genius, isn't it?

With smacking lips he puffed. One minute, two minutes, five minutes. Then:

"The press is great. Some people believe that the press manipulates others. And they're right. But what they don't know is that the press itself is manipulated. And the most beautiful part about this is: it doesn't take much effort. Put a heavy ball on the track and it will roll. And take all the others with it. No one asks if what you write is true. They simply take the notes from colleagues - if it is scandalous enough. And what eliminates people most effectively of all are rumors. And you know why?"

The eyes turned to him with an amused sparkle. "Because it's the same as with fame. Maslow's hierarchy of needs ... social affiliation ... they all want that. A rumor can split people off from the social network. And people can't stand to not be loved. Love - all strive for it ... Nobody gets that it's the true cross of humanity. That is the cross they have to bear... they'll do anything for love."

Michael and I agreed to take a break for two days, then we would continue.

We stayed at home and locked ourselves into the fireplace room. It was warm outside, but Michael had a fire going. He loved fire and he loved the nights.

Nothing happened

If one thing remained in Michael's memory after this night, then it was Tito saying: "Nothing happened, nothing happened."
Those were the words that were hammering in his head when he was afraid to fall asleep, that Tito pounded into his brain stereotypically when he woke up from a nightmare and which he recited during the day when he felt something inside him coming up - in the form of cold sweat, trembles and fear. 'Nothing happened ... nothing happened' ... his only chance in his present position was to do what he did: he repressed the experience until it was no longer visible.
And so it sank into the depths of his soul, where it was dark, where even he could not find it after a time. However, he could not control his dreams. That's when it swept up, and sleep became something that led him back to the hell he had experienced, a hell from which his brothers had had to rescue him.
Michael was afraid of adult men. For the rest of his life.

His brothers put their heads together and decided to tell Joe that Michael screamed at night but not the reason why. They were concerned that he would then keep all of them locked up in their rooms. And so they told him only that Michael didn't sleep well and had bad dreams.
This didn't mean much to Joe. That sort of behavior was just wimpy acting up that he had to drive out of his boy.
"Look, pal," he said to Michael, and it was supposed to sound gentle. "There are winners and losers in this world and my children do not belong with the losers."
He wanted to help him with these words, wanted to tell him that there were some things where you just had to look the other way. But Joe's talent was not for psychology or his peculiar notions of pedagogy. He wanted to make his boys strong and able to cope with life.
That is why he did what he had often done before to make something clear to his children: he put on a horror mask and using a ladder climbed up to his children's room at night. Thundering, he hammered against the window, screaming and raving like a madman. The smaller and bigger ones alike leaped up with wildly beating hearts, whereupon Joe tore the mask from his face and broke out in laughter that sounded almost more frightening than his antics before.
He wanted to say: look, everything is just fake! Everything is just an illusion! But he only made it worse.
Michael began to see his father as the epitome of evil. He was the one who caused suffering and fear. The adult man, who beat him who cheated on his

wife and created a toxic atmosphere. He started to hate him. And not only that. He did what many children do in distress: he polarized. The mother was good, the father the enemy. Sometimes just seeing him made Michael throw up because when he saw him, he saw not only him.

After these experiences, he became shy and reserved. Melancholy that he wasn't able to rid himself of for the rest of his life took possession of him.

Since the red curtain incident, he felt dirty and inferior. He longed for his mother, longed to be able to simply play, to give the lighthearted one within him some space, to be able to move about in the world of children, in dialog with stars and the moon, the way it used to be. He looked out on to the street, saw children running around, and a strong yearning dug into his heart. In the carefree faces of these playing children, he could see the awareness of being loved just for the sake of their own selves. That was what he was craving most. What he missed so vehemently and couldn't find anywhere in his life.

But he also wanted to become a star and he loved the stage, because there he could feel a bond that was good for him.

The contradiction of these desires made him despair. But even if he had been able to figure it out - would he have had a choice?

Overnight he'd had to start thinking and feeling like an adult. His heart was overwhelmed. His brain was overwhelmed. All that he could do was to infuse those feelings into his songs, let them flow to the outside and to share them with others. All that he could do was to promise himself to stay child-like because that's the source he drew from. On stage everything was harmonious and safe. Everything that had to do with music was safe ground for him. But outside of this he felt insecure - that was the adult world, the world of deals and racial discrimination - there no longer seemed to be an higher authority there on which he could rely.

He tried to get along in this world. Since he was inquisitive and intelligent, he read everything he could put his hands on. He bought tons of books, and acquired a vast amount of knowledge over time. Soon there was hardly a topic he didn't know about and about which he couldn't talk. Still, he always felt that all the others who had grown up in normal schools knew more than he did. He was afraid to embarrass himself when he opened his mouth. And so he kept it shut.

So many things happened over time that his heart didn't understand. And then his survival instinct was activated: his head told him that he had to play along in order to survive, he had to be the best, he owed that to his talent. Then happiness would come.

But Michael was already pondering the meaning of life in those days, thinking about the value of a talent, which died with the body and became worthless like the money one made in life. You could not take either with you. But he wanted something permanent, a positive reverberation, something that gave purpose and meaning to his existence.

And one day when he and his mother sat in front of the TV, there was a program about Africa, about children who were literally starving to death before his eyes, had mud holes instead of beds and parents lying dead beside them. They had nothing, not even clean water. Shocked, Michael watched the images flicker on the screen, and felt at once he was in the middle of what he saw happening. He felt the suffering of the little ones, their hunger. The desperation in their vast eyes was his despair. He felt the fat flies on his head and the pressure of the unnaturally bloated bellies. This misery pulled readily on his own injuries like a strong magnet, and he associated himself with them, as if he were one of them. He could feel everything: their pain, their hopelessness, their sorrow and bottomless hunger. Floods of tears flowed down his cheeks and he swore, swore with all his might, to fight against this despair for as long as he lived.

Dear God, he prayed, let me do something about it... I know now why I can sing and dance... I will do something about it.

Since that day, he felt the total commitment to use his talents for something good and to never intentionally hurt another person.

And then there was his father, who said he had to give his best on stage and he could never let down his fans. His mother, who told him that he must obey the laws of God. He must be a good person.

Michael was faced with the most demanding challenges - and in his whole life never felt that he met them.

"I'm a perfectionist," he said of himself, "I'm never satisfied with what I'm doing. It could always be better."

He tried to get rid of the sense of separateness, sought the love and joy he had felt in his childhood, when he had listened to the music of the stars. And he sought them, like so many before and after him, in his success and in feelings that others brought him.

"This all sounds so... sad," stated Michael when we were at this point. "It sounds like that because we're concentrating it...but it wasn't all like that. Especially not at this time. To be honest, it was a wonderful time with my brothers... we stood together, we wanted to achieve something together, we were a wonderful team, and when the time came and we had our first number one hit, when we were played on the radio for the first time, we were floating off for months into seventh heaven."

Joe did all he could to advance his sons in their career. They played at the famous *Apollo* Theatre in New York. To perform there was an honor. But *The Jackson Five* bowled over even this audience, known to be very moody and difficult, with their professionalism and their music and the evening was a huge success for the family band. They were just darn good.

They got a contract with Motown, and were the happiest children in the world. Los Angeles beckoned, the world of Hollywood, and they went out of cold gray Gary directly into the sun. Michael felt he was walking on air. The only sad part for him was that he was now completely separated from his mother, who had stayed with the girls and little Randy at home until their future was secured in LA.

Berry Gordy, head of Motown, invited them to his house, and the children's eyes almost popped out of their heads when they were faced with this big name and his wealth. And not only that, Mr. Gordy played together with them and his children. He took the time, was like a second father to them, talked to them, and this was a completely new experience for all of the brothers.

Since Michael was the youngest, he was assigned a substitute mom by Berry Gordy, the most attractive one that Mike could have imagined: Diana Ross. He nearly fainted when he first saw her and fell in love with her on the spot. Diana was beautiful, confident and talented and she had endless style. With elegance unique to her, she moved in the world of the rich and famous with a nonchalance that was unrivaled.

Michael admired her from the first moment. He was with her as often as he could, and under her wing he developed even more a sense of beauty and art - not only in music. Diana introduced him to pen, paint and canvas, and he lost himself in painting as much as he did in his tunes.

Michael loved charismatic women and Diana was a woman who caught everyone's attention as soon as she entered a room. She had that kind of subtle, elegant sexuality that Michael had also recognized in that artist in the club: the "Just look, don't touch" - sexuality. A sensual dignity, or dignified sensuality that fascinated him and that portrayed people as works of art rather than merely as human beings. And he registered subconsciously how much people responded to beauty and how effortlessly it opened doors for them. Everything seemed to be easier if you were beautiful.

The keen observer that he was, his mind tuned for success, he noted how important the external forms were. Beauty always enticed a smile; it seemed to him that beautiful people were loved much more readily.

For her part Diana was extremely touched by the little Michael, not only because he sang so fabulously and was so polite. She felt his sensitivity, the ability to perceive subtleties, the invisible, which spun a fine thread between them.

Michael was filled to the brim of his faithful young soul with gratitude for the love that she gave him. Deep feelings did not let go of him that easily and from then on Diana always remained in his heart, for all his life. She was his star while he was longing for a mother, and Diana tried to be his friend and mentor. She was so different from Katherine, but she gave him safety at an age in which he needed it urgently. He never forgot her for that.

When Katherine eventually moved to Los Angeles, Michael was happy that she was back, but he would have liked to have both women as mothers.

With the signing of the Motown contract, an entirely new world opened up for the whole family: a world full of warmth and sunshine, blue sky and palm trees, beautiful homes and the greatest fame of all. Not only were they out of Gary: they stood in the starting blocks to gain world success.

Berry Gordy guaranteed it.

And it came. It came overnight - as it did for so many who had worked hard for years to get there. They landed one number one hit after another. America loved *The Jackson Five,* the black population more so, since their success was proof, a banner of hope, that even with their skin color you could get all the way to the top.

It was not long before the Jackson-mania broke out. In a short period of time *The Jackson Five* were one of the most popular bands in America, and - to the astonishment of everyone - soon all over the world. They were crossover stars, stars, who reached both the black and the white audience.

At the time Michael was twelve years old, having already stood for half his life on the stage, when he had, along with his brothers, entertained himself right into the pinnacle of fame.

And with this breakthrough his chance for even a touch of childhood was over. Now he had a friend - a permanent, never-failing friend: the camera that henceforth accompanied him like a Siamese twin.

"It didn't just come as it appeared to many," Michael said. "It just got bigger. I'd already had no peace in school at Gary. Fans climbed through the window, disrupted the class, no one wanted to play with me - they all just wanted an autograph."

He looked up into the air. As always, he sat on the floor, knees bent. He was not sad, but rather thoughtful.

"In LA, when we had this huge success in the 70s with *The Jackson Five*, I got to know fame for the first time from this huge perspective – with no idea of what was still ahead of me.

It was ... exciting ... at the beginning ... suddenly bodyguards are around you, you're pushed into the car, the car can hardly move forward ... when it finally collects some speed you see how they follow you with their cars, fans and paparazzi alike, how the fans are waving, how they almost cause accidents just to catch a glimpse of you ... then you're maneuvered out of the car and brought to the hotel room using an indirect route. And then you sit there. You can't even go to the restaurant."

"Did you never sneak out?" I asked.

"Sure, again and again. When I began my solo career, I often times drove around the hotels in a wheelchair, or disguised myself and just got out ... that was great! That was my piece of normality. I felt sometimes like I was on another planet when I overheard people talking, when I heard what was going on in their lives... I just never dared to talk to anyone. I'm not good at disguising my voice."

"Jeez, all these things to think about," I said and laughed, "it's insane."

"It is," muttered Michael. "Like I said, in the beginning it was fascinating to be so desired and it was like a game when we were trying to get to the hotel ... like escaping ... the suspense ... are we going to make it ... can we make it? But after you've done this 100 times and are sitting in your room for the 100th time... well, I don't know ... we had board games, had pillow fights ... but there only so many games you can play in a hotel ... and it's a lot of time that you have to spend there. A lot of time. But at least I wasn't alone." He paused briefly, before he continued telling his story:

"And then ... one day ... we almost didn't make it to the hotel in one piece. At least I didn't."

***

He was about twelve years old when they landed at an airport that was mobbed with fans, who were totally out of control. They had already torn down a barrier and were much closer to the gangway and the limousine than was comfortable. Things were at a boiling point.

The bodyguards had already been warned by radio - there was no way to put up the barrier again and push the crowd back.

"It has to be fast," the security guards told them. "Tell the kids, they have to run as fast as they can."

Michael was tired that day. He hadn't wanted to leave. He had wanted to stay home with his mom. To crawl into bed and daydream. Sometimes, he thought, dreaming is more beautiful than reality. Even if you wish dreams would come true, the reality always feels different, less good. The dream itself is beautiful, he thought. How often had he dreamed of becoming famous! And now they were famous and he thought parts of it were stressful and tiring.

"Mike! Did you hear? You have to run," shouted Jermaine, when the door of the plane opened. Deafening shrieks exploded towards them. The brothers - except for Michael - looked at each other with sparkling eyes.

Wow! What a reception! It was getting crazier from performance to performance! The bodyguards looked at each other, too - with less of a sparkle in their eyes.

"Okay, boys, when I say 'go', run like a devil to the limo over there," explained Malcolm, one of the security guys. "It's still inside the barrier, but we're afraid that it won't hold much longer - and before it's trampled down, you have to be in the car, okay? Got it?"

He looked at each one of them, waiting for the nod. The screeching of the fans outside became even more frenzied when they saw movement at the door and the gangway was let down. Nervously, the bodyguards looked outside. To Michael the incoming noise sounded like an infernal cacophony of wildly screaming hyenas. At other times he was fearless and eager for adventure. Today his heart had plopped somewhere else and more than usual he wanted to get to the safety of the hotel room as quickly as possible.

"We have to go - the fans are going ballistic!" yelled Brother Michael, the head of security. "Hold each other by the hands and ... go!"

The start gun had been fired. The brothers ran. Jackie was holding Jermaine's hand, Tito ran with Marlon and Michael. Tito's hand felt good. Michael grabbed it as hard as he could and ran with him. Down the gangway, he almost stumbled, Tito pulled him up, the arm hurt, but Michael didn't say a word. His ears were flooded by an incredible, never-ending roar. He heard the voice of a girl, who shrieked, as if a knife had been rammed into her body, over and over again the same shriek, as if she were insane. Michael heard her clearly amongst all the other voices. Beside her another siren, hysterically sobbing, screaming his name in complete disarray. In a pitch that Michael could not understand ... how could anyone scream like that? As if a monster was devouring her! As if she was in a horror movie! He clung to Tito's hand, focused on the limo, on reaching safe harbor.

Michael wanted to cover his ears. It was getting even more chaotic. He noticed how the bodyguards yelled something at each other, despite the microphones in their ears. Somehow he felt sick, he couldn't stand this, it triggered something in him ... these screams, so close to him ... so close to his ear ... they were screaming right in his ear! Spittle sprayed him ... it surprised him and he looked up for the first time ... to find himself enfolded by people who had torn down the barrier and had descended upon him in a blink of an eye. Shocked, Michael looked into the throat of a girl who was roaring at full volume and was ruthlessly shoving her elbows into every body that was trying to push her from her spot. Another one threw up, an elbow hit him in the face, and he ducked automatically in pain.

The crowd heaved between Tito and him and he felt how his hand slid an inch from Tito's. The mass of bodies pressed on their arms ... The pressure was so huge, so huge... Michael's fingers slipped out of Tito's hand and he screamed like a madman. He was alone in the midst of this rampaging mob that did not know what it was doing anymore, which was totally out of control, that grabbed for him with greedy hands, tearing at his hair, at his clothes, pinning his arms and legs. Screaming, bawling, hysteria - he sank into the inferno, felt a greedy hand on his head, a jolt, a fiery pain - someone had ripped a bunch of hair from his head, he felt how it was burning, how his legs buckled, and he was falling... he saw legs, many legs ... many feet that would trample him any moment and no hand that would yank him out of this nightmare ... He had no connection ... the connection was cut ... he was alone ... alone ... alone ... open mouths, fanatical eyes ...bodies ... cuffing, pushing, kicking, hands ... everywhere ... everywhere ... Michael couldn't get any air, he fell into paralysis, he was scared to death.

"Where's the little one?" Malcolm screamed. "Tito, where's the little guy? Where is Michael?"
Tito briefly shook his head, he could not get back, the crowd was between him and Mike. He pointed with his finger to the approximate spot where he had lost Mike and Malcolm went pale. Ruthlessly he pushed through like a bulldozer, striking his elbow in bodies that stood in his way, found Michael, who was being heaved back and forth by the fans, semi-conscious with a bleeding head and he hacked at the crowd with his muscular arms and pulled him to his chest. As fast as he could, he ploughed his way through the crowd, literally threw the boy into the car and with engine howling and screeching tires the limousine started through.

"That was a blast, huh?"
"Have you ever experienced anything like it?"
"Look, I even have bruises!"
The brothers laughed excitedly once they were safely in the car and driving towards the hotel. Only Michael sat in the back and did not utter a sound. He was in shock, but no one noticed. He felt terribly sick and *that* they noticed because he threw up in the car.
His brothers groaned in disgust and complained about the stink. No one saw that Michael was bleeding. No one saw how sickly pale he was. No one saw that he had just experienced another traumatic event.
In the hotel his brothers went looking for groupies. Michael got into bed and pulled the covers over his head. He was cold. He was trembling. He was scared.
Longing for warmth overcame him, longing for his mom, longing for someone who loved him, just loved him and showed it unconditionally, who just simply, simply loved him, even without him singing beautifully, without being on stage, even without his talent. He longed so incredible strongly for

it that he thought his heart would break that night. But there was no one there - except for his faithful companion, fear.

It was remarkable that despite all the sadness that he developed, Michael never lost his child-like side. He sensed that this was his salvation. And his personality was also based on good deal of humor - that was his bridge to the bright side of life and he was always up for goofing around or for a joke. Michael loved funny people, loved people who made him laugh and he loved to play a prank on somebody. To devise it, the suspense ... the victim's face - that was divine! He loved good old games like hide and seek, water balloon fights, pie battles ... He loved to laugh and he laughed often. Hardly anyone could lose himself in a game the way he did. It was amazing how deeply he could draw people into his space when he was playing. He was so much part of his fantasy world, so completely immersed in this imaginary story that you suddenly had to ask yourself what the "reality" was. This dedication was a big part of Michael's personality - in his work and his play - which were the same thing for him: he devoted all his senses to the task at hand.
And he retained this ability, which so many adults have lost, despite the all-inclusive drama in his life. Michael was a child, and even more ... he was a child who gladly wanted to be a child. It was not just about making up for something he had never had. It was about never giving up the child-like because that gave him access to his source. He knew that a very special magic lay within.

He was "cute little Michael", twelve years old, Jermaine 16, Tito and Jackie were practically grown up. The latter basked in their success and during the tours they took all they could get. And they got everything. There was not a girl who denied them. They all wanted to have sex with a Jackson and marched with them to the hotel room. The noises were piercing and sometimes did not sound like anything beautiful, sometimes as if it hurt the girls, and Mike wondered once again why they did it.
Lots of the girls came into the room who still had something about them that bore witness to their childhood, but they seemed to lose this in a single night. Michael watched it closely. It seemed to have to do with growing up.
When it was over, the girls were tossed out of the room without another loving gesture. Most of the time they were crying. And Mike suffered with them.

And then there were all the other adults too: people who raged war on one another, cheated, stabbed each other in the backs. Michael observed how adults lied and smiled at each other at the same time, how it was all just about pulling one over on another so they could get ahead.

He saw that with reporters and journalists, too. Motown had taught them that everything must be "marketed," that you couldn't just talk with a microphone in front of your face. There were standard answers to standard questions. But Michael wanted to be honest and at the beginning he answered with what he had on his mind. He was deeply hurt when he read in the newspaper what they printed about him and his brothers afterwards. Things that had been twisted around to make a good story. He noted that reporters also "marketed". That they ingratiated themselves so they could get an interview and then wrote something hot that furthered their career.

Already at this time he began to refuse to talk to journalists, and if so only with proper preparation, or with someone he knew to be okay.

His inner conflict grew. On the one hand he wanted to be what he was, bubbly and full of life. But that did not seem to be possible in the world in which he lived. In addition to the childlike side, he developed a second one, the shy and distrustful kind. And on top of that he was often unsure which one was appropriate.

"And yet I grew up," Michael said, "my body was growing and I couldn't stop the process. I always had the impression that it was going too fast. I had the impression of not having lived my childhood yet ... the feeling of missing something ... it was such a vague, dull feeling and at that time I couldn't handle it at all. My professionalism grew up. Our success grew up. My face changed ... everything changed. It was the worst time in my life. I was so confused, I didn't know how to conduct myself, I had only experienced the stage, studios and hotels ... I didn't know any normalcy. And suddenly I wasn't the little guy that everybody liked anymore.

My skin was blotchy and greasy, I got acne, the nose grew wider and wider. I was so ugly."

That was especially bitter for him, knowing about the power of beauty.

And every evening he had to get on stage, into the spotlight, in front of thousands, millions of people and let them stare at him. But that was still OK. On stage, he was able to wear makeup, tell the lighting techs to adjust the light favorably.

But daily life wore him down. Completely on his own, he was often in despair because he noticed that people suddenly perceived him in a different way.

"Once," he told me, "we were at the airport and there was a woman who recognized us and stormed towards us. She shouted, 'where's the little Michael, where's this sweet, little guy?' And my brothers pointed at me, I was 13 or 14, was already almost 5'8 and she... she made a disgusted face when she saw me and let out a sound of repulsion. I cried for three days. When my father got wind of that, he started teasing me. He pointed out to people my big nose and pimples. He did everything to humiliate me."

These insults served the purpose of keeping Michael's self-confidence down. Michael kept hearing that he was not worth anything, that he was ugly that he could not exist without the family. He internalized this deeply. His previous experiences added the rest.

His voice sank to a whisper when he talked with adults ... if he said anything at all - mostly he evaded them. Instinctively this was also his cry for love: he played a young child because he had been accepted more at this age. However, people mocked this whisper voice, which didn't particularly further his talkativeness. Hardly anyone knew that Michael was able to talk naturally and did not even have an overly high voice. But only children and close confidantes knew about that.

I hadn't said anything about the episode with the woman at the airport. It was so typical.

Often it's the tiny moments, undetected, that push the crucial button within us and initiate a lifelong pattern that colors our thoughts, generates our actions and then in turn determines our personality and destiny. Another person, who grew up under normal circumstances, would not have been troubled for long by this incident. Michael, for whom the outer appearance was a principle of survival, had been shaped by the airport encounter. He felt ugly. And he knew if he were ugly, people wouldn't love him as much. But love was his elixir. Without love, he would perish. Without love, everything was ruined. Love was what he wanted to give because he felt it within himself. Love, he was convinced, was the power that keeps the world and him alive.

He changed his diet for a while and got rid of his pimples. Vegetarianism changed his facial forms and the proportions became harmonious. His voice had recovered better than well from breaking - Michael practiced a lot and his voice teacher was impressed by the range that his voice delivered. Even without the puppy factor, Michael was very charismatic.

The groupies had long since begun to chase him. He was now, too, a candidate for bed. But Michael refused. One day when he saw a girl, who was on her way to be with one of his brothers, he said to her: "Don't go."

"What?" she asked, confused.

"Don't go," he said, "don't sleep with him. Why are you doing this?"

The girl looked at him blankly. "I am going to your brother now and I'll sleep with him," she said, "and I'm going to enjoy it."

"You will regret it," said Mike.

"Why? Is he no good in bed? Are you better?"

"That's not it. You'll regret it anyway."

Half an hour later, the girl came out of the room. She was crying. Michael was standing on the street with the cab when she got in. He pressed a note into her hand. With tear-streaked eyes, she looked at him. Mike closed the car door and she drove away. Trembling, she unfolded the note: 'Believe in Love', it said, 'Michael.'

***

The male, older members of the family, including and especially Joseph, thought that Michael's virginal behavior was a bit fishy.
"What's wrong with that boy?" asked Joe. "He's not right. He is surrounded by sweet things and doesn't want to snack? What's wrong with him?"
"Maybe he's gay," surmised one of the brothers. But Tito shook his head. "He for sure isn't," he replied. "Michael says he'll only sleep with the girl he'll marry. Like it says in the Bible."
"What kind of nonsense is that?" growled Joe. "He needs to gain experience ... what is this holy chatter ... can't you give him a couple of tips?"
"Nope, he's stubborn," they said. "Even if he had the girls naked on his bed..."
Electrified they looked at each other. And they all had the same bright idea. Giggling, they dialed a number and ordered two hot babes for their untouched brother.
Michael came back home in the late afternoon.
"He's coming! He's coming!" called Marlon and they all assumed their position to witness as much as possible of his deflowering. Michael went upstairs and opened the door to his room. The first thing they heard was a horrified scream. Mike squealed like a hysterical housewife who had discovered a spider in the bathroom. "Oh my God! Oh my God!" he screeched. "What is that? What is that?"
The brothers broke into fits of laughter.
Soothing feminine noises and soft laughter was heard. From the ensuing harsh shrieks, they concluded that the women had approached Michael and were probably touching him.
"Stop! Stop!" they heard him call out in a shrill voice. "How did you get in here? You probably wanted to go somewhere else! You've got the wrong room!"
The brothers laughed themselves silly. Again cooing, lulling sounds were heard. The ladies had been forewarned accordingly; they had told them that Michael would be scared. And they seemed to be doing a good job. The room got quiet.
With elephant ears they listened at the door. Now and then voices could be heard saying something like: "Yes, sit down here ... yes, that's good ... here?

166

Is that what you like? ... just like that... come here ... you, too ... uh ... oh, yes...yes ..."

Then it was largely silent. The brothers waited.

"What are they doing?" asked Jermaine. "How far are they?"

"No idea, man," said Jackie, "quiet.... isn't someone moaning there?"

Full of effort they listened with ears to the door. It really did sound like that! And there! A loud groan, something like wheezing, again soft voices, something like sob, a sigh.

"Sounds good..." Tito said with satisfaction, "our little boy is growing up! Watch out, so he won't grab the most attractive groupies!"

They shared a restrained laugh and camped out in front of Michael's room. They had paid for an hour.

Ten minutes after the time had started the door opened. The two girls stood in the doorframe, fully clothed. Just like Michael. He pressed a book that looked like the Bible in one of their hands. The girls nodded several times thoughtfully and didn't touch Michael with a finger.

"Great talk," they said, "really helped... we'll think about it...and about our lives... thank you, brother..."

Then they saw the dumbfounded brothers sitting on the stairs and one of the girls said:. "Your brother is totally nice."

Flabbergasted they looked at each other. Nice? Great talk? Michael hugged them both and sent them downstairs. Then he threw his brothers, who stared at him open-mouthed, a nondescript look and disappeared into his room.

Even if the deflowering of their lead singer had not met their expectations, their careers did: the success of *The Jackson Five* rose to dizzying heights. They were the first black band to acclaim such huge international success and the driving force was Michael's divine voice, his charisma, his choreography, his ideas. But more and more often he felt patronized. Joe decided what he could and could not do, Motown determined which songs he was to sing...everything, everything, was regimented from the interviews to their choice of costumes and hairstyles.

"I was happy on the stage," Michael told me. "I was happy because there I wasn't missing anything ... not in the early years. But there was still so much in me that I wanted to express, so many visions that I had ... and I became dissatisfied with Motown. Berry Gordy had done a lot for us, especially for me ... but I was only allowed to sing what he determined. And at some point I didn't want to do that anymore."

Exactly at this time the sales numbers of *The Jackson Five* crashed vehemently. They could barely land a noticeable hit. While the Jackson-Mania still continued, it was only a question of time before the spinning top of success would wobble. Michael was desperate. He wanted to make a difference in the world! He had so much in him! It had to get out! He was so full! Joe and he asked Motown for permission to write their own songs, but it was denied. They switched to CBS, and only then did they realize how much profit Gordy had made through them and how badly he had paid them for it all. But Michael felt that Gordy had made them big and that was the price to pay. This was the first insight that came from the change. The second was: nothing lasts forever.

Jermaine had married Hazel, Berry Gordy's daughter, and was sitting on the fence now with a massive conflict of interest - but he stayed with Motown and was the first to leave *The Jackson Five*.

"How was it for him?" I asked. "Didn't he miss you?"

"And how," said Michael "And we missed him. He was unhappy as can be. Although he made his own career at Motown, but we ... we had all enjoyed the time with the brothers together. That was really the best time of our lives. We could rely on each other, we were never alone ... and suddenly ... everything was different ...To Jermaine the family and the cohesion of the brothers had always been very important, even today. If there is someone who wants to see *The Jackson Five* back on stage, it's him. Or to be precise: *The Jacksons*... because Barry didn't allow us to keep our name, so we had to rename. Since then we were *"The Jacksons"*.

"And what about you? How did you feel about that?"

"It was hard for me to see the band breaking apart. Although there had been a lot of stink before."

Because over the years the attitudes of his father, his brothers and his own had drifted apart quite a bit.

***

Even back then Michael already began to donate the money he made. He joined forces with Katherine and openly rejected Joe. And Katherine was a woman with strong religious values. In the Kingdom Hall, the church of Jehovah's Witnesses, which he still regularly visited with his mother, he heard a lot about people chosen by God, about only the few, that would make it to heaven - if they were good enough. He was afraid of not being good enough. Things like loyalty, keeping his word, no sex before marriage and the issue of humility surfaced again and again.

"What does humility mean to you?" I asked at this point with interest.

"Humility to me means admitting that God is the source of all accomplishments here on earth," he answered, "not the person. And that's something I can feel every day in my work, during my work and through my work. For me that was never a question. Without God, without this source I would never, never, never have been able to accomplish all this ... I would never have been able to write a single song, so I was incredibly grateful, and I thought: everything must have a purpose... it's to fulfill some sort of purpose."

His brothers, however, cheated on their wives, enjoyed with all their senses a life of luxury, and spent the money they earned on themselves.

Michael was not only the star, but also the driving force in the band. He organized everything - taken for granted over time - yet he had to do it, because no one cared as much as he did that the fans get a good show for their money. And so the entire show up to the smallest details of special effects remained in Michael's hand. None of his brothers was interested in details. They did little for their own development and thought that it would go on like this forever.

And there was Joseph, who did not want to really believe that it was Michael who had the main effect on crowds. For him, one thing was clear: they were a family, and as such they had to stay together. And he could only keep them together by suppressing any kind of individuality. They had become successful as a family band. That was the recipe, and in this he stayed firm. Rather than letting it go when the time was ripe for it, he followed it all his life and at every opportunity. After all, *The Jackson Five* were his life's work - and his livelihood.

He would be able to keep Michael, the family was at the heart of everything, Michael had to realize that, too. Genius or not.

Breakthrough

The pressure was getting greater for Mike. Sometimes he could hardly stand it when he had to sing nonsensical songs instead of realizing his own ideas. His drawers were full of notes and texts and ideas. His urge to find his own fulfillment eventually developed to a level that gave him courage to start his solo career.

"This was certainly not an easy step for you, huh?" I asked him.

"No, it wasn't," he replied in his always silent way. "But in the end I couldn't help it. I felt unsung songs, un-danced dances in me. I wanted to sing what I felt, not what someone else had felt and written. Sometimes so many inspirations were in my head I was ready to burst. They came with the force of a waterfall, they rushed like information through an open data channel, and I only had to retrieve them - before someone else did. Sometimes, even now, there is so much at once that I can't process everything. Then I write it all down as soon as possible. It's already here...it is all there...you just have to listen. Ideas are flying around in the universe, like specks of dust in the sun." Intrigued, I listened to his words. That was pure, pure inspiration. That was the side of him that was so divinely inspired and that he embraced. That was the real reason why everyone was so into him. That was the element that made Michael's presentation authentic and unattainable.

Yet to me the ever-recurring discrepancy in all of what he had revealed leapt out again: how could someone who was so close to God be so far away from Him at the same time?

But it was clear: someone who was inspired in this way, who let his songs and choreography flow into him from above had to have success.

It's the ancient story, one that is so hard to understand. Some people exert themselves, with their brains, their bodies, are diligent and persistent and yet don't obtain the desired success. Or achieve only a poor imitation of it. And those that let it flow, who follow an internal vocation, don't have to chase success - because it's rushing with giant strides towards them.

Michael had everything and more of what was needed for a huge success. Divine talent and the discipline to bring it to fruition. For months - for years - he worked on the completion of his first solo album.

With suspense his producers, his family and the rest of the world followed the sales figures when *Off the Wall* came out. The numbers soared to levels that no one had expected.

Off the Wall made Michael a superstar. Everyone was ecstatic about the mix on the album and about Michael himself. He was on cloud nine. Not only because of the good reviews, also because his real dreams and visions began to come true and his success proved to him that the words of doom and gloom from his father could not be true, that he was somebody after all, that he was talented after all, and that he was much better than anyone had previously thought.

With this success, he felt more liberated. His self-confidence grew. The people who had worked with him had affirmed him in a way that was new to him. They praised his precision and marveled at his musical talent, about his ability to break boundaries and to follow his vision. After the success of *Off the Wall*, to the world he was suddenly no longer only a member of *The Jacksons* ... he was Michael Jackson.

That didn't sit well with some. *The Jacksons* were no longer called for these days, and instead of pursuing their career, Michael began to distance himself from the family, although he was still under contract with his father. The members of his family watched this development with concern.

Michael zealously devoted himself to his second album, was at home lying on his bed in his terribly messy room letting the melodies flow into him.

He danced and practiced until he literally dropped: one day he slipped and broke his nose. The twist of fate! For such a long time he had wanted to have it made smaller and now he put it under attack.

The result of the surgery made his heart beat faster. For the first time in his life he found himself attractive. It gave him a completely new body image, a whole new feeling, and he was so happy, yes, so happy! Finally he could look in the mirror and an image looked back at him that he didn't reject! This joy generated more self-confidence and Michael felt this power to do what he felt like. To be allowed to follow his feelings like he followed the music and the dance. It was a wonderful feeling.

Janet was the one who showed him another way to get along better in this world.

She stood in the bathroom, her make-up case with her where she stored her latest colors. Michael was talking to her about the contract he had with Joseph and his desire to do his own thing. Of the family members he liked Janet best. She was as gentle as he was, and most importantly she could listen ... and keep it to herself. Michael had infinite trust in Janet. He told her about the latest argument he'd had with Joseph and complained about his woes. She listened attentively while she applied mascara to her long eyelashes. Michael watched fascinated as her eyes became more expressive.

"Wow, that's really effective," he smiled. "You women are lucky."

"Do you want to try?" she asked.

"What?"

"Mascara?"

Michael giggled. "I ... I have an interview later - in half an hour," he objected and began to talk about that. He had not wanted this interview, but Joe had forced him into it.

"Come on," Janet consoled him, "we'll paint a different face, then it won't be Michael sitting down there."

The thought struck him. His eyes began to glisten. Janet looked at him invitingly. Mike grinned and surrendered to her hands.

He had sat many times in make-up, had dressed up for the movie, *The Wizard of OZ*, for example, where he'd had the role of Scarecrow. But that was costume. What Janet was now doing with him was something else entirely. It was accentuating. She brought out a brand new Michael. With growing enthusiasm he saw how rouge emphasized his high cheekbones, how his lips obtained a different balance in his face and let his smile shine. And then his eyes! The best part was the eyes. Janet coated the lashes with mascara and traced the inside edges of his eyes with eyeliner. On the lids she put a hint of dark shadows. The makeup was subtle but he felt like a completely new person ... he felt protected ... he was not the vulnerable Michael whom no one understood. Captivated, he looked at himself again and again. The makeup helped him see his various facets. It was protection and an opening all at the same time.

When he went downstairs to give the interview, he felt like a different being. The reporter was familiar, it was not the first interview with him. Once the business side was done, he asked, confused: "Tell me, Michael, is that makeup?"

"Yes," Michael grinned mischievously, "looks good, doesn't it?"

"Uh ... yeah," said the journalist, "it ... looks really good ... different."

It was not just that Mike looked different - he suddenly felt that there was more in him than just the shy boy. For him, the effect was similar to someone who had forever worn jeans and sweater and suddenly changes into an expensive suit. That was one thing. And the next thing was: there was a way to get the beauty that he liked.

What had started with the face continued with his clothes. He developed a completely new style, had red leather jackets and military suits tailored, rhinestone gloves and costumes as if from a fairy tale, almost king's robes. His head was bubbling over with ideas and melodies, and, since his success, he was able to work with the best in the world and got the chance to implement his ideas and visions. Creativity burst from every pore, and seemed endless. He had elevated his dance style into such professional heights that the usual laws of gravity and possible interaction of muscles, tendons and joints did not seem to apply to him. It was simply breathtaking to watch him. His movements had something special about them; it was pure joy to see him. He began to create short movies that accompanied his songs. Choreography that told a story, that sent a message. And from all of this stuff in his head *Thriller* was created.

When it was announced everyone was excited. The music world was waiting for an adequate follow-up after *Off the Wall*, but if there was an expectation that *Thriller* did not fulfill, it was this. *Thriller* was no adequate successor; it was the ticket to the mega-star sky. It would become the world's best-selling album of all times.

It was a breakthrough not only for *him*, but one for all black singers, because Michael had gained them access to MTV. Until then, the channel had refused to play music by colored people, but Michael was so successful that they could not help but air him on the channel. It's ratings rose rapidly after that. A black man entered the realm of whites. The music world was upside

172

down, one success followed the next, one hit after the other - all singles of *Thriller* were number one hits.

Michael made dizzying amounts of money. He won so many prizes at once that one's head spun. He had become one of the most sought after people on this planet.

The Michael Jackson mania outstripped anything of its kind. Millions of people were screaming their throats hoarse for him. Millions of people were running after him. Millions of people wanted a piece of that magic. Of its connection to what we all carry within us.

***

"Were you happy?" I asked him. "Everything seemed to be going well at this time, for you. Man, you were super! That was the time when even someone like me knew about you!"

Michael laughed:

"Yes, in 1982, everything was going well. Sales were higher than anyone would have expected. I remember how my agents told me back then that I should be happy if I sell a million records. I formally freaked out. I called the studio and stopped production."

"Are you serious? Why?" I asked.

"Because I knew how strong faith is. And I knew that if we all pull together and everyone visualizes a certain number, then we could achieve that. I just wanted a bundling of energy ... and it worked. Instead of the one million it became 60, more than 100 to date. And I was awarded eight Grammys! Everyone wanted to go out with me, everyone wanted me here or there ... it was a gigantic time."

"And? Were you happy?"

Michael turned thoughtful. "Not the way I had imagined," he admitted. "I also wanted to prove that more was possible. The fewer the people who believed *Thriller* could be outdone, the more tenaciously I worked to prove the opposite."

"The dear ego," I murmured, "... isn't satisfied with anything. It just wants more and more."

"And there were so many side effects," continued Michael, without hearing me. "Things that gave me a vague sense of guilt..."

"Guilt?" I asked incredulously. "What do you mean?"

"Well ... the Jehovah's Witnesses were of the opinion that in the *Thriller* video I was glorifying the occult and forbade me to release it. The compromise was a disclaimer that we put before the movie ... and then two Jehovah's Witnesses were assigned to me and since then followed my every step, so that I wouldn't do anything unseemly."

My jaw dropped. "And you put up with that?"

"For years," he replied, and I could only imagine what this constant observation and spying for mistakes and missteps had triggered in him.

"Lots of people were jealous," he continued, "there were people who wouldn't even shake my hand! I hadn't expected that. I looked around and saw thousands of admirers, but no friends - and hardly a chance to find one at all. I couldn't relate to the talk at parties. It didn't interest me. I felt stupid because I had nothing to say. I mean, this superficial talk was...pointless. Adults almost never had anything useful to say. The people I made music with were okay - there was common ground, but the others ... it was as if I lost my energy when I was with them, and so I began asking people to bring their children if there was some place I had to be. And that worked. I could play with the kids, they were good for me, gave me strength ... they didn't twist words around. They were my protection."

The downside of success became quickly apparent. Michael could go nowhere privately. And in private he was under surveillance. He was told what to do, with whom he could meet, in which restaurant he had to eat and which people he had to do business with. Pictures of Madonna and him were shot, just for the newspaper, so people had something to talk about; Brooke Shields, who needed the publicity, inquired and many others who wanted to be seen with him.

Madness began.

Everybody realized that Michael was loaded with many millions and he was only just over 20. Everyone attached to him, everyone offered him a deal, a tidal wave of offers, contracts, petitions and commitments rolled toward him. Michael became dizzy. He needed help - he was an artist and had neither the time nor the inclination to take care of all that stuff. So he took the promising attorney John Branca on board, who specialized in the music business, and in addition personal managers like Bob Jones and Frank DiLeo, who in turn put together a staff to handle the job. Michael's entourage increased massively.

There were a thousand obligations, honors, awards, performances, parties and world tours that usually lasted one and a half to two years. The pattern: screaming crowds when he went somewhere with the limo. Screaming crowds when he got out, faces of fans smashed against car windows, screaming masses in front of the hotel. Through back doors, elevators, fire escapes to the room. Cordoned-off hallways. Lonely corridors. Lonely rooms. Lonely Michael.

He could only eat in the room because in any restaurant his presence would have triggered a mass uprising. He couldn't tour any city without producing a riot and needed a schedule that would have done credit to any intelligence agency.

"I had to ask businesses to close for me, so I could get in," he told me. "People said I was arrogant. But I wasn't!" He looked at me indignantly. "They said I was a human being like everyone else and could abide by the business hours. These business owners have never thought about what would have happened if I had visited their shop like a normal person, the fans would have shredded everything to pieces! I could've done that. But I never did − out of consideration." He smiled slightly.

"Was I happy?" he reflected then. "In a way. Yes. I could make my music, make my charity projects happen. And that made me happy."

The recognition made him happy because it seemed to dissolve this curse of not being worth anything. It was a sign that people liked what he did. That they liked him. It made him happy to see that he touched others with his art. And yet he was uncertain to the bottom of his soul when he perceived even the slightest signs of − sometimes only supposed − rejection. That shocked him deeply and it was grounds to shed fierce tears. This was something he simply could not bear. And his all-overpowering success was never even close to a replacement for real, human feelings that nobody brought forward.

***

At just a little over 20 years of age, Michael was the most coveted pop star under the sun. *Thriller* stayed on the charts for 122 weeks. He was invited to the White House, and his schedule was booked solid for the next few years.

Yet he stopped rehearsals to alert his team to a beautiful cloud formation. He was deeply touched by a stunning sunrise, the smell and the perfection of a flower, and enjoyed renting an entire amusement park to do what he loved most with the children of this world: to play and be carefree.

He gave much of his massive earnings to children. How many times had he emptied the shelves of a Toys 'R' Us, wrapped the gifts and delivered them to needy orphans and children's hospitals. His generosity was legendary. If someone came to him and told him that he knew of a sick child, that the parents could not afford the treatment, Michael pulled out the checkbook and made out a check for the sum. And he also visited these children. He never said a word about it. It was a given for him. What else was money for? In it, he saw his mission. In every city where he gave a concert his path led him first to children's institutions. He noted the poor conditions, saw that the children were freezing, that there were not enough blankets, not enough warm and clean clothes, that the food was not nutritious, and the staff overwhelmed. An employee with a clipboard stood next to Michael and jotted down what he specified. The list went with a check to the head of the institution and Michael made it clear:

"I will not perform in this city until this is taken care of."

There were certainly kids who knew who Michael Jackson was, but he was also in countries where they had no idea who was coming through the door – or were too sick to recognize him.

But no matter what the circumstances were: Michael's presence seemed to have a healing effect: he gave his love to the children, he was deeply moved by their gentle, patient energy, patted, cuddled, kissed them and made them promise to get well soon. The children's eyes lit up when he was there, they were still alight even when he was gone. He sparked something in them, which could not be explained by his fame.

When they were in Africa one day, his manager DiLeo told him that it was perhaps not such a good idea to go to the hospital ... for one not to offend the government when he addressed short-comings, and also because the children might suffer from contagious diseases. But Michael just looked at him and DiLeo closed his mouth.

As they entered the hospital, they were met by an animal stench. The kids did not know who all these people were. But when Mike came in, those who were able to, sat up in their filthy sack shirts, full of flies and sores and crusted blood. The children's eyes lit up as if they saw an angel. Michael could sense the wave of energy, the cry for help and then that was all he could feel. All encompassing love and compassion in him rose up and spread throughout the entire building ... he connected with the children, as if he himself were in one of these little beds, and he tried to leave as much warmth and love as possible behind for the children. His heart ached, but he did not show it. More important to him was that they saw his confidence; he wanted them to understand that there is hope and there is a prospect for a life. And it was these moments that reminded him to stay strong, to bear his fate. These moments that made it clear to him that there was logic in the world and that he could use all the gifts he had been granted for this work.

DiLeo was nauseated to see these children, at this penetrating, offensive odor. He couldn't bear the sight of these little faces, disfigured by disease and misery.

Then the doctor brought an especially sick child to Michael. The child was skeletal, covered with some form of disgusting pustules, and he was in pain. He was in so much obvious pain that he continuously whimpered in a horrid cry. DiLeo turned away. Tears streamed down his fat cheeks, he could not

176

stand this ... and ... he was grossed out. Michael sent him out. Then he took care of the child.

But afterwards he lay in sterile hotel rooms somewhere and cried.

He often looked down on to the streets: fans with sleeping bags, banners, posters. "We love you, Michael." He stared at the heaving masses of enthusiasts out there, saw how they hugged, cried, danced, rejoiced when they saw that something was happening at the window. A tremendous surge flooded upwards to him, he could feel their love, their passion for him ... and yet he was so far away from them. So far away from their love. How could it be that one could feel all that and was still not fulfilled? His fans could share their joy with the person standing next to them. But there was no one to share this tidal wave of emotions with him, and all he could do was to throw a pillow down with the word 'Love'. He was stranded up here permanently in the hotel's luxurious rooms, receiving pure love and feeling separated.

With tremendous force, the agony of the children's destinies he witnessed overwhelmed him in his solitude and linked with his own. The deep wounds of the past were always ready to recognize their peers and to latch onto the suffering of others. And when this happened ... when Michael fell into this hole, then the burden he was carrying became so heavy that he thought he could not endure it. Then his own wounds began to fester and no one was there to understand them, let alone heal them. Everybody he knew wanted to talk about money, career, the next event, the next deal, the next tour. It was beyond anyone to understand his thoughts, to even begin to understand them, and he would not have dared tell anyone. People already did not understand why he cared with such commitment about children. What he felt when he was with them.

He became even more vulnerable, the wound in him larger. And that attracted more and more blowflies of all kinds.

Change

In the shower, he saw it for the first time. First he thought it was an abrasion he'd not noticed before. But it grew. On his right calf an irregularly shaped, bright spot developed. It did not hurt, and Michael thought nothing of it. Then he noticed it between the legs - or had that one been there first? That was not nice, but it caused only the uneasy feeling that something was not quite the way it should be. He planned to consult a dermatologist, forgot about it again until the next spot began to form around the neck. And then came the spots on the face that disfigured everything.

It was a time of upheaval. Every day his father was bugging him to renew the contract with him as a manager and perform with the brothers again. Tours brought the most money and that's what they all needed - except Michael. Everyone ran after the money because it was important to them ... it flowed towards Michael because he devoted himself with his heart and soul to his work. But his talent was all of their life insurance. Joseph was not an evil person. But when he wanted something, he was stubborn and Michael was someone who had a hard time saying no because he didn't want to hurt anyone's feelings.

Joe yelled at Mike that he had become famous only because of the family and he owed them. Who did he think he was? He was nothing! Michael avoided him. But that was no easy task: he still lived at home in Encino, Hayvenhurst, and was therefore readily accessible. Whenever Joe felt like it, he just stormed into Mike's room. He was still able to put Michael down.

One cannot help but wonder how someone with such exorbitant success can still have doubt about himself. But the mere fact that it was possible and not unique to Michael shows that success does not build essential self-confidence. Often times it just covers up.
And though there was hardly anyone who did not respond to Michael with glowing eyes, he never felt worthy. Like a madman, he was looking for mistakes in himself: his dance, that could have been more perfect, the choreography that could have been better, the spin that wasn't fast enough, a note that hadn't been sung high enough. Perfection was protection and a demand on himself, because he secretly felt that the people outside were looking for mistakes ... the way his father had always been looking for mistakes, the way the press made mountains out of molehills.
This urge for perfection, from looks to skill, procured him the crown of the pop world - but it also turned into a stumbling block. The feeling to be allowed to exist only without flaw sat deep. Instinctively, he thought that would be the basis for love. To give himself and others no possibility to accuse him of anything. God wanted perfection.

The unrecognized fear possessed him that people, once they saw him in person, would not like him anymore, that they would say he looked very different than in the pictures. The skin disease was progressing further and it made him more and more shy and awkward when interacting with adults.
And the most successful pop star of all time, with the world at his feet, asked his photographer shyly, with whom he visited an award ceremony:
"Mr. ... is over there. Do you think he'd agree to have his photo taken with me?"

And the photographer replied, completely stunned: "Don't you think he's much more interested in being photographed with YOU?"

In a panic Michael sat at a dermatologist's. The nurse almost couldn't close her mouth anymore, when she saw what a prominent patient her boss had and she fanned herself with air in the nurses' room before she went into the treatment room. Michael was sitting in his boxers on the examination table and felt uncomfortable when she entered.

"Michael," said Dr. Klein, "that's Debbie. She is discreet. You can count on her."

Michael nodded. He was still embarrassed. He had zero experience with girls; he was ashamed. But Debbie was friendly and casual. With her dry sense of humor, she took away his shyness quickly and Michael laughed wholeheartedly after his initial shyness about her not quite G-rated jokes.

When he came the second time, he brought her one of his records with his autograph. And a poster.

"Well," said the doctor, looking at Michael over the rim of his glasses, "you have vitiligo, young man." He explained that this disease can sometimes be stopped during puberty - which had not been done with Michael. And now he must expect that it would continue to spread.

"What ... what exactly does that mean?" Mike asked. "At what speed is it spreading? There has to be some medicine ... there must be a way to activate the pigmentation again ... "

But the doctor shook his head regretfully. There was nothing. Michael was faced with the prospect of going on stage looking like a spotted cow.

"If there was something that kept me from relationships and a normal development, then it was this disease," he whispered, "what would the fans think of me? ... I had problems anyway approaching girls. I didn't know how. I never learned how. I've learned so many things, but not that."

At least he knew that girls wanted good-looking guys. All the careful shots, the perfect look that everyone had come to expect from him ... when they saw these spots ... how he really looked ... worse than in their nightmares!

He became more and more uptight. Makeup, previously applied voluntarily, became a necessary evil. The more pigment that left his skin, the more Michael began to withdraw, the more he shied away from people, adult people who regarded him with the sensationalist desire to shine a spotlight through the layers of his makeup and to make fun of it.

For it was his own desire for beauty that forbade him to show himself up close too often. Never again did he want to see that horrified, disgusted look, like back then at the airport. He protected himself against what hurt. Like any of us would. He's not the only one who uses makeup.

Mid-June 2009

When will it end? When will it finally stop? God, my body hurts. It's one big wound. Am I on the wrong path after all? Back to the stage ... I'm longing for it, at the same time I feel that it's killing me. That's the mistake that I haven't recognized all my life. I should have left years ago. Not drive the same old track ... the stage, my curse ... and my life. I long for it and yet ... I feel inside: it is the mind that says yes, my heart says no. There is nothing more I can do. Cannot do anymore. Everything hurts, not just the body, everything. Do you hear me, God? I can't go on. I did what I could. I always did what I could. I've danced my head off, have endured everything. God, I've tried to help as many people as possible in this world, made use of what you gave me. Did I do enough? I hope it was enough. How many more tears? I have no more. I ... I ... can't go on anymore. Please come get me. Get me out of here. Please let it be over. Please get me. I finally want to come to you. I want to go home. Where it's warm. Give me another life. Give me a chance. Please.

***

"No way," said Michael, leaning on the table. "I won't drink that stuff - and I can't stand for something that I don't think is right. I mean, the kids see me with the stuff in my hand - and I'm a role model for them."

On the table was an immensely highly paid advertising contract from Pepsi in connection with a tour they had sponsored for *The Jacksons*. Michael liked neither soft drinks, nor the idea of a tour with his brothers.

Pepsi had promised them all whopping fees, but only with Michael in the lead role. No one said it out loud but they all knew it, and the emotions ran deep. If Michael was there, they, the brothers, were also tolerated. They were brought along only when they were the way to get Michael. And that the brothers had to ask Michael more and more often to accept deals that brought them, the family, money, made them angry. Damn it - they all had a contract with Joseph as the manager! And Mike had to stick to that too, had to fulfill another year, just like they did.

But it took months until Mike agreed to the commercial. They used Katherine, whose influence he could never escape, and lured him with the fact that the clip was to be made with children. Additionally, he was offered a particularly high salary; from the start Michael gave 100% of it to a children's charity.

When it was finally decided, Michael was looking forward to working with the children.

The test shots were running and there were more than 3,000 fans present. His brothers and bodyguards were there, his friends and the Pepsi people. As soon as the music began, Michael was hardly able to hold back. His body began to dance by itself, he knew exactly what he had to do, when to take what step, when lights and fireworks had to come in.

And as always, he wanted everything to be perfect. It was nearly perfect from the start. But with all those fans present - The Jacksons wanted to offer them something and Michael wanted it to be right to a fault. Again and again they were rehearsing the gig and at the sixth take, it happened: a firework display erupted too early and sparks showered onto Michael's thick hair. Fire spread, as he danced down the steps, and by the time he had reached the bottom his head was ablaze.

The crew took a second until they recognized the situation, then masses of people rushed towards him, in front of them all his bodyguard, Miko Brando, who burned his own hands while extinguishing the fire burning on Michael's head.

Michael was taken to the hospital, he had a hellish headache on the outside as well as inside - on his head was a palm-sized, burned away area.

At the hospital, chaos broke out. The news had spread like wildfire, and the administration had to employ additional staff to answer the umpteen thousand people inquiring about Michael's condition. The lines almost collapsed. The entrance was besieged by journalists and fans, hundreds of bouquets were delivered.

"We'll give you a pain killer," said the doctor, looking sympathetically in to the huge brown eyes.

"No ... no painkillers," Michael whispered. "I don't take anything allopathic."

"But ... the pain will become more severe ... Right now a bit of the shock and the ointment is helping..."

"Then continue with the ointment," said Michael.

"That won't do much for the pain," the doctor replied, "maybe think it over ...you should sleep, that's the best of cures."

"I can never sleep anyway," muttered Michael, "for years now."

That grabbed the doctor's attention. "You haven't been sleeping for years?"

"No ... I sleep an hour or two, until I wake up and again, can't fall asleep..."

"How can you stand it?" the doctor asked, surprised. "You've got a tough job ... the training ... performances ... that must make you very tired."

"Not me," said Michael. "After performances I'm pumped up, then I really can't sleep."

And then the doctor said something that made Michael listen up:

"But sleep," he said, "is the best and most natural remedy of all. You should do something about your sleep problem."

Michael looked at him.

"Let me know if the pain gets too much," suggested the doctor, "then we'll see what's next."

He was right. After four hours, Michael couldn't stand it anymore and called for the doctor. He gave him a painkiller that kicked in within a half-hour and let Michael's mood drift smoothly upwards like a balloon. He got so hyper that he visited all patients on his station and it was not long before he was dancing on his bed and entertaining other burn victims with a performance.

In the evening, Michael went through the rooms again, talking to patients. There were people there who'd had their 14th operation, their faces horribly disfigured forever. Full of compassion, he sat and listed to their stories and gave them courage. A woman was totally desperate, she was crying and Michael listened to her as she told about her life, which was, in essence, a continuous depression. He stayed with her until late at night. What he discussed with her, no one ever knew, but the doctor, who was in charge of the woman's care was amazed at how strong her will to live had grown after this encounter and how differently she behaved afterwards.

Michael himself then went to his room and lay down on the bed. After an hour, he turned on the video recorder.

"You should really sleep," came a voice from the door. Michael looked around tired. The doctor stood in the doorway.

"Do you agree if I give you something? It's natural."

"Something natural?"

"Yes," the doctor said, and pulled something out of his pocket, "purely plant-based. Should I?"

And Michael nodded. He did not know what the doctor gave him. He just knew that this night was the first in a long time, in which he slept a deep and dreamless sleep. When he awoke, he felt like a new person, despite his wound. He had not felt this great for a long time! It was a fantastic event for him - a deep, solid, restful sleep - without nightmares or sweats, without any fear. Michael was immensely grateful.

"What did you give me?" He asked the doctor the next morning.

"You can call me anytime if you need me," he said instead and pressed his business card into Michael's hand.

Michael left the hospital with a mix of emotions. He had learned of many tragedies and gained new friends. He felt this vibration that was between him and the people, and he felt the change that happened to them when he sang something to them and gave them courage. He donated the $1.5 million compensation that Pepsi paid him immediately and completely to the Brotman Hospital for burns victims.

After those days, he felt more than ever that he had an assignment. He wanted to use the talent he had received from God to ease the suffering in this world. He saw his mission clearly ahead.

XX / 1986, very close by

"We undermine every aspect of his life. In a subtle way. The safest and most improvable agents are rumors, mistrust ... and dependency. We feed the press. That should be an easy game."
That was the first aspect of his strategy. The network to fall back on was not only huge, it was especially influential and richly branched.
Second point: distrust.
The weapons: human weaknesses. The drive for money, power, recognition, the big deal and ... the desire for love. Dissension and discord grow like weeds, people believe more readily in evil than in good anyway. Once suspicion was sown, you just had to wait for the harvest. In general, people tore each other apart. For the target victim, a deadly combination. Nothing makes a person insane faster than the feeling of being followed, not being able to trust anyone and being lonely.
Third aspect: finances and existence. This was the most tedious.
And the fourth aspect must be prepared most precisely. This was the most tricky.

The brothers were badgering him and made it clear to Michael that he had a moral obligation to perform with them.
"Come on, brother," they said. "We made you famous and now you don't want to have anything more to do with us - how ungrateful you are. We are still *The Jacksons*!"
This rumbled around terribly inside of Michael. To perform with his brothers appealed to him, the old days were too good to be forgotten. But he was working on his solo career and his management made it clear that it would be bad to jump from one to another. He also had concerns about coming under Joe's tutelage again, something he desperately wanted to avoid. Therefore, he tried to stand by his 'no'. But if someone asked for something, he could not be firm - he just couldn't do it. He knew this was a weakness, and so he began to provide refusals through others to protect himself. But Michael's brothers had known him long enough to know how they could crack him best.
Again they put up their heaviest artillery: Katherine, who had talked Michael into many things over the years.
Meanwhile, she had repeatedly filed for divorce - only to retract the papers again. It was a stab in Michael's heart every time. He loved his mother, but

he could not forgive Joe for what he had done to her and them. Sometimes for months there was ominous frustration and tension in the Jackson's home that chased Michael to his room. He ate, slept and daydreamed there. He could not go out anyway. Outside, the fans would have crushed him. Even at home he was a prisoner and felt confined more and more. But Katherine ... Katherine was a force in his life, he needed her as an anchor, and the whole family took advantage of that - all except for Janet.

Katherine herself was in a dilemma: her very sustenance depended on the family band. And it did not look as if the brothers would be successful without Mike. But Michael was not her only child. She had nine. So she engaged herself for the preservation of *The Jacksons* and Michael was persuaded once again to do something that he really didn't stand by.

After her intervention, he was willing to sacrifice a whole year to prepare a world tour with his brothers and perform. He signed the contract for the *Victory Tour* and vowed it would be the last. The brothers, however, hoped to be able to start anew.

Meanwhile, at times Michael was even dubious about his mother. She was his support, but she also limited him. Why did she stay with Joe? Michael would always have taken care of her, as he already did!

But although Joe cheated on her, and even had a child with another woman, she did not leave him. He was not even able to feed her. In the meantime he was broke - not a single one of his deals was working out. The situation was so precarious for Joe that Michael had to buy the house in which they all lived. Joe's only accomplishment was *The Jacksons*, and he held onto that as if it were a recipe for life.

In the planning of the *Victory Tour* Michael confirmed that his brothers' way of thinking was not aligned with his. With very mixed emotions he sat in the first preparatory meetings and offered them the use of his professional management team for the organization - at his own expense. But the brothers declined - with thanks - to put in to practice their own views on making money.

They hired a shady figure, Don King, a violent convicted felon who had transitioned into a career as boxing promoter. From the start Michael distrusted him and it soon became apparent that Don King had no experience planning an event of this magnitude. Important safety precautions were lacking. There were cutbacks when it came to the fans, but where revenues could be generated, he became outrageous.

They invented a preposterous system, a ticket package sale that offered tickets only in packs of four. Together with a kind of lottery, which pulled the money out of the fans' pockets like nothing else. This way millions and millions had already flowed into the bank accounts where it generated nice interest before even one of them had set foot on stage.

Michael was shocked when he heard about it ... and he heard about it when a girl wrote to him saying how much she wanted to see him at the concert, but could not afford the lottery system... his blood was boiling.

Without the consent of his brothers, he abruptly called a press conference and stood - this time without any shyness - very determined and with clenched jaws in front of the mike. Then he explained to the press that the price per ticket would be reduced immediately, that they could be bought individually and that there was no lottery. He also stated that, in addition, he would personally donate his fee to the particular city in which they performed, and for every venue would make a quota of tickets available for underprivileged children, and in addition he would give autograph sessions.

With a deadly glance behind, that shut the brothers and Don King's mouths, he said that the previous ticket strategy was a misunderstanding and he apologized.

And finally the bombshell: he called this tour officially the farewell tour of *The Jacksons*. His brothers went pale.

Then Mike looked up the girl who had sent the letter, thanked her, bought her toys, gave her tickets and a special seat at the concert.

Nevertheless - he immensely enjoyed the tour with his brothers. They all felt transported back to the old glory days and it was wonderful to feel this connectedness again. But from the entire tour, which lasted half a year, Michael did not keep a penny for himself. He gave everything to children's aid institutions.

The brothers were suckered two or three times over: had their ticket trick originated mostly from the fear that the concert halls could no longer be filled, now they watched with horror how the announcement of their little brother made the tickets sell out in less than two days. People bought because Michael was performing. They wanted to see the moonwalk, they wanted to hear Billie Jean.

And when they were on tour, there was usually only one name that the fans called and that was Michael's.

But Mike counted the days until the tour and the contract with Joe was over. He counted every single concert until he was free.

ATV

A short time later his attorney John Branca called him.

"Listen, Mike," he said in his jolly way, "the ATV catalog is up for sale. The "Northern Song"."

It was silent on the other end of the line.

"Mike? Are you still there?"

"Sure, I'm still here. Say that again."

"The Northern Song, you've heard right - the Beatles' rights, Little Richard ... and some more ... ask your friend McCartney if he's bidding. I mean ...for decency's sake."

That was the first thing Michael did after the phone call with Branca: he called Paul and asked if he was bidding. Paul said no. Although they were his and John Lennon's songs that were coming under the hammer, he was not interested because he thought the bids were too high.

Michael asked twice. Twice Paul said no. John Branca initiated negotiations. There were three parties that were bidding on this catalog, and Michael had given his lawyer Branca an upper limit. Just before the bidding was over, he was outbid by Martin Bandier, the CEO of EMI, and Mike was not willing to go any higher.

But Branca used his connections. A couple of people who were involved in the interaction still owed him some favors. He called them and told them that he, personally, was the one who was behind the deal, and would they please take into consideration these personal aspects. The financing, which Bandier had set up and had been accepted, was overturned and so it was Branca, who landed the deal at the last second. For 47.5 million U.S. dollars he got hold of the ATV catalog for Michael Jackson.

This gave Michael a steady cash flow at a minimum of at least ten million dollars per year, this in 1987 alone. Twenty years later, the catalog's worth was estimated between 800 million and one billion dollars. Michael, who at the time already recognized publishing rights as an independent, valuable investment created a fund for his own songs, 'Mijac', that in a short time was valued at over $100 million dollars.

The press went nuts. Michael was now not only the most successful, charismatic entertainer in the world — he was also recognized for his shrewd business practices and for his foresight.

It was success on — almost — all levels. And it was just too much.

Despite this success, in spirit he remained humble ... he was happy about the acquaintance of interesting people who went deep into things with him, such as Deepak Chopra, who introduced him to a world in which God was nothing mystical or vengeful, but rather loving and understanding. Michael talked a lot with Deepak and wrote his book *Dancing the Dream* with him, his true biography as he always insisted.

And there were other adults, people he could talk about his feelings with, such as Elizabeth Taylor and Jane Fonda. These were the first to whom he confided his inexplicable sadness. And who gave him the courage to work on himself.

The success filled him with satisfaction - it had many positive sides to it, even though he was being pushed around by his managers, who planned his days and sometimes treated him like a piece of merchandise. One of these was Bob Jones, who was not unlike his father, and curiously, also treated him the same way. Everyone was surprised that Mike put up with this. But it appeared as if such people created a painful familiarity that he could not disassociate from.

His entourage zoomed up, everyone hired assistants and aides for themselves. They all stuck together in a multimillion dollar company called Michael Jackson and everyone thought they were entitled to a piece of the pie. Everything was getting more convoluted, complicated, impenetrable. Innumerable contracts went back and forth and it was difficult to keep an overview.

But at least Michael could split his time as he wanted because people now followed him. Lately he had made the acquaintance of boys who were really cool and with whom he could play the way he had always dreamed of. His little friends didn't care that Michael was three times their age.

Intrigued, he looked into the faces of these little boys and girls and saw something he had never been able to discover in his own face: this carefree, jubilant joy, free of any obligation. Since he was so receptive to energy, he wanted them to be around him so he could bathe in it. Playing was like making music to him: you had to turn off your mind. Playing and thinking or dancing and thinking at the same time did not work. His success was due to just the fact that he could exclude the cumbersome, non-creative mind when he created something - the true feature of timeless artists and geniuses of this world.

There were redeeming moments in Michael's life, when he could be with his friends and their energies connected. Then he felt like after a night's sleep: fresh, rested and fully inspired, Notes and lyrics struck with the force of a meteor, and he sometimes had trouble capturing them all. Michael was one of the few people in the world who rarely experienced a creative slump.

"I'd be careful if I were you," Branca said to Mike who was sitting in front of him, laughing.

"But why?" he asked back carelessly. "What's wrong with that? I am living my dream and I have the money for it. Everyone buys things when they've earned something. Including homes and property."

"That's not it, Mike," said Branca, choosing his words deliberately. "It is a white area, Republicans, as far as the eye can see. And you are a - black - democrat. The DA there is known as 'mad dog'. That says a lot. And you want to acquire 2,700 acres of land in his district? As a newcomer ... be careful ... it's explosive in that corner ... "

Michael looked at him seriously. "But my presence alone will boost the economy there," he said, "then more money will go into his pocket, than if..."

"That's not it," Branca said again. "You are, forgive me ... you're black. Some people can't stand that."

"Then they have to learn to," said Mike, "we have the same rights. Why should I bow down? It'll be all right."

And so in 1987/88 he bought the Sycamore Ranch in St. Ynez Valley and converted it to his own personal dream.

A 2,700-acre facility with a beautiful house in the Tudor style, guest units with service better than at a hotel, a private cinema, zoo, amusement park, fire department and security, helipad, swimming pool, a railway station and two trains that traveled the entire grounds, with tepees, forests, several ponds and a huge lake with a fountain. He employed 80 people as permanent staff for the house and garden, had fleets of Bentleys and Rolls Royces. It was like an independent kingdom.

Nestled in the beautiful nature were magical places on the idyllic landscaped grounds and there was the huge, mystical Giving Tree.

For Michael it was a place where he could move freely. A place where he didn't have to participate in the silly adult games, an empire that he wanted run by his rules, rules of love and joy. His Peter Pan land. He called it Neverland.

Without much ado, he moved out of his parent's house in Encino, Hayvenhurst. Suddenly he was gone - which was nothing out of the ordinary, but this time he didn't come back. No one in the family knew that he had bought the property - they heard about it through the newspaper. Even Katherine.

Michael couldn't look his mother in the eye and say: "I want to live my own life." Not as long as she was together with Joseph. Maybe she would have tried to stop him, because he, Joseph, had told her to.

Michael was now 30 years old and an icon at the pinnacle of the music world.

He did not drink, did not smoke, spoke out clearly against drugs and violence, produced no scandals, didn't womanize, his sex life was a mystery. He looked great, danced like a god, was personable, shy, polite and generous and had a wonderful smile. He was invited back to the White House and this time received an award for his efforts against violence and alcohol and for his help for the world's children from George H.W. Bush.

It was a terrific time. A time in which his wildest dreams came true. He loved Neverland, invited socially and physically disadvantaged children to his ranch every three weeks and gifted them with a full wonderful day. He always approached the fattest, most unattractive and timid first. Those whose behavior expressed that they were not used to affection. He took care of those most, gave them the feeling of being worth as much as all the others. He always had children as guests at Neverland, romped around with them, ate ice cream and candy and then was just another one of them. Neverland transformed everyone. It was simply magical. And when Michael was around children, he could let go because they didn't reduce him to his high school degree, the number of millions he earned or the art he had in the house. Joy and gladness were the basic pattern of most children. Their stake in the game was imagination with which they invented fairy tales and stories. They were happy with so little, and when children were happy, then they hummed and sang. That was God in its purest form. Michael loved that.

And when they left in the evening, their laughter and their joy was still in the air, and he walked on the paths, and sat on his Giving Tree and inhaled this atmosphere with all of his senses. He effortlessly glided into this flow of positive energies, transforming them into melodies and rhythms.

***

"Mike," said his manager, "you're the first to understand how the press works ... if you want to stay famous, you need to stand out ... with something."

"But I can do that with my music ... with what I'm doing ... give them information about the children's projects..."

"That would be counter-productive ... that ... about the kids. Man, this is America! I mean ... let's see you with some hot chicks! We need something tangible ... otherwise it's boring for the media ... you have to feed them ... have to throw them treats ... you're too clean! You don't even know what it's like to be tipsy! They'll write about all sorts of people, just not about you ... because you're boring ... believe me ... business doesn't work that way!"

Michael paled. He knew that many in the world of Hollywood desperately tried to stay in the headlines. He saw his success as proof that he was on the right track. And so it was important to remain successful. It was important first *that* they reported and second *what* they reported. Why did it have to be something scandalous for people to respond? He'd been having discussions like this more often lately and they did not sit well with him.

But he had been in the business long enough to know that it was, unfortunately, true. Every star created the image that he or his agents thought valuable - and then fired it up with the help of the press.

"Business works like this:" he was told, "you create a scandal, and then you call the paparazzi to let them know where they have to go and set the camera where you want at the same time. Then they report what you want them to report. That's how it's done."

With mixed feelings Michael listened. "But they always write what they want, not what you want," he said.

"Because you don't give them anything! Mike, you're THE giant in the music scene ... and deny interviews! You haven't spoken to a reporter since 1978! What do you think you're doing?"

"But ... they twist around words…"

"Mike," said his manager and looked at him closely, "that was before *Thriller*. Now you are someone. They'll write what you want. Give it a try."

Michael's eyes began involuntarily to glitter. The rascal came up in him. He thought back to the Motown instructions in dealing with media: say this, not that. Be vague, never give anything personal away. Answer this and that. And now he could say what he wanted? And the people out there would believe it? The idea pleased him immensely. He started to giggle, as he thought of all the nonsense the press could be fed. The PR man was watching him and recognized his opening.

"What kind of image you would you like to build for yourself, Mike?" he asked, and with that clicked into Michael's fantasy channel. Immediately his eyes began to light up and he was suspended in visions and ideas that fascinated him. He saw the book of Barnum before him, the man who had created a world of his own in this world, a bubble in which he could live according to his ideas, who had given his imagination free reign and had achieved self-fulfillment ... and he suddenly saw an opportunity to really create a better world ... by living a life he believed to be worth living.

"Okay," he said enthusiastically, "okay ... I'm thinking of ... a world in which children have a say ... someone who gives children a voice ...who ... yes ... exactly! We'll create a Children's Day! We'll show what talent and money can be used for…" he became lost in his descriptions. It was the ideology of a perfect world without war and poverty, where the gaze of a child could stop a tank, and he meant every word he said.

190

His managers looked at each other with raised eyebrows.

"Yeah, Mike, all right," said one eventually, "but we need a big bang ... something crazy ... you know what I mean?"

"Write that I want to buy the bones of the Elephant Man," Michael giggled and laughed himself silly at the idea that someone would actually believe that. And next to the mischievousness was also a calculating thought to use it to get back at the press and also to prove his power. He was Michael Jackson! He would show everyone what he could do!

Again his advisors and agents looked at another. Some of them shrugged their shoulders. "Why not," they said.

"Yes," Michael exclaimed with shining eyes, "and you think that'll make a splash?"

"Will it ever Mike," they replied. "You'll see - that'll make a splash."

***

It made a splash. It was the ultimate backfire. As the headlines went around the world, as Michael realized just how right his managers had been and everyone indeed printed this story. As he noticed how quickly the rumor spread, and nothing else was talked about in the media for weeks, he was at first positively impressed, then concerned, and eventually horrified. Another intentionally generated rumor that started when the press was given a picture of Michael in an oxygen chamber pursued him for his life, too.

What had started as a joke and vindication became serious, and it weighed heavily on Michael over the years. The rumor about the purchase of the bones was not even that far-fetched, he had actually briefly toyed with the idea. He didn't identify with the elephant man himself, but he did with his sadness, and perhaps he sensed that he and this misfit had more in common than he liked. At this time, however, the main kick for his attempt to sucker the media was an irrational desire, buried deep down, that people would see the real reason for this potential purchase: understanding for a human being who never harmed anyone, who had a big heart, and only wanted love. Perhaps they could have put two and two together and understood him better? It was an unspoken, barely perceptible emotion in him that emerged there, and through which he basically revealed something very intimate about himself.

The same with the oxygen chamber: there was a bit of truth, a little bit of fabrication, and the rest was press-intrigue.

This resulted in the elders of Jehovah's Witnesses putting pressure on Michael again and they attempted to dictate how he should lead his life. In 1987 Michael dared the break, and to his mothers horror, left the church.

His film *Moonwalker* was a disaster, too. When the clip was watched with Michael's personality taken into account, it quickly became clear that in a child-like way he was campaigning for understanding for himself: he, who had a reputation as a shrewd businessman and also acted like one, attempted a balancing act that was meant to show people his true self, the infinitely good Michael, who fought against evil. The misunderstanding: Michael *was* a good person, but he wanted to prove it and because he was emphasizing it so much, it turned into a farce that no one wanted to believe.

Disturbed, he read what the media made of all this. A new image was born: from this time on he was not only just Michael Jackson, not only the King of Pop, now he became Wacko Jacko, the mad eccentric, whose success had gone to his head.

These rumors pursued Michael for a lifetime and there was no way to relieve himself of them. No matter how many times he insisted that they were not true. Even when it could be read explicitly in his biography how the rumors had come about, they never left him. Even as he publicly distanced himself from the rumors, the press stubbornly pursued them. More ferociously than with anybody else.

Always at the worst possible time, the ghost surfaced and left foul vapors. The rumors seemed the foundation of an as yet unpredictable plan, the basis of a sinister game.

Even months later hardly any of the media in America reported about his music. They all wrote only about oxygen chambers and the elephant man.

He complained to his PR people: "Why do I have you if you don't know when the shot can backfire?" he raged. "That's the last time that I'll take part in anything like that!"

"Oh, come on, Mike, calm down" was the reply. "Look, how many newspapers you are in! Really, in EVERY ONE! Even the most reputable papers that usually only have news have you in them!"

"Still," Michael insisted through clenched teeth. "They treat me like I'm a psycho! It was bad advice. I should have listened to my instincts - I want to get into the newspapers with positive things, not with such garbage."

From a rational point of view: would it have been such a big deal if he had really wanted to buy those bones? How many people collect meaningless things - and no one takes offense at it? And the oxygen chamber? Everyone wants to stay healthy and live longer. So what was so wrong about oxygen - except that the box in which Michael had been photographed looked so uncomfortable that any person with the IQ of a banana would have hardly thought that this was a space that lent itself for sleeping.

But the press made sure that no one looked at it rationally by continuously portraying the same old news as a scandal. And the majority of people did not ask further. They ate up what they were served.

In Michael these headlines not only raised concern, but they felt like he had a deep-sea drill working in his stomach. A vague feeling crept out of the resulting leak. He started to get suspicious of his managers. But he had to be able to rely on them! It was impossible to control this whole apparatus himself. Nevertheless, he could not resist the suspicion that some of the threads that came to the press were spun in his own camp. It was a bad feeling, but he still believed that the rumors would sooner or later peter out. He gave them no more food ... and the press reported only about the latest scandal ... sooner or later this crap would be forgotten, of that he was convinced.

With a sigh, Michael went back to his day-to-day routine. He had big plans.

He performed one concert after another, attended one event after another, and was often away from home for months on end. A world tour meant two years of preparation. Football stadiums had to be booked to accommodate the crowds he attracted, countless trucks with equipment, the delicate security arrangements, the games with the press, with hotels and sieges wherever he went. The superfluous games of adults that he had to participate in around concerts: a golden key presented here, entry to a city register there, mayors who did not really know what to say to him, and for whom Michael had little words himself. Adults wherever the eye roamed. In time Michael had begun to take children with him on his tour if it was possible. Then he paid for everything for the parents, too - from any necessary extras, up to the five-star hotel rooms and other amusements that his guests wanted. It was not a rare occasions that out of gratitude Michael gave the people who accompanied him a credit card. He was generous to a fault.

Michael was surrounded by people when he got into one of his huge stretch limousines, surrounded by people wherever he needed to enter or exit, surrounded no matter where he was - until he was brought like a prisoner to his room, where he sat like a monkey that was only let out again when it was time for it to be paraded to the public.

And it were these impersonal, always identical, hotel rooms that created the place in him for deathly loneliness. That's why he hated tours. He hated them because he was so alone with himself, alone with emotions like sadness and old experiences, which sent their mental vapors in the form of premonitions and dreams up to him - and that he didn't want to feel.

Ever since the stage had taken everything over in his life, his family had reduced itself to a working team missioned to accomplish something. And when he hadn't delivered, he had been beaten. His mother had not been there in many of those instances and there had not been enough time to take care of him the way he needed it. He was hungry for love, hungry for affection, hungry for a real, true friend.

Surrounded by thousands of people, deep down he felt an omnipresent isolation that could not be quenched by anything, and certainly not by any success in the whole wide world. And he knew it. He had no choice but to throw himself into the work.

He was ready to take on his next album, with which he wanted to surpass the success of the second. Feverishly he worked on the songs, the stage show, the arrangements. He had a firm goal, wrote comments and notes and stuck them to the walls and mirrors.

"I want to exceed *Thriller* ... with the new album I want 100 million in sales and I want you all to believe in it," he told his people. And he wanted it not least of all to stop the false negative reports that still circulated in the press.

"Yeah, Mike, that's great ... but you know ... 100 million is a number that ... no one has ever achieved."

"And that's exactly what I don't want to hear!" shrilled Michael, upset. "Why should I go by what others have not been able to accomplish before me?"

The people at the meeting looked at each other. The sale of one hundred million records was a big enchilada even in this crazy world.

XX / 1988

"Where does this ass want to go next? He's a megalomaniac! I think he has forgotten where he came from! He has forgotten everything. Get him back to the basic facts ... he so readily represents himself as a philanthropist... when in fact he is a selfish, hypocritical bonehead ... one who thinks he can break with his obtuse ideas into a world that doesn't belong to him ... that will never belong to him ... and which is none of his business."

Shortly afterwards, during routine blood tests, Michael was diagnosed with another disease. He was afflicted with lupus erythematous, which could not only cause disfigurement in the form of a butterfly erythema in the face, but also could cause permanent hair loss, inflammation of the heart, kidneys, lungs and brain, in acute inflammatory episodes. Michael's heart sank to the floor when he heard the diagnosis.

With trembling hands he clutched his still thick hair. He closed his eyes and made himself aware of what this meant to him: inflammation of the lungs ... hair loss ... rheumatism and arthritis in the joints ... that was pretty much the last thing a dancer wanted.

Now he had two autoimmune diseases. And the term autoimmune disease spoke for itself. Something in him was directing itself against him. His body was destroying itself.

***

He turned to me and his face spoke volumes. I gulped.

"Over night, since my success with *Thriller*, it appeared that the entire world press had conspired against me. There were hardly any positive news reports. My third album received scathing reviews, especially here in my own country, so I had little chance to reach my goal. In other countries, the press was not as negative - on the contrary, many praised the album, and I had good sales. But here ... here it suddenly seemed there was a power that had decided to cut me off. And the media went along. In any case, since this time there was only shit about me in the newspaper. Just shit."

His mouth was a thin line, his voice rough. "It's said that America is the land of unlimited opportunity, but that doesn't seem to be quite right. What happened to all of those who stood in the way of the money sharks and leaders? It's always the same pattern. I mean, I'm not stupid."

Frowning, I listened. Was he serious? Was this thing around Michael so powerful, so big?

"There's strategy behind this," he continued, "and a method with which you can destroy anyone ... this infallible method is called the press."

He was silent.

"You ... mean, this was all ...deliberate?" I stuttered doubtfully.

Michael turned fiercely towards me. "Chirelle, why don't you look at what the headlines in the tabloids say about me? Look how persistently they have pounced on issues with my skin, the plastic surgeries, my relationship with children! Not one was neutral! Not one was interested in a fair analysis! Not one believed that I suffer from the white spot syndrome! Who owns the tabloid papers? In whose hands do they run together? I mean, look at Cher! She's had tons more plastic surgeries than I've had - and it comes up every once in a while in the newspaper, but they're not taking it out on her! And Jolie and Pitt! How much their dedication is praised! Over and over again! I have donated many more millions than they have and still do to this day! I've been helping children for more than 30 years! And look at my reviews: only nastiness, mockery ... what did *you* know about me before you came here?"

I blushed involuntarily.

"There you have it," he huffed and adjusted his glasses on his nose. He was wearing these bright ones without a rim again, which made him look very distinguished.

"And to fully answer your question: a newspaper is not a person. Why would a newspaper want to finish me off? I know that media folks are manipulated. That someone uses them to manipulate others."

"That would mean that somebody is deliberately trying to destroy you?" I asked in dismay. "Who? And above all, why?"

But Michael said nothing. His eyes were lost somewhere in the room, and his thoughts were ... I had no idea where they were. In any case, no longer with me and our conversation. He was crashing inside - with thoughts that he did not express.

After awhile he turned to me again, just when I'd decided to end for this evening. "Someone wants to destroy me, Chirelle," said Michael, and he sounded very calm. "And so far they've been doing a very good job..."

With a defiant, rebellious smile, he glared at me.

"...but for now ... I'm still here."

Michael had brought me to my door and I would have rather not left him alone. He had fallen into a state difficult to describe. A state between rebellion and hopelessness. I felt guilty because I knew it was our conversation that had thrown him back to these awful memories. And now I also knew that there was more, much more that was putting a heavy strain on Michael. Things that were so terrible that I now wondered how he could stand it.

Not only the celebrity hype, not only the loss of childhood and his traumatic experiences, not just this loneliness that was associated with this insane success ... wasn't that enough? Did there have to be a threat coming towards him in addition to all this, aimed at ruining him?

Again I recalled the book and the sentences in it, which were responsible for these revelations. *Your problem is not greater than you, nor is it smaller.*' It was hard, very hard to see it all in any kind of context given the enormity that had been demonstrated here. And Michael had told me only the beginning!

I buried my head in the pillow. Tomorrow he would tell me about Jordy Chandler. And about his first accusation for child molestation.

Prelude

Michael felt panic rise in him after the last visit to the doctor. The spots were gaining the upper hand and now this second disease ... he held back the tears until he was home. But then he collapsed on the bed and sobbed loudly. He did not want to be sick! He did not want to be ugly! He could not afford to be! On stage, defects were not that apparent - he was too far away from the audience for that. On the big screen, too, the pixels were too fuzzy for anyone to notice anything. On video you could work with lighting and makeup. But what if he had to be with someone one on one?

Horrified, he watched the flight of the pigmentation on his skin, looked tormented at his unadorned face in the mirror.

The wings of his nose were white, while the bridge was still holding the pigmentation. On his cheeks bright spots of varying sizes were forming, making him look like a leper. His body was covered all over with white and purple areas. But the spots in his face were upsetting to him most of all. Sobbing Michael broke down in front of the merciless mirror. Why couldn't he just be beautiful? Why was God doing this to him?

The white spots were getting larger and larger and started to blend together. His skin doctor gave him a cream that removed the pigmentation from the skin. The cream hurt; it was far from gentle on his skin. Michael endured it all. He was being photographed, had performances. He had no other choice than to apply pancake makeup, an action that earned him full cynicism from all the media that said he had a problem with the color of his own skin and with his own looks.

And by God, yes, that's what he had.

Although he looked markedly sexy on stage, he was still, at over 30 years of age, unable to present himself in a credible affair. A point that the press plunged into, just like they plunged into his forced metamorphosis: Michael was gay, he was asexual, he was a woman, he'd had a gender change. They showed digitally altered images of Michael with no nose, pictures in which they put the eyes too high, giving him a stupid expression; images that made his face appear as unfavorable as possible.

Brazenly, the press formed the opinion of the masses, knowing full well that their reports would be read by millions and the truth could not be verified anyway, since only a tiny fraction of the millions would have the chance to get to know their victim personally and form their own judgment.

But Michael's exorbitant successes still stood for who he was, for his musical genius. Even when the media in America started spitefully stomping their greatest entertainer into the ground, they couldn't harm Michael much at this stage.

Every opportunity he had, Michael asked his fans, asked the world, not to believe what was written in the press. In addition, he had also become more wary of his management team.

"Where did this picture come from?" he raged and threw a newspaper on the table. "…And this information? Did DiLeo instigate this? He needs to stop feeding the press like this!"

DiLeo swore that he hadn't done it, but Michael could not help feeling uneasy. What were his people doing out there? What was going on here?

Information about the disloyalty of his lawyer was brought to him and he turned pale. Branca? John Branca who managed his fortune? Who was in charge of supervising his ATV catalog?

"No, I don't believe that," he said firmly.

"Then look at this," said the other, and put a balance sheet on the table. "Here is the proof ... something is going wrong in your camp ... they all want to take you apart..."

Michael's knees were weak. What kind of world was this?

"You're too rich and successful," explained his informant, "that draws vermin. Here ... this contract ... is that your signature? The guy cashed in half a million bucks because he supposedly represented you abroad. Well, the money was transferred ... and we are half a million poorer ... "

The signature was forged and the perpetrator long gone. And that was just one of many cases. Of the smaller cases.

Finally Michael was forced to release DiLeo after the *Bad* tour, when he had announced this had been Michael's last tour, without having consulted with him beforehand. He had the suspicion that he was working for two sides and no longer trusted him.

A year later, in 1989, the contract with CBS expired and Sony bought their music department. Sony insisted the acquisition would take place only if Michael Jackson was part of the deal. And Jackson stayed. Head of Sony Music Entertainment was Tommy Mottola. Michael committed to 15 years and negotiated the biggest contract that the music industry had ever seen. The former chief of CBS, Walter Yetnikoff, whom Michael didn't get along with anymore at all, was friends with Branca. That, and the information about Branca having betrayed him meant the end for his lawyer.

"I tried not to get upset about it," said Michael. "I wanted to do my work, and I had wonderful ideas. I wanted to get ahead. But it was hard. The more the people read the derisive reviews, the more they believed them, of course, and the more everyone looked through the cynical filter of the press. The media influenced their purchasing behavior. I wasn't played on the radio as much anymore, and if at all, then only by smaller stations. Still, I sold 30 million records of *BAD*. In those years I believed in a natural down cycle. And I had my ranch, my Neverland, my little piece of paradise. I felt a strong energy there that inspired me, and above all I wanted to be by myself in my sound and dance studio. Or in my Giving Tree. These nights ... full of work ... full of music ... those were my favorite. I like being alone. But I don't like being lonely."

But Michael was lonely. More than ever he longed for affection. He was now over 30 years old. He'd never had a girlfriend, at least none that could be called one. Who was caressing him? Who gave him the body contact everyone needs to stay sane? Michael's high energy helped him get over a lot, and at Neverland, it was easy for to him to fall into his child's soul, to laugh and be happy.

As before, he still felt a deep bond with children - to everyone's incomprehension, it was from them that he drew the most power. But he was not only a child, he was also a grown man and sought adequate interaction and real friends. He instinctively protected his childlike self as the source of his high inspiration. At the same time, the urge to want to be a normal functioning adult in the world caused conflict in him. His friendship with boys gave him a lot, but not enough. Until he met Jordy.

With Jordy, everything changed.

***

Every morning Grace looked at me with the same unspoken question in her eyes. And the last few days I was able to only answer with a shrug of my shoulders. While Michael's narratives did crystallize into patterns, recognizing and solving things were altogether different matters and the latter being clearly more difficult than the former.

"What are you waiting for?" Grace asked me after the fourth night.

"Dunno. Maybe for a nervous breakdown."

Grace said nothing, but got nervous. Restlessly she put things away, ran back and forth in the kitchen, while I leaned against the sink and watched her. Finally she stood still.

"You're serious, aren't you?"

"Yes," I said, "I don't know if we should go ... I couldn't handle it. Grace ... I am not a therapist or a doctor ... but I also don't want to consult one ... because ... then it wouldn't be personal enough anymore."

"I know, I know ... but why a breakdown?"

"I read about that once," I said, "when people get rid of serious patterns with a bang ... it has a corresponding physical effect - do you know what I'm saying?"

Grace frowned. "But how does it manifest?"

"I assume he'll throw up, scream, cry, rage, break down ... I don't know."

"Oh," said Grace, "*That* I can handle. We've had all of that before."

You could tell that she trusted the approach less and less. And I could not blame her. I had no idea myself where everything would lead. Whether it would ever lead to anything.

A friend for Mike

"I can't take it anymore! You can't get anything together! You can't even feed your family decently! You are sick! Paranoid!"

Jordy knew it by heart. His parents argued constantly. And for a long time. Oh, it sucked so much! Frustrated, he covered his ears and could not do anything except wait for it to be over. As always after the quarrel his mom came to him and took him in his arms. This was particularly bad. She came with all her worries and burdens and clung to him. Then he tried to help her, tried to give her what she needed in such moments: his love. Children are so simple.

"Are you sad, Mom?" he asked.

"Yes, honey. Mommy is sad."

Jordy looked at her attentively. "Make the sadness go away," he said, reaching with his pudgy little hands to her face, lifting the corners of her mouth with his fingers and forcing a mechanical smile from her.

June closed her eyes. "Yes, my angel," she whispered. "Mommy makes the sadness go away. You're so right. I'll make what makes me sad go away."

And June divorced her husband, Dr. Evan Chandler, and re-married. A man named Dave Schwartz, who loved her madly and who owned a car dealership. She thought that Dave was more grounded than Evan and that he would take better care of her little family.

Someday, thought June, happiness will come to me, too. One day, she was sure, something would happen that would propel her life upward.

"But your son misses you," she said in a forceful voice. "He's eleven now, and he needs his father."

"Aren't you the one who complains constantly, I wouldn't get off the ground and not work enough?" snapped Evan. "I'm slaving to make payments. Meanwhile, the least you can do is take care of the children."

"Evan, it's not only about that. I mean, in case you haven't noticed: you have a son. Children grow up fast ... you might regret it, that..."

"Oh, cut the crap!" Evan swore into the phone. "Here comes that number again! Fuck off! And have a nice day."

June stood holding the receiver in her hand for a full minute before she hung up.

Then she went with a heavy heart to Jordy, who was sitting with a small travel bag in the living room.

"Jordy, hun, your father has got an important patient ... he can't this weekend ... but he told me to give you a huuuuuuge kiss and..."

Jordy looked at his mom. He knew that she was lying. Silently he slid off the couch, went upstairs and turned on his play station. At the least he could rely on that.

1984/1985

"God, how cute, look at that!" Michael said, showing a letter to his sister Janet. He had been discharged from the hospital just a day after the Pepsi accident and was at home in his bed. Janet had brought a bag of fan mail upstairs. It was of course impossible to reply to all the letters, but Michael picked out a lot and looked at them. Right now, he had a drawing of a four-year-old in front of him. A sun with a face, colorful clouds in the background, a green meadow with a hospital bed on it, in which laid a stick figure with a ball-round head, huge eyes, a half-pipe mouth and black hair. Next to that it said in touching writing, 'Get well soon, dear Michael!'
Michael was thrilled with the picture and taped it to the wall.
He called the boy and thanked him, as he always did when something touched him. He always took time for things like that because he respected his fans down to the very foundation of his heart. No matter how old they were. This boy was Jordan Chandler.

Nine years later he would get to know him personally. It was May 1992. Mike had a headache - the burn after the Pepsi accident was more difficult to deal with than he had expected, and he had to see his dermatologist even more often than usual. Sometimes the doctor was not even there - if it was a routine treatment, he left it to his assistant Debbie, who got along great with Michael. Michael liked Debbie - he trusted her, something that was very rare in his world.
Debbie's eyes sparkled whenever Michael came - but whose eyes didn't? He was Michael Jackson, that sort of treatment was nothing new for him. New, however, was that Debbie expressed an interesting mix somewhere between veneration and disrespect. She looked forward to seeing him in a way that took away all his shyness. There was something in this joy that told him that she didn't only see him as a superstar. Michael loved to be treated like an ordinary person, just like others found it exciting to be considered a celebrity. He always brought Debbie something, and it was so natural and so sweet that Debbie soon lost her initial awe of his superstar status. They joked and laughed together and Michael began to look forward to his doctor's visits - and to hope that he would be alone with Debbie.
Then he told her about his life, about all the corporate intrigue that he had to see through, about the egos of people who all wanted to be the most powerful and the greatest, and to whom a car or an 'It Bag' was more important than the life of a child. Debbie was a very good listener. What's more, her dry comments on his reports often took away the rough edges and

made him see things differently. And not only did she make Michael laugh, she became a piece of freedom for him.

***

If Debbie wanted one thing from her fellowmen, it was to be left alone and to do her own thing. She wasn't interested in the opinion of other people, she was not interested in material things, and she had something in common with Michael: she did not like adults very much. Debbie had had a difficult childhood and did not have a high opinion of her parents. At some point she realized that it was better to take her life into her own hands - the same as Michael. During the treatments they had intense conversations - the time with Debbie was valuable and enlightening for Michael.

When one day deep in conversation they heard the bell announcing the next patient, Debbie looked shocked at the clock.

"Shit," she said, "you have to go out the back door. You can't see the next patient"

"No problem, I'm used to back exits," said Michael, "too bad, I would have liked to get into this more..."

"Me too," Debbie said, "...but... I'm off in an hour... would you like to have a beer with me?"

Michael laughed, as if she had made a joke. When he looked at her, he realized how serious she was.

"Then I could tell the paparazzi right away," he said, "and starting tonight you'd never have a private minute in your life again."

"Bull," replied Debbie, "your way of looking at this is way too complicated. Let me take care of it ... would you want to join me?"

Her heart was beating in her throat, and she hoped that Michael did not see it. Michael gurgled

"If you want to take the risk ... but you'll see ... it'll end in chaos ... wanna bet!"

"The bet is on," Debbie said, grinning back. "We'll leave from here."

Michael then disappeared out the door to the back staircase.

At the appointed time he was back at the practice. But now he hardly recognized Debbie. Wrapped in black leather gear she stood before him and pushed a jacket, a kidney belt and a helmet into his hands, then went with him unrecognized through the front door, settled him on her motorcycle and drove off with him. Michael felt on that back seat freer than ever before. Laughing, he sat behind her and saw the world with entirely new eyes. The buildings of Los Angeles roared past them, and when Debbie stopped at a red light, he was able to watch the people and nobody, absolutely nobody, recognized him with the helmet. And of course, no one would have suspected it could be him on the back seat of a motorcycle. While still very nervous at the first light, he laughed out loud at the third and began to sing. All this was lost in the noise of the city: he was one of the many, and they rolled out of LA without incident, into the more rural areas, where Debbie bought a ton of food at a drive-up, plus a few bottles of beer and then sat with Michael under a large tree in the country for a picnic.

He was psyched to be there, his eyes lit up, they talked long and hard about God and the world, and finally she brought him home.

"Thank you, Debbie," he said as he returned the helmet to her, "it was a fantastic afternoon - absolutely wonder-wonderful!"

"Yes, it was," she smiled back and took the helmet from him. "This will be a permanent fixture now - with me at the practice ... and whenever you feel like it ... give me a call. I'm here."

They met more often and Debbie had become Michael's confidante. She had been for years now and knew things about him that no one else would ever know. It was a nice feeling to be able to trust someone like that.

***

His family hadn't gotten over the fact that Michael wasn't available for them any longer. And they were relentless. Joe visited over and over again and wanted him to perform with the brothers again. Indeed, the *Victory Tour* had been the last major source of revenue for all the brothers. And so Michael was continuously confronted with all sorts of demands that were made in the name of the family.

Currently Jermaine was bugging him with an idea. Jermaine always thought about reviving *The Jacksons*, as if he wanted to bring back the glorious past, the time in which everything had gone so well for him, Jermaine, too.

The latest concept was around an award for celebrities that would be presented by *The Jacksons*, a TV show. Michael hated TV shows. He liked videos and movies because in them things were developed until they all fit together. And that was very much in line with his desire for perfection.

But Jermaine did not let up because, as so often, the network only agreed if Michael would be part of it. It was strange - as much as the press made fun of Michael, he nevertheless remained the guarantor for filled coffers, for astronomical figures, for huge sales and television ratings. But as always, Michael refused to participate.

And as always they sent Katherine, who spoke for the entire family.

As always, they quarreled and Michael furiously got in some car that happened to be parked just outside the door at Hayvenhurst and fled. Away, away, away! Away from the pleading eyes of his mother, the challenging of one of his brothers who all equally instilled a guilty conscience in him and made him feel as if he were to blame.

He drove and drove, oblivious to his surroundings, a storm of emotion raging in his heart, until he noticed on Wilshire Boulevard that the indicator needle for the fuel tank was pointing unhealthily far to the left and the next gas station was miles away. And then the engine chugged and lurched and Michael was just able to drive onto the shoulder of the road where the engine died.

"Damn' it!" he swore and pounded his hands on the steering wheel. "Was that really necessary? Has everything conspired against me?"

It seemed to him that he had no chance to escape his family. And to call one of them was the last thing he wanted to do now. Inexperienced as he was - he usually had a chauffeur - he called the fire department, the only number he knew. But they didn't want to help him because they said a broken-down vehicle is not an emergency. When he said he was Michael Jackson, they laughed and hung up. Furious, Michael got out and kicked the tires. He was so full of emotion, of disordered feelings, and this stupid latent guilt! Damn - why couldn't he have a family that supported him instead of constantly putting pressure on him! Why couldn't they just leave him alone?

He made for a strange sight in his flashy clothes, a black scarf wrapped around head and mouth, the huge sunglasses on the small nose, angrily assaulting the tires of the car - not knowing that dubious help was already coming his way.

"I'm not kidding! He's on the road! I saw him clear as day!"

The voice on the other end of the line squawked something about the face being covered ... about an impersonator ... that this must be a bad joke.

"But I'm sure!" the woman squealed into the phone. "On Wilshire Boulevard! Send someone over - Jackson will sure be glad to see you."

He was indeed glad to see him: a mechanic from the car rental "rent a wreck," who rushed to the spot and found Michael Jackson in person, swearing and with a useless phone in his hand.

Relieved, Michael drove with the man to his garage. In the meantime the owner of the shop, Dave Schwartz, called his wife June.

"June!" he almost shouted into the phone and stopped himself again, trying for composure and a decidedly casual tone. "June, pack Jordy and Lily in the car and come here as soon as possible! I've got a surprise for you!"

"A surprise?" hesitated June. "What kind?"

"I don't want to say now ... but one that is really something ... hurry up ... get the kids and come here!"

June still hesitated. She did not know what to make of it. Lately, it had not been going too well with her and Dave. They argued more often and Dave had withdrawn from her and the children.

"Maybe you'll tell me what it's about," she insisted. "Jordy is doing his homework and I don't want to..."

"Man!" cried Dave, running his hand through his hair. "...all right ... are you sitting down? In a few minutes Michael Jackson will be here!"

"Michael Jackson?"

"Yes! That's what I'm telling you! Michael Jackson himself! We picked him up on Wilshire Boulevard! With a breakdown! And if you don't hurry, he'll be gone before you and the children caught a glimpse of even a stitch of his clothes!"

June did not need to hear that twice. She ran into the room of her 12-year-old son, screaming ecstatically something about Michael Jackson and mechanic shop and to hurry, dragged Jordy and his half-sister Lily into the car and started the car.

Her cell phone rang. 'My God,' she thought, 'I hope this was not a false alarm and now something came up!' But it was Evan, her first husband, who was on the phone.

"Evan, I don't have time right now," June barked into the phone.

"What's the matter with you?" he asked, puzzled.

"I ... we ... I'll call back later!"

Suddenly it occurred to her that she did not even know if it would all work out, whether they would be there in time.

"I'll call you back - in an hour ... or tonight!" She clicked off.

Jordy looked at his mother. He hadn't seen her that crazy in a long time. But, man, honestly, he could understand it. She had said he would meet Michael Jackson. Michael Jackson! His big dream since he was a little boy.

He was really there. They could not believe it. He was sitting right there. Slim, shy, somehow a bit awkward and incredibly polite. That's what Jordy noticed first: this quiet, restrained politeness. There was nothing show-offy or pretentious about him, none of the egotistical kind of behavior Jordy had seen so often in adults: the 'I am someone' - posturing for recognition.

Michael was someone and was aware of it. But he seemed to find it rather embarrassing. Quietly, he signed the papers that Dave gave him, smiled, nodded and thanked him a million times.

Then he stood up and looked around. His charisma flooded over Jordy and June like a tidal wave.

Michael first saw only June. And June was a beautiful, exotic woman with long black hair, almond shaped eyes and a great body. Slightly blushing, Michael's admiring gaze slid down her and she, all woman, noticed it.

Instinctively he took the black scarf and pulled it like a Burka over his face, as if he were the woman, blushing at the sight of a man.

Then his eyes fell on Jordy and Lily, and his eyes lit up. Jordy felt more than he knew that he was being pushed towards Michael and the two faced each other for the very first time.

"He is your biggest fan!" said Dave Schwartz.

"Yes, you should be friends," June added and smiled. Then she took a piece of paper and scribbled her phone number on it. "Here is Jordy's number," she said, handing the note to Michael. "Maybe you could call him…"

"Mom!" Jordy protested, embarrassed.

"But why not?" insisted June. "You've admired Michael for such a long time…"

Michael smiled and put the number in the pocket of his pants. June and Jordy spent the following days practically glued to the phone, but Michael did not call.

***

"You said you'd call back," Evan said sourly.

"Oh, sorry, I was busy … I forgot."

"And?"

"And what?"

"What was going on the other day?"

"What do you care?" June asked aggressively because nothing had come of the encounter with Michael. Why was Evan so curious when it was about sensations, but not willing to take care of his son properly as he had promised?

"You can ask Jordy should you happen to remember that you have a son," she spat.

Shortly after, June regretted her reaction. 'I shouldn't be so hard on him', she thought, 'he is Jordy's father and I'm making things worse.' And she planned a make up call.

A day later, and about one week after their meeting, Michael called Jordy and invited him to his condo in LA. Jordy could not go because he had a school commitment, but the two talked for two hours on the phone and exchanged views on video games, books, hobbies and ideas. Michael was strangely touched by Jordy. Something was different about him, and it took Michael a while until he had figured it out.

***

"You won't believe who called our boy today!" chirped June radiantly into the phone. She wanted to make up for her cranky call the other day and today it was particularly easy.

"No!! You'll never guess! Imagine: MICHAEL JACKSON! Yes! Exactly! THE Michael Jackson! In person! Dave picked him up when he ran out of gas. I gave him our number and he called…! Our boy!"

June was beside herself with joy. Michael Jackson! Her son was in contact with the most famous pop star of all time! Who was just celebrating unequaled heights of success in music history! The celebrity par excellence! My God! Her son! Friends with the person who all the doors of this world open up to! To whom nothing was refused, who was worth millions, who ... she got dizzy when she realized the full scope of what this could mean to *her*. She saw herself at the most coveted events, along with Michael and her son, meeting other celebrities, Hollywood's crème de la crème, interesting people, movie stars, actors, important people…! Then she remembered the look Michael had given her and she got weak in the knees.

All day June danced around happily. 'Oh, God,' she prayed. 'Don't let it be a fluke!' But she was really the least worried about that. Because Michael was known for his kindness - and for his generosity and hospitality.

During the dreams of all the doors that could open for June, she had yet another, uplifting thought: Jordy had ideas, he was creative. Together with her ex-husband Evan, he had already written a script that was even filmed. Since then Evan hoped to start a career as a screenwriter. He was an unsuccessful dentist and hated his job. For years he'd wanted to break out - one of the many reasons for the collapse of their marriage. Evan had always had great plans but had never finished anything, had never made it. At the end of the day, the ideas for the script had been Jordy's, not Evan's. He had simply helped his son put them into the right form. June knew that Jordy was eager to make something of his creativity. Evan saw that as well.

"Man, June," he said, "if this works out…then it could be possible that we don't have to worry about Jordy's or our future any more."

The sentence was ambiguous. No one would know how much Evan was interested in the implementation of these few words.

Shortly after this, Michael embarked on his *Dangerous* World Tour, which consisted of two legs. That meant being away from home for one and a half years. A life in the crowd, on stage, in hotels, airports, surrounded by at least ten bodyguards and an entourage of 250 people altogether. Already after the first week Michael longed for Neverland and his friends. He took out his numbers and called them: Debbie, Liz …Deepak … and Jordy. His friends were his only connection to some kind of family when he was trapped in his hotel room, where no luxury in the world was a substitute for human connection.

And yet, concert tours were not all negative for Mike, rather ambivalent - when he was in the middle of it, it was divine. It was the anticipation of the performance, this massive consolidation of energy and the simultaneous reverence over its expenditure. He felt as if his human body was not fit for this extreme exchange, this power, which propelled his whole being out into the universe, into an indescribable condition that made him experience his body as a boundary and facilitator at the same time.

The stage was a magical place. The tension immediately before the appearance enlivening, electrifying. Everything oscillates, everything vibrates, is under tension. The atmosphere is charged, powerful, embraces everything, embraces the entire universe.

Michael has just seen off the children who will be with him on stage on *Heal the World* during the final number. Their eyes were shining, so pure, so innocent, so clear, so honest. He is filled with this energy, filled with something that is much bigger than he. This is the energy he needs to get through this effort. It is his opening, his immersion in the source.
The amplifiers are humming, the crowd screams, yells, yells his name, he hears them chanting ... he owes them a perfect show ... he owes them everything ... these are the people who stand by him, give him their love unconditionally. They are his backbone, his support, his everything. A force that he can feel nourishes him. Already behind the stage, in his dressing room, he starts to interact with those people out there. He captures the vibration that creates a strong connection, a bond that forms and with every second grows stronger and stronger ... it is like a power line - he charges up, higher and higher, all the way to the top. Tremendous energy is released, a wave spills over from him to the audience, to the musicians, dancers, singers ... everyone is magnetized, infected, at 1000 volts.
Karen keeps looking at Mike with scrutiny; the makeup is fine, the man with the costumes holds the first outfit out to him. Mike feels slightly sick and he sinks into himself, listens to his heart, concentrates, sinks even deeper. And then ...then he finds the point ... he turns calm. He is in the eye of the storm. He closes his eyes, he hears the frenzied cry of the crowd, it blends into one frequency, is like the rhythm of a beating heart ... the rhythm of his heart, the heart of the fans ... boom-boom, boom-boom ... it is all one ... it is a single heart that beats ... it's as if something new is about to be created... a birth ... these are the labor pains, the painful contractions beforehand that will soon deliver something of amazing beauty.

He feels himself get up, feels his legs move, goes to the starting position, stands on the springboard below the stage, puts his sunglasses on ... closes his eyes, his concentration is at its peak. He is a point of pure, compressed energy ... feels how something makes his heart swell up, spreads over his entire body like a luminous substance, like light that extends from the inside, beyond the outer boundaries of the body and all of it ... boom-boom ... boom-boom ... the pulsation of the stars, overly loud, omnipresent.

The screams get louder, the hatches are opened, Michael's soul is filled completely, he doesn't have any other thought in his mind, he's just full, full, full of what he will soon be able to give, is granted to give. Within him something begins to rejoice, he can feel how the energy rises within him, always higher and higher, it is close to spilling out. At this moment the catapult shoots him upwards and everything, everything flows out into this crowd that screams out in a wild frenzy, wildly greets him, and he feels how it flows, how it floods ... the love for these people, his heart, his energy ... how everything surges back at him with full force...and the stage, the fans, the sky above him melts in a huge explosion into one single energy field.

After these experiences Michael could never sleep. Sometimes he wondered if it was really just the adrenaline that kept him so awake. This energy exchange with this huge mass of people, the exchange of emotions ... he sometimes had the feeling he could fly, wanted to lift off, to leave his body ... but something held him back ... something prevented ... and often he then fell into the exact opposite: into feelings of loneliness and depression - when the hole opened up and devoured him.

The telephone conversations with his friends were like ladders out of this hole, and the conversations with Jordy proved to be the most funny and interesting.

"Basically, we talked for half a year only by phone," said Mike. "You have to know that when I am on tour, I take care of everything - from light and show effects, to choreography and technique — there's not much time for anything else. I was home for Christmas for a brief stop, and my friend Liz Taylor had decorated my entire house for Christmas. I experienced this for the first time in my life - Christmas with lights and sparkling! With a tree and presents underneath! That was so wonderful. Then the NAACP was on the agenda, the Inaugural Ball for Bill Clinton, the American Music Awards, the Super Bowl ... and the interview with Oprah Winfrey ... there was hardly any room to breathe."

"Goodness, during all this time you'd only talked on the phone and didn't see each other?" I asked, amazed.

"Essentially, it was almost a year before I saw him again - but during that time we talked at least once a week."

Jordy was witty and intelligent and had an incredible imagination. They could make up all sorts of stuff on the phone together, laugh about it, build their castles in the air, let them crumble again. They talked about school, about Michael's performances ... about simply everything. Michael found a harmony, for which he had always longed for. It was so new for him and meant so much to him when Jordy asked, "What kind of feeling did that give you? How did you feel?"

It made him feel accepted as a human being, something he desperately missed in his stardom, and his affection for Jordy deepened enormously. And when Michael replied, Jordy either had a sensitive answer or made such a disrespectful comment, that he had to laugh immediately, which let him see the situation in a completely different, less serious light, and that was good for him. It was liberating... it was something that Michael had never experienced before: to be able to talk to someone who had sadness and mischievousness in him at the same time, who addressed the little boy as well the man in him and who didn't see a discrepancy in that but a connection.

Already after the third or fourth call, Michael had a sense of joyfulness when he dialed Jordy's number.

All Evan heard from June, meanwhile, was that she was arguing with Dave about money and that Michael seemed to be calling Jordy every week. But otherwise, nothing happened. Michael was on the road and the first leg of the tour took nine months.

A long time... many months, in which thoughts arose, were further developed, were pushed into a corner ... came out again ... spun around in Evan's head, possessed him until he couldn't get rid of them anymore.

The phone calls with Jordy became an anchor in Michael's life. Sometimes Jordy talked about school, about problems with classmates or teachers. Michael tried to help him from a distance, gave him advice, did what Jordy did for him: without taking on the role of lecturer as so many adults did, Michael participated in his life and advised him to be a good student. He told him:

"A good education is very important, Jordy, you should get out of it what you can and forget about the bullies in your class who think it's cool to get an F..." and then in the next minute he'd discuss whether he should buy a private jet and whether it was possible to flip a switch by shooting it with a water pistol.

Jordy did not feel there was an age difference between him and Michael, and he was able to open up to him in a way he had never known before in his life. His classmates were too immature, the adults too much in their heads. Michael connected both states in a fascinating way for him. And this was what Michael felt, too. With the children he could play, but not have deep conversations. With Jordy he could do both. For Jordy, Michael was the best listener in the world, and in return Jordy confided things he had never discussed with anyone before. Before, no one had wanted to know.

Mike had, as always, the implicit desire to help Jordy in much the same way that Jordy helped him by turning Michael's dramas into amusing anecdotes with his own wonderful combination of depth and humor. Their connection became closer and closer in these months. A comforting feeling surrounded Michael when he thought of Jordy. The boy was really special. And what he felt for him most of all was love and gratitude. For his friendship.

The candles in the lanterns had burned down, their light no longer bright. The crickets chirped in the warm night, but Michael was cold. I gave him a second blanket, which he wrapped around himself. In the shadows of the night, he looked like a hermit, at one with his surroundings. It was as if he was telling his story not only to me, but also to the heavens, the universe, with the eternal question in the background: why? Why did it have to come to this? Why did something so beautiful have to turn into something so ugly? "It was as if I had known Jordy forever, as if I had found someone long-lost at last," Mike said, and his voice was very quiet. "It was like a coming-home for me ... such an ... age-old connection between us, inexplicable. Jordy seemed to feel the same way. He gave me the sense as no one else had before, that he was there. That he was there for *me*. For the first time in my life ..." He paused, aware what he was about to say and was silent for several seconds. Finally, he whispered so softly that I had trouble understanding him:

"For the first time in my life I felt like I had found a friend, a real friend. A *true* friend."

And every week, amidst all of the obligations, rehearsals and performances, he looked forward to calling this friend. He was excited; he had butterflies in his stomach. And he could hardly wait to have Jordy with him at Neverland, to show him everything he loved. Where everyone was allowed to be the way they really are, where children had rights.

***

After Michael finished the European part of the world tour he went home in February '93 for a breather.

He invited June, Lily and Jordy to Neverland for a weekend. When the call came, the Chandler Schwartz family was ecstatic. A whole weekend in the legendary Peter Pan world! June was jumping up and down: she had a ticket into the glamorous world of Michael Jackson!

Again, Evan heard about it from June. Evan was almost more frantic than the rest of the family and felt excluded at the same time. He had not been invited, of course. He was just the ex-husband.

June, Lily and Jordy came to Neverland and were welcomed by a most accommodating staff. They were taken to their rooms, the guest suites where high-profile celebrities had already stayed before. They admired the idyllic landscape as they rode in the golf cart there, the wonderfully laid out flowerbeds, bushes and ancient trees and they were, like so many, immediately charmed. There was such a special atmosphere at Neverland, it was such a wholesome, childlike, joyous world that highlighted the beauty of nature and enticed fun, play and enjoyment. From the beginning, the three were fascinated and so filled with awe that their jaws dropped.

Then they were taken to the main house, to the living room where they sank two feet deep into the cushions, waiting for Michael. He came soon after, giggling with a tray of drinks and apologized jokingly for his delay that he had trouble finding the kitchen because he had been away from home for so long.

Everyone laughed, the ice was broken quickly, and Michael took the whole day to show them Neverland with all its amenities and entertainments. The weather was fantastic, the kids romped around, they drove bumper cars and the carousel, visited the zoo, went swimming - it was better than they had ever dreamed of.

The next day, Michael took them to Toys 'R' Us and told the children that they could have whatever they wanted. The shop owner closed the store for the time Michael was there with the Chandlers, and June watched her children load three shopping carts full of toys worth several thousand dollars. Michael did not bat an eye. He had one of his employee's load everything on a pickup, then they drove back. The children were in exuberant spirits. Their eyes were bright, their cheeks were flushed, as they sat amidst their new mountain of toys and felt like kings and queens.

June could not fight it - she felt the same way. This was a world that went beyond her imagination and she decided to enjoy it to the fullest. Michael was friendly and courteous, funny and generous, and it was touching to see how he played with their children.

And he was handsome. He was more than attractive. He smelled of a pleasant perfume and his body was ... sexy. He radiated something - something she had never felt before with any man, something different, rare, and he was basically glowing with sensuality. June watched him as he put clothes on a doll for Lily, as he joked around with her, built a toy kitchen, which they had bought, fried imaginary eggs ... how he and Jordy were lost in a Gameboy game, and how he squealed like crazy when he managed to reach a higher level. She had never seen an adult unfold this way in a game with children.

He took walks with her, too, showed her old trees that he liked the most, drew her attention to rare flowers ... demonstrated a high level of education in his conversations with her ... he just had these two sides to him and June felt as if she were in another dimension. Which she was. The day had been wonderful and continued to a warm summer night.

And when the color of the sky turned between black and blue, the stars sparkled, the moon stood in the sky, classical music was heard everywhere, millions of lights glowed on the property, on the rides, hidden in trees, shrubs and flowers, Neverland gained charm and magic even more.

And for Michael these days were full of joy, too. He felt infinitely comfortable in Jordy's company, he found June breathtakingly beautiful and was grateful to her that she was so receptive to it all. He was glad that he was the one who was able to give them this beautiful time.

That had always been what he had wanted: to make others happy. But he, too, wanted this happiness. When he saw into Jordy's glowing eyes, he was seized with this liking for his own childhood, for just this happiness that radiated form Jordy and Lily, for this something so absolute, where nothing seemed to be missing.

After weeks of traveling and the loneliness he felt amongst so many people, he longed simply for genuine caring. Oh, and he wanted to be understood so much! Wanted so much for people to like him! Wanted to get away from the loneliness that came over him constantly. With an overflowing heart, he sat with the three of them up there in the big Ferris wheel, which he had stopped at the highest point below this immense sky with its lights, and below they could see Neverland in all its glory. The urgent feeling came over him to share himself, with the sense that this family had something that he was missing. Something that maybe they could give him...that perhaps would take away the feeling of loneliness. The emotions overwhelmed him and he whispered:

"I sit up here so often alone ... so alone ... in spite of everything that I've accomplished ... I always feel lonely ... you can't imagine how lost I often feel..."

Jordy immediately put his arm around Michael. "You've got us now," he said softly, "and you know we love you."

Michael smiled wistfully. Then he looked at June with his deep, painted eyes. She felt butterflies inside.

"Thank you, for being here," he said softly, "I'm so glad that I can share all of this with you..."

June's heart overflowed, she sensed his need for love and hoped from the depths of her heart that she could be the one who could make his loneliness disappear forever. She gently placed her hand on Michael and her arm around her daughter. There beneath the vast firmament with its millions of stars, they were united and everyone wanted only the best for each other.

When the weekend was over, Michael drove with his new friends back to Los Angeles, then on to his hideaway in the center of the city, not without arranging another meeting at Neverland.

***

"And... how was it?" He wanted to sound indifferent, but inadvertently the curiosity crept in his voice, which annoyed him and put Evan in his usual grumpy mood. The advantage was that his feigned disinterest sounded more authentic that way.

"Evan, it was a dream ... a dream ... a dream!" June swooned enthusiastically.

"You can't begin to imagine - and I mean the way I say: it is un-imagine-able, unless you have seen this with your own eyes!"

And she began to rave about what they had seen, how they had been waited on, that Michael employed up to eight chefs and you could have, any time of the day, even at night, a dish of your desire prepared immediately. The masseurs, the landscape, the toys, the zoo and the amusement park, the cinema ...June seemed to come to no end.

"And these were only two and a half-days!" she gushed. "Michael is such a polite and amiable man, the coolest, most generous celebrity I know!"

"That's not too hard, after all, he is the only one you know," growled Evan.

Again he felt left out, without being clearly aware of this. There was just a rumbling in his stomach - he could not share June's happiness.

"When is Jordy coming to visit me?" he asked involuntarily, and wondered about the question himself. But even more surprised was June. She had always had to ask her husband to look after Jordy. Now he brought it up on his own? Life could be beautiful!

"Whenever you like," she said warmly, "you know that Jordy was very disappointed when you canceled last time."

"Nothing I could do ... you know ... the patient ... "

"I know, sure."

The two were silent for a while, then June said:

"I'll ask Jordy to call you, then you can make a date."

***

Michael experienced this time as something very special. He felt that now, after all his successes, after *Thriller*, *Bad* and now *Dangerous*, and especially when the world tour was over, some peace and quiet could come. Time to cultivate friendships, to collect himself. This thought came to him one day with crystalline clarity when he was sitting alone in his tree. For him, the workhorse and the perfectionist, this was an exceedingly great and strange insight. Like the thought of the very first vacation in a stressful working life. Somewhere, he felt that there were other things to discover. He had every right to think so: after all, he had 30 years of hard work behind him.

Of course there would never be a world without music for him, he had to fulfill his contract, to deliver new albums, meet obligations with Sony. Nevertheless, and he promised himself firmly, he wanted to devote himself more to his private life.

Debbie had put him on a completely different track. The first motorcycle trip was followed by many more, and once she had even smuggled him into a movie theater, which had given him particular pleasure. They had been in pubs with such dark corners that nobody had turned their head around to them and since Michael loved disguises, they had even gone out to dinner, drank wine and had talked and laughed a lot. He enjoyed Debbie's company very much. She was so straight and unspoiled. He liked that because he himself was more held back and he thought her fearlessness was quite attractive. Moreover, the meetings with her generated a new self-confidence regarding the female sex. Now, if he met women in groups or parties, he could deal with them in a much more relaxed way than before.

He was successful, he was doing well. He was able to achieve his objectives, help children, donate money, turn visions into reality, and since Michael had met Jordy and went out with Debbie, he had the hope that the nagging feeling of emptiness and loneliness would disappear one day, too.

After he had brought Jordy and his family home he spent the week in LA. His skin ached. Meanwhile, his entire body was afflicted with vitiligo and with the sharp cream the doctor cauterized off the pigmentation in places that were photographed. Face and arms. His skin became very pale, but was still blotchy and needed makeup.

When he came for treatment to Debbie, it always seemed to him as if he came to a secret hideaway. And, moreover, one in which he could talk and did not have to stare at the walls. He enjoyed that a lot. He also enjoyed her hands, they gently touched his face when she examined him and he liked it when she was close, when her full figure came close to his body during the treatment. There was something tingly, something that inspired Michael's imagination in a direction that he had been able to think of only with disgust previously.

And so he sat on the table in a sleeveless T-shirt and Debbie looked at his right arm. The bleaching cream irritated his skin, it often itched and burned, and every once in a while the edges became inflamed. He winced as she applied a soothing ointment.

"Shhh ... " she said automatically in deep concentration, as a mother would have calmed her little child. "...It's almost over ... it'll get better soon."

Michael took a breath and looked at her from the side. Her eyes were calm and focused on his arm. The honesty of her thinking was so apparent in her face that a deep wave of affection swept over him. He exhaled audibly and relaxed.

"Better?" she asked and meant the pain that the ointment had caused.

"Yes ... everything is fine..." said Michael and smiled warmly.

She glanced up and smiled back. Two pairs of eyes, which sank into each other for a brief moment - a gaze intense as a concentrate. Both noticed how something slipped down in them ... to the stomach, where it caused a tingling feeling. Michael felt a slight electric shock run through his body and he shook himself slightly.

"Are you cold?" Debbie immediately asked, worried: "I'm almost done, then you can put the sweater on again ... I can do the face like that and I'll get you a blanket."

The blanket was not necessary, but it was cozy and that was what Michael longed for at that moment.

"Lie down," Debbie prompted him kindly, placed a pillow under his head and wrapped the blanket tightly around his thin body, stuffed it around his sides, wrapped his feet.

'Oh, that feels so good', he thought, and closed his eyes. 'That feels so good...' ... it felt so good to be able to surrender himself to someone he trusted. Debbie sat on the stool beside him and began to examine his face. Her upper body was near. Michael had closed his eyes, but he could feel Debbie. A wave of heat emanated from her. Then she rolled the stool to his right side and turned his face to the left so she could look behind his earlobes. Her touch was gentle but firm and Michael felt himself relaxing more and more - despite the tingling feeling down to his groin. Her upper body was further away now, but still he felt it, felt the primal closeness of the female breast.

"This looks pretty good," she murmured, applying cream behind his ear. "The skin has become a bit thin, Dr. Klein should prescribe something to help rebuild..."

Her breath smelled of mint, he refused to open his eyes. Her right hand was completely on his cheek, covered his face in order to move it gently to the opposite direction and the hand was sure and tender. And then came the other hand that touched him on the chin, turned his head, stroked his cheeks... she mumbled something and then leaned far over him to get a magnifying glass from a moveable cart on the other side of the treatment table. She didn't get up, so that her upper body pressed a little against his face, fleetingly, a brief second only, until she had the magnifying glass in hand. But in this moment, Michael held his breath. One second leaning against the breast of a woman and a thousand longings erupted in him. He could not open his eyes, thought ... 'do that again... get something else from the cart...!'

But Debbie didn't get anything else, and instead he heard a rolling noise: sitting on the stool she rolled away from him to the desk to write a memo. The warmth was suddenly gone, but the tingling feeling was stronger. But before the room could turn back into a normal doctor's office, she had rolled back, an ointment in her hand, which she dabbed at his face and his neck. She leaned far over him to get to his left ear, and he enjoyed this to the fullest. So much so that his body could not help but respond.

Immediately he blushed and tensed up. Confused, Debbie interrupted her work. Michael squeezed his eyes shut as if this would cover up his predicament. She looked along the blanket, saw the visibly bulging reason for his anxiety and began to giggle.

With a bright red face Michael lay on the table. Was she making fun of him? Before this thought could turn him off, he felt her place her free hand between his legs, unabashed. Startled, his eyes popped open.

"Well, you're not gay for one thing," she giggled and grinned at him cheekily. "Don't worry about it - it happens all the time here... a real disadvantage for you men ... right?"

Michael had to laugh. A little embarrassed ... but Debbie was so wonderfully frivolous, without being vulgar - it took away any of his shyness.

"And ... how do you handle it?" he asked, relieved.

"Oh ... I ask them if they have to get to the bathroom ... most of the time they do." Debbie laughed. "And they all have a red face, when they come out again."

Michael giggled. "Are you serious?" he asked, already feeling much less stupid.

"Well, what do you think?" she said, and he realized that she still had her hand between his legs. It was incredibly warm, this hand ... she was getting warmer ... it sent a pleasant flow of energy through his body and Debbie did not make the smallest attempt to remove her hand from there. Michael looked at her. Debbie looked back calmly.

"Well," she said dryly, "we'll have to treat that body part sooner or later..."

To her surprise, he moved slightly beneath her hand. To his surprise, he asked no longer shy and with a far lower pitch in his voice:

"Can you do that?"

"What?"

"Treat a body part like that?"

"I'm afraid..." stammered Debbie, "...something like that should be approached gradually ... so the patient ... isn't ... irritated..."

Her cheeks were bright red and the warmth that radiated from her entire body seemed to be amplified by it.

The clock in the treatment room ticked loudly. They looked at each other. Quietly. Then Debbie leaned forward and kissed Michael on the mouth with trembling lips.

***

The weekend arrived and Jordy was ecstatic to visit Michael and Neverland. He liked this place, it was like the promise of freedom. Michael had been quite right, it was a place where boys could be boys. No parents fighting over money, no father, who made promises he didn't keep, instead a generous, funny and loving person who was able to listen and was ready for any kind of nonsense.

Jordy had overheard his father bragging to friends that HIS son was friends with Michael Jackson, that he called Jordy every day and that HIS son was a welcome guest at Neverland. He thought that was terrible.

Jordy really liked Michael from the bottom of his heart. Michael was the first grown up with whom he could talk about everything. Ranging from video games to showbiz, about school to girls and growing up.

And Michael could play. Had his mother or father ever tried to figure out what made video games so exciting to play? They couldn't understand any of it. Michael did, Michael was cool. At times he did find him super weird with his makeup, his childlike squealing and his sometimes bizarrely assembled clothes. At the same time he liked that Mike was remarkably uncomplicated and often walked around at Neverland with comfortable pants and the oldest T-shirts.

And he gave him a lot of input. He told him about foreign countries, his charity work, and offered to take him along, if his mother would allow. Jordy could still remember a long conversation on the phone, when Michael had called from some country whose name Jordy had forgotten, and had described a visit to an orphanage.

"You can't imagine, Jordy," he had said with a breaking voice. "The children there were lying on the ground on old stinking mattresses or in rusty cribs. Some of them were tied to the beds because they were crying from pain and were trying to crawl away. There wasn't enough medicine, enough food ... enough staff ... it was terrible."

Michael had started to cry, he couldn't stop, and Jordy did not know what he should do. Finally he asked:

"What did you do?"

Michael blew his nose and sobbed: "I wrote a check for half a million dollars and said that I wanted them to buy decent beds immediately, get medicines as well as clothing, disinfectants and all that stuff. I have a guy who specializes in those kinds of things and organizes everything. Then I gave them a deadline - in some countries, you don't know what happens with your money. I said that I'll come back in three days - in that time they'd have to complete most of it - otherwise I'd go to the press and wouldn't perform."

"Wow," Jordy said, impressed. "You said that? Would you have really not performed?"

"Yes, I wouldn't have. My fans would have been the first to understand," Michael said with a conviction that expressed his amazingly deep bond with his fans. "On the contrary, they would have helped me, I'm sure of that. I love my fans ... I really love them - I have the best fans in the world."

Jordy believed him right away.

"You have to join me one day, Jordy. I can pay for a private tutor, and you can see this with your own eyes."

"Yes, I'm in, definitely," said Jordy, resolving to be just like Michael one day: to expand his talent, and work hard on it so that he could help other people. For him it was a beautiful and coherent thought.

"Oh, man," he said then, "if everyone were to think like you ... our world would really be a better place"

Michael was just about thrilled when he heard that.

"That's just it!" he cried excitedly. "That's exactly it! Somehow we have to get people to think that way! Children do that automatically! Children aren't suspicious and don't have this treacherous thinking and none of this 'I begrudge you this and that'. I mean ... at the beginning children are so innocent ... and then, they are spoiled, then the adults teach them that they have to cheat others so they can get ahead themselves, that you have to use your elbows, that lying is legitimate and that money and power are the most important things in life ... and they believe it, and then they are ruined forever, forever conditioned..."

Jordy listened attentively. What Michael said sounded plausible. He only wondered whether it was feasible. When he thought about school and his experiences, there was a lot of meanness, jealousy and envy ... how could you get rid of that? He asked Mike this question:

"If everyone plays this game, how can you stay out of it? Don't you have to participate so you won't go under?"

"Well," he said, "it's hard to uphold your ideals when everyone is laughing at you. Look at me. Look at how the press drags me through the mud ... but I don't want to be changed around... I mean ... if someone steals something from someone else and that person steals something back from him ... then they're both thieves, right? Then who is better or worse?"

"That's true," admitted Jordy. "Still...it's not easy to live such high ideals..."

"No," Michael said, "it's not easy, Jordy. I feel it every day. But it's worth it. Don't let them condition you, Jordy, promise me that you won't get on this track of the adults!"

"Yes," said Jordy.

"And you won't let them influence you negatively?"

"No," said Jordy.

"You have to stay strong ... for your own sake, for the children ... for a better world..."

"Yeah, okay."

"You know what, Jordy? When I come back, I'll show you Neverland ... you'll visit me ... and then you'll know what I mean."

And Jordy had really understood what Michael meant when he had been at Neverland for the first time. The place was just supernatural. There he had the hope of a world where he could breathe and feel that promised freedom. And this was so, because Michael followed his premise not to use his talent for ego gratification.

During these months filled with phone calls, all of which ended with the sentence: "I love you, Jordy," it had become a certainty for Jordy that he had become special to Michael. The first weekend at Neverland, Michael's admission that despite all his successes he was lonely, had touched Jordy's heart. He wanted to be as good a friend as Michael was to him. And so he was looking forward towards the next weekend with his whole being.

***

It had stayed at a kiss between Debbie and Michael. With many words and red-faced, she had apologized and was seconds later horrified at herself.

"Hey, girl, calm down," Michael smiled at her, "it's all right. It was a sweet kiss from you."

"Oh God, oh God ... how could I ... I'm sorry, I'm so sorry..."

Michael sensed no more of the tomboyish Debbie, and he once again realized how honest she was. Touched, he put his arm around her. She did not match his ideal of beauty, but he liked her infinitely because Debbie formed a solid foundation in a world that seemed to consist only of decaying columns, and he was grateful for her friendship.

"Debbie, please calm down, it was nice ... I don't know what I'd do without you."

Debbie looked up at him shyly. She felt his arm on her shoulder.

"Do you really mean that?" she asked.

"Sure, I'm serious. We've already done so many things together ... and there are damn few people I can trust. You are one of them. I'm glad you're here. And I don't want to mess it up ... with sex... because... for one thing I don't want to take advantage of you ... and for another ...another..."

"... You're not in love with me," Debbie finished the sentence for him and curiously regained her composure, as if this statement had brought her back to safe, familiar territory.

"Right," Michael said simply, and now he was the one who looked at her shyly.

"I can deal with that just fine," Debbie replied firmly. "I'm thankful that I am your confidant ... that ... that means more to me than you could ever imagine."

Michael nodded, they looked at each other again, then they laughed and hugged and when Michael left, both of them knew that they had shared something very valuable with one another: infinite trust. For Michael that was an especially rare treasure.

Not without me

"Hey Jordy," said Evan, pressing his son to him, "how are you?"

While he was hugging him, he realized that he had not seen his son for a long time... and that he hadn't spoken with him for even longer. Jordy was a teenager now ... another fact that had passed him by. Evan had not had good times. More precisely, he was still stuck in them.

He asked Jordy about Neverland and Michael and how everything was. Jordy remained somewhat monosyllabic. Evan understood - he had really not taken care of Jordy for a long time. He decided to make it up to him for Christmas, he'd get his son the computer that he had wanted for so long.

But Jordy longed to be back with Michael. At Neverland, where he was safe from adults and their hypocritical ado.

And finally, finally the time had come. Finally Michael's huge stretch limo showed up in the driveway, with all the neighbors gawking out the windows and a bodyguard holding the door for June, Lily and Jordy as they got in the car where Michael Jackson sat. And he, Jordy, was Michael's bestest friend! Disillusionment followed hot on the heels of excitement.

Mike sat in the car wearing a hat, black face mask and - with a ten- or eleven-year-old boy called Brett Barnes on his lap, who had known Michael for numerous years - much longer than Jordy had. Who had been to Neverland far more often than Jordy. Who was bantering with Michael in a way that Jordy had thought was something unique to their friendship.

Jordy's heart abruptly sank to the very bottom and with lightning speed it came to his mind that he was not the only boy in the world. That Michael had many friends, had a past and a future. From the shocked look on his mother's face, he knew that she was thinking the same.

When they arrived at Neverland, Jordy's belief in an alleged special status was completely wiped out when Michael had Brett's luggage brought into his bedroom.

"Brett always sleeps in the lower part of my bedroom," he explained, "...or Cul ...Nicole and whoever happens to be there ... We often watch movies at night and then sometimes they fall asleep. This way they can just stay where they are."

"And you?" Jordy asked anxiously.

"I've got a sleeping bag," said Michael lightly, "my bedroom always looks like a Bedouin tent, because so many of 'em are lying around. I usually sleep on the floor. Make yourself comfortable ... I'll see you at dinner."

Jordy was left with mixed feelings. He slept with his mother in one of the guest units, away from the main house, away from Michael.

It was still a wonderful weekend anyway. There were more children invited and they all had loads of fun with water fights, the rides, lots of candy, movies, picnics, camping in the teepees, campfires and anything a child's heart could desire.

When Jordy finally said good-bye to his new friends after this sunny, happy day and was walking over to the guest units to his mother, he saw Michael sitting by the lake. He wanted to say good night, but when he got closer, he noticed that Michael had his hand over his eyes. Was he crying?

"Are you okay, Mike?" he asked, startled.

Michael winced; he had not heard Jordy approach.

"Sorry, Mike, I didn't want to frighten you," said Jordy, "just wanted to say good night."

"That's sweet of you ... yes ... I'm fine ... it's so beautiful out here, don't you think? And today is such a special night…"

"A special night?"

"Yes ... some nights have ... in some nights something is just in motion…"

Michael stopped short, he was going too far, he felt that and he did not want to scare Jordy off. But the boy sat down next to him, looked at the sky and suddenly Michael felt that Jordy knew exactly what he meant. He looked at him.

"Can you feel that?" he asked.

"Yes ... but I can't access it ... it's as if a message were hanging in the air...like an invisible veil...and sometimes I see it around you ... around your body…"

Now it was Jordy, who stopped because he felt silly. They looked at each other. Both knew about the other, what he thought and felt.

Jubilation sparked in Michael's heart...a disbelieving, abruptly upward surging hope of not being alone with his feelings and his way of seeing the world, to not be alone as he had always believed. He was not alone! Jordy also saw the things he saw! That was like a revelation for him. It was mystical, cosmic.. he was sure to have found back an old soul, an age-old friend from ancient times -his soul brother.

That was a deep irrational certainty. He just knew it. He felt a connection that lacked any logic. He was not alone. He was not alone.

And it was this shared experience that opened their hearts wide, because they both felt something that in these days was accessible to only a few, something that made them allies in a world that seems to be blind and deaf towards such things.

Michael experienced this time as a blessing. It was a time that nurtured his hope for a happy future, for the faith, after years of intense work, to be able to give fate a different twist.

The life of a pop star in the midst of camera light and paparazzi was hard. The life of a megastar was doubly hard, and friendships in this business were not on the agenda. But now...now he had people like Debbie, he had secret friends who were known to almost no one and who also wanted to remain anonymous - a sign of their sincerity - he had Jordy, connected together by something mystical. Then there was another acquaintance who made his heart beat a completely different way: at a dinner with friends sat a beautiful woman with a figure like an elf, a sexy-husky voice, an infectious laugh and a huge helping of wit and humor. Michael was fascinated by her, never left her side and flirted with her for the entire evening. She was rich and famous, so he could be sure that she certainly was not after his money or his fame. She had a lot of admirers and she was married: Lisa Marie Presley.

Michael thought her stunning in every way, and after that night not a week went by in which he didn't call her.

He went through several developments at the same time: with Jordy a childhood friendship, with Lisa his first love, with Debbie a casual camaraderie and with the Chandler family, he learned about the life of a typical American patchwork family.

Fast-paced, eventful, happy days followed. Michael invited the Chandler family for a visit, or he was a guest in their home and enjoyed sitting in the midst of a real family, eating with them, doing everyday things, like cleaning up the house. It was a bit of normalcy, which was so exciting for Michael, as one week of celebrity life would be for ordinary people. Jordy was for him like a brother, a friend and a son ... all simultaneously. He was one of the first to whom he revealed his ideas, his vision of an ideal world, the possibility to believe in the good and to live it. Jordy was his confidant. Like King Arthur and Sir Lancelot. And Michael was so often a guest at the Chandler-Schwartz household that he no longer felt so alone. He was a part of a small family.

"Feel like a weekend in Vegas?" Michael asked, handing the delighted June tickets for a first class flight, a stay in a $ 3,000-a-night suite at the Mirage Hotel, the prospect of a face-to-face encounter with Siegfried and Roy and other celebrities, shopping in Caesar's Palace and much more. Michael paid for everything and for him it was absolutely natural. June felt as if she were in heaven.

After the first busy day, June and Lily fell asleep in their suite as soon as their heads touched the pillow. Jordy and Michael shared the other suite - with separate bedrooms.

"Come on, let's watch another movie," urged Jordy. Michael, as always, was not tired. He never seemed to be very tired, he seemed only sometimes a bit run down, then he disappeared somewhere, but never for very long.

"Sure, what do you want to see?" Michael asked. Jordy rummaged in the archives of the hotel and found *The Exorcist*.

"Uuuughhhh ... creepy," said Michael, "that's not for you."

"It is too, I'm not a little kid anymore," Jordy shot back in the best teenager mode. They inserted the film and lounged on the giant bed.

After about 45 minutes, Michael registered a change in Jordy. The boy was scared. It was night and the movie not an easy subject for a thirteen-year-old.

Resolutely Michael turned it off and said he was tired, he wanted to sleep, they could see the rest tomorrow. Jordy was relieved.

"Can I stay here?" he asked. Michael looked anxiously into his ghostly pale face.

"You're not doing that great," he noted. "Wait, I'll get you something to drink."

Michael got up, fetched a glass of water for Jordy, and was undecided.

"We can't ask your mom," he said. "She's already asleep."

"But I want to stay with you," Jordy insisted anxiously and demonstratively put his head on the pillow. How well Mike could understand that! He had also always felt much safer in the midst of his brothers. To hear someone breathing next to him was reassuring. The truth was: Michael did not like sleeping alone. He got panic attacks. Then memories overtook him and now...now there was Jordy who was afraid. He could not possibly send him alone to his room. He knew what could happen if you are alone in these situations.

Protectively, he covered Jordy. And settled himself on the floor with a blanket. He preferred to sleep there anyway. Jordy was his friend. And he would be there for him.

The next morning, June saw her son slip out of Michael Jackson's bedroom. With horror, she realized that her son's bed had not been used.

"Where are you coming from?" she asked sharply and unnecessarily.

"I stayed with Michael," answered Jordy.

"Are you nuts? I don't want to see that happen again!"

"But why? Michael is my friend!" defended Jordy. "Everyone sleeps with Michael!"

"Jordy!" she cried. "That's just not done! You promise me that you won't do that anymore and that's that!"

But she did not say anything to Michael.

"Man, I can tell you, my mom is so mad at us," Jordy said in a quiet moment.

"Mad? At us? Why?" Michael asked.

"Because I spent the night with you - she really freaked."

Michael got a sickening feeling in his stomach. What was June construing there? After all this time? He could not stand it if someone thought poorly of him, and so he immediately ran to her.

"June!" he exclaimed. "How can you be so suspicious? What's wrong with Jordy sleeping with me?"

June was somewhat perplexed. Michael stood before her, entirely beside himself, a grown man who looked at her with eyes aghast ... like a child who had been accused of something terrible.

"I can't believe you think that way about me, June," Michael said with a whining voice. "I thought you were my family, you are the ones who I can trust and who trust me ... who..."

He broke out in tears and June found herself in the situation of holding a 34-year-old, weeping man in her arms, who she comforted and reassured that they did not think poorly of him, however that it was an inappropriate behavior, that others could misinterpret that. She wanted to protect him and Jordy from that.

"There, you see," Michael sniffed and wiped his eyes. "That's how the world is, that's how adults are. Their thoughts are only dirty and mean, they can't feel anything else anymore. And whenever something innocent happens before their eyes, they tear it down, so that everything is the way they claim."

June didn't know how to respond. Something in her told her that Michael's thoughts were not so far from the truth and another side warned her and appealed to her common sense.

"Jordy and you are the best thing that ever happened to me," cried Michael, looking at June from his huge, black-stained eyes.

"Jordy was scared and I didn't want to leave him alone. You wouldn't have left him alone either! You have to believe me!"

"I believe you," June said with difficulty and patted Michael's back. She had very conflicting emotions. She welcomed the fact that Michael considered them his family. But she also realized - with all the consequences - that not the man, but the child dominated in him and he therefore seemed to be interested mainly in her son...which made her feel disappointed.

As soon as they were back from Vegas, Michael extended an invitation to the entire family for a full five days. Five days in which Jordy slept every night in Michael's room, and June and Lily stayed in one of the guesthouses. Five days in which many children were guests at the ranch and spent the whole day in revelry together. Jordy often made fun of Mike in a very flippant manner, so that Mike pounded his fists on the floor with laughter. The friendship between the two deepened more and more. Their conversations flowed along like a fresh stream, invigorating and lively. Exuberantly they romped around with all the others, but they could also be seen alone, deep in serious conversation. From time to time, June discovered them on a bench at the Lake, Michael with knees pulled up like a teenager, while Jordy sat cross-legged beside him. Sometimes Jordy looked older than Michael;

sometimes it was the other way around. The two shared a really close friendship, and their behavior gave June no reason for worry.

As for the nights: Jordy was not alone with Michael. Many children were sleeping in his room. Boys and girls, they all wanted to be with Michael. And once they were with him, no one wanted to leave. And that was not only because he was Michael Jackson, since the children didn't really care about the celebrity status after a little while. They wanted to play and Michael joined in with a devotion not to be surpassed.

They had slumber parties with pillow fights, watched movies, he read fairly tales to them. Then Michael sat in the middle of the crowd of children - pure happiness on his face. He saw immediately if any of the children did not feel well or was sick, sometimes before the child was aware of it himself. He was infinitely caring. No, the nights weren't what bothered June. But she would have preferred if Michael had shown more interest in her company. Disappointed and grouchy, she often wandered around alone at Neverland. Water fights were absolutely not her idea of fun, and in addition she had discovered that Michael was calling other women on the phone, was almost flirting with them. All of this did not contribute to her good mood. Apparently, only Jordy was the link between Michael and the life she dreamed of.

XX / 1991/92 on the plane

"Take a grain of truth and turn it onto an avalanche. That's the point. Since the grain is the foundation ... and if true, everyone will believe the escalation. And the twisting. People can only see the avalanche. That's the trick"

But Michael was so thoughtful and kind that June decided to simply enjoy all the invites. Since what is not now could still well be. They visited Disneyland and spent the nights at the best hotels in the world and everywhere Michael's status ensured that they received preferred treatment.

Michael gave the children toys and June expensive jewelry. In addition, soon after he invited them to Monte Carlo. June nearly fell over when Michael asked almost casually if they would like to attend the Music Awards in Monaco at his expense.

She was in heaven and any doubts she may have had at the sight of Brett and the other children, or when Jordy had spent the night with Michael for the first time, drifted away like a feather in the wind.

She, June, would sit next to Monaco's successor to the throne! Next to a real Royal Highness! She! And her children! She was at the top! She couldn't believe it - it was just too much, a dream come true.

Evan Chandler could not believe it either. For three months now his ex and his son were intimate friends of the King of Pop. And he had not received a single invitation. And more: his son spoke only of Michael, Michael, Michael. And the other day when Evan wanted to meet with Jordy, his son postponed the meeting because he preferred to be with a pop star rather than with his own father. And the kicker: his ex-wife flew to Monaco? Would meet His Highness Prince Albert of Monaco? On a show that was hosted by Michael Douglas? With Pavarotti, Rod Stewart, ABBA, Tina Turner... all the famous celebrities in the world and a guest list that read like the cover of *Forbes Magazine*? And what about him? Wasn't he the father of this boy whose friendship Mr. Jackson seemed to appreciate so much?

The day his ex-family left for Monaco, in one of these ominous limos that Michael had sent, Evan stopped by unannounced to say goodbye. His heart sank into a bottomless abyss when he felt Jordy's indifference. Who was he to him? How could he ever measure up to a megastar? His son treated him like an outsider! More than that, like someone who was in the way! Evan's heart clenched. He watched the car leave and highly contradictory emotions raged inside him. There was June, driving off to a world that was barred from him. His son drove off to this world, too. Nobody cared about him. Nobody had invited him. And it seemed as if the little that he had left and was so sure of, Jordy's affection, was completely lost to someone who had the money to buy anything. He felt betrayed. He felt rejected. And rejection was intolerable to him. June had what *he* wanted. Everyone but him had what *they* wanted. And Michael Jackson even had his son!
Two days later at a newsstand, a picture of his ex, Jordy, Lily and Michael at Disneyland jumped out at him from the front page of the *National Enquirer*. "Jackson's new adopted family" was the headline, and a destructive feeling awoke in Evan, like a cobra ready to rear itself up to its full size. That was the button in Evan that set a disastrous mechanism in motion. And when hurt, a person much more readily thinks poorly of others ... and lashes out blindly.

Dave Schwartz, June's still current-husband had to struggle with this news story, too. He could not join in on the trips - he had a job. And he had trouble with his wife. All right, his marriage had already had an expiration date before the encounter with Michael Jackson. With a pitying look and many expressions of sympathy over the loss of his family, an acquaintance brought over the *National Enquirer*. Dave stared at the picture. Did June have what she wanted now? And he, too, began to grit this teeth.

As always, when Michael traveled he caused mass uprisings. The family had traveled separately to Monte Carlo because it would have been too difficult to shuttle four people unscathed through the madness that raged on the streets because of him. His fans flipped out when he got off the plane. They screamed their lungs out, were hell bent on getting close to him, had painted banners and pictures, crafted things, prepared gifts, held up signs with slogans and photographs. Mike admired his fans, admired what they put themselves through just to see him. They were so easy to please, were happy with a wave from the window, a smile, his peace sign and a couple of "I love you's" before he was shoved into a limousine.

When his car drove off from the airport, people jumped into their own vehicles and followed him. No matter where he was, at Neverland or anywhere else in the world –. Michael always had fans around him. The detective skills they developed to pay their tribute to him were amazing. When he arrived at the hotel, the big question always was: how could he get in? He could be sure that every nook and cranny was already besieged by fans. Just to get to his suite, often diversions had to be planned, complete strategies developed which had to take into account the equally strategically thinking of the fans. His fans spanned a remarkable network. They had connections with flight and ground personnel, with staff in hotels, with police employees, even with his own people. They cultivated friendships with anyone who could be useful to them with the single goal to shake Michael Jackson's hand once in their lives.

Once there had been no other way to get into the hotel than to spontaneously rent a helicopter that was supposed to land on the roof of the hotel. And still, a few fans had even figured this out and were positioned up there when he had landed. Not many, maybe three or four ... but they were there. How they had received the information and had managed to get through the massive security at the hotel, no one knew. But Michael loved them for it. Okay, there were the lunatics who trampled over him and ripped out his hair but the majority was sweet and respectful.

Michael always took the time for them. He always gave autographs, looked at their banners, replied to letters as best he could, and from time to time opened Neverland's gates for them when he saw them camped in their cars in front of his ranch for hours and days. When he was in the hotel, he bought them pizza and drinks and threw souvenirs down to them. He owed them everything and he knew and appreciated that. But it was not only that: he understood their longing.

Still, he envied Jordy, who checked in at the hotel undisturbed and could look at everything without being assaulted.

Chaos engulfed Michael before and during the trip, and of course at the hotel, where he was brought to the back door to enter via the fire escape to his room. He was tired, the days before had been long and strenuous, and he looked forward to Jordy's company. Michael didn't feel like being with June or the people who accompanied him. More than anything he wanted just to be with Jordy, wanted to savor this feeling that gave him so much at this moment.

When the small family entered his suite, June whined about not having anything suitable to wear for the upcoming ceremony. She was excited ... it wasn't every day you were in such illustrious company and she was concerned about not being dressed appropriately.

Michael seized his chance. He handed her a credit card, told her to fly to a location of her choice - maybe Milan or Paris ... they're not far away after all ...take Lily along and get clothes for themselves, regardless of the cost.

June was thrilled. For sake of politeness she said things like, "I can't accept it, that's too much..." and so on, but Michael insisted that she should not worry, and was glad when they finally left.

He did notice how alarmed his crew looked. Meanwhile, the press had begun to not only make fun of his fondness for children but to put negative connotations on it. He did not understand that. Why where they doing this to him? Yet he was not desensitized by the malicious reports. That in June's absence he and Jordy spent the night in one room caused many of his people to get a bad feeling. And so he told them that he and Jordy had the flu. Nobody believed him. This obvious lie reinforced the uncomfortable feeling that the outsiders had about the whole thing. But the other, the real, the actual reason was something Michael would have been able to explain even less. He knew that. So he stuck to the flu and fate took its course.

The next day June got a call from her ex-husband, Evan. When she happily rubbed it under his nose that she had a new outfit of clothes at Michael's expense he almost lost it.

"And where was Jordy?" he asked through clenched teeth. "Did he get a new outfit as well?"

"Oh no, you know how little boys his age feel about shopping trips - he was with Michael."

"He was with Michael," he repeated sarcastically.

"Yes," June said, surprised, "he always is."

"So you leave your son alone in the hotel, while you're flying around all over the place." Evan's tone annoyed June and she replied pointedly:

"Michael was looking after him - he couldn't have asked for a better protection, he is literally surrounded by bodyguards."

"Michael is surrounded by bodyguards," clarified Evan, "not Jordy."

"But Jordy was in Mike's room and so he was protected just like Mike," said June, immediately biting her tongue after this announcement.

Evan took a whopping three seconds to capture the sensitive nature of the situation. Then he said quietly and seemingly without emotion:

"Jordy was ... in the room with Michael? The whole time? He stayed overnight with Michael?"

"Uhm ... yeah," June admitted uncomfortably. She had to justify her shopping spree, but at the same time didn't want to be perceived as an uncaring mother in front of her ex. "Michael lovingly takes care of Jordy ... you know that," she persisted

"Michael takes care of Jordy lovingly."

The way Chandler repeated it, made clear what he meant with 'take care of lovingly'. June blushed at his unspoken thoughts.

"Evan," she said urgently, "Jordy and Michael are friends, just like boys are friends with each other... you should be..."

"Michael is not a *boy*," Chandler corrected, and the silence that followed his words triggered a stream of bad conscience and unpleasant concerns in June. Abruptly uprooted from her recent perspective, she saw the unnaturalness of the situation: a 34-year-old alone with a 13-year-old in the room! Night after night! For weeks now! Mute, she held the phone to her ear, frantically seeking answers for Evan, while her brain picked over the last few weeks for suspicious moments. Her silence made everything worse.

"We'll have another talk about this," Evan said acidly and slammed down the phone.

June sat on the edge of the bed and gulped.

That evening when Jordy was preparing to spend the night in Michael's suite, June put in her veto.

Jordy got terribly upset. He whined and pleaded and wanted to be with Michael no matter what. Given the recent phone call, this begging suddenly sounded completely different to June's ears. Then Michael was added to the mix, both tried to push her just as hard. He did not understand June's sudden misgivings, he was shocked that she even had any, everything had been fine before! But June was thinking about the phone call and all of a sudden she realized that Michael was indeed a grown man. But the two did not stop pestering her, and the longer they nagged June, the more her previous impression of Michael came back to her: the big boy who enjoyed the company of a friend.

Finally she relented, and overjoyed the two fled back to Michael's suite. Two children, who had successfully persuaded the mother. June watched them with mixed feelings.

She was far from mentioning this episode to her ex-husband. She didn't have to. There were other ways. The day of the awards came. And there, a lot of beautiful pictures were taken of Michael's new family.

***

Michael sat leaning against the tree, looking into space, his fingers were playing with a blade of grass, and I thought how refined his charisma was and how graceful he looked even while sitting - even in casual clothes. There really was something about him that made him simply beautiful.

"I never talked to anyone about it," said Michael, and turned to me with a pained expression in his face, "but I always had the feeling that I belonged to an alien species. I didn't think like most people here, I had other ideas, felt differently, I ... see things that others can't see ... often I really thought that my life on this earth might be a huge misunderstanding ... had it not been for the music and the children. All these years I was looking for like-minded people, for people who understood me, with whom I could simply be Michael. But in showbiz, where it's all about sales, image and money, I had to operate as a music machine, a product of the stage, and the confusing part was that I knew for sure that I also belonged there. It is the only place where I could express myself and find acceptance. The stage is a place in a world that seemed to reject me ... and Jordy ...was just like me ... he ... he..." Michael broke off. He was ashamed to say the next words, couldn't get them out.

I said nothing, just listened. Waited.

He wiped his tears, new ones bubbled out and his mouth twisted.

"Chirelle," Michael said tightly, "...he loved me. I felt it so clearly. He did not admire me. He loved me ... and ... I enjoyed it ... I ... yes, I admit it ... I enjoyed it ... it was an innocent friendship ... and I have been punished so much for it... to enjoy the love of a friend ... I had never experienced anything like it ... but did I ever get punished for it..."

He started to cry. His pain had a hopelessness that choked me up. I imagined what it would have been like for me, growing up for 34 years without having had the important friendships of youth with which one could mature ... as far as his experience was concerned, he hadn't been any older than Jordy. And then this statement, that he had been punished!

When Michael turned forward again and closed his eyes, single tears rolled down. One, two, three. He let them roll. Then with his hands he wiped the wet spots dry on his cheeks and sniffed.

"The time with Jordy was so fantastic..." he said, and a wistful smile came to his lips. "We wanted to change the world together. He understood when I talked about things like universal love. He understood my need to want to help the world, he wanted that, too. He didn't make fun of it like the others…"

I handed Michael a tissue, he blew his nose and continued staring across the lake.

"We talked about the stars, about the universe, about things he read, or that I had heard about. I started to feel lonely when he wasn't there … I longed for him and his understanding."

I didn't have to ask if Michael had loved Jordy. Of course he had. How could you not love someone who gave you this elementary feeling? Even in the best of circumstances? And Michael had started under dramatic conditions. Yes, he had loved Jordy with all his heart, as his soul mate, as the friend with whom you can experience youth. I didn't have to ask the question about sex, it was hardly necessary. Sex was not what Michael had wanted from Jordy. It was as if Michael had silently cried for love and Jordy was the first person who heard that cry in all its clarity and who responded to it.

Michael, meanwhile, naturally picked up on my thoughts.

"You know, it was never physical affection that connected us. Our friendship was on a completely different level. It was … cosmic."

There was a long pause. It was so long that I thought Michael had had enough and he wanted to stop the conversation. Then quietly, in a whisper, barely comprehensible:

"I would have never been able to undress in front of Jordy or anyone. He would have despised me. He would have been disgusted. He wouldn't have liked me anymore."

My heart stopped. "Oh, God," I thought, "Oh God, Michael, please don't…"

"I was so ugly," he whispered. "I couldn't stand seeing myself without makeup, let alone show myself. My skin condition was at its peak, that is: spots everywhere. At that time, I needed full makeup. People saw a product of cosmetic art, but they didn't see me. They would have rejected me … everything about me, and my music too. I have never been able to show myself naked in front of anybody. I didn't even walk barefoot in those days."

My voice was hoarse:

"But Mike … if Jordy liked you so much … if he was a true friend … don't you think he wouldn't have cared how your skin looks?"

Michael was silent for a long, long time after this question.

"You know," he said, clearing his throat several times, because his voice did not want to continue. "He … I was … once… there…"

Again he paused. Our eyes met. Then he muttered, embarrassed, ashamed, as if it had happened yesterday:

"One morning I came out of the shower … with a towel around my hips. I didn't know that Jordy was in the room … I swear … I didn't know it! The towel snagged on the door handle and fell down and for a second I was standing naked in front of him."

In a fraction of that second Michael registered not only that the boy was staring at him, but he also recognized the nature of his look. With a cry, he pulled the towel to cover his lower body and ran back into the bathroom, Jordy's cries of apology in his ears. And irrevocably burned into his brain was his non-definable glance, the lips slightly curled. A look that reminded him of the incident at the airport. It made him sick to see this expression in Jordy's eyes.

"I loved his friendship- that means so much to me – I never wanted more. I was afraid to lose Jordy," Michael whispered. "And I lost him. But differently than I could have ever imagined in my worst dreams."

***

"He's got the boy on his lap," the bodyguard said into his microphone and barely moved his lips as he spoke.

"Tell him to stop doing that, for Christ's sake!" the voice complained from the headset. "Damn, damn, damn – he's being filmed! Where's the mother?"

"Next to him."

Pause

"Think of a couple of nice words. The brat is supposed to sit on his mother's lap!"

They were about to start the trip to the event. Michael sat on the broad back seat of an oversized Rolls with open windows, Jordy on his legs, June and Lily next to him. With his massive body the bodyguard tried to obstruct the view as much as possible from the paparazzi cameras.

"Mr. Jackson," he said to Michael, "we would welcome seeing Jordy sit next to his mother. The press could get the wrong idea."

June looked at Michael. He had just been distracted and did not hear the request.

"Michael!" said June and touched his leg. Michael looked up. The bodyguard looked at him.

"Mr. Jackson, I have Jones on the line ... he thinks ... just a moment ... he's saying something ... please wait a moment."

The bodyguard was listening to his headset. He could not believe his ears.

"Leave the kid where he is," he heard, "tell Michael to hold on to him tightly... we're taking off. It's too late anyway."

The paparazzi snapped pictures. The storm of flashbulbs did not seem to cease: Jordy in the car on Michael's lap. At the awards in the front row, next to Prince Albert of Monaco, on Michael's lap. Lily sat on Michael's lap often, too - no pictures were published showing that, if any were even taken.

When Evan saw the photos in the newspaper, something snapped in him. It couldn't be that they excluded him to this extent. He was getting nothing, absolutely nothing out of the connection to Jackson. And it could not be possible that his son was sitting on the lap of another. Of one who had the advantage of being able to give him anything.

XX / 1993 Europe

"Everything is a matter of interpretation. Give the press a good 'ol push. The guy feels so secure that he's giving us one point of attack after the other. He loves children? That's great. America loves that. You'll have an easy victory "

Not with me

Bob Jones' blood was boiling.
"How could this happen?" he yelled. "I even called you specially! Did you lose your tongue? Can you imagine what kind of shit we have to deal with now?"
The chided one rolled his shoulders in, but didn't feel at fault.
"You radioed twice," he said, "and the second time you said, 'it's too late, I should leave it alone' ... so, what's it gonna be?"
Bob was set to reply, when his answer got stuck in his throat.
"A second call? Not from me," he said finally.
"Bob, that was your voice, I'm not stupid."
Without a word, Bob turned around. He knew for sure that he had called only once. Lately things were completely out of control. And he didn't have the faintest idea who was behind it or what it boiled down to. He just knew it wasn't good. And he hadn't had a chance to talk to Michael about it.

"Michael, you should avoid pictures like this," his advisors told him.
"But why?" he asked perplexed. It was amazing. Michael was such an exceptional artist, was so concerned about his image and was a shrewd businessman. He never missed a meeting of one of his companies, was always wide awake there, alert, prepared, and followed the discussions with thorough interest. But when it came to children, to his ideas of life or

philosophy, he was stubborn; he could not understand why this was so difficult for the outside world to grasp.

"Why?" he asked again, as all those around him fell into embarrassed silence.

"It's simple, Mike," one of them said quite roughly. "Because people take it the wrong way... they see a grown man with a child on his lap who isn't his."

"Yes ... but ... if I wanted to hurt the child, I wouldn't show myself with him in public! Anyone gets that! And what does this picture say other than there is a loving platonic friendship?" Michael insisted stubbornly.

"It maybe says something else," his adviser told him. "I mean, not everyone thinks positively..."

"Well I won't let them take that from me, too," countered Michael and was suddenly angry. "They take away my privacy, they make fun of my face, my skin disease ... they're already pulling me through the mud ... I won't let them take that away from me, too!"

"Michael, you have to think about your image!"

"What image?" raged Mike, frustrated to his core about this additional restriction. "Do you mean the Wacko Jacko image? It doesn't matter what I do - the press writes crap anyway!"

"Michael," said his adviser and looked into his eyes, "there is crap and there is dangerous crap. This here belongs to the group of 'highly explosive crap'. I don't know if you want that."

But Michael was unrepentant. For the life of him, he could not imagine what the world would want to think about him that was even more terrible than what they were thinking now. He was Wacko Jacko, a madman, beauty-obsessed, an eccentric and an enigmatic pop star. The image hurt him more than he wanted to admit because it was so far removed from reality. But he also knew that it helped him to stay in the headlines, being good and free of scandal didn't help ... but it would have been a thousand times nicer if people were interested in his good attributes, in who he really was. But that did not only seem boring but also dangerous - according to his adviser.

And then defiance was added to the mix: he was Michael Jackson. He could do whatever he wanted. Fuck the media!

***

"Listen, if Mike wants his friend to sit on his lap, then let him," he said.

"Man, I'm his PR person! Any idiot knows that will backfire! What do you want?" The two stared at each other.

"That you leave him alone."

"That's not what I am getting paid for! He has to listen to his PR advisor!"

"To you?"

"Among others, exactly," said the other, amazed at this strange conversation, "what does he have us for?"

"He's Michael Jackson, and he can do what he wants."

"No he can't. Especially because he's Michael Jackson!"

"I see. And what are your plans?"

"To prevent him from doing stupid things like in Monte Carlo?"

"And how do you intend to go about doing that? Nobody tells Michael what he can and cannot do. He's the King of Pop, the greatest entertainer the world has ever seen."

"Oh, yeah? He won't be for long - if you continue to let him do stuff like this. He is about to destroy his image. And I'm supposed to watch with a friendly nod of my head? No way, buddy, not me. I like Michael, he's friendly, polite and he needs good advice. And that's what I'll give him."

A short time later a tape was played to Michael.

"He's Michael Jackson, and he can do whatever he wants."

"No he can't. He has to listen to his PR advisor."

"To you?"

"Exactly!"

"Nobody tells Michael what he can and cannot do. He is the King of Pop, the greatest entertainer the world has ever seen."

"Oh, yeah? He won't be for long…"

Scratching, unrecognizable noise, then "…to destroy his image…scratch "…that's …what … I'm paid for…"

Michael turned pale when he heard that. For years this had been happening to him. Since 1983, more and more strange things had been happening. He knew that the business was filthy, dirtier than the average person out there could possibly imagine. He was surrounded by sycophants, cheaters, people who were only out to get a slice of the giant pie that was Michael Jackson. People, who threatened him. With letters, phone calls, false statements and forged contracts. Fairness did not matter. More and more often tapes were presented to him, evidence produced, videos shown, letters and double-contracts that his advisers had with the press and other people... it was a confusing mess of distrust and lack of transparency. He was tired of all this stuff, tired of being presented with proof over and over again of dishonesty, of the meanness in people.

"Fire him," he said sadly and turned away. Situations like this were on the daily schedule. All the more he was attracted to children who didn't have all this insanity in their minds, all the more to Jordy, his anchor, with whom he could talk about worlds that no one else understood.

Three more long months had passed. Months in which emotions fermented like bacteria in a compost pile. Months in which the various press articles, June's rapture, her expensive clothes and jewelry and Jordy's indifferent attitude catalyzed like highly explosive additives the mind muck in Evan's head. But all of a sudden there was a valve that allowed a discharge of the hazardous gases and seemed to prevent an imminent explosion.

Evan Chandler met Michael Jackson.

Michael was often at Jordy's place. And when Michael was in the house of the Chandler-Schwartz's, he slept on a cot in Jordy's room, happy and without any complaint. June often wondered about that. She wondered, just like everyone else, why someone with such a vast amount of wealth and talent and relationships preferred the company of a simple, small family and that of a 13-year-old boy over anything else. There he lay on the uncomfortable cot in old sweatpants and a t-shirt, lay like a child and slept. Oh yes, for many of us in our world it is hard to imagine that closeness and warmth, love and security are much more precious than all the wealth of this world.

It was one of these days that Evan stopped by unannounced and saw Michael Jackson for the first time in person.

Evan greeted June who was preparing a cup of cocoa in the kitchen for his son Nikki from his second marriage, when he went upstairs to say hello to Jordy. What he did not know: he had caused a medium-sized panic attack in the children's room with his arrival When he had rung the bell, Jordy had run to the window and looked down.

"Oh," he said, "Dad's here."

"Your daddy is here?" Michael asked, startled, "you think ... he'll come in here?"

"Sure," said Jordy, surprised at Michael's frightened tone of voice. His eyes grew even bigger when he saw Mike haphazardly and almost with panic grab some toys and cower in the darkest corner of the room like a little child wanting to hide.

"Mike, what's wrong?" Jordy asked puzzled. But then the door opened and Evan stood in the doorway.

"Hi, Jordy," he said and looked around searchingly.

Michael's heart was in his mouth. But he knew he could not stay in the corner - how would that look! So he emerged shyly, his eyes directed more towards the ground than towards Evan and embarrassed, he shook his hand.

No Superstar, no King of Pop, no solid, strong, 'Time to make a bow! - macho handshake'... no: a totally insecure, fearful and shy man stood before him and the poisonous cloud around Evan's heart instantly evaporated. His son Nikki was the one who opened the valve some more, allowing a great release of pressure. He stormed into the room, shouting:

"Wow!!! Michael Jackson!!!" and Evan watched dumbfounded as Michael transformed from one second to the next. He let out a whoop and immediately sat on the floor with the little guy, and within a fraction of a second, with amazing intensity, became absorbed in a game with him, as if they'd known each other for years.

Evan stood open-mouthed at the door and finally looked over to Jordy. He grinned, shrugged his shoulders and said, "Yep, Dad, this is Mike."

Evan needed a moment to process this. This image did not fit at all with the one he'd had before. It had been the same for him as for anyone who knew Michael only through the press or from hearsay.

Flabbergasted, he went into the kitchen to June. She gave him a quick look, then grinned like Jordy had and said: "All of us reacted like that. It's hard to comprehend and impossible to describe. You have to see it for yourself."

At dinner, they sat together and Michael was talking to Evan and Dave in an ordinary way. For him, only the beginning was difficult. Once he had overcome his initial shyness, it wasn't that bad ... even if he still didn't really trust adults. And men even less.

But Evan was friendly, he tried to make conversation and Michael was grateful. Above all, he was thankful that he did not seem to be against his and Jordy's friendship. He knew deep inside what it must mean for Evan - he was the father of the child, and Michael the one who spent most of the time with him.

Evan began to relax completely once he recognized Michael's child-like personality. With complete fascination he observed how again he turned to the children with total involvement after dinner. How he also discussed topics at length and in depth with him, Evan, that revealed his intelligence and his education. Evan was confused. The contradiction between this child-like behavior and this extremely mature mind was a mystery to him.

But the fact was that he got along great with him, which made the most part of his self-made aggression disappear into nothingness. Evan wanted mainly one thing: to be acknowledged. To be part of the whole thing, too. And now he finally belonged.

But that was not everything he wanted - he also had dreams that had taken on form since Jordy's first outing with Jackson. His medical practice was unsuccessful. For years he'd tried to get into the movie business. He had written screenplays, good scripts, that if only the right person would read ... and Michael Jackson knew tons of people like that! So far, his scripts had been rejected, which didn't necessarily mean anything, since that had happened to many now-famous authors. He had to force himself not to rush things, otherwise everything could be spoiled. And this opportunity was too big to risk that.

He practiced patience. He was nice to Jackson, which was not difficult, because Michael was lovable, he was like a big kid when it came to trust and, above all, he was kind, and just threw his money around. On his first visit to Evan's house he gave him a watch from Cartier, which surprised him at first and then was immediately followed with excitement.

He could not know that the company of his son moved Michael to tears of gratitude; he would never have been able to understand this feeling. Michael needed to thank him for having him in his house, for letting him be friends with Jordy. With the excitement from all these emotions, and also because it's proper form to give someone a gift when visiting for the first time, he gave the father the watch.

Chandler was convinced that Michael would be ready for a deal when the time came to talk about business.

Carefully, he dropped a hint from time to time. He was involved in the movie business ...Jordy's greatest wish was to write ... he had certainly heard about it ... education ... expenses ... not much money ... it's tough, not to be able to give your child what he deserves ... and he, too, Evan, was talented ... could support his son ... had already prepared several ...

But for some reason Michael did not take the bait and Evan was forced to become clearer.

You won't get rid of me

Meanwhile, Michael went in and out of the Chandler and Chandler-Schwartz homes, and nobody in the world could have imagined what it meant to him to be able to lead a reasonably undisturbed normal life. He watched June and noted that at Neverland she was trying to take a leadership role by bossing around the staff in an unpleasant way, which displeased him greatly.

But Evan and he got along great. Evan fit him in to his household without fuss. Michael ate the things that were put on the table, helped with the cleanup, played with the children and slept on a cot in Jordy's room. He had become such a permanent member of the family that one day Evan proposed to make an addition to the house so Michael would not be so cramped. The fact that Michael began thinking seriously about it and obtained architectural designs showed how much he had already become part of the family. When the addition had to be dropped because of legal reasons, Evan suggested that Michael build a new house for him. With a superstar on his side, nothing was impossible - not even the realization of his most intimate dreams. Michael became wary.

In a moment he thought fitting, Evan brought up the subject of his screenplays and offered them to Michael for sale. He said it was difficult to get into the movie business - the real movie business - without a recommendation. Once you had grabbed a foothold it wasn't an issue anymore, but until you got there ... and if you ever got the chance, although you delivered first-class work ... Michael knew how it goes. In the music industry it's probably the same thing: there were so many great voices, but for a breakthrough the famous trump card of connections had to be put on the table. And he could surely do this little favor for him, the father of Jordy, Michael's best friend, after everything he, Evan, had done for Michael ...

Michael listened, frowning, Chandler noted with alarm. As much as Michael could lose himself in a game like a child, it was also a fact that he had been in the business for more than 30 years and was in this respect neither blind nor naive.

There were millions of people who wanted a favor from him because he was Michael Jackson. To say no was hard, but in time he should have learned to, if only because of the embarrassment of abusing his business connections for dubious characters and deals. However, he didn't like these kinds of situations, because he didn't like to deny someone his wish. And if someone constantly harassed him with a request that he could not or would not fulfill, Michael simply avoided him. That was his recipe that apparently worked. That's how he had also found peace from his family - by avoiding them as much as he could.

Evan's request was doubly unpleasant to him. First, because he felt indebted to the Chandlers; second, because Evan's calculating side became so markedly apparent. Michael felt emotionally blackmailed by the way Chandler put forward his request. But still Michael said:

"Of course I'll help you. I'll introduce you to all directors and producers I know or I'll pass your scripts on with a recommendation from me." But Chandler did not want to have any of this.

"And then see my idea become a blockbuster, and have to fight for copyright in a year-long trial," he said. "Look, Mike, I'm not greedy. I want to sell these scripts, and I know they are good. I don't have a name yet in the movie industry. You have one. Buy them from me and sell them off to a producer. If you sell them for more than you paid, I'm fine with that. I'll waive the royalties, too ... it's just a tiny deal for you, huh?"

He was so excited over the potential outcome of the conversation that sweat trickled down his back. He wanted twenty million for four books - he could do something with that! And Jackson was loaded! What were a couple of million to him?

To his surprise, Michael's response was vague. He said at the moment he was not interested in screenplays, but he would like to read them so he could get an idea. Chandler knew that this was nothing more than a polite refusal. He tried a few more attempts, but Michael remained unexpectedly firm. The always-eager-to-please Michael, who paid thousands of dollars for clothing and jewelry for his ex, for toys, travel and hotel stays for the kids, denied him, Evan, his rightful share. It took a while until the reality sunk into Chandler's brain: Jackson was not going to support him.

The friendship between Jordy and Michael gained dimension. Jordy had not forgotten Michael's anxious reaction at the first sight of Evan and spoke with him at the first opportunity.

"How come you were afraid?" he asked. To his amazement, Michael began to tremble. "I ... I ... don't know..." he said in a quivering voice.

Jordy attentively observed his friend. His foray had triggered something, he sensed that clearly. And when Michael looked at him with teary eyes, desperate, that's when Jordy suddenly recognized that something must have happened in his life that had traumatized him deeply. Silently he put his arm around him and urged him to tell him everything. And Mike spoke for the first time to another person about the fears of his childhood days. It turned into a long night. Jordy held him and listened. And even when Michael was crying, he was not shocked, didn't let him feel the age difference, because for him it simply did not exist. He just held him. Michael never forgot him for that.

In the following weeks, Evan made many more advances. Over and over again. Every occasion he saw Michael, he rushed up to him.

"Come on, Mike, you know millions of people ... it's no big deal for you..."

"Evan, I'll pass them along on your behalf, I'll be happy to do that for you," Michael said in his soft voice: "If you want, we can have my lawyer handle it to protect your copyright so you're on solid legal ground... I'll pay for the lawyer..."

Chandler didn't want to hear anything about it ⁻ he wanted the money right away. But Michael was not willing to pay $20 million for screenplays he didn't even know. Evan became intrusive, with the consequence that Michael began to steer clear of him.

Once Chandler felt that he was being shunned, the production of toxic feelings and thoughts was reactivated. No Jackson, no money, no entry into the glamorous world of Hollywood. No future, no options. Thrown back into the old, sad world. He started to panic. He did not let up. He dug in.

Michael was uncomfortable with having to constantly put out rejections. Finally, he avoided Chandler entirely and stopped coming to his house. He did not call and did not respond to Evan's messages. He didn't give him his new phone number - which he changed weekly. There were no invitations to Neverland for Evan. Michael no longer trusted him.

After weeks of waiting, Evan realized: Michael Jackson had disappeared from his life. With the blink of an eye, he became completely isolated while June, Lily and Jordy remained guests at Neverland. The brew in him boiled over.

If Jackson kept refusing him the money for the screenplays, he would just deny him his son!

"You're gonna stay home today and study!" he roared at Jordy. "You're not going to this Michael!"

But Jordy yelled back, which dealt Chandler quite a shock. His son was yelling at him? Because of Jackson, who was too stingy to buy his screenplays? Hadn't he just spent thousands of dollars on useless, stupid clothes for June? And he came away empty-handed? Evan was fuming and the straw that broke the camel's back and caused the decisive click in his brain came shortly thereafter: Michael, unsuspecting, gave his friend Jordy just the computer that Chandler had planned to give him for Christmas.

Jordy's friendship warmed Michael's heart to its darkest corners. It was a real love that demanded nothing in return and it was for him, Michael the person, and it was this that he needed most. He reveled in it and for the first time in his life he was really happy.

"Jordy," he said emotionally, as they sat together on the end of a bed. "I've never met someone like you before. You are my first, best friend."

"Same here," said Jordy and yawned. "...you're my best-ever friend, too."

He was tired. They had played for a long time on the console, but as was so often the case, Michael was still wide awake. Jordy's words brought tears to his eyes.

"Promise me we'll always be friends no matter what happens," he said suddenly, and an inexplicable fear arose in him that he might lose that love. He sat up. "Promise me, that ... that you won't be like the others, please, please promise me that you'll stay true to yourself, that you won't lose this light... that you ...won't be seduced...by this adult world that destroys everything ..."

Michael suddenly burst into tears.

Fully awake now, Jordy sat up. He felt Michael's despair and his own heart was heavy from it. Awkwardly, he put his arm around his sobbing friend.

"Michael, why wouldn't I want to be your friend anymore?" he asked quietly. "I love you. Since you've come into my life, I understand some things much better. You're so right, when I see my parents arguing, how it's always about the same stuff ... and all the others ... I don't wanna be like them. I want to be like you!"

Michael's heart opened wide, and pure love poured out of him. He didn't have to defend his own feelings, didn't have to justify himself, because he felt something that others deemed ridiculous...or dangerous. Tears of gratitude streamed down his face, and he hugged Jordy long and affectionately.

"You can't imagine how glad I am that you are there ... you can't imagine ... I'm so glad, so happy..."

Jordy held him, feeling despite his young age, that this was a very special moment for Michael. And Michael cried in his arms, he cried his eyes out, God only knew what experiences were washing out, and it was good for him. Jordy simply held him just as he had done before.

Then, when the stream of tears subsided, Michael blew his nose and sniffed:

"I will never let you down Jordy, never. I'll do anything for you, will always be there for you, I promise you that."

"You're already doing that," said Jordy and rubbed him awkwardly across the back. "You've already given us so much."

"And it'll be even more," Michael promised profusely and meant every word. "You, you and June and Lily, you are my family ... You are my true family."

They were both silent for a while.

"After I graduate, I'll work for you," said Jordy. "Then I'll write the storyboards for your videos ... I ... I'll be director and produce your films ... your and my ideas ... that'll be so awesome!"

Michael was delighted and said, "I'll take you with me on the second leg of the *Dangerous* tour, then you'll see other countries, other people. I'll hire a tutor for you ... and we'll have a fantastic time! That's going to be so great ... so wonderful ... and then I'll show you the children's hospitals and how much you can help, how important that is ... and ... if you're with me, they can't condition you!"

"I'm not sure if my parents would let me," said Jordy, becoming a little hesitant. "I recently overheard a conversation between them ... my father was kind of funny..."

"Funny? What did he say?"

"He said that I shouldn't latch onto you so much.. He thinks it's too much... Dad said I should grow up like a regular teenager, go out with girls ... and that it's not good to hang out with a grown man."

Hurt, Michael closed his mouth. He looked exactly like a little scolded child at that moment. Involuntarily, he pressed his lips together.

"Jordy," he said imploringly, "I've seen in real life what happens when you get involved too soon with women. I've seen whores and striptease dancers, saw the men...how they couldn't think straight anymore from sheer lust, how these whores used everything to twist their minds...and then they have sex with them. Without love, without gentleness, without any tenderness...it's degrading. First my father did it, then my brothers...and since then, our family life has completely fallen apart, they've changed ... Before we all stuck together ... then they dragged the groupies into their room ... who sleep with anyone who is famous in any way ... My brothers only wanted that anymore. They lost their creativity, they make music only for the money, so they can buy everything, sex, too ... I've seen it ... it turns out like that for everyone ... they fall for the wrong things, they lose their innocence and they get into the game of adults ... It's all over!"

"And they can't go back?"

"I haven't seen anyone who even wanted back!"

Jordy was silent for a long while. They were both lying on the bed and staring at the ceiling. Then Jordy suddenly began to talk about his childhood. About his parents' divorce, how Evan disappeared from his life after a time, how he had really never been there and for years had behaved as if he, Jordy, did not exist. How his parents had fought...Evan's uncontrolled outbursts of anger, his mother's fear, the poisoned atmosphere in the house ... how June then hooked up with Dave, who after a time behaved just like Evan: he pulled back and suddenly he was hardly there anymore. Now it was Jordy who was crying and Michael who held him.

"What do you think was the reason?" he asked. He was calm, he was there to listen and to help his friend.

"I don't know," sobbed Jordy. "Maybe it was my mother. She is very ... bossy. Everything has to go her way and she doesn't really tolerate other opinions. I don't know ... but only since you came into my life, Daddy came back ... and I can see exactly what the adults are doing ... one stupid thing after another ... and they can't get anything done…"and then Jordy turned with a quick movement to Michael and said sharply:

"I'm not gonna let them condition me!"

"Oh, Jordy," said Michael, overwhelmed. "I love you, really ... and I won't let you get into that rut... I want to help you ... I promise that I will always take care of you…"

With the deep sense of their unique friendship, they looked at each other. Then Mike had an idea:

"You know what? We'll make our own laws and promise each other to abide by them. We'll put them on paper and put them in our pockets and every time we feel the paper, we'll be reminded!"

No sooner said than done. Alight with zeal they fetched pen and paper, sat on the bed and phrased what was most important to them. In the end, they had six rules, which they swore they would follow.

First: No wenches, bitches, heifers or ho's.
Second: Never give up your bliss.
Third: Live with me in Neverland forever.
Fourth: No conditioning.
Fifth: Never grow up.
Sixth: Be better than best friends.

Jordy wanted to seal the whole thing with blood, but Michael didn't want to cut his own skin. "It'll be fine without that, too," he said. They solemnly looked at each other, then burst out in laughter over the gravity of the situation. Their bond gave them the certainty that they could endure anything in this whole world.

***

The part about denying his son wasn't so easy, Evan realized quickly. Jordy pouted with every trick in the book when his father informed him that he wouldn't be seeing Michael Jackson so much anymore.

"Why not?" he cried indignantly. "Why are you suddenly against it?"

"You think only about Michael! Always just Michael! Think a bit about school for a change!"

"I am! My grades are good! Michael even got someone to help me in math!"

Chandler was steaming. Whose son was he actually? And why was Jordy so fervently interested in this friendship? In his rage he completely forgot that before he had been fervently interested in a relationship with Michael himself.

He began to raise concerns. He completely excluded Michael's personality and saw the relationship between the two the way it appeared to the outside: an unnatural friendship between a 34-year-old man and a 13-year-old teenager.

But his ex-wife did not share the concerns that Chandler suddenly expressed. She poured more gasoline on the fire by stating:

"Michael is a lovely person. The relationship between the two is so close because Michael cares for Jordy in a way in which you've failed completely to care for him for years."

After these incidents the previously blessed connection became an eyesore that poisoned for Evan what had been before and what might come after.

Jordy wanted only Michael. And Evan's ex was the one who allowed his son to become more and more distant, while he was kicked out as father. No wonder, Michael could buy the kid anything he wanted! Michael was the superstar! Who was Evan? A puny dentist who fought for survival and had to ask this black fucker to help him, who then had the cheek to coldly turn him down? Feelings of inferiority and jealousy clouded his perception, then escalated to bottomless rage, and he saw things in a totally different light.

What interest did a 34-year-old man have in a teenager? That was strange and inappropriate. And it couldn't be explained away solely by the eccentricities of a pop star, on the contrary - that made the relationship even more charged.

Why does Michael always look at his son as if he were in love? Why did he follow him to the kitchen? What were the two always whispering about? And why did Jackson want to take his son to Asia? Have the child part of a 250-person entourage for months? No way. Why did a superstar loaded with millions prefer to sleep on an uncomfortable cot in the room of a 13-year-old? Why did he prefer a super-soaker battle over a party in Hollywood? Why did he invite so many children to his house?

The world was proving Chandler right. Too much had already happened in this world, too many unexpected crimes, too many nice uncles who had turned out to be criminals. And the explanation that Michael was recovering a piece of his childhood with Jordy, a piece of life that he had always been missing on his path of maturing, was much too tenuous.

Chandler became extremely suspicious. This situation was a chain of complex emotions. What was crucial, in any case, was that Chandler worked himself up to a kind of holy rage. This Jackson, this black ass, was taking his son away from him! Was methodically working against him!

And not only that - he even begrudged him, Evan, a future! Jackson didn't want him to become big so he wouldn't be competition for his own son! He didn't want Evan to become manager of his son because he didn't want to have Evan in his life! And why didn't he want Evan? Because he wanted Jordy all to himself? Why? Because he had something to hide? What? What in heaven's sake was Jackson doing to his son? Evan's thoughts were spinning, inflaming each other and putting everything under a toxic, stinking haze.

Meanwhile, Michael and Jordy were in seventh heaven. Their lives were carefree, unconstrained and Mike's feelings for Jordy, indescribable. He was so happy about his friend, nothing more, nothing less. They talked about girls and Michael wanted to know how that worked in Jordy's world, and he soaked up everything like a sponge, since he himself would never be able to experience any of this, he was already far too old for that scene. But as far as relationships go, he was still a 14-year-old boy, and Jordy and he were living the strong bond of two youths who exchanged their experiences about the world and its inhabitants, and rebelled against the adults. Michael's heart was big and happy, and he vehemently dismissed the concerns of his team, who kept pointing out the possible effects on the outside world. He had given up so many things in his life. He would not let anyone talk him out of this wonderful relationship. No way.

June, however, was of course very interested in the Jordy-Michael connection. Her marriage to Dave was not doing well and he also didn't like that a stranger was butting into their lives and spoiling any chance for reconciliation. And that June let herself be kept.

"You're taking away all my dignity," Dave said bitterly, "I specifically requested you not accept clothes or jewelry from Michael...and you've maxed out a whole credit card!"

"It's really simple, Dave," June replied, "...just give me the same card."

"June!"

"What? What do you want? We haven't led a married life for a long time now!"

"At least we had a chance before Jackson!"

"No, we didn't!"

Dave looked at June sadly. "It's over, isn't it? What are your plans, June?"

"For me, first and foremost are the children. Can you imagine what Michael could do for them? And for you? You need this loan for your business. I'll talk to Michael...he's very generous, and I can't imagine that he wouldn't help you out, as much time as he has spent here. Then you don't have to go to the bank."

Dave was silent. He really liked Michael. But he also had his pride and was not sure whether he wanted the advocacy from June. And he also did not want Michael's money. But to be principled and stay principled was hard when the water was up to your neck. Especially with such an obvious solution right under your nose.

The day came when Jordy informed his parents that he wasn't going to his school's prom. Before he had met Michael Jackson, that day had been the most important day in his life for an entire year.

Because of this reversal that amounted to the rejection of a normal teenage life, even June became uneasy. For weeks she had already been under the negative influence of Evan, who kept making her feel guilty. And it was of course unavoidable that these constant repetitions, nitpicking and threats (you are the mother, you will be held responsible!) penetrated her thinking. She tried to convince Jordy that the prom was something unique - it was just one evening, whereas he could see Mike so many other times. But Jordy remained stubborn.

"These are all stupid, conditioned people," he told her, and June felt uncomfortable hearing this word. She had already heard it in connection with Michael several times before. Michael was meddling in Jordy's upbringing in a way that went too far. When Chandler found out, he went ballistic.

"What's going on between you two?" he wanted to know from his son. "Something is fishy there! Are you gay?"

"Dad!" protested Jordy, blushing all over. With surging emotion, Evan walked over to his son and hugged him.

"Jordy," he said. "Please ... please tell me ... is Michael doing something to you? Are you having sex with him?"

"No!! I'm not! Michael would never do something like that!" cried Jordy and burst into tears. "You don't understand! You'll never understand! You adults think only of bad things! You're all conditioned!"

Both parents were left with an awkward, vague feeling.

Evan stubbornly tried to prevent his son's visits with Michael. But June resisted the injunctions and Jordy, as a result, refused visits with his father. Evan could feel how he was being pushed aside, how he was losing not only his closeness with Jackson but with his entire family, too.

"June, that's not normal what's going on between those two!" he shouted. But June countered: "Michael is nothing but a dear friend for Jordy! At least be happy for him for that! Considering he didn't have a father for years!"

The words affected him more than she could know. But the effect his ongoing dispute triggered was indeed that the family began to withdraw from him. The calls came less frequently, until finally no one called him anymore at all. No Michael, no June - and for sure no Jordy. Only Dave stayed in touch to some degree. Evan's head was spinning. It couldn't be that Michael took everything away from him! They shunned him! They did not want him! And it couldn't be that his long-awaited dream turned out to be a mirage so quickly.

Evan called June. She didn't call back. He called Jordy. No call back. He learned from Dave: he was with Michael. For days... weeks - no response, nothing. Evan was being completely ignored. As if he didn't exist.

Deep anger and pain broke through. Each unanswered call was like a whip that drove him further on the barren path that effortlessly bridged the fine line between love and hate.

So Evan went to a lawyer and asked about his rights. And there he learned about things he had not thought possible in life.

After these initial meetings, he applied for custody of Jordy, arguing that June did not adequately fulfill her supervisory duties, was blinded by the glitz and glamor of a pop star and was endangering his son through the company of an eccentric and possibly pedophile individual. Evan knew one thing for sure after this appointment: he had enough leverage to get what he felt was his due.

June was furious when she learned that Evan had sought custody of Jordy. When the lawyer's letter landed at the house, she turned pale. Evan was trying to take Jordy away from her...and with him her connection to this wonderful world!

"What's he doing?" she muttered, grabbing her hair. "What the hell is he up to?"

She talked to Dave about it. It was clear to them that Evan was just mad because of the screenplays. If he had gotten the money, he would have left them all alone, and then he wouldn't have cared about Jordy either. Evan's only chance for a better future was through the boy. So he had to have him. June doubted very much that the concerns that Evan worked himself up into more and more each day were justified.

She told Michael what was going on and, to her surprise, he dismissed the whole thing with a flick of his wrist:

"June, that happens to me all the time! People are always trying to stick me with something!"

June was not happy about Mike's reaction. It may very well be that he was used to this kind of crap - but she wasn't. And it ate away at her.

Shortly afterwards Evan called Dave, the only one who was still communicating with him, and proposed a meeting between Michael, June, Jordy and him.

But June was so mad at Evan because of the custody issue that they refused to talk, let alone see him.

***

His lawyer sat silently behind a monumental desk when Evan told him about all this.

"Listen, buddy," he said, after Evan had finished. "This has to be fought with a vengeance. We need proof. No matter how. Otherwise, nothing goes."

"How can I prove anything if I can't even get close to my son!" Evan yelled uncontrollably.

"Then we have to create this closeness," his lawyer explained and leaned forward. "People like Jackson are surrounded by corrupt crooks, from time to time he needs people from the outside ... it's not cheap..."

"How ... what ... what do you mean?"

"The technology in this area is well developed now, my friend ... and there are people who are always ready to help uncover a crime. Just think of reporters ... and others ... it's about your son after all. How much is he worth to you?"

The pain forced Evan to take all the steps his lawyer suggested. After taking these actions, he felt much better, and he felt a need to let the other party know just *how* good he felt. He wanted it to be clear that he was by no means the dim bulb they had dared to project him as being. Above all: he would let himself be heard, he would show them not only that he existed but that he existed with a force that they had significantly underestimated.

And so Evan went to see Dave, to his shop, where everything had begun.

"Look, the thing with the custody was a big mistake," said Dave. "What can you accomplish with it other than riling everyone up against you?"

"The question is: what you can accomplish if you keep going along with things the way they are?" Evan replied with cold excitement.

"What do you mean, 'accomplish'? Jordy is friends with Michael. They like each other a lot. That's all there is to it."

"Yes, they like each other a lot. Maybe that's exactly the problem."

"Oh, come on Evan, you know perfectly well that's nonsense...you're getting yourself worked up about nothing!"

"How would you happen to know that?" Evan said heatedly and fixed Dave with sparkling eyes. "Are you in the bedroom with them?"

"No ... of course not ... but June watches the two of them closely. I mean ... she would see if something was going on there."

Evan threw Dave an ambiguous look. Dave became uncomfortable.

"I'll just throw a completely different point of view into the balance," continued Evan condescendingly. "One that you and your stupid wife have yet to come up with..."

"Evan! Don't talk about June like that!"

Evan simply dismissed this. He smugly leaned back in his chair, crossed his legs and studied his fingernails.

"My version of the story," he explained, "...is far more realistic than yours: why do you think June is so interested in the friendship between Jordy and Michael? Out of pure motherly love? Come on ... you know June... we both know what to make of her. Don't you think in the long run she couldn't bewitch some celebrity - if not Michael himself - with her looks, her body at one of those events that she attends? She's off the hook - she uses Jordy for a springboard for her own life! What this means to you, you can imagine yourself — you're financially screwed, and one thing I know for sure: a Michael Jackson wouldn't give a shit... and of course, you'll lose your wife. In grand style. Or rather, *to* grand style."

Evan laughed at his own joke and leaned forward. Dave was silent and Evan knew he got to him with every damn word.

"But what is even more in the range of a possibility, and what June and you completely disregard, is the fact that Jackson may someday have enough of Jordy. And then what? No director-training, no support. It suffices if Jordy had the honor to be 'good company' - in whatever way - for Mr. Jackson."

With these last words Evan's voice rose to a falsetto and his words were dripping with mockery:

"Maybe one day he can even write an awesome book about this black motherfucker...my fucking time with Jackson's ass ... with the hope to finance a college education ... My God, Dave, you're both so stupid! So near-sighted! In a year at the latest this bastard will have a new, pretty face and scrap Jordy! And you know why? Because this pervert surrounds himself with *little* boys! Ever noticed? But Jordy's going to be 14! And 15! And 16! Then he'll be out of touch with the appropriate age group and he'll be completely alone! And by then he'll be completely spoiled! He is already now! Is that what you want?"

Dave was still silent. Evan's arguments could not be dismissed entirely. Jordy was really more than crazy about Michael, and this affection had become a kind of life insurance for June. It was not so far-fetched to point out that this was an extremely flimsy foundation for the planning of a future. And the thing with the little boys...

Finally, Dave asked: "And what do you suggest?"

"Suggest?" Evan laughed sardonically. "It's too late for suggestions, Dave. I've talked with absolute experts. I have a solution. The question is: What about you? Anyway, I've decided to let you tap into the shit for a bit ... just a tap ... so you get the taste ... and I can imagine that then June will be more ready to negotiate."

With a satisfied look at a deeply shaken and agitated Dave, Evan left the room, slamming the door behind him. There! He had given them a sign of life! He was alive! Yeah! And how he was alive!

Two days later, he gave Michael, Jordy and June an ultimatum: either they would meet with him on Friday, July 9, 1993 or he would kick loose an avalanche.

After this threat, he firmly expected a frightened June on the phone. But the phone did not ring. Okay, he thought, and ran around the house like an animated bull shortly before the gates open to the arena. "Okay...they're stupid. They don't understand that I'm *here*... they haven't understood anything, nothing ... it's their own fault." And he thought back to the incident that had supplied him with additional explosives...that he hadn't wanted to ignite yet. Well...now he couldn't help it, they gave him no choice! His hatred blazed fiercely. And what Evan didn't realize was that he had long ago lost control of the game.

A week earlier

"Listen, old boy," said the husky voice of his lawyer. "I wasn't lazy... I'll get you together with the right people who can make sure you get what you want. But I want to make one thing clear: no squeamishness... got it?"

The way he said it made clear exactly how these people did their work - and what kind they were. Evan nodded apprehensively. At the appointed time he arrived for the meeting.

Several men in suits were sitting at a conference table. His lawyer introduced them. An intense period of questioning followed. Then there was silence. Evan felt uncomfortable.

"Now we'll tell you something that should...interest you..." a drawling voice from the end of the table reverberated. Evan turned his attention there. It was quiet in the room - every word fell loud and gravely like a boulder to the ground. The men were all wearing sunglasses, despite the dim lights that prevailed in the office - it was a surreal scene.

"Mr. Chandler, before we continue... we assume that nothing leaves this room. Do you understand?"

Evan understood.

"You're not the only one who has an axe to grind with Jackson...there are people who he has angered tremendously ... with his arrogance."

Evan stayed quiet. It was palpable that something big was going on here... something much bigger than his own little story.

"To express it more clearly: sooner or later, the man will fall, in fact, fall endlessly far. We don't need you for that. That's a process that has already been initiated."

Evan's gaze was fixed intently on the man's mirrored lenses, as if he were hypnotized. He felt the hairs rise up all over his body. The voice carried on:

"You, Mr. Chandler, would, however, be a catalyst... a very attractive catalyst that would give the whole thing a push...and not be to your detriment. The only thing you have to decide today is whether you want to assume this role or not. Jackson *will* go down. What will then happen to your son should be clear: he'll fall with him. You are a caring father - you prove that by being here. You would certainly want to get your son out of there before it's too late."

"What is this?" Evan asked, confused. "I'm not sure, if..."

"Mr. Chandler, for more than one-and-a-half years you have been observing and allowing Jackson to conduct an unhealthy relationship with your son. What do you think social services will have to say about this negligence? Do you not understand that your son's life has been irreparably damaged? Do you think he can now, once he has been with Jackson, resume the normal life of a student? What psychological, if not physical, damages have you already permitted?!"

"But ... but my wife has custody!" Chandler ventured to interject.

"You are the father...it's equally your responsibility, and you have been silent for too long. However, you can now step forward as the responsible parent you are - as opposed to your wife."

"What's the deal?" Evan asked through clenched teeth.

"The deal is: you go public."

"No way," Evan said immediately. Deliver his son to the press? As the toy of a pedophile pop star? He sat up.

"Listen, I thought I'd get a...I mean...I wanted a legally acceptable solution here ... I want to protect my son, not sacrifice him!"

"You also want other things, Mr. Chandler, that you will never get if you do not accept our proposal...and by the way... it's your son Jackson is abusing."

"I don't think he is," Evan heard himself say. The sweat trickled down his back.

"Mr. Chandler - you promised not to let anything of this conversation get to the outside - I want to remind you of that now. We want to show you something, something that we will use - if you don't want to protect your son yourself - we will in any case. Like I said: it'll be faster with your help, but it'll happen without you, too. It's your decision."

Surprised, Evan looked up at these curious words, as the twilight of the room quietly humming turned into clammy darkness and the new, uncomfortable silence was cut by noises of a videocassette being inserted. In front of a completely mute audience pictures began to flicker over the prepared screen:

A large lake, a bench, two diffuse shadows of people from behind. His son and Jackson? They were whispering to each other.

Jackson puts his arm around Jordy, Jordy his head on Mike's shoulder.

Next scene:

An idyllic place. Neverland? The two are taking a walk. Jordy has his arm around Michael's narrow hips.

Next scene:

The two, along with other children in a super-soaker water battle. Michael falls on Jordy, the two are lying directly on top of each other for at least ten seconds in soaking wet T-shirts and shorts. Michael is doing something to Jordy. Is he tickling him? Or...Evan tries to make it out, then the scene changes.

Monaco. Jordy on Michael's lap in the car. Jordy on Michael's lap during the awards...

"What's that supposed to be?" Evan interrupted angrily. "You're not going to knock off anyone's socks with that. These pictures are already published."

Nobody said anything. The picture of Michael with Jordy on his lap hovered frozen on the screen. It stood there like a silent reproach when a tape started to play. Someone turned up the sound. The whispering voice of Michael, unmistakably, was heard:

Promise me we'll always be friends no matter what happens...promise me that you won't be like the others, please, please...scratching noises... seduced...

Jordy: Michael, I love you. Since you've come into my life, I understand some things much better. You're so right: When I see my parents ... I don't wanna be like them... I want to be like you...I love you, Michael.

Michael: You can't imagine how glad I am that you are there ... you can't imagine ... I'm so glad, so happy ...

Jordy: I love you, Michael.

Michael: ...*Dangerous* tour ... if you're with me, they can't condition you!

Jordy: I'm not sure if my parents would let me. I've recently overheard a conversation between them... my father was kind of funny because...

Michael: What did he say?

Jordy: He said I shouldn't latch onto you so much... he thinks it's too much ...Dad said I should grow up like a normal teenager, go out with girls...

Michael: Jordy, I've seen in real life what happens when you s... with women...

Jordy: ...and I can see exactly what the adults are doing ... one stupid thing after another.

Michael: Oh Jordy, I love you, really ... and I won't let you get into that rut...

With a colossal racket the blinds drew up - Evan's ears were ringing. I love you, Michael. And what about him? With unbelieving eyes, he looked into the lenses of the sunglasses that mirrored his gaping mouth.

"Well, Mr. Chandler," the voice said. "I believe it essential for you to gain custody of the boy."

Evan nodded silently. I love you, Michael. I want to be like you.

"First you'll insist on your visitation rights - at a time after you haven't seen your son for a while, let's say... for a week... that will be difficult to deny you ... then we'll turn this week into forever."

And they laid out the plan to him. Detail by detail. Day by day. Minute by minute. Everything was already happening. And the best Evan could do was to get the most out of it for his and Jordy's future. It was impossibly difficult, based on present circumstances, arguments and emotions, to see a different way forward than this. I love you, Michael.

"Dave! What is he doing; what he's up to?" June kept asking. She was starting to get scared. Like before, she was still planning to go along with her children on the *Dangerous* tour, but now there was a tension so unbearable that she feared her plans were in jeopardy. Dave called Evan, hoping to learn more, and taped the conversation. That was on August 07, 1993.

The recording has since become accessible on the Internet to everyone in its full length. I listened to it. It wasn't always perfect in quality, sometimes scraping was heard, but the main thing came across loud and clear.

The phone call was long and enlightening. The theme that stood out most was Evan's frequent repetition that the family had broken off contact with him. In almost every other sentence he mentioned that no one had responded to his calls, no one spoke to him, no one cared about him. "June said to me, 'Go fuck yourself'"

That was the fundamental tenor and provided the essential basis for this escalation. Aside from that, Evan said other things, too. For example Dave asked him why he insisted on the meeting on July 9th.

Excerpts from the original [2]:

Evan: The only reason that I'm meeting with them tomorrow is [...] because of Monique (his second wife). Monique begged me to do it. She said: „You're out of control."

Dave asks about June, if he (Evan) doesn't care about her at all.

Evan: „You tell me who June has who really loves her, who she really loves back, you can't think of one person."

More excerpts after Dave pushes and tries to learn more:

Evan: I have a set routine of words, that I'm going to go in there that have been rehearsed and I'm going to say...okay? Because I don't want to say anything, that could be used against me [...] ...you don't understand... it isn't up to you to decide, whose fault it is. Other people are trained to [...]
and by the way...they're not going (to Asia on the *Dangerous* Tour). They don't know that yet, but they are not going ... tour (inaudible) ...get cancelled...I am not allowed to say anything more [...] right now he'd (my attorney) like to kill them all. I picked the nastiest mother-fucker I could find...and all he wants to do is get this out in the public as fast as he can, as big as he can and humiliate as many people as he can [...] he's costing me a lot of money...
Dave: Do you think that's good?
Evan: I think that's great. I think it's terrific. The best. Because when somebody tells you that they don't want to talk with you – I'm only going there because of Monique [...] Dave it would be a lot of easier for me and a lot more satisfying ... to see everybody get destroyed ... like they destroyed me [...] it's a matter of life and death ... This is life and death for my son ... I have to get their attention [...] And you know something? I even have somebody after him if he doesn't (tape irregularity) [...] I mean, it could be a massacre if I don't get what I want. [...] He (attorney) is nasty, he is mean, he is very smart and he's hungry for the publicity (tape irregularity) ...we will totally humiliate him (Jackson).
Dave: You don't think everyone loses?
Evan: See, the issue is that if I have to go that far... I can't stop and think: who wins and who loses? [...] All I can think about is ...I only have one goal, and the goal is to get their attention [...] I have to go step by step, each time escalating the attention-getting-mechanism. Unfortunately after that, it's totally out of (tape irregularity) ... it's going to be out of all our control [...] It's going to be monumentally huge, and I'm not going to have any way to stop it. I mean, once I make this phone call, this guy's just going to destroy everybody in site in any devious, nasty, cruel way that he can do it. And I've given him full authority to do that. [...] I have done every possible thing in my individual power to tell them to sit down and talk to me...and if they still (tape irregularity) ... I got to escalate the attention-getting-mechanism [...] ultimately, is that their lives are over, if they don't sit down. I am not stopping until I get their attention.
Dave: So wouldn't you sit down with me and we could discuss it first?

Evan: (inaudible)...totally ignorant of all the issues [...] there's really no way you could relate this to somebody, you know.... it's not going to be up for me or you to decide. [...] what if I told you their house was wired?...I'm not saying it is...

Dave: [...] the way you've sounded is completely different than when I talked to you the first time...why do you have to have Jordy there...?

Evan: [...] I want him to see how I'm behaving.... want him to see, how I'm acting....

Dave: And why do you have to have Michael there?

Evan: What's that beeping going on? Do you hear that? Are you recording this?

Dave: No.

Evan: Do you hear that beeping? ... Well, let's hang up.

Alarmed Dave tried to get a hold of Evan again and succeeded. Evan felt good that he suddenly appeared present again even if it annoyed him that neither June nor Jordy talked to him. The conversation turned to Michael and why Evan wanted Michael to be there personally, not just one of his representatives:

Evan: Michael has to be there, Michael has to be there. He's the main one. He's the one I want. He's an evil guy, he is worse than bad (…) I have evidence to prove it. (…). Nobody in this world was allowed to come between this family of June, me and Jordy. That's the reason why he's evil. Now there's no family anymore. Jordy is my life. He is my life. Period.

Dave: How does it help it?

Evan: It doesn't, it doesn't, that's why I have nothing to lose ... I have to force them to the table...if they don't sit down and talk to me they're gonna get hurt. They can't keep telling me to fuck myself anymore [...] I still love Jordy, but I do not like them because I do not like the people that they've become [...] If I go through with this, I win big time. There's no way that I lose. I've checked that out inside out....

Dave: But when you say „winning," what are you talking about „winning"?

Evan: I will get everything I want and they will be totally − they will be destroyed forever. They will be destroyed. June is gonna lose Jordy. She will have no right to ever see him again. ... Michael's career will be over.

Dave: Does that help Jordy?

Evan: it's irrelevant for me. ... June is harming him, and Michael is harming him. I can prove that, and I will prove that [...] I will be granted custody. She will have no rights whatsoever. [...] If she wants to tell me to 'go fuck myself' after that, she's welcome to do it...

Dave: (tape irregularity)... the custody?

Evan: Forget the custody thing. It's gonna go further than that. [...] you see, I love him (Jordy) so much that I'm willing to destroy my own life to protect him. [...] but I've been so convinced by professional opinions that I have been negligent in not stepping in that now it's made me insane [...] (tape irregularity) ... if the kid's more important that you are, and they are more important than I am [...] staying away from the family is not a good way of indicating that you care about your family. It's a copout... my feeling is that when you have really good communication with somebody, you don't have to stay away from them. [...] when the talking stops, that's when people get hurt...[...] that's what happened with me. They won't return my phone calls. [...] My opinion was formed by (tape irregularity) you're wrong automatically if you don't sit down and talk about it... in the opinion of these experts, I would be a negligent father if I did not do what I am now doing. [...] I happen to agree with them now. I didn't agree with them first. Michael...(tape irregularity) nice (tape irregularity)

Dave: So why do you think he's not nice?

Evan: Why? Because he broke up the family, that's why. ... I mean, that was the worst thing anybody could do to me... I mean, you (Dave) came into this family and made it better. It was great. Someone else comes along and breaks it up ... Michael divided and conquered, Dave. [...] Michael Jackson (tape irregularity) the smartest, streetwise people that I ever met ... that guy is extremely bright ... I think he's totally insensitive. I think he's sensitive – I think he's an extremely selfish person.

[...]

Evan: [...] I have harmed my son greatly. I believe that.

Dave: Well, are you talking about harmed him in the relationship with you?

Evan: Well, that's for sure. [...] I'm going to tell you what. There is no excuse in law for June having done what she does.... my son is being harmed greatly [...] he could be fucked up for the rest of his life (tape irregularity) [...] I have the evidence [...]

Dave: ... I don't know what evidence. I don't know what you're talking about.

Evan: You show up in court and you'll see it on the big fucking screen ... and you'll hear in on tape recordings. [...] you'll hear it all [...] it cost me thousands [...] ten thousands of dollars [...] to get the information and I – you know I don't have that kind of money... and I spent it, and I'm willing to spend more and I'm willing (...) to go down financially to ...

Dave: Do you think that's going to help Jordy?

Evan: Dave, Jordy's – I believe that Jordy's already irreparably harmed.

Dave: I mean, do you think that he's fucking him?

Evan: I don't know. I have no idea.

Dave: But harmed in – in just being spoiled?

Evan: No.

Dave Just tell me...

Evan: You know, you gotta forgive me for one thing, but I have been told by my lawyer that if I say one thing to anybody [...] He said: ... you open your mouth and you blow it...just don't come back to me."

Dave: Yeah, okay. ...

[...]

Evan: and let me tell you this, by the way: what harm would it be to you, what harm would it be to your relationship to June, if Michael wasn't around anymore? ... she is going to come back to you. [...] she doesn't need you anymore. She doesn't want you around anymore. [...] that's the best thing that could happen to him (Michael), that people think he's interested in June. The fact is he doesn't even care about her. He doesn't even like her.

Dave: You don't think he likes her?

Evan: I know he doesn't. He told me he doesn't. He can't stand her. [...] He told me that when he was in my house [...] yeah [...] at that point he liked us better than... Jordy too [...] and until I had a talk with Jordy one day at (tape irregularity) they were gonna come live with me. They were gonna pack up, leave June's house, and come here. [...] they simply divided and conquer...

[...]

Dave: [...] did you ever pull away from your parents when you were a teenager?

Evan: I hated my parents.

Dave: Do you think Jordy hates you?

Evan: If he doesn't, he's gonna hate me tomorrow.

[...]

Dave: do you want that?

Evan: I doesn't matter what I want ... because all I care about is what happens to him in the long run.

Dave: ...is that going to be healthy in the long run?

[...]

Evan: ...according to the experts, If it goes on the way it is, he's (Jordy) doomed. He has no chance of ever being a happy, healthy, normal human being [...] he will definitely hate me tomorrow... because I'm taking Michael away from him. [...] So I mean, what reason would he (Michael) want me out of the way, unless he has something to hide? I happen to know what it is... but I can't tell you. [...] my approach to the whole thing is that... the person who doesn't talk is the one who's wrong, period. [...] I mean Michael is very seductive, without even trying [...] he's so damn good at it. [...] Dave, he fooled me [...] there is no reason why they would have to cut me out [...] I had a good communication with Michael [...] there was no reason why he had to stop calling me. He could have called me ... in fact, Dave, I - you ask

260

Jordy. I sat in the room one day, and I talked to Michael and told him exactly what I want out of this whole relationship, what I want (tape irregularity), okay?

[...]

Dave: why couldn`t we talk it over?

Evan: Because the thing is already – the thing is already set in motion ... it's happening at 8.30 tomorrow [...] it`s out of my hands. [...] It's all automatically set in motion [...] I'm not even in contact anymore [...] you have no idea, what's going on [...] you'd have to have lived it. You'd have to have witnessed it. Myself would never have believed it – [...] the evidence is already locked up in a safe place [...] that's it. If they don`t talk to me tomorrow, out it comes. [...] This man (Michael Jackson) is gonna be humiliated beyond belief. You'll not believe it. He will not believe, what's going to happen to him [...] beyond his worst nightmares (tape irregularity) not sell one more record. [...] I've tried to make it really clear on the answering machine [...] the fact is so fucking overwhelming – [...] that everybody's going to be destroyed in the process. [...] It's gonna be bigger than all of us put together and the whole thing's just gonna crash down on everybody and destroy everybody...

Dave: Yeah. And is that good?

Evan: Yeah. It's great.

Dave: I mean, is that how you're –

Evan: ...because June and Jordy and Michael have forced me to take it to the extreme (...) to get their attention. How pitiful, pitifuckingful they are to have done that. I've tried to get their attention [...] I've cried on the phone, I've talked on the phone [...] I have begged on the phone and all I get back is, „Go fuck yourself."... they leave me no choice [...] everything's their fault, one hundred percent [...] they will gonna be destroyed and I'm gonna get what I want [...] there are other people involved that are waiting for my phone call, that are intentionally going to be in certain positions ... (tape irregularity) ... paid them to do it. They're doing their job. [...] Everything is going according to a certain plan that isn't just mine. There's other people involved [...] my instructions were to kill and to destroy (tape irregularity), I'm telling you. I mean, and by killing and destroying, I'm going to torture them, Dave. [...] let them show me how Jordy's benefitting and not being harmed. They got their chance...

On the Big Day, July 9, 1993, one day after this phone call, Evan Chandler was on time and present at 8.00 o'clock. He was the only one there. That opened the last floodgates, and like acid burned any residual doubt and any remainder of conscience.

Storm warning

In a panic June and Dave played the tapes to Michael. Michael turned pale.
"The man... is sick," he said, shaking his head. But now...now things had
become very, very serious for him too. He had to respond.

The Jackson camp immediately activated the private investigator Anthony
Pellicano and one of the best lawyers in the country, known to have never
lost a lawsuit.
Pellicano cornered Jordy alone.
"Okay kid, now sit right there and look me straight in the eyes," he said in a
very intimidating Mafioso way and stared into Jordy's face. "Tell me the
truth now. And by the way ... I've worked years for the Army Intelligence ...
I can tell right away when someone is lying."
Jordy remained calm and serious, looked Pellicano unflinchingly in the eye
and swore that nothing inappropriate had been going on between him and
Michael.
Pellicano asked him more than once and observed the response closely. He
also studied Michael.
"If I see as much as a twitch from only one of them and get the impression
that there is something fishy, they'll have to go find someone else," he
announced.
But both Michael and Jordy were open and natural. They had nothing to
hide. And they didn't hide their affection for each other either.

Pellicano had barely left when they hugged. Jordy was shaking.
"Michael," he whispered, "my father is going nuts...he...I don't know what
he's up to...but these tapes...are terrible...what he's saying...he says he loves
me and then he does this to me!"
Michael pressed Jordy to him and gulped. "I'll protect you, Jordy. I gave you
my word that I won't let you down and I'll stick to that...you and your
mother have to get away from here...I don't know...if your father gets his
hands on you...what is he going to do to you?"
But he knew he had no right to act against the will of the father. Jordy was in
the same situation he had been stuck in as a child. Michael looked at Jordy.
And Jordy burst into tears.

***

June's phone rang. An LAPD officer was on the line.
"What's this about?" she asked timidly.

262

"Ma'am, we have a boy here who was sexually abused by Michael Jackson. He does not want to give his name for obvious reasons but because your son is in the same situation…"

The color drained out of June's face. Her knees shook, she had to lean against the wall.

Evan, meanwhile, insisted on his visitation rights. June could not withhold the father from his son.

The lawyers of both parties, including Pellicano, set up an agreement whereby Evan could have his son for a week. A place and time for the transfer and also when Jordy would be returned to his mother was determined.

"Don't go there, June," Michael implored. "You can see how Jordy is suffering … He doesn't want to be with his father! How can you let him go after everything Evan said on the phone?"

On top of it all, this was the day he had set up a huge party for Jordy's half-sister, Lily, at Neverland and that was the direction they were heading instead of driving Jordy to Evan.

For Jordy one thing was clear: he would never let himself be surrendered to his father. Both children had seated themselves demonstratively in the car with Michael, and June had followed reluctantly. The reason she came along was: she had to talk to Michael about Jordy's and her future. But Michael was angry with her because she hadn't taken a clear position for him and Jordy and he let her know it.

June's indecisiveness went down to the bone. Evan had spoken of proof, and June had just come out of a meeting with two LAPD officers who had presented credible evidence of a former sexual abuse allegation against Michael. She had heard Evan's assertion on tape that Michael hated her. Michael was here today and for the first time openly pissed with her. Where was her future?

The drive was tense. Meanwhile, Michael got an angry call from Pellicano. Where was the child? They were breaking their word!

Michael tried to explain that Jordy couldn't go there because he had big doubts that Evan would keep his word.

"He won't give him back!" he predicted heatedly, "Why can't you get that?"

"One thing is clear: We will not be first to break our word," Anthony replied and, in a harsh tone, ordered Michael to immediately surrender the child.

Michael was angry, he yelled at Pellicano. Pellicano yelled back, and June watched it all as if in slow motion. Then she had the car stopped and told Michael they would take a cab back. Michael would never forget the look that Jordy gave him when he had to climb out of the car. It was his last in freedom.

June rode back and surrendered Jordy to his father.

Then she decided to call Michael and talk everything over with him. But emotions were running high in him too:

How could June have handed over the child? All she'd have had to do was play the tapes to her lawyer! He was not sure what to make of June, something was not honest about her, he could feel that. And in addition, he had now received strict orders from his lawyers:

"Michael," they had said, "this thing is hotter than you think...we don't know yet who is on whose side...and who else is involved. Don't talk to anyone unless we are present."

Michael had nodded in dismay. An exceedingly sickening premonition spread through him. And when June called him, he could only tell her what his lawyers had advised him to say:

"I'm not allowed to talk to you, June, or see you either ... things have taken such a horrible turn ... I can only talk to you in the presence of my lawyer."

June had little understanding. The police were constantly in her head, the child claiming sexual abuse, Evan's threat that because of her negligence she could be charged, should a crime be proven. She was scared.

The Authorities

"Going well, so far. The child is here. And stays. Good work. Knew that an officer always scores! Now full steam ahead with the dad. We have to catch this guy before he leaves. We need something tangible"

"June, you do realize that the child will be taken away from you forever if it comes out what you have let happen? And it will come out - you can be sure of that. Your name will be on every damn tabloid in bold print - you always wanted to be famous...now you can have it!"

Evan was on the answering machine: "I think it's better if we can reach a reasonable agreement."

This time June went along. The day after, she signed a contractual agreement that did not permit Jordy to leave Los Angeles County. With that, not only had the *Dangerous* tour died for them, but also visits to Neverland, which was out of this district. In addition she also gave her consent that Evan could keep Jordy not only this week, but 'for a while'. God alone knows what Evan had told June.

Michael's departure for the second leg of the *Dangerous* tour was planned for August 20th.

264

It was the last week of July when June gave her son to Evan. Michael's team informed him that this one week of visitation had been extended to an indefinable period of time and they threw Michael into an abyss with this message. He couldn't believe it. Couldn't June see the weapon she had given Evan with that? Wasn't it predictable to her that he would never give Jordy back to her? The only thing Evan wanted was money for his crappy screenplays, and now that he had Jordy, he would make just this demand and blackmail him!

Michael knew that Evan's greed was stoked by infinite jealousy - because he had the kind of relationship with his son that Evan wanted. What could come out of a meeting with him? They would negotiate only about scripts and money - and not even talk about Jordy! For Evan it wasn't about his child - otherwise he would never have instigated this multi-pronged assault. Concerned parents would have tried to resolve an issue like this and it would not have been lacking honor, respect and protection for their child!

And still Michael did not believe that Evan could harm him. He had a clear conscience and Jordy loved him. What, then, could Evan ultimately do to him? He could only bluff and he wanted to scare Michael so he could extort the money.

Instead, Michael despaired over losing this wonderful friendship, and over having to do the *Dangerous* tour without Jordy. And he was worried about Jordy...how was he? Now his friend was precisely in the situation that he, Michael, had promised to protect him from.

"Oh, my God," he thought, "Jordy will never forgive me..." It appeared to Michael as if he were reliving his own fate all over again. A boy who wanted to retain his child-like self, his connection to above - and the world that snatched it away from him by force.

And June? She had betrayed him! After everything he had done for her... the travels, the clothes, the jewelry ... and now ... nothing but ungratefulness, even more, betrayal on every level! She had just surrendered Jordy! Her own child! His friend, his best friend! He buried his face in his large hands. Jordy...what were they doing to Jordy? He missed him with every fiber of his heart. Now he was gone and it did not look as if it would ever be as it once had been. No friend for Michael. No love for him. Depressed, he sat under a large tree. And sorrow and despair, as if wanting to remind him of their lifelong companionship, flooded him in such a tidal wave that he thought his heart must burst.

He was alone. Again.

Thunder

"I hate you! I hate you! I hate you! I hate you!"

Again and again the boy screamed at his father, who stood facing him, and waited, provocatively quiet, for the end of the outburst. But Jordy was not about to stop. The zero reaction of his father drove him to escalation, as did his father's arrogant 'I-know-what-comes-next-face', and made a fuse blow in Jordy. With a cry of rage he stormed towards him and raised a hand against him. Evan propelled him to the floor with a single blow. Blood dripped from the nose of the boy and he howled even more loudly.

Evan was shocked. The experts had indicated to him that Jordy would not be thrilled by the sequence of events, but he never would have expected such an outburst! The hatred was almost palpable, and with his child-like intuition Jordy knew exactly how he could hurt his father most:

"I don't want to be with you! I want to be with Michael! Michael is the best friend I ever had! He understands me! He is there for me! And you...you're just cruel! You just want money! You're an…"

"Don't you dare…!" threatened Evan and raised his fist at the boy lying on the floor, bleeding. "Don't you ever dare to raise your hand against me, or else…"

"Or else? What? Are you going to kill me then?" With fiery eyes, fueled by disgust, Jordy scrambled up. "Just so you know...that would be a thousand times better than to be with you!"

Evan could not control himself. He hit him again.

Jordy fell to the ground. Hatred smoldered hot in him. Hatred of this father. Hatred of the mother, who had abandoned him as soon as she saw her goals at risk. He would never forget the moment...the moment in Michael's limousine... his mother's voice, the driver should stop, he should call a cab... the rumbling feeling in his stomach, the fear shooting upwards, the look on Michael's face, watching him get out of the limo...suddenly in the back seat of an ordinary cab...just beginning to comprehend that he wasn't going to Neverland...and then the stone, heavy as a ton of bricks, that sank into his insides when he heard his mother call Evan, the conversation dribbling like slime through a funnel, slowly, slowly translated by his synapses and transmitters, as he understood: he had to go to his father.

But the hope had not yet died, he still had the feeling that it would all turn out all right, everything would still be OK...until the next day, when June and Evan sat together, telling him something about a boy Michael had allegedly sexually abused, about police, psychology, educational contracts and experts, risk and protection, and finally showed him the agreement saying he wasn't allowed to travel beyond Los Angeles County. He was a prisoner.

Jordy turned numb inside and for minutes could not hear what else his parents were discussing. It oozed only in fragments into his brain, and maybe that was a good thing.

"Think of something. That's your part."
Evan looked discouraged. "We did manage to get the boy, but he doesn't want to testify."
"That's your part!"
No answer.
"And don't forget- we have a deadline: August 20th."
Evan had a meeting in his lawyer's office. He was nervous. Jackson was not aware of any wrongdoing and not willing to negotiate. The 'experts' were putting Evan under pressure. His lawyer was not really helping; instead, now he got to feel his wickedness and malice for himself.
"Why don't you use the video and the tapes?" Evan asked him irritated.
"As long as you don't have a handle on your own son and he'll shout the opposite from the rooftops?"
"But ... on the tape ... that IS a statement!"
"It's not enough," rumbled the other, "because…it's ... ambiguous. Don't you have enough balls to stand up to your own brat?"

***

Evan was under pressure, and it came from all sides. June had instigated a custody battle after she had realized that Michael's prediction had come true. Jordy was defiant and didn't want to play a part in Evan's game. Insisted on Jackson's innocence. But Evan could not turn back - the 'experts' had made it clear to him what his life would look like if this thing went wrong. They'd made it very clear that they now had some things against him in their grasp. Very clear. More clear than he would have liked. He could not turn back. He had to come up with something.
Should he tell Jordy that it was a done deal to bring Michael down? That he couldn't have done anything about it anyway? That forces were at work that would crush them all? Make him aware that at least they still could milk some money out of Michael, while he still had it, in order to secure Jordy's future at least? That he, his father, could at last take care of him the way Jordy had always wanted once he had enough money?
Because of the pressure, and as events had progressed, Evan had become less and less perceptive. He tried to tie Jordy to him at an age when children naturally separate from their parents, when the outside life becomes more important. And he thought money was the solution to everything. Evan had never really been present in Jordy's life and now forced himself on him in an impossible way and at the worst possible time.

Jordy could not warn Michael, could not speak to him, could not reach him. He was not allowed to call, to write, to go anywhere on his own. He was far from wanting to support his father. And the clock was ticking.

In their distress Chandler and his attorney sent a hypothetical letter to a psychiatrist...What if...a 34-year-old man slept with a 13-year-old in the same room, although plenty of other beds were available...etc. ... They described the affection between the two, said that they often walked arm in arm...
The psychiatrist wrote back that, should the case be true, he would consider it an absolute danger to the minor, and he would forward the case to juvenile court.

"What good are hypotheses? We need facts! Is the guy getting finicky now? Make it clear to him what the consequences are if he messes up. Make him aware of the deadline again. Maybe he forgot."
And they made Evan aware of the deadline with extreme clarity.

On August 2, Evan administered a general anesthetic to his son - to extract a bad tooth. But he inexplicably used a barbiturate with little analgesic effect, known as sodium amytal or amobarbital.
This drug had been used by intelligence agencies as a truth serum, but was later rejected because it had a strong hypnotic effect that allowed implanting anything that was wanted in the mind of the treated.
Its effects:
Influence on the central nervous system, suppression of its functions, in particular of the sensory cortex, acts as a sedative, and capable of causing a change in the original state of the central nervous system on all levels. Causes fatigue, slows thinking and attention, can impair clear and logical thinking, causes distorted vision, anxiety, depression and suicidal thoughts. Can be addictive.
In high doses it acts as an anesthetic. However, all other effects are then amplified, too. The half-life is surprisingly high: between eight and forty-two hours. In addition, the effect is cumulative.
The most important effect: the administration of this substance allows facts and acts to be implanted into people that they will emphatically swear to be true. Sodium amythal has been recognized as a suggestion drug, not as a truth serum.
While even under normal circumstances it is already a fact that the constant repetition of a lie can make people believe it, the use of a drug results in a potentiated effect.
Every one of the professionals who were questioned about the use of this agent for tooth extraction shook their heads in disbelief. Many pointed out

that the drug was extremely dangerous and entirely inappropriate for this purpose.

What happened during the time of anesthesia, God only knows.

In any case, immediately after administration of the barbiturate, Jordy claimed to have been sexually abused by Michael Jackson.

Evan broke down crying and hugged his son. Finally! Jordy had finally confessed! The pressure was off. Certain of victory, he arranged a meeting with Michael and Pellicano. This time Michael agreed to be present.

"I expect nothing from the meeting," Mike said to Anthony, "but I have to see Jordan. I promised never to let him down. I have to do something for him. I have to see him."

"What do you mean, he made a confession? Verbally! And only once, when the father and the anesthesiologist were present! Tomorrow the brat will deny it and claim the exact opposite! We are exactly where we were before! How stupid is this man? We need ironclad proof, and unless there is something in writing, there will be not a word about it. Tell him that! That'll only warn the other party"

Michael thought of Evan only in connection with the scripts and the extortion. Until now, Evan had not made noises about anything else. Up to this point the tapes in which Evan spoke of wanting to destroy Michael were the most threatening.

He did not want to pay Evan the money, but he missed Jordy terribly and he hoped to perhaps find a solution in this meeting.

When Michael came through the door of the hotel room, Evan got up and hugged Michael - the man he claimed had abused his son.

Michael focused on Jordy, the boy did not look good at all, seemed apathetic. Distraught, he ran to him, pulled him to him and asked over and over again:

"How are you doing? Are you all right? God, Jordy, I miss you!"

"I miss you too, Michael," said Jordy, "but ...Michael...I..."

There was no time to make insinuations. Evan was charged and drooling to see Michael tremble. He hurriedly pulled a document from his pocket and Michael expected it was a contract for the scripts. But then his jaw dropped.

With great satisfaction Evan read him the hypothesis of a doctor who wanted to involve the juvenile courts and file charges, because he saw an absolute danger in the relationship between an adult man and an adolescent. Evan had a hard time keeping himself from mentioning Jordy's confession.

Michael froze inside. Evan really wanted to harp on this crap? Slowly the scope of the proposed indictment seeped into his brain.

He said no more. A cloud of cold, hate and anger built up in the room. Unlike Michael, Pellicano was beside himself and the conversation between him and Chandler escalated in no time. Evan screamed at Michael:

"Are you having sex with my son? Admit it already!"

Anthony asked the man to leave. Michael was still sitting there, frozen to the spot. With increasing clarity he began to recognize the interrelations that even Anthony couldn't see yet; he realized the extent of the instigated catastrophe. And that there was not the slightest chance to protect Jordy. Why wasn't Jordy saying anything? He looked at him. The light around Jordy was gone.

Tony demanded a second time that Evan leave. Evan got up. Triumphantly. He pointed his finger at Michael, and uttered an oath:

"I'm going to crush you like you won't believe it, I'm taking you down...I will ruin you... you won't sell a single CD anymore!"

Jordy followed his father to the door. Turned around. Cast Michael a long, sad look.

Michael burst into tears when they were gone. Terrible fear enveloped him. Everything he loved was in danger. Now it wasn't just about this extraordinary friendship anymore but about his goals, his career...his music… his entire life.

And yet Evan shied away repeatedly from coming forward to the public, seeing his name and that of his son in bold headlines in every damn newspaper. He knew that then all of their lives would be completely destroyed. Their identities would be erased. There would be no Evan or Jordy Chandler after that affair. They would have to move. Hide. Give up everything. And until then: having to run the gauntlet through the destructive forces of the press and angry fans. He turned hot when he thought of this colossal scenario with him and Jordy in the lead roles. Could he do that to his son? Evan was not even sure if anything inappropriate had happened between Mike and Jordy. In honest moments with himself, he knew that it was disappointment, jealousy and greed that had driven him to this point.

And the other day...the other day he had found a drawing in Jordy's room - of a boy who had jumped out the window and lay in a pool of blood on the sidewalk. Jordy wanted to kill himself! One of the listed side effects of this barbiturate! Oh, God, sometimes he himself did not know how he had gotten into this horrible situation, how it could have come to this.

Furthermore, in the meantime, charges had been filed against him for extortion - the first thing Michael's lawyers had responded with. And since they had the tapes, Evan's odds were poor in every conceivable way. Evan started to get scared. The 'experts' had not been pleased with the tapes, and they had threatened him because he had become carried away in those discussions and didn't realize that the conversation was being recorded. By now he had gone so far, was so involved in the whole thing...he could hardly breathe. His heart ached when he thought about Jordy. That's not what he had wanted! Not like this! Not at this cost! They had prepared him for the fact that Jordy would hate him...but it was hard...this hatred...he had not wanted this hatred. Perhaps it would be better if he would back off...the pressure was so tremendous and ... especially ... what would happen afterwards? They would have him in their grip...always...forever...and he knew that...and hadn't they told him that they would do it without him? Maybe he could still get out.

He ventured to make an advance.

"The whole thing...is burdening Jordy too much," he made it clear to his lawyer at the next meeting. "Maybe it's better...to look for another type of agreement..."

He thought his idea was pretty good - it was probably worth quite a bit to Jackson to avert the catastrophe...Evan could make do with lesser prospects. The main thing was to get out of this disaster, make a bit of money to start a new life, to pay off his debts...

But his lawyer virtually freaked out when Evan suggested that, and finished him off.

"It's my head I'm sticking out!" Evan screamed back. "I'm the one who has to bleed when things go wrong! The rest of you are keeping yourselves so conveniently in the background! You lose nothing! I lose everything!"

He convinced his attorney to make a lower offer: from $20 million down to $350,000.

But Michael refused even the 350,000.

"I'm not going to pay this person anything," he said. "I didn't do anything wrong."

The 'experts' gnashed their teeth when they learned of it. The lawyer was replaced. And they made it unmistakably clear to Evan Chandler that in their circles "pissing in your pants" is not looked upon kindly. And that it was indecent to stab one's own legal team in the back; not only that, but dangerous.

Evan's brief departure from the plan had impeded the timing of the process considerably. And what was worse: June won the custody battle with flying colors. Evan couldn't tell the judge anything about the sexual abuse allegations, because then an investigation would have been ordered, in the course of which Jordy may have been separated from him, and he could not afford that. So he didn't say anything. And lost custody.

The child was supposed to go back to June, Jordy drew hope, and Evan was losing his mind with fear.

June still did not quite know what to make of it: if Evan was really convinced that his son had been a victim of this crime, why did he want $20 million instead of going to juvenile court? Why hadn't he told the judge about it? Why did he want to go to the media instead of protecting his son from them?

Meanwhile Evan's nerves were raw. Once Jordy was removed from his influence at his mother's…and his powers of suggestion…what would happen then? For how long were thoughts anchored in his brain? The clock was ticking. With no mercy seconds were ticking away and Evan's head was a morbid darkroom, no light, no way out. He was afraid of the day when he had to give Jordy to June…then what would 'they' do to him, Evan?

And then this day was there. There was only one night in between. Sleepless, Evan tossed and turned until the morning dawned. He only had a few hours until everything was too late. He got up. And went in Jordy's room.

The day on which Jordy was supposed to go back to his mother had arrived. With a heavy heart, Evan put his son into the car a few hours later and drove him to a psychiatric clinic, where Jordy made a voluntary, detailed confession about Michael's sexual activities with him, including a vivid, detailed description of his genitals. Jordy explained that Michael had threatened him, saying he would be put into a foster home, should he ever reveal anything.

And so Jordy was delivered not to his mother, but to a youth representative of the Los Angeles Police Department. Jordy had also testified that he did not want to go back to his mother, but wanted to stay with his father. It was August 17th.

"Put the fucking bureaucracy in motion. We need the whole thing by August 19 or 20 at the latest"

The documents were finished on August 20 and forwarded to the appropriate parties.

Michael had set out on his World Tour. Just in time.

"Okay," the voice growled. "This is not really a point for him. The tour may not be canceled at the start, but it will be canceled, you can bet your life on that. He won't make a penny from it. We have enough ammunition in stock."

***

A torrent of sensations pelted down on Michael when he heard of Jordy's wish to stay with Evan. His vision went black. That could not be good. Panic crept up on him. The diffuse feeling of having done something wrong, without knowing what it was. The way it had always been with his father. Punishment for nothing. Beatings because of seeking love. And having to pay a high price for three seconds of happiness.

Michael gave no sign that he was not well at the beginning of the trip. Since the meeting with Evan and Jordy, he had cried through the nights. He had been looking forward so much to go with Jordy, to see countries, together, to introduce him to his charity work...now he was alone again. Loneliness surrounded him, amid all his advisors and employees, and there was no one with whom he could share anything.

The time with Jordy had freed him briefly of his nightmares. He'd been able to sleep fairly well. But now it all came back.

Despite claims of his eccentricity, up until that time Michael had a wonderfully clean reputation. For many young people he was a role model, more than their parents. His clear refusals of alcohol and drugs were believable. No one had ever seen him drunk, no paparazzi, no fan, no friend. He was religious, believed in God, read the Bible. His sexual abstinence was a mystery - but the fact was that he neither produced scandals nor screwed around. In the meantime the skin on his face had a uniform color, it still had to be smoothed out with makeup, but Michael was also beautiful up close and without touch-up. He looked much more natural than the media represented him.

He took his image very seriously; after all, he had grown up with it and it was part of his job. He felt a need to be a role model for youth; he had seen for himself how his brothers had imitated other adults, including his father. Image was close to his heart. Even the stories about the elephant man bones, the oxygen chamber and his allegedly countless plastic surgeries hurt him.

But what was rolling towards him now was a hurricane of an unimaginable scale.

Storm

The news leaked out from America to Asia, like drops from a drip infusion. Because he had to deliver an exhausting performance almost every night, his crew tried to convey only pieces of the facts or none at all, which was a mistake. Had Michael been able to suspect from the beginning how great the earthquake was that Chandler had unleashed, he might have reacted differently.

At first he could not believe what he was told. He called Lisa Marie, who, with her black humor minimized the whole thing.

"Hey, Lisa, what's going on in good old America?" he asked, trying to suppress his fear.

"Dude, I'm telling you, a real Jackson-Mania, like we're used to from you! How'd you do that, that everything always assumes such dimensions?" asked Lisa and laughed. "Fuck, that's so cool, you're a real superstar, you're in every newspaper again!"

"I can do without that kind of superstar status," Michael replied sourly. "What are they writing?"

"My God, Mike, the press is digging itself a big hole just...it's like always, they don't know a thing. They're only speculating. They' ve got nothing. Nada."

Her words calmed Michael, but then Debbie and Liz Taylor called him and told a completely different story. Debbie reported, in accordance with Liz, that his advisors were obviously not in agreement and conveyed a very dubious impression to the media, as if they themselves were not convinced of his innocence.

"They contradict each other, slow things down...there is something fishy going on," Debbie said. "Mike, some details from your camp are always leaked at the wrong time. One of them said that you spent days in bed with Jordy in Monte Carlo...you have a couple of rotten eggs in your ranks!"

Liz Taylor played the same tune and made him realize the immensity of the disaster that was brewing over him at home. And that this was ready to spread throughout the whole world.

The Chandler camp's strikes were set to hit the mark: on August 21 Neverland was raided. The officers confiscated anything they could get. Hungry for scandalous revelations, they grabbed diaries, videotapes, magazines, bath articles, cosmetics and makeup, documents...anything they could get their hands on. With arduous efforts they broke into the safe - to find nothing. They ransacked and photographed all the rooms, the entire property and nothing was left the way it had been.

Michael became ill when he heard about it. His Neverland! They vandalized his home! Greedy hands on his stuff!

Thus, the media was enabled to give a genuine factual report and strike two: on August 23 television reported the search, and it was revealed that of all people, Mr. number one squeaky-clean, who had received awards from two presidents of the United States for services to children, was suspected of having committed a disgusting crime. A day later, they unveiled the crux of the investigation

274

Michael Jackson, the mysterious superstar, had a revolting secret: he was a child molester. And Jordy, his best friend, had accused him of it.

An inferno broke out in the United States. The scandal was dragged powerfully and at length through all media.

***

"The press did not report," explained Michael. "They did everything to distort things. They showed stupid digitally altered pictures of me, they fished around in the gutter...for guys who could be bought and who made outrageous statements - they finished me off with every trick in the book."

Instinctively, he delayed the effect of the shock as much as possible by displacement. In the U.S. everything that could go wrong was going wrong. His PR department was making one mistake after another, while Chandler delivered solid work: within a few weeks, Michael Jackson's name was irrevocably tarnished.

Michael registered with horror how the prosecutor Tom Sneddon swore eternal vengeance, vowed to take him down. Dimly, Mike remembered how Branca had tried to prevent him from buying the Sycamore Ranch and all that land. He had pointed out that he, Mike, a black democrat, was settling into a predominantly white Republican nest. Sneddon hated that nigger, who had moved into his district. Who moreover enjoyed such status! Who was richer than most whites! You could see from afar Sneddon's satisfaction over this scandal.

People surfaced whom Michael had never spoken to or seen before, who initiated private investigations to convict Michael. People, who analyzed him from afar, cheekily imposing their headlines on him, devoid of any truth, just so they could appear in the newspaper themselves.

Strictly speaking, it was all still about a mere suspicion. The media could only publish the subject of the investigation. Nothing had been proven. But then the psychiatric report of the Child Services Department was leaked to the trash reporter Diane Dimond in a bar, on a silver platter, that is, in a cleanly organized binder.

Slobbering, the woman pounced on this tidbit, oblivious to anything around her other than herself and her career, and the very next day the content was already published.

Jordy's statement was a bomb that tore Michael's life apart. Stunned, he stared at this image of his friend, his own, distorted, schizophrenic looking face next to his, read the discriminatory headlines, saw the lies in black and white. Jordy...Jordy had made a confession. A confession! This was not a confession! It was a poisoned knife that Jordy had plunged into his back. Michael could not breathe. His eyes were dark black.

Headlines proclaimed that children had been found that Jackson had held captive and had tortured for years in his basement. Frantically more victims were sought...after all a lot of money was at stake. That's worth a false statement or two.

In huge letters these children were presented by the media. But none of these alleged victims had any evidence. None of them testified. All of them disappeared from the scene again - something the media took no note of. What were the people out there supposed to believe?

Everyone jumped onto the band wagon in the name of reporting that had ceased to actually report a long time ago. A wagon that drove Michael into an actual never-land.

It was sensationalism - and fabrication on the lowest level. Before long, half the world was convinced that Michael Jackson was a child molester. Michael's emotions and image plunged into the abyss. No one, absolutely no one, could comprehend how he fared in those days. He lay on his bed and cried the soul from his body. And couldn't tell anyone why he was actually crying. The pain tore his chest apart. Any contact with a human being cost him superhuman effort.

"Jordy," Michael whispered into his pillow, "Jordy, why did you do this? Why?"

There were so many emotions that took possession of him that he was unable to master, that he could not even imagine ever being able to overcome. His best friend was no longer one. His soul mate had betrayed him for the proverbial 30 pieces of silver. The person he thought he could trust with his whole heart. That was the paramount pain in the first few days. Madly he wrote wherever he came across something to write on - wallpaper, sheets of paper, mirror - his words, inspirations and thoughts.

"I love you, I love you, I love you..." how could a genuinely perceived love receive such an answer?

He felt sick. His blood pressure was going crazy. It was hot and humid in this country. He vomited. He had to vomit all the time. These accusations tore his soul out, and unprocessed emotions flooded out like feces and polluted every second.

Like a heat wave the ugly realization drove through his weakened body with the thrust of a sword: he was accused of being a *child molester*. He! Who loved kids more than anything, who saw in children the greatest sacredness! He did not want people thinking badly about him, he could not bear that. He had no love from childhood days in reserve. He was starving for love. Now he was a child molester! One of the most disgusting people on God's earth!

Michael was nauseous, everything was spinning inside him. He could not eat, the pain hooked like a razor blade, permanently in his heart.

With inhuman effort, he dragged himself through the concerts, traveled from one country to another. Some performances were postponed because on some days he couldn't do anything. Without resistance Michael fell into depression.

The sharp pain of loss and betrayal by Jordy was the primary problem he had to deal with. He could have coped with that. But now suddenly - worldwide - instead of admiration, he was met with revulsion. It was a loss of love on all levels and it hurt like hell. The mountain seemed insurmountable. He wanted to forget, wanted to sleep...but that's exactly what he could not do. Panic attacks kept him awake permanently, and he began to take painkillers so he wouldn't go mad.

His opinion of adults experienced an irrevocable push deep into the abyss. Everything had fallen victim to the dubious values of the adult world. Michael knew once again how important it was to never grow up. He wanted to remain innocent, he didn't want this bullshit, this stinking muck, with which the adults pelted one another, the cruel games of those who had lost their inner child. No, never, never in all his life did he want to turn into such a person.

"Dear God," he prayed, "grant that I may not be as they are. Let me be strong. Let me be strong, please help me. Do not take everything from me. Help me so that the children of this world have a chance."

That was the thought that kept him going. The thought, that this was a test for him. That love will ultimately prevail - even if the road was long and hard.

Nevertheless, his heart seemed to have suffered irreparable damage. His eyes would light up like before only in special moments, and he mistrusted adults more than ever.

From the world of showbiz Liz Taylor was the only one who backed him up regardless of the risk to her own reputation. She was also one of the few people in the world who dared talk about Michael's high energy. But in this situation, that sounded even more bizarre, and it didn't help. That kind of thing never helps in the public eye. Moreover, everyone knew that Liz loved Michael like a son, and her opinions did not matter much in this disaster.

He called Debbie and he spoke at length with Lisa. His family was there and stood beside him, but he was now careful on all levels: so far they had only used every situation to get him to agree to another *The Jacksons* tour.

He lay awake, days, nights, his body found no rest, his spirit least of all. He popped sleeping pills that did not help. And then he remembered the doctor who had injected him once and made him fall flat on his back and feel nothing anymore. No pain, no agony...just rest.

He called him and had him flown in. The doctor gave him the drug, and Michael slipped into a dreamless sleep. When he awoke, he felt at least a little better physically, and the doctor left him with numerous pills that he downed too quickly and too often.

He called Lisa and waffled about meaningless stuff on the phone. Alarmed, across thousands of miles, she tried to bring him to his senses.

"Dude, you're totally out of it! Have you been drinking? What did you take?"

"Llllisa..." he mumbled with the package of sedatives in his hand, "ffflllly here...I can't read...it...fly... here..."

His head became heavy, and he dropped it down toward the table where the phone was. His knees sagged, his chin bumped on the edge of the table, he toppled over and on the other end of the line Lisa heard a crash.

"Mike!" she cried. "What's wrong? Why are you alone? Why isn't a bodyguard with you?"

"Alone, alone," Michael sang and held his head while tears streamed from his eyes. His whole body felt like rubber, only the head was so heavy...a hammerhead of stone on a rubber handle...hanging down...the head...oh...it moved rapidly towards the carpet...and then he noticed that his body was already on the ground. Ah!! He was already lying on the floor! He could stretch out...stretch the legs... ah...yes...that was good...the ground held him. But the head...what was it doing...? He felt as if it was drilling a hole through the floor...the entire ground would collapse and he with it...the head was heavy...so heavy...so heavy...

"Mike!" someone yelled right in his ear and made him grimace in pain. "Mike! What are you doing? Where are you? Where, damn it, are your people?"

"People..." he mumbled weepy, "...people hate me...they hate me...Oh, I feel sick ... Lisa? Is that you...? Lisa...I have to tell you something...I feel sick...I... my heart hurts so much...it hurts so much...Lisa...do you hear me...I..."

Michael began to cry. Lisa spoke to him insistently, grabbing a second phone, called the front desk of the hotel, demanded to speak to Michael's security and made sure that someone came to the room.

And there was this doctor, thank God, injecting this heavenly stuff that made him forget...a mini-death, a reset...until he had to power up again...to look into worried faces that had a lot of bad news ready for him. Who didn't know what to do...and in some faces he saw doubt. Doubt about him.

It made him sick.

The next day he picked up the phone again.

"Lisa...thank you," he said. "I don't know what I would have done without you."

"You're welcome, buddy," said Lisa. "I know the feeling...I was there once too, was perhaps even worse than you."

And she did exactly what helped Michael the most: she told him of her childhood, of her drug problems, the death of her father. She gave him the feeling of not being the only one with problems, and he felt that he helped her by listening as well. And Michael was a good listener. He was a world champion in it.

"Your father loved you so much," he said.

"Yes, he did," she said warmly, "but...he could not deal with himself. And because children learn from their parents or caregivers...I learned just the same thing. Subconsciously, of course...but I couldn't deal with myself either. I did what he had done. He took pills, I took drugs...same thing. Just that I saved myself at some point. Rehab...cold turkey...is not for the faint of heart. Thank God I found people who helped me."

Michael took the hint. "Scientology," he said.

"Yes... it was the best thing that could have happened to me..."

"Lisa, I don't want to be a Scientologist," he said frankly.

"You don't have to. It's enough if you realize that you need help."

Lisa was compassionate and unsentimental. She liked Michael a lot. During the six months of their occasional meetings and frequent phone calls, she had come to know him as a warm-hearted, spiritual, humorous, and above all, normal person. He was gentle and polite, a man of the sort: I'll open the car door for you and put a coat around your shoulders if you're cold. He could be charming in a cheeky way and he was intelligent. She enjoyed the conversations with him. And his eyes, these so deep, dark lakes, sent a tingle through her body. Lisa could feel Michael's charisma and his fate draw her in more and more.

In America, meanwhile, the media storm raged unabated. Although no really new reports were added, the fire continued to be stoked for his cremation. For a quarter of a year the media reported with unvarying fury about this case. It was not even clear whether it would come to a trial - merely unproven accusations stood for debate - but only a few individual's viewpoints were hammered into the brains of the masses through constant repetition of incorrect facts. The opinion that Jackson was weird, that something was wrong with him, was a foundation already established. For many, it was an easy-to-believe fact that Jackson was a child molester, too. Sodium amytal for everyone. Disintegration time: zero.

Refuge

The few rays of light that helped him build bridges to the other shore in those days were his close friends who proved themselves in the crisis, his humor, which often pulled him out of this sadness - that was the healing connection between the light and dark side in him - and, again and again, Lisa.

Her smoky voice tickled his ear pleasantly, in a way that sent shivers down his spine. Her not-entirely G-rated expressions, her disrespectful manner, amused him, activated his life saving cheerfulness and allowed him to perceive his unhappiness as not so drastic in these moments.

The phone calls to her during the tour were like vitamin shots, and he was incredibly grateful to her for her support. In Hollywood circles it wasn't popular these days to know Michael Jackson, and so everyone who paid attention to career and reputation kept their distance. And since everyone was in Hollywood to pursue a career, there was no one left who admitted associating with him.

Michael suffered greatly from this social ostracism. The part of being called a freak, he could cope with because this statement did not have a criminal intonation. But Evan had crossed a line that was literally below the belt. And so Michael was more than ever grateful to the last fiber of his heart when someone showed sympathy for him - and, in addition, publicly like Liz did or...Lisa.

"Fuck the media!" was their shared slogan. And Lisa predicted: "The exact opposite of what they are expecting is going to happen...they think they can dunk you under...but you're like a rubber ball, you'll pop back up again just like that...they're not going to crush you that easily! And then you'll be even more famous than before! Fuck! That's pure publicity! Chandler's going to kick himself when he realizes that he's only helped you get even more famous!"

Michael grinned when he heard her talk like that. Only after he had hung up, when her voice, the effect of her words and his medication fizzled out, did he realize that he could have done without this level of fame and that it was too serious a matter to crack jokes about. But his gratitude remained - and more - Michael became aware that he had an effect as a man on Lisa, and that made him weak in the knees because he had never experienced this in such a form before.

He had been ashamed because he had to ask friends like Brooke Shields if he could name her as his current date in an interview. When he took off with

Thriller, she had used him to be noticed by the public, and because he really liked her, he'd had no objection.

In the Oprah interview, it had been her turn to return a friendly favor because he knew that Oprah would ask if he had a girlfriend. He just had not found an opportunity in his life to start an unburdened affair in which neither his money nor his position played a role. There were many women - before the Jordy debacle - who wanted to be seen with him because he was successful. But...that was business. Where was the romance? Where was genuine, uncalculating love?

And then, suddenly there was Lisa. Such a beautiful, humorous and unconventional person who seemed to be interested in him as a man? That was a feeling that made Michael's heart beat faster. Lisa was famous herself; she was a $300-million heiress. She did not have to be seen with him - on the contrary - in those days it was very courageous to be seen with him at all. And a dream woman like her was interested in him, just as his career was on the brink? Conflicting emotions were swirling around in him: the continuing threat from Chandler, and the unknown and tender romance that had been developing between him and a very exciting woman. Her star shone so brightly in his consciousness that he knew at once where fate would lead him:

"A family," he said softly to me. "I wanted a family of my own. Suddenly it came to me like a revelation that that was exactly right for me. *My* family. And that Lisa came into my life precisely at this time I felt was God's providence."

But that was only one reason to enter into this relationship. There were a thousand reasons — and the most important was that Michael sincerely loved Lisa.

***

"Lisa, I want to thank you for standing by me...that you..."

He was still on tour, called from abroad, his voice wavered. Not just from emotion, but also because he was pumped full of pain killers so he could make it through the day.

"Thanking me for nothing dude! Fuck the media!"

"Yeah, fuck the media!" said Michael weakly and suddenly he felt terribly nauseated. He thought, "Oh, God, not again..." and held his hand over the receiver so that Lisa could not hear his wheezing. Sweat broke out on his forehead; he concentrated on keeping the contents of his stomach down.

Lisa was telling him something. Her words flooded around in his ear, up and down, louder and softer...he understood them...did not understand them...understood them...did not understand...with a supreme effort, he threw in a comment from time to time to create the impression that he was listening. His hand clutched the receiver so firmly that the knuckles turned white. His head was spinning, and he forgot to press his hand over the mouthpiece.

"Michael?" Lisa stopped abruptly. "Michael, is everything okay?"

"A... all oookaayy..." he gasped, then all Lisa could hear was a loud bang, heard how Michael pulled something with him on his way to the floor, heard him whimper and she closed her eyes in horror. A bodyguard took over, hung up the phone, left Lisa alone with her thoughts. This was the third of their conversations that had had this outcome.

She could no longer banish Michael from her thoughts. There was something about him that beguiled her, something she had not expected. In the entire world she had not encountered any person who was more of a contradiction.

When in February 1992 a mutual friend had invited her to dinner and revealed that Michael Jackson was her table partner, she had laughed. What had she expected? What the press had professed? The choice of someone either asexual, gay, a male virgin with child-like behavior or a bizarre egomaniac, who built up his quirks as his image? Unexpectedly, she had been faced with a man with a deep gaze, a man whose sensuality exuded from every pore, who with one glance had made her heart flip.

Well, what had she expected? Anything but that. And more, Lisa could feel in Michael what many sensitive people felt in his presence: something high, something great, something resonated within him, something that intrigued her to no end. At the same time he appeared fragile and vulnerable to her. He was like something precious, something that needed to be protected in this very aggressive and loveless world. Her heart beat with his, and awakened a desire for and a belief in the power, of preserving this treasure from all evil.

Scenes from her childhood spooled in her brain like in a movie. Her father and the bathroom closet full of tubes, jars and packets. Thousands of pills. Oh, this closet! Her father in front of it leaning on the basin. The water rushes. Disregarded, useless, from the source to the drain. Her father does not notice. Stands in front of this closet, looks at himself in the mirror. Bloated. Staring at the pills, stuffing a handful into his mouth. Crashing to the floor. Vomiting. Writhing in agony. Moaning. Her own screaming. How she had hoped that this groaning would come to an end! And it had come to an end. All of a sudden. Arms and hands, that had held her so safely, fell without resistance to the sides of the body. Lifeless, the soft lips that had kissed her lovingly. And then suddenly, the certainty, that so damn certain knowledge: In front of her is merely inanimate matter, not able to give her one more word, one last gesture.

She had been a little child at the time. At that time she hadn't been able to help.

But now...now she was not nine anymore. And she didn't want the same thing to happen again. She didn't want to feel powerless again. This time she would be there on time. This time she would know what to do to prevent what had happened then.

Evan was still far from being finished with Michael. To Mike the stress, the threat of his career - what he had slaved away for so hard his whole life long, and had cost him his childhood - was increasing exponentially and even with Lisa's phone calls he could not release the amount of pressure that was added anew.

It was not long before Michael could no longer live without pills. Already since the Pepsi accident he hadn't been able to because the pain had been so severe. But now he was already afraid when he woke up, and sometimes he would rather not have woken up at all. He bravely tried to forget on stage, gave everything he had, but it didn't work. His body was not able to regenerate itself to the extent it consumed energy. And worst: his psyche, his confidence was affected and left in the pits.

When he collapsed after his last show in Mexico, his crew had no choice but to cancel the rest of the tour.

***

And again he called her. Locked in his hotel room, lonely, with people all around him, the choice between dull stupor when he took painkillers and murderous fear in the heart when he didn't take them. Today he had decided in favor of anxiety. He wanted to be clear. Closed his eyes as he waited for a connection. With the third possible number he got a hold of her.

"Lisa, Lisa...!" he cried, and almost choked with excitement.

"Michael!" she said happily, and for just that joy in her voice he could have kissed her feet.

"Lisa..." he stammered, "I...I'm so sorry, I...I promise not to break down on the phone today..."

Lisa laughed. "That's okay, dude, relax. We've been through it all, you know?"

A wave of tenderness flooded up and oscillated through the ether to her. Immediately the mood shifted and they both fell silent. It was a pleasant silence, full of expectation, knowing. Finally, Lisa asked:

"How are you doing?"

"I feel...as can be...expected under the circumstances. In two days I'm going to rehab."

"Good for you," she said.

"I'm a bit afraid of it."

"That's OK. It'll be good for you"

Michael took a deep breath. "Lisa...it...I am eternally grateful to you, that you're there...that you talk to me...you are..."

"It's all right, kid," she said, and with that response Michael almost lost himself in love. He felt protected, solely through these few words, so much so that he did not know where to put so much emotion.

But emotions travel faster than the speed of light and they arrived almost instantly at Lisa's side. She felt that she was activating something in Michael. That gave her strength because she so desperately wanted to help him out of this crisis, be there for him. And these thoughts too bridged the thousands of miles and found Michael's heart, kindled a fire there of gratitude and love.

"Lisa," Michael responded spontaneously and asked with a husky voice, "If I asked you to marry me, would you say yes?"

His advisers urged him to come to America, but there he would have been immediately incarcerated by the police. It only took one look at the emaciated, gaunt body, to know that he would not have survived it.

They took him - despite all the sneering headlines claiming that Michael only wanted an easy way out - to the UK, to a rehab clinic. Where he belonged.

As justification to the court and the world, Michael admitted his dependency for painkillers. That hurt him most. Because it was true and he would have liked to have been a better example for his fans. He would have wanted to be stronger, the true perfectionist he was. Somehow he could still not believe it: he had crashed completely, his image in the outside world was sullied and destroyed. Like him.

And it was not over yet. The disaster reports did not stop. Everyone tried to make money from the persona of Michael Jackson. Reporters, journalists, producers, consultants, self-appointed managers... and then his family.

La Toya, Michael's sister, turned to the camera and publicly accused her brother. He was a pedophile, she could no longer remain silent, because her silence would be a crime against all of the children that Michael had used already and who would have no life anymore, because of her brother. She had seen the checks, checks for exorbitant sums...and she saw it as her duty to prevent further atrocities. Michael had to undergo psychiatric treatment.

La Toya did not just proceed with this performance against Michael. Among others she sat down with conservative Swiss housewives in cardigans at the table, railed via TV against her little brother, and claimed his crotch grabbing on stage was evidence of his perversion.

"Man, don't be so squeamish! You've seen it! You saw it! With your own eyes!"

"I saw how he wrote out checks, but not for what," she hissed back. Her large eyes were full of tears.

"You said he gave the parents these checks! That's no lie, La Toya, no lie!"

She did not know what devil had possessed her when she told her husband Jack Gordon that Michael gave large sums to the parents of children. Fact was that she really had seen those checks. She had seen first-hand how Michael had signed horrendous amounts.

She had asked him what they were for and he had replied: "That's none of you business Toy."

Michael had recently denied her a large amount she had requested from him. He would have given her the money, but he mistrusted her husband from the depths of his soul, and he knew that La Toya had been sent by him.

Michael often made out checks for that kind of money. A bone marrow transplant, an organ that was hard to find, expensive drugs, surgeries or treatments that could save a child's life. The case was reviewed and then presented to Michael. He never even batted an eye, took a pen and signed checks with six figure sums. He did this without speaking even a single word about it.

If La Toya had known that he refused her money, which he then in the next breath gave for an unknown child, would she have understood? Michael had always kept quiet about these matters.

But still, red-veined eyes were staring in La Toya's face. The eyes of Jack Gordon who hated Michael abysmally.

"You saw it," he growled. "You saw it."

La Toya said nothing. A fist slammed into her stomach. Groaning, she sank to her knees. Out of control, he shouted, "You do what I say!" and punched her so hard against the back of the head that she fell down and lay on the floor. Brutally he yanked her up by the hair and pressed a note into her hand. "You're going to read what it says...you know what will happen if you don't." Jack squashed her hand. She didn't utter a sound. He stared at her, a look out of mad eyes, and she did what he told her to do.

It turned black before Michael's eyes. If one thing was for certain, then it was that people out there would be given the entirely wrong combination of individual scenarios and conclusion by the media. It was a hydra that seemed impossible to fight against.

Rehab was a short breather. His attorney who had been re-hired in these days, John Branca, wrapped up a fabulous deal for him during this time. He sold half of the ATV catalog to Sony for about $90 million. Since Michael had paid only 47.5 million for the whole thing, it was a huge deal and everyone hoped that it would cheer him up a little. And it was not just that Michael had sold half of his part. What many people did not realize was the fact that Michael had thus established himself at Sony because 50 percent of the shares of the Sony/ATV catalog still belonged to him. And Sony could not do anything with it without him.

But in the end Michael had to finally face the allegations. He had no time to recover properly, he had to return to America - and step into the ring.

Chandler and the brains behind him did not leave anything out. Evan wanted the money. He wanted to see Michael on the ground because he was responsible for his own son hating him. Evan's oath, to humble Michael to the very foundations of his soul, had become true and - now in the wake of complete success - he wanted more.

He had helpful support. The District Attorney, Tom Sneddon, had been after this black pop singer for a long time, who earned money because he wiggled his ass, and, what's more, grabbed his crotch in such a vulgar way. If he deigned to become famous with such things...well, then he, Sneddon, had an adequate retribution ready for him.

Michael had barely set foot on American soil when he received the summons to an investigation of a special kind: he had to be photographed naked, in particular his genital area so it could be established whether Jordy's description matched the reality.

Sneddon and Chandler were all about humiliation. And they succeeded. Michael suffered unspeakably when he had to undergo this procedure that, in addition, made it to the press. The knowledge that the officials of the district had looked at his genitals turned into his own personal nightmare. He felt defiled and polluted.

And with horror, he remembered the scene when Jordy unexpectedly had come into the room and the towel had slipped from his waist. A lump formed in his throat and remained there. A lump of fear and powerlessness.

***

Michael looked around and could see only people who accused him of awful things. He spent these first days in America almost in a trance. On TV he saw his own dance scenes where the crotch grabbing was shown in slow motion, the lifting of the pelvis, how it pushes forward, the hand before the sex, his open mouth, the ugly headlines next to it. He painfully noticed how people avoided him, how radio stations did not play his songs anymore, how the American people had sentenced him and regarded him with hostility.

A tsunami of negative, hateful emotions washed over him.

And the modern Inquisition, the media, full of sensationalism, bloodthirsty, played the lead role in this drama. It is unconscionable, what is allowed to pass in journalism, which supposedly prescribe itself to reporting.

Michael Jackson had been branded, tarred and feathered in the public eye forever - for the sake of entertainment. So people had something to read about at home in their boring living rooms. So some could climb a bit higher on the career ladder. So some reporters and moderators could fill their empty lives with the mission of imposing their own inner hatred onto another. So that they could make a carefree life for themselves with the money and through destruction of another. Reason enough to torture and destroy a human life.

Chandler had made good on his promise: He humiliated Jackson to the deepest recess of his soul. And an ending was nowhere in sight.

Emergency Exit

"I knew that Chandler wouldn't back off until he had the money," Mike told me quietly. "And then I began to realize, and the informants let me know, that there was much more to it than it seemed."

With disillusioned eyes, he looked at me.

"They said there was a campaign launched against me in which Evan merely played the figurehead. Everything was so confusing. Every day new suspicions, different rumors, new acts of viciousness were reported to me, that could be true or not. I ... I was stuck in a swamp, didn't know what to believe anymore, who was right, who was wrong. Nobody knew in those days."

He bit his lip, turned to look straight ahead.

"I... was running the risk of losing everything."

Again, he pressed his lips together. Unspoken words, thoughts from his past etched visions into the ether. "My heart hurt so much," he whispered. "It wasn't beating regularly anymore. That's when ... when it started..."

He swallowed hard, his neck muscles went rigid, then he let his head drop. Involuntarily I held my breath. Michael said nothing for a long time. I had to strain to hear him when he continued.

"...since then...death threats have been coming to the house. Someone swore to kill me, me, the child molester. Nobody knew how these letters, notes, scraps, sometimes messages in lipstick written on my bathroom mirror were able to get to me. It could, in principle, have been anyone from my crew. I didn't know anymore who I could trust, who I could turn my back to without worry, who was telling the truth or who was just saying what I wanted to hear, even whether my advisors were real advisors...it makes you insane."

Blind to the beauty of the night, he looked stubbornly straight ahead.

"I wanted it to go away," he said, tortured. "I just wanted to get rid of it...I couldn't take it anymore."

"Is that why you paid?" I asked, and he sighed.

"Chirelle...I wanted the lawsuit, absolutely. But the judge at the time quashed that...because there was no official accusation. Instead, he approved an accelerated civil suit so that the 'memory of the child would not fade'. If Jordy really was under the influence of a drug and I'd have lost the civil suit, I wouldn't have had a chance in a criminal trial. Chandler knew that. That was his move. My former advisors felt it would be best to settle. If it had been only about Evan, I would have fought it...but there were these uncertainties, this suspicion that behind this demon Evan...Hades loomed...an underworld that scared me. And ... like I said ... I didn't have any strength left. It's easy to give good advice in hindsight. Although lots of people said it was the same as a confession of guilt ... there were several reasons why I paid."

One aspect that made the decision easier mentally was that the payment was covered by an insurance company. So for Michael, it was not really his money that was tapped.

And then... there was Lisa. Lisa, who was waiting for him, and for whom he wanted to be free. And she wanted, too, to put an end to this, so that their developing relationship was not overshadowed by a lengthy lawsuit.

Michael leaned back against the tree trunk, his fingers playing with the blade of grass.

"There were clear indications that Chandler had drugged his own son with sodium amytal... if Evan had really done that...what choice was there for Jordy?"

Michael's voice sounded bitter, so bitter that it cut the air like a knife.

"Do you believe that?" I asked. I had a lump in my throat, speaking was difficult.

Michael was silent for a while. Then he said in his so gentle way, without any remaining trace of resentment:

"Yes, I believe it. There were a couple of other things that helped me survive after this case."

"Which ones?" I asked, eager for a little bit of positivity in this darkness.

"Pellicano," Mike told me, "… found a crumpled piece of paper in front of Evan's house. He picked it up and brought it to me. It was a note from Jordy."

"From Jordy? What did it say?"

Michael's lips trembled, his voice trembled, he started twice before he whispered:

"'I don't know who I am anymore. I don't know what I am doing anymore. Can't take it anymore. Please pay the money. Make it be over. So it's finally over. I love you.'"

The words were etched into Michael's memory, you could feel that. I on the other hand, was at a total loss for words

"Why didn't you go to the police with the note?" I asked him, stunned. "That's proof of your innocence!"

"A boy who writes that he loves me?" Michael shot back mockingly. "Then I'd really have had it. What makes me feel better was: I knew then that Jordy was being blackmailed, too. I remember how Chandler asked if he could have the computer I had given Jordy. We were all shocked by his audacity. But later, too late, it occurred to me that Jordy may have wanted it, so he could send a message to me on this computer. He was being monitored. But to your question: What counted in the end was his testimony. If a hypnotic drug was involved, Jordy would have sworn later that he hadn't written this piece of paper or anything else. And another thing: Jordy has since lived only with his father, for ten years, he never saw his mother, June, again...what had Evan told him? What had he really done? These are all questions that I ask myself...and the note...was a small consolation, an indication that Jordy's love...was not fake. I paid. And kept my mouth shut. For him."

***

Life went on. Michael was only left to process this multitude of pain with songs. He dressed his anguish in hard rhythms, aggressive electric guitar solos and raging videos. Music was and remained his true expression, and so every one of his songs felt mercilessly authentic. But the thorn was deep, like so many others. Thorns that told him: "No friend for Michael. You are alone. No happiness for you". There were no happy songs from Michael. There were the aggressive ones and the ones filled with melancholy. In between, there was nothing. In his lyrics his whole life, his thoughts, his fears could be found and ... his cries for help.

I often wondered how Michael managed to remain so loving, with this open wound called heart. For despite all of these experiences, he was more than ever ready to give love.

"Because love is everything," he replied to my unspoken question. "I wanted to forget and move on. At that time, however, I hadn't seen through the full extent of the scandal. Only guessed at it without wanting to believe it. I thought if you're successful, you simply elicit envy and jealousy; I thought I'd just start from scratch. And there was this love...the love I felt inside, I didn't want to give up. It was... is, my support, my lifeline."

Michael sat under the tree in this quiet way I loved so much. Oh, my God, what a wonderful aura this man had around him! His eyes were closed, and I saw single tears well up beneath his eyelashes. But there were only a few. He was imbued with a strange restraint, one that forbade him to give completely in to tears in the presence of another. But his body was shaking, and it was not because of the coolness of the night. He was already covered with two blankets while I still had only a T-shirt. To quiet him somewhat, I put my arm around him. To my surprise, he dropped his head on my shoulder and took my hand. This time I was the one who breathed out, deeply releasing the pressure from the heart when he leaned onto me. It was easy to see that such gestures were alien to him. But tonight he was a child, a child who does not understand. A child who is beaten by his father and does not know what for. Something that had happened to him physically in childhood, and he had encountered in the Chandler situation psychologically again.

"So, Chirelle?" Michael whispered. "What are you thinking about?"

I could smell the scent of his hair and saw his pointed nose that emphasized his child-like character so much. I gently pressed a kiss on his hair.

"Michael, I don't think I want to tell you tonight," I mumbled.

"But I want to hear it, Chirelle," he said firmly.

I pulled my arm away from around his shoulders and smiled. "You are such a wonderful soul, you know that? You could have become the most bitter person on earth after all this crap, with this whole past - and everyone would have understood."

"Oh!" he exclaimed. "Maybe that would have been a way to gain public approval for once?"

I laughed. "Unfortunately that's not so far from the truth! But I think your way of dealing with it is so much more heroic. And more noble," I hesitated.

"Come on, Chirelle," he urged. "Spit it out!"

"I think," I began quietly, "with Chandler you encountered someone who matched your inside."

He winced. With his huge eyes, he looked at me. "Do you really think that?" he asked, hurt. "This evil... inside of me?"

"No," I replied. "Not the way you're interpreting it now."

Alarmed, I saw Michael's eyes wander towards the house.

"Stay here, Mike," I asked him. "Please... you were the one who asked..."

He sighed, his shoulders slumped down.

"Mike, you know my belief that what we encounter on the outside, is the mirror of our soul. So... ask yourself, what was the whole situation mirroring: you were defamed, dishonored, humiliated - what is the pattern that corresponds to? What does Chandler represent? Why did he flip out? I mean, what did he really want?"

Michael was silent, but I could see that he had understood. His head sank down.

"You mean... he wanted ... love," he whispered.

"Yes, he did. And money, of course. He couldn't find it inside and so he projected all shortcomings to the outside. And thought he could heal it with external things, with money. He suffered terribly when he felt excluded. He lost Jordy to you. He lost everything. He did not realize why that was. You were his fate and he was yours. But he chose a completely wrong path. And: to understand why he did it doesn't mean that you have to *approve* it. He... drifted off, became lost in hate, something you didn't do. You could say now: Okay, perhaps that was *your* test. Then God could have said: Good job, you've passed! But I think this story goes deeper. The question is, when you meet people like Evan, when you are humiliated so much... what, dear 'Man in the Mirror', did that show you? What would you have needed to change, so that it wouldn't happen again? And ... it *did* happen to you again..."

God, Michael's eyes and their expression at this moment were so beautiful, to die for. I could only stare at him, unable to take my eyes off him. His charisma was so immense, so intense, and the whole time this light energy was radiating from his every pore. My hand moved carefully to his face and I gently stroked his incredibly soft white skin.

"Such a beautiful person," I mumbled. "You are such a beautiful person... believe me, Mike, you're just a stone's throw away from your happiness."

He was upset, more upset than I had ever seen him before. He asked for patience. "Give me some time," he said. "I have to think ... I need to think ... give me some time."

We had packed up our things and were heading back to the house. Michael in large strides, as if he could not wait to be alone. I knew the feeling. As always, he brought me to my door. As always, I turned to face him. Leaned against the doorframe. We looked at each other. My heart was once again spilling over, and I could feel how words bubbled up and wanted out. Bravely I suppressed them. I forced myself to smile at him.

"Just tell me when you're ready. I'll be there."

He nodded, hastily made his 'Namaste' greeting, and left.

I was convinced that he would go into hiding somewhere first for a couple of days... until the questions that crystallized out became so insistent that he returned. Hopefully. He could also steer clear of them. That was what he had been doing so far.

If that were the case, it would be time for me to go, too.

XX / 1994

"If he thinks he can get out of it like this, he's wrong ... why don't you have more victims? Find victims! He's always surrounded by them. Whatever it's going to have to work without victims, too ... Get moving."

Puzzle

That night I could not sleep. I was dog tired, we had talked through many nights, and this time too it was early morning when we had separated, but something was going around in my head, or rather, it was not going around in my head. It was something I wanted to remember, and I just couldn't get it. It was something important. I had missed something... but what? Was it something about Michael? With the conversation? No ... it was something else ... had I missed someone's birthday ... forgot some formalities...? Restlessly I tossed and turned in bed.

I wondered what Michael would do with today's still unresolved message. There was such a huge range of options: from rejection to applying it to the rest of his life. I wished so much that he finally could solve all this ... I wished that he could spend the second half of his life in happiness and contentment ... that he could finally fully enjoy his life... and with this desire it suddenly hit me what everyone meant when they said there wasn't much time. Everyone, who had accompanied Michael for so long, Grace, Karen, Jason, Bob ... they all were afraid that he would not live much longer.

And then, in the afternoon of the next day, it finally occurred to me: Tom. He had said: "I want you to *think about it* ... that you *think about* it..."

That wouldn't leave me. Out of the blue the sentence started an infinite loop in me.

I googled Tom. There was nothing to be found about him. No law firm, sure, but no editorial office, no career as a failed writer, journalist, reporter, freelance writer or camera man, no Facebook, no references, no club activities, newspaper reports, nothing. Simply nothing. I remembered that the check was issued by one of the famous tabloids. So he had to work for them. But ... did he really have to?

I typed his name and that of the newspaper, was directed to some interesting sites and was shocked to see how much the press was concentrated - so many newspapers and news channels were in only a few hands! But Tom: Nothing. There was no Tom Cevicz. Neither here nor elsewhere. He had acquired a name that seemed to be unique. After I had spent two hours just searching for Tom on the net, I started to doubt myself. What was I doing? He was a guy who had offered a dubious deal using a false name. Had he really meant with 'think about it' only the amount and the offer?

It was pointless to inquire at the editorial office about a Tom Cevicz.

I did it anyway. He did not exist. Neither in the editorial office nor in any other department. At least that's what they told me. Never heard of him.

The second option: the check was fake ... then Tom was an even bigger scumbag if he had expected to get the story for free - or ... had it not been about the story? And if the latter was true - what was it about to him then? A blender whirred in my head.

What was I supposed to 'think about'? Why and damn it, about what?

In the meantime, things in the house were going crazy. Important looking men came and went. Meetings were held, whose participants left the room with anxious and stressed faces. In addition Michael was frequently away from home - also for meetings. Grace walked around depressed and didn't want to say anything. Linda also hung her head. I missed Karen - but she didn't show up.

Uncertainty took hold of this house and drove me out. To the city, to the beach. I thought about Michael, about Tom, about so many things and could not rest. I asked Linda to give me work, and since I had gained her trust now, she let me clean the entire lower floor. I started with the library.

The mechanical work was good for me. Man, did this man have books! Linda had said it was only a tiny part from Neverland. The rest was in storage. Michael had a reputation as a bookworm, devouring everything, even medical books, and there was scarcely a subject, which he could not talk about. Systematically, I worked myself towards the middle of the huge wall of shelves.

After three hours, I took a rest. Got myself a cup of coffee from the kitchen, sat down in the library on the floor warmed by the sun, leaned my back against a shelf, and looked out the window.

That was a combination that I found immensely appealing: sun, books and coffee. The stacks of books around me were like living figurines that wanted to tell me something. I grabbed a book from the pile and read around in it. Put it away, picked up another. But today I did not have the peace to read. My hands were barely idle, the thoughts in my head circulated again. Unfocused I flipped through a book when a photo fell out.

Three people were looking at me, a pretty girl was laughing into the camera, standing somewhere in the sun, accompanied by two young men, all around thirty years old. The girl held her thumb demonstratively into the lens. I turned the photo over. 'For Michael' it said. 'Love of my life'.

Further down, with a different pen and flying letters, as if it had been added in haste: 'Who taught me that love is everywhere. Regardless of time and place, body or form – I'll wait for you.'

On the back was yet more: two large FFs in the middle. That was the common abbreviation for fan fiction. Everywhere were the kinds of doodles you do when lost in thought during long calls: ornaments, circles, squares, flowers, plaid patterns, and in between letters that were barely decipherable. I held the photo a bit further away to get an overview of the writing from a distance:

'Joey'. I looked closer. Okay - yes, that said 'Joey'. The name of one of the three? Next to it three unidentifiable letters, the first could be a G or S, the second letter, lowercase, offered more alternatives: an i, a c, an s, an r, or a blip of the pen? Take your pick, Chirelle. And also the third letter was so unclear that it could have been anything. The only clear part was in the middle: an unmistakable 'gg'.

All in all: illegible. But still the photograph and its inscriptions appeared significant. I put the books back on the shelf and memorized which book the photo was in.

***

"Do you think… could you …I mean … maybe he likes my music?"

Just as I was leaving the library, I heard his voice. It was Michael talking on the phone. I paused in my step, not wanting to disturb him.

"Maybe you can find out?" he asked. "If it's the case … I could give a free concert … just for him … if he lets the women go."

Which women? A concert? For free? He had only recently rejected $10 million for a gig in Vegas … he did not want to perform any more … what was he talking about?

"Call me when you've found out," Michael said, and hung up.

He went back to one of these meetings that seemed to be permanently held here recently.

"Grace, what's going on?" I asked her when I finally caught her alone. She let out a sigh.

"Everything is going on! These people are going to kill Michael yet!"

Frustrated, she kicked the fridge, something I was not at all accustomed to from Grace. I looked at her, nonplussed. She had tears in her eyes.

"They want him to perform again," she said. "But that's his death sentence, definitely. He hasn't recovered from the last trial yet, he needs to go on a really long retreat... he would have to do so much ... and for the first time he is ready to take time to heal... but they're not letting him, they're not letting him ... they're putting so much pressure on him!"

"Perform again? Do you mean the benefit concert?"

"Benefit concert?" Astonished, she looked at me.

"Yes, he recently mentioned two women ... and ... "

"Oh, oh, that!" she cried sounding no less desperate. "That's our typical Michael! He saw on the news that two Asian women are being held hostage... now he is trying to find out if the dictator of this country happens to like his music so he can sing the two women to freedom ... but he can't... he is ... health wise... and otherwise ... oh ... fuck!"

She raised her hands in despair, let them fall again, eyes rolled to the ceiling. Then she turned to me so abruptly that I flinched.

"This Tohme Tohme is working in Michael's name like a madman! We have no idea what kind of havoc he's creating out there! His so-called consultants are not able to sort out his finances, and I'm not sure if they even want to. He's just supposed to make even more money for these shit heads!"

My eyes followed her as she furiously paced back and forth. All of this wasn't new - where did this enormous frustration come from?

"And his family is stressing him again, too! For the 500th time they are thinking about a revival of *The Jacksons*... nobody cares how Mike feels!"

She emitted an angry, frustrated noise, slammed her fist on the refrigerator, stood frozen in front of it and gritted her teeth.

"And me ... he's sending me away", she said so softly that I could barely hear her. I thought I must have heard wrong. Dismayed, I asked:

"Pardon?"

"He's sending me away again." She still stood in front of the fridge, motionless, stiff.

"Send you away? But why?" I heard myself ask aghast, "... again? Away again? What does that mean?"

"He does that every once in a while ... always when ... when he thinks that the children are getting too close to me ... he says I'm not their mother, and he doesn't want them to feel that I am. He doesn't want them to love me too much. He wants them to love *him*!"

The veins in her neck swelled in her vain attempt to suppress her tears. Startled, I walked up to her and touched her shoulder. As if this were a switch meant for maintaining her body tension, she collapsed, fell into my arms and cried her eyes out.

***

In these days many things were happening that I could make no sense of and no one talked about. Michael met often with some people, there were serious discussions with his family, too, whom he met at the hotel and not at home. Did he not want to have them here? Or was he not sure if he was being wiretapped here?

Grace argued with Michael in the living room. And almost every day this Tohme Tohme showed up, asking for Michael. Every day he was more worked up. He said that Michael would go down if he did not listen to him. The conversations were often loud, loud and clear, and they charged the atmosphere in the house. Michael meanwhile refused to talk to the man. That went on for a whole week.

At the end of this week, Grace yelled at the man to piss off and never come back. He yelled back that it was not the concern of a baby-butt-wiper. He had the upper hand, and she would soon see what her inappropriate behavior would get her. Grace literally flipped out and in turn put him in his place. Furious, he crumpled a piece of paper in front of her eyes and threw it at her. Grace dodged to the side a bit; it bounced off the wall and fell down.

"Tell him that I won't accept this!" he snarled.

"I'm not going to tell him anything! Take your rubbish and get out!" Grace's icy voice echoed through the house. Doors slammed. Then there was silence.

I heard Grace go upstairs to her room. Linda and I looked at each other. No one said a word.

The crumpled note lay where it had fallen. Surreptitiously I picked it up when I was alone in the entrance and could not resist. I smoothed the paper and read the words. It was a termination letter. Michael formally terminated Dr. Tohme Tohme with these words and without much ado, thanked him for his services and made it clear that they were no longer required, effective immediately.

Grace instructed security to no longer admit Tohme. When she said that, I had a rumbling in my stomach. This man did not look as if he would put up with that. He appeared extremely dominant and intent on his cause. Until 2005 it had been Bob Jones who, Grace told me once, so convinced of his own importance, treated Michael like a schoolboy and was addressed by Michael during his time of service with 'Sir'.

"He behaved like a gangster..." Grace told me, "and Michael obeyed like a child, as if he found some kind of security in it. Bob could scold him and he stood there and put up with it."

Frowning, I listened. Bashir came to mind. 'Take a glass for Christ's sake!' 'Don't yawn like that!'

He had treated Michael the same way, outrageously and without any respect. But why? As Grace continued to talk, she provided me with a possible answer:

"Often times Michael did not even know how and with what Bob had scheduled the day for him. It was Bob who let business partners and fans, who had won a meeting with Michael wait for hours. But Mike found out about that only when he sat together with the respective people and often not even then. Most of them were happy to even see him once in their lives - they didn't complain about four hours of waiting...but of course it was always Michael who had the reputation of never being on time for any appointment."

"But didn't you say that Michael hated exactly this kind of ordering around?" I asked in surprise.

"Yes, that's the strange thing. But with Bob, he put up with it for decades. And as soon as Bob was gone, there was Shmuley Boteach, this rabbi, who took over Michael's life. He meant well - but at some point people don't know their boundaries anymore, because Michael doesn't set any. Because he doesn't want to hurt anybody, can't say no. Everyone tries to change him, dictate his life. Shmuley at least had good intentions, but when the relationship ended, he was no better than others and talked poorly about Michael. And as soon as he was gone, this Tohme shows up ... another one of these characters. All of these guys behave in a more or less modified form like Joseph, Michael's father. It's as if Mike can't let go of the past."

"But I thought Shmuley has been helpful for Michael, had worked up a lot..."

"I don't know," said Grace, and pressed her lips together. "It ... was bad timing. *Invincible*, Sony, death threats ... his existence threatened, Michael's health was way down, he had an attack of lupus and his hair was falling out in clumps, he had to have his nose operated on because otherwise he wouldn't have been able to breathe, and he was totally depressed in those days. Shmuley dragged him in front of the public, at a time when Michael would have liked to crawl away and hide. Because of him he popped tons of pills... so he was able to talk with him. Still. At least Shmuley didn't act out of greed. But anyone who directs Michael in a way that does not fit with the business is eliminated anyway."

"What do you mean by that?" I asked, worried.

"Simple," she said. "When Shmuley's influence on Michael was getting too much, his advisers made it clear to Shmuley that he was no longer considered good company for Michael - and they simply removed him from his life."

***

In the evening I sat by the pond. Alone. With only the moon and the clouds. The wind blew through my hair, and I breathed in the air deeply. Enjoyed the breeze and held my face in it. I longed for peace and simplicity, longed for my family. To be precise: I was awfully homesick that night. I'd been here for four months now. I had seen less of the States than I had expected. And still, I wouldn't have wanted to miss a single second. The night was so beautiful, and involuntarily I thought of Neverland. To be in Neverland on such a night must be the ultimate dream. To sit on the Giving Tree with the knowledge that humanity is not everything that life has to offer here on earth. To feel this more-than-ness, detachment from the body, and troubled thoughts ... on nights like this you could see the true freedom, when you felt no bonds, no desires, no needs, when you were happy with only yourself and what you feel deep inside your heart. I thought of my children and my husband at home, and streams of love and longing flowed from my heart. I imagined how these flew without time delay across the ocean, into my little village, into my house, into the hearts of my children and my husband and I closed my eyes. A smile came to my lips - all three of them were with me.

I sat by the water for a long time, in this bottomless, all encompassing happiness, and restlessness left me, all of that anxiety, all that uncertainty, all of those disturbing thoughts and brooding. To attain this state of being, I knew, was our goal.

The conversations with Michael gave me a lot, but they also inevitably pulled me into this tangle of intrigue and manipulation around money, power and greed. It was impossible to withstand it. I longed for my quiet life in the countryside, for walks with my friend in German fields and meadows, for a super-boring cup of coffee by myself on the terrace. For almost nostalgic reasons, I packed a basket of snacks in the afternoon and provided the guards with coffee and biofood, like I used to do for my children.

"Man, Chirelle," Jason chewed. "What are we going to do when you're not here anymore? My wife wants to have your recipes, because otherwise I'll just stuff myself with donuts again. My digestion…" Jason rolled his eyes meaningfully. "…I'm telling you ... great digestion because of your health food stuff ... and the ginger ... I've really lost some weight…"

"Where?" asked Bob, who was sitting with us. "In your brain? It's definitely shrunk, you can see that clearly from the outside."

While the two were squabbling, I headed with my empty basket towards the park, I had seen wildflowers growing along the fence, and I wanted to put a couple of them in a vase.

All around the grounds there were secret entrances and exits, small doors camouflaged by lush shrubbery, and of course all locked - you needed a key from the guards. My flowers were growing close to such a door – that's how

I discovered it. I crouched into the bushes and began to cut purple and white flowers, unknown to me, with a small knife. I was just putting the first ones into my basket when I heard voices. Instinctively, I squeezed tighter in the bushes until I was completely hidden behind them. No one could see me, but I had a good view of the little door through the branches.

Greg was there, the old gardener; it was said that he had been with Michael forever and he kept him on because Greg did not want to leave and he could still do light work in the garden. I'd had almost no contact with him during my stay here. He was very taciturn and rarely joined the company of others.

Now he stood at the gate and was talking to someone who stood in the shelter of the trees. Someone with jeans, t-shirt, three-day stubble, a cap that covered his very short hair and the inevitable sunglasses. The age was impossible to make out. It could have been a teenager around 20 or a vital 40-year-old. I couldn't make it out clearly.

The boy/man gave Greg a small envelope. That alone roused conflicting emotions in me. Greg took it, looked at it briefly, nodded. They talked. Straining with effort, I tried to understand some of what they were saying. "…support …" said the boy/man. "…slowly time … he has to … could blow up …personnel … prepared … but time … limited … definitely dangerous for him … delivered … got off this stuff … impressionable … "

The wind rustled in the trees, and the noise made it even harder to understand. The softly spoken snippets of conversation drifted over to me. What remained in my memory was 'blow up', 'got off this stuff', 'impressionable' and 'not much longer'.

With bated breath, I crouched in that bush like a stupid spy. The boy/man raised his hand in farewell. He smiled. My heart stopped. I knew that smile. I knew that smile really well. It was Tom's smile.

***

"I saw you," said Michael, looking at me with a peculiar look.

"Saw me?" I asked, thinking first about my spy position in the bush.

"Yes, last night at the lake."

"Okay." I did not know what he was driving at and looked at him confused.

This time he was the one who stroked my cheek, and he smiled an incredible smile. I hadn't seen him smile like that for a long time. It was an untroubled, joyful smile, free of all worry.

"Chirelle," he said, sounding in really good spirits, "tonight. We have to continue. I've made up my mind about something."

"About what?"

"Well, I'll tell you then. We'll start earlier. 6 pm?"

"Sure," I said, surprised at his very different mood. There was something fresh about him, something dynamic, something I associated with Michael from the 90s and 80s, something he seemed to have lost and had now recovered.

"Why are you so different?" I wanted to know.

"Like I said, Chirelle, I made up my mind about something. And I have the absolute feeling that you're right, that the garbage has to get out of me ... I need to see things differently and take them on in a different way."

Downright excited he paced back and forth in the room. Surprised, I tracked him with my eyes.

"When we are through with it, I'll share something with you, Chi," he promised. "But for now I just want to keep going."

Again he stroked my cheek, eyes shining, then he hugged me.

"Get ready for a long night," he warned me and grinned again with this more than charming, irresistible smile. And I began to suspect that the fascination I'd felt up to this point for him was nothing in comparison to the Michael free of burden and obstruction. He was intoxicating, enchanting. A light and an incredible power emanated from him. And all of that without a stage.

XX / 1995 In the mountains

"He'll never get back on his feet ... he'll never get rid of that reputation... that's screwed on ... implanted ... w"re going to the next step ... keep working on his image ... that's so important to him ...since he likes to be so special ... he can have that! The more irresponsible he appears to the public, the less they'll believe his statements ... Nobody will believe anything he says. Is he still being a good boy and taking his medicine? Great, he's riding himself into it ... what can you do ... really sad ... hehe..."

***

I stored the scene with Tom a little further back in my brain. I was neither a strategist nor criminologist and had little talent for research. To follow him, spy on him or the like were not options for me. I had hardly any time at all to try to put two and two together. It was 5 p.m. and too late to ask Grace. In one hour Michael wanted to meet and he was usually punctual.

Effortlessly we sank into the period when Evan Chandler's sad remnants smoldered on the horizon.

Lisa

As soon as Michael was back in the States, he met Lisa. She was still married to Danny Keough, and they had two children, so they were as discreet as possible. At first no one knew of their affair - except Debbie.

"Debbie, she's wonderful!" Michael raved as he sat on the table and Debbie as always quietly performed her work. She smiled slightly, let him rave, and did not comment on his remarks. Michael was, in spite of the recent disaster, happy - for the first time since he had come to her in the practice - because of a woman.

She was sincerely happy for him; she was quite aware that she could not elicit such feelings in him - she was not Michael's type. She did not even stop to think if she would have liked it to be different. It was the way it was. Michael loved Lisa, Debbie loved Michael, and she was grateful to the last cell of her body that she was allowed to be his friend because she knew that friendship lasts forever. A marriage... not necessarily. Whether Lisa would ever be able to give Mike what she felt for him was at this time entirely uncertain. Lost in thought, she pursued her work.

Only after a while Michael noticed that Debbie was unusually quiet.

"Debbie?" he asked. "Is everything all right?"

"Yes, of course. Sure. Everything is fine." But her eyes avoided contact with his, and she pretended she was busier than she was.

"Debbie," said Michael softly. "I hope it doesn't hurt you when I talk about Lisa?"

"No, Michael, not at all," answered Debbie and glanced up briefly. They were both silent and after a while, she said: "You must never forget one thing, Michael: I'm your friend - forever and ever. You can rely on me 100% in every situation, and because that's the way it is, my only wish is that you're happy - no matter how. That's really all I want."

Michael had at this time at least two women who were central to his life. One born into the world of Hollywood, beautiful, desirable, talented; and the other sturdy, from the world of one bedroom apartments on streets with heavy traffic, overdrawn bank account, motorcycle outside the front door, a bottle of beer in her hand. The similarities: Both were straightforward and open and did not mince words. Both stood behind Michael. Both gave him support.

1994

"Lisa, would you come to Neverland tonight?" he asked, and the questions made his heart pound so hard that it felt as if the stereo was turned on.

"You mean over night?"

"Yes, overnight. Will you stay with me?"

Lisa was silent for a few seconds - with closed eyes Michael pressed the phone to his ear. Then her voice said:
"I'm coming. I'll be with you in three hours."

It was a moonlit night when, after dinner, they went outside and sought out the quieter corners at Neverland. Michael showed Lisa his favorite places and gently grasped her slender fingers. Hand in hand, they walked and talked. They never ran out of topics of conversation. Lisa had the same sense of humor as he did, and he could laugh with her so wonderfully. Oh, and she was so worthy of adoration, so beautiful, so exciting and so sexy! Michael stopped and looked at her with his huge, deep dark eyes. This gaze alone made Lisa's heart drop into a chasm. Fascinated, she lost herself in this sensation, felt his body, the narrow hips, the slim, muscular legs, smelled his scent. Michael wrapped his arm around her and pulled her to him. Gently he put his hand in her hair, bent her head back slightly, stared at her with these so unfathomable, deep eyes. Her heart began to pound wildly.
"You're ... so ... incredibly ... sexy," he whispered hoarsely in her ear, sending shivers down her spine. Michael felt her trembling in his arms and pressed her lithe body tightly. He felt her heart fluttering in her chest like a little excited bird and could not believe that he was the one who caused it. Animal instincts came up in him, shut off his mind, letting him feel only this arousing body in his arms and the almost painful longing of wanting to touch it everywhere.
With no holding back he pressed his lips on hers, consuming her. Lisa's breath caught in her throat and she felt as if she were plunging down for miles. The surroundings were completely wiped out. What Michael was doing to her was neither shy nor asexual. Hungrily, he pressed her against him, whispered in her ear, pushed his lean body against hers. Lisa let out a gasp, both of them were under a spell and could barely take the desire.
They hardly made it to the bedroom, where they descended upon each other as if he were the last man and she the last woman on earth. Michael was in a state of euphoria he had never before experienced. He found in her passionate response, complete oneness. Lisa and he harmonized in a way he had never thought possible, and the way they made love was so beautiful to him that all the grossness that he had experienced around this topic was pushed far into the background, where it partially disintegrated. It was fulfilling. It was gigantic. It was the best thing that had ever happened to him in life. Love flamed up in his heart, grateful, indelibly and ever-lasting.
And that night he repeated his marriage proposal, in a really romantic way, with roses and champagne and all the bells and whistles. Lisa said 'yes' and made Michael the happiest man in the world.

302

The more Michael got involved with Lisa, the more he fell in love with her. A feeling of elation came over him, one that let him hope: He could make it again, there was a new beginning, moreover, on a completely different basis. Evan had been a test and God did not want him to give up. He owed it to the children of this world that he would keep helping them, that he didn't give in. Life went on.

And Lisa...she was simply everything! She was the glamorous diva, gorgeous in evening dress, jewels and big makeup. She was the tough biker chick in a leather jacket, ripped jeans and tousled hair, sitting in a bar and making sassy comments. She was soft and tender, and she knew the world in which he lived.

Michael loved beautiful women, he loved their shapes, their bodies, and sometimes he got magazines in which he traced the perfect curves with an admiring finger. Lisa had a body like that. She had her father's intense eyes, his sensual lips, a cute nose, and she was bubbly and independent. Oh, he loved her, he loved her! She had turned to him at a time where everyone else had done the opposite. What better proof of their love? And yes - even the fact that she was who she was, that he could prove to the world that he was normal and man enough for a woman like Lisa, played a role. The King of Pop and the daughter of The King! It couldn't get any better than that! It was second nature for him to give image a high priority. His bruised reputation hurt him and his marriage to Lisa Marie was definitely a possible way to not only eradicate the Evan business, but also the hated Wacko Jacko image. He loved Lisa from the bottom of his heart, but at the same time he could not resist calculating thoughts, they were the icing on the cake of his love. He had been in this business for too long not to think that way, and his advisers were tooting into the same image horn.

This true love between them, the wonderful outlook for a family life - his own children! - restored his old enthusiasm.

To his own astonishment, Michael was an almost happy man, so shortly after the Chandler affair, despite the expected negative headlines that cruelly pleaded him guilty because he had paid an eight-figure sum. He faced his life with a new courage, a life in which he would not be alone anymore. He would have children, he would have a family - there was a life after Chandler, whose predictions didn't all have to come true.

"We'll have a real small ceremony," she said, and suggested a place in the Dominican Republic, where they could get married by a justice of the peace without much bureaucracy.

"No, if we get married, then it should be big," contradicted Michael. "I want a fairy tale wedding, with you in the lead role! This wedding will move the world and overthrow all prejudices!"

"What prejudices?" Lisa asked suspiciously. "Michael, this is all about us, and I don't see this wedding as a means to improve your image."

Michael blushed.

"But Lisa," he said, and felt stupid. He loved her, but he also loved a huge production ... and yes ... this wedding would have had this super side effect that would have benefited them both, but still ... he was ashamed. He didn't want Lisa to think it was his main reason, mostly because it simply wasn't. He would have just liked to take along the side effects, already had visions and ideas to make this wedding the dream wedding of the century. He would compose a song specifically, a show just for Lisa ... fireworks and rainbows...a video... a new CD... this wedding was going to be bigger and better than Dianas' and Charles'! Something the world had never seen before!

But he didn't want Lisa to believe that he was wanting it only for this reason, and so he gave in. They had a very ordinary wedding in the Dominican Republic, without any pomp, without the press and without anyone else hearing about it - neither his family nor Lisa's mother Priscilla. Michael could not help feeling disappointed and the entire ceremony was awkward to him. Katherine was the only one they called later.

All the other family members heard of the marriage through a press-release as did the rest of the world. Lisa's mother, Priscilla Presley, was horrified. She was completely convinced that her daughter, who was afflicted with the helper syndrome, had fallen victim to a strategic move by a quirky pop star with a tainted image.

Lisa and Michael's entire social circle met this news with suspicion and skepticism.

Life with Lisa was refreshing. For Michael it was like a holiday, far away from the usual stress, but after the first exciting weeks he gradually returned to the daily routines, worked zealously at redoing his life and rehabilitating his image. Thousands of new tunes came to him, lyrics, videos, arrangements and ideas. And not to forget, visions of a happy family with their own children.

Initially it was a shock for Lisa to see the tenacious way that Michael was attacked by reporters. A shock because now she was involved, too. And so she found herself in a situation where first and foremost she was faced with combatting Michael's whacko-image, rather than unraveling his soul life in peace and quiet, which burdened her over time more than she wanted to admit.

But Lisa was one-of-a-kind; she rolled up her sleeves and jumped into the action.

She sat with Michael in TV interviews and intervened when he was trying to say things that he could never adequately convey, because the journalists jumped onto every twistable and re-interpretable word. She defended him and his love for children, instinctively doing the right thing: brushing over the mystical and simply portraying Michael as someone who just happened to have a special talent in dealing with children, as this so happens to be the case with some people. She stood behind him and showed it at every opportunity.

Yet it was exactly this that caused the first conflicts in their marriage, because Michael was still talking openly about having children sleep in his bedroom. After this Jordy-shit? The implications should be the first to occur to someone who was so concerned about his image!

"Michael," she said angrily, following an interview with a reporter, who, although describing herself as serious, at the same time had no problem manipulating Lisa's decision for Michael in front of an audience of millions, with nasty questions - as if she had married a sea lion! (How could you marry Michael Jackson? And you go to bed with him? - while Michael was sitting right next to her). Lisa was appalled at the way journalists felt that they could treat him - and now her. The anger about that was as strong as about Michael.

"Stop talking about your children bedroom stories," she raged.

"Why?" Michael asked, puzzled and hurt. "It's something completely innocent!"

"I know that. And you know that! But it's something that no one out there will understand! Never! Not in 100 years! You're just hurting yourself!"

"But for me it's the most important thing of all!" cried Michael. "The host asked me and I had to answer! Should I have lied? And I don't want to deny what is most important in this world: namely to give children a home and security! I want to set an example for that!"

"But you are not an example because people interpret something bad into it! Why is that not clear to you? I just can't get that into my head!"

"But I don't want to give up what the essence of me is! What I live for!"

"Nobody says that you have to give it up. But it's stupid to talk about it!"

Michael closed his mouth, hurt. The word that reached him above all was 'stupid'. Lisa felt it. Conciliatory, she put her arm around his shoulders.

"The host was so awful," she said. "She just wouldn't let up until ... until she had at least a little of what she wanted ... what is it with you, buddy, that they harass you like this?"

Michael smiled thinly. That was not something he was proud of. Lisa laughed at his face and said: "Fuck the media!"

Michael started to giggle.

"Hey, little one," he said and grabbed her. "Before I do that with the media...
I think, you're a much more attractive subject..."

He jumped up and wanted to grab her, but Lisa screamed and ran off.
Laughing, they raced through the garden, until Lisa pushed Michael into the
pool and jumped after him, screeching like a banshee.

Then: a warm bath, cozy blankets and a hot night. And Michael fell asleep,
with the knowledge that she would be next to him when he woke up. His
heart still fluttered when he thought of all this, as if this heart didn't dare
consider this good fortune its own.

With fervor he processed the events of recent years in 'Ghost' and 'Blood on
the dance floor', and was away a lot for business. Lisa, however, got to know
some people from Michael's camp and had a bad feeling. These were people
with whom you had to count your fingers after you shook hands with them.
An uneasy feeling crept over her. Her father had had similar vermin around
him. Yes-sayers who did everything the boss wanted, whether it helped or
hurt him - as long as it was to their advantage. Intriguers who consciously
spread lies in order to sow discord in the own ranks, with the aim to become
the sole confidant and thus have the power - and double players who fed the
hyena named media and themselves by promising them juicy mouthfuls of
human flesh in return for huge sums of money.

When Lisa had planned to get Michael out of his predicament, she had
counted on herself only ... and not to have to stand up to an army of
arrogant egomaniacs and schemers, not thought to be treated as a
commodity, as part of the 'Jackson business".

It depleted her faster than she had thought. Closely she snuggled at night to
Michael, uncertain who needed more protection and advocacy: he or she.

"Lisa?" he asked softly and lifted her chin. "Is everything okay?"

She nodded, she did not want to dwell on this that evening and fell asleep
after a while in his arms as he was watching "The Three Stooges" for the
1000th time and laughed at the same slapsticks that even she already knew by
heart.

**

Noises traveled through her outer ear, pushed through the ear canal to her
eardrum, were converted and translated into chemical and electrical signals in
her brain, formed words into a vague idea which in turn led to various
emotions in her ... that sank into her consciousness, signaled danger, and
then finally pushed her internal alarm button, awakening her abruptly from
sleep.

Lisa jumped up. Disoriented, she listened in the darkness.

"Noises," announced her brain: "not locatable noises. What is that?"

Michael was not next to her. Some of the sounds came from the flushing toilet, but her brain had not declared these disturbing - there were also other sounds. Choking, gasping noises. She got up and tried to get into the bathroom. The door was locked.

Lisa went back to bed. When Mike came out, she turned on the light and looked at him. In a split second, he hid his face behind his large hands and ran back into the bathroom. Lisa knew he would put on makeup before he came back to her. After that, he still looked terrible. Pale and haggard. Pain in his eyes. Wordlessly, she patted the place next to her.

"Come here, babe," she said, smiling with worry in her eyes. "What's the matter?"

Trembling, Michael lay down beside her and pulled the covers over his head, in another attempt to hide his face. She gently pulled back the blanket, took his head in her hands and forced him to look at her.

"You have the most beautiful eyes in the world," she whispered tenderly, and breathed a kiss on his lips. "Bad dream?"

"Yeah..." Michael whispered, resting his head on her chest. "I ... I'm sorry ... I didn't mean to wake you up..."

"It's all right ... tell me ... what did you dream about?"

And Lisa let him tell her what had happened in his dream. Haltingly, the first time in his life, he told another person about the walls that pushed in on him and monsters that wanted to eat him. In every nightmare he was supposed to die, with someone after him, wanting to kill him. And he ran and ran, but his legs were like lead, moving in slow motion, he could barely lift them, while the pursuers were getting closer and closer. Until he woke up screaming and drenched in sweat. Alone in a hotel room, he was unable to fall asleep again afterwards. But today ... today, he heard a soothing voice, there was someone there. Lisa stayed awake with him. Many nights. For that reason alone Michael loved her. There was someone who would wake him up before the pursuers could kill him.

***

"Are you afraid I wouldn't like you without makeup?" she asked him one night when he again sank onto the mattress fully made up.

Michael's sheets were changed daily. Thick traces of makeup covered the pillows and duvet after every night. And in the morning he always tried to get into the bathroom before Lisa.

The eyes of a child yearning for love looked at her. A child that believed only beauty would be loved. Only accomplishment and perfection. He didn't answer her question.

"I think," said Lisa, "...everyone feels like that. I mean, you get made up so great when you go out with someone ... and everyone is afraid of the moment when they show themselves to the other without makeup."

"I'm not beautiful," he said softly. "But I would like to be."

"You *are* beautiful," said Lisa moved. "You just think otherwise. Is that why you've had so many surgeries?"

"Lisa," he said and he propped himself up. "I didn't want to have so many surgeries. I had to. The first nose job wasn't done right ... in the 80s the doctors weren't where they are today. It had to be re-operated. When that happened I requested the nostrils closer. I had exactly two cosmetic rhinoplastic surgeries. All other surgeries were compelling necessities. The nasal septum began to dissolve and a couple of other problems appeared that you don't really want to hear about ... I mean ... I'm not ... not healthy ... Lisa."

He stopped abruptly. The reason for this was so apparent that Lisa's heart turned heavy.

"Are you afraid of death?" she asked straight out.

"No," he replied spontaneously. "I'm more afraid of being old and sick, in an ailing body. Lisa, I think I'm going to die like your father ... the pictures that you've described ... those are my pictures..."

"Why do you think something like that?" Lisa asked, agitated. "Please don't believe that! You want to live forever ... you always say that you don't want to die!"

Michael smiled. "Being immortal has many meanings," he said. "You don't have to be alive for that."

"But this is connected with the fact that you don't want to look old? Are you afraid of that?" she pursued, stubbornly.

"Who wants that?" he sighed. "Come on, Lisa, in our business? Who can afford to age naturally? Hollywood is a plastic surgery capital. The pressure to look good is enormous. How else can you survive?"

"I don't believe that," said Lisa. "Look at Mick Jagger ... and others, too ... you don't have to submit to this expectation ... and anyway ... what keeps you from breaking out from this madness ... to live somewhere else and lead a completely different life?"

Mike was silent at the question. Then he said:

"The idea is not far-fetched ... but the time is not right yet. "

"What do you mean by that?" she asked.

"They wouldn't let me ... I mean ... I ... there's still so much to do ... and I don't want to go yet, not with this image..."

"But ... why don't you talk about what you told me?" Lisa interrupted. "Don't you think the public would understand that?"

"Nope," Michael said with conviction. "With everyone else, but not with me. The tabloids would make something completely different out of it. I'm not going to even try."

Lisa paused. What he said was not to be dismissed. She had seen for herself how hopeless his efforts were to achieve something positive in the print media or on TV. That was unsettling to her. She had never encountered hostility in such a form before. And it was now clear to her that she was also being mercilessly processed by this meat grinder, the press. She wanted to start a career for herself, but without Michael's help because she was too proud to have people say she had made a breakthrough only because of him. And that was exactly the first thing that the writers had reported: the marriage was one of convenience - career in exchange for image.

The largest bond between them was created by their nightly conversations - which were the best moments she and Michael shared. In these nights, they were infinitely close. If Michael could not sleep, Lisa was there. If he didn't awake from a nightmare, she pulled him out. Then she held his flailing arms, pressed them down, gave him support. She firmly held his narrow body and rocked him back and forth. Regardless of her own fatigue and her still healthy need for sleep, she talked to him, stroked him, kissed him. They talked about his fears, about his past, his father, his family, about everything they could bring up from the depths of his soul. For hours they lay on the big bed, talked and talked. Often these conversations ended with them holding each other in their arms and falling asleep, sometimes with them breaking out in laughter over some silly thing, and Michael would then chase Lisa around the bed and they would throw pillows at each other. Or they got dressed, roamed through Neverland and fell asleep somewhere where it was cuddly, like children.

"Hey, Michael," she whispered in his ear during these nights and snuggled up to him. "You're not alone ... never again... you're not alone."

"Yes, Lisa," he said happily. "I know ... and it's so beautiful. And soon we'll be even more."

Lisa was the best thing that had ever happened in Michael's life. He loved her more every day. And looked forward to having children with her.

It was a night by the fire, when Lisa - this time in great detail - told him about the death of her father. Michael had an uncanny affinity for the suffering of others. He was involved 100% in her story as if he were the one who had gone through all this. Silently he listened to her.

"Something's gone, that you had deemed secure," she said quietly. "I was nine, you don't really think about death then. But ... sometimes when I was sitting on Daddy's lap, I thought I felt a shadow, and I begged him not to die, not to leave me here alone. He had given up internally ... maybe that was what I felt. I wanted to ask him so much, I wanted so much to give him courage to live...I mean, there was me...why couldn't he want to live for *me*?"

Tears poured from her eyes, and Michael, who was sitting behind her, held her to him as gently and firmly as he could.

She pressed her lips together and stared into the fire. "I ... I didn't really believe ... didn't really believe that this was the end ... and when the ambulance came up the driveway, these people all pushing around on him, attaching machines, injecting things, everything became chaos, I was just standing there, screaming. That's when I swore that never in my life would I endure such pain again. And that's just how my life turned out after my father's death. I avoided potential pain, which really means: I avoided responsibility for my life. I was afraid to do things wrong, so I didn't even try them. I numbed myself. All day long. From booze to drugs, I took everything, was always in a daze. I was no longer living, just vegetating and maybe barely even that. I imitated my father even after his death: in the end he was just matter, with no soul in him that made him alive. And I was just as empty. He hadn't wanted to stay with me. I hadn't been worth it. I was just a body and my soul was ... I don't know where it was. I couldn't feel it."

Michael cried, and his tears dropped on her hair.

"What triggered the change?" he asked hoarsely.

"I wanted to live," she said simply, and turned around in his arms. The iris of her eyes were the color of a mountain lake and incredibly intense.

"One day I was so far down that I felt the ground under my feet again. These are moments full of ... grace, because they inject you with a thought that has the power to pull you out. I realized: I didn't want to be the product of others' mistakes. I realized I have *my* life, and no one else can live that for me. In that second, I understood that life is a gift and that it's not right to treat it the way I had."

Michael did not respond for a long time to her words. Tightly, he held her in his arms, this very delicate and yet very strong person. With immense gratitude he grasped that this person would stand behind him. That this person had promised before God to be there for him, in good times and bad.

It was almost creepy how the two had sought and found one another. Lisa was paralyzed by a father with a painkiller addiction and drug problems and since she still hadn't fully processed it, she attracted another man just like him, so she could finally solve it.

And Michael was called to solve his father-childhood problems and bound himself to someone who had to make peace with the past - just like he did.

They were a perfect fit. The only question was whether they could work through it. There were a lot of unpredictable variables in this game - which Lisa hadn't guessed at yet.

***

Michael observed this; his image had suffered, but his fans were still there. People's fascination with him continued unabated. He caused riots wherever he went. Everything as usual! He had survived the storm not entirely intact, but still. It could go on.

His crew jabbered that he needed to show the world that he was a man, a real man ... they told him that it was his duty to restore his reputation after the Chandler mess, that he owed that to Sony, too. With these demands, Lisa fell into the clutches of his PR machine, not for the first time. Michael and his advisers wanted them to kiss after her first performance in front of his fans. She refused to serve as public proof of his masculinity. But Michael wanted the kiss, too - and he prevailed.

And when he introduced Lisa to his fans as his wife, walked down the catwalk with her, dangerously close to a screaming inferno of enthusiastic, crying and screaming fans, and gave her their widely discussed public kiss, he was proud and happy to have such a woman at his side.

But Lisa felt used - and not for the first time.

Michael didn't give it much thought, however. His beautiful wife seemed terribly straightforward, independent and she loved her freedom, so he let his life simply continue the way it had been.

The prospect of having own children after a time defined the essence of the relationship. It was clear to him that when Lisa was finally pregnant, everything would be even much more beautiful. However, discrepancies were inevitable: Lisa had experience with relationships and had matured in them as opposed to Michael who was in his first-ever partnership. He had no idea about living together and all it entailed. Had he been in the situation with Jordy, a 13-year-old boy in search of his best friend, then his relationship age now would have corresponded to that of a 17– or 18-year old at most. He was an inexperienced young person, clumsy and awkward when it came to the psyches of women - a condition in which many men remain because the souls of woman seem too complicated. And so he hung out like teenagers like to do, with former friends, and with those he had previously enjoyed - with children. Ever since he had become a superstar, he didn't have to be considerate of other people's daily schedule, and he didn't even notice when he bulldozed over Lisa with his routine.

Another important issue was: what model for a relationship could he have followed other than his parents? Katherine had basically always followed his father's wishes and supported him, even with things that she did not fully approve of internally. And reinforcing this pattern: He was Michael Jackson. He had only to say his name to get what he wanted. And so he firmly believed subconsciously that Lisa would align herself with him and his lifestyle.

Lisa, for her part, had to overcome her own childhood trauma, and the commonalities between Elvis and Michael were too apparent for her to ignore. She wanted to be his helping angel and do what she thought she had failed to do for her father. The misconception they both had was that nothing gets better if one looks for the solution in a change of circumstances or people.

And their surroundings did not make it easier for them.

Lisa was pressured early on from all sides. Her mother was extremely suspicious of Michael. She did not like him and had little willingness to open up to him in order to understand his essence. She was convinced that he was using her only daughter for prestige purposes and was not really interested in her. And Lisa's friends, her entire circle responded with incomprehension to her marriage to Michael. A woman who had ten men wrapped around every finger chose Wacko Jacko? For he was not a real man for them - rather an alien, strange and not normal - and the timing of the proposal too obvious to be sincere. And in addition this persistent desire for children!

"What do you think is going to happen once he has the children?" asked an acquaintance pointedly. "Is he going to divorce you because then he got what he wanted? You said yourself that Michael thinks he can get anything he wants."

The constant repetition of these evil suspicions made their mark on Lisa, especially since she saw that Michael was not willing to give up certain things.

His friends lived in his house, as if it were theirs, they came and went as it suited them. Like in a hotel they had 24-hour room service and a restaurant. Michael often hung out with them, and then he was like a teenager who needed his buddies more than his wife because they understood him better. And then...children...children again and again! Unknown children, adolescents and young adults from all over the world were standing all at once in Neverland's kitchen and identified themselves as Michael's guest. When she asked him about it, he shrugged his shoulders and said:

"It's just a few days... we're happy for them from the depth of our hearts, right?"

In front of the gates were fans, at any time of day or night. They were lying in the bushes, sleeping in their cars, followed the limos that left Neverland, if there was only the slightest chance that Michael was in one of them. And occasionally he opened the gates for them and let them in.

"Look, Lisa, how happy they are!" he said then, and his face glowed when he could give them that joy. "They always have gifts, and sometimes they wait for weeks in front of the gate. Would you not let them in?"

Lisa sighed. That was the part that was still the easiest to understand and to endure, especially since Michael didn't mingle with the fans and at most watched them from the window.

But thank God there were the connecting moments in their relationship, especially the nights that made Lisa think of what had moved her to say her 'I do.'

And it was one of those nights that inspired Michael to make a short film about this miracle of their relationship. Lisa was lying in the dim light of the bedroom on the rumpled sheets and blankets, stretched out like a statue by Michelangelo, adoringly beautiful. The lanterns placed tastefully in the bedroom cast shadows on her curves and played with the reflections of her necklace. Her very beautiful, iridescent eyes glittered with a light that made Michael absolutely speechless. Lisa said something, lolled on the pillow and closed her eyes. His eyes went from her feet to the slender legs, the curve of her hips, the waist, which was so narrow that Michael could circle it entirely with his big hands, to the full upper body where he loved to nestle, up to her chiseled face.

God, she was so beautiful! And he felt that what he experienced with Lisa was so unique that he wanted to share it. It urged him to show the world how much they loved each other. When R. Kelly offered him the song 'You are not alone', Michael knew he had to turn it into a very unique video that showed the aesthetics of their relationship to everyone. Lisa initially agreed, but after the clip was published, she felt that it came across the wrong way ... in an exhibitionist way. What actually belonged to only the two of them had been made public.

***

"Lisa, can you pick me up when you're in town?" Michael asked after breakfast.

"Sure, where should I be?" she asked, and wiped toast crumbs from her mouth. He gave her the address of a doctor. She didn't ask any further.

But soon she had to pick him up from this, then that, doctor. Michael did not like to drive by himself, and he used the opportunity to see Lisa.

"Why are you seeing so many doctors?" she asked him, alarmed.

"Because everyone is a specialist in his field," said Michael. "Internists, dermatologists ...routine check ups... I have to get them because of the insurance ... because of the concerts ... you know, I have to go on tour again…"

Lisa was satisfied with that.

Until she picked him up one day and Michael's coordination was obviously off. Alarm bells rang. Frantically she turned them off. Michael said they had put something in his eyes, so they could examine them... everything was fine. Lisa forced herself to think of other things. Face to face with her deepest fears, she tried to avoid the confrontation for as long as possible.

But then more and more things occurred that she did not understand and that cast an unexpected light on Michael.

He was preparing for an event appearance and was in the hotel room with Lisa. After breakfast countless people showed up and Michael suddenly became someone who maneuvered them around in an extremely professional way. Lisa, too.

"Bob, you have responsibility for her," he said, and told him exactly the complicated plan that would bring Lisa safely out of the room and into a limo.

"Call the paparazzi. Give them a tip that we are leaving via the freight elevator. Tell the others that we are taking the back door ... and tell them that Lisa could already be pregnant ... Lisa ... you could stuff a small pillow under your dress, what do you think, that would create a stir!" he giggled. "Or ... I know something better! You collapse - into my arms ... that'll look great! I'm the worried husband ... and then we say it's because you're probably pregnant…"

Speechless, Lisa listened. He made quite a few more instructions in this direction, some pretty crazy, like a hoax for the press, which denomination the not-even-yet-conceived baby would adopt ... then she intervened.

"Are you out of your mind?" she snapped at him.

Michael looked at her dumbfounded. He had almost forgotten that she was in the room. Then he smiled.

"Lisa, sweetie ... we have to give them something to nibble on, or they'll write a lot worse things," he explained.

"But ... I'm not pregnant!"

"That's not the point ... it's just a rumor we can live well with, right?" Michael giggled, but Lisa did not join in.

"And what are my children supposed to think when they read that in the paper?" she asked indignantly.

Without thinking Mike handed her the phone. "Call them," he advised, "and…"

"Forget it," she hissed, turned and simply stalked out of the room, regardless of all the previous strategizing.

She did not understand. Michael complained constantly about the lies of the press ... and then created some himself? What set of values was that?
She did not know then that this was his only chance to keep the proliferative reporting in check, at least to some degree.

That Michael was so looking forward to having children quickly became counterproductive. He could hardly wait for Lisa to get pregnant. He asked her every day about it ... and he asked her so many times that it was gradually becoming annoying and the suspicion crept up in her slowly and sneakily that Michael had married her only for that reason. What was she to him? A birthing-machine? An image-polish? She saw how he lived his life, saw him with these slimy people around him, and sometimes she did not know where he was, he never asked her how she had spent the day. He worked around the clock, was home less than she had thought. Lisa wanted, just like Michael, to be loved for her own sake.
That's probably why they had met in the first place.

"What is that?" he asked disappointed when he found a box in the bathroom containing unmistakable feminine hygiene products. Lisa felt guilty, something she couldn't stand. Aggressive because he made her feel shitty and she felt reduced to the role of a stud mare, she turned around and said coldly:
"Michael, I'm using birth control. I don't want to have children yet. I already have two - they are having a hard time coping with the fact that because of you I divorced Danny so quickly ... I can't present them with a half-sister or brother right now. You should be the first person who gets that."
But Michael didn't get it. He was boundlessly disappointed... He longed so much for children and Lisa was his wife. A woman who controlled birth! Lisa didn't want children with him! He couldn't believe it.

He repeatedly brought up the issue with her. The more he brought it up, the more she resisted.
Frustrated, she met up with her ex-husband, and cried herself out. It felt so good to be together with someone who wanted nothing from her ... and certainly no children. At the end of their meeting, she hugged him long and intimately.
"Thank you, Danny," she said. "It's so good that you're there."
A photo was taken and sent to Michael. He gritted his teeth and felt a hole in his stomach. Not Lisa, he prayed. Please not Lisa! I love her. Please let me have Lisa.

After that they argued vehemently because Michael still had his pictures taken with children.

"Is your head full of straw?" she yelled, frustrated with him and his inability to respond to her arguments, although it had looked as if he could at the beginning of their relationship.

"Lisa, this is something ... something you cannot understand," he defended himself. "But I want so much that you understand it ... do you have any idea what children give me? You know, I want to…"

"This helping-thing-a-ma-jig - you can stick that!" shouted Lisa. "With all this sheer helping, you forget that there are people in your immediate vicinity who would also be very happy with your understanding! And who you are harming with all that!"

"Does that mean that you don't want me to continue with my charity work?" asked Michael.

"That's not what I'm saying! But it would be nice if you could see beyond your own needs!"

Michael was silent. Upset, Lisa continued: "And I don't know if you can get it into your head that you are putting me in a bad position with all this baby stuff."

"What do you mean?" Michael asked anxiously.

"By that I mean that I, as your wife, have to share your image. And until now mine was pretty much in one piece. I don't feel like being the wife of a…"

Michael went pale. Lisa as well. Quietly, he said:

"If your image is so important to you, it would be one more reason to have children. So many things would be out of the way then."

"Your image is not a reason for me to have children," she said icily.

"But ... I would really like to have them with you, Lisa," said Michael, close to tears. "With you! I mean ... I really love you! I…Lisa!"

But Lisa turned away.

"Leave," he thought. "I have to go, I need distance."

"Don't run away," she begged him.

"Lisa ... I…"

"Michael, about ... the other day I'm sorry."

"Lisa, you know ... I love you ... all I want is for us to be a real family…"

"Michael, I'm not ready. We have been married for just six months ... I mean…we've time!"

"But I'm ten years older than you! You can't imagine how I long for our own baby!" Michael looked at her with tears in his eyes. Her admission that she did not want children pushed him to deep despair. If he wanted something, then he wanted it right away.

316

"Yes, but you've got me," she said provocatively. "Isn't that enough? Do we have to start with baby making? Why can't we just enjoy ourselves as a couple, before we get red eyes from crying babies?"

Michael did not recognize the call for help behind this. For him his happiness would have been completed with a baby, and he could not understand that Lisa thought differently. His desire made him terribly insensitive.

***

"Why doesn't she want children?" asked Debbie and put the beer bottle to her lips. Mighty gulps swishing down her throat. Michael watched as the liquid ran down her throat in pulsating movements. Debbie put the bottle down and wiped her hand across her mouth.

"Because she already has some," he replied. He sat beside her on the grass. They had driven around and chosen a piece of grass with shady trees for a rest.

"If I were your wife, I'd give you everything," Debbie said, and took another sip of beer.

"Even children?"

"Especially children. If that's what makes you happy."

Michael was quiet for a long time.

"Maybe that's the solution," he said then. "If Lisa doesn't want children, maybe we can do this with a surrogate mother."

Debbie looked at him doubtfully then stared straight ahead at the burnt grass.

"And you think she'd agree with that?"

"Would you agree with that?"

"Don't ask me," said Debbie. "I don't work the same way."

"I don't want to lose Lisa," said Michael. "Debbie, I love her. But I also don't want to put her under pressure ... maybe a surrogate would really be the solution ... then I wouldn't have to insist on my wish for children ... I can tell how annoyed she is."

"Yes, exactly," agreed Debbie. "Then you could take care of her alone again, just like she wants."

Michael pressed his lips together. "Do you think she'd accept a child from a surrogate mother?"

"Dunno. Could be a solution: She gets what she wants, and you get what you want. Ask her."

"Yes ... I probably should do that," Michael sighed. "But ... even still, I'd have to find one first."

Debbie sat with her back leaning against the tree, her arms loosely on her knees, the beer bottle dangling between her hands.

"Can't be that hard," she said.

"Oh, yes it is," replied Michael, "it's hard."

Debbie took another swig from the bottle.

"Don't make it so complicated," she said, almost snidely. "I'm here! Okay? You've just found one."

"Lisa, finally open your eyes," said her friend and nudged her. "He does not want you. He wants your good reputation, your looks, your sex, your uterus and otherwise his peace and quiet. He does whatever he wants! And where does that leave you?"

Her children grumbled. They loved their biological father, Danny, and wanted the parents back together. They didn't accept Michael, thought he was weird, were teased by their classmates because of his reputation and appearance, and they refused to speak to him. Lisa's mother Priscilla was still suspicious and watched over her daughter like a hawk. Many people advised Lisa to leave before it was too late. Too late for what?

Lisa had to realize that it wasn't a piece of cake to be the wife of Michael Jackson. Some of the fans hated her. Female and male alike, because she had taken away their idol. The public in general, but also her social circle made no secret that they considered her marriage to Mike grotesque. The malice of the press and the negative effects of the Chandler affair also affected her. She constantly had to defend Michael because he still showed himself with children and because to the public he was so screwed up. And then his god-awful advisers who told her what she had to do and what not to do! Who did these dickheads think they were?

She realized how tied up Michael was, how much of his life was spent fighting on many fronts. And he ... he lived for children and music. That was what he was trying to concentrate on, regardless of her! Couldn't he see that it was not so easy for her either? Why did he have so little understanding? And what was with these doctors? She had believed he was clean, he had rehab behind him! Reluctantly, she felt that she had perhaps been mistaken: she could not bear to emotionally attach herself to someone with a painkiller addiction a second time. Her insides resisted the repetition of her greatest drama and trauma. Because it still hurt, it still held power over her. Every day the situation escalated for Lisa a bit more.

Together they sat by the fire. The mood was tense. Michael tried to approach her. Lisa made herself rigid. She was emotionally exhausted and Michael could feel it.

"Lisa," he ventured, "if you don't want to have children ... right now at the moment ... then…"

"Oh, leave me alone," she snapped. She was sick of hearing about this topic. Michael hesitated, hurt - and scared.

318

"I just wanted to tell you that I ...Lisa, I love you, I don't want to lose you."
Silence. Michael's throat tightened.
"Please, Lisa, talk to me."
But she could not. She had been through too much in the last few months that had affected her self-confidence. She was 26 years young. And she did not know if she would have the strength to endure a life alongside Michael in this swamp, where he lived.
Black despair spread through Michael's heart when he saw Lisa's reaction. Deep fear overcame him. He had lost Jordy. The person, whom he had loved so much. And now he loved again, even more so, and it looked as if he would lose again.
He looked at Lisa for a long time. She looked straight ahead, ignoring him. Discouraged, he went to his room, hoping she would follow. But she did not come. Instead he heard the front door close and her car drive off. Hot pain shot through him. After an hour of futile waiting, he ran around aimlessly through Neverland. He settled, as so often before, on his big Ferris wheel and rode to the highest point, the place where he was so close to heaven. All alone he sat in the gondola, empty seats around him.
An engine approached. He raised his head. With a beating heart he listened into the night. The sound came closer. And closer. Quickly he rode down, ran to the front door: It was only employees who delivered something to the house. Michael slowly turned around, went to the bedroom, lay down on the bed. Pressure in the abdomen, head, throat, heart. And there ... there it was again. This sickening feeling in his stomach, that crept upward unstoppably. After about an hour he reached into the drawer and pulled out a packet to prevent it from reaching his heart.

She came back. Two days later she stood in the bedroom, crushed. But this time it was Michael who exercised restraint. He, too, was afraid to get hurt. He, too, knew no other way than escape or putting up walls.
"Michael, let's talk," said Lisa, when she had finally tracked him down at the pool at Neverland, where he sat like a little kid, curled up and waiting to be found. He was grateful to Lisa that she had come looking for him. She sat still beside him. For a long time they didn't say anything.
"Can we talk?" she finally asked, looking at him from the side. Michael nodded silently.
"Openly?"
Before he could agree, it burst out of her:
"Michael, I miss you ... I don't want us to treat each other this way ... I..."
"Neither do I, Lisa, I really don't," Michael sobbed and threw his arms around her. "I've missed you so ... I missed you... please ... don't leave..."

Weeping, they held another in their arms. It felt so good to feel each other, knowing this was a real feeling ... and yet they were careful.

"Mike..." Lisa began, "I will be frank. And I want you to be as well. That's our only chance. I mean, our circumstances...all that...the media, our position, our environment is ... hard enough. That alone is able to destroy a relationship. Look at Hollywood and count the couples that make it, are happy over years ... you know what I mean."

Michael nodded again. He was happy and scared at the same time.

Lisa opened her mouth and closed it again. After a few seconds she took a deep breath, looked Michael straight in the eye and asked:

"Michael, are you still addicted to painkillers?"

Heavy as lead, the question hung in the air. Michael lowered his head. That was answer enough. But Lisa was waiting.

"...I take something so I can sleep ... and when I feel bad," Michael finally whispered.

"And how often do you feel bad?"

"I hoped that with you...with children...it would get better...I'd have a chance to get out." Michael cleared his throat.

"We'll talk about that ... I mean, about family ... but first I'd like to know ... who's giving you all this stuff?"

"I ... I can get it..." muttered Mike. "You know, in America ...especially in Hollywood, it's not so hard to get these things."

"But you went to rehab in England!"

"Yes, I did, but ... I can't live with this pain in my head... this burn ... I always have to take something against that ... and ... when I feel bad, they call a doctor ... or ... when I'm on tour ... if I can't function ... can't sleep..."

"But you can understand that that frightens me?" Lisa asked fiercely. "That that's one reason that keeps me from starting a family with you, having children with you? What kind of father will you be for them if you're addicted to this stuff?"

Michael swallowed. "Lisa, I swear, if I knew that we'd have children ... I would go to rehab ... I would ..."

With wide eyes Lisa looked at him. "And you think 'they' would let you? Wouldn't it be more likely that they ...would provoke situations, so they could give you something that you wouldn't get off from?"

"Lisa," he cried, and became nervous. "Where did you get that idea...?"

"I was not idle these past days," she said. "Imagine, I'm interested in you."

Michael's eyes gazed silently at his beautiful wife. She said:

"I know more than you think. And don't ask me how I found out."

"It's the system," whispered Michael and something like hope swung in his voice. Lisa was the first one who believed him. Everyone else thought he was paranoid when he voiced his speculations. "Lisa, a global system…the whole system sucks…"

"Anyway," continued Lisa. "…it's a total lie to say that you'd come off the stuff if we had children. You're fooling yourself and me if you believe that."

"No!" cried Michael. "No, Lisa, that's not true! I'm serious ... I really want it - I mean, I know it can't go on like this, but I have to fulfill the Sony contract... have to make the album ... go on tour again ... then I'm done ... and then I'll rest and I'll have time ... some things you don't know about ... please believe me ... you just have to believe me!"

Lisa looked at him angrily.

"Believe you? After you lied to me? Massively? I mean, that's not a trivial thing with the drugs, dude."

Michael dropped his head. "I didn't lie to you, Lisa. I have to take medicine. I'm not healthy. But it's clear to me that I have to change my way. Only ... I was just really sure that it would be easier with a family."

Lisa's eyes turned slightly upward. "Okay, to the family. If I asked you to move away with me, somewhere where the world is not so crazy, where you can make your music, where they don't have such a hold on you ... Michael, you are surrounded by assholes! Can't you see that? They plot like there's no tomorrow! They make you sign things, they're robbing you ... this is a circus! You have to separate from these people! That's the only way you can do it! You need reliable people around you, not yes-men who grin in your face so they can pull the money out of your pocket. And then go to the press so they can collect the same amount again, because they have insider information to give out? Helloho? Where's Mike, the business professional?"

"Which of my people do you mean?" Michael asked, worried.

Lisa named them.

"Lisa, I can't vouch for everyone, but a few are not as bad as you think."

"Man! Just believe me!" Lisa said in despair. "I know that it's like that! I...as I said, I wasn't lazy ... come with me! Go for a treatment! You have a chance for a good life ...*we* have a chance!"

"But Lisa ... I'm in the middle of a huge story! It's too early! I can't just leave! I have obligations! I have a contract with Sony!"

"Yes, I know, but you can produce somewhere else, you don't have to be in LA, and your musicians will fly to wherever you are! And ... you're talking about the system. Why you don't you simply vamoose from the system if it stresses you so much? That's your decision to make!"

She was so right. But he did not want leave his beloved Neverland, and was it really as easy as she thought?

"Lisa," he asked, "you say that it's so easy. But would your kids want to move with me to another continent? They don't like me because they make me responsible for your separation with Danny ... and then I'm supposed to be the one who pulls them out of their environment?"

This time it was Lisa who remained silent.

"And I have another question," continued Michael. "If I were to do that and - by God, I'd do it ... for you Lisa I would do it! - what would then become of having our own children?"

When Lisa didn't respond to that for a long time something began to sink in Michael. Finally, she cleared her throat.

"Like ... like I've said many times, Mike ... at the moment I don't want any more children. I want to wait and see how everything develops before I take that step with you. I need certainty."

She lifted her eyes and looked at him. The disgusting thing in his stomach now completely rushed down and caused a heavy, clammy feeling.

"And then I'm somewhere in the boonies while Lisa jets back to her children in Los Angeles?" he bit back. "Is that how you imagine it's going to be?"

"We can both jet anywhere we want," Lisa said with forced calm.

"What sense does that make? If we can't make it here, we can't make it anywhere else either! We'll always be taking our problems with us!" exclaimed Michael angrily. "No change of location in the world could bring about a solution!"

"It would!! Because you need distance so you can see clearly again!" she said defensively. "You're in a muck of negative people who are strangely all related to another, by marriage or with other dubious connections ... along with your doctors! Doesn't that make you suspicious? Or can't you see clearly anymore because you're so doped up? Danny also thinks..." She bit her lip.

Michael paled.

"Danny?" he asked angrily. "You talk with your ex about me? Were you with him in the last two days?"

Lisa paused.

"You were with him." Michael said unhappily. "You were with him, right?"

"We talked. This situation concerns him, too. We have children together."

Lisa could literally see how this response put something in motion in Michael. He stared at the small pond and seemed to be thinking.

"The thing with having our own children is out of the question for you?" he asked, without looking at her.

Lisa pressed her lips together and took a deep breath before she answered quietly: "Not unless a couple of things change first ... and I hope you can understand that."

They walked slowly back to the house, lay in their bed together, each on their own side. Neither touched the other.

322

"Debbie, the other day, did you mean that for real?" Michael asked. Excited he paced up and down in the treatment room.

"The thing about the surrogate mother?"

"Yeah!"

"Sure, you know me, when I say something, I mean it."

"Debbie ... it may be that I'll approach you sooner than you think."

But Lisa and Michael weren't giving up on their marriage just yet. It went on, albeit slowly.

Michael thought the extent to which Lisa's first husband was present in her and his lives was horrible. And how much she let him be present. He tried to focus on his work, to shut out these sort of thoughts, but it was hard. His stomach was going crazy and he no longer tolerated some of the medicines, so he had to resort to other ones. He hadn't been adjusted to those properly, so that he was high sometimes, appearing dazed and drunk. As much as he could, he tried to hide all this from Lisa.

And the more he got the impression that Lisa pulled away, the greater the fear was that he would lose her, the stronger the desire for unconditional love grew. Offspring would not leave him. They would simply love him and he'd love them back. And he would be the best father in the world to them. This wish became the branch to which he clung, one that would be strong enough to pull him out of all this mess, one that would not break.

He had not asked for it, but some members of his team presented him again with pictures of Lisa and Danny.

He felt inferior, was disillusioned. But with his desire for children, he put Lisa under pressure and that was exactly what their marriage tolerated the least of all.

Lisa was in a miserable situation. Her ex-husband Danny now understood her in a way he hadn't during their marriage. Their children clung to him, and they took that as justification to spend as much time as possible with him. Danny was so wonderfully ordinary. There were no games of hide and seek, no complicated battle plans just to get from a hotel room to a car.

On top of that there was no end for Lisa to the quips from her so-called 'friends'. (So, do you put on Mickey Mouse ears in bed to turn him on? Where are you going to spend your next vacation? Let me guess: Euro Disney? From one roller coaster to the next? It goes up and down with Michael Jackson, quite a bit, huh...?)

Lisa was never at a loss for words herself, but she was mighty pissed at her friends for throwing these things at her. She was angry with Michael because he always just seemed to think about his own issues and had zero consideration for hers.

And the stuff with the kids... she was convinced that he wasn't doing anything wrong, but the world still wasn't and everyone was waiting for the slightest misstep by him. And she would be stuck with this image forever, too - as his piece of advertisement and as the wife who put up with these things. Could she, did she want to afford that? She had children! And they were also drawn into this! But Michael could not be swayed from his opinion that he needed to help children.

In this respect, she was sure, she would never be able to change him, because for one thing he saw it as his vocation, and for the other he was simply used to getting his way. And that's why he surrounded himself with people that made everything possible. While his business decisions early in his career were marked by clarity and vision, Lisa had the impression that now, because of the constant use of analgesics, he was losing his intuition, his sense of what was good for him. The only exception was his music, his art. There he could fully immerse himself into his spirit, and that seemed to be a constantly replenishing source for him.

But otherwise he was stuck in a sticky spider web, listened to people who were so obviously insincere that their sight alone disgusted Lisa. When she spoke to Michael about it, he said he couldn't do anything about it, or she was seeing it too one-sided. He explained that these were people allocated to him, not people he had hired. People from the record company, who dictated which events he should go to, what he had to do, which restaurants he should visit, etc. He liked it as little as she did, and he often boycotted it all by showing up in a wheelchair or on crutches or by pretending he was sick, just to annoy them. These signs of his rebellion eventually fell back only on himself. He was just Wacko Jacko, creepy and moronic, but Lisa was understandably not delighted to be the wife of a lunatic. She wanted to be proud of her husband. She wanted a mature relationship, but Michael's way to deal with certain things reminded her too much of a defiant child, and the question came up for her more and more often as to whether she could deal with all of this. Aside from that Michael was nevertheless soberingly realistic: "At the end of the day," he had once said to Lisa. "...You are the slave of the record company. You are the means by which they make money. And that's how they treat you. They say that the artist is nothing without them because they pay for public relations. If no one knows about your album, it won't sell. They've got you in their grip. Of course everyone is interested in good sales, but they try to control you, to make you their property. It's not like you have liberties without end. Actually, it's the other way around: You have to fight for everything, even for your music, for every song you want to have on the album, for every costume you like. You have to read every contract over ten times, and still they have some loopholes in there that can break your neck. You're nothing but a puppet, nothing but a means to line their pockets."

Lisa was frightened by all of this. She was not naive - she had put her own career on hold for just these reasons; she did not want to be an asset of a music company. It was not just the celebrity hype that raged around you when you had succeeded in becoming "it." There was a strict dictate of 1001 commitments that barely left any room to breathe. But above all, you were dependent and vulnerable to blackmail because artists do not want to be without their fame. Being famous was a dangerous drug - and Hollywood was capable of anything.

And with Michael, everything seemed to be exponential. Lisa realized that he was a willing prisoner, one who rebelled against this exploitation, but at the same time needed his fame in order to get what he really wanted.

He swam against it. And that made her afraid the most.

With the purchase of the ATV catalog and the founding of his own publishing company, he had started to build up enough power to provide a dangerous counter-weight - one that could make him fully independent. With that he would be the first artist to have escaped the clutches of the music industry. And not only that: he would be the first *black* artist who accomplished this - and he firmly believed that he had been given his talent for that reason, too. He was the first black artist with this kind of fame, the first black with such gigantic sales and earnings, the first who could create his own image. He was dangerous.

Lisa was dizzy when she thought about it. He fought against forces that were not to be trifled with…against powers that already had many peoples lives on their consciences and would not be afraid to add another.

And in this situation Michael wanted children?

Didn't he realize that he was making himself vulnerable? That the children could be used as his heel of Achilles?

She was scared. Had tried again talking to Michael about it, but he was stubborn, he wanted it his own way, thought he was untouchable despite the Chandler affair, because he was still a shining star in the pop scene like before. He believed in his fans, believed that they would always stand by him. He believed that love would always win, believed in his vision of a better world, in getting around the machinations. But Lisa was a mother and had to think rationally.

In addition, Mike was inexperienced in relationships, and aside from these horrendous threats she found herself confronted with having to develop his maturity in their marriage and get him through his adolescent crises.

And: he was not healthy. Would a family of his own really pull him out of all this? What role did he really have in mind for her? Michael had been quite distant lately. She had no idea how fervently he wished it were otherwise, had no idea that his coldness was born out of fear.

When she arrived at this point with her thoughts, she stopped. Her ex-husband was standing in front of her. She smiled at him. He was serious.

"Hey, Lisa," he said. "It's about time you made a decision."

***

Michael was not well. He suffered tremendously from Lisa's spending so much time with Danny; more precisely: It made him sick.

Since his success with *Thriller*, he was used to having his wishes granted by mere mention of his name. 'I'm Michael Jackson!' was the 'open sesame' to get what he wanted most of the time. Lisa was the first person in his life this catchphrase did not work with. But at that time, immature in relationships as he was, he did not understand it. He just saw something that had started in such a romantic and wonderful way suddenly going wrong. Was it his fate to remain without happiness? In his training to be a superstar, the topic of partnership had not been covered. To make matters worse, the painkillers made his emotional vibrational frequency considerably flatter. He did not notice how he ignored Lisa's needs and saw what she said and did as an attack on his person and on his lifestyle. Naively, he thought that she would share his life with him and it would then be even better. But none of this had happened.

He longed for her endlessly. And after long thought, his desire outweighed his pride and he called her.

"Please come tonight," he requested

"You come to me," she replied, but Michael saw himself incapable of being confronted with her children. He felt confused; the doctor had not yet been able to optimize a drug combination without these side effects.

"If you wouldn't mind...", he said. "...I would prefer if you'd come ... I'm in town ... if you could pick me up...?"

He spoke slowly, as if he had to think about every word, but Lisa blamed it on their current crisis. Again he gave her an address she did not know. Suspiciously she looked it up in the phonebook. A doctor's office.

With mixed emotions she picked him up. Michael tried to get into the car and bumped against the doorframe. He seemed drunk. Lisa was shocked.

"What did this doctor give you?" she asked, frozen in her seat.

"Dunno..." Michael said with a thick tongue. "Oh, Lisa ... I'm not doing so great ... without you ... not good at all..."

He was trembling while she drove and had his eyes closed, gasping at times. Her eyes were dark with thousands of thoughts in her head. The analogies were appalling; the past had caught up with her and Lisa felt panic rising in her. She brought him to his city apartment and put him to bed. With desperation she looked at the sleeping Mike. She knew, he would not sleep long. He could never sleep for long, no matter what they gave him. She stretched out her hand and stroked his pale face.

"God," Mike, she whispered, "I don't know if I can do this, I really don't know if I'm strong enough for all this crap."

She stayed over and Michael was so happy to see her.

Lisa, he said. "You're here..."

"Yes, Michael, I'm here. Unfortunately we haven't been seeing each other that much lately."

"No ... no, we haven't..." Unhappy he looked at her. Then he said:

"I'm going to Disneyland for a couple of days with Frank. Why don't you join us?"

Something in Lisa slumped down.

"No thanks," she replied, and her voice was colder than intended. "Disneyland is not my thing."

Michael was only gone for a few days. But when he returned, he was told that Lisa had gone on vacation with Danny for three whole weeks.

The pain shot through his whole body. Weeping, he lay down on his bed and did not get out of the bedroom for the whole day. Grace, who attended him even then, became worried. He didn't want to eat, and no other signs of life could be heard either.

A few days later, he left. No one knew where he went.

Lisa went looking for him. She knew she had affected him deeply. But damn it, he had hurt her with his behavior as well! She was worried. But Michael could not be found.

***

"You're sure?" she asked in her quiet, firm way. Blue-gray eyes looked into dark, fathomless lakes and called out a warm glow from them.

"I should ask you that," muttered Mike.

"No, you shouldn't. I said, yes and coming from me that means yes."

He hugged her tightly. "Thank you, Debbie. I know what you have to go through ... and I hope it won't be as bad as they describe."

Since he had learned of Lisa's vacation, it was clear to Michael that he would fulfill his desire for children independently of the development of his marriage. He did not want to give up Lisa, but right now it did not look good for the two of them. And he was reluctant to be sensitive towards Lisa in regards to Debbie's possible pregnancy. Lisa had rejected him, and to prevent this pain he had no choice than to do what he always did: put up walls and feel deserted. Outwardly, he was charming Michael; inside the storm raged.

Michael had disappeared for four whole weeks. He was well hidden, traveled disguised and with an assumed name, but Lisa found out where he was. The sole confidant that Mike had with him told him that an agent Lisa had commissioned had located him.
"How did he find me?" Michael asked, amazed.
"He specializes in things like that. He finds any and everyone. Do you want to press charges?"
"No," Mike said, "I want to meet him."

Eventually he returned to Neverland. She was there.
They spent chilly evenings together, never coming close to each other the first few days they were there together. Each of them wounded, each in their own world. During breakfast one morning he let the bomb explode.
"How about having Debbie carry a baby for us?" he asked her straight out.
"Excuse me?" Lisa stared at him open-mouthed. "Debbie? Isn't she the chubby nurse? You're kidding, right?"
"Lisa, I haven't changed my mind about children. And if you don't want any - I can accept that. Debbie is ready for it. She'll act as surrogate mother so to say."
"A surrogate mother? We're married!"
"Yes, but you don't want to have children! Lots of married couples use that approach!"
"And then you just get what you want from someone else? What am I to you?" Lisa asked upset.
But Michael was unforgiving in certain ways. She had hurt him; that was all that mattered to him. That this could be mutual never occurred to him. And he did not realize that they could have had a chance if Debbie had not butted into their relationship with her devoted willingness.
Lisa was dumbfounded. Silently, she sat at the table. Michael just abandoned her and went to somewhere else. Along with the front door, a door slammed shut in her heart, too.
His reaction threw a heavy black stone in her innermost being and swirled up mud clouds of old traumas: the feeling of failing, of being worthless, not enough for her father to want to live for, not enough for Michael to wait for... to have no weight ... all of that stretched out in concentric circles, turned into anger and spite and made her shut down.

***

Debbie called him. It had worked! She was pregnant! Michael was beside himself with joy. Only the thought of Lisa and the status of their relationship swam like a fat fly in the ointment.

Six weeks later, Debbie on the phone: she had lost the baby.

Michael's physical and mental condition became disastrous. He tried to function, overcompensated, but he had performances, he had to practice, he had to prepare for another world tour. As always, he went to the extreme and nothing could be good enough. As always, he handled everything. He didn't drink enough, eat enough, sleep enough. Thoughts revolved incessantly in his head. He missed Lisa, missed those very happy, carefree days, and emotional pain returned to its all-encompassing basic pattern.

HBO had plans for a concert with him and Marcel Marceau in December '95, and together with the world-famous mime he worked on four of his songs. The work gave him pleasure. Let his mind forget the darkness for a while, but his body could not.

He was dizzy and nauseous. Inconspicuously, he sought support on stage walls; his head was booming. He had put on white makeup; no one saw that he didn't need it because underneath it he was paler than death. With an iron will, he tried to follow Marceau's executions, forced his body to work, to somehow survive this training. With dread he thought about tomorrow's gig - the drugs did not work the way they were supposed to. A sharp pain tore through his forehead, and he grabbed his head. Michael stood on the stage like a statue, trying in vain to cope with the inner turmoil in his body. Then dull emptiness filled him, and he collapsed and fell hard onto the stage floor.

A short while later he found himself back in the hospital and various rumors began to circulate. He had a virus, he was dehydrated, he had fainted, it was a PR stunt, he didn't want to perform.

Lisa refused to see him. But then she got calls from Michael's staff, who suggested she show herself; they both were public figures and she couldn't just do whatever she wanted. It was her duty as the wife of Michael Jackson to pay her husband a visit, and she should act as worried as possible. For the press. Otherwise the speculation could go the wrong way, and unfavorably affect her image as well… hadn't she just been on the road with her ex-husband for weeks? Wouldn't that make for a media feeding frenzy?

Michael had no idea about the nature of the phone conversation. He was told merely that his wife had been called - and she was coming. He looked forward to seeing her with very mixed feelings.

An extremely irritated Lisa swept through the main hospital entrance in front of an army of fans and paparazzi. Clearly no sign of a loving or anxious wife. The phone call had enraged her, Michael's coolness had made her angry, and she cursed his PR people who treated her as if she were an arbitrarily deployable means for purpose of image posturing. Was Mike now playing sick to elicit her pity? The current headlines, that he had a liaison with Karen Faye, his makeup artist, made Lisa no less aggressive. But the worst of it was the confirmed news that Debbie was pregnant. He had really dared!

A short time later she came out again. She had already filed for divorce. The relationship was over.

***

I had to swallow hard. Eighteen months. That was too early, way too early to give up in the face of the tight knots that had to be undone.

"Why did you let her go?" I asked sadly. "You were such a good fit. You both had the same problems, you could have solved them so well together…"

Michael sighed.

"Oh, Chirelle, it's not as simple as it looks. We both got stuck on the wrong track. Today I see lots of things differently. But don't you always want to do things differently in hindsight? I was stubborn. And ignorant. And mean. I hurt Lisa so much. But Debbie wasn't pregnant when Lisa left me - I don't know who told her that."

We were both silent.

"But what about the pills?" I asked. "How are you with that today? And how were you back then?"

"It's not that I didn't try to get off of them," he said. "I've had several rehabs. But in the end something always gets in between. Things like the back injury I suffered when a bridge collapsed on stage ...or when I broke my foot ... you go to the hospital and the first thing they do is give you painkillers. And I'm back on them just like that."

When I said nothing, he added: "I don't take much. I need sleeping pills, lots of people do. And I need something ... when I'm afraid, when my body hurts... I mean, lots of people take pills for far less of a reason ... I try to use them in moderation ... but ... I'm not ... healthy, Chirelle. You're talking with a sick man."

"This may sound naive," I said, "but ... there are so many wonderful things in the world - why not addiction-free health for Michael Jackson?"

"You mean it's a matter of faith?"

"I believe that all medical problems are influenced by one's attitude. And what I can't get into my head: you yourself are able to heal, have this power...

and: you have your children who you love so much ... and for whom life is worth living ... to live long…"

With this statement, I somehow locked his mouth. The conversation did not get going again. After several unsuccessful attempts, I rose unsteadily.

"Do you want to continue tomorrow?" I asked him. He nodded with much hesitation.

And suddenly I was the one who felt there wasn't much time. Sentences and words pressed forward in me and I opened my mouth as if by remote control, to let them out:

"Michael, you've had the option several times in your life to choose the easy way out, and that ended in bitterness and left you with even greater suffering. Don't let it happen this time. Go through the pain. Look at your responsibility. If you really want to change something, you don't have a choice."

Dead end

Grace came to me and excused Michael for the next couple of days. He had meetings that could not be postponed, she said with a worried expression. Then she left too quickly - I barely had the question on the tip of my tongue if she could tell me what it was about. And if it was true.

The next days, Michael seemed very tense. He left each conference with an even paler face. Where his appetite during the past weeks had not been outstanding, it now dropped to nothing. He ate hardly anything, and even in dealing with his children he seemed strained. We saw him walking around in the park, lost in thought, and Grace and Linda seemed to be paying special attention. It was a strange atmosphere. Critical. Hopeless. Hopeful, desperate. A mood like shortly before jumping off a cliff, from which you did not know if you would survive.

Michael did not come downstairs for dinner. The children ate with Grace and asked for their Daddy. Grace explained that he'd had a hard day and needed to rest.

A man came into the house, apparently a doctor, at least according to the shape of his bag.

Grace took him to the top floor to Michael's bedroom, tried to act calm, but everyone noticed that she was very alert and suspicious. She did not leave the doctor's side and attempted to enter the room with him.

"Are you a family member of Mr. Jackson?" we heard the doctor ask.

"I've been his caregiver for over 15 years." Grace replied, and I could literally see how the veins in her neck swelled with anger.

"I'm sorry, ma'am, but I was called by Mr. Jackson. You are not allowed in here."

"That's ridiculous," said Grace, getting herself all worked up. "I am the one who has to deal with the consequences of your unconscionable treatment ... I make sure that everything is done properly."

Her barely disguised aggression provoked her counterpart to similar behavior.

"Listen, I'm a doctor," he said coldly. "I know what needs to be done ... You are not next of kin and therefore you stay outside."

BANG. The door slammed shut. Linda and I exchanged glances. We both envisioned Grace with gritted teeth at the door, as if she were standing next to us.

Then, after three long minutes we heard her steps coming slowly and heavily down the stairs. She came into the kitchen, dropped into a chair and said: "Be prepared for a crazy night."

She was right. About five hours later it began. I startled from sleep and listened in the darkness. Choking noises, cries and sobs penetrated muffled through the walls. With the speed of light I threw on my jogging suit and ran towards the noise. It led me out into the garden.

Grace stood there with a convulsing Michael who was trying to lean on her. Grace had grabbed his left arm and had pulled it over her shoulder, but Michael's legs gave way, he collapsed and fell on the hard stone path. Horrified, I ran toward Grace and jumped in to help. The grass beside the path was trampled like after a battle, and it smelled of stomach contents.

"He's thrown up, he's thrown up!" Grace cried desperately. "Oh, this fucking asshole!"

My mouth dropped open so far that Grace took time to explain:

"I mean that bastard of a doctor," she hissed. "He gave him too much ... and I don't even know what he gave him…!"

We grabbed under Michael's armpits and pulled him up.

"He can't throw up again ... we need to get him upstairs…" She wasn't looking at me at all. Michael's head was dangling between ours. He was so skinny that he posed no appreciable weight. Then Bob came running; he had seen the whole thing from his cubby. His burly figure inspired confidence; we let go of Michael and he just about fell into Bob's strong arms, who did not seem to even notice the weight. A minute later, Michael was lying on his bed and for the first time since my arrival I found myself in his bedroom. No one seemed to be bothered by it.

"Should I get something to drink?" I asked helplessly.

"Goodness, no!" cried Grace. "He can't drink, and he must not vomit!"

"But he has already thrown up…" I said and watched Grace leave.

332

She rushed to the phone and called someone. A few routine, short answers followed, then she hung up. Looked around and saw Michael lying deathly pale on the pillow, saw me standing helplessly there, staring.

"Go to bed, Chirelle" she said, "real help is on its way ... and ... thank you."

With mixed feelings, I went to my room. About an hour later the front door doorbell rang. I was awake, so I opened the front door. A very personable-looking man with a warm expression stood outside. Grace smiled broadly, was utterly relieved when she saw him and fell around his neck. He hugged her tightly, pressed a kiss on her cheek and followed her upstairs. Immediately a different energy was present in the house. Confidence, trust and dependability spread, and it was liberating. From Linda, I learned that the man was a kind of surrogate father to Grace and the person who had connected her with Michael: Mr. Deepak Chopra.

He stayed all night and the next day. I met him only in passing, a little smile, a friendly nod, but that alone was heart-warming up into the last tiny cell of my body. Everyone felt as if an authority had finally arrived at the house, who could be trusted without a doubt.

The evening of the following day Mr. Chopra spoke with Michael for a long time. Michael also seemed to trust this man unconditionally. He was feeling much better and he seemed to enjoy his treatment.

For me it posed the question of why Michael would ever let anyone else near him with support like that.

"He wrote *'Dancing the Dream'* with me," said Mike, once he was able to talk again. With some surprise, I'd heard from Grace that Michael wanted to continue our conversations, a recommendation from Mr. Chopra.

"What did he say?" I had asked Grace.

"That it's a chance. Just a small one. He said that Michael has previously always defended his drug addiction. His standard statement was: 'You don't understand'. He gets angry when someone wants to take away his painkillers. He avoids anyone who wants to stop him. Even Deepak. In his opinion no one can understand the suffering that brought him there and makes him hold onto it. He simply can't stand a life without painkillers."

"And he still wants to continue with our conversations?"

"You're letting him keep that stuff after all."

I was silent. Then I said, "Grace, he told me that he knows he has to come clean. He said it the night before ... but shortly after that first doctor was here and…"

Grace turned to me: "What else did you say?"

With seething heat I remembered my last sentence, and I blushed.

"Well?" Grace prompted.

"I ... I asked him why he couldn't find a way to stop ... for his children ... that they would be worth living a long life for... and that he must finally walk through the pain instead of constantly avoiding it..."

Grace made a sound I couldn't place, whether it was a moan, groan or sob.

"Well," she said. "His touchy point. That of course, hurt."

"You wrote these lyrics with Deepak?" I replied to Michael's words. "They're beautiful."

"Yes, they are. They are the expression of myself. Deepak has given me a deep understanding."

He looked haggard, his face was pale, he was wrapped in a blanket and lay in front of the fireplace, staring at the wall, quietly, almost fatalistically, as if no longer interested in his fate.

"Michael," I asked gently, "why don't you leave this place? Are you afraid?"

His body wrapped in the blanket turned to me.

"That's not so easy Chirelle," he said again. "If it were easy, I would have done it already. But it's definitely not easy for many reasons."

With this answer, I had to be content. He said no more. Again I had the feeling - from wherever - that there wasn't much time. And so I asked him about the children, how their births and existence had changed his life - topics of conversation that he loved and were more innocuous than the malicious web in which he was suspended.

Next Attempt at Happiness

"Michael and I are connected in a way that is very different than usual," Debbie explained to her friend. "I don't think I'm attractive to him. He likes me because he can trust me. And I'm proud of that. I love him endlessly - and that's enough for me. He can marry another woman - as long as that makes him happy. I just want to be his friend, nothing more."

Her friend listened to this altruistic declaration of love without commenting. She wondered, however, how long Debbie would be able to uphold that position. But Debbie was a tower of strength. And when she said something, she meant it.

Her solid, straight personality was good for Michael. She neither interfered in his life, nor did she plan to. Debbie knew that Lisa's divorce petition pained him infinitely, that he was now defiant in order to protect himself. And she was the one who gave him what Lisa had refused to give. She wasn't doing it so she could play a greater role in Michael's life; she was too realistic for that. She just did it, and for no other reason than that she loved him. In May 1996, she became pregnant again.

That she finally had to play a bigger role than wanted, they owed Michael's mother Katherine.

Mothers often mean so well. They have no idea how their eternal defense statement: 'I just mean well!' often provokes exactly the opposite: that out of a sense of duty mixed with some guilt, one does what is supposed to be 'sensible', but in the end completely contradicts the heart. And ultimately only crap can come of that.

Michael and Debbie had been in agreement. But Katherine convinced Debbie that it would be better for the child if they got married, awakened in her the hope that they could have a good marriage. They talked about God and sin, then called Michael and let him know their views.

It was strange: for such a long time Michael had lived his own life and had retreated from his family. But that separation did not mean liberation; now that became clear: Katherine got what she wanted. Was he afraid of committing a sin? At any rate, further malice from the press was inevitable.

The marriage to such a plain woman, who appeared out of the woodwork so suddenly, shortly after his divorce from Lisa, and who was moreover obviously not a "real" wife, delivered another sharp angle to Michael's bizarre image and was grist for the mill of the media.

"I don't know how my mom convinced me," Michael sighed. "I love her, but when I had to go through the damn hype about the relationship between Debbie and me, I vowed to listen to my inner voice in the future. And Blanket came to the world like it should have been with Prince and Paris already: no one knows who the mother is and the mother doesn't know us."

But for now it was about the first child. And this time Debbie carried to term.

Michael was not a big cell phone user. As a rule, he didn't need one, and if he wanted to make a phone call, he simply borrowed one. But when Debbie was pregnant with his child, he carried a cell phone around with him day and night and meticulously made sure it was charged. He was still in the middle of his *HIStory* World tour, which included 82 concerts - 19 in Asia, 11 in Australia, 6 in Africa, 45 in Europe and only one in America. It consisted of two legs and he had left a gap between the beginning of January '97 and May in order to take care of his first baby.

He decorated a nursery, picked out wallpaper, bought loads of toys and arranged them in a special room at his ranch. He read magazines about babies and text books about bonding, breast milk and strollers - in short the baby magazines piled up next to his bed and the kitchen was perfectly equipped with bottles, sterilizers and pacifiers. Michael was entirely focused on the birth of his child. And he was looking forward to it like mad.

And then it was time. Michael's phone rang one February night. Michael was still awake, and when he saw the number on the display, the heat rose up in him. It was Debbie.

"Michael," she groaned. "I think the baby is coming ... I have ... contractions ... the ambulance is coming any minute…"

"Debbie! Debbie, Debbie!" he cried frantically. "Oh, God, how are you doing? Be careful! Don't move from the spot, I'm coming, I'm coming, I'm hurrying! Wait for me ... no! Go with the people from the ambulance ... I…!"

"It's all right, Michael," gasped Debbie, caught in a further contraction. "I'll see you at the hospital."

Michael raced out of the room and alerted his chauffeur. "It's time, it's time!" he shouted. "Debbie is having our baby!"

He was already crying and couldn't wait until the driver rolled up the garage door and was ready to go. Frantically, he jumped into the car and was wringing his hands continuously. His lips were pressed together and he was praying. He prayed that God would grant him this joy, that everything was going to be OK, that mother and child were healthy, that it wouldn't take much longer.

He was so excited about the moment when he would be allowed to put his son in his arms that he almost couldn't breathe. A baby! His baby! That would live with him here in a couple of hours! A baby for Michael.

The nurse kept throwing a glance at the black-clad bundle of nerves, who was walking back and forth with his pregnant wife and supported her in the corridor, which was cordoned off from everyone else. Michael Jackson, here in the hospital! And it was her shift. What luck! She watched him as often as she could. The entire staff had been forced to sign that they would not hand over any pictures, other material or other information to the press. A helicopter was on the roof that would bring Jackson and his baby home afterwards, as he was afraid to be unable to leave from any of the exits unseen.

The administration of the hospital had shaken their heads over all of these safety procedures - how would anyone know when Mrs. Jackson was going to give birth? But Michael knew the game - in situations like this, people had always been bribed. And that's exactly what happened. Someone had made the call and within the first half hour of Michael's appearance in the hospital, reporters besieged the building, and Jackson had by no means exaggerated when he had requested the helicopter. It turned out that he had even approached the situation rather temperately because the uproar that prevailed in the hospital was incredible. The tricks that the paparazzi used to get closer to Jackson and his baby ranged from risky to distasteful. Freight elevators, fire stairs, disguises as a doctor, nurse or cleaning staff were used...

everything was happening. They had their hands full just stopping the hydra-headed reporter corps - and all that just because a woman was having a baby! Because Michael Jackson was having a baby!

The nurse looked back at the couple, who like so many before them and after them, walked up and down the corridor, and at this moment wasn't different from other expectant parents.

Michael encouraged Debbie and every half hour they staggered back to the midwife, who checked how far the cervix had dilated. Michael waited outside as the nurse reached with experienced hands between Debbie's legs. Then she came out, looked into this child-like face and said, "All right, Mr. Jackson, we're taking your wife into the delivery room now."

Michael's eyes were huge as he followed the midwife and Debbie, who was lying on a gurney. A sheet was draped on her stomach, so he could only see her quivering upper body and face. Debbie screamed in agony and tears flowed from Michael's eyes. He never would have thought that women had to endure such pain! His heart overflowed with love for Debbie and he kissed her hand. He loved her because she was so selfless, because she was giving him the greatest gift of all time. He would never forget that.

Then Debbie screamed one more time, long and shrill, and her cry blended together with another one - the first cry of a new earth dweller.

"He's here!" shouted Debbie and tears of relief and joy ran from her blue eyes. "He's here! Oh, Michael, he's finally here!"

Michael's knees were so wobbly that he had to hold onto the bed frame. His child! That was the voice of his child! He tried to peer behind the sheet. His heart pounded as if he had just finished a sprint. He sensed the angelical, the energy, the innocence, Holiness ... Michael briefly closed his eyes, tears tumbled from under the lashes, he reveled in this vibe when the nurse came out from behind the sheet and put his child, his baby, his greatest treasure, into his arms.

"Congratulations, Mr. and Mrs. Jackson," she said. "You've got a strong little boy."

Michael completely broke down in tears then, and with infinite gentleness pressed his baby to his chest.

"My baby," he whispered, overcome. "You're my baby, my angel, oh, you little angel ... my baby..."

Happiness flowed through him to his very last cell, and he bathed in the awareness of holding a miracle in his arms, never again to be alone.

A year later, his daughter Paris was born. Three years later, Blanket.

Raising his children gave him back a piece of childhood. With ardor, he adjusted his life to theirs and enjoyed every moment.

He was the most loving father imaginable, but he did not allow them everything. With the upbringing of his children began a healing and maturation process that lent him a completely different point of view in many ways. With infinite patience and his unique gentleness, he instilled in his children the values he thought important: respect for others, courtesy, justice, compassion and commitment to put one's talents to the service of humanity. He drew their attention to the misery of the world and at a young age taught them to take this on. To be grateful for life, grateful for opportunities. With them he was happy. With them he was able, for the first time, not to put so much value on his grief and self, to let go a little. The best years of his life were from the birth of his first son until around 2001.

A short time. Four years. I hoped for him that there would be more.

He was working on his new album, *Invincible* - it would be his softest, one that perfectly represented his paternity, and, as always, his thoughts and the events of that time.

Debbie and he had agreed not to live together. They both knew she was not the woman he was waiting for.

"Were you waiting for someone at that time?" I asked.

"Yes and no," replied Michael. "My children gave me fulfillment. And they gave me the feeling of being untouchable. That was ... too bad..."

"Too bad?"

"Yes ... when Prince was born ... I squandered another opportunity with Lisa... Man, I was so stupid!"

Inevitably there were touch points in Debbie's and Michael's marriage, especially in the time between the birth of Prince Michael I and Paris, when Debbie learned about the life of her husband. Within a few weeks she felt completely paralyzed from his camp. Michael gained facets. There was the side that she knew: the sensitive, humorous and loving. There was the Michael who knew exactly what he wanted in his music and art and got it. But now she also saw a man who let himself be ordered and bossed around by others without resistance. Debbie was an exceptionally clear and practical-minded, an especially free-spirited woman, and she was shocked to see Michael turn into a small, defenseless child, as if his father were still in front of him and threatening to beat the crap out of him if he didn't do what he was told. Michael suffered from these encounters with others, and that could be felt, too. Debbie couldn't understand why he put up with it.

It seemed as if despite everything, Michael was looking for an authority, who gave him direction in his life. Stunned, she saw how contracts were pushed under his nose, how Michael even read them, but then what he ended up signing was not what he had read. Almost everyone around Michael was out to enrich himself; these people were not interested in supporting Jackson but in exploiting him - he was surrounded by bloodsuckers.

Nonetheless, she agreed to have a second child with him. She began to hope she could free him from this enormous mess.

***

"Hey," she said.

"Hey," he replied. Couldn't help that his heart fluttered. She cleared her throat.

"I ... I wanted to congratulate you on your baby."

"Oh ... thank you. Thank you, Lisa."

"How are you doing?"

"I'm great. I've never been better! The little one is pure heaven. I can't tell you how much I love him."

Lisa pressed the receiver to her ear firmly and forced herself to say appropriate things. She missed Michael. She missed him terribly. She had never thought she would miss him so much.

"Can I see your baby sometime?" she asked.

"Of course, Lisa, anytime. When would you like to come?"

In the weeks following the separation, Lisa was terribly confused. She had sought and found a change and she'd had a lot of time to think. She thought of Michael, the lovable sides to him, the hours of harmony and understanding, of the pillow fights and the fun they'd had together, of Michael's tenderness and his efforts to keep up with her far greater experience in relationships. But also that they had hurt each other and that she was another adult who had, in Michael's opinion, disappointed him. At some point the decisive thoughts flashed through her mind: he's alive. You can still get him out of there. You shouldn't give up this easily. We both can change. Why shouldn't it work? Her father had died. Michael lived. And she loved him. She knew that now.

Like many times before, she stepped into the living room at Neverland Ranch. Michael stood up to greet her. She had brought a present and her eyes lit up when she saw Michael. He noticed and it warmed his heart. He hugged Lisa deeply.

But a short time later, the guardian in his head reported, warning him not to be too open, reminded him of the old hurts, and anxiously he shut down. He now had his baby, who would never, never, ever betray him, and that was all he needed. So he was distant when she tried to approach him in a certain way. Lisa noticed it, but she had made up her mind to not give up so quickly this time.

She showed up everywhere where she hoped to find Michael, deepened the friendship with his sister Janet, who she liked very much, talked to his mother and worked to eventually penetrate his armor.

Lisa's overtures were good for Michael, but he did not reciprocate. Caution and memories were effective shields against her newly inflamed interest for him. She had appeared several times after their marriage on Oprah and had not left a very favorable impression of him.

He was in a: 'What do you want from me anyway? I have everything I need' - mind frame that did not suit him and made him arrogant and stubborn.

After months without any success, it was Lisa who pulled back with a newly wounded heart, determined to never again in her life engage in such a meaningless game. Michael noticed it too late.

Only when she was gone, he realized with a shock how much he missed her calls, her voice, her laughter.

As if someone had switched on a light, the scene came into his mind when she had visited him to see his baby. When they were together, very close, standing in front of the cradle, Lisa lifted out the little Prince, held him in her arms, and with shining eyes had looked into his. It was a picture of perfection. It was exactly what he had dreamed to see. And he had blown it! With a groan, Michael buried his head in his hands. Oh, my God, when he thought of how he had treated her! So rejecting and know-it-all! And realized suddenly that she needed encouragement and caring, just as he did, that it was not only about his own feelings, but that a relationship was something reciprocal that needed to be developed.

He realized how much he loved her, still loved her, and that he had behaved like a sulking teenager. He wanted love from her, she from him. Two drowning people clinging to each other. And he made a decision, too: he would do anything to get this woman back to his side.

And now he was the one looking for her.

At the same time he was planning a second child with Debbie, addicted to this miracle, these angelic beings, their purity and innocence. But for the first time since he had known her, Debbie had a condition.

She was not blind; she realized that Michael's heart was set upon the children... and Lisa. Hope and hopelessness in equal parts made her put forward her claim.

"Mike," she said in a trembling voice, while her face started to turn red, "I want to go to Paris with you ... I've never been to Paris, you know?"

"But of course, Debbie," said Mike, stroking her cheek gently, surprised at her pained voice. "Anything you want…"

"Don't get ahead of yourself," she said, and tears streamed down her face. "I want to ... give you ... a child…"

"I know," he whispered. "And I am so grateful, so grateful."

"But Mike," she whispered back. "I am ... your wife ... just once I want to really be your wife ... you know what I mean? Just one time ... just for one night…"

They flew to Paris, the city of love. And she came back pregnant. It didn't make things any easier for Debbie.

Gradually she came to see how fragile Michael's health - and his psyche were. Often he had the shakes, then sweats, then he was cold again. His nose acted up and he had to have another surgery. Because of the many medications he was taking, that posed a considerable risk a void suddenly appeared before Debbie that she had not been aware of when she had agreed to carry his children.

Michael looked miserable - even though he was so happy with the kids. But the Chandler claim was only three years back, his image was damaged as ever and would remain damaged forever, the press was relentless and full of spite, the failure of his marriage had affected him more than he wanted to admit, his financial situation was unclear and his body weakened tremendously.

Shortly after their marriage, Debbie had her first encounter with hate mail. Michael had warned Debbie that disturbed people were out there who sent this kind of stuff. But this time they threatened to kill the children. And not only that: they described how they would do it, and it made Debbie sick. Some of this dirt had been directed at her and the hair on her neck stood up. Then right before Paris' birth, a horrible letter arrived that implied that the baby would be murdered while still in the hospital. Debbie was beside herself and could not help it: she began to understand Lisa - and she began to meddle.

"The children will be veiled," she said and there was nothing pleading in her voice anymore. "Michael, I have brought these children into the world so they could live - they are your children, but to some extent they will also always be mine - although from a distance," she added quickly, seeing the expression on Michael's face.

"I don't want to ask anything of you, Mike, you know that ... but I'm scared! My God, how can there be such sick minds?"

She began to cry. She was not well either. She'd suffered from postpartum depression after the birth, her breasts were swollen, they felt as if they would burst, and although the agreement to give Michael the children was absolutely firm, she had not taken into account how much emotional pain would follow. Motherly love that was now her duty to suppress erupted like lava from a volcano, and she could not control it. It was a divine mechanism that made life difficult for her now, but she was determined to keep it to herself and to tell Michael nothing about it.

Michael put his arm around her and hugged her. "I'll protect the children with my life, Debbie," he said.

"That's just it," she sobbed, "Which one of you are they going to kill first?"

The fear remained - for Michael and for the children. And the feeling that she had consented and now couldn't do anything about it.

Debbie noticed how Michael began to block her off when she tried to talk to him about his situation. Carefully, she broached the subject of going to rehab, reshaping his management team and his life and she felt she was talking to a brick wall.

"You don't understand," he kept saying. "Don't try to tell me how I should live my life. My whole life, my whole childhood was wasted because I had to do what others told me."

"But Mike!" exclaimed Debbie. "Surrounding yourself with suck-ups who pretend they are doing what you want, but ultimately maneuver you where they want you to be, can't be a solution!"

"They're not all that bad," he replied. "And sometimes you have to run with the pack."

The answer, more than vague, nevertheless left Debbie with some hope that Michael was not regarding the situation quite as naively. This seemed to be a deadly game of chess, where every opponent was waiting for the other to make a move.

She couldn't do a thing. She had no voice and little influence. She had no other option than to accept things without complaint, and she continually repeated her oath that it was about Michael's happiness and not about hers.

She moved into a large house that Michael gave her, bought horses and tried to forget the pain of being separated fully and completely from her babies and from Michael.

"It's safer for you, Debbie," Michael told her. "At least you should be out of the line of fire."

But he wanted her out of the way not only because of that. There were so many people who put him under pressure. He tried to prevent that at least with those he had a chance to influence.

The children changed him. They changed his values, his priorities, made him more compassionate and soft. For hours he sat at Prince's crib and watched him sleep, admired the rosy, round cheeks, the pudgy little hands, the miniature feet and was dazed with happiness. Yes, he had nannies, but he insisted on doing a lot himself. When he was at home - and during these times he was often at home - he changed diapers, gave Prince the bottle and sang good night songs to him. He felt less and less of an urge for business, and he felt how his ambition waned to the extent that the love for his children and the desire to remain close to them grew. The outside world with all its problems and challenges became not only uninteresting, but an annoying intruder into a protected, simple life. He felt self-sufficient with his children, because their love filled him completely. He thought about many things.

He was still looking for Lisa. She did not appear. It was said that she was ill and had withdrawn for treatment.

He was only able to locate her again after she was better. Carefully, he began to establish bonds, called her, invited her, took walks with her ... it was starting off on a good note. His heart drew hope - she was still there. For now she was there. Carefully, cautiously this time he nourished the seedlings of their relationship, and he learned a lot. His babies were his teachers when it came to fully opening up to another person. They simply trusted that he was a good person and did the best for them. To live under such a premise had never crossed his mind before ... and changed his perspective enormously. He began to think about what would have happened if he, too, had simply trusted. If he had opened up completely to Lisa. What would he have discovered.

And he was ashamed of how he had treated her. He saw how she had done everything for him, how much she had supported him and how he had wasted his good fortune. And so he was grateful for every small gesture from her, for every time she agreed to visit, and it was everything to him when one dark blue night she let him kiss her again.

Debbie was watching all this. Michael's love for Lisa was very obvious. And she drew the only right consequence: if Michael wanted Lisa, he had to be free. She filed for divorce.

Got it?

He had to make money, he now had an entirely different responsibility. The main income of an artist consists of recorded music sales, and he was working on a new album, *Invincible*, six years after *HIStory*.

In between, he had created *Ghost* - a remarkable video with brilliant dance sequences and a CD called *'Blood on the Dancefloor'*.

For the promotion of *Invincible* a tour was planned, as always, and Michael wanted to charge into promotion. But when the album was released, several things loomed over him: he suffered from arthritis and chronic bronchitis now. Besides that fact his insomnia was impeding his healing process, and he lost weight massively during tours ... he felt ... old.

Sometimes he looked at himself in the mirror, discovered alarming signs of aging, and was worried. His self-image kicked in, which wanted him forever attractive, which made him not want to ever stand in front of his fans with wrinkled cheeks and a sagging jaw. The fear of not being liked once again easily took prime position.

But there was nothing to be done, in the truest sense of the word. In the shower, he had his hands full of hair, and the inner structure of his nose was a disaster. In another function-preserving operation, the doctors had to severe some nerves. His upper lip was paralyzed, and it looked awful. He appeared unnatural when speaking, especially when he laughed, and every public appearance became torture.

But his record company urged him to keep doing exactly those. He could not shut himself in at home and hope that his CDs sold by themselves! This was understandable, and Michael knew that the sale of recorded music itself would not bring in enough to maintain his standard of living and his ambitions. He had already long since diversified when it came to his fortune, bought a lot of art and wanted to get into film, as the movie business would offer him variety and an extension of his creativity.

The ATV catalog and his own company provided consistent royalties and effortless revenue, and that was the track that appeared the most profitable to Michael. Sony was constantly adding new catalogs and Michael went along. The music - and publishing rights were his way forward. As soon as new opportunities to acquire music rights came up, he took them. He bought them and tried for a real chance for himself and his future.

Michael was rich - very rich in assets - but he was not liquid in cash. Six years without significant performances and the damage to his reputation through Chandler had taken their toll. His cost of living, because of Neverland, his luxurious lifestyle and especially his generosity when it came to donations were higher than his current income. He had to take loans using the existing ATV shares as security. And this made his life a gamble.

XX / 2001 Somewhere in the world

"Do I understand correctly that you want to play music of a pedophile on your stations? That you are advertising for a lunatic so he can put even more money in his pocket? Which planet are you from, man? Why don't you use your budget to support people with a flawless image? The amount of money that this psychopath needs for a video clip is downright outrageous! At this point the question comes up quite simply whether you are the right person for this position ... and one more thing: characters like him have no business being in the film industry."

Michael put his whole soul into *Invincible*, as he always did when he made music. Defiant songs were coupled with deep melancholy in the style of children's songs and ballads, sung by Michael's angelic voice - it was a timeless album. And with the title song 'Unbreakable', it was a declaration of war.

The album spawned controversy because Sony began to refuse him everything that was important to him. He was not allowed to include the songs he liked and not allowed to omit the song that seemed most dispensable.

And then, mysteriously just the song that had been planned as the first single from the album appeared on the Internet. Nobody knew how it could have happened. The song was on the net and could be downloaded and this created a significant loss of income.

Michael paled when he heard about it. It was a warning shot, aimed at his existence.

To his horror, *Invincible* was - in comparison to the other albums - hardly promoted. There was no money for his famous short films, so that Michael was forced to finance them himself. But he knew that a video was instrumental for sales, so he bit the bullet and took the money out of his own pocket in order to boost sales of his album. There were angry confrontations with Sony, who stubbornly refused to pay for promotion. They suddenly said that his video productions were too expensive, that no other artist asked for this kind of money, and that it wasn't justified by anything.

In all this, Michael found out that Tommy Mottola, the CEO of Sony, had tricked him. Instead of getting the music rights for his songs in 2001, as negotiated, they stayed with Sony until 2009/2010 - another tender loss.

Then came the disastrous September 11th, 2001, and all American musicians canceled their concerts because it was not justifiable to crowd droves of the umpteen thousand fans together and subject them to a possible terrorist attack.

Michael was willing to go on tour later, but Sony didn't buy into his arguments for a second, demanded that he should go on tour now, that he did what they wanted, and Michael fought it. He did not want to be blackmailed and would not jeopardize his fans. As a result Sony suspended any future promotion of *Invincible*, especially since Michael was threatening not to renew the contract with them.

Michael's threat presented an unpleasant reality for Sony, because he owned 50% of the shares of the Sony/ATV catalog. And if he left, he would be the first major free and independent artist. He would be the first significant free black artist.

Something that did not sit well with some people.

As always the press acted as the sidekick: the album received poor reviews, especially in the States.

His songs were not played on many broad stations - yes, there were others, especially the small stations, that sided with him, that played Michael Jackson at all, but it became more and more clear every day, every week, every month that not only his music was not being promoted, but it was being boycotted. *Invincible* with $10 million sales took the last place of his solo albums, sales that had been made mainly abroad.

And that was what was reported gleefully: Michael Jackson was the loser of the year - from nearly $100 million sales with *Thriller* down to a ridiculous ten! Madonna had at the time $11 million sales with her album - the media spoke admiringly of her superstar status and of immense success.

And then when Michael wrote his song 'What More Can I Give' to help the victims of September 11, he had to witness Sony shooting down even his relief effort.

In exactly this difficult time, the press publicized his debts. Suddenly almost every newspaper wrote that Michael Jackson wasn't making sales, was the on the verge of bankruptcy, lived beyond his means, was a nutcase who had succumbed to megalomania, and that his latest album was amateurish. Next to the headlines his dumb-looking face was printed.

Frantic, Michael saw his hopes dashed. His confidence crashed, the CD was a flop, he could not polish up his image by artistic recognition as planned, and in addition to the Wacko-Jacko and child molester image he was now also considered a failure in business.

He understood the intention: he was being trimmed down to the paranoid, uncreative ex-superstar, was supposed to appear not creditworthy. Piece by piece, they took away everything that was important to him. And when he thought about what else was important to him and what they could therefore still take, his blood turned cold. At this time he really understood the plan and the full extent of what they were doing. And that they were serious.

When the next threatening letter came, it gained importance for Michael.

And so he lived in constant fear. He told me that so far the threats had not been followed by actions, but then again he was well protected. In addition, according to Michael, it was clear to him that the letters' primary intent was to demoralize him.

"Seriously," he said, "if someone wanted to kill me ... who could prevent that? An overdose, an accident... if someone is really plotting that, then it's not an issue. I didn't see my life as such endangered at the time. But my existence was. And when my kids were there, it burdened me terribly. For the first time I really thought about how I could escape all this."

Michael looked at me and he actually winked at me. As if it were a game of hide and seek!

"What do you mean 'escape'?" I asked.

"Wait," he said, "the story isn't over yet ... not yet." For a few seconds, he stared straight ahead, then he continued.

These threatening letters appeared in his house, and made it clear that they had to be from someone in his immediate vicinity, but the identity was never uncovered. He had, again and again, replaced his teams with a few exceptions - without success. They made him insecure in regards to his legal advisers and managers, everyone denounced the other and substantiated it in the usual way: a (cut) video, tape or document. It was impossible for Michael to distinguish what was fake, who told the truth, who lied. That also served to wear him down. It was years of psychological terror. Michael did not trust anyone.

"There were always facts," he said. "…but twisted in such a clever way that it was hard to see through them."

They brought him papers that proved that his lawyer Branca was working with that same Tommy Mottola who had tricked him with his music rights. Branca represented the rights for Sony and for Michael - which was basically a conflict of interest. And then an offshore joint account in the Bahamas belonging to Branca and Sony was discovered into which apparently money from Michael's ATV assets flowed. Michael was beside himself and fired Branca - for the third time.

"Why did you keep hiring him?" I asked.

"Because he was ultimately able to prove to me that someone else was screwing me. And under his watch my money was always growing ... but the thing with the account was so real ... everything was so real ... you have to constantly assume that you are getting ripped off. I once had a friend I trusted endlessly, I shared everything with him, everything, you know? My fears, worries and troubles with Sony ... my finances ... I asked him many times what I should do. Until one night I overheard a phone call. He spoke with a board member of Sony and told him hot off the press what I had shared with him. God, it's so tiring! That's why I love children. They are in the here and now. They play. They don't think about finagling something today that will help them tomorrow. It's just awful to live in this corporate world, and it frustrates me to no end. Chirelle, my entire staff is infiltrated. When my second baby was born, I found a threatening letter in my pocket, saying they wanted to kill my little girl while still in the hospital! I mean, she was there - in a room with doctors and nurses, covered with masks and gowns up to their eyes ... and ... after so many years of permanent terror, you're just scared. You're scared. I grabbed her and ran when she was barely out of Debbie's belly. You've just been through so much that you're always second-guessing everything. And you trust no one. Nobody."

"But Mike, that ... that's ... there must be..." I croaked.

"My God, Chirelle," he said, almost impatiently. "It is a hydra. You can't verify it. I mean, I can't sit down all day and uncover these things. I'm an artist."

"But others *do* have a functioning management," I said blankly. "Sure you can't prevent that you'll get suckered by the one or other, but when you have a handful of reliable people at the top, then..."

"Chi," Mike said insistently, "everyone is corruptible. The longer they're with me, the more interesting they are to others. The higher the prize money ... and the temptation."

He looked at me and I could see the millions of thought loops he had already spun. And again in his words, the silhouette of a mastermind could be sensed. Or did *he* just think so? Was he stuck in something? Anyway, he seemed to be more than an ignorant victim.

Michael had to lay off people constantly. He had as many lawsuits as a dog has fleas, because most of the people he dismissed were suing for settlements - and of course in million dollar figures. Everyone was trying to carve out a bit from the giant Michael Jackson - just a tiny bit! He could surely afford it!

"You come to terms with it after a while," he said. "But to answer your question: since *Invincible* I know for sure that I am supposed to be destroyed. And with that I wouldn't and couldn't want to come to an arrangement."

"Sony?" I asked. "That is what most people think, a lot of your fans."

Michael looked straight ahead.

"That's what I thought in the beginning, too. I mean ... it makes sense. But honestly - Sony isn't that stupid to play such an obvious game."

"But it would be only logical that they wanted to have the whole ATV catalog," I countered surprised, "...that you are too powerful for them!"

"It's logical," said Michael. "That's the trick. It is so obvious that I've come to the conclusion that, if at all, it's not Sony alone."

My jaw had dropped again. I closed it. Someone had once told me that you could not think with an open mouth.

"The fact is," continued Michael, "my image was destroyed, my sources of income reduced, my children threatened, and according to the press I'm broke, not able to feed my children."

With an ardent movement, he turned and looked at me with those huge eyes. "I'm far from broke," he said. "But what the press says is taken for granted. And if I were to deliver a counter reply, it would go down miserably - like all my justifications. If I were to say I'm being threatened by something that is larger than you could imagine, the media would be the last to print it because they are in the hands of precisely those people."

Now my eyes were huge, "Michael, what's going on here? What do they want? And who are 'they'?"

"Well," said Michael, "'They' ... are the ones who determine what happens in the world. I'm telling you, it's dangerous to be successful. It is dangerous to be black and successful. And it's particularly dangerous to be successful and black and to have something that ... embodies a certain amount of power."

I sat there as if slapped and did not know what to say. How had Michael been able to survive all these years with this going on in the background? So many were shattered by the pressure to succeed alone! Without this Mafia stuff! And he could still be normal? Because that's what he was: a completely natural, friendly person.

"Oh, God," I said, shocked. "Is there really no solution? The police…?"

"The police!" Michael scoffed. "Quite honestly, they could have intervened a long time ago, why haven't they done it? Instead…"

He quieted. And gritted his teeth together so hard that his jaw muscles stood out white.

I stopped, startled. We had arrived at the main massacre. Bashir. And the 2003 to 2005 trial. Two agonizing years, years of misery, those years that had destroyed Michael completely.

XX / 2002/2003 on the phone

"He has plenty of enemies. Activate 'em all. Short notice will do, hold out some bloody meat and they'll pounce. What about that old broad, who wants to take the kids from the nigger ... and this crazy woman who is after him, as if she had nothing else to do in her life... she'll be happy when her favorite subject is brought up again! Light a fire under his ass.

And the main card, our best friend, who is eager to lead his personal vendetta ... a nudge with a feather... and he'll go like the energizer bunny!

Got any bait? Yeah? Who...? Ah, great, money grubbing, dumb rednecks ... a teensie ... like last time ... the guy just doesn't learn ... huh? You can spit easier into big hearts ... 'cause you can't miss ... hehehe ... All is well ... that's settled. Cast unbeatable. Good work"

***

Almost as expected, Grace came to me and extended her apologies on behalf of Michael for the next few days. While she was otherwise a reliable seismograph of Michael's condition and mood, this time nothing could be read from her physiognomy. To my surprise, Grace put on a poker face and didn't take it off for the next several days.

I was restless. I wanted a solution for Michael, wanted something to resolve, wanted something to happen. And I wanted to go home. But I had promised Michael to see this thing through with him to the end, although nothing really significant had happened so far. The one small issue we had been able to solve had only been a drop in the bucket. Grace was right. At the moment I saw no promise in advancing even one inch further. Instead of helping him out of this disaster, I was slipping into it more deeply.
Well, now we were faced with Bashir and the 2003 trial. That was his most intense and recent disaster. And I had completely forgotten to ask how things had turned out with Lisa.

1993

Thoughtfully, the official put away the file and locked it in the safe. In the file there was a report, and usually the desk sufficed for storage. But that was not the only thing that was odd about it. The whole case was odd.

2008

Thoughts, crazy ideas, fiction ... they all swirled around in my head in the next couple of days. I tried to put logic to the events.
The in-itself illogical nosedive after *Thriller* and the purchase of the ATV. Bad press, which prevented not only an increase of its sales, but revenue from advertising that many other stars had in abundance. His albums after '89 were mostly a mix of old and new songs, which infuriated the audience: they had to buy old songs if they wanted to hear some new ones.
Which company does things that would predictably annoy customers? Any average person would have been able to foresee the reaction - why not a top company specialized in public relations?
And even the argument that after the 1993 trial Michael's image was not clean anymore didn't hold. Because: how many stars were there with scandals? How many lived through scandals? And they were all systematically rebuilt because they promised profit. And with a talent like Michael there was no question that he would have continued to be profitable had he been supported. What would have happened if favorable reports had been published in the newspaper? Why didn't anyone report on Michael's unprecedented charity work? It did not want to get into my head that it should not be possible to refurbish his image with the united forces of his

management and the record company. Had they tried and nobody wanted to print it? Something didn't seem right. It smelled too much like method.

That day, Karen came to me in the kitchen and grabbed a coffee from the machine. She looked at me in a strange way, as if she was overcome by different feelings and did not know which one to follow. The conversation dragged on, which was quite unusual for both of us. Finally, she asked:
"Chi, you're talking with Mike about the trials?" It was not a question; she wanted to find out if I was subjecting Michael to foul play.
"Yes, he told me the Jordy story," I said.
"He talked about Chandler?" she asked with such immense surprise that I realized how large Michael's concession to me was.
"Yes..." I said hesitantly. "Yes ... he did. Among other things."
Karen exhaled loudly.
"Karen, let's not beat around the bush," I said firmly. "I know what you're thinking. I know that the girl who had my job last stole letters from Michael. But that's not me. And I can't do anything to convince you that you're way off!"
"Just tell me why are you having these conversations with Michael! What is the reason?"
"I don't have a reason! It just happened! I would never have approached Michael on my own account! I'm just kitchen help here, nothing more!"
"A kitchen help who went to college and has a degree," hissed Karen.
"Karen! What's that supposed to mean? You know how I got here! It was a coincidence! What's going on with you?"
Karen gritted her teeth and said nothing. She stared at me, and I was tremendously unhappy about the thoughts she must have spun together. Her suspicion tainted everything.
"And tonight, you want to talk about the trial," she said with an immovable face.
"Yes ... that was the plan."
Karen abruptly changed her approach:
"Don't do it," she whispered, looking at me pleadingly. "Please, please don't! If there is a heart beating in your chest, you can't want Michael to go through this shit again!"
And suddenly I knew she was right. Although Michael was prepared for it, the murderous look on Karen's face made me realize instantly that the conversation would not be good for him.
"Yeah...okay," I gave in. "I'll tell him that we'll talk about something else tonight."

"I'll tell him that you are indisposed," interrupted Grace, who was suddenly standing at the door. "In three days you can talk to me. I will tell you the story."

Karen threw Grace an indefinable look. And when she left, a clear threat was to be seen in her eyes that she didn't have to voice, I understood it anyway: "Don't you dare to even touch a hair on his head; if you do, then you're toast."

In these three days, when I had nothing else to do but wait for Grace, I sat in front of my computer. My fingers clicked again on the Bashir documentary. It was the cause of the second trial. But the question I was asking now was: was it really? Or would Michael have gone through this hell in any case? Because somebody wanted him to run through hell?

Grace's story

Grace exuded the charm of storytelling of her African ancestors as she sat down with me to unveil the most bitter part of Michael's life. We sat on the terrace, each in a chair, and Grace's silhouette stood out sharply against the twilight. I hung on her every word.

The years from 1997 to 2001 were for Michael ones of relative harmony. He made music, and he had the children. These were basically the two main activities that almost filled him. It was a life he had always wanted. Michael was a good father. He did not spoil his children. He had not forgotten where he had come from and that wealth was not to be taken for granted. He taught them respect, for man and nature, for the earth on which we all lived. They could only sometimes use the attractions of Neverland. At Christmas, they got oodles of presents from all sides, but were allowed to keep only two, and the others they donated to poor, destitute children. He taught them humility. When his son once stood before the mirror and commented that he looked good, he corrected him gently by saying, "You look okay."

He learned a lot in those years, about himself, too. His fatherhood brought a soothing normalcy to his life, let him reflect on his own childhood differently. He could have wept for joy when he saw the sweet faces of his children, in those honest trusting eyes, in their shining hearts, which were surrounded by the shimmering aura so familiar to him. When he was with his children, there was only love. His love, the love of his children. It was so easy.

To the bottom of his heart he was grateful for these little souls who had decided to walk with him in this world. For nothing on earth would he want to shake this trust, this love. His children were his jewels, the apples of his eyes; they compensated him for all that he had experienced in the past.

And still, he opened the doors to his huge ranch for hundreds of children, who he wanted to give a bit of happiness. He still rushed to every hospital in every city he stepped foot in. He still bought toy stores empty and gifted the toys to orphanages, hospitals, kindergartens and other organizations.

He never neglected a call for help from a child.

So he had taken on the case of Ryan White, the child who was infected with AIDS by a blood transfusion at a time when the disease was just announced and people were terrified of a contagion.

Ryan was expelled from school - and not only that, he was socially excluded in every way - because he was sick.

But he began to defend himself. Although he knew he was dying, he wanted to learn. Michael stood by his side, the same man who reportedly suffered from a paranoid fear of bacteria and infection, and supported his case, invited him to Neverland, chatted with him, let himself be filmed with him, to show that a person with AIDS does not have to be shunned, that social contact does not cause infection, but that these people needed help.

A sensational trial followed, one of the first HIV trials, and Ryan won: he was allowed to go to school.

Michael cried often over Ryan who knew that he had to die and who could still boisterously enjoy a spin on the carousel or when Michael fulfilled his very simple wishes.

At the age of 18 he passed away and Michael wrote a song in his honor: 'Gone Too Soon'.

Still he sat in church, thinking of this terribly brave boy who, although death was looking him in the eye, nevertheless was filled with such a love of life and optimism. People like him made Michael humble.

The endless list of his official donations was nothing compared to the countless unknown cases in which he simply wrote out a check when he heard that a child needed help. He had the cost researched and gave the money. And no one would ever know where it had come from. He did not care to boast about this act. Through his global charities he organized organ donations and saved countless children's lives, unheard, unseen. He was the one who held children's hands in orphanages and hospitals, children who no doctor in the world could offer any more help, and who had no parents at their side. Michael was the one who did not let them die alone. How often had he seen children leave this earth, and every time a light was extinguished, he wept and vowed to stay strong, to endure everything so he could make it a bit easier for at least a couple of little souls.

So many times, calls came from hospitals, from desperate parents or staff. Or directly from the children. Children who had no more hope and were allowed to express one last wish. And sometimes the children's wish in their lives, where the clock was ticking, was to meet Michael Jackson.

Michael never said no. He always responded to these calls. Loaded with presents he traveled to the hospital and visited the young patients.

And so he also visited Gavin Arvizo, who had an unknown type of aggressive cancer, from whose body the doctors had already removed a six-pound tumor, along with the spleen, a kidney, and other organs that were affected. Gavin was condemned to die and he wept. His parents were unable to pay for the expensive treatment and other surgeries, though his mother tried to organize donations from everywhere. But the doctors said it would make more sense instead to plan the funeral. There was nothing more they could do.

On the deathbed wish list of the boy were three celebrities, including Michael Jackson.

Michael came. And he saw more than the boy. He saw that he could become healthy and told him: "Once you're through with the chemo, you can come to Neverland. There you will get well again."

Without another word, he took over all the costs of hospitalization, surgery and medications and then brought Gavin to Neverland. The boy arrived with his siblings and his mother. Emaciated and bald, he sat in a wheelchair, desperate, despondent, because despite the treatment he was given, he had no chance of survival.

But Michael would have none of that.

He took Gavin in his arms and carried him to one of his magical trees, he fed him, talked to him and made it clear to him that he could be cured if he wanted to.

"You have to tell your healthy cells that they should eat the sick ones, like in Packman," he told the boy. "You have this light around your body, a white light. I can see ... you will get well."

Michael pounded that message into him until the vision was anchored in Gavin, until he could not help but think about it all the time - when he ate, when he drank, when he heard music, when he went to sleep. After several weeks, Gavin, to the amazement of the doctors, was completely healed, and Michael was beside himself with joy and gratitude. He patted his head with hair meanwhile regrown and said:

"Good job, you've done well, Gavin."

Gavin took Michael's hand and cried with joy. He was healthy! He was allowed to live! And he was in Neverland, where everything was good and wonderful.

Those were the moments that made Michael happy. Love and music, he often thought, are so inextricably connected. Both are vibrations... and people, they vibrate too, and therefore music heals them. He could see it. He could see how the colors changed around a person when they heard a beautiful song. He could see how music made them softer or more vital and, more than ever, he was inspired, now that he had his own children, to lift this world to a higher level, thereby helping to ensure that all children of the world had a chance for a good future. He was often occupied with thoughts of God, with the Bible, and other scriptures. He meditated, and was in touch with people whose thoughts swung in unison with his own. It was a time in which he developed the desire to regenerate both mentally and physically. He underwent drug rehabilitation treatment, he didn't want to surrender to threatening letters and to someone unnamed, unrecognized, who wanted to destroy him for whatever reason. And he believed firmly that the power of love was invincible. But he was not naive and began to make provisions in the background for all possible scenarios.

After *Invincible*, it was clear to him that his future was in serious jeopardy. But at least he had success and revenues, despite insufficient advertising, that others achieved only with high-profile promotion. He would come back again - if only for his children. That was the reason he was generally interested in an improvement of his image, and gave in to the now five-year-old insistence of Martin Bashir that he do a documentary. This time the letter came at the right time and his friend Uri Geller, the mentalist, encouraged him.

Bashir had written Michael numerous times how much he admired his commitment to children, how much Michael was doing for this world, and he wondered why no one was writing about it. What is the reason, he wanted to know, that you would do this in secret? Why should the world not know what a great benefactor you are? Wouldn't that be something that would make the events of 1993 fall into oblivion? Wasn't it about time that someone reported in an exclusively positive manner about him? Authentic, open ... show the real Michael Jackson?

Michael was pleased by these words, but journalists were not to be trusted, and he said to his friend:

"I'm not going to do this. Who knows what's behind it."

"But he is serious," argued his friend. "And Diana has trusted him. He told me that he wants to be the first to show an entirely positive picture of you ... and he'll broadcast first in the UK, so you will not face the American stations. Maybe that's the solution - to choose a different starting point."

And when Michael still did not respond:

"Remember what I told you ... if you carry distrust in you, you'll bring it to the outside and it will come back to you. Now you can try it with the opposite."

Michael turned thoughtful. He felt refined and more matured from these past years. And since he needed love, very badly needed it, like all people of this world, Bashir's flattery did not miss its mark. He had so long been pounded ... since 1993, almost ten long years. Bashir seemed to authentically admire him. It was balm to his soul and stirred the wistful hope of finally finding recognition in the world again. He saw it as the end of the lean years, as the start of a real new beginning. Excited like a child, he accepted.

February 2003. The disastrous Bashir documentary flickers in millions of living rooms across the screen. A strange man in his mid-forties is shown, a shopaholic, who climbs trees, disfigures his face, dangles his baby out a window, masks his children, holds hands with a 13-year-old boy and sleeps in the same room with minors.

The result was devastating, ruining Michael's reputation around the globe - it was irreparable damage.

And once again he fell into a big black hole. Michael locked himself in his room and cried for three days. He cried afterward, too. He could barely calm himself.

But the hole was deeper than he could ever have imagined. It was an abyss.

XX / 2002/2003 in the back room

"Oh, what a naive asshole!" he cried, clapping his hands elated. "What an incredible dumbass! He hasn't changed! He's still hard at work digging his own grave! Hehehe ... yes he's doing all the work without us! How nice of him!"

With mixed feelings, the receiver of the orders listened. With mixed feelings, he looked at the screen. He knew them both well. Michael and the healed child. And - he knew the original recordings, of which little had remained in this so-called documentary.

"You've done a great job! My respect! And now: activate the press, infuse them; they are horny anyway for this fucker ... there, too, we'll have an impossibly easy job ... law and order has changed ... anything goes. Fantastic.

He was not the only one who had watched the documentary with obvious pleasure and excitement about upcoming opportunities. A whole army of dark demons gathered in the background, ready to descend on Michael Jackson.

Lisa called him after the disaster, and it was good to hear her voice.

"What a vicious motherfucker!" she shouted into the phone and had a fit of laughter. "This idiot dug his own grave! No cow will want to be interviewed by him after this documentary!"

Michael smirked - for the first time in a week. And missed Lisa even more. She was his star in the dark sky. She always managed to cheer him up a bit.

Chasm

"Mr. Jackson, I do not like to mention it, but the boy is really outrageous. He... broke into your wine cellar, and Julie caught him and his brother drunk in the garden ... throwing rocks at the fish."
Michael tuned with disbelief to his property manager.
"He broke into the wine cellar? And was ... drunk? Where did he get the code?"
"Nobody knows," his manager cried indignantly. "The two brothers are brash. They give cheeky answers and won't listen to anything!"
"But ... but where is the mother?" Michael asked. The entire Arvizo family had been guests at the ranch for weeks now - which didn't bother him. He was delighted that Gavin was healthy again, and he should recover as long as he wanted. But this? That did not sound good.
"She ... is getting ... she is at the Beauty Farm," the manager reported sourly. "Getting her legs waxed."
And as Michael looked at him, he could not resist adding: "The bills from the beauty farm and from Mrs. Arvizo's shopping sprees will surely, as always, show up in accounting next month."

But Michael had other worries. Even though the New York Times condemned Bashir's methods vehemently and Lisa's prediction began to come true, Michael suffered from the consequences.
Two days after the Bashir's broadcast several complaints were already filed with social services by the well-known trash reporter and the lawyer who was infatuated with protecting children, in addition to anonymous plaintiffs. Tom Sneddon, the district attorney, excited like Nero before setting fire to Rome, pawed feverishly with his hooves. A complaint against Michael Jackson was raised - charging child molestation. Although no victim had come forward.

Meanwhile Gavin, the 13-year-old, holding hands with Michael, and his family were aghast at how Bashir had disfigured them, too, in his documentary, and the mother, Janet Arvizo, complained that she had not given Bashir permission to publish material about their family.
They made themselves available immediately for a rebuttal, where she stressed repeatedly and passionately how grateful they were to Mr. Jackson for all the things he had done for them.

He had saved them, Janet Arvizo said in the recording. He had been like a father, an angel to them, had healed Gavin. Had paid for the drugs, for the treatments, had taken them in. He had helped them when others slammed the door in their faces. He had restored in the children the joy of life and had given Gavin his life back. They could not thank him enough!

And Gavin: Michael was like a father to him, had never done anything sexual with him. Had never touched him inappropriately. Michael had never been anything but wonderful.

The sister: "Michael took care of Gavin when he could no longer eat, when he could not walk anymore ... the doctors told us to make arrangement for the funeral..." her voice dies away in sobs.

The children's father was interviewed separately and says there is not the slightest reason to accuse Michael Jackson of any offense. On the contrary: if Gavin had anyone to thank for being healthy again, then it would be Michael.

February 2003

The charges were examined. They covered the period from February 14 to 27, implying that the offense had taken place during this period.

That a prosecution without a victim could stand at all was possible because, after 1994, the law in California had been changed accordingly: a victim was no longer necessary for an accusation.

All together three investigations were conducted, Gavin repeatedly questioned, and his insistence that Michael was like a father to him, a wonderful person, recorded several times. There neither was a victim nor a justification for action. The file was closed with the remark 'unfounded suspicion.'

February until April 2003

The District Attorney Tom Sneddon was in a rage. He had the case investigated by his own office, which was not at all their job. That he uselessly squandering taxpayers' money was never held against him. But to his great anger, even his own people closed the case in mid-April as 'unfounded suspicion'.

File closed again.

Michael had traveled with his children to Miami to distract himself from the Bashir story and to see a circus that toured the city. He was sitting with friends over a cup of tea, when suddenly the door opened and the Arvizo family strolled in. Not invited, not called for. A friend of Michael's, Chris

Tucker, had brought them here from Los Angeles because they had pestered him for so long until he had given in. Nobody knew what they wanted here. Janet Arvizo had said absurd stuff on the plane and whispered with her children. Chris felt she gave them instructions. He was visibly uncomfortable and nervous.

Worried, he pulled Michael into a corner of the room.

"Hey buddy," he said, "something is wrong here... something is terribly wrong. Watch out for yourself."

Michael became aware. He began to distance himself from the Arvizos. Not only because of Chris' statement but also because it displeased him how the boys behaved on his property. Janet Arvizo started to panic. Did he no longer want to support them? Push them back into poverty? She instructed their children to call Michael "Daddy", whined constantly about how bad she was suffering, how much the Bashir documentary had destroyed her life, and did everything to make Michael feel guilty and responsible.

Michael responded with even more distance. His head was full of his own worries. Bashir upset him a lot, his advisors just told him that Branca was cheating and double-crossing him together with Sony, and he saw his future at extreme risk. Branca was the most important person; he managed the ATV catalog and all of his assets. He had neither time nor nerves for Janet Arvizo's whining. Moreover, he was suspicious of her and he remained vague about a renewed invitation to Neverland.

Faster than expected the Arvizos were back in their squalid shack again. No more full-time service and luxury. No more beauty farm and shopping at Michael's expense. Janet raged.

But then she got a call and a visit that showed a very different perspective - and put her under severe pressure. But still: it was a door that was open to her, should Michael actually withdraw support.

And fate took its course.

Another two months later the psychologist Stan Katz, who in '93 had written Jordy Chandler's evaluation, and the attorney Larry Feldman, who had represented Evan, now represented the Arvizos in public and announced that the boy whose life Michael had saved had turned against him.

Father, mother, Gavin and his siblings insisted now that Michael hadn't contributed anything to cure Gavin. Instead Gavin had been sexually harassed by Michael. They gave a time period between the February 7th and March 10th instead of the February 14th to 27th as originally indicated by Sneddon.

The reason: the Bashir documentary had been aired on the February 8, and this had supposedly been the trigger for the sexual harassment. Nobody noted the change in the time period, nor did anyone think the explanation was what it really was: illogical.

Michael's attorney, Mark Geragos, also noted that Mr. Jackson had an airtight alibi for this period: he hadn't even been on the ranch during the time that Gavin had given as the dates of harassment.

This should have closed the case for a third time and this time conclusively. But wordlessly the time of the crime was once more changed to February 20 through March 12.

After three lawless pushes the accusation finally took hold.

None of the super-smart reporters, committed to objective reporting, or other responsible people appeared to notice this.

They all wanted to see Michael hang. And of course, the Arvizos wanted damages in the millions.

Tom Sneddon, the prosecutor, who in his district had the nickname "mad dog," swung his first blow against the real victim. With a police force and press contingent - that would have even seemed ridiculously oversized for hunting a mass murderer - for the second time he raided Michael Jackson's ranch and did not appear to be conducting a search, rather a destruction. They slashed mattresses, demolished art, furniture and personal items.

Michael was in Las Vegas at the hotel Mirage when his manager broke the news: they had ransacked his home again, the devastation was being filmed and Michael's name stood in shredded letters in every newspaper and ran on every screen. The blood froze in his veins. In his mind was a landslide, everything fell into his stomach, causing a crazed feeling. Then he did something he had never done before: he cried out loud, long suppressed anger shot up like a rocket and he pushed over the breakfast table with full force, demolishing the furniture in an aggressive outburst. Silently his children stared at him. Breathing deeply, Michael turned around and ran, with tears streaming, out of the room.

An hour later he was thrown out of the Mirage. He was no longer wanted there. They drove to the nearest hotel. His limousine stood waiting before the entrance - they were not admitted. The disgusting thing in Michael's stomach knotted itself more and more, grew into an evil entity, wrapped itself up to his heart, clasped it, held it captive, crawled into his brain with black, all embracing tentacles. His breath was short and flat, needles in his throat, eyes covered behind the XXL sunglasses, biting back tears with effort.

Frantically his managers called all the hotels in Las Vegas. None was willing to host him. The news that he was again accused of child molestation ran on all stations. Michael's new album *Ultimate Hits* had just come on the market.

That would literally go up in smoke. Instead of a fair chance for a fresh start, Bashir had built the trap door to hell and led him there. And the backers of the Arvizos - he knew exactly who they were - dragged him into the deepest darkness, into their underworld. Within seconds, Michael had become a persona non grata.

"Who is this Tom Sneddon?" I asked hoarsely. "I thought the justice system in your country was fair? How can something like this happen?"
Grace shrugged.
"Tom Sneddon," she said, and there was no word to describe the look in her eyes. "is ... oh, look it up on the Internet! He is guilty of so many cases of racism... but since he is a white man, nothing is ever…"
Frustrated and angry, she looked at me. "There is this case with an Indian doctor," she said. "Sneddon didn't want a doctor from India practicing in his district, and so he used various illegal methods to get rid of him. The Internet is full of his crimes. He unjustly put a young black man behind bars for four years because he refused evidence proving his innocence. Santa Barbara prosecutors stood by their conviction until the case was taken to a higher court, where the man was exonerated. Sneddon has been charged with human rights violation on several occasions. But at the time it didn't have any consequences. The most macabre case was when a white man was indicted on charges of child *abuse* - and that is much different from *molestation*. The victim speaks out and the defendant confesses. Both statements are consistent. Sneddon closes the case, stating 'lack of evidence.'"
Angry, Grace looked out the window; her eyes were dark black.
"Sneddon is accused of malicious prosecution, civil rights violation, things like illegal taping, witness intimidation, death threats, and attempted attacks against persons."
I sucked in some air. "How can such a person still be in office and walk around freely?" I shouted.
"Well, anything is possible," said Grace. Her voice was monotone and she had to control herself even now, three years later.
"It was said - and we now know it's true - that the naked photos that were made of Michael during the Chandler case were handed around at parties."
I was speechless. When I finally found my voice again, I asked: "Why didn't Michael sue him?"
But Grace just looked at me, and her dark eyes confirmed everything I had already heard from Michael too in the meantime. I could answer the question myself.

Michael was accused of *molesting* a minor, Grace told me, not of *abuse*. Most newspapers, however, placed no value on this very important distinction.

"The term, 'molestation' is very elastic," I learned. "Michael was accused of 'lewd and indecent acts with a child under 14'. That could mean anything. That includes even a coquettish glance, or what is called a 'lewd or lascivious look' if made for satisfying a sexual need. And that is determined mainly by a credible testimony from the victim."

"But ... how can one prove, a 'lewd look'?" I asked outraged. "You can twist it into anything! Ultimately it depends then on how credible the family's acting skills are?"

"Something like that."

"What kind of theatre is this? How could Sneddon abuse his power like that?"

Grace was silent for a moment. Then she continued:

"Initially, there were two counts to the indictment, one count of attempted child molestation, the other of intoxicating a minor in order to molest him. The second count was brought up intentionally - it resulted in Michael losing his right for possibility of parole. Had he been found guilty of both charges, he would have ended up in the slammer for 20 years."

I closed my eyes. Twenty years. Because he had lovingly cared for a kid with cancer, and this child out of sheer greed for money now had nothing better to do than to pay him back this way?

Angry tears flooded my eyes, and I did not notice that Grace was watching me carefully.

"In early May the charges were expanded," she said. "The time period in which the alleged crime had supposedly occurred, was changed, without anyone out there thinking it odd, and Michael was indicted on several more counts of conspiracy to commit extortion and child abduction, and one count of conspiring to hold the boy and his family captive. Ten and then later fourteen counts."

"Excuse me?" I groaned. "Hold them captive? Michael?"

Grace stood up and leaned against the railing. Her profile stood out sharply in the dusk. With a blind look in her eye she looked at the tree outside the window and crossed her arms.

"The thing was designed so that nothing could go wrong for the prosecution," she said flatly. "The accusation of child molestation was based on Michael supposedly once briefly standing naked in front of the boy, that they had looked at pictures of nude women together, that Michael had indicated sexual acts on a doll, and got Gavin drunk twice until he passed out. Gavin said he was afraid of Michael, totally intimidated and didn't know what this was all about. Remember, we're talking about unfounded accusations of a 13-year-old rowdy who was cocky as hell to the staff! Who broke into the wine cellar, drove cars without permission, demolished them and wasted Michael's money! I mean, a statement from a kid like that could have resulted in a sentence of 20 years! And Michael carried this child in his arms when he first came to Neverland because he was too weak to walk! The same boy! Oh, he should be ashamed…!"

She turned to me. Only her eyes revealed what was going on in her.

"They set Michael's bail at three million dollars. That's about forty times higher than the usual bail. They drove up with 80 police cars - eighty! Even the FBI was there! The FBI! To investigate a case of alleged child molestation? Because of allegedly looking at a naked woman in a magazine? For 14 hours 250 policemen turned everything upside down! And they found nothing! Nothing! Not a thing! They slashed mattresses, tore down cabinets… they created havoc! So much that was dear to us, just … ruined … destroyed! Why are they allowed to do that? Why do you have to break a man who saved thousands of children's lives? Including the life of this unscrupulous brat?"

Tears of rage sprang into her eyes, then her hands clenched into fists and she began to sob as she thought of Michael who was so vulnerable and so gentle and could not bear this. I rushed to her side and put my arm around her. Grace dropped her head on my shoulder and gratefully took the handkerchief that I gave her. With tears in her eyes she looked back at the trees. Her voice was shaking.

"Michael was admirable. After his one and only outbreak, he was as calm as calm can be. It was almost as if he had seen it coming. He didn't freak out; he did not even appear upset. He consulted with his lawyers and they decided that he should surrender himself. He flew in with his own jet, and didn't even incur any expense to the DA's office - unlike Sneddon's pack that squandered millions of tax dollars for their slimy work! Oh, how I hope this Sneddon gets a just reward for his deeds!

And then they put handcuffs on Michael. He was taken in handcuffs to their office! Can you tell me why? He had come to them. He had voluntarily surrendered. He had only to walk another 10 feet through that door but these assholes put handcuffs on him! For the press! For his humiliation! They didn't miss any chance to disgrace him. And everyone played along.

She dropped into the chair. Wordlessly, I handed her a glass of water.

"The Santa Barbara County set up an 'open casting call' for anyone who had been molested by Michael Jackson or who had any information against Jackson. Pedophiles are well known to have many victims - and again they did not find even *one* far and wide. Amongst the thousands of children Michael had met during his life, there was no one. Not one."

Bitter, she continued through clenched teeth:

"More tax dollars were squandered when the district hired a whole PR firm, allegedly in order to meet the media storm, but we guessed correctly that it was only there to feed the public with distorted information from the courtroom. And that's how it was: there were suddenly these rumors that Michael had converted to Islam, which especially warmed the hearts of Americans after the September 11 attack. They did all that and more to take him down."

I remained silent. My heart was racing, even though the case had been closed more than three years ago.

"In my opinion - because of him they even amended state laws in California. Twice. They used loopholes that allowed them to bring up a sexual abuse charge even after the seven-year statute of limitations had expired. This way the old Chandler case could be brought into the present case. And in 1994 the law was amended so that the presence of a victim was no longer required to press charges. Want to know what I think? Michael goes through the Chandler shit. He comes out still kicking. That was in 1993. In 1994 the law was amended and Bashir begins to drill Michael for the documentary. He films him with Gavin and it's all set."

Silently, I looked into the darkness of the night. With Michael's claim of a large-scale operation in my mind.

"The video," continued Grace, "in which the Arvizo's affirm Michael's innocence, was not admitted. It was not considered evidence. This was an interview. At every possible place they choked the air from him. He lost his right to a preliminary hearing, where both sides, prosecution and defense, bring forward evidence to the judge, so it can be determined if it will even come to a trial. Instead, a grand jury indictment was obtained, a clear strategic disadvantage for Michael because evidence is presented to the grand jury only from the prosecution, and not from the defense.

Our defense had crates of defense material – but it was useless because it could not be considered by the grand jury. In addition, 'hearsay-evidence' was allowed. Admitting hearsay arguments is to my mind nothing more than taking hypotheses as facts."

Upset she paced back and forth, let her anger run wild.

"Since they wanted to bring up the Chandler case again, our lawyer at that time, still Mr. Geragos, called Pellicano, who perhaps had evidence that had not been used because they had settled out of court."

Seething hot I remembered Jordy's scrap of paper. But after what Grace had told me, my enthusiasm over that was limited.

"So," I asked anyway, "did he still have mitigating material for Michael?"

"Yes," she said. "He did. But what a coincidence: the day before the raid on Neverland, he was incarcerated for alleged drug abuse. How easy is it to slip someone drugs?

But the real highlight was that, even if Michael had been acquitted on the first counts of the sexual molestation, which no one really believed in at that time, then the counts of conspiring to hold the boy and his family captive and conspiring to commit extortion and child abduction would still have been valid. And here the law says that even *conspiring* and the *intent* of one of the counts is a criminal offense! Can you explain to me how to prove someone had 'the *intent* of an offense'? Or the opposite? Do you notice a pattern?"

I stared open-mouthed at her. "But..."

"Exactly. Michael was already as good as in jail before his lawyer had even once opened his mouth!"

And when I remained silent in disbelief:

"Sneddon put himself in the public eye and announced that Jackson would get eight years in jail for every count. And there were 14. The count for conspiracy, which is the most difficult to refute, coincidentally comes with the highest penalty: 70 years of jail... aside from the molestation and intoxication charges, which prevent the chance for parole ... can you imagine how we all felt when we saw that black and white in front of us? Can you imagine what it looked like for Michael? The trap was perfect. The noose tightened. Not even his lawyer saw a loophole."

Grace returned a quick glance. I was speechless with horror, could not bring out a word.

"Michael was dying of fear," whispered Grace, "dying of fear. He had been threatened his whole life ... but now ... now he got letters from inside jail - from inmates. From felons. From murderers. He ... you need to know ... child abusers are smuggled into American prisons with false identities because they are considered absolute scum inside, and otherwise the chance of their survival is zero. How was that supposed to work out for Michael, one of the most famous people in the world? Everyone knows what goes on in these high-security penitentiaries ...guards are trained to mistreat prisoners, make their life a living hell ... and Michael ... Michael got these beastly letters and we couldn't prevent him from reading them. And ... they described what they would do to him ... they described ... how to torture a man ... ... until he begs to die ...he... I..."

Grace broke off again, squeezed her eyes shut, held the handkerchief to her face.

"The truth is: it was not just a lawsuit, not just about destroying his reputation. This time he was fighting for his life. And he knew it."

It tore my heart apart. How could there be people who did things like this to other people? How could people like Sneddon and Bashir and all the others ever answer before God for what they did here? What kind of miserable tests had Michael been submitted to? I moaned loudly and started bawling. This time it was Grace who put her arm around me.

After a time we walked to the kitchen and got some coffee.

"I have to go, Grace, take a walk," I said. "Otherwise I can't stand it anymore."

Grace just nodded, fetched a jacket, and together we went to the water and sat down on a bench.

"Things went badly from the start," she recalled. "Michael was late the first day, which didn't sit well with the judge, but of course worked fine for Sneddon. But...Michael's fans were there - they had come. From everywhere. They arrived from every continent of the world. From Africa, Asia, Europe, Australia ...America ... they were there. Michael could count on his fans. They spent their own money to pay for the airline tickets, sacrificed their vacations, camped out under horrific conditions, endured the treatment of the law enforcement officers. They weren't allowed to wear Michael Jackson T-shirts, were threatened by dogs, and people listening to Michael's songs in their cars were questioned and arrested on the slightest pretense ... it was as if they were in a prison camp.

But they endured it all to show him their love. They besieged the streets in front of the building, and Michael took time for them, touched their hands and threw them a kiss. This was not only a handful of fans. It was what we were used to from Michael: masses. And those who couldn't come prayed at home for his release. There were chains of beacons, prayer circles, silent demonstrations.

But the judge was not happy about all this commotion. Or the press frenzy - that wasn't Michael's fault at all. And the media..."

Grace stopped. Now, when it came to the press issue, her body stiffened with anger. "The media was biased against Michael from the beginning. I don't know why they showed up at all, since they already seemed to know what they were going to write. I mean, there are millions of reporters out there, and all of them deemed Michael guilty from the beginning? All of them? They were so biased. They picked Michael to pieces. There was hardly anyone who objectively reported about the trial, especially when it came to the last 40 crucial days. To them, Michael was a criminal. They drooled for his execution, greedy like the plebs at the Colosseum in Rome. No one presumed him innocent."

"They way Sneddon put it together, it looked bad," I mumbled. Back then I had taken no notice whatsoever of the trial. To withstand this wave of scorn and malice was in itself a feat.

"Yes, it looked very bad." Grace looked up, her throat was constricted. She tried to pull herself together, but the tears were stronger, finding their way out again.

"They were pummeling Michael. They outdid themselves with adjusting the camera lights, so that they showed his nose and eyes in the most unfavorable way. Took pictures with distorted lenses, just to get a particularly stupid picture of him. This trial was the largest in American history. It was a circus. A media arena in which Michael was supposed to be thrown to the lions. A modern Christian persecution. NBC alone had a 4,000-square-foot platform for its TV broadcasters, producers, reporters and cameras. CNN was allowed to build a several-feet-high base so they could film from a bird's eye view. All the others staked their tents with their equipment inside, around the Santa Maria Court. FOX, ABC, CBS ... it was a huge media village ... everyone, everyone was there ... a total of about 2,500 reporters, with the sole purpose of putting Michael Jackson down for every move he made. And I repeat: for child molestation! Because of a possible 'lewd glance'! They were all so disappointed when they saw how civilized Mike was and what good manners he had - in contrast to those vultures."

Grace's eyes flashed with fury.

"As if he didn't have enough on his plate! Michael had to wear a bulletproof vest because every day his murder was foretold. None of these fucking reporters could have survived an hour of Michaels's life – they should think about that, before they judge him. And even if there may have been one or the other who did want to report objectively, the producers of the TV stations broadcasted only bad news. Why? How in the world is it possible not to think of conspiracy and corruption when you see something like that?"

I was silent at her gaze. The extent of his tragedy was terrible. It was even more terrible knowing of Michael's gentleness and the vulnerability, which are such a part of who he is.

"The trial started and it was lengthy although the jury selection happened rapidly. It was not easy to select unbiased jurors; try to find 12 people in America who don't know Michael! There are scarcely a dozen people on this planet who haven't heard of him! Surveys showed that black citizens tended to believe in Mike's innocence. But none of the jurors were African-American, despite efforts by his defense team to secure at least one black juror. But blacks make up less than two percent of the northern part of the county where the bulk of the prospective jurors were drawn from and Sneddon used his veto to dismiss several of the black jurors. In the end Michael did not get a jury of his peers, which would have been people of his age and people of color, a mixed diversity."

I closed my eyes. His chances of survival dwindled with every sentence Grace uttered, and her words almost hurt physically.

"We had to assume that even the jury was influenced from the outside ... but I'll spare you the details," she said. "I'll jump ahead to the most important time, before the verdict in the Spring and Summer of 2005, the last 40 days. The prosecution gave their opening statements first; then the defense. Both called their witnesses. It was brutal for Michael to have to listen to the lies of the witnesses. It got worse every day. Every day he became more discouraged, he was being gutted out, and it was awful to have to witness that."

"But how come the Arvizos changed their minds so suddenly?" I asked roughly. "They had already testified to the opposite! And what kind of bullshit is this 'conspiracy and abduction'?"

"Sneddon had already been in touch with the Arvizos in February, before everything took off," said Grace. "Our two employees who had tended to the family found the business cards of Sneddon and the Chandler's lawyer, Feldman, at the home of Janet Arvizo. From the nearly 200,000 attorneys in LA, the exact same team as in Chandler's case was assembled. Why didn't that make anyone suspicious? And Sneddon wanted to dig his nails into even our two employees. He promised full immunity - and what not else - if they testified against Michael. But thankfully they were both loyal. They decided to testify on their own behalf and on Michael's."

"On their own behalf?"

"This is your second question: Sneddon threatened to report Janet Arvizo for welfare fraud and because of a few other tricks she had been playing. But if she went along, he promised her protection; she could then sue Michael for damages in the millions. Dumb thing for Arvizo though, that she had already stated several times that nothing had happened.

So they constructed a case. They said that Michael and our employees had held the Arvizos and had threatened them. That they were prevented from leaving the ranch. Further, that Michael had given them a script and ordered them to speak a fabricated text to the camera to exonerate him. According to that, Michael wanted to take the Arvizos to Brazil so they would be neutralized. He had supposedly summoned them to Miami in order to deport them from there out of the country. And there you've got the charges, conspiracy, kidnapping and false imprisonment."

"That's ... outrageous!" I cried.

"Isn't it ever. At least now it was clear why they persuaded Chris Tucker to bring them to Miami. Meanwhile Janet Arvizo wanted to go on vacation at Michael's expense and had actually booked a flight to Brazil ... and so she presented the scheduled flight as part of her intended abduction."

"Who believes this kind of crap?"

"Everyone believes this crap as long as it was dirty enough," Grace said. "And then Sneddon claimed he received a call from Tokyo."

"From Tokyo?"

"Exactly. A call that said Michael was totally broke. That Michael was penniless. That he had hoped to get back up through the Bashir documentary. That a lost trial and its costs and consequences would completely ruin Michael. And that he had therefore begun to molest Gavin. So Michael was anxious to force the Arvizos to make false statements in his favor, and to get them out of the way."

I looked at her blankly, "You don't give the impression that you believe that."

"I don't. Sneddon gets a call from Tokyo? Why should Sony call Sneddon? Anyway: what weight does an unverifiable call carry? If Michael had to go to jail, he would have been finished regardless ... think about it. They used Sony to cover up the real mastermind ... that's my opinion."

"Michael has indicated all along that a bigger force was behind all this, that someone's pulling strings…"

"Oh yes, someone is seriously pulling strings," hissed Grace. "And that someone is too powerful to ever get his shoes dirty!"

"Who?" I asked, gagging.

"Even if I knew," she said. "I would never be able to tell you."

I nodded nervously.

"I admired Michael so much throughout these days," whispered Grace. She clasped her cup with both hands as if she could transfer the pressure onto the porcelain.

"He was so strong, he mobilized all the forces that he still had ... but still ... it wasn't possible without pills. He controlled himself, day after day. He endured everything without complaining. He never spoke of himself. His interest in the welfare of other people had not been reduced an iota. He asked his lawyer every day about his sister, who was going through brain surgery, asked everyone with whom he spoke: 'How are you?' rather than talking about his own misery, and he was always sympathetic. Not for one second did he give up his love. The trial proceedings... he took it ... like ... a performance. He was standing on the world stage and he would hold out until he collapsed. That's what he had always done. He'd danced with pins in his foot ... with a fractured vertebrae... until the show was over.

But when the end of the trial approached and the closing statements came, he was only a shadow of his former self. Inwardly, he was completely eroded, entirely finished. His insomnia had risen to its highest level. I asked myself every morning how he managed to sit in this courtroom for a full day, stared at by people who hated him and judged him - for nothing. And the prosecution, mainly Sneddon, dug around in the dirt. They had brought in witnesses that made your blood run cold. They brought the mother of Jordy, who wore clothes like a model - paid for with Michael's money. She said that she had not exchanged a word with her son in 10 years. The prosecution would naturally have loved to have Jordy as a witness, but he was abroad. Maybe his father had managed to get him out of the country, we don't know. But still ...Jordy is a grown man...he would have ... it would have been a good opportunity for this..."

Grace bit her tongue to hold back the insult, which was lying on her tongue ready for release.

"Wouldn't Jordy have indicted himself if he had suddenly admitted that it had been blackmail back then?" I asked.

"Sure, it would have required a display of greatness..." spat Grace, paused, tried to regain her composure before she continued:

"Anyway, the prosecution's witnesses didn't look like much: there were former employees, dismissed for dishonesty, who God knows would have claimed anything to hurt to Michael. They even called the staff of the private jet in which Michael had flown back to surrender himself. And guess what: they had bugged the jet and installed hidden cameras to record anything that might incriminate Michael! It's illegal! Why can they get away with smearing him like that when crates of exonerating documents are not allowed? Where were these super-clever reporters who were supposed to inform? These vultures were all ready to push a man and his family into the abyss for the sake of profit, sensationalism and their careers! If at least one of them had thought about the children! Oh, I wish so much for these people to come into such a situation even once! So that they feel who is the actual criminal! The plaintiffs and the press dug up every sleazebag out of his hole who still had a bit of dirt to throw. The prosecution called it a 'strong case' against Jackson - but the whole thing was nothing but an evil, despicable farce."

"But ... tell me how..."

"Our rescue was God," said Grace, "and the lawyer Thomas Mesereau who took over the case in April 2004. Michael's brother Randy had asked him earlier, but at the beginning of the disaster he was busy with another major trial, and said he couldn't handle two large cases. But for the first time we were lucky: six months later, Mesereau was not convinced of the innocence of his former client, handed the case off and came to us. And with him everything changed."

It was easy to see Grace's opinion of Tom Mesereau. I had seen him on YouTube. He was a very handsome man. And he had shown integrity, was very clear, very straight and personable.

"The reason why we had a chance with him, I believe was, because of a statement he made," whispered Grace. "He said, 'This case is about one thing only: it's about the dignity, the integrity, the decency, the honor, the charity, the innocence, and the complete vindication of a wonderful human being named Michael Jackson'."

Briefly she pressed her lips together, her eyes were moist.

"Mesereau had recognized Michael's soul. He looked into his eyes and knew that Michael was innocent. More than innocent. Tom Mesereau simply captured the character and essence of Michael."

I said nothing. The significance of Michael's drama made it hard to breathe.

"Mr. Mesereau completely took apart the prosecution's witnesses," Grace said grimly. "The most important witnesses. The ones that were supposed to incriminate Michael the most, he unmasked as vile liars. When Gavin Arvizo came to the witness stand, the prosecution could have peed in their pants they were so excited with anticipation. But he was cocky, slouched around in the witness stand and reeled off his memorized text. He was so obviously insincere that it made your toes curl.

After that, it was his brother Star's turn, and strangely the statements of the two did not coincide at all - on the contrary - they contradicted each other, and the first stirrings of disbelief were apparent in the faces of the jury. And even more: when Mr. Mesereau drilled them, it turned out that the two boys had been instructed prior to their testimony by the prosecution! That didn't come across well to the judge, even less for the jury. Fortunately for us, they were so stupid they couldn't agree on the same story!"

With a forceful movement that revealed her anger, Grace set down her cup

"And the mother ... this ... Janet was the pits! This woman embarrassed herself and the prosecution completely! Oh, how I thank God for that! You have no idea how thankful I am! Mr. Mesereau shredded her to pieces! He uncovered her as a professional scammer. There was nothing more to quibble about, not even for our dear Sneddon. Mesereau proved how she had extorted large sums of money from a department store with lies, claiming she had been sexually harassed by security personnel. And that, after they had stolen thousands of dollars worth of clothes! Her boys were trained to seek out celebrities and live at their expense. One of them spoke about how Gavin attached himself to him and how he couldn't get rid of him. How he constantly begged for money. He and his father! And the mother! They claimed to have forgotten their wallets in the house of celebrities when they were invited there, and when the host returned the wallets, they claimed that there had been $300 in them, which was now missing. They just used the cars of these people and became more and more brazen. And they did that to many kindhearted stars! And the most kindhearted of all was of course our Michael!"

I almost laughed a little. Most likely Grace had already fought often with him about that. At the same time, I wondered why Michael attracted these dark, awful energies.

"Janet Arvizo was really something," spat Grace meanwhile. "She kept contradicting herself and had no credibility to speak of ... she snapped her fingers at the jury and turned herself into a caricature - nobody believed an iota of what she said. In the end she stated with completely inappropriate drama that she had wanted in desperation to flee with a hot air balloon from Neverland! She and her children were the star witnesses and had been expected with anticipation. And they were an absolute disaster for the prosecution."

"Thank God," I cried, relieved. "Did Sneddon ever have believable witnesses?"

"Oh, there was Debbie Rowe ... he was after her! He hoped for the most crushing statements from her!"

"From Debbie?" I asked, astonished. "She was Michael's wife! How could she even be a witness for the prosecution?"

"Because she was fighting for custody of the children, and Sneddon was convinced that she was interested in hurting Michael."

"But why did she do that? Hadn't they agreed that she was merely a surrogate mother?"

"Yes, and she stuck to that until... umm ... I mean, she was worried about Michael. About his health, especially about his environment ... she felt the children were endangered and wanted them out of the mess."

Grace bit her lips.

"Debbie is still deeply concerned. She thinks Michael surrounds himself with the wrong people who take advantage of him and are only interested in his money."

"Which is obvious," I mumbled. "What do you think?"

"The same," she growled and bowed her head. "If we could only convince Michael ... but he won't listen."

"After everything that's happened to him?"

"Well, at the time he was also following someone's advice!"

"Hmm ... tricky. But this means that you and Debbie must get along well if you are on the same page here."

"Debbie is great," said Grace. "She is straightforward, and that feels wonderful in a world like this. But I think she hadn't ever imagined that after the birth of the children she would become so uninteresting to Michael. The children became the absolute center of his life — nothing else was important anymore. Before, they had gone out, rode the motorcycle, had talked. That wasn't much, but now even that was over. Moreover, she saw the swamp he lives in, and that he can't tell who is good for him and who isn't. Yes, he is suspicious, but the heart of this suspicion is that he lost his sense of who is still trustworthy anymore. And then there's his pills ... the years of long term use... that makes him hazy... he wasn't thinking straight anymore. I mean ...Debbie is sharp. And she saw it all. The danger Michael was in. And along with him the children. She thought if she had custody, the children wouldn't be threatened to this extent ... but Michael is uncompromising when it comes to his babies ... they are what he lives for, and if someone tries to take them away ... that's a bit too much. She hurt herself a lot with that."

"Too bad," I said. "Michael had a real friend in her."

"He still has. People like Debbie don't cross over even if they've been hurt." Grace smiled and it was good to see something positive in this mess.

"Sneddon questioned Debbie in such a smug way, so confident of victory that everyone thought he was winding up for the blow to Michael's destruction. Debbie was his last witness, which means that her impression would be the lasting one. Sneddon asked these subtle and sneaky questions so she would just say anything that could be used against Michael. But right at the beginning she cut him off and told him that she wouldn't let him dictate what she has to say, and she always says what she thinks. She was so damn honest and straightforward that she shone like a beacon in this charade. And in the end she broke into unrestrained praise about Michael."

Grace giggled.

"You should have seen the face of this scumbag Sneddon when she suddenly got going! In such a blunt, direct manner that nobody could oppose. She was so irresistibly personable! Everyone in the courtroom had an entirely different image of Michael after that - one that was true!"

"Oh, that's so great! For this alone, I could kiss Debbie in hindsight!" I cried. "Again something positive for the press!"

Abruptly Grace's smile died again. "The press?" she asked sarcastically. "You don't believe that even one of those damn reporters out there had one good word to say about Michael? To them he was guilty!"

"But Grace! You said earlier that none of the witnesses of the prosecution had held up! And there was no question that Mesereau was able to take them all apart! And exposed the Arvizos as liars!"

"Do you think they care about that?" spat Grace. "They all reported only scandalously, just like before! When Michael once came to court in pajama pants ... that was fodder! That was important! They said nothing about how unbelievable Gavin was. After his statement, they wrote in big headlines: 'the victim confirmed the statement! Jackson as good as convicted'. I mean, what is the public supposed to think? And when the mother was on the stand ... not a word about her scams! No, they repeated the charges! 'Mother of victim afraid of Jackson!', 'Mother of victim accuses: capture and kidnapping'! 'Janet Arvizo crying on the witness-stand over Jackson's cruelty'! THOSE were the headlines! These bastards! And of course, they pounced on the statement that Sneddon supposedly got from Asia: that Jackson was broke! This was the news that went around the world! I can remember when Michael was accused for the first time because of Jordy, the press was presented with a boy said to have been detained since his third year of life by Michael in a basement and abused sadistically. Six years! And Michael supposedly filmed the whole thing! How sick can people get?"

Distraught, she paced back and forth. "They printed that Mike had had 42 cows slaughtered in Asia to put a curse on Steven Spielberg! That Jordy allegedly couldn't bear to see Michael and that's why he hadn't come!

That was what the public heard about - no matter how good Mesereau was, no matter how many witnesses were taken apart, and no matter how many witnesses testified on behalf of Michael! None of that was printed! They were all biased, infiltrated, primed!"

I was dizzy with the thoughts from that time. What had been going on in Michael's head in those days? How much faith could he have had in the judgment of the jury after all these manipulations? How big, or rather, how tiny, was the hope of coming out alive from this drama? How, damn it, had he been able to stand up to the pressure?

Tormented, I looked at Grace. Sisterly, she took my arm, squeezed it and we took a quiet stroll through the park.

"Are you holding up?"

"Yes, please. If you are up to it, I'd appreciate if you'd continue."

Next scene: kitchen.

We had prepared a bite to eat and it was nice to be with Grace. The story, however bitter it was, connected us.

After dinner I made us a cup of cappuccino, we sat at the kitchen table and lit a lantern in a red glass. The flame was burning quietly and without flickering, and Grace set out to talk about the last part.

"The prosecution began in late February with the examination of their witnesses. Did I already mention that our most beloved Mr. Bashir was there, also?"

"Oh, no!" I cried in horror.

"Oh yes! And he showed who he was: coward, coward, coward. He denied virtually every statement. Then they showed his film..."

"What for? What does his documentary have to do with proof?"

"Nothing. But it portrayed Michael as mentally ill! To millions of people around the world! Could be that it would have the same effect on one of the members of the jury!"

Outraged, I snorted out some breath. "I hope it didn't, right?"

"Who the hell knows? But you see - they didn't leave anything out. The video statement of Gavin that indicated that nothing had happened between Michael and him was not allowed. But the shitty film of a career mad journalist..." Grace broke off furiously.

"How did you feel when you first saw the documentary?" she asked me then.

"Umm... weird," I admitted. "I didn't want to believe it, but at the same time I felt my mind tell me: but those are real pictures, that's Michael in person, these are words he is saying, things he's doing ... I mean, he *did* dangle Blanket from the balcony... he seemed ... strange."

"You see," Grace snorted again. "There you have it. And you'd seen the documentary after you already had personal conversations with Michael! Now try to imagine that someone sees it who, up to that time, has seen him only portrayed by the press as a crazy psychopath! Or a member of the jury, who thinks, there is a man who has every reason to be a pedophile!"

I realized that the chances for Michael were, despite the excellent work of Mesereau's, minimal. More than slight.

"Mr. Mesereau," continued Grace, "then proceeded to do exactly the right thing. He showed the cut scenes, everything, in full length. The unabridged statements from Michael, all the good things, his faith, his belief in love ... The whole thing was accompanied by Michael's music and ... what can I say... it was ... touching ... it felt so good, to suddenly see something so sincere, honest, warm-hearted. It felt so good to see the real Michael. And ... his energy spread out in the courtroom like wings of an angel. He seemed so open and innocent in his child-like way, in his need to help. Some members of the jury even cried."

"Oh, thank God," I whispered. "Thank God, that they were so sensitive to capture the true message."

"Yes, it changed a lot. Michael is right. Music heals. And some of his songs especially."

"Yes," I said. "They do."

"After May 5, the case went to the defense. As I mentioned, Mr. Mesereau was able to discredit all of the witnesses who had testified against Michael. Most had personal reasons, revenge, jealousy, and so on. Staff who said they had been dismissed unfairly, while most had actually stolen something and had been caught. One of Michael's housekeepers even bribed her friend to make negative statements about Michael. With money that she then wanted to get from Michael. But the girlfriend didn't go along, she recorded the call and it was played."

I shook my head in frustration. Here they fought in such absurd and unfair ways, I wondered why a judge stooped down to allow things like this at all.

"Who testified for Michael on the witness stand?" I wanted to know.

"Other celebrities who had been harassed by the Arvizos confirmed Gavin's audacity. They said that despite his age Gavin knew exactly what he wanted and that he was by no means the small, poor victim he was portrayed as on the witness stand. They said how the Arvizos had repeatedly extorted money from them and when Janet, the mother, claimed she had been abducted by Michael in Miami, Chris Tucker bluntly stated that that was not true. The jury did not like it at all when it saw the crude lies that were used here. Tom Mesereau had shaped this magnificent phrase when Janet Arvizo claimed that they had been held captive on Michael's ranch. But it could be proven that she was on the road, going anywhere she wanted! With Michael's limousine! Tom asked her, 'How many times did you people escape and go back voluntarily so that you can escape again from Neverland'?"

Grace laughed herself silly over this sentence, and I laughed too. The rest was unfunny enough.

"And then the now-grown child star Macaulay Culkin testified, who, when he was a child was allegedly molested by Michael. Cul finally said what had needed to be said by someone for a long time. He said he did not find it funny when innocent people are accused, and without any regard to their social circle, including himself or other friends, who are included in the affront. He said he was a man of dignity, just like Mr. Jackson, and he wanted that to be respected. He couldn't understand why people went about their dubious interests while denouncing people wantonly. This is a young man of character!"

Grace was quite excited.

"But," she said then. "Of course we had to assume that all those things were not significant. Nothing that the voracious giant that wanted to see Michael hang, was interested in."

"Here's a totally different question," I interrupted. "How did Michael's children react? Did they know?"

"Yes and no. Blanket was too small. But Paris is a bright child and Prince, too. They caught on, even though we told them as little as possible. Paris and Michael wished their Daddy the best of luck. Every day. Every damn day. The whole thing went from the end of February to mid-June. On June 2 the lawyers had their closing statements... then the jury retired and we had to wait until they had reached a verdict. The call came on June 13."

I quietly said, "That is, the hot phase lasted three and a half months, and then you had to wait an entire eleven days for the judgment?"

"Eleven days, yes," whispered Grace. "Eleven terrible long days. Eleven days in which the media did nothing but rile up people still out there by saying Michael Jackson is going to prison."

"God, Grace, how did you all survive this time?"

"We prayed," said Grace. "Day and night. Those were the days when Michael went from bad to worse, worse and worse ... no thought of sleep, we all slept poorly during that time. I remember that Michael was awake the first five of these 11 days, without a second to regenerate. His brain must have been like a carousel. On the sixth day, a doctor came and gave Michael something that made him sleep for almost one and a half days. While I don't like it when he gets pumped full of chemicals, in this case I was pleased. A day and a half in which he slept like a dead man. No nightmares, no sweating, just quietly and deeply. And when he woke up..."

Grace's voice faded. She had wrapped her hands together and bit her knuckles. Her eyes filled with tears, her lips pushed forward and her eyes rolled to the ceiling. Tormented, she rubbed her forehead with her fingers, closing her eyes.

"I happened to be in the room because I wanted to check on him. And he was just waking up."

Full of suspense I looked at her.

"He ... he had slept so long," she whispered. "And ... he ... he could not remember in the first few minutes ... he was fully in this blissful feeling of having slept well, to feel rested ... In those few minutes, he was ... he was ... simply...happy..." Her voice broke. "Do you understand? It was the first time I saw him completely happy! Completely happy."

Tears rolled down her cheeks as she remembered a happy Michael, a picture that was so rare. Much too rare.

"He was so sweet in this innocence, so open.... like a little child. He lay with this blissful smile beneath his blanket and beamed at me ... like ... well, like a baby who wakes up happy, full of trust in a new day ... oh God..." cried Grace. "It was two minutes ... two minutes! Two measly minutes!"

Suddenly she sobbed, and burst into tears. Startled, I put my arm around her narrow shoulders, she clung to my hand and cried her soul out of her body. I had trouble holding her, she was shaking so badly form her crying fit, which seemed endless. When she had finally quieted down a little, she blew her nose. In a hoarse voice she said:

"I'll never forget his eyes as the memories slowly came back. How slowly the light went out again, as the agony and sorrow flooded him. That's when I knew for the first time that he ... that he no longer wanted to live ... it was too much ... that he..."

She broke off and fell silent.

"And there were still four days until the ruling," I said softly.

"Yes, four more days," whispered Grace. "Michael did not eat. Finally, we had to force him. And the fear grew. The fear grew. We could see it. We could feel it. The days became more and more tense, tighter. Time stopped and sped by at the same time. On the one hand, this uncertainty was unbearable, on the other hand we sensed how small our chances were and we tried to hold onto every minute. It was an eerie atmosphere. In those days Michael appeared no longer human. He was a nervous wreck, he was an open wound. He talked on the phone every day with the co-attorney Susan Yu and Mesereau came by often.

Three days before the ruling, Michael suddenly asked him what exactly would happen if he were found guilty. He wanted to know what would then take place in the courtroom. Never before had he asked that question. He hadn't wanted to deal with it ... but ... then ... then we found out that Sneddon had given a party. That he had made a toast with champagne to Michael's sure conviction. It was clear: this trial was openly unfair, an execution. We could not hope for justice. We couldn't trust that the jury was not tainted. And we knew: even a single charge would bring him twenty years imprisonment.

Sneddon was celebrating. Michael was dying of fear. And now he wanted to know how they would proceed with him after a guilty verdict."

Grace's face was ashen.

"Mesereau was very direct, and Michael was grateful. He said that the officers would be standing right next to him when the verdict was read ... and if it was so ... if he was found guilty, then the officials would yank him up within fractions of seconds and drag him away. In less than a minute he would be dragged into a waiting armored car and driven straight to the high-security prison."

My heart stopped.

"Grace, that means he wouldn't have seen his children? He couldn't go home and say goodbye to them?"

"No, not seen them anymore. No, no going home. It had to be this way because of the press, because of the risk of flight ... Michael almost collapsed when he heard that."

I felt a wire in my throat. A stone in my chest. Grace had her eyes closed when she continued:

"That was around the time when the children caught on. Michael was with them every minute, but he cried a lot, he hugged them tightly, he never left their sides. He went from one room to another at night, to see the children sleep. He patted their cheeks, he kissed them gently so they wouldn't wake up. And he prayed. God was his only hope ... his only hope ... but since this whole disaster was a controlled production, we didn't know ... I mean ... it was hard to believe that the jury ... these 12 people ... would decide in favor... of Michael's fate..." Grace's voice had become softer and softer. Then she stopped.

For a long time no word was spoken until Grace had regained a reasonable composure:

"The bad thing was that we all knew there was still something bigger out there that wanted to destroy Michael. Something we had no control over. Something incalculable. Since the day of the final pleadings, Neverland was besieged with police cars at every entrance, every exit and the helicopters were circling in the sky. Michael was besieged in the truest sense of the word."

She told me how he had become almost mad with fear and pressure and stress in the last two days. Another note was found – in Blankets crib. A piece of paper on which was written, in Michael's handwriting:

"We got you. You don't stand a chance! You never had.

"On the morning of June 13, Michael was a wreck. He knew that the call was coming; he could feel it. He tried to meditate, but he was still a wreck. His nerves were raw. We sent for his doctor, so that he could give him something. He injected some meds, but it couldn't be too strong, because Michael had to be mentally alert. The last day he was as stiff as a steel rod, every muscle tense, his whole body ached. Everything hurt.

Then the phone rang. The jury was ready. We had to appear in court within the hour. When he was picked up by Tom Mesereau we all stood in the foyer. Karen was there, his friends, his siblings, his parents ... and his children. We were standing there like a formation of honor guards.

We ... we shouldn't have done that. That was ... that was ... when Michael saw his kids standing there, knowing that it could be the last time for a very long time or even forever, he dropped to his knees. He cried, oh, my God, how he cried ... he cried his heart out. He was on his knees, in this foyer, and the children embraced him, pressed their little mouths on his lips, on his cheeks, told him that they loved him and that they were thinking of him and were sending him lots of energy, and Michael could hardly breathe, he whispered, over and over again how much he loved them and that they must never forget, that they must never forget ... that love is the most important thing, no matter what happens ... no matter what happens ... He couldn't stand up. Again and again he hugged them, whispered: "My children, my children ... you are everything to me, everything ... I love you, I love you..."

His father finally grabbed him under the arms, picked him up like a doll, and he let himself be led away without resistance. They hauled him into the car and from then on he was composed. He concentrated. We all concentrated. We all sat and prayed. Although it was already too late."

The Ruling

June 13, 2005. Michael is in the back of the black SUV that takes him to court. He feels cold sweat on his skin, shivering inside his body, where no one can see it.

His heart is stiff and he tells himself to stay that way. Calm, calm. Only a few more minutes ... in half an hour it will all be over. Maybe literally over ... Stay calm, pull yourself together ... the internal commands have an effect. He freezes into an artificial calm, feels dizzy, barely registers his environment, phases it out.

The SUV stops. The engine shuts off. The heart starts to beat independently, no longer obeying his commands, hammering against his ribs. Michael gets out. Like a punch the heat strikes him, relentless sun, hot air that makes him weak. Someone opens the umbrella. A shadow falls over his eyes. Something is different from usual.

It's quiet.

Ominous silence. Not a good quiet, eerie suspense. Here and there a ray of hope, barely perceptible. His fans are silent. Like birds in the forest before the storm, before danger. He feels their fear, as he feels his own. He feels the hearts of his fans that race with his. Feels their prayers, this unspeakable pressure and all of a sudden he realizes that this could be his last minutes in freedom. He thinks of his children and tears want to stream down his cheeks. He wants to throw himself into somebody's arms and cry, cry, cry, wants to scream out all this agony, scream out this pain, to finally, finally be free of it. An iron hand strongly squeezes his arm, lifts him, pulls him up, gives him power. His father stands behind him, has felt the brief collapse. His hand is there. At that moment, Michael is grateful for this force, even if it hurts.

The short walk into the building where it is cool. He feels a lump in the throat, which pushes up to the palate. He cannot say anything. Hangs on from one second to the next. Arms outstretched. An official. Metal detector over his body. Michael closes his eyes. There is his mother. She looks at him, her eyes a pool of compassion, love and care. He looks away. He wants to be a little kid again, wants his Mama, to throw himself into her arms and bury himself there, knowing that everything will be fine. But ... nothing is fine. He is here. No air, aching heart ... his children, his children...!

Keep going. Keep going. Go on. His legs function strangely. One foot moves automatically in front of the other, until it's in the right place.

Until he is seated in the chair. At 2 p.m. all are gathered in the courtroom. Ten minutes later, the verdict will be announced. Mute, the officers take position next to him. Michael lowers his head.

Like a statue, he is sitting in his seat. More than ever all eyes are on him. More than ever his feelings exposed, exposed to everyone. His heart beats and beats, like a panicked bird that thunders against the cage.

A door opens. Wildly his heart leaps. The jurors enter. Serious, composed. Looking down, one after another, impenetrable expressions. Quietly, almost silently they sit. In the courtroom, it's so still, you think you can hear the dance of the dust in sunlight. Michael slowly raises his eyes. His accuser, the District Attorney, stares at him and in his face is triumph. The knot in Michael's neck swells, thick, firm, threatening to suffocate him. He bites his lip. Painfully he tries to suppress the ever-increasing panic. Intolerably long seconds tick away in the room.

A female member of the jury stands up.

A document in her hands.

His life in her hands.

Outside his fans standing, sitting. The tension is palpable, cruel. Many have their eyes closed, clutching the people next to them. Many pray. Many cry. Speakers are set up to pass the judgment directly from the courtroom to the fans outside. A woman has a cage of white doves with her. It's so quiet...so quiet ... even from the reporters, prevailing outside, no more sound. No coughing, no scratches, nothing.

Then the speaker crackles. Rustling of paper is heard. The voice of a juror sounds who, with a clear voice, reads the verdict:

Count # 1: Not guilty ... Count # 2: Not guilty ...# 3: Not guilty ... not guilty ... not guilty ... not guilty ...not guilty...they find Michael not guilty of all charges.

The fans erupt in frenzied jubilation. Everybody screams the pressure from their souls and cries with happiness. While for the duration of the trial they had been bossed around and harassed by the district police, there are now no bounds. They hug, leap and jump and yell madly. They sing Michael's songs like a hymn of victory, turn the stereos they brought up to full volume and dance the dance of liberation. In front of the courthouse, within seconds, all hell breaks loose.

The white doves fly to the sky, one after the other − to freedom.

***

Inside the courtroom, the reporter and the prosecutor sat in their seats, stunned anew with every 'not guilty'. And after the last official word of the jury, the emotions exploded.

Despite their one-sided reporting, Michael Jackson was a free man.

Everyone yelled at the same time, the family members embraced, the reporters yelled around, the audience raged in wild turmoil; chaos broke out, the officers of the court called in vain for silence. The noise was deafening.

Michael stood in the midst of this pandemonium, as if in the eye of a hurricane. A single tear rolled down his cheek. He pressed a handkerchief to his eyes. For seconds. Then he looked to the jury, the 12 people who had braved the long months of manipulation and pressure, who had upheld and taken seriously the dignity of the American justice system, and his lips formed the silent words over the chaotic screaming:

"Thank you."

The relief in him did not come. The show was not yet over. He had to get out of this chaos. No opportunity to let the feelings out. The agony of having to control himself almost killed him. But he went outside with his family, who all hugged him. He did not wave. He had just enough strength to raise his hand in greeting to the fans. Dutifully, he climbed onto the roof of his SUV, but he did not jubilate. There was nothing to jubilate about. He counted the seconds until he got into the car and counted them again until they were at Neverland when he finally, finally was able to give free rein to his tears. He knew it was not over.

"The media was upside down," said Grace. "They had been so sure of a guilty verdict - and they wanted to be right to the very end. Nobody had given the facts even lip service. But now that a truly independent jury bestowed justice, God bless them, they looked at one another, the madams and monsieurs of the press and this one or that probably wondered what they had been fabricating for all those weeks. Some said openly that they felt 'used' ... by whom? They had all failed their mission of objective reporting, everyone single one of them."

"And Michael?" I asked quietly.

"Michael..." Grace said, and her voice was stricken with grief. "Michael went home. The others wanted to celebrate. He was quiet. He let them hug him, he accepted the congratulations, but he pressed his children to his chest ... pressed them so tenderly to himself, as if he wanted to say goodbye ... and then he went to his room and cried. He was broken. You could see it. It was over ... it had ... just been too much. They got what they had wanted."

The faucet was dripping. In intervals as regular as a second hand ticking on a clock, the drops fell into the sink. It was the only sound in the big kitchen. For one last time that night Grace made her voice heard.

"We had packed up within a few hours and flew away as soon as Michael had his passport back. He knew that America would hate him as before. He left his ranch for good. Neverland had been just as dishonored as he had been. He didn't want to stay on a property that bore the spirit of destruction, or sleep in a bed that had been shown to millions of people. The kingdom of the children was dead. Sneddon was rid of Michael. He was homeless, broken and ostracized. A pariah. The press did not want to expose themselves and admit 'wrongful reporting'. They said that Michael was guilty and the jury incompetent. He had only come off free because he was a celebrity. Some went so far as to claim the jury had been bribed. It was ... over and out ... everything was over and out."

With a monotone voice Grace conveyed the last ugly bits.

"We traveled around in the world, rootless. Michael's self-confidence ... there was nothing left. He didn't understand why he'd had to experience this, and to be honest: no one did. Nobody who knew what a good person Michael was.

Eventually he settled back down here. I wish he would have gone to Europe and stayed in Switzerland as he had originally intended. But he moved back to this country that had dealt him such a miserable hand and even moved close to his parents. God only knows why..."

She sighed deeply. "The gossip columns and even the more serious newspapers spread rumors that Michael was broke and lived on credit from some sheikhs. They said he had to sell the ranch. But he didn't want the ranch anymore. He started therapy and that was good for him. That was only about three years ago. And I just wish, for him, just for Michael above all else, to get to a place where he can laugh again. The way he laughed before. But that's ... that's..."

Grace fell silent.

The acquittal had not changed the fact that Michael was outlawed in his country. Journalists often began their reports with sentences such as, "We are so sorry to have to bother you again with disgusting news about this Michael Jackson..."

He was the laughing stock of the country, a prime example of paranoia, the grotesque poster child of failed plastic surgeries, was elected "dumbest person in the world" three times in a row, was freaky, weird, and still a pedophile.

There seemed nothing, nothing, nothing left of his former greatness. Inside *him*, there was nothing left. Inside him was just a black hole.

Broken, full of hot desire for a person who understood him, supported him, loved him, to whom he was still worth something, he called Lisa. Lisa, whom he still courted. She had put him back together in her usual way after the Bashir story, and was a quiet observer of the trial. Michael had been hurt when she had married Nicolas Cage in 2002 and was relieved when the marriage had ended after only three months. As before, Lisa was the woman of his dreams, and he still hoped to win her back. But after the trial he felt a change in even her. Lisa couldn't bear the morass he was stuck in, saw that he couldn't free himself from it, saw that his reputation was destroyed and that it was not over yet. She was disgusted by all this dirt, this world of intrigue and dubious doctors with Michael sitting right n the middle of it all.

"But I'm not sitting there, Lisa," he tried to make it clear to her. "Look, I'm free, I have my children, I have my life, I…"

"But you … you have … Michael, let me be blunt … at the moment you have… no future…"

Michael's heart slipped damn far down.

"What do you mean by that?" he stuttered and this disgusting, depressing lump, which he knew so well, formed in his throat again.

"Mike," she said, "get over this thing first … then we'll see…" She dodged, and for Michael it was like the thrust of a knife into his chest.

"Lisa," he whispered, "…you know that I love you. I … I've made so many mistakes … I've told you so many times … you were so right … about so many things. Many of my people … aren't good for me. Some of them really are bloodsuckers and vampires … like you said … I wish I had trusted you then … I'd give anything for a second chance … with you I was so happy … and … Lisa … I would move to Europe with you…" Michael's voice cracked with suppressed tears, with loneliness, with longing for her. "…no matter where … wherever you want … where we could live in peace…"

"Michael…"

"Lisa, I'm scared, scared for my life … they want to kill me … they want the ATV catalog … you know these people, you know I'm not making it up…"

"Michael, why don't you just give it to them?"

"Because … it's too late … they're counting on getting it anyway. If I offer it now, no one would buy it. They already destroyed everything else for me. It's all I have to keep me alive."

Lisa paused.

"But … if we were out of the States… I…"

"Mike, stop it. You know that you don't really want that."

Michael bit his lips. His heart ached horribly. Not Lisa, not Lisa, too … please, God, let me … let me keep Lisa! Everyone had left him. There was hardly anyone left. Nobody wanted to have anything to do with Michael

Jackson. The pressure of the tears squeezed his throat, his voice was thick and very quiet as he asked his crucial question. The question that he really didn't want to ask, because he was so afraid of the answer.

"Tell me honestly, Lisa ... what are your feelings for me? You know I love you ... But what about with you ... tell me honestly…"

Lisa was silent for a while. Michael's heart was pounding and tears ran down his cheeks. He knew what she wanted to answer and hoped she wouldn't. Hoped he was mistaken, the way he had been mistaken with so many things in his life.

"Michael ... at the moment I'm rather indifferent towards you," said Lisa, and he could no longer control himself. A loud sob burst from him, and he gave his tears free reign. Lisa clutched the phone, pressed her lips together.

"I don't like that word," he whispered hoarsely. "I don't like that word, Lisa. Tell me it's not true."

"I'm sorry, Mike," she replied softly, "but I can't tell you anything different."

"Is there someone else?" Michael croaked distraught.

Silence. Then: "Yes, Mike, there is."

"What ... what's his name?"

"His name is Michael, too. I met him in Japan."

Michael bit his lips, his heartstrings severing by the blade of a guillotine. It hurt so much, so much, so much ... until something broke in him completely. He hung up. Weeping, he collapsed in his bedroom. Opened the drawer, popped pills. It was all so much more than a human being could bear.

***

With an awful pressure in my throat, I kissed Grace on the forehead good-night. I could hardly look at her. I was so grateful to her for this story, grateful that she had prevented me from having Michael tell me himself. In light of the misery that he had gone through, our initial conversation and the views that I had so strongly held then seemed outright ridiculous.

I professed to be unable of having any more words of wisdom for him about this issue in the future. Stiffly I went to my room, fell on my bed and cried my heart out.

Michael sent word that he was traveling the next couple of days, and I was thinking about finally taking a plane home. I was already emotionally exhausted just from hearing the story, and could not imagine how one could survive such an ordeal. Michael lived. He wanted to live. And not only that, he could still laugh. As before, he still believed in love.

That had now become quite a miracle to me.

Since he still was not here, I was surfing the net. This time I was looking for pictures of him between 2005 and 2007. There were only a few. A couple of meaningless photos. Then I came across a little video that showed him as he had appeared at the birthday of a well-known personality, a year after the trial. My heart ached at the sight of him. Dark sunglasses, oversized, were sitting on his dainty nose. He moved uncertainly, slowly, as if in pain, as if he could not believe that people tolerated him here, that there were still people who showed themselves in public with him.

He seemed visibly uncomfortable, craving the company of others and at the same time wanting to escape from it. The worst, however, was his smile. Michael smiled with clenched jaws and there was no need to look behind the glasses to know that the smile did not reach his eyes. That smile was so full of pain, so full of feelings of inferiority that I shut down the computer, shocked and depressed.

XX / 2008 on the desk

"Put more pressure on the kids," squawked the voice and it sounded angry. This man was still standing! This shithead just wasn't giving up!

"The children are his one and only. If we get to them, he'll be completely destroyed."

The other who had been executing so many orders hesitated.

"The children?" he dared to ask. "Isn't it enough already?"

"I hear he's planning a comeback. There will be no comeback. Who, Goddamn it, on this fucking earth wants to still hear this snotty, black fucker?"

"Then…" ventured the other further, who usually accepted orders without question. "…there is actually no danger…"

"We will not allow one," snapped XX and grinned diabolically. "…we won't allow it to be one." And then he leaned forward with a sudden movement and stared coldly into the eyes of the other:

"Prepare for everything - for the real thing. He's protecting his children? Remove the protection. We don't have to do anything … a threat will do it. Fear will take care of the rest."

The ordered one nodded casually. Avoided swallowing.

XX: "What about the doctor? Were you in Vegas?"

"Sure," was the reply. "We have somebody."

"There's nothing like a fall guy," XX smirked, and his lips curled "Always make sure that someone else takes the fall for you. There are enough corrupt idiots in this world."

The ordered one left. He had a big problem. One you were never allowed to have in his profession, in his position, with his rank, his reputation: he had long since developed feelings for the victim. Good ones.

The official

He sat on the couch, a beer in his hand and stared thoughtfully at the screen of his television set. On all channels Jackson's pale, tormented face flickered across the screen. Each of these reports were commented on by an eager reporter who was selling the world a monster that indulged in his abnormal appetites under the guise of a gentle disposition, with supposed generosity and kindness. No one noticed the ludicrousness of this case. No one its absurdity. Most people believed the written word, the transmitted images and commentaries.

Carefully, he analyzed the manner of the reporting. The deliberate selection of distorted images, obnoxious repetition of Jackson's metamorphosis, his alleged obsession with plastic surgery, his unnatural fatherhood, his strange marriages, the ranch with the zoo and the amusement park, all of which was illogically misappropriated as valid indicators of pedophilia and crime. And again and again: the Chandler case. The masses had no chance to think anything differently.

Sky Blumfeld leaned back. He knew the Chandler case. It had happened right in front of his eyes. And he knew Jackson.

He had met him ten years ago. At that time he, Sky, had been just an unimposing official. Now he was ... a bit more than that.

His wife's voice carried to the living room. He got up and helped her with the barbeque. They wanted to spend a nice evening with friends and there was still much to prepare.

Although Sky was only around 40, he was already afflicted with what his friends called "pre-senile bed escape." His bladder, no longer able to hold its contents for long, sent a feeling of pressure to his nerve cells, which forced him at least once per night to the toilet.

Sighing, he got up and shuffled to the bathroom. As he walked back down the hallway, he thought he heard a noise from his daughter's room. Although it was a long time ago, he winced, and then he calmed himself by saying: "It's okay. It's over. She's healthy."

He quietly opened the door anyway. Her luscious, brown hair was spread across the pillow, her round cheeks were slightly flushed, her lips beautifully shaped and curved. Sun was a stunning girl, 15 years old, on the way to womanhood. When she opened her eyes, a bright green struck the person she was addressing. Sky thought that without Michael Jackson, nobody would have been able to admire this green. Without Jackson, these eyes would have closed forever 12 years ago.

"Honey, what's wrong? Can't you sleep?"

Beth turned on to her left side and looked at her husband, tossing restlessly.

"Sorry, Beth, did I wake you up? I'm sorry."

"Never mind. What's the matter? Is something troubling you? Trouble at work?"

"Oh, no ... no ... just the usual ... it's nothing ... no."

Beth looked at him doubtfully.

"I don't believe a word you're saying," she said.

Sky turned to her, put his arm around her waist and pulled her to him. He gently pressed a kiss on her hairline.

"No darling, really," he muttered. "It is not the job. It's just that I was thinking about ...Jackson ... and I was thinking that without him our daughter wouldn't be alive."

The old fears made Beth freeze for a brief moment. She, too, had to remember that it was really, really over. She looked in her husband's eyes.

"You're thinking of the trial?"

"Yes, Beth. This man saved the life of not only *our* child. And look what they are doing to him. Even if we hadn't had the problem with Sun ... look at him. Look at those eyes. That's no criminal. I know that for sure."

Exactly those eyes ensured that the thoughts in Sky Blumfeld's head would not rest. They followed him. And the agony in them did not leave him.

1993

"Blumfeld!" shouted an unpleasant voice. "Bring me the file!"

Blumfeld got up. He had just been in the process of typing a very obscure report on exactly this file when the order reached him. He brought what had been requested, tucked in a gray folder, into the office of his boss, who was sitting together with an unknown man and discussing something. The man looked very proper and inconspicuous. When Blumfeld entered the room, he pulled a folder from his briefcase, and Blumfeld could see clearly the thinning at the back of the man's head. The man put the file folder on the table. The metal reinforcement was dented at the bottom right corner, as if it had once been dropped and had landed right on that part.

Blumfeld returned to his computer to write a letter of receipt for an expert's opinion.

A hypothetical case. Anonymous. An expert who had been asked: what if.

What if an adult was sleeping with a juvenile in one bedroom. If this adult spends a lot of time with this young boy and the boy prefers his company over that of his peers. What if. A lot could be construed from that. Apparently it had been decided to construe the utmost from it.

His boss approached and tore him out of his thoughts. He placed the gray file on the desk and rasped:

"Lock it in the safe."

Usually files of this kind were not put in the safe. As far as Blumfeld knew the gray file contained only an opinion. There were lots of expert's opinions lying around there. They were piled up in the input and output baskets and were kept in a lockable drawer at most. But not in the safe. It had to be an important expert witness report.

His boss was in a hurry. Over his shoulder, he called to him:

"Oh, Blumfeld before you go: replace the black toner in the copy machine. The cartridge is empty."

The gray literally jumped out at him from the usual manila, which was always used. When Blumfeld was sure that he was the last one in the office, he opened the file and studied it.

This time it was a real opinion and not a 'what if' scenario. This time, names were mentioned, and everything got a very ugly face: there was a report from Jordy Chandler, who described in detail how Michael Jackson had molested him.

Blumfeld nearly fell over. Jackson - a criminal? With mixed feelings, he put the file in the safe, saved his documents, and was about to leave. At the last moment he remembered the copy machine.

Cursing, he put his coat and keys on the counter, pulled out a toner cartridge and went into his boss's office. He changed the cartridge, and ran a test page on the copier. Patiently Blumfeld waited until the paper came out. With incomprehensible frustration he crumpled up the test page and tossed it fiercely, together with the empty cartridge, in the trash. The force made it rock back and forth precariously. Blumfeld watched the trashcan as if in slow motion, as if his fate depended on it, and finally it toppled over. Paper and garbage spilled out onto the floor.

"What kind of shit is this!" Sky shouted uncontrollably, wondering about himself. He was always a model of calm! Since when did a toppled trash can make him lose his composure? Angrily, he stuffed the papers back, when he realized suddenly what was bothering him: he did not want to believe that Michael Jackson was a pervert. He felt as if someone told him that Beth was cheating on him with his best friend. He did not want to believe it. But the report was so clear! With two or three papers in his hand, he paused thoughtfully for two seconds in front of the trash. Then he shook his head, stuffed the papers into it - and pulled them right back out. They looked familiar. It was two pages from Jordy's statement, only half legible because the cartridge had run out of ink. The file had been copied.

And then he acted quickly. He went to the safe, removed the document and made a copy for himself.

Sometimes, he thought, a series of coincidences determines the fate of people. He was confused and upset that night and decided to take a little detour to have some more time to think before he came home.

The form of the coincidence that he encountered in this detour consisted of two gray-clad legs, which he stared at as he waited for the bus. Before he recognized the man, he recognized the folder. It was the one with the dented corner.

As if directed by remote, Sky followed the man with the light hair into a bar. He squeezed into a corner with a clear view of his target, ordered a beer, bummed a cigarette and stared at the beer glass, perking his ears.

A woman in a dark blue suit entered. She seemed nervous, jumpy, excited. Unpleasantly and greedily she grabbed the folder, as if it were her diary. He knew who that was. It was Diane Dimond, the well-known trash reporter noted for her overzealous ambition - to express it kindly. She pressed the file like a baby to her chest.

The very next day the story was on "Hard Copy" and from there spread throughout the whole world. He could imagine that the woman had made a lot of money with this. What he could not understand was why his boss had shared this file. It was illegal.

Two, three years earlier, 1990/91

Gaunt, emaciated down to 110 pounds, Beth clung to the cold tube frame of a hospital bed. Her eyes were filled with tears, as she stared blindly into space, trying to process what she had heard. Sky stood next to her. His knees trembled. He could not help his wife. His legs were so weak that they buckled. He had to sit down.

Before them stood a stocky man, clad in green surgical scrubs with resigned, sad eyes, who was obviously feeling uncomfortable. Who would have liked to escape from the whole situation. Everyone in the room would have liked to do that.

"I ... I'm so sorry that I can't tell you anything different," the doctor said helplessly.

"How much longer?" Beth whispered hoarsely.

"Maybe a week, maybe two. If the kidneys fail, it'll be faster."

Beth made a sound as if it were her last breath and burst into such a violent torrent of tears that she could not breathe. Sky rushed to her, they both literally sank to their knees and, while dropping to the floor, clung to each other, weeping with open mouths and loud sobs. The pain tore apart their hearts. In the crib lay their dying, terminally ill daughter Sun. She was two years old.

The doctor fled the room.

"Hey, Mike, the parents can't get the money fast enough from the bank. They can't afford the surgery and there's no kidney to be found."

Frank, Michael's closest friend, handed him a small picture. A cute little brown-haired girl was lying in a hospital bed, connected to all sorts of devices and transfusion tubes.

"The parents are already in debt because of the high cost for the hospitalization. The little girl has cancer and she needs an organ transplant."

"Oh, my God, the poor little thing! What's her name?"

"Her name is Sun, but her parents call her Shiny ... kind of an endearing nickname…"

"When can I visit her?" Michael asked. His hand, which held the photo, trembled. He felt that he must go immediately, before it was too late. He could see things like that. He could recognize even with strangers how sick they were.

Frank had arranged for a visit the very next day. The Blumfelds could not believe their ears when they heard that Michael Jackson was going to visit their daughter and wanted to pay for all the necessary procedures.

To this day Sky was not able to really comprehend what had happened then. He was a level-headed, disciplined officer, known for his sharp mind. But this encounter he could not comprehend to this day.

They had rushed to the hospital. A shy man stood against the wall, wearing a surgical facemask, together with Frank. Sky walked over to Michael and had the impression that he was inching a bit away from him. He really did seem as shy as he had been told.

But that changed when they walked into Sun's room. The little one lay listlessly in her crib, and Michael's eyes were focused intensely on the child. His gaze turned infinitely soft when he looked at the little girl. He pulled down the mask and asked:

"May I touch her?"

Beth and Sky nodded silently, overwhelmed by their feelings and the tiny hope that had emerged as a cautious, almost imperceptible sunbeam with the go-ahead for the operation, and with the presence of this slim man sitting at the bedside of their daughter. His eyes were full of love and he was persuading her that there was still a lot to do in her life and that it was her duty to get well. He whispered into her little ear, ran his fingers over her soft cheeks and gave her a kiss on the forehead. And Sun relaxed. Where her eyebrows previously knotted together with pain, she now looked intently at this man with the huge eyes. A trace of a smile was on her face.

"God, what a sweet kid," said Mike as he looked up, and noticed the surprised looks of the parents.

Beth could not say anything. She had to cry again. Michael walked up to her and hugged her, and Beth felt how she drew strength from him. Sky was watching all this, incapable of a clear thought.

Michael talked to the doctor, who was very reserved, as if he did not know what to make of it all, and Sky could not blame him. However, Michael seemed to be accustomed to this behavior, and he seemed knowledgeable, as the nature of his questions proved. Then he turned around to Beth and Sky:

"I read a lot about this disease ... I think there's hope. My organization is connected to a database that locates organ donations across the whole world. We have already set all the wheels in motion."

Beth was the first one who collected herself.

"Mr. Jackson," she said, sobbing. "Thank you! Thank you! I ... don't know how we..."

"I'm Michael," Michael said simply. "And don't thank me yet. Let's wait and see. It is still too early to say anything."

"But still," Sky added in a hoarse voice: "Thank you for your help. Thank you for giving us hope."

Sky talked to Michael on the phone several times until everything was arranged. He had the impression that he was dealing with a sensible, down-to-earth person. But above all, he knew that he was dealing with a man who had an exceptionally big heart.

Then the redeeming message arrived that Michael's organization had located a kidney match. Sun was flown to a specialist clinic. Over the course of one year she was operated on several times. Mr. Jackson covered all costs. Sun became healthy.

Beth and Sky saw Michael only one more time, when he visited the already recovering Sun. He did not want any thanks. He was embarrassed. He had only come to make sure that their daughter was doing well.

After that all they heard about him was what the press reported.

And now the Chandler report. The more Sky got into the case, the more certain he was that something was fundamentally wrong. He began to educate himself about the drug sodium amytal. Alone the so-called confession ... there were several inconsistencies ... was not real. The more he read it, the more certain he was. The discrepancy between the previous statements and the ones after the drug were too big. Finally, the connection ... the attorney ... Sneddon ... the authorities, Evan constantly talked about ... and then during his research Sky found a document that stated that Jordy hadn't wanted to sign this report - and in fact had not signed it at all, that he had refused, and Sky uncovered names that confirmed that.

He looked these people up and interviewed them. They testified that Jordy had been forced by his parents, that he hated his parents for it and had sworn never to speak to them again.

Meanwhile, Sky knew that Michael had saved thousands of children's lives. Had made out hundreds of checks. That he was a regular fixture in hospitals and orphanages.

He had helped so many children and their parents. And not one person stepped forward to help him when he needed it? Not one? But when he worked out the background, the people who were involved and their network, he felt dizzy. Mr. Jackson had powerful enemies.

Carefully, he brought up the issue to a colleague with a friend who also had been able to benefit from Michael's money and his caring for their child. The answer confirmed what Sky had figured out for himself:

"Hey, man, can't you see who's all involved here? Do you want to lose your job? And honestly: what weight does your opinion carry? Just imagine the picture: someone much bigger than you wants to destroy someone else. And a little runt, you, goes running to the press, blathering something about the truth. Guess what happens. Leave it alone. This is a fight meant for Jackson."

Sky launched several more attempts anyway and met with a press person, baiting him with a hot story about Jackson. But even as Sky began his story, he noticed how the man abruptly lost interest and leaned back.

"Man," he interrupted Sky. "You promised me a hot story ... this is crap ... total crap ... no one is going to believe it."

"I have proof," said Sky

But the journalist wasn't interested.

He was not the only one Sky tried. The third one gave him the crucial advice: "This is making the rounds, man," he explained to the disillusioned Sky. "You're gonna make yourself very unhappy, if you don't quit ...don't you have a family...?"

And so Sky hadn't said anything. He had seen no way to preserve his livelihood, to protect his family and at the same stand up for Jackson.

And ultimately Michael had gotten out of the story, although the nature of the settlement had harmed his reputation enormously. Still, Sky had been ashamed. He was still ashamed today.

And now, ten years later, they were again choking the neck of the man who selflessly and, expecting nothing in return, was constantly saving lives. This time around was so obviously absurd that one's cheeks burned red with shame.

He sat in front of the television. He walked past the front pages of newspapers. Michael's tortured eyes followed him. Everywhere.

Finally, he made a decision. He was 10 years older, his job no longer the same. More so, he didn't want to lose this job. And without a job he would not be able to benefit anyone. Perhaps there were other possibilities.

Sky bought a pay for service phone and applied for a number using a fake name. As soon as the phone was activated he placed a call.

***

"It's in every newspaper – he's not here. He is in Bahrain."

"I know. But maybe ... you can tell him ... that I would be happy if he called back. Tell him my child is well - because of him. He saved her life back then...tell him that we never forgot..."

"Hey, man, what do you really want?"

Sky took a deep breath. "Please let him know that if he should ever need help, he can count on me ... that I can do something for him..."

The other end of the line was silent for a short time. "Who are you?"

"Tell him greetings from Shiny. Tell Michael to call me if he needs me."

That was 18 months ago. Michael had never called. But still, Sky had not canceled the service and the phone lay forgotten in the drawer of his bedside table.

***

Knowing about Michael's fate made me sleep poorly. But he was living with this fate. He was living with constant blackmail, amongst schemers and sharks, and with the knowledge of an all-controlling threat. I felt thoughts overrunning me, how they began to dominate, could not be switched off and I fought against them. With huge effort I tried to get back to the mindset I'd had before I came here. And in this endeavor, I was overcome with a deep longing for Neverland, for Michael's noble vision, for his ideal world as a balance against the evil that surrounded him. But this world, Neverland, was no longer his, it had long been boarded by Captain Hook and fallen into disrepair. But I felt an excessive desire for this imaginary oasis of peace and happiness. And I realized that precisely these feelings were the driving force of his being: to escape from this left-brain, business-driven world and to find a counterbalance.

Before I went back to Germany, I promised myself I would visit Neverland one more time.

The days went by, and it was impossible for me to talk to Michael. It was impossible for me to read my books. Now and then I picked them up only to put them away again, discouraged. Individual thoughts circled in my mind, beginnings of ideas arose. But ultimately, everything swirled around confused: the philosophical doctrines, his destiny, his immense threats, his fear of being killed, fear for his children, the frustration, that despite or perhaps because of all these divine gifts, despite all his wealth, he could not find happiness.

I thought about how everyone said he was crazy and that nobody believed him when he said he was being threatened. Nobody believed him anything. They didn't buy the white spot syndrome, his true love for Lisa or that Paris had been conceived naturally. It was all so perfect, it shot through my head. For decades, the media had printed that he was nuts and that, because of his antics, the drugs, the lack of treatments, he was paranoid. Who would believe someone like that? Wasn't that the best cover you could have? The devilish thing was that he really was being driven to insanity, so that in the end what "they" said was true. Whoever they were. But the relationship between cause and effect was the other way around, not that it mattered anymore. Taken too much, suffered too much, possessed by megalomania, sick, unsuccessful. A logical explanation. For all possible outcomes.

In the night I dreamed violently. I dreamed that Michael and I were locked in a room filled with instruments of torture and with gruesome creatures that wanted to kill us. They were everywhere, invincible, each creature a hydra whose heads multiplied the more we cut off. Our view was obstructed by scrolls that flew about in this chamber of horrors. Thousands of them were buzzing around us, lit up when they came close to our heads, only to vanish again, while their lights extinguished.

We were both so absorbed in the battle with the monsters and in defending ourselves that the scrolls were quite a bother. They smacked against our bodies, obstructed our vision and increased our fear that someone would ambush us from behind. Michael and I were completely panicked, totally absorbed with warding off the monsters.

A chorus of whispers arose and grew louder and louder.

"Find the answer, find the answer, find the answer…" it chanted from every nook and cranny. Michael and I were suddenly like one person, even though we had two bodies, but we were so fused that each could feel and hear the other's thoughts.

"Find the answer, find the answer, find the answer…" The chorus swelled and ebbed, sang, screamed, sometimes menacing, sometimes demanding, sometimes gently.

In the exact same moment, Michael and I realized that our struggle was in vain, that we could not win - there were too many monsters, we could not destroy them all. We realized that we were both trapped in a world filled with terror and horror. And we gave up.

With dread in our hearts, because we knew that now we had to surrender to the monsters, give our lives to them, we crept into a corner, backs to the wall, quietly holding hands. The chorus of whispering voices swelled one last time ... find the answer, find the answer, find the answer ... and died.

Then it was quiet. Deadly quiet. The monsters were moving toward us. As if in slow motion they approached, expectant grins on terrifying, hideous faces, giant spiders stretching their slimy fangs out to us, stinking, rotting, decaying bodies, with a paralyzing stench.

No chorus. No shouting. Only silence, emptiness, a black room. Like dying elves the scrolls fell, one by one, slowly, silently to the floor, sank into the greasy morass.

Michael and I were one and waiting for death. In our minds the message of the fading away, whispering voices echoed stereotypically. Find the answer. Find the answer. Find ... and with a last rebellious thought we both jumped up and grabbed the last scroll, just before it fell on the swampy ground.

At that moment, the ground beneath our feet gave way and we fell with a cry. We fell and fell and fell ... the scroll in our hands, endlessly, eternally.

Screaming I jumped up. Awakened by my own voice. Slowly my consciousness of the dream world penetrated back into this one. Realized that it had been a nightmare. A nightmare. One that had followed Michael in this world and materialized in a terrifying way.

Grand Finale

And again, I was sitting at the computer. Again I was scrolling through interviews and performances, clicking random scenes, known, unknown, always the question in mind: why? Why him? Why so viscously? Why so long? The 'light-attracts-shadow explanation' was too meager, certainly it played a role in this ... but something told me that this was not everything. Click, close, click, close...

Restless, I looked at scene after scene, jotting haphazardly on a piece of paper anything that jumped out at me.

"God," it read. "Humility, gratitude, giving. Love, sharing... his values. Need, wanting to be happy, he cries so much. His humor, his laugh. Then... such sensitivity. The raw eyes that hurt so quickly. Lasting pain."

He says he does not trust anyone and then trusts just the wrong people too quickly. He draws from the eternal source when he dances and sings and yet, he is so unhappy.

My fingers slid through interviews that I already knew. But today I saw and heard things in a different context, and arranged them differently.

And that night something began to crystallize distinctly.

Again, I noticed how the statements about his father always sounded the same. He often complained about the harsh behavior ... the endless yearning for childhood, for something whole and happy was palpable. His longing for love. Although he was so filled with it. He said that childhood was the key to happiness and at the same time it was something he believed he had lost forever, which no one could give him back, because the time was simply over ... and in reverse, that means he could never be happy because in his conviction this essential element was irreversibly lost. And despair, resentment and anger ran deep - a thorn in his soul.

Statements summed up, statements that he had made over and over again: Michael told reporters that he had often cried during the first years of his career because he thought he was not good enough. But he cries to this day.

Michael thinks he is ugly. Michael is never satisfied. He isn't happy about successful events. There is always something that could have been better. He has to be perfect. What is behind this desire for perfection? The child-like: I've done everything right! There is no reason not to love me! I was good!

Michael is always afraid that others won't like what he does. That others won't like him. That they might think badly of him.

After one of his grand deliveries of Billie Jean in 1983 at Motown 25, when the audience had gone wild over his performance, when his magic had been so evident in the hall, he had cried because one of his turns had not been perfect.

Michael loves perfection, he wants to create things, he says, for eternity and therefore they have to be perfect. No mistakes for Michael. Mistakes are bad. Mistakes are punished.

He identifies with the sadness of the elephant man. Someone who came to this earth as a monstrosity and was always regarded with disgust and with repulsion and yet precisely that was the attraction for others.

He tells Oprah that he models himself after Jesus, he wants to be as good as Jesus, give like Jesus did, help like Jesus did. What is the role he feels for himself? Does he feel perfection within him, but cannot attain it? What separates him from it?

He wants to be a good person. And if people have the desire to be a good person, it's often because they want to be loved. We all do so many things just because we want to be loved.

And then I looked at his video *Teaser*.

Content: crowds cheering him. They want him, are consumed by him. He is shown as a giant statue, adored by thousands of people. *Teaser* - that is his cry for love. But is that the kind of love he really wants? That he really needs? Is he misunderstanding something here?

Frowning, I read quotes from him:

I am an instrument of nature. My mission is to make other people happy.
"Gandhi, Christ ... if it was their fate, why not mine?"
"If you enter this world knowing you are loved and leave this world knowing the same, then everything that happens in between can be dealt with."
He says, *"I love what I do and I would be happy if people would also love what I do and if I am loved. I just want to be loved wherever I go. All over the world, because I love people, people of all races, truly love them from the depths of my heart."*
A scene from the Bashir documentary where he is asked if he feels lonely:
"If I'm stuck in the hotel and there are these thousands of fans calling out to me ... love is everywhere, but still you feel trapped and alone. And you can't get out."
And in his song about his childhood, one of the chorus lines, his eternal plea: *'Try hard to love me'.*
That was his challenge. All these statements defined his longing, his mission and his misunderstanding here in this life: love me! Finally love me! Give me this love that I give to you! Give me your love. Look what I'm doing for this love! How hard I try, how I torture myself, how much you torture me ... what have I done to deserve this? All I want is your love ... only your love, your love.
The misconception of our world, the misconception of most of us people on the planet.
I sat back and focused on the laptop. A final quote from him flickered across the screen:
"You want to be touched by the truth and want to understand that truth, so that what you feel and experience, be it despair or joy, you can use to give purpose to your own life and hopefully that of others. This is art in its highest form. For those moments of enlightenment I want to live now and in the future."
Something exploded in me. I turned off the computer, deleting everything about him that I had collected on the Internet. There was nothing more to research or to do. Finally, I felt no more conflict within me. It was all clear.
Night after night I went to the pond, watching the water. And I knew that this was the quiet before the storm.

Calm and still, he sat next to me on the bench on the fifth night. Neither of us said anything. I closed my eyes and enjoyed this wonderful aura around him. Still he had retained this innocence, still there was this light around him and given the knowledge I had now, I was gripped by a wave of respect, love and admiration for this fawn-like man, for his willowy strength. But more prominent than on the first night with him I sensed the antagonism of his soul.
For a long time we just sat. For a long time we felt the vibrations of our lives and those of sentient beings around us. The lake was calm and smooth as a mirror, not a wave rippled the surface, no bubbling fountain that would have

destroyed the transparency of the water. From the shore we could see all the way to the bottom. The small lake was quiet, just like we were.

And it was the water that attracted us and taught us the greatest wisdom. Every drop of the lake was so individual and yet made everything one. Water is so versatile. It is solid, liquid and gaseous. Invisible, visible, within us and outside of us. Water was everywhere. And a great teacher.

Michael was cold. I felt him shudder beside me when a gust of wind sped through the trees like an invitation.

I pulled out the blanket I had been sitting on, unfolded it and draped the fleece, warm from my body's heat, over Michael's gaunt shoulders. Gratefully, he snuggled into it and, as so often, I let my arm rest around him for a while until the warmth reached him.

"Yesterday I had a dream," I murmured softly. His eyes were alert and serious and so beautiful and so deep. Silently, they prompted me to continue. In a halting voice, I told him about it. I still remembered all the details and when I finished up with our bottomless fall, the answer in the form of the scroll in our hands, Michael asked: "We didn't open the scroll?"

"No," I muttered, "not yet."

He looked at me: "Can you open it?"

"Together, with you. I think the answer is for both of us."

Michael understood. Silently he leaned back, pulled up his knees, wrapped himself tightly in his blanket and closed his eyes. This time I was the one who told a story.

"What I remember most from my childhood is my mother standing in front of the mirror putting on makeup. She was very pretty, had a good job, and was away a lot. My father was home and yet he wasn't. Mentally, he was always somewhere else. At first he had a job, but later he didn't. When my siblings and I were kids - I have two brothers, both are younger - my parents pretended they were the perfect couple. But somehow we all felt that it wasn't true. Still, it was vital for us kids to believe it. It's what happens in many marriages: the parents play a game and the kids can feel the masquerade. On a subliminal level they know what's going on. But the parents are constantly telling them what they feel isn't true, and at some point there is a shift: children no longer trust their inner perception.

We all model our parents, so we also start to play make-believe. We no longer listen to our inner selves or believe what we see or what we are told. We learn that it's all about what we accomplish in the outside world, learn how to function in society ... this whole misery. Most people define themselves by performance, praise, recognition, and appearance ... and that's how it was with us.

I learned from my mother that it's important to look good, and I spent a lot of time on myself because instinctively I was afraid I wouldn't be accepted if I wasn't beautiful. She taught me that social acceptance and an acknowledged profession are crucial. And as if to prove her wrong, my father lived in the exact opposite way. He sat at home, started to drink, and in his drunken stupor he often beat my siblings and me. The police had to come and ... they were obviously not discreet - they drove up with sirens blaring, so that all the neighbors caught on, and it made me feel like a leper. If I went to shop at the butchers' or bakers' after a night like that, people avoided me. That hurt terribly.

Then my mother left my father - and us. There are so many moments in our lives that make us swear unholy oaths or vows, born from pain. Oaths, binding you to your mind, to your ego. Because mind and ego are the two that want to save you when it feels like your heart is deserting you. Ego and mind were my protective functions that told me: "So that this misery never happens to you again, you need a serious profession, good income, social acknowledgement and acceptance. Nothing else is of any importance. If you get that, you'll be happy."

Michael looked at me from the side. I did not want to return his gaze. He was entirely engaged in listening, and I knew that, with his deep intelligence, he had already transferred my words to his own situation.

"So I set out to attain a career and money," I continued, "in the hope of becoming happy. And I made money and had a career. I rose quickly through the ranks. I studied education and then headhunters from a business enterprise found a job for me. There, I went through some more training and soon earned more money than I had expected. I was a successful woman, but I wasn't happy. I had an important position with an important-sounding title. But oddly, that didn't make me happy, either. I met my husband, fell in love with him and we got married ... and that made me a little happier. But not the way I had imagined either, because to live a life and grow old together means you have to develop together. We had found each other because he had pushed my buttons and I his ... and so I was afraid to lose him again. Not be good enough. Not deserve this happiness.

Both of us worked around the clock. The success proved us right ... our ego right ... but it felt ... empty. Yes, exactly, that's probably the perfect word. And we wanted to fill that void with happiness, and so we decided to have children. I got pregnant right away, as if our decision had been the starting gun, overdue for some time. Within two years, we had two children, a girl, and a boy."

"Oh, how wonderful," whispered Michael next to me, and our eyes met.

"Yes," I smiled, "they are the best thing that could have happened to us. Suddenly I could access the child-like, the intuitive inside me again. Your baby can't speak and so the mind doesn't stand a chance. You have to immerse yourself in it's world and, believe me, it was damn hard. I had spent so many years in this other world, in the business world, and now was thrown back into the original, into … if you will …into "being". A baby simply 'is'. It can't do anything other than give you love and trust. That was a life-changing experience for me. But this change of course did not come all at once. It came gradually and it was fraught with many obstacles.

For in spite of my love for my children my ego was still there … and my patterns, after all, I had cultivated them for years. Happiness, my ego declared, comes with social acceptance, and this contradiction seemed unsolvable to me."

I breathed deeply.

"I encountered this problem in all areas of my life, in business and at home. I wanted to be popular and be loved, belong, you know … but … despite the success at my work, despite my best efforts at home, people never gave me the affection I longed for. They admired me. They asked for advice. They gave me compliments. They wanted to be seen with me. And they talked behind my back."

Michael looked at me. A wonderful deep look from beautiful eyes.

"Why?" he asked quietly.

"I didn't understand for a long time. I thought something was wrong with me. Then I thought something was wrong with other people. I thought maybe they were jealous, which they often were. That's the tricky part about the ego: it presents you with a plausible explanation. Ultimately, I felt excluded, like an outsider. I had felt ostracized as a child, and then as an adult as well. I had tried to learn how to behave so I'd be popular, and of course that backfired. But I just couldn't figure it out. I was friendly, I was nice, I helped everyone, I even gave money to some people; they were always pumping me for it. I gave expensive gifts … nothing helped. They took my money, used my influence and my contacts and trash-talked me."

Michael was silent and listened raptly.

"And then came the last straw," I said. "My husband and I had built up a small, medium-sized company. Nothing major, you can't measure this by American standards, but for our area and for our little Germany, it was a big accomplishment. We had started from scratch and within a relatively short period of time had grown our operations to steady sales levels. A level that allowed us to build a nice office building. We were doing well, the money was pouring in. And people started thinking. But they weren't thinking good thoughts. And then at some point we read in the newspaper that we supposedly belonged to the Scientologists and received financing from them. Now you have to understand that to Germans, Scientology is scarier than the mafia. It's considered one of the most dangerous, most unlawful and most hated sects."

Michael stared at me with wide eyes.

"That was almost the kiss of death for our business," I continued. "We couldn't get anyone to work for us after the rumor made the rounds. Nobody wanted to work in a Scientology organization. Revenues decreased. I mean, we had just built the building and had financial obligations. It was ... it was just awful. Soon, we weren't sure if we could even survive another day financially."

"Couldn't you defend yourselves?" asked Michael.

"Against a rumor? How can you defend yourself against a rumor? You know that best from your own experience! You never know who put the awful gossip in circulation! You can't get to it! Everybody knows about it, everybody talks about it, just not with you! If someone had approached me in person ... I would have been able to deal with that. But this way ... this way it was like a bag of feathers in the wind. Of course we tried lots of things. We even initiated an investigation by the minister of the interior government, and that officially confirmed we were *not* Scientologists ... but to no avail. All it takes is an evil person saying that someone is possessed by the devil and you've got the Inquisition in your house."

"Oh, my God," said Michael, "why are people so cruel! Why do they do this kind of thing? What for?"

"That's just what I wanted to know," I said. "And I went looking for an answer."

Michael sat up, all ears: "Did you find one?"

"Yes," I said, "because of you." And when he looked at me with surprise, I added:

"You gave me the clearest of answers. The final one! You are my liberating resume, my final result!

But...at first when I was still at home, my realization was: everything we are looking for from the outside is not happiness. Anything that can be taken away from you is not happiness. They can take away your money, your career, your reputation, your relationship, even your children...happiness is still somewhere else."

"Do you realize what you're saying?" asked Michael. "Children?"

"Yes," I said quietly. "...without wanting to go into detail at that moment... and, please, Michael ... don't think in black and white like so many others do. This doesn't mean that all of these things *don't* make you happy. Quite the opposite! And it doesn't mean that you have to trade them in for this independent happiness, or that you have to abstain from them - no, definitely not! You know what I believe: that everyone deserves an abundance of happiness here on earth!"

402

Michael nodded vigorously. He seemed reassured, had been afraid to hear something he didn't want to hear.

"My husband and I stopped looking for purpose from the outside. Believe me, we were shaken up in those days. You know how it is when you're ostracized. People who do things like that don't know what they're doing. My children didn't understand why they couldn't make friends. Parents wouldn't let their children play at our place and vice versa, my kids were not invited over to theirs. They got the feeling that there was something wrong with them and that shook me up even more. It was bitter to see that they suffered from the same exclusion I had suffered from all my life."

"Oh, your poor children!" Michael cried. "Why are there always such idiots in the world? Why can't they just leave you alone?"

"Yes, but Michael, remember our conversation! They are all only playing a role. They are all only responding to us! To our signals. We've called them. If you change, your surroundings change. If you change your signals, other things come your way. But I admit, I know that today. At that time I wasn't aware of these things. I just suffered and felt the others were to blame. I found this pattern everywhere in my life. Even in my family. You have to know that I'd taken care of my younger siblings. I paid for their education, wrote their job applications, went apartment hunting with them, and used my connections to get them jobs. If they needed something, they always came to me first."

"Your siblings must love you very much," Michael said in his soft voice.

"Oh yeah, they love me very much," I said cheerfully. "They loved me so much that they convinced my father to disown me and leave everything to them when he was in a drunken stupor. And just at a time when our company was not doing well because of the rumors. We even found out that some of my family was behind the rumors."

Outraged, Michael groaned. He was so sweet with his concern. Despite the fact that my stories were nothing compared to what he had gone through.

"What did you do?" he asked.

"At first I was incredibly offended and lashed out uncontrollably. I hurt people, too when I did that ... that ... it wasn't pretty…"

I stopped for a moment. Michael didn't say anything. Then I turned to him and said emphatically:

"But I recognized the pattern. I was always confronted with the same theme in green, red or orange. It was simply incomprehensible to me why I seemed 'odd' to people. Why they didn't really like me. And they even spoke badly about me behind my back. Sometimes, thoughts helped like: people don't understand me ... I mean, what do they want? I haven't done anything awful! On the contrary, there was hardly anyone who was more engaged than I was – for the community, for school, kindergarten and on and on!"

Michael gulped.

"Yes, exactly!" I cried. "The number of guests we welcomed to our home! I hosted them, cooked for them ... for nothing! It didn't do *any* good. The rumors didn't become any less, but more!"

Michael looked almost frightened. His body was now slightly strained and he had planted his feet on the ground. Confused, anticipating something, he looked at me.

"There was no way out except to be honest with myself. So I asked: Chirelle, what do you think about yourself? And all my 'good deeds' came to mind and I answered: 'I'm really nice.' But my inner voice was not satisfied with that answer and asked me: 'Why are you doing all these nice things? To prove to yourself that you really are? If you were sure of it, if you really knew deep down inside, would it really be necessary to do all these things you do?' I was shocked. I realized I was doing everything with the wrong premise. Not because I really wanted to do them, but because I had an intention ... and that attracted the wrong people.

This was an insight that didn't yet offer a solution ... but then again ... it's said that God will always save you, often in original ways, and yes, ... then he saved me; I met a wise man."

"A wise man?" Michael repeated. "How did you know that he was a wise man?"

"I didn't. I didn't recognize it until much later, after I'd worked with him for years already. Before, I was not perceptive enough to get it."

For a while I was still. Michael respected my silence.

"Many, many conversations followed," I remembered, "for years. I discovered how many patterns I had adopted from my parents, how many oaths I was unconsciously bound to; oaths, that made me believe I didn't deserve all the happiness. I had to function and everyone had to like me, so I would get the love I longed for so much. Isn't it funny that just the opposite happened?

We began to take it apart. We blew away all the black fog that made up my mental world. Layer by layer, I came closer and closer to myself, my real self, to this light in me. And sometimes I was completely immersed in it. I could see then what you can see in children, Michael, see in the way which you have preserved, despite all your pain. I was getting better and better and the best thing was to understand that I didn't have to transfer my bad patterns onto my kids, like my parents had transferred theirs onto us ... it was relief with more far-reaching implications than imaginable at the time."

These words brought Michael to complete attention and I expanded my explanation.

"Whatever you solve for yourself, you also solve for your children, and that's why it's so important to take care of yourself - that's not selfish. That's the best way to conduct yourself in life: I didn't pass on my garbage to my kids, or ... to the world."

"And then, were you happy?" he whispered.

"Yes, more and more often; my thoughts changed, I met other people, and those people who had upset me moved away - disappeared from my life. The rumors died away, eventually no one gossiped anymore about us. I made real, deep friendships ... but I still felt that I hadn't reached my goal. Things that bothered me were still happening. I started meditating so I could be close to myself. It helped a lot, but I kept falling out of that state of happiness ... there was a disparity between my state in the meditation room and in everyday life."

Michael stirred next to me. I knew this was not news to him. He was in this same bliss when he was with children and made music. His question hovered silently between us: "How can you anchor yourself in it?" I closed my eyes.

"Pain is something that disrupts this connection over and over again," I replied softly. "And I have invited pain over and over again, Michael, ... and you are doing it, too. I nourished suffering, it become a habit and is the raison d'être of the ego: the need to create problems and dramas; I had barely solved something before a new "problem" arose and it turned into a vicious cycle. I held onto my misery. I complained about how mean people were, how nasty my family was to me, that I'd had such a shitty childhood ... and even when I stopped talking about it, I continued to *think* about it ... and since I hadn't separated myself from my drama, it kept presenting itself to me in the form of external circumstances. My question was: 'Why did I cling so tightly to my own shit, to my painful story, if it burdened me so much?' I still had negative feelings about my past, and those caused the same old responses from the outside world."

"Okay," Michael said, rubbing his face with his hands. "Okay, wait a minute, hang on."

Wheels were turning in his head. Motionless, he sat there and tried to organize the thoughts in his own mind:

"That means that years of hard work still didn't get you what you'd hoped for?"

"No," I said and flashed him a broad smile. Michael looked at me truly aghast. "Then ... there is no real solution?"

"Michael, there *is* a happy ending," I assured him. "Because all of this work brought me to you, to my final unraveling ... oh, and I'm so grateful to you for that! Because of you I was able to solve it! But to be clear right here: it doesn't mean that people admire you, that everyone loves you or the papers say you're the best person in the world. That's definitely not the goal and not what you and I consider to be unconditional happiness."

Cautiously, I looked over to Michael. He had inched to the edge of the bench and the atmosphere changed. It became tense.

"I just want to live!" he cried, and burst into tears. "I want to just live! I want to be with my children and have a good life!"

"And that's your prerogative, Michael," I said urgently, and put my hand on his leg. "…let me tell you more. Since I still felt excluded, I realized that I still had some kind of signal in me that encouraged people to hurt me."

Large dark eyes looked at me. Hope burned in them and I took a deep breath. The culmination was to follow.

"Michael … if someone is humiliated in life, then there are deep, deep reasons. It has very deep reasons. For one: high energies, like yours, are always suspicious. This energy is strange to people, they find it disconcerting; they fight it because it makes them afraid. It was the same way with Jesus. That's why its crucial to surround yourself with the right kind of people … and you're not doing that."

Michael's eyes looked at me sarcastically.

"Yes, I know!" I cried impulsively. "This is your very special cross, your suspicions! That you're surrounded by sharks, but why are they there? Why?"

Confused, he opened his mouth for a question.

"Okay, okay," I said, touching my temples with my fingers. "I'm going too fast, my thoughts are all over the place. Just let me continue."

Michael nodded, nervously, I thought. He felt the increasing tension, just as I did, and he was not comfortable with it at all. Undeterred, I continued:

"Ask yourself: why do people come to you who aren't good for you? Why can't you find the right people? How come I got suckered, too, by those people who talked poorly of me? And I realized - oh, it was so liberating! - I realized that I was thinking poorly of myself. That I was doing all the nice things to prove to myself and to the world that I'm a good person. That's why I also talked so much about my past! So that they'll feel sorry for me! Why did I think poorly of myself? Because I identified with my ego, with my mind, and not with my inner light. And ego and mind had never thought I was that great! I realized that that's exactly why people existed in my life: because they mirrored just this! And that is the underlying reason for humiliation: not loving oneself! To not love yourself, and instead, to identify with the mind … it's the mind that is humiliated, not you! Only that can be hurt! And, Michael, you don't love yourself. You don't look to your light, the piece of God within you that tells you that you're worthy of everything in this world. You're worthy of every bit of happiness in the world! Just as every person is!"

He winced and had an almost hostile look on his face. The countdown was on … and I was talking faster and faster:

"People who do not appreciate themselves cry for love, just like I cried for love and you cry for love. Boy, and how you cry for love! You've been humiliated in your life because what you carry inside of you was mirrored: You make yourself small. You are cruel to yourself. And that's what happens around you: people make you small and are cruel to you! Every damn scumbag thinks he can pick on you! Because you allow it! Because you think too little of yourself! Because you don't give the sweet, perfect Michael within you a chance! You love children because they are far enough removed from ego and mind! Because you know that that's what is authentic! Do you have to be with them because you don't trust your own source?"

Michael sat upright in front of me as if he had been slapped. His mouth was slightly open and I felt how everything in him rebelled against what had been said. He wanted to run away so visibly that I instinctively looked around for something to tie him to the bench with.

"You are one of the most loving people in the world," I said quickly, trying to keep him there. "But the urge for the love from others is messing everything up. That cannot be compensated for with the next music success. If you give so much love, the force will fade if it doesn't come from your source! Maybe that's why you're sick!"

Set like a statue in stone, he sat in front of me and I continued relentlessly. We had no other choice, and I had a clear sense of urgency to finish before he would flee.

"Michael," I whispered and looked into his wonderful eyes. "That first night when we were sitting together, you revealed to me the secret of life. Through you, through your aura, everything became clear to me: you sat there and love was pouring in streams from you ... from this inexhaustible source within you ... and it flowed from the inside out, and only in that direction. Love is a one-way street. I recognized it by your own presence!

Nobody can give you what you are looking for because everything is within you. And the solution is so simple! It is: stop to demand love! You especially have such a high spiritual vibration, the energy of an angel, but you have a mighty problem because you give this energy to everyone but yourself. You love all people, but not yourself! Be honest: how strongly do you really believe that you deserve to be happy? Rather, don't you see your role in suffering? What chance does your fate have if you program it in only this direction? What's the chance it can fulfill itself? This is your own free will! You know yourself from quantum physics that electrons behave in accord with the observer's intent... what then can the result possibly be if you think the way you do?"

Michael's eyes had narrowed to slits, and several times he had tried to interrupt. Involuntarily, my voice had risen, had not allowed it.

"It's only a step, just a small step, not to look for blame in the evil world outside, but to go inside. You hold on to your lost childhood ... you do that so you get a bit of compassion and love! And all the while you're busy trying to save the world! Believe me, the world will be fine. It would be even better if it had a happy Michael in it! You can't save the world, if you can't save yourself. It's bullshit! The more you cry for love, the more you're being shown that you won't get it that way. That's the reason why all this is happening to you! You're like someone in a crashing plane who hands oxygen masks to everyone else and doesn't put one on himself! How long is that going to work out for you?"

"Where did you get the idea I don't love myself?" Michael asked, with a cold and distant voice. He had completely shut down, but verbally I forced my foot in the door to his soul.

"Because you say so yourself! Because someone who loves himself is not as unhappy about rumors to the extent that you are! He wouldn't be so vulnerable! He wouldn't need to be a perfectionist! Look at the Dalai Lama! Everything he's been through! What disasters he might expect in his country every day. And he has a happy tranquility anyway; he knows that he wouldn't help anyone by being miserable! But you suffer! You exacerbate your own suffering! To this day you think awful thoughts about your childhood, about your father, about all the injustice! Forget about your story! That story is not what you are!"

Michael made a funny noise, one that showed me that he still had to hear more, but didn't want to, no matter what.

"You don't understand me," he said strangely controlled. "This is all complete nonsense. It's totally unfounded. I was always grateful, was grateful to God for ... everything ... always giving, never showed it off..."

"It is true, Michael," I interrupted him softly. "It is not unfounded. You said it yourself. To Martin Bashir you said, 'I love what I do and I would be happy if people also loved what I do and when I am loved. I just want to be loved wherever I go' ... you said that it's most important to be loved when you're born and when you die, then everything in between was bearable."

Full of hostility, he stared at me, wanted to get up. I moved, leaned towards him, the black of his eyes almost covered my entire field of vision. We were staring at each other and I breathed my words in his face.

"Mike, it's okay to want to be loved. The idea that children who are loved, turn into loving adults is true, but..." I bit my lip. "... but it's a wrong point of view to think: if others love me, I am lovable. Love cannot come from the outside. Never. It only comes as a response to your own love, the one felt inside. Everyone has to redeem his or her own self. That's why we are here. And if you say it's important to be loved, then I say: It's *not* important. It's important that you love yourself! That you connect with what everyone feels when they are close to you! They are all taking your love! And you are taking, too! You need your fans because they give you the love - could you exist without them? But fate has shown you: you can't be on stage forever and recharge ... it even showed you: you can't draw love from children forever."

"Chirelle," said Michael, and pushed me away. He almost growled. "You have no idea what you're talking about."

"Oh, yes," I said grimly, "you say, 'Try hard to love me!' You *sing*: 'Try hard to love me!' Sing instead: 'Love yourself!' Finally stop trying to draw it from the outside! Damn it, I've never seen anyone who is so close to God and yet so far!"

The conversation had tilted. Michael's posture was frozen. Stiff and immobile, he was sitting on the front edge of the bench, ready to leap up, ready to run away. But undaunted, I hammered him some more. I desperately hoped for a revealing crack in the armor he had built over a lifetime, a crack that would finally, finally destroy the defensive shield and open his heart.

"You've even written a song about this theme - that people may finally understand you and finally love you! The trials from all these vicious people were there to demonstrate to you your own worth! If you knew your own worth, no one would dare drag you around in the dirt! They dragged you through the dirt so you can see how you think about yourself ... so you finally see your light, the source from which you draw your songs! This source is *you*! It is not just there for your music! Oh, God, and you *own* it. You've been using this source for so long now! You don't have to look anywhere else!"

With sparkling eyes, I looked at him. His body twitched, rebelled.

"Mike, damn it," I said trembling because he was about to run away. Incessantly he rubbed his leg, and now he really did get up, determined to avoid the daggers. I blocked his way. Through clenched jaws, I pressed out:

"You escaped the last trial - this is your chance, your ever reoccurring chance to understand, to realize that you deserve love ... not for your looks, not for your performances, not for your image or popularity! All of that was taken from you so that you realize: it's only about loving yourself, for your own sake. Your true refuge is not Neverland but your own heart! What damn programming in you prevents this?"

My voice had risen, I was almost shouting ... wanted so badly for Michael to understand, so badly that the switch would flip, the enlightenment come, the breakthrough.

But Michael shook his head fiercely and I almost despaired.

"Michael," I tried again, "you said once: it's happened to Gandhi and to Jesus ... why not to me as well? What is 'it'? Are you convinced that you need to repeat the fate of Jesus? Does that give you justification for your suffering? Don't you see the blasphemy? Do you really think that God sent you to this earth to make you suffer? Do you believe that? You read the Bible: it says: your faith determines your fate! And if all these things fester inside you - can you tell me how your children will feel if you think like that? What legacy are you passing on to them?"

Michael turned infinitely pale, as much as could be seen given the color of his skin. But something palpable began to crumble in him, while his ego rebelled like crazy against the words that had been spoken. Upset, he raged: "I love my children and that's all that matters!"

Snappy, I hissed back:

"If you love them so much, then show them what real love is! Do you want to make martyrs of the little ones? Didn't Jesus say: love your neighbor as you do yourself? You love your neighbor - but do you love yourself?"

"Shut up!" Michael snapped and backed away from me.

"But I won't shut up!" I cried with a wildly beating heart. "I am not your employee! Sure, you can send me away! But the message is the same! And will be until you understand, goddamn it! Until it finally penetrates to your poor, tormented soul! To the young, poor Mike inside of you, who for so long has wanted to be freed of all this crap! Who loves you the way you are! Without you dancing the damn moonwalk!"

"Be quiet!" cried Michael. "Be quiet, be quiet, be quiet!! Damn it, be quiet!"

"No, I don't want to be quiet!" I cried, tears of despair dripping from my eyes. "You've lived your whole life with a misunderstanding! With a misunderstanding that so many have! You want so badly to be a nice person, the good boy, the boy who believes in God and you're so cruel to yourself! You let any crook come close to you! Why did you let people like the Arvizos into your home? Which person with any self regard would bother with people like that? But you, you need to be loved! You are a good person, Michael, but if you put yourself down like that you will attract energies that will drag you down! You are the cause! You have to change something! You don't have to receive love - you *are* love! Stop demanding it, damn it!"

"Stop!!!" he cried hysterically and at full volume. "Stooopp! Stop! Stop! Stop it! Stop it! Enough!" His voice turned over. Frenzied, I shouted back:

"And you know what your biggest crime is? That this love flows so openly and uninhibited from you! Any moron can see it - except you! You swim in love and you let your heart starve!"

With eyes wide open, he stood before me. He wanted to scream, his mouth gaping with a strangled cry. For seconds. And then ... then a bestial sound came out of his mouth and he began to shriek, like in a horror movie, so loud, so hard, so shrill that I could barely understand the words:

"That's not true!!!" he cried shrilly. "Not true! It is not true, not true, not true... it's not true...!"

"And if you die over it," I hissed into his tirade. "It is true! Whether you like it or not!"

But he could no longer hear me. Incessantly he shrieked in this high, inhuman tone, as if to drown out any further word from me.

"Be quiet! Stop! Stop! Just shut up, shut your fucking mouth, finally be quiet! Stop it! Just stop it! Stop it! Stop it! Stop it ... It's not true ... not true, it's not true...!"

Shocked, I held my breath. He was in uncontrollable hysteria. Eyes rolling in panic, glaring at me half mad, and he screamed, screamed... oh God, he screamed in such a high pitch, so garishly, so shrill ... indefinable things that I stopped even trying to understand. He had pressed his hands to his ears, had squeezed his head, sank to his knees, crouched down, and in a panic shut out any additional explosive input.

Shaken, I stared at him, not knowing what to do. Everything in him was in resistance and confusion, immobilizing him as firmly as Pompeii's lava had solidified its residents in its volcanic eruption, unable to escape. Whimpering, he held his head as if he were afraid it would burst. Beads of cold sweat collected on his forehead, he was trembling, was filled with enormous pressure, a reflection of extreme, mad tension.

Involuntarily, I let out my bated breath. The arrow was launched, I could do nothing more.

I could sense, how I fell inside, how only this massive external voltage kept me upright. Mike stood before me, trembling, panting, piercing me with his eyes filled with hatred. He was breathing hard and heavy, his chest rattled as if he had asthma, abruptly his hand drove to his heart. The panting became louder every breath was a groan, and he was panting in and out, in and out, faster and faster and faster. The escalating force of his hyperventilation increased my panic. I knew that people who were confronted with their inner selves too abruptly could go insane. It is as if the heart thunders against the mind and causes a crash. It is as if the dark energy of the unfortunate pattern escapes the body's cells with a loud bang ... but, damn it, what could I do? Horrified, I stared at him.

Michael was gasping even louder and suddenly seized up, as if he was having a heart attack. Alarmed, I took a step toward him and froze again. He screamed, fell to his knees and raised his hand as if I was Lucifer himself. Then he seemed to have chills. With arms wrapped around his body, rubbing his legs, he chattered and whined like a little boy in complete shock.

I could not move, not a finger, couldn't wrap the fallen blanket around him, couldn't put my arm on his shoulders, not a word of reassurance crossed my lips. Petrified I stood facing him, watching him inflate like a balloon to its limits, with an outer skin so taught it moaned and groaned from the pressure. Involuntarily I pulled up my shoulders in anticipation of the violent discharge, the consequences of which neither of us could imagine, and which I instinctively hoped for nevertheless.

And then he exploded. Shrilly, he cried out and collapsed. My arms reached out and wrapped around him, held this slim, fragile body. Tears streamed in a monsoon rain down his face. He moaned and sobbed and cried and shook spastically. He was so rattled that I had trouble holding him. Michael sobbed and cried the soul from his body. He babbled like a child, scraps of words from the past, stammering from past experiences, innermost fears. He bellowed the misery from his heart and from each individual cell, and the wetness of his tears washed out his eyes with thousands of black streaks. Oh, he cried for so long, so hard, so heartbreakingly, liberating himself. For hours.

I had wrapped the blanket, as best I could, back around him and was holding him. We both sat on the ground. Convulsive fits of weeping shook him again and again, and the tears flowed and flowed. He had stopped shouting, was just sobbing, whispered, lamented, curled up to me, like a baby. All I could do was hold him.

And finally, finally, something changed, became lighter. He softened, his crying sounded different, cathartic, cleansing, his body began to relax. We were crouching on the ground, I was holding Michael like a child in my arms. At the beginning of dawn, his tears were still flowing, but I felt happy like after the birth of a child. I kept gently stroking his cheeks, whispering soothingly, and was so thankful that Michael had possessed the tremendous courage that allowed this to happen.

It was his birth. It was an opening and I hoped he would walk through to the other side of life.

Grace appeared. Suddenly she was there. Still, she stood like a guard beside a tree; I don't know how long she had been standing there. Her eyes and cheeks were streaked with tears, too. Isolated sobs erupted from Michael now and a leaden fatigue overcame him. When I looked up, I saw Bob, Jason and a few others, standing at a respectable distance behind Grace, sniffling, helpless, still.

Grace and I took Michael's slim body between ours and brought him to his room.

"Grace, he needs to take a shower … and please stay with him," I whispered, "he will need you."

Exhausted, I went to my room and looked out the window.

The night was gone for good. The light was dominating. The sun was rising.

***

The next day, Grace came into the kitchen before breakfast. And as always when she did that, Linda stiffened because she knew that this occurred only when something unpleasant had happened. Uncomfortably, she registered how Grace's gaze settled on me, and how I, anxiously waiting, responded to her look.

Then she rushed so quickly towards me that Linda let out a sound of surprise. I put down the dishtowel and looked into Grace's eyes with the question that had me in suspense all morning. Grace's eyes glittered with tears, she spread her arms and we fell around each other's necks.

"He's sleeping," she whispered in my ear. "He's sleeping!"

I squeezed her more tightly and buried my face in her hair. Then we pushed away from each other at the same time, smiled knowingly at another with teary eyes and we laughed.

Linda was dumbfounded, staring open-mouthed after Grace when she went back into the dining room.

"The issue ... uhm ... with your room ...that has been fully resolved?" she stuttered.

"Oh yes," I replied freely, "...that has been fully resolved."

XX / 2009 Everything that counts.

He had always said of himself that he'd achieved everything he'd aimed for in his life. Everything. Almost everything.

"Think ahead, my son," he had these words in his ears still. "Foresight and patience. Foresight and patience. Conduct yourself so that no one can retrace your lines of thought. Act with thoughts about the future, of eternity. Begin to spin today and you'll have fabric some day in the future. And nobody can connect you with those first threads."

Wise words, which he had assimilated, which were his creed and that had made him into what he was today. Powerful. Encompassing. The man in whose hands all the threads came together. Who could pluck a string and make everything move. Who could tear threads, could cut them if he wanted to send the one hanging on the other end to hell. How long had he been spinning for this fabric! It was an almost flawless fabric. One that covered the whole world. One no one could recognize him behind or suspect him beneath of. If he wanted something to happen, then it happened. If he wanted something to take a certain direction, then it did. If he wanted to guide the destiny of a person, he did. He was equal to God. He was huge.

And things went badly for anyone, anyone at all who opposed him. Too vast was his power, too powerful his contacts; too many were dependent on him.

That was his adrenaline, his happiness. That was his substitute for love. He was stuck in the same hierarchy of needs as everyone else. He just didn't know it. And it didn't interest him anyway. But the consequences of his actions he, too, would have to bear - sooner or later.

The days following Michael's breakdown were marked by gentleness. A pain in the air hovered like fog in the rooms. Everyone was moving with a strange caution, as if they did not want to disturb these wisps.
Even the children were playing more quietly than usual, and Paris, who intuitively grasped the situation, whispered sometimes, even though it was not necessary.
It was a strange atmosphere.
Michael was in his room. He wanted to be alone. The first few days he had slept a lot, to all our joy, but then his anxiety returned. We heard him pace. Back and forth, back and forth. Steps during the day, steps throughout the night. For days he stayed in his room, ate little, was not to be seen. Talking to no one, not even to his children. Sometimes Grace looked at me, worried. And I looked back just as worried as she.

XX / 2008, not enough

"You forgot the kids." Dry, scratchy.
"Didn't forget. Just didn't think necessary…"
"That was the order." He looked up briefly. A look from dead eyes. From unpleasant eyes. Another pair of eyes came to the mind of the one who always listened and had executed so many commands. He tried hard to chase the image away, but it stubbornly captivated his senses. A pair of hurt, big eyes full of life and intensity and suffering. Suffering he had caused. Whose path he had paved. And would pave again. Should. Briefly, he lowered his eyes, so as not to give himself away. And was not sure if he had not done so long ago already.

"Grace?"
She turned around. "Mike!"
"How ... how are the kids?" Michael stood before her in his pajamas. He was without makeup, his hair disheveled. He looked like a little boy who had just crawled out of bed. Involuntarily, a tender smile appeared on Grace's face.
"They're fine, Mike," she said warmly. "Of course they are asking about you."
As often, he asked his question without a word. Grace understood him.
"No, of course not. They wouldn't have been able to understand. We told them you had the flu and didn't want them to catch it."

414

They stood facing each other, 10 feet between them. They stood silently, and looked into each other's eyes. Then they started to run at the same time and fell into each other's arms.

His tears flowed in Grace's hair. Michael pressed her firmly. She stroked his back and held him. She held him as tightly as she could.

"Grace," he whispered. "I hope I can still turn it around."

***

Michael appeared serious and introspective. Our intense experience was still recent and we had not discussed it. He had spent a lot of time alone and I had stayed out of his way, more or less. Neither of us had felt the urge to talk.

But today, for the first time, Michael sat with the kids in the living room and had them tell him what they had done during the day. The kids enjoyed his presence and seemed to want to crawl inside him. Paris had snuggled into his lap and he stroked her back. Prince played with Blanket and kept looking over to his father with uncertain glances. Michael noticed.

"Come here, big guy," he said, and Prince came over next to him. Michael, with Paris on his lap, put his arm around his oldest son while Blanket was clinging to Mike's leg.

"I love you," Michael whispered. "I love you so much ... so much ... so much..." And the children hugged him. Their little mouths covered him with kisses and like a raging river Michael's love poured into them and through the whole house. This love was worth everything to him. Simply everything. And he felt it was there for him, too.

Cool Down

"How are you?"

"A lot of questions."

"Shoot."

When he turned his face to me, it seemed for the first time not tortured, and the beauty of his eyes was all the more evident.

"You really think my fate will change now?"

"Yes, I do. If you keep at it."

"What do you mean?"

"If you finally look for someone who helps clean out the rest of your disastrous patterns."

"I don't know if I have that much time," Michael whispered.

"Oh, Michael, please take the time! It's your engine, if you want to swim against the current to get to calmer waters."

"And you really think that if I had thought differently, this wouldn't have happened?"

"If you are referring to auto-suggestion," I said. "No. If you constantly tell yourself the world is paradise and your subconscious tells you something else … then the subconscious wins. And that in turn is, as with all people, affected by unfortunate vows and patterns. So you have to heal things, otherwise pus will flow from the wound and those projections are not pretty. Go inward. Search there."

He was silent, but the silence was filled with a doubting hope. One, that only partly believed in a promised land and did not dare to be too enthusiastic.

"Why don't you grab the kids and go somewhere where you can more or less live in peace? Go to Switzerland! Or to Germany! Things aren't as crazy there."

Michael grinned.

"Why don't you leave? What keeps you here?"

"So far they have found me everywhere," he said.

"So, what?" If you live in a remote place, off the beaten path … don't you think that the wheel will slowly stop its turning? You told me that you're not broke. Maybe after you've paid your debt you'll no longer be so rich - but you could cut back some. And lead a peaceful life."

"And still go nowhere."

"Time will tell. What's holding you back? The faces of your children are changing. You could put them in a regular school. Under false names. Or in a boarding school. You would have peace."

"I'm … just thinking about these things," he said to my surprise. Frankly, I was so surprised that I didn't know how to respond. But Michael continued:

"We … we are not done with this issue," he said and looked at me. "There's still something we have pushed back."

"Yeah…" I said, surprised that he remembered. "The subject of distrust."

"Exactly! My special … cross."

"Oh yes, your special cross," I nodded and smiled. "But what about the main theme? What do you think about it?"

"I … I think you're right," he said hesitantly. "I always thought it was normal to want to be loved."

"Most of us do, almost all of us do. And it's so fabulous to be loved," I mumbled. "It's a natural, human need. I wish that for no one more than you! You'll see that'll flow to you now for sure! And as for your double misunderstanding: look, it's really quite simple. You want to be loved and you long for it. But inside, you reject yourself. So you encounter situations in the outside that point it out to you. So you can see how cruel and nasty humanity is. So you are suspicious of it. But why should people trust you if you don't trust them? And if you distrust even yourself? Why should people

416

love you if you don't love yourself? And why should they treat you fairly if you walk around with a sign that says: 'I don't trust you! Betray me, so my prophecy is fulfilled!' That is the double cross. With your mindset towards adults, you keep the right people from coming to you. Only people who confirm your assumptions come to you, but it does not help to simply trust people as long as you haven't resolved the basis for the distrust in yourself, and that's how the cat is biting its own tail. Nasty people *do* exist out there; the only question is whether they have to cross your path.

And as for desire to be loved: the paradox is that you'll probably be lavished with love once you stop looking for it ... that you'll enjoy it, but don't need it anymore. Oh, Michael, you're so connected to love! All along, you have already owned what you are looking for. Your gift to write songs, to be so present on the stage, that's the presence of God, you've know that for a long time. You draw constantly from this source, but primarily it's there to make you happy. And you will see: then you won't need either recognition, or applause or anything else. Then you're free. Trust in that thought. So far you have been looking only in the wrong places."

"Oh, God," said Michael, and put his hands to his face. "Oh, God ... if that's true, what you say, Chirelle, then ... then ... there would be such a simple solution!"

"Yes," I smiled. "All you have to do is to always remind yourself - until you never forget."

Late in the evening he came back to my room one more time. "But if nothing changes ... what if you're wrong..."

"Michael, it's not about being right," I said, "and it won't change right away. You've been thinking for 50 years in one direction. Imagine that you are filling half a glass with black ink. How much pure water do you think you will need to pour in the glass before the water becomes clear? But don't forget: currently you have a waterfall in you. Let it flow."

Later he asked me: "And how do you deal with those who've hurt you?"

"They have not hurt me, basically. *I* was hurt. My ego. They just showed me what I thought."

"Were you able to forgive them so readily?"

"Oh, no, not at all. I was ... completely flustered ... I was angry, frustrated, sad. I cried a lot during those times. It was a process, like everything in life."

Michael said: "I remember, when you said at the beginning of our conversation, that ... that the people who have hurt me ... that there was an agreement ... it had been agreed to. If that's the case, could I have been able to prevent it?"

"Sure, Michael," I said, "once you understand then you don't need any more teachers. You would have probably never met certain people."

"People like Evan and Gavin," said Michael bitterly. "Bashir. And Sneddon."

I put my hand on his bony leg. "Michael, it's a long way to your own love, but the most important thing is that you forgive yourself, that you're not cruel to yourself anymore. The past is gone. It's important to know that you can forget your story. You are not your story. You are not your mind. You're much more. Stop! No more stirring stuff up, okay?"

He smiled. "How do you know all this?"

"I was the champion in stirring up stuff myself. Believe me, for years stupid me was wading in the same old shit. What a waste."

"But sometimes ... often ... I still feel…"

"That's okay, give yourself time, Michael," I replied, "that's only natural. Perhaps just the thought helps that even a Gavin Arvizo is crying for love. I can't imagine how he must have felt when he thought you were leaving him. Or Martin Bashir."

"Bashir? But he got what he wanted."

"No, he didn't," I said. "He also had to bear the consequences of his deeds. It was a costly victory. And look closely: what do you think is the underlying reason that he wanted to have a career so much, and wanted to get to the top so much, and wanted to be recognized so much... just like you?"

Michael smiled weakly. "Okay, I get it. He wanted to be loved, too."

"Bingo. And there's two guys running around in this world, - one needs a victim and the other one plays one. Both for the same reason. Both, because they think that way they will reach their goal. Perfect, isn't it?"

"Oh shit," Michael giggled.

I admired Michael to the depths of my soul. He was and remained an extraordinary man, an angel, who had little trouble to forgive and continue to do good - no matter how much he was harassed, no matter what anyone did to him: like a strong spring he bounced back to his paradigm, to who he was - a wonderful man, generous, kind, humble and loving.

Our last conversations gave him the breakthrough. It became lighter in Michael's soul and lighter around him. He began to shine in a way that warmed all our hearts and made Grace's eyes glow. Finally, hope and confidence flowed through the whole house. It was in the air: something was changing,

The next day I called my family. I wanted to come home. It was time.

Neverland One More Time

My last days here were approaching. I was sitting at the computer, twiddling with a pen and planning my return trip. Soon I would be thousands of miles from here. The thought made me jump up quickly. I had planned for one more thing. And I would do that now.

Impulsively, I rented a car with a navigation system, left LA and drove to Neverland filled with reminiscence as if I were the one who had lost this piece of paradise.

It was late afternoon when I arrived. I had set out without a plan. The only plan was to come to Neverland, but how I would get in, without a key, without any permission, I hadn't put any thought into.

And it happened as it had to happen: I walked from gate to gate and found them all locked. Some were even guarded. Two security guards were standing there and I guessed they would be there all night.

Discouraged, I drove into town and bought something to eat. In front of the store stood two rickety, round plastic tables and a couple of chairs. I put my sandwich, coffee and water on the table and sat down. The owner of the store had nothing better to do, so he came out and asked if I needed anything else.

"No thanks," I said and then it occurred to me that he might be asking because he wanted to close his store for the day.

"Are you closing for the day?" I asked him. "I can eat my sandwich in the car."

"Oh no! Just stay! I leave the tables out here anyway," he said kindly. He hesitated. Then he pursued: "Do you want to see Neverland?"

Surprised, I looked at him and could not help but grin. "Does everybody who buys food from you and isn't from here want to?" I asked.

"Well, most of them," he said and joined me. "Most of them. But it's quieted down a lot. Hardly any more fans come here. What for."

"Yes, what for," I repeated sadly.

"Some still try. But everything is locked."

"I noticed."

He raised his eyebrows. "Okay - so, you were already there."

"Yes, once I was even inside ... it wasn't too long ago. I was with a ... friend of Mr. Jackson's and he had the key," I explained.

The shopkeeper nodded. He was a man around 40, personable, the typical American, strong chin, broad smile, brown hair, gray eyes, powerful build and ready to roll up his sleeves.

"Yes, Michael," he sighed. "Too bad he isn't here anymore. He's such a pleasant person. Always friendly, extremely polite, way generous and without much air about him. We miss him. Everyone in Santa Maria liked him. We liked having him here."

And when I looked even more surprised than before, he said:

"The community here is not the DA."

I nodded, unable to express anything meaningful. I took a sip of coffee, waiting for more, and looked at the man. He looked back.

"Nobody thought what they did to him was right," he said. "Everyone suffered with him. But no one had the courage to stand up for him."

"Why is that?" I asked plaintively. "Why didn't anyone have the courage? Almost everybody who knew him in person describes him as a loving, down-to earth-person ... but no one stands up for him. Why?"

The man was silent

"Well," he said then, "he moves in a tough crowd ... not much say there for people like us ... but much to lose."

This time I was the one who didn't reply. After a while the man went back inside his store. I wrapped the rest of the sandwich in plastic wrap; my appetite was gone. After throwing my coffee cup into a trashcan, I raised a hand in goodbye to the shopkeeper, when he hurried out from behind his counter.

"Hey, Miss," he said. "You still want to see Neverland?"

"It's closed," I said. "I..."

"I could get you in," he interrupted me.

"Get me in?"

"Yeah," he grinned, "if you've got a bit more courage than we have... I know a hole in the fence, it's overgrown, but you can slip through easily ...Feel like a little adventure?"

"Always!" I beamed and watched happily as Sam, that was his name, locked up the store and got in his pick-up. I followed him.

He led me around just about all of Neverland. The downside was that I had to walk a bit, Sam explained, because this hole in the fence was quite a ways from the main entrances. And of course I couldn't get in the house, just on the property.

"No problem, Sam, thank you," I said and smiled at him happily. "Thanks a million! That's so kind of you!"

He held both thumbs up and left me behind, in the wilderness, between reality and wonderland.

As soon as I set foot on Neverland, I was seized again by its immeasurable magic. Oh, it was beautiful here — it was still so beautiful here! I easily found my way around to the buildings, quickly caught my bearings. Up ahead was the Giving Tree! Happily, I ran up to it and stopped abruptly. Someone was sitting in the tree. It was unmistakably Michael.

Startled, I looked around for a hiding place and darted into the bushes. Under no circumstance did I want Michael to see me. But I could not help looking at him again and again.

He had something in his hand, which he was staring at incessantly. It was not a book, but rather a single piece of paper. Then he pressed this paper to his heart. It disappeared underneath his large hand.

"Mike!" a soft voice whispered suddenly. I jumped. Someone else was here?

"Mike, we gotta go! The guards will make their rounds any minute!"

Guards, rounds? Michael was here secretly, too? Was he no longer permitted here? Or did he want to avoid people hearing that he was still sitting in his Giving Tree?

Michael nodded and jumped down with practiced movements. In doing so the note fell from his hand. A gust of wind caught hold of the wispy piece and swept it away. Michael suppressed a squeak. "Oh shit!" I heard him swear softly. Frank I've lost something!"

"Mike, we don't have time, we've gotta go!"

God, were the guards so close? What about me? Instinctively, I pushed myself deeper into the foliage, involuntarily gaging whether I was safe here. But what if they had dogs? Wasn't that one of them barking?

The other two seemed to have the same thought. "Oh, shit, shit, shit," Mike moaned. "Frank, I have to get it back!" Frantically he looked around, in the direction it had flown, but the grass had not been mowed in a long time - it stood high.

"Mike, I'll come back tomorrow during the day ... then I'll look for it," Frank hissed.

"That's a bad sign," whispered Mike, "...a bad sign, I can't lose this..."

But Frank dragged him away as fast as he could, into my direction, past me - obviously they had used the same entrance. Good thing I had parked my car out of view!

Then everything was quiet again. No Mike, no Frank. No dog. No guards.

Carefully, I scrambled up. With ears pricked, I crept to the Giving Tree and there ... there it was ... halfway there, trapped upright between the blades of the grass. A picture. Again, three faces. This time, two girls and a young man. The face of one of the girls and the young man were the same ones in the picture I had found in the library. I turned it over, "Love" it said. And a word that I could not make out in a hurry. It looked like, "innocent!" I tucked the photo into my pocket, then I listened to the night.

I heard noises further back, two voices in conversation. But the photo made me braver than I really was. Despite the danger of being caught, I continued to walk towards the Giving Tree. I touched the bark with both hands; I wanted to feel it one more time before I had to leave again. And as if its magic transferred over to me, my eyes looked downward. Tonight was the night of treasures! There was a legal-sized, blue folder approximately half an inch thick. In it were lots of single, densely printed pages.

The voices were nearing. Straining, I listened into the night. And heard voices from two directions. Michael and Frank had noticed their loss and were on their way back here. It was crazy, I know. But even though the voices were getting closer, I opened the folder and tried, despite the darkness, to decipher something.

"Frank"…and something else, it said. An address maybe. Damn, it was too dark! Frenzied, I shuffled through the pages. Everything was in handwriting, not legible in the dark. Before I could think twice, I nervously pulled my camera out of my pocket, moved around the gigantic trunk, put the folder on the ground and snapped a picture of the first page. The hissing from the flash seemed infinitely loud. But I snapped pictures of the second and third page anyway. The voices were coming closer. Fourth page. It was the first of many that was covered in writing. The flash needed time to recharge. Frantically, I clicked the shutter. Nothing. The flash did not want to work. Damn it. Abruptly I closed the folder, swayed briefly, instinctively placed it down a bit further back, so that the guards walking by could not see it, scratched a couple of leaves over it and hurled myself into the bushes.

Not one second too late. Frank crept forwards, snatched the folder, looked around hectically and disappeared. I heard him and Mike running off and giggling like two little boys.

I grinned. Then I remembered that I still had the photo with me. Now I snuck to the exit, heard Frank and Mike's car drive off. I waited a bit, then drove as fast as I could to LA, gave up the car and had Bob chauffeur me home. I felt like I was Zorro in person. Casually, I asked Bob if Michael was home.

"Nope, he left with Frank," Bob said yawning. He had night shift and I promised to bring him coffee and dateballs.

When I got home, I assessed the situation: Grace with the kids in the living room, the staff in the lounge, no guards in the house.

I had some peace so I could look at the back of the photo more closely. The word with the exclamation mark that I had incorrectly read as "innocent" was "innocuous." Michael had pressed it to his heart - but since there were several people in the picture, I had my pick of whom he had meant it for. It was indeed innocuous!

In a sudden burst of mischievousness and intuition, I reached into the drawer and pulled out a hand-painted card that I had brought with me from India. Picture in hand, I ran as quietly and as quickly as I could to Michael's room and put it, together with the card, on his turned-down bed.

Then I went back into the kitchen, made coffee for Bob and was rather pleased with myself. After I had delivered my goodies to Bob, I put the camera chip in the computer, copied the images to the hard drive, deleted it from the chip and turned off both devices. It was enough for today.

***

Michael returned disheartened from his trip. He thought it was a bad omen that he had lost the picture. Nobody except Frank knew what it meant to him. Given the challenges that had been presented to him before, and that were currently intensifying, he had followed his intuition to go to Neverland again and get the answer to all his questions at his Giving Tree. To lose the picture right there was simply too much for him. It felt as if Sneddon had snatched it greedily, as if he still wanted to say: "No happiness for Michael Jackson," even after the fact.

He went to his room, looked around. This was just no comparison to Neverland. It was true he did not want to live there anymore; he still could not forget; and he was afraid they would come after him again, and pictured DA officers everywhere, heading towards him with handcuffs.

He missed it anyway. He missed the original Neverland he had created. Tired, he was about to throw himself on the bed - and could not believe his eyes.

There was the picture. And something beneath it. Something black. Oh, my God, he thought, shocked. His heart stopped for a second. Please, no. Don't let their claws get into this, too ...

With trembling hands he took the photo and card. The background of the card was black, but in the middle was a heart that pierced the blackness of the background with warm colors; red to orange to yellow. Below it said: "Believe in Love."

Michael's knees trembled. He sank in front of the bed, pressed both the card and the picture to his heart and did not know what to think.

A sign. Believe in Love. He cried. That was exactly what he felt called to do.

Sky 2008/2009

His bedside table rang. An unknown ringtone. It was Saturday. The day he could sleep in.

"Beth," he mumbled sleepily. "Your cell is ringing."

"That's not my phone," she said. "Did you set the alarm?"

"Sun!" he cried indignantly. "Your cell!"

No answer.

Sky reluctantly opened his eyes. Then he jumped up. His bedside table was ringing! The phone, that had been in there for a good two years and had never been used.

***

There he was again. Tom. Back at the gate. With Greg.

Since I had seen the two there the first time, I had often come back to this place and now my perseverance was rewarded. Tom was there. He handed something to Greg. Greg put it in his back pocket and shuffled back to his garden shed.

I had known Tom was playing a double game for a while now. But Greg? Was leading a double life? I had to tell Grace. I should have done that a long time ago.

Greg was so quiet, seemed to speak more with his plants than with people. What was he up to? Oh, God, I was getting as suspicious as everyone else here. You didn't stand a chance.

What I also noticed: I developed a pronounced taste for pursuing things. Maybe it was because I wanted to protect Michael, or because I thought it was suddenly exciting to solve a puzzle. Whatever it was, an hour later, I grabbed a basket and strolled over to the greenhouse.

Greg had already finished work for the day. His work pants were neatly folded on a wooden stool in the hall. Before I knew it, I searched the pockets for the piece of paper. I found nothing.

"Grace ... how long has Greg been with Michael?"

"Oh ... for ages. He was there before I came. I think Joseph, Michael's father, brought him back then from Encino to Neverland. He had been working there for many years, too."

I chewed my lower lip.

"What is it?" Grace asked, looking at me with a furrowed brow.

"I saw ... I mean ... this Tom ... Cevicz ... who made this offer to me from the newspaper... do you remember? You showed me the video…"

"Video? ... oh ... yes! Tom! *That* Tom! Uh ... yeah ... right…" Grace drawled. "What about him?"

"I saw him," I replied tersely, "with Greg. Twice already. They exchanged something, words and something in writing."

"Did you hear what it was about?" Grace asked worried.

"No, I was too far away. But I recognized Tom - and you know, he's a double-crossing ... but Greg ... I mean…"

"Don't worry about it, Chirelle," Grace interrupted me. "I'll handle it. Thanks for telling me."

I don't know - I was really disappointed with Grace's lack of interest. Shouldn't this information have struck like a small bomb? Or did she already know or suspect something, and I had kicked in an open door? I was surprised at her reaction. Tom's bequest, his prompting for me to "think about", appeared more relevant to me than ever.

***

On the last remaining days, more from laziness than real interest, I looked at the three pages I had copied. They did exactly what I expected them to: they incited confusion.

"F. Ahearn" read the first page and there was an address.
Next to it: *"Alternatives."*
Then, in a vertical line: *"CH, A, D, EU, UK."*
On the next page another list:

"The BEST, underlined in thick pen.
SK. Joey
Sky
Tom
Friends D / U
Family?
L.
D.
Dr. ... that I could not decipher.

Then, clear again: the word *"clinics."* At the edge of it: *OMG!*
Period of time: min two years to three years .
A non-smiley face with pulled down corners of the mouth next to it.
And very clearly: *JAKE,* underlined three times.

Third page: sloppy, barely legible.

Photo, Heli?
Amb Vehi. - Photos, Mon.
Large, clear: *MEDIA, Fuck them all!*
At the edge of it, too *OMG!* And a smiley face.
French fries.

Everything was adorned with ornaments, absent-minded doodling. Paisley, flowers, mandalas. It was a brainstorming session. Or a table of contents. Or both. I thought of my previous discovery from the library. It was covered in doodles just like this one. Where I had put that picture?

I went through the file folder on my computer. It had been a while, I couldn't actually remember where I had saved the file or the name of the file folder. That was so typical of me. Quietly chiding myself, I went through the files. Linda called me. Reluctantly, I got up and went into the kitchen. Then I remembered that I had not made a copy. There was only the original- the photo in the book in the library. If it was still there.

Man, it occurred to me with a surge of seething heat. Now you're snooping around again! But the whole thing was too exciting, so much so that I could not have been able to stop it.

Tom

Linda looked out the window. A car pulled up and a man got ejected from it. He did not appear, as expected, at the front door. For a minute Linda waited for the doorbell to ring. Nothing. She went to the door, opened it and looked right and left. Nothing. The man had long since gone around the property, vanished from her sight.

I was on my way to one of the secret exits. Grace had asked me what I was doing tonight and I had replied: "Staying at home and getting ready for my trip." In a week I would go back home and it felt odd, despite my longing for my regular life.

But then I became restless. I had booked the ticket online, given my husband the details of the flight times via email ... and it was too early to pack. And so I decided spontaneously to go out, took a shower, put on some make-up and something pretty to wear, and made my way to the exit. There I had to let the guards know. I did not want a chauffeur. I would walk a ways and then take the bus.

When I arrived at the exit, the guard stood there with Greg. Both raised a hand in a surprised greeting. I returned the greeting, and let them know about my change of plans for the evening. But something in their eyes made me suspicious. I took a few steps down the street. Then I instinctively flattened myself against a fence behind the branches of an overhanging tree so they could no longer see me. There was a sudden movement of the gate. A couple of men approached the security guard and Greg. One of them held something out to be viewed. I could see everything clearly. Greg looked back towards me and chased the men inside.

The gate closed.

I went back inside by the front entrance and made my way to Greg's garden shed.

They came back out individually. I'd had to wait for a long time. For such a long time that I was beginning to think about how stupid it all was. Several times I was tempted to simply take the bus and go to town as I had planned. But I didn't. I crouched instead in a dumb bush under a stupid window and could not understand a word of the conversation. Then I got up, went out again to the main exit and posted myself under the overhanging tree again, waited forever and didn't even know what for and why.

He wore a baseball cap and sunglasses, even though it was night. He walked a few feet and then stopped. The black-haired man craned his face to the stars, as if looking for the moon, which tonight presented itself as a sickle in the sky. I almost got the impression he was sniffing the air and was picking up a scent. And before I could even think, I was shoved with lightning speed into the fence, a warm, muscular body pressed against mine, one hand on my mouth, stifling my cry. The hand slid from my face, grabbed my hair and yanked it down so that my head was bent backwards. Only now I registered that he had effortlessly pinned my wrists behind my back with his second hand. Dangerous glittering eyes looked into mine.

"Well, you hobby detective," muttered Tom behind clenched teeth. And when I opened my mouth, he pressed his lips to mine, and hissed, "Don't scream" before he pushed his tongue into my mouth for an incredibly passionate kiss.

After about ten seconds we heard the voice of a police officer:

"Hey, piss off! No smooching around here!"

In a completely foreign dialect and with vocabulary I could only guess at, Tom cussed into the direction of the officer, grabbed around my waist, grinned at me mischievously and dragged me towards the bus stop. The grin made the penny drop: *that's* what I was supposed to "think about"! Grace had said back then, "It (the check) was not made out for much." *That* was the explanation for Grace's lame reaction towards the information about Greg, the reason for Tom's pleading expression when I had torn up the check, the real reason why Grace had the complete video, and had known how much the check was for and had opened up to me after this situation!

The reason why Michael had begun to talk to me and Tom had the key to Neverland - he worked for him and the check part had been my test. I felt beyond stupid.

"You encouraged me to think, and that's what I did."
"So?"
"Your name is certainly not Tom."
"Call me Jake."
"That's just as meaningless as Tom."
"Maybe that's my real name."
"Yes," I answered sullenly, "maybe." I stared at him angrily.
"Hey," he said, grinning his irresistible smile, "that was a good kiss!"
I had to laugh. "Yes ... delicious! You kiss almost as good as my husband."
Tom/Jake laughed. "You're really funny, Chirelle!"
"Who says my name is really Chirelle?"
"Who says I don't kiss better than your husband?"
"Have you ever kissed my husband?"
We looked at each other and then burst out laughing. Something like that I really could only experience with Tom/Jake. We found ourselves in a situation, the seriousness of which I could only guess at, and we had nothing better to do than goof around. Despite or perhaps because of it, it felt good.
"So," asked Tom/Jake. "What else did you find out?"
"That the check-scene was staged."
"Cool. What makes you think that?"
"Grace knew how much the check was issued for."
"Oh!"
"And you're not an editor, a journalist or a publisher or otherwise known to any newspapers."
"That doesn't have to mean anything."
"True," I said despondently, "there is so much undercover stuff going on that nobody can make head or tail of things anymore. Should I really call you Jake?"
"I prefer it over Tom."
"You work for Michael?"
Jake was silent. Something in me deflated.
"Jake ... do you work for Mike?"
"I'm all *for* Michael," he said.
The thing in my stomach sank a little deeper. "Is that a good thing for him?" I asked.
"I hope so," he replied.
"You don't know?"

"Who can know that?" he said, and looked at me mysteriously. "I told you back then that I like him. And that's true."

"Michael needs people who are 100% behind him and show it." I replied more heatedly than intended.

"I don't see it that way," Jake replied. "It's better if he has people around him, and it's not known how they feel about him."

Inconspicuously, he looked around. We were standing close to each other in a crowded bar in the far corner, and every once in a while Jake put his arm around me to whisper something in my ear that he didn't want to say out loud. We seemed like lovers. And just like now he looked around ever so often, the baseball cap low over his eyes.

I nodded slowly. Someone unwavering and transparent who was faithful to Michael was, if his fears were justified, really no help.

"But what are your plans?" I whispered.

"Chirelle, what kind of a question is that!"

"Sorry, Jake ... I ... I'm naive, I know."

"You tell me, what did you talk to him about? He's different."

"Is that reason for hope?"

"Hope for what?"

"That he can get out of this mess?"

"What do you mean get out?"

Sighing, I exhaled: "That he goes somewhere, detoxifies, heals physically and mentally, that he can make music the way he wants to, make his videos... he's written so many songs ... he wouldn't even have to produce new ones... couldn't he make a living with that?"

"That sounds as though all of his problems would be solved if he removes himself from the public eye! You're really naive."

"Maybe his problems could be solved if there were no more Michael Jackson in the public," I retorted angrily, "so people would finally leave him alone!"

Jake's response was caught in his throat. "No..." he lowered his voice to a barely audible whisper, "...no Michael Jackson ... anymore?"

His eyes flashed. This was not a flash of insight, but one of caution.

"How is that supposed to work?" he asked warily.

Right, how was that supposed to work? Of course I didn't have an answer for that. I said nothing and stared defiantly at Jake.

Jake. The name on my photographed list, underlined three times.

***

Already the very next day seemed to belie my words from my previous conversation with Michael. A picture was haunting through the newspapers. A picture that put Michael back into his old state. It showed not only him, but also the unveiled faces of his children. It was a picture that had been taken during a visit with a friend, approximately four/five years ago. As almost always, no one knew how it could have gotten to the press. Like a manifest scorn, the cover stared at anyone who walked through the hallway. It lay there like a living protest against the subject of our conversations. I was ill-at-ease.

"May I borrow a book from the library?" I asked Grace.

"Yeah, sure, go ahead," she said, and sent me out with a nod. She didn't have to tell me twice. As soon as I was in the library my eyes roamed over the bookshelves and made out some books with interesting titles. I chose three of them. The third was the one with the picture. Without opening it, I went into the kitchen, showed it to Grace.

"Is it okay if I take these to my room?" I asked.

Grace threw a quick glance at the top two titles and grinned.

"As for spirituality, you definitely have the same taste, you and Michael," she said indifferently and turned around. "I need you today for a picnic," she said. "We need a basket for five people in about an hour. Can you handle that?"

I nodded, took the books and went to my room. The photo was still there.

Familiar scene: I could not sleep. Old recipe: glass of wine, blanket, lake. Staring until thoughts choke on their own toughness, until tiredness sets in. When I was walking to the lake in this moonless night there sat a form. A few steps later I recognized from the posture and stature of the person that it was not Michael. Hesitating, I faltered in mid-step and then stopped altogether. Just when I wanted to turn back, the man looked at me. It was Jake.

He looked at me for a long time. For so long that my legs continued moving and I finally sat down next to him at the shore. Without saying anything I held out my glass of wine to him. He took it and drank a long sip.

"Are you a permanent fixture here?" I asked.

"I've always been."

"Ah, all right, sure." He handed me back the glass of wine. Began to gather flat stones that were around him in the grass and that he stacked neatly beside him. With a practiced move, he skipped one across the water's surface. My eyes were keeping count.

"Wow!" Five times. Cool."

He looked at me with a grin. "Not my record, I can tell you that."

"Even cooler." It sounded sarcastic.

"Mad?"

"Oh, not at all." I nipped from the glass and looked at Jake fleetingly. "It's just, you live in a totally strange world," I told him then. "What madness."

"Yes, what madness," he confirmed with a force that made me pause. Surprised, I looked at him. For him, the meaning went deeper than I had meant, of that I was sure.

Again he skipped stones across the water. Six skips. Five skips. Three skips. Six skips. Jake looked tense. Suddenly he said: "You love him, right?"

"Yes, sure" I said. "I love him very much. He is one of the most loveable people in the world."

"Yes," he murmured. "There's something about him ... he's like a little kid ... but believe me, he's also smart ... and pigheaded."

Depressed, he looked at the last stones that lay next to him on the ground.

"Tom ... I mean Jake ... what's wrong? I mean, what's troubling you?"

He turned to me with a crooked grin, with an incredible look in his eyes, as if he were amused by my question. But the despair in this grin suggested a monstrosity, one that shut his mouth. And so he said after a moment's hesitation:

"You really don't want to know."

I was quiet. He was quiet. The last stones skipped across the water. Then silence enveloped us.

"Michael seems different," he said then.

"Yes ... you've said that before."

"What did you do?"

"Me? Nothing. Michael did it. But I don't want to talk about it."

"Grace told me a little bit. She doesn't want to talk about it either."

"Did Michael tell you anything?" I asked.

"Yes ... he did ... a few words at least."

"Well then..."

"And now," he asked, his voice dripping with cynicism. "Now what? Do you really think that his life will change now? It'll be better?"

I opened my mouth to reply, but Jake turned to me with such a violent movement that he nearly knocked over the glass of wine. He did not even notice.

"This is dangerous nonsense, Chirelle," he growled. "You have no idea! No idea! How can you... make him have hope like that?"

I saw into Jake's eyes ... into this mix of resignation, anger and a few drops of uncertainty ... what was the matter with him?

"Still," I said carefully, "...yes, I believe in it. If Michael manages to break away from these awful patterns ... then his life has to change."

"Chirelle, that's the biggest bullshit I've ever heard," he said angrily. "Michael is the most generous and kind-hearted man in the world, and what did this altruism get him? A straight path to hell!"

"But there's got to be a reason!" I shouted rebelliously. "I'm not claiming that..."

"Listen, kid," Jake snarled. "There are forces ...that are ... strong, networked, powerful and greedy..."

"I know what you're trying to say," I interrupted him. "Michael told me about them. Everybody talks about them here. That someone is trying to destroy him."

"Don't you think that someone doesn't give a shit about your spiritual chatter?" he remarked sarcastically.

"He probably doesn't," I said, "but it takes two to tango. Maybe now Michael will make other choices because he can base them on different ways of thinking. A game can only take place if everybody cooperates. What if he gets out of this damn game? What if he suddenly doesn't accept the rules any more? Mental turns real, Jake."

Jake snorted derisively in response. Then he said:

"But you don't really know ... because basically you don't know anything."

"Maybe," I retorted defiantly, "but if I take stock of his disasters, and you ... as you already said ...are a permanent guest here, then your previous measures couldn't have been so hot either! Just treating symptoms! How about fighting their cause for a change?"

"Those are useless hopes and stupid, theoretical babble!" Jake insisted angrily. "It's no good for anything!"

"How do you know if you don't give it a try?" I spat, furious now myself.

"Quite simply, Chirelle," he bit back, "it's not logical! You say that the cause of his disaster is that he doesn't love himself ... which implies that self-love prevents personal suffering and everything is fine and dandy just because you like yourself? What kind of..."

He bit his lips, it was obvious how moronic he thought this point of view was. His break gave opportunity to set something straight that was close to my heart.

"Jake, self-love is something very ... deep ... it doesn't mean the adulation of one's self the way it's often said in workshops ... my opinion is that we're all plopped down here to find that source in us ... and if you have that, then everything..."

Annoyed by my talk, he interrupted angrily:

"That's the naive talk of a simple-minded German housewife who's read a couple of esoteric works of shod and whose main problem is that she didn't program the washing machine right!"

Hurt, I closed my mouth. Jake's eyes burned as he continued:

"Your chatter is not only illogical, it lacks any substance! Think about it ... smarty-pants, what about Gandhi? What about Jesus? Was, in your opinion, Gandhi someone who didn't love himself? Or Jesus? Jesus did not love himself? Or Mandela? Chirelle, realize: Gandhi was shot. Jesus was crucified. Mandela was innocent and rotted in prison for decades. How does that jive with your bullshit theory?"

I stared at him with an open mouth. Jake was in a rage, and when I could not oppose him, he took advantage of his momentum:

"There is a completely different assumption," he said angrily, "one that is just as philosophical as yours! Since you like to cite scriptures so much - the first rule of Buddhism says: 'Life is suffering.' I hope this'll make you shut your face!"

He breathed deeply, expelled a breath. There was such an uncomfortable feeling in me, one that wanted to alert me that possibly I had made a huge mistake.

"And what is your theory?" I asked apprehensively, trying to maintain my composure.

Jake gave me a look, took a stone in his hand, played around with it. He calmed down a bit.

"Always, before things changed in this world, there were martyrs," he said emphatically. "People who were willing to suffer to bring things to other peoples attention. Maybe it's just that Michael is one of the last martyrs of this world. Maybe he's someone who draws attention to the state of this world with his very own personal suffering. So that people will change something after he's gone. Maybe he's one of those who've come into this world for just that purpose. Have you never wondered why he endures it all more or less without complaint? Why he doesn't defend himself, like others would in his situation? Wouldn't one explanation be that he has clearly recognized his role and destiny and lives it without complaining? How many people do you know who are capable of this greatness? Of this conscious suffering? Who recognize that all of us are the puppets on the strings of a few power obsessed people! And say, 'I will persevere ... for a better world' ... or at least the *prospect* of a better world?"

My mouth stood open and I paled. Jake's views literally bowled me over - and they sounded conclusive. God ... had I been so wrong? But something seemed out of sync ... some aspect Jake had not considered and my brain rattled trying to figure it out.

"Jake," I said in a husky voice, "you're right in so far as ... Michael is something like an ambassador. You can feel that very clearly, if you get more involved with him... and the thought of the last martyr ... it all sounds ... right at first ... but ... I don't know..."

I broke off, desperate because I couldn't get to the heart of the matter. For a little while I was silent. And then it burst out of me:

"The point is that Michael *wants* to be happy! And God has given us free will - he doesn't force us into roles that our ego thinks we should play to be a good person! Because this ego thinks it has an ace in God's hand that way! Damn it, I don't believe in that kind of crap! Michael has the right to be happy just like anyone else! And the martyr talk is total rubbish! If he had set out to be a martyr, he'd be happy even in this role! And he wouldn't have put children in this world…because he wouldn't have needed them for his cause. Michael wants a happy life and he is permitted to have one! Everything else is bullshit! And he thinks he's not worthy!"

Jake stared at me with an inscrutable expression.

"And as for your example of Gandhi and Jesus - well, yes, of course - their lives don't appear to have been easy. But were they unhappy? To me they are rather examples of how one can experience happiness even in horrific conditions…and untouchable happiness - because they didn't need circumstances to make them happy! And while we're at it: I interpret even your Buddha's teaching differently: life is suffering, if you cling to the outside. And if you equate living with the outside, then you suffer. That's it! In all the scriptures you can read that life on this planet is a cycle of birth and death - and that we can liberate ourselves! Yes - seen that way life is suffering because we're not where we could be if we realized that there is a form of happiness that is independent of external things! Stop the talk about martyrs! Michael wants to be and should be and can be happy - and he is the first to deserve it."

Jake let out a short, scornful sound, and turned in the opposite direction, away from me.

I said no more. Anger clouded my eyes. Irritated, I took the glass of wine in my hand and tossed a good portion of its content down my throat.

"And if you're already on this martyr track and find everything so illogical," I added grumpily, "…then pray tell how he can be an example for the world when everyone says: 'I'd never want to be as unhappy as he is!' He is here to live his own, very own happiness! And if he can do that, then he can demonstrate just that to others, because he can reach people with his gifts and his charisma!"

Jake was silent. For a long time. After a while he stretched out his hand for the glass. I understood the gesture and offered it to him.

"What makes you think he would have a chance with your theory?" he scoffed and I could not say whether sarcasm or hope outweighed the other in his voice.

"Because … because he is changing," I said and he looked at me critically.

"He's changing his course, he's exploring new waters … look, it's like the Titanic. You're going the wrong way because you and others think it's the right one And then there is the iceberg. You kill the engines. That's what Michael is doing. He's in the process of stopping patterns of thinking that he's been thinking for 50 years. Reprogramming belief systems that have determined his fate for 50 years. That doesn't happen so quickly. These thoughts have momentum. Everything they have created has momentum. Even if you stop now and turn the rudder as far as it will go, you don't know if it's enough to avoid a collision with the iceberg."

Jake sat on the bank as if chiseled to the spot. His expression betrayed nothing.

"And if it collides?" he retorted. "What if it's too late?"

"Then there are lifeboats," I replied. "Even if you fall into the sea, you can still be saved."

He stared at the water. After a while he said:

"Fact is: the Titanic sank. And most people drowned. The only ones who were saved were cowardly, rich, arrogant assholes."

"Not all of them," I said, trembling. I did not want to think about such things.

***

In a few days I would have to say good-bye to Michael, to his children, Linda, Grace, Karen, Jake, Jason, Bob and all the others. My heart was heavy when I thought about leaving them, and at the same time I was incredibly looking forward to arriving home.

"You'll come visit us, Chirelle," said Michael, patting my shoulder. "...and then you'll bring your family."

They threw a party for me. A true American kitsch party with garlands and cake with gaudy colors (which I had not baked myself), table fireworks, paper hats and clown noses. The children raced around and screamed wildly, the adults danced to Michael's songs and shared anecdotes, we drank champagne and enjoyed the evening's fabulous catering, including wait staff that Michael had ordered in my honor so that nobody had to think of being in the kitchen and such.

Michael danced a piece for us, then he danced with his children for us, and that looked so cute that we all squealed with excitement. Then he sang. It was incredibly beautiful. It was just a wonderful evening and Grace suggested a drink in front of the fireplace at the end, an idea that we all embraced with enthusiasm.

In the best of spirits, we gathered in front of the huge fire and Grace poured velvety red wine into large, bulbous glasses.

Michael approached me with a glass in his hand. He wanted us to toast this last evening and he was standing in front of me and looked me in the eye.

My heart was in my mouth. The King of Pop. One of the best people I've ever met in my life. My heart was overflowing and I was so grateful that I had met him. In his presence so much had become clear to me, and now I carried so much with me as a model for my own life at home: his kindness, his way of playing with kids, his way of opening to God when he was creating something ... and most of all his graciousness that he had preserved despite all his suffering. With shining eyes, I looked at him and raised my glass.

"Thank you, Michael, for everything," I said, feeling the tears come. "I love you, and the time I was here with you was one of the most beautiful times in my whole life."

"It's for me to thank you," he said softly and embraced me for a long time. It was like a merging together, like the union of two drops of water, we felt each other's being and were happy.

Two days later I was in Germany, at home, and thought with warmth and love back to this very unusual, unexpected time. I was happy that I was able to stay in touch with Grace, Karen and Mike. Jake hadn't given me his contact information.

Every day I prayed for Michael, I prayed that Michael's ship, his great soul, could circumnavigate the iceberg. No one deserved it more than he did.

I crossed my fingers until they turned blue.

XX/2008/2009 Change of course?

The appointment did not take place. In the last twenty years that had never happened, even once. Never. Even when XX had been sick, he had received him, he had passed on his instructions and expected reporting. But now ... the date was cancelled.

Behind closed doors, there was talk of a heart attack. He's not responsive. XX will contact you.

Suddenly there was time. Time, that could be used. No one else could give him commands. Time. Time to think. Time to do other things. Who knows ... time to make amends.

***

Grace's letters reached me. She sounded cautious and skirted around about different things. She wrote that Michael had received concrete offers that he faced with mixed emotions. His creativity was running at maximum output, she had the feeling that he felt the need to let it all out ... but that he simply wasn't ready yet. He needed a 'regeneration phase', which he was currently strongly considering. There hadn't been hate mail for a while now and they all saw this as a good sign for a better future. The children were fine, just the other day they had celebrated Paris' birthday and the girl had wished to see Michael on stage.

"They love their father infinitely. They would do *anything* for him."

436

I could not help myself. Somehow I read a silent concern between the lines. I bit my lip. Why had she emphasized 'anything' that way?
And then I never heard from her again.

The iceberg

For several days fear was back in his face. Old torment demanded its right to exist, attempted to pave its way. There had been several meetings with his bank and his managers. The old challenges stood before him like a wall, ready to be overcome. His lips trembled when he sat down with the directors of the bank to discuss his debts. His people tried to explain that Mr. Jackson would sell some property and other assets to reduce the mountain of debt, but the bank was putting pressure on him. Everyone was shaken by the recent financial crisis; they wanted the money right away and everyone knew what that meant.

"We've been waiting for a long time for repayment, Mr. Jackson," they said. "Time has run out. We want our money back. With interest."

His managers countered with documents proving that effective measures had already been initiated. But the bankers knew no mercy. They demanded something tangible.

"Your most valuable asset is your own person, Mr. Jackson," one of them said. "Get some work done and give concerts, as befits a musician ... or sell the ATV."

It went back and forth. After hours they parted without having reached an agreement.

Michael was desperate. Tours. The ATV! A foreclosure would mean a total loss of value. And sell it on the open market - what would he even get for it? Did a buyer even exist who was able and willing to pay a reasonable price? He remembered Branca's words when he had considered selling once before. He had said, "If there's one thing I wouldn't do. Mike, I wouldn't sell the ATV. Under no circumstances"

But the thing was like a curse. And since Sony had taken join ownership even more so.

***

"Jake."

"Mike." The two sat across from each other. For over twenty years, Jake had always stood by his side − he was his closest and most secret confidant. Mike took a deep breath.

"Jake ... how ... how far are you along with your ...baby?"

Astonished, Jake sat up straight. "Is it getting current for you?"

"Not sure ... I just want to know ... if there was a chance ... maybe I won't have to take it... I just want to know if there is one."

"Opportunities pass. They are bound by time," Jake replied, almost angrily.

"Just tell me, Jake," demanded Michael flatly.

"It's ... it's not entirely ... done ... but we.... it could be done. Why don't you do it?"

"You, of all people ask me that? What about the, 'you take your problems with you everywhere'? Isn't that what you always told me?"

"Times change," Jake replied. "Sometimes ... the time comes for things that didn't make any sense before."

Michael slowly took off his glasses. The ensuing silence was as meaningful as a page-long dialogue. Michael was the first to break it.

"What does it hinge on?" he asked.

"On you," Jake said, "one word."

The room was deathly silent. Even the fire, burned down to embers, still glowed subtly, cast ghostly shadows on their faces.

"Would it be a real solution?" Michael asked, trembling.

"Mike, this hunt is not complete until there is no more Michael Jackson."

Michael turned his head and looked at the embers. The large eyes filled with the familiar expression of despair.

"It's the only way out," Jake said with emphasis. "You know what will happen if you try to tell the truth: your reputation is destroyed. *Vanity Fair* and other magazines just recently featured you as psychotic ... no one would take you seriously."

Michael swallowed. "Jake, the only thing that is keeping me is the finances. I need to settle this somehow."

"How they will ultimately turn out, no one knows, Mike. Everything is a risk – no matter what you do. But there's a chance that it'll work out. You know you're being threatened from many sides, not just one..." Jake hesitated. "...and not just because of the ATV. They could have snagged that a long time ago considering your debt. If they force you to repay the loan, you are through with it. See it as it is: everyone is trying to make money off of you – either off of what you own, or your potential or what you represent. Or off of... I mean ... think of scenarios ... where your heirs are considered more willing to negotiate than you are."

Michael winced. Jake went on relentlessly:

"Where is your last will? You should specify that no one can sell the thing ... and as far as our baby is concerned: there is the chance that our deal will work out ... and this offer for the concert comes at a good time...maybe it's useful for our baby…even if your life is in danger by performing. But your life is in danger either way. Whether you … have the baby or not. But…"

Jake hesitated again. Then he leaned forward and looked Mike deeply in the eyes.

"*If* you do decide to go for it − be clear: There will be no King of Pop. No superstar status. No fans. No applause. No special treatment. No Glory. No more anything. You'd be out. Forever. Can you do that?"

Michael's huge eyes stared like ET's at Jake. He stared back in silence.

***

"Why is a concert such a big deal?" asked his manager. "Michael, a concert! Two hours! Or for all I care only one and a half!"

"You know that it's not only two hours," Michael said nervously. "The rehearsals, the program … the choreography … people want new songs … there's no time to mix my ideas and rehearse. I could only fall back on an old repertoire … nobody is into that … and I don't want to dance the moonwalk when I'm 50 years old."

"Who cares in this situation?" snapped back the manager. "There's not much room for negotiation. When was the last time you performed? Almost 15 years ago! People would sell their household to see the legendary Michael Jackson again on stage!"

Michael smiled thinly. And still … something stirred in him. Quietly, coming from below, the memory of the revitalizing, sparkling feeling of the stage … the electricity and … his fans! He quickly pushed it down, turned his eyes back to his manager and said:

"I can't go back on stage. My body can't take it anymore."

"Oh, come on, you haven't been as fit as you are now for a long time! Since this summer, you look really good again! You seem sound! You feel all right! ONE concert, Michael, man, that would be the ultimate, if Michael Jackson came back on stage! We'll sell the recording, we'll print exclusive tickets, we'll think of special events … we'll promote a new CD … Michael − this is money, money that the bank wants NOW. We need a plan they can believe in! And if we provide a signature, a signature from AEG - the largest concert promoter! - then the guys from the bank will hold back! They said so themselves! One more time on stage, Michael, a brilliant comeback! Your… farewell! Exactly! Give your official farewell concert! A finale! The most grand finale the world has ever seen!"

Again, something stirred in Michael's belly. A farewell concert. One more time on stage. One last time! He remembered his little girl. Her birthday wish had been to see her Daddy singing and dancing. In front of thousands of people.

Michael agreed. "Okay," he said. "One last concert. I hope people will come."

XX 2008/09 Revival

A man walks along a row of shops. Past many people who walk up and down the street. He pauses before one business or other, but only briefly, only if an item in the window attracts his attention. But he never really stops. Three or four seconds at most. A lot of people do it that way.

"You're busted. You should have known that he never relies on just one person."

Between two puffs of a cigarette, words wrapped in smoke.

"Plan continues. Without you."

And now the man is gone. A fleeting message. The one executing commands has no illusions about his future.

But he wouldn't have been an agent either, if he had only one person to rely on. Now it's time to go into hiding, to take necessary action. Chances are 50:50 for everyone involved.

On stage – the final performance

Michael's hand was on the mouse, and with the index finger of his right hand, he scrolled through one posted message after another.

His manager had announced in a mini press release that Michael Jackson was planning a concert. Now he had entered in Google "Michael Jackson comeback" and had clicked on the relevant pages. With a lump in his throat, he looked at what people thought about him and his comeback.

"Where is Jake?" Mike asked. Nervously, he raced through the house and his restlessness increased from day to day. With every minute he was waiting for him.

But Jake did not come. He had disappeared without a trace.

An familiar, ever-increasing feeling he didn't want crawled up from his stomach. He felt torn. His mood ranged from enthusiastic to discouraged. He had the feeling of being at someone's mercy, was afraid of the concert. The concert, the concert! Oh God! They would boo him out! They would put him down! He longed for Chirelle. He would have liked to talk just now. Where was Jake? Now of all times, he wasn't there!

His unrest increased. His heart felt pierced. Involuntarily, his hand went to the chest area. What was wrong with him? Old, familiar fear crept up. Was he being poisoned? What had he eaten today? Where had he eaten? Who had been there?

"I'll never be happy," he thought, as he had thought a million times. But ... he want to stop thinking that way! He had been so successful with that the last few weeks! Day after day he had consciously reprogrammed himself and he could feel the progress. And on some days he had felt really free. He had embraced deep happiness that made it clear to him where he needed to go. Again he thought of Chirelle. Remembered that she had told him he wasn't his mind, not his thoughts, and that his thoughts could be directed. He got better at it every day ... but sometimes ... he suddenly felt weak, no longer able to tame these wild fabrications, get a grip on this fear, a fear that seemed again to be taking on a life of its own. Why, why? When had this started? Why wasn't it working anymore?

He went to the music room. Turned on the music. Let it flow into him. His feet began to move, his arms, his midsection, his whole body. For a short time his consciousness dipped into another dimension, and he was liberated from thought. But when the music stopped and he stood in the darkness of the room, he felt the immediate tribute his body demanded for the exertion: pain.

Groaning, he stumbled into his bedroom. His shoulders ached so much that he was barely able to get out of his shirt. When he sat down to take off his pants, he felt like an 80-year-old man. His knees burned like hell.

Discouraged, he collapsed. His anxiety level increased several notches. How in the world was he supposed to survive all the rehearsals and the concert? He would be a wreck even before the first rehearsal was over! He shouldn't be walking this path again. It was killing him.

He pulled himself together. The next day he contacted his manager and concert promoter:

"I can't do the concert," he told them sadly "I'm sorry, but my health is too poor ... it's not going to work."

And directed to his managers, aware of the paling organizer in the background. "I need another solution. There has to be one."

Turmoil after his statement. Michael had simply got up and left. His manager hastily insured the promoter, AEG, that this was not the end of the story and hurried after Michael. They talked to him, made it clear to him that this would be his financial way out. Wasn't he thinking of his children? Finally, they brought him back home with Michael's commitment to reconsider the whole thing.

The next day a meeting took place at Michael's house. They raised his hopes, gave him courage. They promised him anything he wanted, said they would take special care of him, consider all of the circumstances.

"We'll provide all-around support," said the concert organizers. "In the meantime we can fall back on your doubles. We'll provide a doctor to take care of your needs. We need a health report for the insurance anyway, and a check-up. In three days, we'll start the medical exams."

Michael thought of Jake. He had said his life was endangered one way or the other. He took a deep breath. Better this way. He would do it. One concert. And having made the decision, he finally started to look forward to it.

XX/2008/2009

"I'll take a shit on his comeback! Does he think his head is out of the noose with this trick he's pulling off? Nobody in the world wants to see this wreck anymore! He's hanging in the web and he knows it. Take care of the children. That other one slacked off with that."

***

Again Michael's long finger lay on the touch pad of the computer, moving from line to line. Google: comeback Michael Jackson.
The following posts were in the forums:

"That old dog? He's so mega-out!"

"Who wants to see him, this monster!"

"Whassup? Is it a girl? God is he ugly."

"Do you know anyone who'd spend money on a transvestite?"

"No, really, how uncool can you get. When was he on stage the last time? He'll fall down wobbly as he is. He's from the last century."

"Isn't that the child molester?"

"Seems to be the trendy recipe of the music industry: take a wrecked star and lure with times long gone. A sick obsession! Right now revivals are mass produced, but to at least say something accurate about the comeback: the term 'revival' is a good fit for Jackson, but the revival of a guy like that is doubtful."

"Uaahh, he looks like a 70-year-old diva who picked the wrong plastic surgeon!"

"Ain't dat related with the whacko from Tokio Hotel?"

"Maybe he needs to stock up and he'll get a couple of new victims on the stage, that's where he plays with kids, too…"

"Wanker!"

"Gay pig!"

"He should take a look around in today's music scene. Not quite up to date anymore."

442

"Heard he sticks a new nose on his face every day. Freak!"

"What happens when a new song of the former "King of Pop" floats through the Internet? Well, nothing! And no one knows who Michael Jackson is anyway…"

"Rare thing to see a guy so over the hill - even Pete Doherty is the picture of health in comparison! Can't help but feeling sorry for Jacko. Meaningless comeback anyway."

Michael's heart stopped. His finger froze on the pad. No one would come to his concert.

It would be the ultimate disaster.

Doctors examined him, injected him with something. An hour later, Michael felt like a different person. He was euphoric and didn't feel any pain. The anxiety was gone, too. GONE! Disappeared! He felt so free, so infinitely free – after these tough, fearful days, he felt liberated. God, so liberated! So free! Of course he could do it. One concert! He would do it, he would get out of this mess. He *needed* a comeback. He had been working on one for years already. And it was part of his plan. The words he most hated from his father came to mind: "There are winners and losers out there, and none of my children belongs to the losers."

Oddly, for the first time the words gave him real power. He would somehow manage. He was not a loser. And this here … was definitely the last battle. He could clearly feel it.

The Examination

The doctor who was supposed to deliver the expert report, saw this extremely slim body on the table and thought involuntarily: "Oh my God."

The patient's eyes were closed. The doctor gently poked and prodded and asked the usual questions. "Does it hurt here, or there? And when I do this?" There were some places that hurt, alarming places, that didn't point to anything good. And although the examination was not pleasant for the patient, the doctor could not help but feel that this person on the table was enjoying the treatment. Not sexually – nothing was going on there with him, no, but because it was a soft touch and he did not seem used to those. This body lay before him in surrender and seemed to ask for more connection, for gentle hands, for relaxation filled with trust. The doctor's eyes went dark with compassion. Bruises, sprains, inflammation … old scars. It was an old body that lay before of him, a ruined body, one that told a long, unhappy story.

The doctor was used to a patient's desire for touch. Old people sometimes came to him, not because there was anything wrong with them, but just to have someone touch them, generate a feeling of closeness. And these days it was not only old people who were looking for that.

And this patient here... My goodness, he thought ... what I would prescribe for him would be 24 hours of stroking without sex, seven times a week.

He did not have to wait for the results of the blood tests, X-ray, ECG and CT to decide on his diagnosis.

The call came in the night. Half-asleep, the doctor picked up the phone. A hoarse voice announced itself.

"It's about the patient from this afternoon," rasped the voice. "The man is finished. I know what you have been advised to do. But I beg you in the name of the medical oath you swore to: declare the man unfit for work."

Confused, the doctor held the receiver in his hand.

"Listen," he managed to say in spite of his surprise, "said ethics tells me that a) this is none of your concern and b) I'm impartial. Who are you?"

"A friend."

"Name?"

"How naive are you?"

The doctor swallowed. He thought of the emaciated, depleted body this was about. He was not naive, no, he knew what it was about.

"Listen, mister," the doctor said succinctly, "if you mean the same person I do, then I can assure you that in this case I will recommend for a compulsory extended vacation with withdrawal and rehab for at least five years. And not because of your call, but because of said ethics. Happy?"

Clack. And the night was as still again.

After that experience, Coleman could not go back to sleep. He went to a bar and grabbed a whiskey. Sitting on the stool, he was thinking.

Two nights later and one day before the results of the medical exam were to be announced, he was torn again from sleep.

"Mr. Coleman?" croaked a cold, sexless voice. A computer-distortion. Technical and tinny, it created an uncomfortable, surreal atmosphere.

"Who is this?" Coleman asked alarmed.

"Doesn't matter. We know the result of the medical report. And we want to appeal to your compassion. If this person is no longer able to make an income, he'll bite the dust."

Pause.

"Did you get that?"

444

Coleman was silent for another three seconds. The other one joined his silence.

"Whoever you are," he then replied in a husky voice, "if ... 'this person', as you call him, is to undertake this feat he'll also bite the dust."

"No, he won't."

"What makes you so sure?"

"We know more than you do. We protect him in our own way."

The metallic voice had an almost pleading tone, which made the nature of the call even more bizarre. As if an alien from outer space was calling and exhibiting unexpected human emotions.

"How is that supposed to work?" Coleman asked. "Based on medical criteria it's simply not possible."

"Guess you'll just have to believe us."

"That's not enough for me."

The metal voice paused.

"Believe me, you'll kill him for sure if you don't let him on the stage. It's his only chance."

Coleman was silent.

The voice: "Do you want money? How much?"

"I don't want money," Coleman said disgusted.

Then all he heard was the busy signal.

The next morning the patient was standing before him. Bright face, subtle makeup, red lips, oriental eyes. A painting. An expression of peace. He sat on the chair in front of the desk where Coleman had invited him to sit. Although Coleman knew that his patient had undergone surgery he was still fascinated by his beauty. Something about him ennobled him, an inner beauty that reflected the outer. His elfin stature had something regal, and yet he appeared modest.

"Mr. Jackson," began the doctor. "I regret to…"

Michael leaned forward and looked intensely into the eyes of the medical doctor.

"Let me do the concert," he said. "It's my only chance. Tell me what I have to do to survive it."

Silently Coleman looked at him and shook his head. With an imploring look Michael leaned forward.

"Please," he whispered.

Still the doctor said nothing.

"You don't have to treat me if you don't want to… but let me on stage. Please. Please let me perform one more time…"

"Why?" Coleman burst out. "Can't you do without the fame? Don't you realize that that's what is killing you?"

Michael looked out the window and then turned his gaze to the doctor. "Sometimes you have to run with the pack," he said. "...I want to do it ... for my kids, you know?"

Third night. Coleman grudgingly snatched up the receiver.
"Damn it!" he shouted into the phone. "Can't you call during regular hours?"
"Oh, sorry... no, couldn't be helped," said another unfamiliar, quiet, confidence-inspiring voice. "But at least I have a message about how we can relieve you of your pangs of conscience ... in regards to your patient."
"Oh," groaned Coleman. He nervously ran his hand through his thinning hair. "Great! I assume something illegal, eh?"
"No, not at all. Something life-saving. Listen, this call is not a threat. I just want us to meet. Then I'll explain everything. If you don't agree, I'll respect that and you'll never hear from me again."
Coleman hesitated. The voice was kind. Although he knew it was silly to allow it to influence his decision, Coleman said yes.

Iceberg: Visibility

The news about Michael's concert went around the world. As a test, an Internet site for pre-orders was set up.
"We'll keep it open for a month," said the managers. "Then we'll see what dribbles in."
The employee nodded. He set up the site and activated it. Then he left to grab a cup of coffee. When he returned five minutes had passed. He looked at the screen. The coffee spewed out of his mouth: all seats were sold.
Speechless, managers and concert promoters stood facing the monitor.
"Five minutes!" croaked one of them. "Five minutes! For 15,000 tickets! The man has a market draw others can only dream of!"

Then everyone was upside down.
"Michael, you are in such high demand, you're so unique, people are crazy about you!" they shouted enthusiastically at the next meeting.
"People are not crazy about me," Michael said. But he had just come from his doctor, the meds were kicking in and a euphoric feeling began to set in. As if his senses were accentuated, he noted that suddenly everyone was looking at him quite differently. With more reverence and respect. Despite this, he repeated: "People are not attuned to my music anymore, they..."
"They are! They are too! We ... "
"Why don't you sell this one concert first?" Michael interrupted them. "Then we'll see."

"Michael, this concert *is* sold out. Completely sold out! To the last standing-room only ticket!"

"Sold out? But ... there is still no official sale, no tickets…" Surprised, Mike looked at the people around him.

"We opened a sales site on the Internet. For non-binding pre-orders," one of them grinned. "Yesterday at noon, the portal was opened. Five minutes later, all the tickets were gone!"

"Five minutes, Mike!" implored another and something swung in his voice that Michael had not heard for a long time: absolute admiration. And it warmed his heart.

Speechless, he looked at the excited faces. They all sat in front of him, nodded, smiled, rejoiced and Michael began to be happy, too, slowly, carefully ... people still wanted him? They spent money to see him? On him?

"Five minutes?" he stammered.

"Yeah! And that's not all of it!" they shouted. "As a test we just left the portal open ... and…"

"And?" Michael asked. His heart fluttered, he was excited ...how many tickets would the concert have sold?

"Within the next 20 minutes..." said his manager, and looked in Michael's eyes significantly. "Michael, listen carefully: within the next 20 minutes, another *150,000* people reserved a ticket!"

"150,000..." whispered Michael and felt something big in his heart. No pain, no fear. People loved him, they loved him and he loved them ...oh God, how grateful he was to his fans! They had gone through all the hard times with him, and they had never, ever left him. They were still there! They helped him, as always, had been waiting patiently for him.

While the people at the table were cackling wildly, excitedly, psyched, Michael composed a huge 'thank you' for his fans in his heart, for the people who still after all these years, stood closely by him.

Then more words made it to his ear:

"That'll be ten concerts ... ten concerts ... with that you're good! And the bank can kiss your ass! *Michael – Jackson – is - back!* That's going to be the greatest comeback of all time!!"

It happened what had to happen: they made it clear to Michael that the rehearsals would be the most difficult part. Once the program was in place, it wouldn't be so bad. Then he would only have to do the same thing over – he didn't have to travel, everything was taking place at one location, and with sufficient intervals between his performances so that he could recover. They would get him in shape, keep him fit, yes, they were convinced that psychologically he would be feel better than ever after these concerts ... that this was the true therapy. His reputation would improve again! The old accusations would finally sink into oblivion! And his financial situation would totally relax, if not even resolve!

They looked at him, at this quiet man, with a deep look, and suddenly they grasped almost with reverence: twenty years of targeted malevolence, foulest slander, and all the crap in the world hadn't managed to destroy the myth around and the greatness of Michael Jackson. His light shone through it all and was, consciously or unconsciously, perceived by a great many people out there. By people who were ecstatic to see that light shine in all its brightness again.

He couldn't sleep. Wandered through the house. Kissed his children. Thought about things.

Ten concerts. Was his body up for it? The meds made him feel good. When he took them he believed he could do it. But he could not sleep. Certainly not after concerts. Was not able to regenerate.

He did not fool himself. All these manager guys could not care less how he felt after the concerts. But he did care. He wanted to live with his family, wanted to be there for them. Did not want to be an irreparable wreck at the age of 50 because others wanted to make money off of him ... his health was affected even now, and this was the time he should be disappearing behind the scenes ... but right now the banks were directly in front of him and putting the gun to his head. He knew why. As always, it was about the ATV/Sony catalog and about himself as a money-making machine. One of the bankers had clearly stated that following the country's financial crisis he, Michael Jackson, was the best investment ever. And Randy Phillips, an AEG concert executive, had explained to him that it was a "do it or die" situation.

Michael thought back to Jake. That would be the only way out. But Jake was not there.

***

The managers just about flipped out over the ticket sales. They were wringing their hands, their eyes were shining, and they were enthusiastic and treated Michael like a king. Which, after all, is what he was. He was the King of Pop. He was the king of hearts. And the slave of his underlings.

They showed Michael the press reports, the resonance in the detested printed media. For the first time in years, there were positive reports. As if the reporters could not believe it themselves — that he was still alive, that he was still standing ... that he had survived the scandals, the disgrace and deadly wounds ... and most of all that the people out there were so euphoric about him...despite their reports. For the first time in a forever-long time, there were words between the lines that held him up with respect and in high esteem ... and it brought tears to his eyes.

The tension, the excitement to see Michael Jackson, the legend, back on stage increased more and more.

He told the people that one concert would be the utmost he could do.

But they worked him again, did the math and showed him how he could get everything, everything back if he were on stage for only half a year. Half a year, Michael! What's half a year! You'll have downtime between concerts! We'll plan it out just in case. There are the playbacks, there are ways ... we'll provide for medical assistance around the clock. Finish your stage career with a success! Then people will remember *that*. Your success and not the last scandal! Then not one bloody soul will talk about Bashir anymore! Show them! This is the opportunity of your lifetime! Don't give up! You're the greatest!

Michael hesitated. To finish with a success. Conclude his career with a good conscience. That sounded ... good. He could start a new life afterwards, reinvent himself ... how often had he prayed to God to get him out of this life ... this was his chance. And something in him wanted to know. Wanted proof, was consumed with a need for recognition, for social rehabilitation after all the meager years.

"Okay," he said. "Open the Internet portal and see what you can sell. I want it open for just one week. What's sold then is sold. But after that not one more ticket is up for grabs, do we understand each other?"

Reluctantly, he agreed to ten concerts.

The managers nodded, pleased, set up the contract. And planned the press conference where the concert tour with Michael would be officially announced. This in itself would be a performance after a very long time, a performance in which, after nearly 20 years, Michael had to market himself.

The spirit of new beginnings, the planning of something big was in the air. The meetings with producers, choreographers, musicians, technicians and all the necessary people started. They all met Michael with shining eyes, shook his hand and said how proud they were to be allowed to work on a concert with him. Michael could not believe his ears. But, God ... it felt so good! It felt so good! After this constant disrespect and abuse, it felt so good! His confidence grew, slowly, haltingly, and his irresistible charisma added the rest.

Chastened by the overwhelming agony of the past, he had developed a subtle depth that made a strong impression on the people around him. His love for people flowed and flowed. He was so grateful for every good thing that happened to him, felt alive again after a long time.

His managers hired a personal trainer who exercised with him every day. And it had its effect. Michael became aware of his body again. The training revived him, he could feel his muscles, how they were building up, how his body changed, was becoming stronger. That also gave him a new sense of vitality. He walked in a different way, his appetite increased. He felt good. Michael began to shine again.

The casting for the backup dancers was announced. On the monitor Mike observed the throngs of talented dancers and singers who were dying to dance with him. They had come from all over the world. As soon as the announcement was out, they had hopped on planes, had given up their jobs, just for a chance to be on the stage with him, with Michael Jackson. They formed a huge line in front of the gates of the Staples Center, and Michael was speechless. No one was ashamed to perform with him: just the opposite was true: they craved it.

They were interviewed and they all had tears of longing in their eyes. They said it would be the greatest honor in the world for them to be allowed to dance with Michael Jackson. They said that he had been their role model from the time they could stand and walk, their role model for life and for art. They said that he was the biggest star in the world for them. Not a word about him being a child molester. These young people were in awe, full of respect, full of love for him, and described the positive impact he had on their lives, how he had influenced them and made them what they were today: the best dancers in the world.

Then the winners were announced. The chosen burst into tears and rejoiced. Their voices trembled when they spoke into the journalists' microphones that the biggest dream of their careers had come true. They would dance with Michael Jackson. The greatest entertainer in the world.

Michael could barely believe it. Stunned, he sat in front of the monitor and saw how peopled responded to him.

He was shaking before his first appearance: the press conference. He hid in his room, filled with fear. The press people had to wait hours for him and that always put them into an ungracious mood.

Michael had not slept for several nights. He told his managers. He said he couldn't sleep, that was his problem. He could not deliver what was expected of him. They wanted high power, the power he had torn the stage apart with in his earlier days. But he couldn't do it, not anymore! People would be disappointed in him — after the press appearance, after the concert at the latest, they would talk poorly of him again ... he would collapse, it would be embarrassing ... he did not want to make a fool of himself. His self-confidence fluctuated depending on the intensity of his pain, which in turn was determined by the dose of his meds and the proper tuning of an antidote.

Doctors. Needles. They reassured him. They told him he didn't have to talk much. Just a bit, just so people knew he was serious. It was clear to Michael: his biggest and dirtiest critics would be there: journalists, the breed that had ruined his life. Could ruin it again. Into whose clutches he was just returning. What would they write about him? He vowed that if this first public appearance were a disaster, he would call everything off. The tickets were not actually sold yet. It was not yet too late. The tickets would not be offered for binding sale until after.

He was made up, he dressed. Put on the darkest sunglasses he could find. He looked damn good.

Masses on the way to the conference. Masses, that surround his car, fans banging on his window, people screaming. What year was this 1980? 2009? It is like it always had been. When Michael Jackson shows up, chaos ensues. Back entrance, bodyguards, plowing through the crowd. Microphones and cameras thrust in his face already here. The moderator, glad to finally see him, a crowd of journalists and fans outside the red curtain. A speaker's podium. Michael's heart is beating like mad. He is excited, nervous. He has no problem with crowds when he is on stage ... but a podium! The people around him encourage him, Michael takes a deep breath, someone is holding the curtain open. He collects his courage and walks with wobbly knees through the opening towards the podium. His presence is immediately effective. With him something greater has entered the space, something that fascinates people, that beguiles them, that they crave. He is met with a deafening roar. He cannot believe his ears and eyes. Even many of the journalists and reporters are excitedly calling his name. Everyone is stomping, screaming, their eyes are shining as if Michael had just delivered an over-the-top performance. But he just stands there. He smiles quietly. Waiting. Feeling.

And… there.

There it is. The connection. This something, this power, that connects everything, merges everything. He can feel it distinctly, feel how this something takes a hold of the people around him and sweeps through them. His love for the people of this planet overflows, fills the room and the people scream even louder. But all he had done was wiggle the microphone. Overwhelmed by the response, he goes up to the moderator and hugs him. His feelings are so mixed, he had not expected all this. Goes back to the microphone. Feels how the adrenaline takes hold of him, adrenaline, which he feels when he's dancing, that makes him alive and focused; he feels how invigorating it is to be on stage again and that feeling, too, overcomes him so completely that he walks over to the moderator once again and asks him something meaningless. The moderator points at the podium. Michael knows he has to say something now. And the decision matures in him to get through this and then really, really bow out. Just one more time, he thinks. Just this one more time. They are right. People will think differently about me. I'll do my best.

He goes up to the microphone, says the first words, but as soon as he opens his mouth and people hear his voice they shriek, as if the Holy Grail were before them. Michael's charisma cannot be described with words. Again, he just stands there, but it seems enough for the audience to simply see him. He laughs quietly and calls to the audience: "I love you more!"

His voice is deep, deeper than usual. It is the voice that he usually only has when he's talking to friends. Today he is in a position to use it in public. And again, they respond to this announcement with thunderous cheers and screams. It does not seem possible to deliver the message, but then Michael raises his hand and the noise level drops down enough for him to begin his short speech.

"This is it," he says. "This is the final curtain call."

He can say no more. The audience goes wild. They cannot believe that Michael Jackson, the greatest entertainer in the world, is standing in front of them. No one knows what he means with this first sentence. Michael finishes his speech. He says that this will be the absolute last time to see him on stage. He makes clear that there will be no new songs, but that he will perform the songs his fans want to hear. That's enough for them — they are in total ecstasy. Michael shines like a star, and no one can escape his charisma. Two minutes — then it's all over.

He turns around and starts to leave. The audience roars, wants to keep him. Don't leave yet, Michael! Michael! Michael! We love you! We love you! We love you more! Michael! Stay with us! Please! Stay here! We want you! We love you! We need you! Michael, we love you!

It is so powerful, it is so light in him, oh, he feels this radiance, he feels the love in him and lets it flow. That is what he lives for, what reconciles all this torment: this infinite love.

Michael turns around. Euphoric. He is still a superstar. He survived all these years of darkness with less damage than anyone had thought possible.

He goes back again one more time. Makes a few small, subtle dance moves, food for the camera, holds out his fist, makes his peace sign, turns and vanishes through the curtain.

The sales begin after the interview. The Internet is running hot, is overloaded, hard to get through.

Within four hours 750,000 tickets are sold. 53 tickets per second.

The manager shouts: "Close the counter, close the counter!" They shut it down as fast as they can. But still, nearly one million tickets are sold.

A number that translates into fifty concerts over a period of one year. That's back-breaking work – even for a completely healthy person.

Michael almost passes out when he hears this. Another new record for Michael Jackson. The fastest sold-out concert series the world has ever seen.

Michael Jackson stands for records.

XX - 2009

The success stories did not unsettle him. "Where's the problem?" he asked. "He's between a rock and a hard place. He usually always plays it so smart. Fifty concerts! That's his death sentence one way or the other. Our man is in the starting blocks. It's simple."

Today he was talkative. That's because he knew he would win. This made him peaceful.

"His only way out is to survive the 50 concerts – that's what he thinks! Has he learned nothing after 45 years in showbiz? Even that wouldn't help him ... he thinks he can change something with his blather about love? He is hemmed in. He can turn wherever he wants – we'll get what we want. That's how I love it. Checkmate and game over."

***

Grace was in Europe with the children.

She called him. "Michael," she said. "What's going on? How will you get through 50 concerts? You're not healthy!"

"Grace, I signed up for 10 concerts ... and when I woke up the next day, there were 50! But the contract is good for 10, I can insist on it ... and if ... if things go well ... if my first concerts are successful, then I can ask for what I want ... they are the ones who are greedy, then they can't do anything without me, and then I'll have the upper hand ... don't worry..."

Michael grinned into the phone. And when Grace remained silent:

"Man, Grace! Rehearsals are going great! Just this tour, then I'll have recovered financially ... I have to get out of this hole, Grace, you understand that, don't you! My children need a future! And the contract even includes a movie! Just what I've always wanted! After that, I'll be at a totally different starting place! And ... for the first time in years, the press is reporting good things about me!"

She could not be quite happy about it. But at least she knew how much it meant to Michael, for once not to be completely pulled through the mud and to read something good about himself in the tabloid press.

"Where's Jake?" she asked, worried. "He isn't getting back to me. What does he say?"

"He ... he's not there. I don't know where he is. We have to do it without him. Did you find a place, where…?"

"But we need Jake! What does Greg say? Doesn't he know anything? You know that the financial threat is not the real one!"

But Michael was under the influence of psychiatric drugs.

Grace could not do anything from a distance and she got scared. Terribly scared. And she condemned these greedy people who did everything just so that Michael would dance for them. So they could get what they wanted.

At night the effects of the meds wore off. At night the demons came crawling out of their holes. And at night he clearly saw the danger he was in. Even a single concert could mean his downfall. And he knew that even with a potential recovery of his finances, nothing was gained. That the intended outcome of this game could be very different. He did not know if Jake's plan was operational, should he need it. And whether Jake was still available. He had to hope, that was all that was left for him to do.

But in the meantime, he decided, he wanted to enjoy the stage.

He wanted to enjoy finally being someone other than Wacko Jacko.

After a long time a note found its way to him again.

"We need a doctor. For my baby. Critical condition. Risk of miscarriage. Should labor be induced?"

His heart pounded when he held the message in the hands. It had been scribbled in haste. It was now clear that something was going wrong. Critical condition. He, Michael, had not yet made a decision. He longed to be able to make the tour ... to give it what he had. But how much strength did he have to do the tour? He swayed. Sometimes he was up, sometimes down. During the day, he felt confident, felt he was in his element ... oh, he wanted this great show so much, to display this gigantic event to the world — with its inherent message and so much more! He was itching for that. He wanted to pass on his love, his art and he knew he would reach millions of people with this tour.

The note had an address. He knew the doctor. It was Conrad Murray, who he literally stumbled upon in 2006 in Vegas. It would be all right, everything would be fine. Jake was still out there, somewhere.

No one wanted to be officially responsible for their plan for how he could make it through the year. Therefore it never really became clear who had actually hired the doctor. Murray was supposed to be part of the contract with AEG, but in the end it never happened – he hadn't signed a contract with Michael, nor with AEG. Michael was responsible for his own health.

AEG cared about only one thing: he had to perform, the show had to go on, and everything else was secondary. Jackson was in good health – that's what the insurance company had documented. That alone was important. But AEG concealed that they had been able to get insurance coverage only for half of the concerts. They were good for $350 million themselves. Randy Phillips, CEO of AEG, was sweating. He was under tremendous pressure, too.

***

But Mike knew exactly what he needed in order to function.
The first thing he let Murray know, was: "I need to sleep. I can handle everything else. But I need to be able to sleep."
And if there was one thing Murray accomplished in the beginning it was to keep Michael stable. The physical therapist who worked with Michael not only built up specific muscles, but also used targeted training to make some of the problems that had plagued Mike disappear.
Mike's appetite increased, although he did not eat much, he ate healthy food and drank a sufficient amount of water to prevent the risk of dehydration. With astonishment, Michael found that he was growing stronger physically. And mentally he felt better, too. Suddenly he realized that he could just let go of certain things, that many things didn't affect him as much. He felt that when his past emotional traumas were no longer fed, they let go of him. It filled him with joy. And working with the dancers and musicians filled him with even more joy. He enjoyed the admiration and appreciation that they brought towards him, and he read and reread Chirelle's words that she had sent him:
"If people now show you a lot of respect and love, that's a great sign! You deserve this respect more than anyone else does! The important thing is that you don't slip back in believing that this recognition is the source of your happiness ... it's the other way around: recognition and love from outside are things that you can receive and that you can enjoy when you nourish the love within yourself…"
That gave him strength, he thought he was on the right track. He felt mentally and physically good and sensed how the old creativity was breaking though in him, gaining traction and pushing outward.
He was inspired and felt like taking on new projects. The universe was open to him – thousands of ideas were now within reach, buzzing around, and he only had to reach out for them. He wrote them all down, captured them.
He was excited about the concert's theme, its composition, artistic expression, its message: love…and healing the world. And then the costumes, the show, novelties such as 3-D animation, the huge chandelier

with acrobats, all of these so incredible dancers and singers, the pyrotechnics – they would give their fans a fantastic performance! All this revived him, enriched him, and ideas spouted forth like fountains from him. He began to initiate classical projects that he wanted to take on after the concerts, called directors and producers and discussed ideas for films. His creativity demanded expression in all its forms. People who met him during that time experienced him as happy and fulfilled.

Michael danced, Michael sang, Michael was in the sound and editing studios. He was completely back in touch with his inspiration, with God. During those hours, he felt neither stress nor pressure. He could have stayed in the studio forever.

They recorded a new song, a remake of the Band 'America'. Michael gave the song a name signifying his hope, his glimpse of a light, which was always with him, even if Jake was not reporting. The song was about an unknown place somewhere in the world. His place. A place with no name.

He did not give up hope that all would turn out well.

Excitedly he phoned Deepak and asked him if he could help him with the lyrics for "Place with no name." He was full of life and optimism. It felt good to do something, and he wished he could do it with full awareness, without these painkillers. The days in which he believed he could do it were in the majority, and then increased. His doctor, Conrad Murray, had found a combination of meds that kept him reasonably stable. It was clear to Michael that after the concerts an equally difficult time was ahead of him: the withdrawal, and the treatment of his insomnia. And he was determined to give his life a new direction.

Deepak was very pleased with Michael's new vigor, was so relieved to have his friend back again, who he had thought was forever lost after the last terrible trial.

"I'm back, Deepak!" Michael said to him on the phone and Deepak could literally see how his eyes light up. "No one could believe it, but I'm back … I'm back!"

"Yes, you're back," confirmed Mr. Chopra and was so happy for Mike. "Michael Jackson is back! You're back!"

Michael felt good and he enjoyed it to the fullest.

He loved working on the stage and enjoyed working with the people. Murray was proud to be able to build him up and strove to give Michael only a minimum amount of Western medicines. But it did not always work out, and sometimes the fear of failure outweighed in Michael, and the adrenaline raced through his body during the rehearsals and prevented any sleep and thus any chance of regeneration.

With the knowledge that drugs were being administered to Michael that were possibly not legal, it was agreed that it would be best to dismiss all the people around Michael who were close to him and could sound alarm bells.

The entire staff was replaced. And first and foremost: Grace, Grace, who would have informed Mr. Chopra and others, who would not have allowed this under any circumstances. It all happened so quickly. Grace, who was still traveling in Europe, received a letter, which stated that Mr. Jackson no longer needed her and thanked her for all the years of reliable service. Signed by Dr. Tohme Tohme. She could not even say goodbye to the children after 15 years of employment.

The headlines read: "Paris Jackson fires longtime nanny" with the explanation: because Grace Rwamba insisted Paris do her homework."

***

It took a while before it dawned on Conrad Murray that he could possibly be the fall guy in a very chaotic and dangerous plot. Then it took a while before he was willing to believe it. He hadn't quite succeeded with that so far. Too great was the opportunity, too tempting the pay-off. But the suspicion was there, fed by many clues.

He had hardly been able to believe his luck when he had been approached by a stranger on the streets of Las Vegas, and asked if he would like to consider a private, lucrative contract.

He could not believe his ears when he heard who it was about and there was no question in his mind: it was a once-in-a-lifetime opportunity, and he did not deliberate for long. He was in a precarious financial situation. He could not afford to think about it for too long.

The concerns came only later. Then, there were actually a lot of concerns he hadn't foreseen. Conrad Murray was not a bad person, and he didn't want to become one. The contract, which had seemed doable at first, turned into his own personal nightmare and into a matter of his conscience. Loaded up with medical books, he gritted his teeth and was determined to steer them, Michael and himself, out of these dangerous waters. If he could do that, so much was to be gained. For him and for Michael.

Initially, he thought along the same lines as the organizers, the managers and Michael did: one year, it's just a year. Then he would be through. He would be the doctor who would make this achievement possible, the personal physician of Michael Jackson. This way he would be forever anchored in the celebrity world and the earnings alone from this year would repair his finances. He was fiercely determined to get Michael through this. For his own sake and for Michael's.

He could not know that there were people who were expressly not interested in precisely this outcome.

***

The nights became a problem for Michael. Sometimes he slipped into a fitful sleep, into a lucid dream world and the brief dip into seemingly real images exhausted him more than they helped him recover.

He jumped up screaming from his sleep and then needed Murray and his meds to get back to sleep.

He dreamed ... how the audience at the O2 Arena was screaming his name, calling him, could hardly wait to see him. He is put into the 45-pound suit consisting of individual pieces each completely covered with thick, sparkling Swarovski stones.

The helmet is placed on his head. The visor is closed. Michael stands as heavy as lead and cannot move. The suit itself compresses, becomes tighter and tighter ... the visor in front of his face locks hermetically shut. Panic floods him ... he wants to tear it open - he is suffocating! But his hands are stuck in clumsy gloves that sparkle and glitter and every damn crystal on this glove pulls him down, makes him unable to raise his hands to his face, and even if he could have moved ... he would not have been able to open the visor, not with these super-sized hands. He can no longer breathe, the suit scrunches his ribs more and more, is getting tighter and tighter. Michael turns blue in the face, wants to scream, but all that happens is that the helmet on the head compresses too, crushes him ... incredible pressure ... there ...the cracking ... his skull breaks, he feels how his blood flows, everything becomes wet and sticky. Michael screams ... feels the metallic taste of blood in his mouth ... until he looks into the face of Conrad who is shaking him awake and talks to him soothingly.

"Give me something, Conrad," he sobs, he pleads. "I can't stand it. Give me something so that I can sleep without these nightmares, otherwise we both don't stand a chance."

A few weeks earlier

AEG was not the only offer Mike had at this time. 'Allgood Entertainment' from Texas wanted him, too, together with his brothers. Someone wanted to promote another revival, and everyone in the family - except, of course, Mike - jumped at it. The legendary *The Jacksons* on stage! With Michael Jackson! Leonard Rowe was commissioned to negotiate the deal. But everyone knew how Michael felt about his family, especially about performing with his brothers.

It went back and forth. Rowe suddenly claimed publicly - and supposedly without Michael's consent - that he was his manager, which infuriated Mike. Why did everyone on the face of this earth try to take control of him? Katherine finally persuaded Michael around March/April 2009 to sit down with Joseph and Rowe. It was the first time since 2005 that Mike saw his father again.

"Mike," he said, "AEG is screwing you. Look at the contract! This is a contract for slave labor! You have to pay for everything, everything! They charge you for the rent for the 02-stage ... for every cable, every backup singer, to the last Swarovski stone on your costume! And they don't do things for cheap! They're already throwing *your* money out the window. They couldn't care less! They're making a killing because you have to bear all the costs! How could you sign something like that?"

Mike became worried. The arguments of his father could not be dismissed. Joe was no fool. He had gathered information and talked a long time with Michael.

"Think about it," urged Joe. "Try to think like AEG does! They have a miracle kid who sells out every concert. Now they have to put the thing together so that nothing can go wrong for them! What are they going to do if you can't come through?"

Joe looked at him. His son looked tired ... and he *was* tired of all this stuff, this back and forth. And Joe said:

"Take Rowe, let him talk to Phillips, let him make sure that nothing happens."

And to Rowe he said:

"We have to get the boy outta there, Leo. I've done a lot of things wrong in my life ... and now ... my son needs help. He has to come back to the family. That's where he's safe. We have to get him out. They're killing him."

But Rowe made himself extremely unpopular with the CEO of AEG. Who did Jackson think he was, to send someone after him who is supposed to nitpick the contract apart? Now that the rehearsals were already going! He did not see why he should be controlled, and was pissed off accordingly. He called Michael and told him to get this monkey off his back, or the deal with AEG would fall apart and they would pull the financial plug. He did the math for Mike, showed him how much money had already been spent, and Michael almost passed out because he began to understand the plan which seemed to be behind everything.

Rowe, who drew a salary from Michael, would in addition collect a commission if he managed to hire Mike for 'Allgood Entertainment'. Alone his mother Katherine had been promised two million dollars for a closing of the contract because it was believed that Michael would surely want to support his mother. They argued that the family shows were far less strenuous than the planned 50 concerts.

Putting aside the fact that Michael was not inclined to engage with the family for a common cause, suddenly even DiLeo, his old manager, appeared on the scene who would have also cashed in a hefty commission if he could persuade Michael to a contract with Allgood.

But then DiLeo apparently switched sides, was now working for AEG, and was therefore paid by Michael - who had to bear all the costs associated with the concert. No one knew why DiLeo had suddenly showed up again and if Michael had even wanted him.

Rowe was fired - by Frank DiLeo. But Rowe claimed he had never been terminated. The engagement letter that Michael had written for Rowe had sounded friendly and just like Mike. The termination letter was formal and impersonal. It sounded as if stern parents had dictated a letter to their child, which forbade him to mingle with someone inappropriate. Rowe claimed the signature was forged.

But because he so strongly pursued the interests of the Jackson family his intentions were also questionable.

But even that aside, Rowe would not have had the slightest chance. Not against this music mafia who used their network and connections that spanned the globe to push Michael Jackson into the only role that was of interest to them: one of an investment that could make them many millions of dollars. Regardless of whether he survived the concert series or not.

The undeniable fact remained: the contract with AEG was binding. But it was not signed by Michael. The executor of the contract was Dr. Tohme Tohme and it was his signature on the contract, not Michaels. Although, allegedly, he had already been fired also. It was all very peculiar.

***

Murray received calls. Just one day after he was so fortunately picked, he realized that the coincidence was no longer a question. He had been chosen because he fulfilled certain criteria. Which were: he needed money; and just like any other person in this world there were a couple of things in his past that could destroy him ... if they were properly presented. The decision, it had been made unmistakably clear to him, would be entirely up to him.

He was promised that he would be left in peace as long as he stuck to the rules. Should he choose not to do that, they would have - in addition to the necessary connections - enough against him to get everything rolling.

And besides, in principle, nothing was asked of him.

Conrad Murray was asked to do nothing.

"That's all there is to it. When our call comes, you'll leave the room for half an hour. Talk to your girlfriend. Or go shopping."

It sounded terribly simple. But Murray knew that it was definitely not that simple. This "nothing" had hung like the sword of Damocles above his head every second since the call.

"What if I don't do it?" he asked back, trembling.

"Wouldn't advise you to do anything other. Don't tell anyone. Don't even try."

Then there had been a second call. About one or two weeks after the first one. Blocked number, different voice.

"All I ask is to make yourself invisible for at least ten minutes."

Murray was confused. "I was already advised," he replied.

A short silence was the answer.

"Then I'll phrase it differently: all I ask is that you call a certain number after you've received said call and then to make yourself scarce."

Murray raised his eyebrows.

"Tell me what your plans are," he demanded. "Who are you? Who are the others?"

"I can't."

"Why should I do what you say?"

"Will you do what the other ones say?"

"I don't know."

"Can have a bad outcome."

"Is the outcome any better if I believe you?"

"Why should they let you go, even if you do what they ask of you?"

Murray suddenly understood. The second one was not blackmailing him with his past. And he wasn't promising anything. He knew intuitively that this was a small chance for him and Michael. But he couldn't be sure.

All, that he could do for now was to focus on Michael's health. And foolishly, he hoped never to get any of these calls.

From the first one he heard nothing further. From the second one he received a text: "Hey, sweetie," stood on the screen. "You wanted my number ... save it carefully...call me if you need me. Miss you..."

Murray stuck his cell phone in his pocket with a bad feeling.

The rehearsals took their toll: Michael became weaker. He lost weight. He could not eat. He could not drink.

Crisis meeting. Doubles were considered. The show was rearranged so that with the help of backup dancers, effects, karaoke and film inserts a more reasonable level of physical activity for Michael was required. That put them considerably behind schedule. The mangers began to grumble. And everyone knew: they had a handle on these things - but the mental attitude, the mental condition was up to Michael alone.

Another meeting. This time it was Michael who was trying to reassure them. "I'm fine," he reassured everyone. He knew he had to endure. Randy had made it crystal clear: it was a "do it or die"- situation. But he was worried. He did not know where everything was heading. He just knew that 50 concerts would definitely do him in. He had to get out. Somehow.

Strangely, many of Michael's confidants were fired during this time. All sorts of contracts and dismissals were circulating around - inscrutable, no telling what was fake and what was real - besides, nothing was checked properly. And Michael seemed to be the last one to hear of these things ... if he even heard about them at all.

Grace had been fired by Dr. Tohme Tohme, by a man who himself had already been dismissed, but for some inexplicable reason signed legally binding contracts, such as the one with AEG, issued checks, and executed changes to staffing and who was listed in the AEG-contract with a salary of 100.000 Dollar per month. Dr. Tohme, who was demonstrably not a doctor and had family ties to Randy Phillips, CEO of AEG, and who Michael was scared of - as he confided in a (now public) call with his spiritual adviser, Rev. June Juliet Gatlin. In this phone call, he told her that Tohme separated him from all his friends, from everything he loved, did not grant him access to his files, and kept everything in his tight control.

In April 2009, Michael's business and tax advisors, Cannon & Co, were terminated by an assistant, which was very strange, because a notice of this magnitude was supposed to take place at the highest level, and in writing.

Michael did not know about it. Instead Arfaq Hussein was engaged, whose company, Crystal Miracles, offered exclusive clothing and who had landed in jail for credit card fraud in 2002.

Jackson was surrounded by a completely unfamiliar crew, his finances so entwined that even hard-core financial experts would not have been able to see through, his health a silken thread from which the fate of many people hung. But above all his own.

***

The family tries to reach him. His father tries to warn him
"Michael, you can't handle 50 performances," he says. "AEG is sucking the life out of you! What's with Rowe?"
But Michael is uncertain.

He is concerned that Joe only wants to force him into the family show. He'll have to sing and dance there, too. They say they are all concerned about his health, but ultimately everyone wants him to go on stage. He is bombarded by the Jackson-business and by AEG.

With 50 concerts, he believes, he would have at least a financial future. But does he really? There is truth to his father's words - he has to pay for everything, everything, from the printing of the tickets to the smallest light bulb in this gigantic set-up.

It may well be that he'll come back from London without a dime. But can Rowe do anything about it? Nobody has a clue what the threat really is.

In mid-May 2009 a meeting comes together between Randy Phillips and Paul Gongaware, who represented AEG, as well as Joe and Katherine, Rowe, and Michael. Tempers are heated.

Rowe yells at the AEG people:

"You're screwing Michael over! Already months beforehand you've got the money for the concerts at your disposal. You're paying Michael in pounds, not dollars! And you're shamelessly scalping tickets, selling tons on the black market and Mike won't see a dime of it! But you've loaded all expenses onto him. Mike, the contract lists your assets as security - the ATV, your own music catalog and your fortune, and a promissory note for 6.2 million dollars- are you out of your mind? You're accumulating even more debt with this concert, because they're anticipating that in the end you'll pay with the catalog! *That*, exactly *that*, is what they're after!"

And when Michael looks at him silent and terrified, Rowe rushes along undeterred:

"Why does the insurance policy cover an overdose? Excuse me? An overdose? In an insurance policy you pay for, and whose payout goes to AEG! And why do you have to pay for the 02 Arena through December 2011, when the concerts are only until February 2010 – for an arena that is owned by AEG? Man, Mike, wake up! Wake up! They've caught you in a trap! Remember - AEG also sees how you're feeling. They have to have a plan B. AEG is a business! They are not your friends! No matter what happens - they always win."

Michael is unhealthy pale when he leaves the meeting.

***

"Conrad," Mike asked, "have you ever thought about running away? Simply starting a new life somewhere else?"

Startled, Murray looked at Michael. Did he suspect anything? Did he know about the calls? Now would be a good opportunity to talk about it... but would Michael still trust him after that? Would he be able to keep this job? Was he being bugged, and they would finish him off after he told Mike about it?

"Um ... to be honest ... no," he replied. "Why would I want to do that?"

Michael was silent. He sat on the edge of the bed, medical equipment around him. He looked at it. That was his world. Drugs that enabled him to live, meds that sent him into an artificial sleep so his body could function for an industry that took advantage of him, for which he had to make money, because they had him cornered.

Devoid of emotion, he looked at Conrad, who was eyeing him with alarm.

"Because this business is a trap ... for all of us ... you know ... how about ... you adopt a different name ... go somewhere where no one suspects you. I know that I have money. I have more than they all think ... you know ... it's not only the ATV catalog I own ... I have assets. And I was not nearly as extravagant as they say. What I have is enough for a good life with my kids."

"But where would you want to go? Everyone knows your face! And the faces of your kids too! They have to go to school, eventually take a job..."

"There is only one photo of my children," said Michael. "And then they were young ... they're growing, changing ... it could work..."

"Michael!" Conrad Murray cried aghast. "You can't do that to ... your children!"

"What?" asked Michael unusually sharp. "Lead a normal life? Do you know why I'm so exhausted? Because I was never able to live a normal life! Do you know how nice it is to be allowed to lead a normal life? You know that, Con? I can just spit on the glitz and glamor! What did that ever get anyone? Name one friggin' star who doesn't have a screw loose!"

Conrad was appalled. Michael was suddenly talking in a very different way. His voice was different. What had happened to him?

"But you," he croaked, struggling for composure. "You! You will always be recognized even if you're on the highest peak of the Himalayas!"

"I could change," Michael said quietly. "I would love to change..."

"But Michael, what about your fans? Your God-given talent? You are the biggest star on God's earth! You sold one million tickets in three hours! One million! How many people would give their right arm to see you on stage! They're waiting for you! How many stars would sacrifice a limb for only a fraction of your popularity! Your fans would never forgive you!"

"I think my fans would be the first to understand," Michael said softly. "My fans are my friends, they do everything to help me."

"But..." Murray stammered helplessly, trapped in his unfinished thoughts, "the wheel is spinning. You can't stop it."

He wanted to look into his eyes, but Michael turned away and stared out the window.

"Leave, Conrad, please," he said. "I want to be alone."

Next day.

Michael had breakfast with his children, which meant he watched them eat something. His stomach was tight, there were too many worries in there. To divert his attention, he asked them about everyday things, their experiences, the progress in their lessons.

He cuddled with them and wished even more to be able to stay with them. But he had to go. He had to go to the studio and he would be gone all day. Sighing, he got up and put on his sunglasses.

"Daddy," Paris piped up. "Please, may we come along? We want so much to see you at work ... please!"

"Oh yeah!" cried Prince. "That would be great! We want to see you dance!"

Until then Michael had shown the children little of his rehearsals. He'd wanted to just surprise them with a bang, just like he wanted to surprise his fans. But now he was not even sure if he was going to be able to give them a concert, so reluctantly he said yes. He felt good that day and the energy of his children added to that feeling. They went to the studio together and the kids were so proud to see him in action.

Singing and dancing was wonderful, when his body allowed it. And, oh, he loved it and it felt so good! On that day everything went great, his voice was perfect, his movements soft, he blossomed in the music. God, it was so beautiful! This afternoon was solace for him, and at the end of the day he walked cheerfully towards the exit with his children.

A battery of people was standing there. Bodyguards, security, all coming in motion at the sight of him. Michael greeted them, smiled, and, flanked by his bodyguards, moved toward the car, which, not as usual, had its doors closed.

He thought nothing of it. When he arrived at the vehicle, still no one made a move to open the door. He stretched out his hand to open the door himself.

"Excuse me, sir," said one of the people, and Michael, with his son Prince next to him, looked in his direction. The man sprang forward, cleared his throat loudly, as if he were embarrassed to have neglected his duty and opened the door.

Michael turned his head in alarm: the cough had not been enough to completely drown out the well-known hissing of a camera flash. Or was he just imagining it? Was he hallucinating? He got in his car and urged his children to get in quickly behind the blacked-out windows.

Again he heard the noise. A second later, Prince and Paris were sitting next to him. Intuitively he slammed the car door shut by himself, just in time.

A never-ending lightning storm of camera flashes rained down on the darkened car.

Stunned, Michael looked out the window. As if from afar he heard the barking voices of reporters.

"How are you, Michael?"

"Where are you going?"

"Are you already excited about the concerts?"

"Will your children be there?"

"Who, dammit, let this crowd in?" someone shouted at the top of his lungs. "Move! Move! Right now! None of you have any business being here!"

But the reporters paid no heed. They shot useless photos of the car, bombarded the closed car door with questions and in a single, protective movement Michael turned towards his children and froze. They were unmasked.

Frantically he ordered masks and shawls and when they got out, the children were veiled as ever.

It was too late.

The very next day close-up pictures went around the world. Michael Jackson and his children on the way to the recording studio - unveiled.

Something broke inside him. That was too much. It was simply too much. That was the day when he made the call that he had shied away from making for such a long time.

"Greg," he says, his hands trembling as he held the phone. "I know you currently don't have any help in the garden. Maybe a few professionals would be good ... and when you see Jake, tell him I would like to see his baby."

Greg is as taciturn as always. Michael hangs up.

Then he has a long talk with Paris and Prince. They look at him with serious, compassionate eyes. There are old souls, he knows that, oh God, how he loves them! This feeling is so strong that he knows for the first time that what he is doing is right. He wraps up several calls. And then there is Branca, his on-and-off-attorney, John Branca, who has the latest version of the will. He does not know if he can trust him, he doesn't know that of anyone, so he hesitates.

But he has to make sure that his children are well provided for - no matter what happens. And anything can happen. Still his hand wavers. Can he trust Branca? His gaze falls on the photo of John's wedding - where he was best man. He can only hope that this is not something that is meaningful only to him. Hopes that a back door is opened for him. He knows neither if it will be there, or if it will be there on time, or if he will be physically and mentally capable of going through it.

***

Over many long years Jake had built a huge network that was now supposed to save his life. He was professional enough to know that he could never be sure where anyone stood with him. Ultimately, everything was a gamble and would always remain one.

He shared the view of his most important client - that suspicion was justified - even though, paradoxically, he was the one who always believed in people. With amazement Jake had watched this client and how his position, when it came to love, was unwavering. He had been humiliated, abused mentally and still believed in love. His eyes still went warm with compassion for other fates, love for humanity, for the earth. Something was in this dainty guy that gave him a strength that allowed him to get up over and over again.

At the beginning Jake had considered this attitude terribly naive, but the tenacity with which his client maintained this sentiment eventually ennobled it, and his respect for this man had grown infinitely.

"Why don't you hate those people?" he had often asked, after his client had been dragged through the sludge again. "Why not just hire a brother and do away with this awful guy?"

But his client had never wanted to hear that. He believed in the good, in God, and he was never dissuaded. When he talked about this and when he was playing with his children, a noticeable glow was around him. Jake had been able to feel this warmth ... it was contagious. And over the years, in spite of his resistance, some of it had passed onto him and become his own personal stumbling block: he had learned to love his client, despite having been deployed for his destruction.

"Love," his client had always said, "love, Jake, is the greatest power in the world, the greatest power in the universe. It is what we are made of, it is what we all are ... it is what is left when everything evil leaves ... and so I believe in the good, I believe in God, I believe that good will ultimately always win. I take care of children because they carry the good so visibly within them, and because they are our future."

Jake was not only skeptical of these words - he scorned them. The world was corrupt, it was bad, money and power reigned over everything. He should know! People were addicted to success, fame, beauty, sex and money. No matter how much they had, they always wanted more, and that desecrated everything. The best attitude you could have towards all of that was indifference. To stay out, to not be engulfed by all these lower impulses that dominated people. The constant babble of love and the like had driven Jake crazy. He could not hear it anymore! Esoteric, meaningless, unworldly gibberish!

But for his client love was, and remained, the law. At first Jake had observed with almost grim satisfaction how that faith had been constantly undermined and refuted. With most clients that he had had, it barely took half a year before they changed course and they themselves ended up corrupt, frustrated and filled with hatred. But his client remained stubborn. He continued to believe in this nonsense.

He believed while he was being dragged through the mud by the media. He believed while professional measures were being taken to destroy his reputation and his career. Yes, there were moments in which he said that the world is corrupt, that people are bad ... but he believed that only of adults, of certain businessmen. His basic idea that every person is good, especially as a child, was steadfast.

He never stopped helping children, never ceased to support environmental causes. He'd get a beating, take it, fall and get up again. Bleeding, wounded, crying, but he would get up. Over and over again.

Jake had started to admire him. His strength, his faith, his attitude. The gentleness with which he eventually parried the attacks. The only rebellion he could recall had been against Sony. And when he was indicted for the second time and a journalist asked him how he was feeling, he managed just a soft: "I'm angered."

Oh, he was so gentle, so soft! And yet, over the years, it was inevitable: he became weaker. He was losing his life force.

Jake saw him waver, saw him become dependent, watched as he tried to lead a happy life, how he kept trying to get to his feet, how he slowly understood the method behind the madness, saw that he could be stubborn and he fought - in his refined way. He had been so incredibly disgraced, humiliated and slandered. But he had never countered with the same despicable manner.

They took his reputation, riled up the media against him, stripped him of his credibility, worked on his financial ruin. When he tried to save his fortune through consolidating his debts, only vultures surrounded him, enriching themselves at every step, so that in the end he had more debt than before. People were shameless. They took advantage of his gentleness, tried to control him, set up contracts he did not want, hired people he did not want, messed around in his affairs like the 40 thieves in Ali Baba's cave.

It wasn't surprising that he didn't trust any adult, since almost everybody he had trusted had betrayed him.

And despite all that, he still ran to every child, helped people in need, and fought his battle against the exploitative methods of those, who, with their attitude, destroyed the world.

But one thing, one thing they had taken from him, and this, it seemed, for good: his self-respect.

Almost wistfully Jake watched how his client faded away both mentally and physically. How he wasted his strength in this fight. But, he wondered, was it really wasted? Wasn't he setting an example with this stubbornness, with this strength to not be corrupted? He exuded his love... he changed the people around him with it ... but he was not able to grant that love to himself. For some reason he felt he was not worthy.

It was the real trump card of his tormentors. But his client knew about his opportunities.

"Jake," he had once said. "I know who you are. Everything in life is a choice. A free choice."

It was not easy for either of them. For both of them, everything was at stake. Ultimately, it was something Michael said that tipped the scales. He had said: "If we cease to be good, just because others are bad ... where does that lead us?"

And Jake had made his decision.

Secretly, he had built a second network. He spoke with people considered to have high integrity. Who had values. And it felt good to negotiate with them. It felt good to know that there seemed to actually be things like honesty and respectability. And when, after the boycott of *Invincible,* Michael realized the significance of the danger, he was in he and Jake started to make plans to escape. Years of preparation now lay behind them. Everything had been planned meticulously. Especially since 2005, people had turned up who were willing to help anonymously. It only needed Michael's okay. And so far, he had struggled to make up his mind.

***

Michael found the pictures of his children, even before their release, on his pillowcase. He remained strangely calm, revealed to his children that they could do without the masks starting today, and their reaction gave Michael more to think about: they were relieved and happy. They did not want to hide behind a mask because they believed in the future.

He called Greg and asked him how far he had come with the staff for the garden.

"Sir," Greg replied with his thin, quavering voice, "I placed an ad and a lot more people than expected reported. Half the world wants to work as a gardener, it appears."

"What ... what does that mean?" asked Michael, and a hot sensation spread deep down inside him.

"This means that everything is on, Mr. Jackson."

And after Michael said nothing, he added. "It's going very well, sir."

"Thank you, Greg," Michael said flatly, and hung up. He slowly sat down on the side of the bed. Closed his eyes. Suddenly a deep peace caressed him, penetrated every cell, culminating in a point in his heart. He was there. God was there. There he was ... and a small smile appeared on his face. A smile that grew wider and wider, which filled him with joy and made everything seem easy. And at that moment he was in absolute peace about his future. He thought about how much he had so far been trying to steer everything, to control everything in order not to fall into the trap. How exhausting life had been because of it. And now ... now he did not want any of that anymore. Yes, his situation was still difficult, but all of a sudden he realized what the word "trust" meant. He understood that the same substance that guided him when he danced would guide him in his life - if he would allow it. It would manifest through the people he trusted. And he wanted to allow it. Not out of fear as before, which had always pointed him in the wrong direction, but from this tangible source. All that he could do was to trust that everything would turn out for his own good. This realization washed with the force of a tidal wave over him. And made him free. At least for the moment.

The next day during the rehearsal and also at home, he found himself in a detached, joyful state of mind. He enjoyed everything that came his way, was pleased with the development of the stage show, was delighted to be part of it. He got into it with great zeal, made jokes, and was in very good spirits. He knew that no matter what might happen, he would never fall lower than into God's hands.

***

Murray was getting nervous. He was being followed. He clearly noticed a car persistently following him. Twice already it had demonstratively flashed its signal light to the right when a parking lot had been in sight, but Murray had taken no part in that.
The third time he pulled himself together and turned into a spot on the right. The car parked closely behind his. An unfamiliar man got out. He looked friendly, which didn't have to mean anything. They were all very nice. But what they wanted of him was just not always so nice. The hair of the man was a bland brown, his eyes hidden behind mirrored sunglasses. He seemed to be young and muscular – that was all Murray could say. He leaned against the fender of his car, crossed his arms and watched the sunset. Murray got out of his car, walked up to the man and stood silently next to him.
"You should be clear about what you have gotten yourself into by now," began the other without transition. And when Murray made no response: "What is not so clear is whether you thought the story through to the end."

"Which version do you have in mind?" Murray snapped. But the stranger had hit the mark. So far he had refused to draw any conclusions, although it was foolish. But the idea that he was trapped in any case and served the role of a fall guy was too uncomfortable for him to want to acknowledge. He was not sure if he wanted to be confronted with it. Staring straight ahead just like the man next to him, Murray asked:

"What do you know anyway?"

"For example ... that nothing was asked of you," replied the other. "From several parties."

"Do you belong to one?"

"Knowing that wouldn't make a difference for you, would it?"

"Maybe that's the heart of the matter, and it would make a big difference."

"Why should it?"

"Because ... because..." Murray felt his lips trembling. The conversation was an outlet for his suppressed fears and he tried to control himself. But the other one had already recognized his emotional state. Ever so slightly, he turned his upper body towards him.

"Because...?"

"Because I like him. Because I don't want anything to happen to him. And because he is not the only one who wants to see it happen ... and has something to lose."

The man nodded.

"It should be clear what will happen in your absence during this half hour."

Murray swallowed. So clearly said, it felt like a punch in the gut.

"Force yourself to think the whole thing through to the end: the call comes. You leave. You come back in. What will you find? And who will be held accountable?"

Naked, the truth lay splayed out in front of Conrad Murray. Naked, the whole thing did not look appealing whatsoever.

"Second assumption: the call doesn't come. It happens on stage or wherever else. An autopsy is performed. The question that everyone will ask is: how can it be justified that someone who requires 24-hour medical attention is allowed to go on the stage? How long has he been taking this stuff already? As a physician you know better than I do that the side effects of respiratory depression range from apnea to metabolic and cardiovascular disorders. And you also know that propofol does not induce REM sleep and he therefore doesn't get any real rest. He's just in a coma. And you want to go through with that for a whole year? The half-life is short - is that what you're counting on when he keels over? That propofol will no longer be detectable? But what will the world think? There's this doctor who supplies him with meds. What kind of meds? Are they legal? What do you think AEG will do?"

"Why does only the doctor get accused?" asked Murray defiantly. He had already arrived with his thoughts at that point as well.

"Because it's the easiest. He's of the least interest. Maybe he has less to lose in the opinion of others, the perfect scapegoat! With the perfect motive: greed! Especially since he would have to know what he was getting himself into. Why did he accept the job? Where were his principles of ethics? Wouldn't it have been more responsible to say: 'My patient cannot perform the required work'? Come on, what's his weight these days? Wouldn't it be more ethical to quit the job?"

Murray swallowed. The fall guy. Now it was sure.

Unsure, he looked at the man. A muscle twitched in his face but he didn't look back at Murray.

"And if it works?" Murray asked.

"Man of God, what are you hoping for?" asked the other one cynically. "For the jackpot in the lottery?"

Yes, that was what Murray was hoping for. To hit the jackpot in the lottery just once. Once in his life to walk on the side of good fortune! For once with a single step to move to the sunny side of life.

"I ... I'll quit," Murray said, trembling. "Is that what you want?"

"As if you could! No, don't quit ... we need you."

"What...what is your suggestion?" asked Murray with a trembling voice.

"Let's sit in the car," the stranger invited. "In mine. Then I'll explain everything to you. But I'll tell you right now: It's probably your only chance ... and it's not pretty. And not foolproof. You have to go through a long, unpleasant phase. But we have important people on board ... who can make success a possibility. We can get you out."

Murray remained silent. The other ones had promised him that, too.

The men talked for a long time. What the man said to Murray was tough. He did not know if he wanted to accept these conditions. But the worst thing was: he did not even know if he had a choice.

***

Barely three weeks until the start of the concert in London.

The performance still gave Michael joy, he loved being with the people, he reveled in the magic of melody and dance. His condition was stable on a day to day basis, and in that shape he craved to do the concerts. At least a few! He wanted to be on the stage, wanted to see his fans again, wanted to show his children what he had in him, wanted to feel this huge sensation again, the magic of the stage, the energetic connection between audience and artist.

Then there were the nights that showed him otherwise ... and he had now set things in motion whose schedule he had to submit to. He had no idea if anything was even going to come out of it. The only connection was Greg. And he wasn't saying anything.

There were days he spent suspended between hope and fear. And he knew he had to talk to AEG - he could not do 50 concerts, not be on tour for one and a half years. That much was for sure.

He dreamed so repeatedly of standing on the stage, all of these extraordinary talents around him, the audience staring at him and expecting an over-the-top performance - the kind he was famous for.

But he stood there paralyzed. His brain empty, everything dull, like wrapped in cotton wool. His legs were heavy as lead, they did not move, he did not know how to do the moonwalk anymore, he had forgotten all the dance moves. The music played and played ... always the same bars ... they were all waiting for his entrance, which did not come. The gaping time span was dotted with the first boos, then grew louder, and more and more people chimed in the longer he stood frozen in the spotlights. The disappointed murmur of the fans, the desperate eyes of the team, the background crew behind him. The headlines in the press: Jackson, the loser.

Michael was hoping so much to be able to do the first concert. All the efforts that he had already undergone! All that work! The incredible dancers and singers! The show was top class, so extraordinary ... it met all his ideas and expectations and he felt enormous joy in participating, in giving everything this spectacular form. He was a fish back in the water again ... and yet he was terribly afraid. It did not make him happy to know that he was the greatest uncertainty for the concert series. But his children would be at the first concert.

That was ultimately the thought that brought out his positive thinking again: after the concert, he would not be alone. His children would be there. They would give him energy during the show. It was going to be wonderful. His children would be there and hug him with glowing eyes. And with that thought his confidence and this burning desire to make it happen returned. He thought about the expressions on those people's faces who had heard him sing during the rehearsals. This - his! - voice had driven tears to so many eyes. He saw the admiring glances of those who had seen him dance, although they were acrobatically so much stronger than he was. As before, his magic was still there. It flowed from every pore, and he knew its origin. It would all go well. It had to go well... no matter what ... if he had to go on stage, he would do it! And oh! He was so much looking forward to a happy end, to this great feeling of knowing it had been a fantastic performance. Michael breathed deeply. He had to move with it. There was no other choice. Sometimes he thought he had one concert in him, sometimes ten, sometimes none at all.

But he hoped very much to make his exit with what he was known for: a gigantic Michael Jackson Show.

And if Greg or Jake should get in touch with him ... then he had to let go of everything. To hopefully win it all.

Every day he was waiting for Jake, for his way out. And hoped that he could hold on long enough.

The rehearsals were long and tiring, and Michael's condition deteriorated dramatically on some days. Sometimes he was in great spirits, other times he did not know if he had even enough energy to make it through the next day. But more often he suffered unspeakable pain after training, his body was rheumatic, the skin of his feet torn, his lungs did not provide enough oxygen, and the adrenaline kept him awake. He was getting more nervous; his fear of failure was increasing. And nobody could inject self-confidence into him. Slowly, what no one wanted to see because it was so uncomfortable became obvious: the fact that Michael was very ill.

But everyone put pressure on him because they were under pressure themselves. They started yelling at Michael, he was ordered around and treated like a piece of merchandise. No more admiration, no respect, only functioning, delivering, performing, and if it did not work out, punishment followed in the form of sarcastic remarks.

The nights where he cried from physical pain and fear increased. His heart tightened. But he wanted to be brave. Endure the year. He had to persevere, but each rehearsal drained energy from his thin body, and since he could not regenerate in a natural way, no fresh supply was in sight.

Despite higher doses of medication, which Conrad Murray gave him reluctantly now, he could not sleep. His body ached. His head ached. He was confused.

Murray on the other hand was in a terrible dilemma. He tried to reduce the doses to a level that was medically acceptable, but to his horror he found that Michael appeared to have additional sources. He saw his work undermined ... how could he know what they gave Michael? It could well be that these unknown drugs had antagonistic effects or potentiating interactions. Murray's fear increased at least as much as Michael's agitation and panic attacks.

Again, threatening letters found their way into Mike's home, while the pressure over not being merely good, but absolutely top class, built up immensely. He was tired from the meds, although Murray swore that wasn't possible, not from what he had administered ... he could no longer concentrate, missed one or the other rehearsal and drew the ire of those responsible.

And there came the day when he was suddenly no longer fully aware of his children. Yes, he saw them, but his eyes worked only selectively ... the kids came running up to him and he could not look them in the eye, they were a blur, their faces blurred together. He felt as if he were stuffed with batting, the head, the brain filled with glue ... he could no longer feel his children. The fear injected itself into him that, due to the sedative effect of his medication, he would no longer be able to reach his audience, no longer capture their energy, no longer make this psychedelic, blessed connection. It began to seem hopeless. Without painkillers he could not see it through. But with them he was at risk, less proficient, impaired. And dependent.

Michael fluctuated between hope and fear, between awakening self-confidence and pre-existing inferiority, between letting go and holding onto old patterns of thought, and his body stumbled with him.

The days went by. And the atmosphere at the rehearsals changed completely. Those responsible became indignant and angry. They'd already had to postpone the first concert by a week and were still behind in time. It was not Michael's fault, but it was good to have someone they could blame and whose reputation justified anything.

Despite frantic efforts, the show was still in an unrefined state. Nervousness spread, the organizers were stressed, and everyone's nerves were raw with the approaching of the first concert.

Phillips made it clear that the schedule had to be met, and he started yelling at Michael in front of everyone else, and others adopted this voice. More than anything, they were furious when he did not show up, thus signaling that the workload was simply too much.

The medications did the rest: Michael fell into an infantile fear of punishment, seemed increasingly shy and insecure. When AEG insisted on the 50 concerts, and when Mike could not get out of bed with pain on some mornings, he said for the first time that he had not signed a contract that required him to honor such a number.

He had lost a huge amount of weight - even before the concerts- where he then lost many more pounds. Pain stretched over his body like a second skin. He often trembled and above all, he froze terribly, at home and at the rehearsals.

But the tickets were sold. The money had been taken in and massive costs accumulated - the organizers made it clear that there would be no turning back and they were not at all polite anymore. Tongue-tied with embarrassment, Kenny Ortega and the other dancers watched how Michael was treated. With horror they watched his physical decline. Michael saw everything in their eyes.

No Jake in sight. No message, no hope, nothing.

Michael cried. Michael froze. He, too, was betting everything on a risk.

He knew now for sure: fifty - that was his death sentence.

The strength leaves his body in giant flares. All at once. As if he has a leak in him. When Michael recognizes it, it becomes quiet in him. He does not have much time, not much time at all. The clock is ticking on all levels. Maybe he can survive one concert. He stands on the stage and Kenny Ortega has tears in his eyes when he looks at him. Mike's body is emaciated to a skeleton. Often he sways and sometimes he can't manage the smallest muscular effort. "Mike," Kenny says helplessly, and pats him on the back because he knows he has to go through with it somehow, Michael has to perform, that is his only chance. He has his own opinion about this ... and he is terrified for him. "Mike," he says again, "you have to eat, look, I've got something here ... we can share ... look ... just a bite ... just a bit to eat..."

And he feeds him like a little child. Michael opens his mouth, unhappy, chews a bit, swallows, and is grateful that somebody cares, longs so much for this...for a little bit of tender loving care ... For someone who is kind to him.

Daydreams are haunting him. He plays with his children. He nods off briefly. He is suspended in space above the stage. This time, the space suit is comfortable, it is big, there is enough room inside. The fog machines are on full blast, obscuring the view to the stage ... the bass drones, music sets in. Strings, drums... generating expectations.

He feels the energy in his body, looks forward to his fans, to offering them something. Everything is ready. The fog is so dense that nothing can be seen ... then a blinding ray of light on which he is beamed down in his heavy glitter suit. He hears people shrieking, screaming, feels the familiar, his world ... feels invigorating adrenaline ... he touches down on the floor ... the suit opens ... Piece by piece, part by part, it exposes Michael. The crowd rages anew, shouts, screams his name, stretches arms out to him ... pines for him and he for them. He stands on the stage and charges up. His battery is full, overly full. Wow, he feels gigantic, abundance everywhere, it pours and flows and gushes.

Michael dances, his legs move, his mouth moves. He feels God's energy in him, feels how it flows forth. He dances like he has not danced for a long time, sings like he has never sung before, he knows his children are sitting down there. His children, who are seeing him for the very first time on stage. They have bright eyes. They can see what a big star their Daddy is. They clap

476

and are happy and marvel at the thousands of people who are screaming their heads off for their Daddy, who give him all their love.

And then ... he feels his heart. A stab, an electric shock, a sudden pain... Michael falls down in slow motion. He looks for the faces of his children. There... there they are ... in the VIP lounge, surrounded by bodyguards ... next to his mother ... his kids ... their mouths are gaping open in horror. Paris screams madly, tries to get to him, Prince's eyes are frozen in shock and Blanket is crying. He still wants to tell them so much, wants to shout so much to them, wants to tell them not to be afraid, that everything will be fine ... that he loves them, that he loves them so much, so much ... but he cannot speak, cannot move. His heart has stopped beating.

With a gasp, Michael opens his eyes and looks into the faces of his three children. They look at him anxiously, and Paris puts her arms around his neck. "Daddy," she whispers, "we're here. We will always be there for you. Like you are there for us."

One thing becomes clear to him since that dream: he does not want that. Not to die on stage in front of his children. But that is a possibility with every concert. Even with the very first one. He realizes that this price is too high. In there, in his heart, the light shines. That's what he wants, that's the only important thing in life. It is simply too early for these concerts ... maybe it would have been better in two or three years. Maybe. He is sick. He is very sick. He cannot wait any longer.

He picks up the phone and calls in a meeting.

Michael is now sure of one thing: The only way to get out of this disaster and to save the ATV for his children... is... to leave this world.

On June 20th a meeting takes place between Kenny Ortega, Randy Phillips, Frank DiLeo, Conrad Murray and Michael Jackson. The outward reason for this meeting is Michael's repeated absences from rehearsals. The folks from AEG read Mike the riot act, threaten him again; they will pull the financial plug and he will lose everything if he does not do what they say. Lose everything. Does he know what that means? They really mean: *everything*.

In a week they are supposed to go to London. The show is not finished, and five days of intensive rehearsal wouldn't make much of a difference.

Michael has his back against a wall. He takes a deep breath and tells them his story, a story that is already over. He tells them about his hopes, his fears and shows them his body. He tells them everything. He needs their help. He has a plan.

Shocked, shaken, they sit before him, tears shoot into Kenny Ortega's eyes. Unbelieving faces. They'll think about it – that's the only thing they will concede to. Michael has to be satisfied with that. And once again everything is up in the air. Crying, Kenny goes back to the Staples Center and tells the participants of the show: "Pray for Michael."

**

On June 21st Michael calls his former nurse, Cherilyn Lee. He complains that one half of his body is hot, the other is cold, that he was not doing well, was not feeling well. Cherilyn is very concerned and…surprised. Doesn't he have a 24/7 doctor around him? What Michael is saying doesn't sounds at all good.
"Go to the hospital," she urges him. But he doesn't go.

On June 22nd Michael visits Dr. Arnold Klein, his dermatologist and longtime medical doctor. His health is at its absolute limit. Michael is in terribly bad shape.

But none of the parties - Jake, Greg, or AEG - gives a positive signal, any indication. The first concert is approaching fast. Michael paces in his bedroom restlessly back and forth. Tears run down his gaunt cheeks. He reaches into his pocket, fumbles for a handkerchief and finds a note:
"We'll shoot you on stage — in front of your children."

June 24, 2009 / The Followers

His fans always sat around the gates of his house or in front of the Staples Center. Always the same ones. They were the so-called "Followers", those who followed him everywhere, no matter where in the world he was. He never knew how they managed that, but it was good to see their faces. And every time he went into Staples, he greeted them, went up to them, talked to them. Every time. It was a ritual. He respected every fan and these ones especially.
On that day, despair and the need to share this immense pressure with someone drove him to his fans.
"I wanted to do only 10 concerts," he tells them frantically. "But I woke up the next morning and they had turned into 50. Help me. I can't do 50. Help me. I gotta get out of here."
The followers were horrified. They promised to do something. But, what? It had to be quick. And it had to be effective. They asked Karen Faye to intervene and many others more. And they went to the press.

"What is this guy doing?" the people at AEG shouted angrily. "That's impossible! Make it stop! Immediately!"

And the following day Michael was not allowed to talk to his fans anymore - he waved at them, but when he walked over to them, several bodyguards went with him - who would drag him away at the first wrong word.

Michael did not say a wrong word. The number of his bodyguards had mysteriously increased from two to ten.

Nobody could afford for this gigantic project to fail - least of all Michael and the managers.

The call did not come at night. It came late in the morning. Michael had not slept all night - Murray was exhausted. He had given him several drugs, none of which wanted to kick in.

At first Murray had hesitated. Michael took them too often. Every night. Already before the concerts! That night he had tried a different approach first. He had given him Valium. Nothing. Lorazepam. Midazolam. No effect. Michael was a nervous wreck. Finally he injected a small amount of propofol diluted with lidocaine. According to him, 25 milligrams, an amount far too small to induce a coma. In lower doses propofol has an euphoric effect.

10:45 a.m. Los Angeles, local time, June 25, 2009.

And then the call came. A friendly voice said:

"Why don't you take a break for half an hour?"

Murray took a deep breath. He knew he was being watched and the room bugged. Slowly he walked outside, the cell phone in his sweaty hand. He had made a decision long ago. If Mike had a chance, he would give it to him...and to rescue his own life. With trembling hands, he dialed the number of the woman.

"Hey, sweetheart," he said in a husky voice in the phone. "I'm on a half-hour break ... and wanted to hear your voice."

A happy, almost relieved sob was the answer:

"Oh, God, honey," she said. "You can't imagine how happy I am that you called!"

There was a brief pause, then she started a harmless conversation with him.

A few seconds later, another phone rang:

"Mike!"

"Jake! Jake ... " Michael's voice sounded dazed, weak.

"Mike, no time for questions: they are on the way over to you. I don't know if I can get there first. Be ready. Do you have money?"

"I ... I always have something here," Mike stammered. He was deathly pale.

"Take the money and pray."

"But Jake ... who...?"

An impersonal busy signal was the response. Michael stood up shakily. He took the money, put it in a bag. Nonsensically he also grabbed a small kit with a toothbrush, toothpaste and a few cosmetic articles. He didn't close the bag properly and the toothpaste fell out, without him noticing. Trembling, praying, he lay down on the bed and closed his eyes. Now he had to leave everything to God.

10:52 a.m., Los Angeles, local time. June 25th, 2009.

The clock is ticking ... and ticking ... and ticking ... slowly, sluggishly, painfully.
Murray was fidgeting on his seat. After what felt like an eternity, he went back to Michael's bedroom. His heart was beating furiously as he put his hand on the wooden frame. The door was ajar. Slowly he pushed against it.

12:22 p.m. Los Angeles, local time, June 25th, 2009:

A manservant calls 911 and says that a gentleman needs help. No name is mentioned. The voice sounds calm and with no sign of agitation.

12.35 p.m. Los Angeles, time: TMZ posts the following message to the world: Michael Jackson has been hospitalized for a serious heart attack in the UCLA hospital.
Some are worried, most believe he faked it - just as he had done many times before when he did not want to perform.

Two hours later, his death is announced.
Mr. Michael Joseph Jackson died, according to the official report, on June 25th, 2009 at 2:26 p.m., from an overdose of propofol that caused respiratory arrest.

A legend had died.
Michael Jackson was dead.

Reverberation

I had not told anyone other than my husband about what I had experienced. I called my mother, who lived a few miles away from me, to ask how she was doing. Oblivious, I was chatting to her about trivial stuff and just before I was going to hang up she asked casually:

"Oh, have you heard? Michael Jackson died yesterday. I think you always liked his songs."

The receiver fell out of my hand. Heart pounding, I was sitting in front of the TV moments later and saw my mother's news confirmed. As if this could change anything, I surfed the Internet. The sites were filled with news of his death. Michael was dead. He was dead. This great man, this wonderful big boy ... he was dead.

I could not believe it. Not for days. I did not want to believe it, refused to believe it. Michael ... this very wonderful, gentle, gifted person was no longer among us? And suddenly I realized how much I had enjoyed him, just knowing that he existed, that he was there somewhere in the world. Just there. The earth missed his energy. All the more painful was the loss - I could not really imagine a world without him. It seemed so empty to me. Less dazzling, less loving, less valuable. A world without Michael seemed like a sky without stars.

I saw him in front of me, his face so gentle, his deep, huge eyes, his slender body with the big hands. And when I recalled the expression on his face when he had said goodbye to me, with this always shy and yet very loving look, it broke completely out of me.

I lay in my room on the floor and could not stop crying.

"I miss you, Mike," I whispered to the carpet. "I miss you, oh, my God, how I miss you. I miss you ... I miss you ... please come back ... you can't leave…please, come back, I wish you were still here!"

The irrational feeling that evil had triumphed over good seized me. The feeling that something monstrous had occurred before our eyes. That he had called for help and no one had heard him. The feeling that he had not accomplished 'it'. But what was, 'it'? What had he not accomplished? I had felt the joy he had experienced in the rehearsals, heard the happiness in his words when he had briefly called. He sounded so confident, so positive, optimistic, and I thought I could sense that a knot had pulled apart. Why, why could he not live that? He had just turned 50 and could have spent another 30 years on this earth in happiness and with joy. And I would have wished him that more than any other person.

I remembered his words: "Gandhi, Christ ... if that was their fate, why not mine?"

I felt hot. And nauseated. Gandhi and Jesus had been murdered.

The following days I walked around in a trance. I turned on the TV more often than was good for me and spent hours surfing the Internet. Michael's death had evoked something that I could not understand. An irrational sadness seemed to capture the entire world. People were crying everywhere - all over the globe they mourned for him.

His fans were there as always and forever. And he had more than had ever been imagined. Hundreds of thousands danced for Michael, danced for what he had fought for all his life, danced for him, for his ideals, for his love, his gentleness. They came together and did what he had always wanted to accomplish with his art: to unite people of all ages, all races, all faiths.

Around the world, people went on the streets for him. Stunned, I watched the reports on TV. Japan danced, China danced, Africans, Koreans, Germans, English, Spanish, French, Dutch ... everyone, everyone, everyone, even in the depths of the Congo, even in prison, they got up for this quiet man who had enriched the world so much with his presence. They were there; every step they took was a non-violent protest against what Michael had to endure all his life, a silent cry against the music business, the ruthless business world, against the media, against all those who unscrupulously sacrificed their professional ethics for profit, headlines and their careers.

Fans of all nations flew to LA. They visited Neverland, the Staples Center and Carolwood Drive where he had last resided.

They organized their own shows and sang for their star, whom they had been faithful to for his whole life and whom they would be faithful to even in death.

There had never been a greater tribute to a pop star in the world. Never one so lasting. Never a greater entertainer, never one with a bigger heart.

Michael broke all records, even in death.

Mourning

It was strange. I had buried my grandmother, buried my father, who had died too soon. The mourning had been intense, but not as painful as it was now with Michael. Then - seven days after his death, as if he had now left the earth forever - I became buried in another mountain of grief. I could not understand.

My friend, who had certainly never voluntarily heard a single song by Michael, shed tears for him. "I don't know," she wailed. "But it's so close to my heart ... as if they had killed an innocent child..." She even had a picture from a magazine in front of her, and pointed at in now: "Look at this person! Those eyes ... oh, what did they do to him?"

And that was the strong voice that was suddenly heard in the room, in the world: what did they do to him? What had they done?

My husband sat at home and cried for him, cried for someone he had neither admired nor seen in his lifetime. He had never been a fan of Michael. But his death affected him in an inexplicable way.

And it was like that for a lot of people. For millions.

Oh, my God, I thought, what could his children be feeling?

Everywhere I looked, I saw people who were touched by Michael's death. It was such a strange, deep coherence.

I remembered one of his biographers who had crudely predicted, after the trial 2005, that if Michael should die, he would not be remembered as a brilliant pop star, but as Jackson, the child molester. Exactly the opposite had happened. Suddenly the darkness had lifted, his star shone brighter than ever, and hardly anyone could imagine that even one of the suspicions had been justified.

Almost lethargically I calculated the average number of his birth – and death day: both resulted in the number six.

In tarot that was the card of the "lovers." He was born and had died under that sign.

Weeks later, I forced myself to do business as usual, although there was not a day when I did not cry for him. I kept myself busy with automatic and physical things: gardening, cleaning out the basement, and organizing drawers. These unpleasant and long overdue tasks came just at the right time when I frantically needed distraction.

When I took apart the bookcase in the gallery a folder dropped down with loose sheets that sailed soundlessly through the house. Silently cursing I set out to collect everything again. Some of the pages had fallen through the railing to the lower floor. Restless, I bunched the sheets together on the top floor and walked downstairs to gather the three or four remaining pages.

A big FF jumped out at me. The name 'Joey'. The indefinable letters. The names on the list. The pages copied with the camera. It felt like a shock. I left the bookcase in the state it was in and sat down at the table.

The first page was the easiest:

F.Ahearn, Alternatives: CH, A, D, EU, UK.

The abbreviations were country codes, that was clear. Switzerland, Austria, Germany, Europe, England. All right. A selection of countries.

The name Ahearn was the only word spelled out on these pages. When I typed it into Google, my jaw dropped:

"Frank M. Ahearn – "How to Disappear," it read.

For a moment I stared at the few lines that stood under the name:

"Frank M. Ahearn is one of the leading skip tracers in the world."

Feverishly I surfed on and came to an article from the "world online" that described that Ahearn had been commissioned to track thousands of people. Including - in the old days - Michael. When I read further, I was overcome by an insane hope: Ahearn had eventually changed sides. He now worked out exit strategies. Instead of tracking people down, he helped them disappear.

My heart was pounding. Frantic, I picked up the second page.

The BEST, heavily underlined.

SK. Joey, then: *Sky, Tom, Friends D, U Friends, family? L., Dr. D.* ... clinics... *OMG!* With an un-smiley face with downturned mouth, time period: min two years to three years. *JAKE*, underlined three times.

At least the last name meant something to me. But then who was Tom? Who was Sky? Had, "Sk" in Sky something to do with the Joey in the first line? Probably not; otherwise he would not have divided it into two distinct points. Again I typed combinations. Together with the information from the back of the photo from Mike's library, it was not difficult. With the "sk" the very accentuated double "G" and "Joey" I typed "Skggs Joey" into Google. And was again speechless.

Did you mean "Skaggs, Joey?" asked Google.

Joey Skaggs, the search engine informed me, is an American prankster, who has organized numerous successful media pranks, hoaxes, and other events.

And further down was an entry: Joey Skaggs, the ultimate hoax master. A hoax master? I clicked on the site, got to his homepage, couldn't make much of it on the fly ... until I hit pay dirt with the third click: 'Who is Joey Skaggs?'

And that made my heart skip another beat. It read:

"This is your final curtain call."

Michael's words at his press conference: "This is it. This is the final curtain call." Everyone had wondered about his choice of words.

Trembling, I read through the pages, through the first paragraph probably three times because I could not believe what was written there:

"The Final Curtain (2000): Skaggs' creation was a combined funeral company, virtual graveyard and theme park. It was meant to satirize showmanship in places like Forest Lawn cemeteries. Final Curtain's website is still functioning."

As fast as my fingers could, I typed "Final Curtain".

I read that Joey Skaggs had distanced himself from malicious pranks, such as fake anthrax letters, but that he had repeatedly tricked the media so effectively with his hoaxes that they had broadcast false information. He was also known to organize fake funerals.

The FF was not for fan fiction, but for Fake Funeral.

There was more in this article, but these few sentences sufficed. Thunderstruck, I stared at the monitor, closed my eyes.

"Oh, God," I prayed. "Let it be true. Let him have disappeared…"

Somewhere between hope and shock, I researched further. Sky. That was too meager. Tom - millions of people with that name. Nevertheless, I thought automatically of the Tom who Michael had dealt with. Tom Mesereau. That was of course a guess. Friends D could refer to his friends in Germany. It was known that he had many acquaintances there. Friends U for USA or UK?

L., D or DR … for doctor … D…for Deepak? And then the note: minimum two years.

A sad smiley. Two years clinic, minimum. The OMG was clear: OH MY GOD! Oh my God, two years clinic!

I vacuumed. I vacuumed the whole house from top to bottom. The thoughts rattled, the frantic energy flowed into the vacuum cleaner and reached every place in the house. Movement was the valve to release the tension from me that was triggered by this news before it become entangled in a confusing knot in my brain.

After vacuuming, I was able to take a look at the third page.

"Photos, Heli, Amb.Vehi., Mon, MEDIA" - At the edge also an "OMG" and a smiley, "French fries".

I knew that Michael often referred to money as "French fries." For whatever reason.

'Heli' was helicopter; he had been taken by ambulance to the hospital, and from there was transported via helicopter to the coroner for an autopsy. And Mon? Monday? No, he had died on a Thursday … what could "mon" mean…? *Montage*! It was "montage". When I went online, I was even more amazed: his fans had been busy. They had already discovered that the photo, which TMZ graced us with, the one that showed Michael on the stretcher being pushed into the helicopter to bring him from UCLA to the forensic medical office, could be a photomontage.

The contradictions piled up. I tried to get a picture.

Many found it odd that when it all happened, there had not been a single fan in front of Michael's doorstep. It was noon, broad daylight. Michael was standing at the threshold of the greatest comeback of all time. Where were his fans? Where were the paparazzi, who otherwise always intercepted every emergency call, and often arrived ahead of the ambulance? Wouldn't they have immediately confirmed the address with their otherwise so sophisticated forensic skills, even if the employee had only cautiously spoken of a 'gentleman'? In the video on the Internet the ambulance seemed to have been in no hurry. Because Michael was already dead? But then they wouldn't have needed sirens.

Exceptionally strange: five minutes before the coroner officially pronounced Michael dead, TMZ had already reported it.

Murray refused to sign the death certificate in the hospital. On the Internet three death certificates are currently posted, all of them issued to Michael *Joseph* Jackson, although his passport and all other documents spell Michael *Joe* Jackson.

First it was said that the children had found Michael in the kitchen and thought he was playing dead, like he had done often before.

Then suddenly he had been in his bed, where Murray tried to improperly revive him on the famous soft mattress, and in doing so broke three ribs.

The children would have been crying in the hospital and would have been terrified. When DiLeo delivered the news of Michael's death in the hospital, they screamed and were inconsolable. Then they supposedly went to their dead father's room and had come out calmly. I don't know - if I lost my dearly beloved father and saw him lying dead in front of me, the irrevocable confirmation that he will never come back - I would cry all the more. And the children were calm? What had really happened in that room? But ultimately, no one would ever know exactly. Ultimately no one would know how many tears the children had shed and how many more there would be.

And there was more, much more.

The statements of Mike's hired-again manager DiLeo were mixed up. He had said to the children in the hospital: "I'm sorry, your father is dead. They are trying to resuscitate him until Katherine arrives." Was he so confused that he did not know what he was saying?

And Murray disappeared after Mike's death for full three days? Was he in a panic? Where had he been? A doctor whose world famous patient dies takes time off?

At 10:52 a.m. respiratory failure was determined, but not until 12:22 p.m. does Murray call 911. He says nothing of propofol, repeatedly makes contradictory statements about what he had given Michael.

La Toya claimed that Michael had looked "beautiful" when he was buried in an unidentified place about three months later. But at the public memorial service, *one* month after his death, where his brothers carried the gold coffin inside, it was not opened as would have been customary ... too terrible was the disfiguration of his body from the autopsy. A several times autopsied corpse looks better after three months than it does after one month and an autopsy?

The paramedics who had taken Michael to UCLA, stated that they did not recognize Michael. They had believed that this was a bald-headed old man.

In the photo that was shown to the public, the Michael who was pushed on a stretcher into the ambulance, was not only in possession of a full head of hair, but also looked fresh and unmistakably like Michael. No sunken cheeks or baldness. Furthermore, there is only this one picture of him when he is lying on this very stretcher and put into the helicopter, and that was broadcast by TMZ. Not one other single picture, snapped with a cellular phone or whatever other way? One of the most famous people in the world dies and there is only one picture? When otherwise they could not contain themselves when it came to celebrity images and the associated profit?

His sister Janet refuses for a long time to make a statement. When asked where she was at the time of his death, she said she had been in New York, then in Atlanta. And when asked about Michael, she answers shortly and says only things that everyone already knows.

The father appears not particularly depressed shortly after the announcement of the death, and hastens to announce that he is doing very well and has started a new record company.

At the time of the funeral the mother did not want to go into the mausoleum. The children hardly shed a tear - not at the funeral in September and not one when Michael was buried at Forest Lawn cemetery weeks later. No one knows his exact site of his grave - so that it cannot be desecrated.

And the contradictions did not stop.

Michael had been healthy, Michael had been a wreck. Michael had normal weight, Michael was totally malnourished. He had popped painkillers like candy, he was not at all addicted. He had repeatedly collapsed in rehearsals, he was physically fit and in extremely good spirits.

Michael had mixed the deadly propofol in orange juice himself and taken it. But propofol is fat-soluble, and in order to be effective, enormous amounts would have been required if mixed in juice. Definitely propofol does not lend itself to self-administering.

The Internet, the media, all these mind bogglers did full work. We only had the right to decide what we wanted to believe. I could only hope that this time it would be to Michael's advantage.

Soon after announcement of his death Michael's CD sales soared to never-before heights. Even the most well-stocked stores had temporary problems with their supply, and Michael was number one with his songs for weeks. His fans kept him there, and cried for him with each song. Most of them did not return their ticket, personally designed by Michael. They kept them as a memento to a final concert that Michael had never given.

His ATV catalog's worth is now estimated at a billion dollars, the catalog of his own songs between 250 to 500 million dollars. His memorabilia sold like hotcakes.

And then his movie *"This Is It"* was announced. All video recordings of the rehearsals had been filmed in HD, which was not surprising, but very practical, indeed.

The film shows what the fans would have seen had the concert taken place. It would have been huge, that's for sure. But Michael is always in different costumes. He sang not one complete song wearing the same outfit.

I saw an interview with Kenny Ortega and a reporter who rewound the film to a specific spot where Michael sang with his angelic voice, "human nature."

"Hear this voice!" said the moderator, completely overwhelmed. "Just listen to that voice! It's unbelievable…!" As if he was only now aware of how Michael could sing.

The movie and DVD sales generated huge revenue. The organizers reported that enough money went to Michael's account for his debts to be repaid.

Eight days before the departure for England he had died. The day before he fittingly gives a closing speech. Even though the show was not finished? Even though on June 20th a meeting over missed rehearsals had supposedly taken place? And suddenly it hit me: why had they prevented Michael from greeting his fans, the followers? Because it wasn't Michael, who stood among the new crew of bodyguards?

There are so many clues. As always, his fans were busy and cleverly working away and on the Internet more and more suggestive facts were gathered. But ultimately, that's what they remained. There were suggestive facts but no evidence. Hints that could be interpreted any way.

Michael was never found. And it still hurt.

"Chirelle," said my husband, "you interpret too much into things. Only the Gods know what happened on June 25th. How do you know whether the children were crying or not? And the reason why the ambulance was driving so slowly was probably because Michael was already dead. You know he took pills, I'm sure they'd given him more than was good for him … but you know he was not healthy. You know about everything he had to bear. He endured more than a human being can take. Maybe it was just that he was broken, that he asked so much of himself that his heart couldn't take it…maybe death protected him from something even worse. When I see how the music business goes … I mean, how much can a person stand…?"

I could only nod to this silently and unhappy. Anything was possible. That was just it.

And where was Grace? There was not one word, no sign of life from her. Simply nothing.

The rumors, reports, news were all over the place and did not improve my mood. The Jacksons sued AEG for having caused Michael's death. They said that it was all a ploy to get the ATV catalog, and to get at Michael's assets. La Toya claimed that Michael hated John Branca and would never have appointed him executor of his will. She hinted at a tangible crime around Michael and implied that Branca himself had enough connections to nudge himself into a position where Michael would never wanted him: in charge of his fortune. The debt would not be repaid, said La Toya, so that someday, when no one thinks about it anymore, the ATV will serve as security. The whole thing was a giant conspiracy. And that was what Michael had always said.

He was trapped in the business world - as he had shown in his video, *Who is it*, which featured people who raked in money for others and when they tried to break out, were held back by threats and fear. A world that prostitutes itself and had lost all morality. Is that the reason he had chosen the theme "High end call girl"? In any case, the text did not fit with the video. Rather, it seemed to me that he wanted to equate the music industry with a pimp business.

The one camp of fans that formed railed against the Jacksons, saying they themselves had only money in mind and now did everything to gain access to it. Who were pissed because none of them had been considered in the will - except for Katherine. After all, everyone other than Janet urgently needed cash. Branca had been employed by Michael exactly for the reason that the money would be managed for his children and could not be accessed by anyone else.

The family again, first and foremost Randy Jackson, let it be known that fake information was leaked to the press that made fans believe that everything was fine and Michael's fortune was not only secure but would be grown for his children.

But most railed against AEG and the 50 concerts, saying that the organizers should have known that Michael was too sick for that. They found it odd that the owner of AEG, billionaire Philip Anschutz had a relationship with the Bank of America and that he had people like Diane Dimond on his payroll. They were also suspicious about Martin Bandier, the man whose nose Michael had snatched the ATV out from under in 1985, was now CEO of Sony.

And then there was Conrad Murray. Murray, who supposedly was not even a doctor, but an actor. Murray, who administered Michael the lethal dose of propofol and had violated his duties in many ways, if he really was a physician, because he neither followed the golden rule to always stay with an anesthesized patient nor did he have the proper equipment for the administration of propofol. Was Murray really sloppy enough to give someone whom his own livelihood depended on, propofol and then foolishly leave the room?

Everyone wondered what had happened in the time span between 10:52 and 12:22. Perhaps Murray had really just given him the stated, more or less harmless, 25 mg propofol. And someone else administered the lethal dose...?

The report in the media: "Strange fingerprints on the propofol needle" substantiate the monstrous suspicion that Michael may have been murdered before our eyes.

Many believed in a conspiracy, but no one knew from which direction it came. Michael had always mentioned "names." Lisa Marie also said in an interview that he called her, sobbing, saying they wanted to kill him because of the ATV: "I know the names, but I will not say them."

Why was nobody saying them? Were they really so dangerous, so mighty, that no one dared?

And why had Mike not kept the names somewhere for his protection? Because he knew that nobody would print them, since the press ran together in certain hands and was manipulated for us common mortals anyway?

These thoughts stole my already faltering peace of mind these days, and the pain of never talking with Michael again did not lessen.

Chris called me. He cried his eyes out.

"Chirelle," he sniffed, "they broke him, these greedy bastards ... they always wanted to get more out of him. And the fucking media! First they kill him, then they want him to dance for them ... Chirelle, some say that he made the leap, do you believe that?"

"Chris," I said tortured, "if *you* don't know ... you were close to him! I'm thousands of miles away!"

I heard Chris sobbing.

"They've fired all of us, Chirelle, Thome fired us...immediately on the day, he died...they killed him ... they killed him ... oh, those bastards ... those bastards..."

My heart was sore, and oh, it hurt so much. Whenever I thought about Mike, I missed him terribly, terribly. Chris's words felt like a barbed wire stuck in my throat.

"Chris," I said hoarsely, unable to comfort him, "he's gone. Whichever way. There is no more Michael Jackson."

Then I just hung up. I hated that last sentence of mine.

***

In my desperation, I called one of my teachers in India. He was clairvoyant and even though I knew he would hardly engage, I wished that he would give a word to support the hope of many people.

"A great person. A truly great man!" said my teacher and sounded as proud as if he were the father.

I started to cry. As always when I recalled Mike's being.

"I miss him so," I sobbed, "I can't tell you how much I miss him ... he was such a fine man, so good, so noble, so loving ... he just was not ready for this tough world."

"Oh, no," my teacher replied warmly, "rather, the world was not ready for him. Eventually we will all be like children again, what he wanted so much... isn't this the goal for each of us?"

"But he's ... gone too soon!" I sobbed. "Much too soon!"

"Nobody goes too soon, my little one," my teacher said gently. "Everyone goes at the right time. And if Michael wanted to go - wherever - then send him your love. That's what he can always use at any time and in any place. That's something all of us can do. And that's exactly what he showed you, right? Now prove that you understood."

But what, for now, overpowered all my thoughts was my own sentence: there is no more Michael Jackson.

And so, for the first time, the words of my teacher brought no comfort. It took me a while before I could accept them. There is no more Michael Jackson. He was the child in all of us, our fascinating partner in our universal quest for happiness, and now he was dead. We would have liked so much to see him happy. There is no more Michael Jackson.

But...there is his music. His lyrics, his feelings, his messages. There are his amazing children who love him so much and want to carry on in his spirit. And now they are the ones from whom we can take an example: we can all carry on in his spirit. We can all live our inner child, like he had done all his life.

Slowly ... slowly ... the words of the wise man from India seeped into my heart, began to softly and gently heal. Love - this is what Michael has taught us. He left us his legacy. It is in every note of his songs, in every letter of his words. And it is time for us all to live it. To let the child rise up in us - against all odds.

***

Four months after his death, a letter with no return address was delivered into the house. Grace! I hoped that it was Grace. With nervous fingers I tore it open.

"Chirelle!" stood there in spidery script.

My heart stopped. That was Michael's handwriting - this typical jumble of cursive and print letters, his habit of suddenly writing the first two letters of a word in capital, or one or two in the middle of a word...

My knees buckled ... I held a piece of Michael in my trembling hands. Tears clouded my eyes, I knelt on the hard floor, heart pounding and with eyes racing to read what it said:

"Chirelle! I'm doing fine. It is wonderful to work with these people! Kenny Ortega is great and all the others, too. It will be everything I had imagined! Everything, as I had planned it! However, we had to postpone the start of the concert. I want to go through with it, I want to do it ... for my children, for a different life.

I will be too busy to write to you in the near future, but I wanted to thank you one more time - for the talks, for all the insights.

I feel very free - I love! That is all that is needed and it is so beautiful! Really, for the first time in my life, I feel free of any burden.

As before I still want to use my talents to do good in the world. And everybody should do that - if you talk to people about me, Chirelle, then just tell them this:

'Go for your dreams and make this world a better place.' That is still my dogma and now I can live it, at last, I realized how important it is to appreciate the inside, to honor oneself.

If you should come into contact with fans, then tell them that I love them, I am grateful to them and I will carry them forever in my heart, no matter where I am. Tell them what to me is so very self-evident: that love lives in us. That God lives in us. And that there is no separation. Tell them, my life, my insights, my music should serve the world. No one should suffer ... and certainly not because of me - that would just mean not to have found your own love inside.

492

That is what I stand for and those who love me show me their love precisely this way: that they live their love. No grudges, no hate, we have no time for that. Love always triumphs. Love is forever. I know it.

I love you, Chirelle, I love you more, I love you all.

Michael
Los Angeles, June 1st, 2009

"Mike," I whispered. "Mike ... where are you?"

Again and again, I listened to the closing speech of the *This Is It* movie, where Michael stands together with his team, ready to go to London, ready to take on the challenge. Michael reminds everyone that love is important, that we must take care of our planet, that all this - and especially for him - is a great adventure.

Then they played him again at the end of the film, at the end of his life, in *"Man in the Mirror"*, where he sings in his so unique way, with his unequaled interplay of body and melody. He sings the lyrics and appears relaxed and free.

"I make this ... CHANGE today..." he sings, "...stand up and *live* yourself - now!"... and these words are pounding in my head, do not leave me. I stare at the screen.

Michael in the spotlight. He is calm and relaxed. The choir sings the refrain to "Man in the Mirror." Over and over again.

Michael stands and feels. Twice he touches the area around his heart with his hands, holds them out to the audience. Then he spreads his arms for his final gesture. He raises his head, tilts it back, flows into the music, into the beating of the stars, which he already perceived as a young boy and that he again perceives, clearly, powerfully, mightily, gently ... the stars calling him, who say we love you, come home, get some rest, come back now ... you've done so much, it's time to come home. And he enjoys the vibration, as he has always enjoyed it, gives in to it, while his persona is immortalized on screen in his so characteristic pose:

Michael in the spotlight. The arms spread, his heart open, for us, for the world, and finally for himself.

The Last Tear

...

How strange, that all these tears could not wash away the hurt!

Then one thought of love pierced my bitterness.

I remembered you in the sunlight, with a smile sweet as May wine.

A tear of gratitude started to fall, and miraculously, you were back.

Soft finger touches my cheek, and you bent over for a kiss.

"Why have you come?" I whispered.

"To wipe away your last tear," you replied. "It was the one you

saved for me."

From, Dancing the Dream, Michael's true biography.

References

1. Quote: *Courage and Contentment, A Collection of spiritual talks by Swami Chidvilasananda*, Chapter One
2. Vindicatemj.wordpress.com/2010/03/05 Evan Chandler - Dave Schwartz phone talk, full transcript.

Literature

Jackson, Michael Moonwalk, München, Wilhelm-Heyne Verlag 2009

Jackson, Michael, Dancing the Dream, Goldmann Verlag, München, 1992

Taraborelli, Randy, The Magic, The Madness, the whole story; New York, Grand Central Publishing, 2009

Jones, Aphrodite, Conspiracy, aphroditejonesbooks, 2007

Guest, Lynton, The Trials of Michael Jackson, Vale of Glamorgan, Aureus Publishing Limited, 2006

Jackson, La Toya, Starting over, Beverly Hills, Ja-Tail Publishing Company, 2011

Jefferson, Margot, On Michael Jackson, New York, Random House, 2006

Rabbi Shmuley Boteach: Honoring the Child Spirit, New York, Vanguard Press, 2011

Rabbi Shmuley Boteach: The Tapes of Michael Jackson, New York, Vanguard Press, 2009

Rowe, Leonard: What really happened to Michael Jackson, Linell-Diamond Enterprises, LLC, 2010

Kuenzler, Hanspeter, Black or White, A 6604 Höfen, Koch International Gmbh/Hannibal, 2009

Sky, Rick, The bad year, London, HarperCollins Publishers, 1994

Ebmaier, Jochen, Das Phänomen Michael Jackson, Hamburg, Rasch und Röhring-Verlag 1997

Bloemen, Dobler, Lohr, Winterholler, It's all about love, Norderstedt, Books on Demand GmbH, 2010

Jackson, Jermaine, You are not alone, London, HarperCollinsPublishers, 2011

Wiesner, Dieter, Die wahre Geschichte, München, Wilhelm-Heyne Verlag, 2011

Cascio, Frank, My friend Michael, The Story of an ordinary friendship with an extraordinary man, London, HarperCollinsPublishers, 2011

Thank you to all the fans, who have never ceased to live Michael's legacy and continue to do so. Without you, this book would not have been possible.

Thank you especially to those people who opened their inner selves to me and shared deeply personal stories, who through nights with intense talks, tears and memories, revealed to me the wonderful soul of Michael Jackson.
Thank you from the bottom of my heart.

www.ingramcontent.com/pod-product-compliance
Lightning Source LLC
Chambersburg PA
CBHW022111080426
42734CB00006B/90